Blood on the Bayou

Blood on the Bayou

Vicksburg, Port Hudson, and the Trans-Mississippi

Donald S. Frazier

State House Press
Buffalo Gap, Texas

Library of Congress Cataloging-in-Publication Data

Frazier, Donald S.
Blood on the Bayou: Vicksburg, Port Hudson, and the Trans-Mississippi
Donald S. Frazier
p. cm.
Includes Bibliographical references and index.
ISBN 978-1-933337-63-0 (pbk. alk. paper)
ISBN- 933337-63-X (pbk. alk. paper)
1. History United States 2. History / Civil War Period (1850-1877) 3. United States: History-20th century. 4. HISTORY / United States/State & Local/Southwest (AZ, NM, OK, TX) 5. HISTORY / United States/State & Local/South (AL, AR, FL, GA, KY, LA, MS, NC, SC, TN)

This paper meets the requirements of ANSI/NISO, Z39.48-1992 (permanence of paper)
Binding materials have been chosen for durability ∞
I. Title.
"Cataloging-in-Publication Data available from the Library of Congress"

Manufactured in the United States

First Edition

State House Press
P.O. Box 818
Buffalo Gap, Texas 79508
325-572-3974 · 325-572-3991 (fax)
www.tfhcc.com

Printed in the United States of America
Distributed by Texas A&M University Press Consortium
800-826-8911
www.tamupress.com

ISBN-13: 978-1-933337-62-3
ISBN-10: 1-933337-62-1

Book Design by Rosenbohm Graphic Design

Contents

For Sue, Kay, and Sarah, thank you for making life fun.
Also, for Jack and Pat Buckley, for all the joy, love, and support.

Foreword and Acknowledgments

This is not the book I intended to write. I had different aspirations for the *Louisiana Quadrille* and believed that I knew what payload this book needed to carry. However, as I opened myself to the sources, I felt compelled to go where they led; this is the essence of history. Now, instead of a tidy—and conventional—telling of the U.S. Civil War in Louisiana and Texas from June 1863 to February 1864, the voices from the past took me on a journey of social, military, and economic upheaval that was more compelling, but it definitely broke the narrative in my head. I learned much and, in the end, felt driven to share this new knowledge.

As with the other books in the series, the military campaigns remain front and center. I trace the movements of obscure regiments and battles fought on unfamiliar Trans-Mississippi landscapes in June and July of 1863 and tell a little-known aspect of the sieges of Vicksburg and Port Hudson. I examine the evolution of Federal and Confederate strategy and sketch the leaders tasked with carrying these plans forward. There is enough combat to satisfy even the most ardent student of campaigns and commanders.

However, the sources revealed an almost obsessive concern over slavery. Actually, these soldiers, civilians, and politicians did not fret over the *institution* of slavery as much as control over the slaves themselves. Both Federal and Confederate authorities seemed preoccupied with who physically controlled the enslaved population. This led me to review Republican views on this subject, and especially those held by President Abraham Lincoln. The tug-of-war over people—whom some considered persons held in bondage and others considered human property—also caused me to reexamine the peculiar institution as a salient feature of Confederate national identity. A greater appreciation for the causes of the war emerged. Although states' rights certainly provided a framework and context for the argument, slavery caused the war, not vice versa.

Many friends and colleagues will consider this common knowledge. I am not sure, however, that the urge for abolition was as altruistic as many hold. I began to discern a cynical undertone to the motivations for, and the accomplishment of, emancipation. I also became convinced that provoking a war over the issue of slavery was part of the Republican plan all along. The Southern fire-eaters had been correct; electing Lincoln meant a relentless march toward the liberation of slaves. The Northern abolitionists were also correct; slave owners sought to create a nation that protected the right to own people. I freely admit to being influenced by James Oakes's important book *Freedom National*, for guiding me toward these conclusions.

Physical control of the slave population impacted how the Federal government conducted its military campaigns. When war broke out, slaves emerged first as "contraband," then morphed into "self-emancipated" persons, before becoming the raison d'être of the Mississippi Valley campaigns in 1863. The blacks became plunder, if you will. I came to the conclusion that the gathering of these persons drove, in part, Union military strategy in the Mississippi Valley. Lincoln wanted slaves removed from Southern owners, concentrated in areas convenient to Union logistics centers, and then redistributed to serve as soldiers or farmers on behalf of the United States. The longer the military campaigns in the Mississippi Valley dragged on, the more Federal officials could feed liberated slaves into the system. For a fresh look at intentional emancipation and black conscription into the U.S. army, I recommend William Dobak's *Freedom by the Sword*.

This strategy held that once Union troops had removed slaves from bondage and repurposed them to other tasks, it would be nearly impossible for their former masters to re-enslave them. No matter the outcome of the war, the Federal government set out to break slavery—forever. Fearing a rapid collapse of the Confederacy, abolitionists intended to make sure that readmitted states did not reestablish slavery. Remember, slavery was then a state prerogative. Passage of the Thirteenth Amendment still lay months into the future.

Concurrently, Lincoln believed black troops would help achieve victory and then secure the peace. Once the shooting ended, these black regiments might serve as an army of occupation. One of the largest concentrations of slaves lay in the Mississippi Valley and this population needed to be under Federal control. The Rebel forts at Vicksburg and Port Hudson were impediments. Despite the presence of these Confederate citadels, U.S. troops could remove the black population of this region into zones of their choosing with increasing impunity. The fall of these positions facilitated commerce and navigation on the Mississippi. Yet, the great gathering of blacks began—and continued—notwithstanding the Rebels in the earthworks.

I became fascinated with the mechanics of this redistribution of Louisiana's black population. Where did they come from? How did they arrive at their points of concentration? What became of their families? How did General Nathaniel P. Banks organize and deploy his *Corps d'Afrique*? How did slave owners respond to this transition? How did Union soldiers view this project? Most importantly, what did the slaves think about being thus used by the Federal government? I used these questions to comb traditional military sources, soldiers' letters and diaries, and civilian accounts. I also listened to the voices of the slaves themselves, discovering their accounts rich and intriguing. I am indebted to the Works Progress Administration (WPA) writers, the *Slave Narratives*, as well as the editorial work of Professor Ira Berlin in his multivolume series, *Freedom*.

Readers unfamiliar with these sources should be aware. Emancipated slaves, kept in ignorance and illiteracy by the institution that consumed their labor, did not write well, or clearly, if at all. Modern audiences may find their quotations jarring. White officials, attempting to communicate on their behalf, often projected their own biases. Similarly, writers gathered the WPA Slave Narratives as oral interviews and often felt obliged to transcribe these conversations in the speaker's own dialect—or at least what they *interpreted* as the speaker's own dialect. What a modern audience might find racially offensive, the original interviewers believed vital to keeping the warp and weft of the voices of these former slaves. As a historian, I chose to quote these sources as they presented themselves. For example, "I am going to" became "Isa gwine ta" in some of the WPA Slave Narratives, "river" became "ribber," and so forth.

In addition, writers and observers in 1863 used language that modern sensibilities consider offensive, racist, and provocative. I concur. I employ these terms only in direct quotations. If a reader finds cause for complaint, I chose to use the quotations as a way of recreating a difficult place and time.

What emerges in *Blood on the Bayou* is, I hope, a presentation of cause, conduct, and effects of the war on the lower Mississippi. I tried to fix the battles in a larger context. These troop movements and small Trans-Mississippi battles had ramifications that rippled across the country. With luck, students of military history will make a connection with the role that these campaigns played in reweaving the national fabric. In this same vein, students of social history may gain a greater appreciation for the role military decisions played in this story.

The interpretations in this book are mine. I may have been inspired by others, and certainly influenced by their scholarship, but my application of their broad interpretations to the narrow field of Louisiana and Texas was a way of testing their conclusions. This book will add nuance and, in a few cases, exceptions, to their conclusions.

No work of this nature occurs in a vacuum. My first debt is to the many great librarians and archivists. This book has been twenty years in the making. Many of those who helped me two decades ago have retired, or in some cases, passed on. Others, thankfully, remain. My greatest allies have been Mary Linn Wernet at Northwestern State University in Natchitoches, Louisiana, and Germain Bienvenu at Hill Memorial Library at Louisiana State University. Both patiently assisted me as I read through their collections and pointed me to sources that I may have otherwise overlooked. They epitomize professionalism and help make Louisiana's research libraries among the best in the country.

I also owe a debt to my academic home, McMurry University in Abilene, Texas. Keith Waddle proved tireless in processing interlibrary loan orders. A large state university apparatus does not support my research. Instead, I labor at a small, liberal arts, teaching institution. Administrators and trustees perhaps appreciate scholarship, but it is not their priority. That said, a number of people encouraged me as I wove my way through the *Louisiana Quadrille*. Sam Taylor fellowships, a program of the United Methodist Board of Higher Education, and Kiva Grants, a program of the Kiva Alumni Association, provided needed funds to underwrite this work.

In addition, I received a sabbatical leave to do nothing but research and write. This came about from a deal I struck with my then-Vice President for Academic Affairs, Dr. Beverly Lenoir. Awarded a half-year sabbatical in 2006, I negotiated for a deferment for seven more years in exchange for a full year's leave. She agreed; then she retired. Her successor, Dr. Paul Fabrizio, and the president, Dr. John Russell, kept the bargain. As a result, I enjoyed a year unfettered by teaching concerns to travel, write, and edit. I greatly appreciated this gift of time.

Others assisted in the processes of turning a manuscript into a book. Caty-Jane McSpadden, our able History Department student worker, took a first pass at the index. My colleague Dr. Gary Shanafelt, an expert on the Austro-

Hungarian Empire in its waning days, brought his potent and penetrating eye to the work and asked important questions that I had not considered. He has a gift as well for proofreading as does Paula Clowdus, my second set of eyes. Thanks for seining my prose.

This appreciation also extends to my family. My wife, Susan, and my daughters Kay and Sarah patiently endured my headlong tumble into the past. For months I have communed with the dead and have only imperfectly interacted with the living. Susan accepted all this weirdness with amazing grace. She endured the long hours I sequestered myself in my office, tolerated my quick dashes to eat dinner with the family only to return to tapping away on a narrative about people, and days, long passed. She made no mention of me showing signs of battle fatigue and war weariness as I spent my days, and many nights, refighting a conflict long ceased while wrestling with slippery concepts fraught with controversy. Thank you, Susan, for enduring your yearlong Civil War widowhood.

Several readers hacked their way through iterations of this book. I want to especially acknowledge Dr. Light T. Cummins at Austin College, my brother, Rob Frazier, and Michael Marshall of Hammond, Louisiana. There were other readers and evaluators chosen by the Press that weighed the book on its scholarly merits. Thank you for taking the time to work this book over and ensure its suitability for publication.

I owe Dr. Stephen L. Hardin a huge debt. He offered to read this book word by word, line by line. Even though he explained to me that, "this isn't my war," this world-renown scholar of the Texas Revolution has committed to memory the tenets of William Strunk, Jr., and E. B. White's *The Elements of Style*. He is a gifted writer, and the nineteen days we spent combing this manuscript made it profoundly better. The gift of his time and talent I can never repay. That said, the Civil War in Louisiana became "his war" as a result.

State House Press is an imprint of the McWhiney History Education Group. This organization intends to continue introducing new scholarship to the public. They understand the expenses, and limited returns, of writing history, yet endeavor to press on in the venture for the greater good. That is rare. They also rely on many talented people. Most notably, I must confess a debt of gratitude to Claudia Gravier Frigo, a multitalented project manager, copy editor, and history intellect that pushes, pulls, and cajoles until the project is ready for release.

Gary S. Zaboly, the magisterial military illustrator of Riverdale, the Bronx, took a difficult subject and crafted amazing cover art. Thank you, Gary, for your patience and commitment.

Many people played a role in encouraging and supporting the project. However, any faults, omissions, errors in fact, or other lapses are mine alone. The interpretation is mine. I understand that this book contradicts traditional narratives. I expect that many will find fault with my conclusions because it challenges many deeply held preconceptions.

So be it.

Good history is, by its nature, revisionist. Good history also begins with new questions. I asked mine, and the answers I uncovered are found in this book.

INTRODUCTION
A Quiet and Sane Life

Ah nebber want to see anudder war.
—Catherine Cornelius, 103-year-old former slave
New Orleans, Louisiana

In the late1930s, two laborers in the Federal Writer's Project of the Works Progress Administration (WPA) called on 103-year-old Catherine Cornelius, a resident of the Lafon Old Folks' Home in New Orleans. Hazel Breaux, a white woman, and Robert McKinney, a black graduate student at Xavier University, had come as U.S. government employees to record the centenarian's life story, being careful to capture her black dialect and accent in their notes. They yearned to record the lives of ordinary Americans, but especially craved stories of Cornelius's life as a slave on a Louisiana plantation.

Cornelius, clad in a black dress with a blue-and-white dotted apron and wearing a black *tignon* headscarf that matched her shoes, walked into the dining room to meet her visitors. The interviewers noted she was "comely and surprisingly energetic, dark complexioned, and weigh[ed] about ninety pounds." After exchanging greetings and learning the purpose of the interview, Cornelius began her story: "Ah was a slave and raised on de *Smithfield* plantation, and came to N'Awlins, an bin hyar ever since."

Cornelius was the daughter of two Virginia-born slaves—Frederick and Nancy Brown—who arrived in Louisiana before 1830. By May 1862, Cornelius was a married woman working among the cane, cotton, and cornfields of the Smithfield Plantation in West Baton Rouge Parish. Her entire world was this considerable agricultural colony. She remembered, "Ah worked in de field cuttin' cane. Ma ma and pa and de whole family was dere too." The massive farm operated on the labor of more than a hundred enslaved people and annually shipped tons of products downriver from its sugarhouse and landing. Her master, Dr. W. J. Lyle, inhabited the large house fronting the river. Behind his home stretched rows of whitewashed cabins, a slave family housed in each. Beyond the fields, stretching in long narrow tracts away from the river, a small grove of willows marked where generations of slaves, including Cornelius's mother, lay buried, most of them having lived their entire lives without any sense of the larger world outside of Smithfield—and bondage.

A former slave, Tante (aunt) Pampiers of Cloutierville, Louisiana, had served the Fontenot Family of Natchitoches Parish, Louisiana, who had freed her prior to the outbreak of the war. She lived to be more than one hundred years old and wears the tignon *and apron typical of elderly black women of her generation living in Louisiana.*
Northwestern State University, Natchitoches, Louisiana.

From her limited experience, Cornelius believed that Smithfield provided her a good life. Although her existence as a slave consisted mostly of the drudgery of cane cutting and cotton hoeing, she believed Dr. Lyle treated his people relatively well, especially compared to the gossip that flowed along the Mississippi. Black couples could freely marry on Smithfield, and she wed a fellow field hand, Wylie Smith. Black midwives helped them deliver their children that their masters then baptized into the Episcopal Church. When ill, Lyle and another physician, assisted by black nurses, saw to their care at the plantation hospital. On special occasions, such as Christmas, Lyle provided his slaves money. The arrival of itinerant peddlers allowed the residents of Smithfield an opportunity to spend their coin on trifles and luxuries. When traveling showboats blew their whistles, Lyle gave his hands a half dollar and time off to enjoy the performances. "Shucks, we didn't need no money in dem days," Cornelius remembered. "We had plenty of clothes to wear. We had everything de white folks had, all de meat and vegetables we wanted."

Like most plantations, hard discipline and firm control lay at the heart of Smithfield's daily rhythms. Work began and ended with a clanging bell.

Laborers had weekends off, but Cornelius explained, "we had to go to church." This orderliness depended on emotional distance between master and slave. Merriments remained segregated. "De people from de big house didn't come down to our cabins and our celebrations. Dey would come down sometimes to see us, but on no special day." Cornelius remembered few instances when her aloof master ordered cruel punishments. "If we was bad dey would whip us and put us in stocks," she continued, "but we never had no trouble on our plantation."

On a spring day in 1862, Cornelius stopped working and looked up, responding to the hollers and shouts of women atop the Mississippi levee. Her curiosity piqued, she moved toward the big house to see what had caused the commotion. Amid the tumult, her master, Dr. Lyle, behaved strangely. He ordered some of his hands to nail a bed sheet to the porch, the length of the white cloth fluttering and flowing in the wind. Confused, Cornelius continued on, scurrying up the earthen berm near the river to investigate the hubbub. When she crested the rise, she beheld a craft unlike any other she had seen. "Lawd . . . Ah didn't know what dat was comin up de ribber," she chuckled. "I knew it wasn't no house or showboat, but ah didn't think it was a war boat, cos ah had nebber seen one."

Cornelius could not have known it, but the arrival of this vessel doomed the only life she had ever known. A Federal naval officer hailed the women atop the levee. "He said, 'girls, what town is dis?' You know it was a big plantation," she laughed. The women yelled back. "'Dis ain't no town, dis a plantation.'" Before long, Union troops came ashore, setting up camp near the plantation bell. An officer and a handful of men stomped heavily up the porch steps at the big house and ripped down the white sheet—refusing to acknowledge Lyle's neutrality. The soldiers left the next day, heading upstream.

That visit by Federal soldiers foreshadowed hard days for Cornelius. Unshared with the WPA interviewers, Cornelius certainly examined shadows of times, places, and people that had faded away. The upheavals inaugurated by the Union "war boat" some four-score and seven years before roiled for many months and concluded with her family scattered, her brother a dead Union soldier, and Cornelius a refugee. Before the war ended, a Federal steamboat carried her to New Orleans and away from the fields—and captivity—of her youth.

How could she describe those events? Where would she find the words to illuminate those days? What was the point? Those days were long past, in a

This painting by New Orleans artist Charles Giroux remembers antebellum life as orderly, bucolic, and simple. War and its attending horrors—destruction and displacement—erased places like this Louisiana plantation from the American landscape.
Charles Giroux, American, 1850s-1880s, Cotton Plantation, 1850s, Oil on Canvas, 55.56 × 92.07 cm (21 7/8 x 36 ¼ in.). Museum of Fine Arts, Boston. Gift of Mexim Kerolik for the M. and M. Karolik Collection of American Paintings, 1815-1865. Photograph © Museum of Fine Arts, Boston.

different country, far away. No doubt Cornelius recalled more than she related and opted for simplicity. "I was a grown woman when dat war broke out," she told the interviewer. "Ah nebber want to see anudder war." Fatigued by recounting her life's story and summoning shades from her past, Cornelius excused herself and returned to her room.

The government interviewers seemed pleased with the session and jotted some final notes before leaving. "For a person so advanced in years, Mrs. Cornelius has an unusually keen mind," the WPA writers concluded. "The only apparently infirmity from which she suffers is a slight deafness, this being due to her age."

Notwithstanding the succint stories of suffering, death, shattered fortunes, and the upending of a civilization, the interviewer missed the point. So many questions had gone unasked; so many details had gone unshared. Before closing out this oral history, the WPA writers added a last, patronizing line.

"She has apparently led a quiet and sane life."[1]

1

Apocalypse

And I saw a new heaven and a new earth: for the first heaven and the first earth were passed away.
—Revelation 21:1

The war that Mrs. Catherine Cornelius endured sprang from many causes. Ultimately, though, the armies of the United States and the Confederacy contended for control of four million people like Cornelius who would be the final beneficiaries of so much chaos, death, and mayhem. Citing the U.S. Constitution of 1787, the Confederacy correctly claimed the legality of slavery and its immunity from Federal regulation. Its politicians—and many of the men in its regiments—fought to maintain this regional entitlement. If the Federal government could intervene in state affairs regarding slavery, where would this intrusion stop?

The Republican Party, growing in strength and influence in the late 1850s, wanted to end slavery but strained against the constitutional leash. Even so, this issue dwarfed all others in the national elections of 1860. Men are born free, abolitionists protested; the Declaration of Independence and Constitution of the United States enshrined this idea. This latter document, though, also left a great deal of authority to the states. Legislatures across the South exercised their prerogative and maintained slavery and "property in man" that they had inherited from their days as British colonies. Republicans detested this colonial shadow on national progress and argued instead that freedom was the natural status of Americans everywhere, and slavery an artificial imposition. By 1860, secessionists correctly believed that although the legality of owning slaves lay beyond Federal jurisdiction, a Republican-controlled government would manipulate its authority to legislate or regulate slavery out of existence. Regulation of interstate commerce, control of the territories, and Federal fiscal appropriations might all become political cudgels in the hands of abolitionists.

The Southern states left the Union, ostensibly to protest the direction the nation seemed to be taking. After declaring themselves a new country in 1861,

Confederate lawmakers enshrined the "peculiar institution" in the Confederate Constitution. Slavery became a bedrock principle. A successful war for Southern independence would create a nation in which slavery was national. Free states could never exist—by definition—within this new entity—a strange contradiction for champions of "states' rights."[1]

On coming to power, the Republicans indeed planned on using the entire array of the Federal government to first limit, and then, end, slavery. A cordon of free states would quarantine the South, buying time for years of economic incentives and market penalties to convince Southerners to naturally abandon slavery to protect their own revenues. Perhaps, abolitionists hoped, the end of slavery might occur in their lifetime. Only a war—and attendant national emergency measures—could expedite that timetable. Secessionists played into abolitionist hands. When eleven slave states left the Union, Federal armies gathered to impose a Republican view of the national destiny on them in the name of saving the union. The government naturally declared a state of emergency.

As the war gathered momentum, slaves naturally flocked to U.S. troops as they marched south. At first, Federal officials hesitated to declare these slaves "liberated." Four slave states—Delaware, Maryland, Kentucky, and Missouri—remained loyal to the Union. Not wishing to antagonize these reluctant citizens further, war planners provided escaped slaves the quasi-status of "contraband of war." Like mules, horses, and cattle taken from the Rebels, the army could detain slaves to prevent their use by the enemy. Despite a year of Union triumphs, the future of slavery remained in question.

By spring 1862, Southern claims of independence became increasingly incredible. U.S. forces broke the shell of the Confederacy on the battlefield in Tennessee and eastern Virginia, devastating Rebel morale. General Benjamin Butler's Union army occupied New Orleans, which was then the largest city in the South, after it had come under the guns of Admiral David G. Farragut's fleet. Secessionist enthusiasm faded; so, too, did Confederate enlistments.

The Union war effort was almost too successful and too swift to meet the ambitions of many abolitionists. Radicals feared an early death for the Confederacy might effectively preserve slavery. Once defeated and restored to Union control, the former rebellious states might go about their business. Under the U.S. Constitution, only the radical redrafting of state laws (or a national constitutional amendment) could abolish slavery. Southern voters would never willingly embrace such drastic measures. Instead, the longer the war lasted and reliable government remained in abeyance, the more unfastened slavery became from its prewar guarantees. The continuous disruption of invasion and occupation would eventually wreck slavery and make Southerners swallow their caustic medicine, accomplishing by the bayonet what democratic process might fail to achieve in peacetime.

The Rebels again played into abolitionist hands by prolonging the war. Tottering and desperate, the Richmond government instituted draconian statutes that forced all military-aged male citizens to defend what the lawmakers declared universally adored national principles. Rebel regiments, once teeming with secessionist hotspurs, now lay battle-ravaged and bullet-scarred and desperate to fill their ranks. Conscription laws and home guards plucked reluctant Rebels from their families and packed them into the Confederate army. The unraveling Confederacy stirred back to life that summer. Union attempts at capturing the Mississippi Valley fell apart and Rebels dug in at Vicksburg and Port Hudson. General Thomas J. "Stonewall" Jackson humiliated Federal armies operating in the Shenandoah Valley of Virginia, and General Robert E. Lee repelled an attempt to capture Richmond. Northern forces had stagnated in Tennessee and General Braxton Bragg planned a Condederate invasion of Kentucky to come to the aid of their fellow slave owners.

The war dragged on. The U.S. Congress reacted by ramping up additional measures that linked the abolition of slavery to the successful prosecution of the war. On July 17, 1862, the Federal Congress passed retaliatory measures against the Confederacy. The Second Confiscation Act broadened the processes whereby Union armies could free slaves and allowed the punitive seizure of private property—including persons held in servitude—of those unwilling to swear loyalty to the Union. The Republicans might claim slaves were people, but they now treated them as "property" just as their masters had long claimed. The Militia Act authorized service in the U.S. army to blacks. Self-emancipating slaves would no longer be "contrabands," but free people subject to Federal interests.

President Abraham Lincoln applauded these measures. "That those who make a causeless war should be compelled to pay the cost of it," he declared to Congress, "is too obviously just, to be called into question." The president

At first, U.S. officials did not know how to handle slaves that came into Union army lines. In the absence of an official policy, officers often put the people to practical tasks. These men served as teamsters with the Federal army in Virginia.
Library of Congress Prints and Photographs Division, Washington, D.C.

correctly assumed that Southerners would resent the loss of their slaves and would correctly recognize these new laws as the next steps in the steady, intentional march toward national abolition. The Southerners would fight even harder; they would prolong the war, and with it, the processes of abolition could grind on.[2]

Southerners declared Northern radicalism unmasked. Louisianan Julia LeGrand, writing from Federal-occupied New Orleans, observed, "the radicals, knowing that they have the reins of Government in their own hands, are determined to press the war and overwhelm us." Their ruthlessness mirrored the French Revolution's Reign of Terror. "These dreadful radicals are the Jacobins of America and their cry is like the old one, 'More Blood.'"[3]

Many Southerners believed the Federal government had turned leviathan, trampled the Constitution, and spawned a radical revolution that they must resist. Radical politicians yearned to blot out state sovereignty. Northerners, especially

Republicans, sought to impose a national order on a country composed of regional—and state—distinctions. If successful, secessionists argued, Federal power would have no limits. This homogenizing influence, these Southerners held, ran counter to the framers' arguments promulgated from Independence Hall in 1787. It betrayed the cause for which the patriots of old—their grandfathers' generation—had fought. "The black Republican Party," trumpeted the New Orleans *Delta*, "is, in fact, essentially a revolutionary party."[4]

This late-nineteenth-century image imagines Major General Benjamin Butler standing on the portico of a marble building with the U.S. flag waving overhead. With a stern expression and arms folded, he appears before a mob of angry, violent men clenching their fists and brandishing weapons. The vitriol of Louisianans toward Union occupation still resonated three decades after the end of the Civil War. Library of Congress Prints and Photographs Division, Washington, D.C.

Republicans did not shy from the label. Horace White of the Chicago *Tribune* embraced it, writing Illinois Senator Lyman Trumball: "We live in Revolutionary times and I say God bless the revolution." Bostonian Charles Francis Adams, grandson of patriot and President John Adams and son of Secretary of State and President John Quincy Adams, confided in his diary. "The great revolution has actually taken place," he gushed. "The country has once and for all thrown off the domination of Slaveholders."[5]

The actual mechanics of the emancipation revolution proved sloppy. During the summer of 1862, officers leading U.S. troops in occupied New Orleans recognized the need for some immediate national policy regarding the future of blacks in war zones. Although they had advanced past a status as mere "contraband," these people remained to be organized, clothed, fed, housed, and employed—in essence all of the actions once attended to by their masters. General J. W. Phelps believed the military could help and urged the commander of the Department of the Gulf, Major General Butler, to raise black regiments in the city. He wrote his commander on June 16, 1862, suggesting that not only would former slaves and free blacks be strategically useful, but also with the application of military discipline, "our slaves might be raised in the scale of civilization and prepared for freedom."

General Phelps believed Butler would agree but reiterated his point a month and a half later after receiving no response. Arming slaves would be good for the *entire* nation and the future of the race, Phelps argued. "Society in the South seems to be on the point of dissolution, and the best way of preventing the African in becoming instrumental in a general state of anarchy is to enlist him in the cause of the Republic." A large population of landless and unsophisticated laborers with no means of support might fall into brigandry otherwise with bloodshed and resentments that would echo through the generations. The U.S. army needed to secure the reigns of this runaway social experiment or the nation would suffer the consequences. "If we reject his service, any petty . . . chieftain, by offering him freedom, can have them for the purpose of robbery and plunder. It is for the interest of the South, as well as for the North, that the African should be permitted to offer his block for the temple of freedom."[6]

The exchange sparked a verbal dual between Phelps and Butler. Although Butler ordered his subordinate to turn away all unemployed persons, regardless of race, from his camp and to quit pressing the issue of arming slaves in Louisiana, Phelps merely established a refugee camp nearby and siphoned off government rations to keep the newcomers fed. Using the pretext of the recently passed Militia Act, Phelps organized a battalion from among the men gathering there. When he sent a letter to the garrison quartermaster asking for uniforms and equipment, Butler ordered that officer to dodge the request, being neither willing to admit blacks into the army—with the accompanying political cost both locally and in Washington—nor turn them away and invite the rancor of the more radical abolitionists. He ordered Phelps to put the men to work felling trees and cording firewood. "I shall have trouble with Phelps," Butler confided to his wife in early August. "He is mad as a March Hare on the 'nigger question.' My respect for him will lead me to treat him very tenderly but firmly." Phelps, not satisfied with Butler's answer and pressing the issue to the point of insubordination, resigned and returned to his farm in Brattleboro, Vermont.[7]

The protean Butler changed his mind within days. In August 1862, when Rebels attacked Baton Rouge, Butler abandoned this forward position in Louisiana and recalled his troops to the defense of New Orleans. He prepared to meet any enemy advance with an army reinforced by black regiments, just as Phelps had suggested. Amid rumors of renewed Confederate offensives and an advance on the Crescent City, Butler remained steady. "If it becomes at all imminent, I shall call upon Africa to intervene, and I do not think I shall call in vain."[8]

Butler had the Louisiana Native Guards in mind. Two militia regiments of free blacks had existed in New Orleans before the war, but the units had largely collapsed after secession. Butler reconstituted them as a way of dodging opposition to raising black regiments, but he also added newly liberated slaves to their shriveled numbers. Even so, he maintained most of their black officers and the regiments ballooned. Within weeks he raised a third regiment of Louisiana Native Guards from the overflow of recruits.[9]

New Orleans and the surrounding region soon became crowded with black refugees. They overwhelmed the system. Heat, disease, and poor sanitation began to carry away the young, the old, and the weak. Commissary officers watched their surplus rations vanish into contraband camps. Medical supplies ran low, as did tents and housing. Butler, unprepared for this influx, reported to Lincoln that Louisiana, indeed the whole nation, would have to endure a period of unpleasant chaos. "We have some ten thousand negroes to feed, besides those at work on the plantations, principally women and children," Butler explained. "All of this has thus far been without any draft upon the treasury, although how much longer we can go on is a problem of which I am now anxiously seeking a solution." Butler's "problem" grew more acute: Southern planters within his lines threatened to quit raising crops, which threw even more blacks onto the mercy of the Federal government.[10]

In mid-September 1862, radical voices in the government of the United States began to bugle for an even harsher and uncompromising stance against the secessionists. Having promised to do so with the passage of the Second Confiscation Act, President Lincoln issued the Preliminary Emancipation Proclamation. If the Confederacy did not capitulate by January (which, of course, they would not), all slaves in areas still in rebellion would be forever free—*free*, that is, to run into Union lines. This pronouncement, in reality an echo of previous legislation,

New York artist Francis Bicknell Carpenter lived in the White House for six months in 1864 while working on this painting. The result, unveiled in 1866, shows a reenactment of Abraham Lincoln signing the Emancipation Proclamation on July 22, 1862. Depicted, from left to right are: Edwin M. Stanton, Secretary of War; Salmon P. Chase, Secretary of the Treasury; President Lincoln; Gideon Welles, Secretary of the Navy; Caleb B. Smith, Secretary of the Interior; William H. Seward, Secretary of State; Montgomery Blair, Postmaster General; and Edward Bates, Attorney General. Former Secretary of War, Simon Cameron, and President Andrew Jackson are featured as paintings on the wall. Library of Congress Prints and Photographs Division, Washington, D.C.

unfastened the foundations of American black slavery forever. The War of the Rebellion had reached a point of no return. Any slaves arriving in Union lines could never once again lose their freedom. These liberated persons would become wards of the state and put to uses in harmony with the further suppression of the Southern rebellion. It remained to the Union armies to bring more and more Rebel territory under national control and with it, more emancipated slaves.

A month later, President Lincoln received a visitor. General Daniel Ullmann, a New Yorker and veteran of the Army of the Potomac just released from Libby Prison in Richmond, urged the chief executive to take the next step beyond mere emancipation. "To arm Blacks was the most direct way to crush the rebellion," Ullmann urged. It was also, he believed, "the surest path to the extinction of slavery" and that "it was clearly within the war power." Besides, the New Yorker added, it made good financial sense. "It was a mode of greatly reducing the expenses of the

Daniel Ullman was one of the architects of raising an army of liberated slaves to help conquer and hold Louisiana.
Library of Congress Prints and Photographs Division, Washington, D.C.

Godfrey Weitzel, a Cincinnati German engineer, tangled with the Confederates in southern Louisiana more than any other officer in the Union army.
Library of Congress Prints and Photographs Division, Washington, D.C.

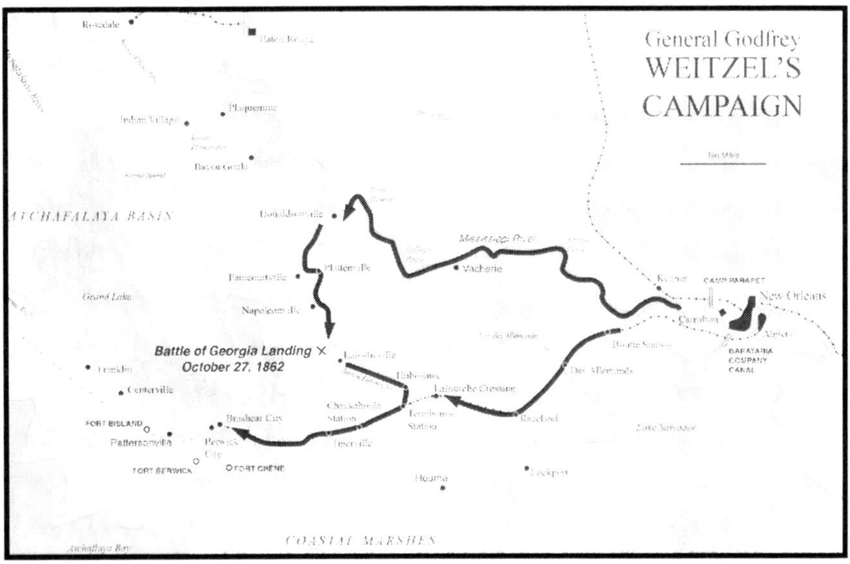

Personally courageous and cool under fire, Confederate Brigadier General Alfred Mouton failed to keep the Federals from overrunning the Lafourche country in 1862 and fell back to the Bayou Teche region. In 1863, Major General Richard Taylor, his superior, lost confidence in Mouton as a strategic thinker.
Photo courtesy of the Acadian Museum, Erath, Louisiana.

war, especially as now it was difficult to raise troops, except by a draft or by offering ruinous bounties." He believed the United States could raise an army of between two and four hundred thousand men without the cost of inducements. They merely needed to be *gathered.* Lincoln listened to him pitch his idea but interrupted. "Ullmann, would you be willing to command Black soldiers?" The president asked. After slight hesitation, the general insisted he would consider it his duty as a soldier. "Well, well," Lincoln mused, "it would have to wait until after the proclamation."[11]

In fall 1862, the contest to control territory took on greater significance. Control of the Mississippi Valley, and with it, the conquest of a region crowded with slaves became a Federal priority. When the rebels assumed the defensive at Port Hudson, Butler ordered his army into active operations on the West Bank of the Mississippi and into the slave-rich interior of Louisiana. This October offensive, led by Brigadier General Godfrey Weitzel, swept a small force of Confederate troops and local militia under the command of Brigadier General Alfred Mouton out of most of the Sugar Parishes. The prizes of this campaign included a territory of large plantations and dense populations of enslaved people. The black 1st and 2nd Louisiana Native Guards were among these U.S. columns invading the region, which was a military reality well in advance of national policy.

Slaves naturally swarmed every movement of the Union army. At Brashear City, the Confederates abandoned some four hundred wagonloads of black

General Godfrey Weitzel is portrayed in this editorial cartoon as the hapless winner of an elephant raffle. "The Question is, what am I to do with the creature?" he asks. The liberation of slaves, an outcome pursued and welcomed by the Lincoln administration, posed many challenges to military commanders in the field.
American Antiquarian Society, Worchester, Massachusetts.

laborers they had attempted to move beyond Union control. These liberated blacks now turned to Weitzel and his command for succor. Federal officials had to feed, house, and employ this self-emancipated throng. Reports arrived at Weitzel's Thibodaux headquarters of rampant and predatory plundering by this ever-growing mass of refugees. This chaos retarded what had been the lightening successes of the army. It also again raised the larger issues of slavery, war, and reconstruction in Louisiana. How far should the army go in remaking the South? Lincoln might wait until January to issue the official Emancipation Proclamation, but for U.S. troops between Bayou Lafourche and the Atchafalaya, the question

This engraving in a popular newspaper was among the first images Americans saw that portrayed black soldiers.
Frank Leslie's Illustrated Newspaper, March 7, 1863.

stared at them from a thousand eyes that October.[12]

"Now, what should I do with them?" Weitzel wrote to Major George S. Strong, General Butler's assistant adjutant-general and chief of staff. Weitzel's frustration bled through every page of his dispatch. "I already have twice as many negroes in and around my camp as I have soldiers within." The United States, in its haste to capture this slave-rich region, had no definite policy on how to deal with the inevitable multitude of liberated people who would hail the arrival of the Union troops as the "Year of Jubilo." Once these workers left the plantations and lived outside of the Southern labor system, they naturally turned to the government to supply their needs. "I cannot feed them," Weitzel wrote, mindful of the rations needed to sustain his army. "As a consequence, they must feed themselves."[13]

With no means of support, this meant theft, scavenging, and the concomitant unsettling of the white population. To slaves tasting the first sweetness of liberty, there was no such thing as loyal or rebel slave owners. There were only former masters, and there was only vengeance. "The community, of whom already quite a number have taken the oath of allegiance, is in great terror," Weitzel reported. This frightened populace came to the headquarters in turn hoping for some same-race sympathy and begged for weapons to defend their homes. The beleaguered general, now deep in enemy territory, remained unenthusiastic about this suggestion.[14]

Neither did he agree with the national drift toward arming former slaves. He believed it would engender a long-term race war and servile insurrection.

The presence of the Louisiana Native Guard in the Lafourche District proved disruptive and distasteful. "I cannot command those negro regiments," Weitzel carped. "The commanding general knows well my private opinions on this subject. What I stated to him privately, while on his staff, I now see before my eyes." To this German-American engineer, the sight of black troops only emboldened the masses of displaced slaves. Once they had seen men like themselves, armed and participating in the fight, these former hands would never be content to go back to their fields. For the first time, they felt empowered.

"Since the arrival of the negro regiments symptoms of servile insurrection are becoming apparent," Weitzel warned. He could not police the entire region without scattering his command. Was he to defeat the Rebels or become a new master? Black troops, he argued, were a bad influence. "I cannot assume the command of such a force, and thus be responsible for its conduct. Its moral effect in this community . . . is terrible." He noted the defenseless nature of the population. "Woman and children, and even men, are in terror. It is heart rending, and I cannot make myself responsible for it."[15]

Weitzel's regiments agreed. "They keep the jail full most of the time with a motley group interspersed with negro soldiers of whose behavior there are endless complaints of burning, stealings, ravishings and lesser crimes," wrote Lieutenant Dana W. King of the 8th New Hampshire Infantry. "They are termed 'The Louisiana Native Guards,' ostensibly freedmen of color, but we know that slaves are in their midst." Certainly, the officer reasoned, Union leaders would soon "disband them or put them under iron rule, or [use them] to garrison some fort away from civilization."[16]

Back in New Orleans, neither Benjamin Butler nor his chief of staff shared these concerns. The Union forces, whether white or black, were not to blame for the dangers facing the civilians in Weitzel's jurisdiction. "The responsibility rests upon those who have begun and carried on this war," Major Strong lectured. It was not the passage of black troops that had upset this social order but secession. "Does not this state of things arise from the very fact of war itself?" Major Strong queried. "Did you expect to march into that country, drained as you say it is by conscription of all its able-bodied white men without leaving the negroes to show symptoms of servile insurrection? You are in a country where now the negroes outnumber the whites ten to one. Upon reflection, can you doubt that the same

As General Benjamin Butler's chief-of-staff, Major George C. Strong cared little for the consternation of Louisiana's white population when it came to fear of liberated slaves. He embraced this terror as being good for the Federal cause.
Library of Congress Prints and Photographs Division, Washington, D.C.

state of things would have arisen without the presence of a colored regiment?"[17]

Strong even had a specific case in mind that illustrated his impatience with Weitzel's squeamishness. Near Thibodaux, Union troops confiscated Bivouac, the home and estate of the Confederate commander of the Army of Tennessee. "General Bragg is at liberty to ravage the homes of our brethren of Kentucky because the Union army of Louisiana is protecting his wife and his home against his negroes," Strong snorted. "Without that protection, he would have to come back to take care of his wife, his home, and," he added, "his negroes."[18]

Weitzel's superiors urged him to revisit the conclusions he had drawn from the scenes he had witnessed. "You say that there have appeared before your eyes the very facts, in terror-stricken women, children, and men which you had before [only] contemplated in theory. Grant it," wrote Strong, "but is not the remedy to be found in the surrender of the neighbors, fathers, brothers, and sons of the terror-stricken women and children, who are now in arms against the Government within 20 miles of you?" Once these Rebels surrendered and returned peacefully to their homes, he argued sarcastically, "you will be able to use the full power of your troops to insure their safety from the so-much-feared . . . servile insurrection." If the Confederates refused to yield, Strong warned, "whatever may ensue is upon them, and not upon you or upon the United States. You will have done all that is required of a brave, humane man to avert from these deluded people horrible consequences of their insane war upon the Government."[19]

Safe at headquarters, Butler and his staff seemed baffled. Why should the plight of these inhabitants impact Weitzel's military operations in the region? Strong, for one, saw the social disorder as something to be desired. "When was it ever heard before," Major Strong continued, "that a victorious general, in an unsurrendered province, stopped in his course for the purpose of preventing the rebellious inhabitants of that province from destroying each other?" He considered Weitzel's compassion misguided, and terror a Union ally. "As a military question, perhaps the more terror-stricken the inhabitants are that are left in your rear the more safe will be your lines of communications." At the urging of Butler, Strong ordered the field commander to continue his active campaigning and to ignore the social issues churning in the wake of the army. "I do not see how you can turn away from an armed enemy before you to protect and defend the wives and children of those armed enemies from the consequences of their own rebellious wickedness."[20]

This said, Butler instructed Major Strong to provide Weitzel with a policy for dealing long term with the issue. "Of course there will be no more difficult subject for you to deal with than the negroes," the chief-of-staff wrote, his tone softening. Congress had already declared that slaves fleeing Rebel masters were free once they arrived within Union lines; after January 1, 1863, all slaves in unconquered Rebel territory were free to come and go as they pleased. "But the question recurs," Strong mused, "'What shall we do with them?'" Butler's solution, as expressed by Strong, was simple: Put them back to work. "It is our duty to take care of them, and that can include employment. Put them as far as possible upon plantations; use every energy to have the sugar crop made and preserved for the owners that are loyal," he advised, "and I do not mean by loyalty [mere] lip service." After the initial rush of freedom, these former field hands would be heading back to the fields.[21]

Weitzel's experience, and Butler's solution, illustrated a growing need for some fashion of national policy regarding freed slaves. General Butler wrote Major General Henry Halleck, General-in-Chief of U.S. forces, urging some sort of ruling. "General Weitzel brings up the interesting question of the war," Butler wrote. "The President and yourself are aware that I am wholly without guide on this matter." In fact, Butler was making his own policy in south Louisiana based on the immediate local needs. He had written to his government requesting a ruling.

General-in-Chief Henry Halleck had to interpret the vision of President Abraham Lincoln and Secretary of War Edwin M. Stanton and see that his officers on distant battlefields carried them to fruition. This often led to contradictory and confusing orders.
Library of Congress Prints and Photographs Division, Washington, D.C.

Halleck responded with silence. Without an answer, Butler had already decided on his own to arm blacks. "No communication disapproving of that organization has been received, I must therefore take it to be approved."[22]

Although the Lincoln administration urged freedom for all slaves, it clearly had not established mechanisms and policies with which to actually deal with the processes—and consequences—of instant emancipation. In this vacuum, local commanders like Butler improvised. During the six months that U.S. troops had occupied New Orleans, local planters south and east of the city found themselves behind Union lines and abandoned by their slaves. Most signed the oath of loyalty and then promptly petitioned Butler for help in recovering their human property. To address these needs, Butler negotiated an accord between planters and their former chattel that established a system of wage labor, including rules regulating length of workweek, wages paid, and restrictions on punishments. Military provost marshals augmented by civilian and military patrols regulated the arrangement and responded when insubordination or agitation warranted corrective measures. Butler ordered this system adapted to the conditions of the conquered Lafourche Country.[23]

Butler remained pragmatic and optimistic. He wrote Lincoln, "it cannot be supposed that this great change in a social and political system can be made without shock, and I am only surprised . . . that it can be made at all. Slavery is doomed. I have no doubt of it." He would have preferred a more systematic process of gradual emancipation, but competent military authorities could still handle the sudden collapse of slavery.[24]

Weitzel, instead of finishing off Mouton's Confederates and pursuing them deeper into Louisiana, stopped his advance at Brashear City, built fortifications, and spent his energy and that of his army reorganizing the labor system in the conquered Lafourche Country. "Let the planters make arrangements to pay their negroes $10 a month for able-bodied men," Major Strong advised Weitzel, "$3 to be expended in clothing, and so in proportion."[25] Sergeant George Smith, a Union soldier in the 1st Louisiana Infantry at Donaldsonville, reported that the former slaves were returning to work, and their employers were paying and feeding them. "This was a nice arrangement," he added, "and opened the way for self-support to thousands that otherwise would be an expense to the government."[26]

There remained, however, the additional question of what to do with the plantations that the government declared abandoned by their secessionist owners, as well as those seized by force. The Treasury Department, authorized by the Second Confiscation Act, brokered this real estate to leasing and finance agents who located tenants interested in operating the farms on behalf of the United States. These contractors would have access to black labor to bring in and sell the crops to government-approved agents and ship them to government-supervised warehouses, thus reviving the plantation economy.[27]

Butler's plan promised to yield multiple benefits. After establishing a tense but workable accord between landowner and laborer, the fields of the Lafourche region would once again be productive. Produce useful to the Union war effort would funnel out of the region and through New Orleans to market. Freed slaves would be settled. Abolitionists would have a missionary undertaking by which they could test their theories about a black wage labor system in the South, and the proceeds of the sale of commodities would help finance the entire operation. All told, there were fifty to sixty thousand former slaves in the Lafourche District who formed the backbone of this arrangement.

Observers believed that this new order would sweeten support for the Union cause. "This sugar would contribute to friendly relations between the people and their true government," trumpeted a writer for the New Orleans *Delta*, now under Union management. "It serves to make loyal men out of planters who can bring their produce to New Orleans, obtain unprecedentedly high prices, in good money, and purchase in return there for such goods as they need for their families at low prices." This ability to sell and buy would keep these Louisianans peaceful. "If the Confederates can not stop this trade," the writer predicted, "their cause will be damaged in the Lafourche country."[28]

The key, then, was to prevent the Rebels from disrupting the new order. Militarily, Butler organized the conquered region into the Lafourche District of the Department of the Gulf with Weitzel in command. Butler's staff directed Weitzel to construct stout earthworks at Donaldsonville and Brashear City; these two points guarded the most likely invasion routes. Butler next ordered civilian employees put back on the job to rebuild the railroad from New Orleans to Brashear City and keep this vital supply link open. Weitzel tried to refuse the command of the Lafourche District to protest the presence of black troops. His superiors ignored him. "The commanding general does not doubt that everything that prudence, sagacity, skill, and courage can do will be done by you, general," Strong wrote, "to prosecute the campaign you have so successfully begun."[29]

At Donaldsonville, scores of soldiers and liberated slaves commenced the creation of Fort Butler across Bayou Lafourche from the city. Lieutenant John C. Palfrey, a West Point–trained engineer with family ties to the region, arrived to design the redoubt. Soon, white soldiers of the 1st Louisiana Infantry (Union) lay down their spades and picked up their rifles, leaving the task to an army of black laborers earning government wages to raise the ramparts.[30]

Weitzel transformed the ambitiously named hamlet of Brashear City into a fortified depot and base for future operations. Workers attacked the mud of Tiger Island to build a line of redoubts stretching from the north shore bordering Grand Lake, along the margins of Berwick Bay, and ending in a stout star-shaped fortification that covered the town and approaches by sea from the Gulf of Mexico. There were bastions along the railroad, as well. New earthworks marked the crossing of the tracks at Bayou Ramos a few miles behind Brashear and at the trestle spanning Bayou Beouf connecting Tiger Island with the rest of the Lafourche District. This outpost, surrounded by swamps, bayous, and river, and connected to New Orleans by rail and water, became the most important Union stronghold in southern Louisiana.

While Weitzel built forts in Louisiana, the U.S. Navy captured Galveston, Texas, against surprisingly light opposition. "Patriotism was high in Texas," sneered Marine Private Henry O. Gusley aboard the USS *Westfield*, which was anchored off the docks of the largest city in the Lone Star State. "Most decidedly they do not love the Yankees as well as they professed they did in '46." Delighted, Butler asked Weitzel to spare some of his troops for occupation duty in Texas.[31]

Texas Unionists would certainly rally to the national flag and reassert Federal control there. The problem, though, was that many had fled to Mexico. "It will be improper to enlist even Americans as soldiers on Mexican soil," Butler wrote to U.S. Consul Leonard Pierce, Jr. Instead, he should transport them to New Orleans to join the army. "There can be no impropriety," Butler added, "in sending Americans to do their duty to their country." These loyal Texans might form the nucleus for a Union army at Galveston.[32]

Butler saw Texas as his next priority. He wanted to drive hard into the state, capturing the Confederacy's "beef barrel." He asked for reinforcements but was particular about the soldiers he wanted. "Please therefore send me New England troops. The newspapers assure me that there are thousands waiting in Massachusetts," he wrote. These right-thinking Yankees would be just the sorts to drag Texas back into the Union.[33]

Butler organized his expanding fiefdom. In the Lafourche District, speculators swarmed in, and playing on the locals' fears of government confiscation, offered to buy crops and properties at deep discounts to keep them from being forfeit to the Federal government. Huge profits followed these speculators, and some of this money became bribes paid to local military officers so that army transportation and equipment might move tons of sugar to eager investors. Butler claimed a desire to combat these opportunists and issued General Order No. 91 on November 9, which effectively placed a government lien on anything of value held by residents in the Lafourche District. "Property," he wrote, "was taken away from individuals, and held by the Government to be returned according to the loyalty or disloyalty of the owners." In short, he as the Federal commander in the Department of the Gulf would be the arbiter of all aspects of life, from the redistribution of property to the allocation of labor. Although his scheme would benefit some, it would ruin others. Butler would decide.[34]

The Lincoln administration, growing cold to Butler's shenanigans, secretly removed him from command. Although the scrappy Massachusetts general had returned a portion of Louisiana to Union control and established some sort of

Secretary of War Edwin M. Stanton had to balance the goals of his president, Abraham Lincoln, with the realities on the battlefield.
Library of Congress Prints and Photographs Division, Washington, D.C.

One-time governor of Massachusetts and Speaker of the U.S. House of Representatives, Nathaniel P. Banks went to Louisiana intending to burnish his political credentials with an eye toward the White House. Instead, he found himself building on the successes of General Benjamin Butler while trying to interpret the often contradictory directives of the Federal government.
Library of Congress Prints and Photographs Division, Washington, D.C.

law and order, he had also proven obnoxious to his superiors. Secretary of War Edwin M. Stanton considered his continued tenure as potentate of the Department of the Gulf to be counterproductive. In short, officials sacked Butler because of the persistent whiff of cronyism and corruption, but also in part because of his success—and speed—at implementing sweeping changes to race, class, labor, and military policies ahead of Lincoln's timetable. The War Department tapped another Massachusetts general, Nathaniel P. Banks, to take an army to New Orleans, replace Butler, and expand on his system.

The growing population of liberated and displaced people presented both problems and opportunities for Federal authorities in Louisiana. Public works received attention and muscle under the new regime.
Frank Leslie's Illustrated Newspaper, May 9, 1863.

On December 8, 1862, Lincoln offered up another executive order. To some, it seemed a last ditch effort at an amicable peace with the secessionists. In reality, this ploy attempted to sidestep the dodgy proposition that Southern states might abolish slavery on their own or support such an amendment to the U.S. Constitution. His *Proclamation of Amnesty and Reconstruction* allowed states to rebuild Unionist governments providing they could prove that 10 percent of the voting population from 1860 had taken the oath of loyalty to the United States—*and also outlawed slavery*. In exchange, officials would return confiscated property and states could determine their own racial policies, providing they did not compromise the freedoms held by newly liberated slaves.

Louisiana, without the nettlesome Butler, might still be the best place to try such a plan. General Banks, Lincoln's personal pick as Butler's successor, arrived at the head of a thirty thousand-man army in mid-December 1862. Most of his troops had committed to only nine months of service, which put his efforts on an

As president of the Confederate States of America, Jefferson Davis presided over a nation that enshrined slavery in its constitution.
Library of Congress Prints and Photographs Division, Washington, D.C.

accelerated pace and signaled a growing confidence that the war might soon end. Upon arriving, Banks discovered a region pacified under Union control, a black population that had settled into new routines after the bewildering spasms of spontaneous emancipation, and conditions generally in order. In terms of labor and economic policies, Banks simply picked up where Butler left off. Militarily, his orders directed him to expand on the successes of the previous few months and bring vast slave populations under Union control.

The Federal reshaping of the human landscape of southern Louisiana infuriated Confederate officials. On Christmas Eve, 1862, President Jefferson Davis issued a proclamation of his own, which declared Butler and his officers war criminals. The former Union commander of the Department of the Gulf was to be captured and immediately hanged "as an outlaw and common enemy of mankind." Davis's justifications included charges that Butler meted out harsh treatment to political prisoners, committed outrages against non-combatants, tolerated graft and corruption, and inflicted cruelty to slaves by forcing them from the "only homes they had ever known." In addition, Davis proclaimed, "the African slaves have not only been excited to insurrection by every license and encouragement but numbers of them have actually been armed for a servile war."[35]

Even if unappreciated, the efforts of men like Butler allowed the Lincoln administration to reframe the quarrel more to its liking. Abolitionists applauded the advancement of their cause—the destruction of slavery—and the remaking of the South. Politicians, pushed by this momentum, allowed the original constitutional questions of the war to soften into an ambient noise; success on the battlefield would provide those answers in the end. In the meantime the armies of the United

BATTLE HYMN OF THE REPUBLIC.

BY MRS. JULIA WARD HOWE.

Mine eyes have seen the glory of the coming of the Lord:
He is trampling out the vintage where the grapes of wrath are stored;
He hath loosed the fateful lightnings of His terrible swift sword:
His truth is marching on.
CHORUS—Glory, glory, hallelujah!
Glory, glory, hallelujah!
Glory, glory, hallelujah!
His truth is marching on.

I have seen Him in the watch-fires of a hundred circling camps;
They have builded Him an altar in the evening dews and damps:
I can read His righteous sentence by the dim and flaring lamps:
His day is marching on.
CHORUS—Glory, glory, hallelujah, &c.
His day is marching on.

I have read a fiery gospel writ in burnished rows of steel:
"As ye deal with my contemners, so with you my grace shall deal;
Let the Hero, born of woman, crush the serpent with his heel,
Since God is marching on."
CHORUS—Glory, glory, hallelujah &c.
Since God is marching on.

He has sounded forth the trumpet that shall never call retreat:
He is sifting out the hearts of men before His judgment seat:
Oh, be swift, my soul, to answer Him! be jubilant my feet!
Our God is marching on!
CHORUS—Glory, glory, hallelujah, &c.
Our God is marching on!

In the beauty of the lilies Christ was born across the sea,
With a glory in His bosom that transfigures you and me;
As he died to make men holy, let us die to make men free,
While God is marching on.

An abolitionist anthem, "The Battle Hymn of the Republic" framed the Civil War in apocalyptic terms and glorified retribution. Southerners bore the sin of slavery and would receive their divine punishment.
Library of Congress Prints and Photographs Division, Washington, D.C.

This image from 1863 portrays a woman (Columbia) holding a document (perhaps the Emancipation Proclamation) standing between two kneeling slaves. The slave to her left, a man, holds a U.S. flag, and the slave to her right, a woman, is draped in the U.S. flag. Images such as this supported the national shift toward the liberation of the slaves as a worthy, almost holy, Union war aim.
Library of Congress Prints and Photographs Division, Washington, D.C.

States might transform—some said, reconstruct—the nation anew.

In this vein, Unitarian preachers, abolitionist crusaders, and evangelical devines viewed the war in apocalyptic terms. Borrowing images from the *Bible*, and especially Revelation 19, Julia Ward Howe's "Battle Hymn of the Republic" became a national anthem, and crowds enthusiastically warbled about terrible swift swords, of trampling the vintage from the grapes of wrath, of crushing the serpent with their heels, and of trumpets never calling retreat. To the delight of radicals in the North and abolitionists everywhere, the complete destruction of slavery—that foundation of rebellion and perceived Southern decadence—became the *national* aim, not merely the aim of Republican politicians.

These righteous warriors also recognized the serpents that guarded these bitter vines. Confederates—perhaps all Southerners—must be crushed like a rattlesnake beneath a boot heel wherever found. Everyone from President Davis to the humblest Rebel private carried the guilt stain of an unholy war to perpetuate slavery. They were minions of the antichrist. Once evoked, biblical imagery doomed any hope of peaceful national reconciliation. The only way for Southerners to avoid being recast as second-class citizens and permanent villains in United States history was to win the war.

On January 1, 1863—the exact day the Emancipation Proclamation went into effect—a shift in the tides of war on the Texas coast offered the first serious check

The Confederate recapture of Galveston, Texas, resuscitated the secessionist cause west of the Mississippi. The removal of the Union threat to the western Gulf of Mexico allowed Rebel authorities to reinforce Louisiana. The USS Harriet Lane *is shown in the center, under attack by the Confederate gunboats* Neptune *and* Bayou City. *The USS* Westfield *is at the far left, being blown up to prevent its capture.*
The Soldier in our Civil War, *Volume II.*

to Union ambitions in the western Gulf of Mexico. In this remote corner of the war, Confederate forces led by an obscure Texas colonel named Tom Green struck back—viper like—and recaptured Galveston from Federal forces. With Texas now clear of Union forces, Confederate General Richard Taylor ordered these victorious Rebels to join him in Louisiana. There, they would strike again.

2

Emancipation

I thinks it great to be with the Yankees, but I wishes I hadn't after I got there.
—John Ogee, *Corps d'Afrique*

On January 29, 1863, Massachusetts Senator Charles Sumner of Boston held forth to his colleagues concerning the recently issued Emancipation Proclamation. The time had come to take the next step, he declared. The U.S. army should enlist liberated slaves to fight against their former masters. Some in the audience believed this measure—a common wartime practice throughout world history—seemed in opposition to U.S. law. Sumner blasted back: "Slavery is the stronghold of the rebellion, therefore emancipation is a war measure, as constitutional as the raising of armies or the occupation of a hostile territory." His speech echoed across the country. Officers in every Union military department and command from Virginia and the Carolinas to Kentucky and Louisiana saw changes coming. President Abraham Lincoln desired it, and officers braced themselves to accept black troops into their armies.[1]

In New York City, General Daniel Ullmann heard that Lincoln would authorize the raising of black regiments. He enthusiastically accepted a commission to recruit black soldiers in the lower Mississippi Valley and sailed to New Orleans, eager to be part of history. "The first gun that was fired at Fort Sumter sounded the death-knell of slavery," the New York officer observed. "They who fired it were the greatest practical abolitionists this nation has produced."[2]

Many Southerners also conceded the inevitability of liberty for the nation's four million enslaved people. Louisianan sugar planter and Confederate congressman Duncan Kenner urged Confederate Secretary of State Judah P. Benjamin and President Jefferson Davis to trade freedom to its enslaved men in exchange for military service, arguing that independence was dearer than protecting the institution of slavery. His attempt to beat the Yankees at their own game gained no traction. Other Southerners maneuvered for peace and reunion based on gradual, and compensated, emancipation, but found few backers for the scheme in the

North. A few months later, Louisiana financier Martin Gordon reported that, based on his observations across the South, "all agree that slavery is to be ultimately destroyed, as the first result of the war." Still, Confederate officials refused to liberate, much less arm, slaves. "If adopted," Gordon cautioned, "it is likely to be rather for local defense, than for general purposes of war."[3]

The Federal government had no such qualms. At his headquarters in Washington D.C., Union General-in-Chief Henry Halleck nervously observed this shift. He heard the talk in the halls of the War Department, in the gathering places of the national capital, and also read the scrawled missives of a hundred different voices that described a new war—a different war—than he had helped manage to this point. National currents now swept him toward uncharted shores.

Conservative by nature, and a Democrat, Halleck had once been master of the U.S. science of war. The Lincoln administration had credited him with saving the Union the previous July. As a respected strategic theorist, Halleck's western armies drove the Rebels from Missouri, Arkansas, and Tennessee; had captured their depot at Corinth, Mississippi; and had nearly collapsed Southern fortunes in the West. After other Federal commanders had failed in Virginia, Lincoln brought Halleck to the capital hoping to bring his bookish and calculating genius to bear against the crisis and panic in Washington. Halleck now commanded *all* of the nation's armies.

He did so with characteristic caution. The General-in-Chief operated as a prudent protégé of venerable and aged General Winfield Scott might. Like his mentor, Halleck believed the South could be knocked to its senses using methods that, although painful, fell short of the societal homicide that Radicals craved. Even so, Halleck merely led the nation's armies; he could not command its political mood.

Despite his reservations, Halleck understood where the task of raising black regiments must commence and have its greatest success. The general's thoughts once again returned to the Mississippi Valley. General Ulysses S. Grant, whom Halleck had always distrusted, remained bogged down on the Louisiana shore north of Vicksburg, Mississippi, with some forty thousand men. Despite several attempts to approach the Southern fortress through conventional means, the U.S. army remained inert and encamped amid a tangle of bayous, gumbo mud, levees, and cotton fields. On the opposite shore, thirty thousand Rebels under General John C. Pemberton waited—defiantly. Well to the south, General Nathaniel P.

Banks—a political general whom Halleck only tolerated—faced a similar dilemma in Baton Rouge. Banks seemed convinced that his force of thirty thousand mostly inexperienced troops would be inadequate to crack the citadel of Port Hudson and its garrison of fourteen thousand. Perhaps the addition of armed, liberated slaves (as many as one hundred thousand lived along the lower Mississippi River), would provide the necessary strength to finish off these Rebel strongholds.

These Union armies sat poised like the jaws of a great vice. To economize their strengths, Halleck had ordered them to cooperate with each other. He envisioned a combined movement involving hundreds of gunboats and transports, tens of thousands of soldiers, and hundreds of thousands of horses and mules, first against one citadel—probably Vicksburg—and then the other. He urged caution on both of his commanders in that theater, and insisted that, together, this great army might carry one or the other of the Rebel positions, but probably not both simultaneously. Both Federal forces could take their time and supplement their numbers with black recruits.

At that particular moment, militarizing the black population seemed more important than quick conquests. Halleck wrote Grant, whom he considered to be capable, but intemperate and cloddish: "The character of this war has very much changed within the last year. There is now no hope of reconciliation with the rebels. The Union party in the South is virtually destroyed." Circumstances had forced Halleck to contradict his own theories, and he knew Grant, blunt and pugnacious, would take some delight in his boss's discomfort. "There can be no peace but that which is forced by the sword. We must conquer the rebels or be conquered by them." The Lincoln administration believed arming slaves to be the surest path to victory, Halleck explained.[4]

Halleck resigned himself to this distasteful task. "This is the phase which the rebellion has now assumed," he explained. "We must take things as they are. The Government, looking at the subject in all its aspects, has adopted a policy, and we must cheerfully and faithfully carry out that policy." The time for finesse and stratagem, which Halleck preferred, had passed; the age of societal war had arrived. Slavery must be broken by every available means. Militarily, capturing the Mississippi would split the Confederacy, but the end of slavery would sunder the connective fiber linking the South's economy, society, and might. Union planners would spool this manpower resource on a Union spindle, allowing the

This political cartoon captures the plight of slaves in the United States during the Civil War. Uncle Sam argues with a woman (the metaphorical Confederacy) in a violent domestic dispute while a slave on the right tiptoes by the couple hoping to escape notice and avoid being drawn into the fight. Uncle Sam holds a newspaper marked "united," and the woman has a newspaper behind her back marked "states."
Library of Congress Prints and Photographs Division, Washington, D.C.

various parts of the experimental Confederate nation to unravel. Slaves, once mere symbols for to the majority of antebellum Americans, now become instruments of, and the *raison d'*être, for the war.[5]

Doubting Grant's mental acuity, Halleck explained this new landscape in the simplest terms. "It is the policy of the government to withdraw from the enemy as much productive labor as possible," he wrote. "So long as the rebels maintain and employ their slaves . . . they can employ all whites in the field." The men in Washington believed that slavery, nearly alone, buttressed the rebellion. Destroy slavery, destroy the Confederacy. Slave labor fed Rebel armies, built their forts, and sustained their cause. "Every slave withdrawn from the enemy," Halleck continued, "is equivalent to a white put *hors de combat*." Because slaves fueled the Southern insurgency, they could just as easily drive Union war engines. "They can be used to hold points on the Mississippi during the sickly season," Halleck suggested, and "it will afford much relief to our armies." What the white soldiers bought with bullet and bayonet, the new black army of occupation

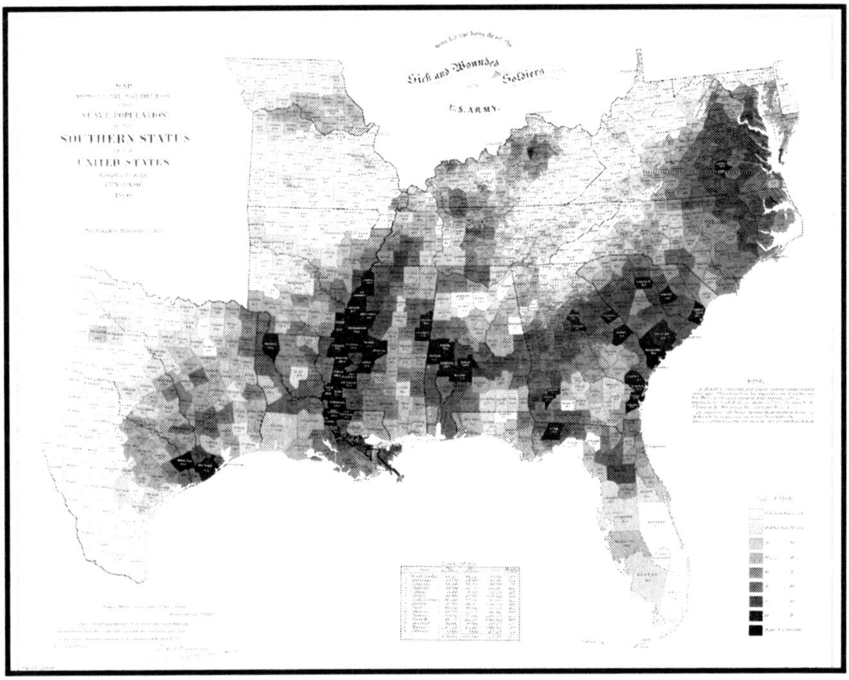

Federal planners consulted this map when planning the strategy to forcibly remove slaves from bondage. Compiled from census returns, it clearly shows the largest concentrations of enslaved people to live along the lower Mississippi. This reality in part dictated Union strategy in the region.

E. Hergensheimer, Map showing the distribution of the slave population of the southern states and the United States, 1861. United State Coast Survey. Image courtesy of the National Oceanic and Atmospheric Administration.

would hold with patience and perspiration.[6] Halleck assured Grant that liberated slaves could make useful auxiliaries. "It is the opinion of many who have examined the question without passion or prejudice, that they can also be used as a military force," Halleck wrote. "It certainly is good policy to use them to the very best advantage we can. Like everything else, they may be made the instruments of good or evil; in the hands of the enemy they are used with much effect against us, in our hands we must try to use them with the best possible effect against the rebels."[7]

Halleck acknowledged the new political mood in Washington. Grant would ignore the shift at his own peril. Halleck's conclusion was, perhaps, somewhat disingenuous: "I write you this unofficial letter simply as a personal friend, and as a matter of friendly advice. From my position here, where I can survey the entire field, perhaps I may be better able to understand the tone of public opinion, and the intentions of the government, than you can by merely consulting the officers of your own army." Do not listen to the mutterings of your brigadiers and colonels, Halleck enjoined. Do as I say. "It is expected that you will . . . thoroughly carry out the policy now adopted and ordered by the Government," Halleck reiterated, repeating it still again. "That policy is to withdraw from use of the enemy all the slaves you can, and to employ those so withdrawn to the best possible advantage against the enemy."[8]

Halleck left nothing to interpretation. A week after he sent the letter, General Lorenzo Thomas, Adjutant General of the Federal Army, arrived at Grant's headquarters at Lake Providence, Louisiana. On April 8, 1863, Thomas addressed two divisions of this forty thousand-man army. "The Administration has determined to take from the rebels this source of supply—to take their Negros." One Union soldier remembered that "instead of being turned out of the Union lines he was to be taken in; and the black arms of iron and fingers of steel that had lifted the burdens and held the hoe for the Confederacy were to be converted to the service of the United States Government."[9]

Although Halleck had helped craft this new policy, Thomas arrived to talk about the practical processes of arming liberated slaves in the Mississippi Valley. He wanted to raise twenty regiments from black men who had already fled to the Union camps, supplementing them with laborers who had remained loyal to their masters in the area. Officers would press able men into the ranks. Officials would put women, children, and "men unfit for our military organization" back to work on government plantations for wages in the manner of the Department of the Gulf.

These emancipated people—groping their way through the twilight of slavery—would have no choice in the matter. The recently passed Conscription Act of March 3, 1863, applied. The army could draft blacks, as well as whites. As quickly as officers could form companies of black soldiers, mustering officers would enroll them in the army; as these companies took the field, commanders would combine them into numbered regiments as a formal unit. "Many unwilling negroes are conscripted into the ranks," sneered Henry T. Johns, a Massachusetts soldier. "I do not object to that."[10]

The recruitment of black regiments would reinvigorate the campaign to capture the Mississippi. "When I get regiments raised," Thomas exhorted, "you

This Harper's Weekly *image was an attempt to portray General Lorenzo Thomas addressing the throng of liberated slaves gathered around Major General Ulysses S. Grant's army on the Louisiana shore near Vicksburg. Clearly the artist had never been there. Most of the men of military age are depicted as already in uniform, whereas the women and children continue to mingle among them. This would soon change.* Author's collection.

may sweep out into the interior with impunity." Halleck wanted these black levees to secure supply lines and strategic positions. Then Grant and Banks could hunt down the Rebel armies. "Recollect, for every regiment of Blacks I raise, I raise a regiment of white to face the foe in the field."[11]

Union General John A. Logan fully understood. After General Thomas left, Logan addressed his division in more colorful terms. "You must hurt the Rebels in every way possible," he urged. "Shoot them with shot and shell and Minnie balls and cold steel, and, damn them, shoot them with niggers. Take their corn-raisers and women-protectors and fort-builders from them, and set them to stopping bullets for us, and the thing is done." His troops liked his tone. "From that day we heard but little against negro troops," confessed a soldier in the audience. Logan finished with a flourish. He declared the time had arrived to put "the one who is the innocent cause of this war, who has everything to gain or lose in this war, in

After the Emancipation Proclamation, U.S. policy in the Mississippi Valley turned to recruitment—by any means—of able-bodied black men for military service. This often overlooked family relationships and cast many women, children, and elderly people into uncertainty because their male protectors and providers disappeared into the ranks of the Federal army.
Author's collection, *Harper's Weekly*.

the front rank." For soldiers in Grant's army who had been hammering away at the rebellion for months and years, this seemed sensible—and welcomed.[12]

The notion played well back home, too. In Wheeling, West Virginia, the *Dailey Intelligencer* put the argument in blunt terms. "The war will use up a certain number of men, and we think white men are more valuable than black ones," an editorial postulated. "If any lives must be sacrificed let it be those of the least value to the country."[13]

Commanders in the field still voiced concerns. How effective would liberated slaves be as soldiers? Would they be worth the trouble? Would black regiments justify the expense and effort? Politicians hoped to find answers. General Benjamin Butler, still smarting from his sacking as commander of the Department of the Gulf, spoke bluntly to the Boston-based American Freedmen's Inquiry Commission. "They are good soldiers," Butler expounded, "precisely in proportion to their intelligence, like anybody else. If I was getting up a company of soldiers, I would like in the first place, the Senior Class of Harvard University." Barring

A veteran soldier, Lorenzo Thomas helped organize the Union armies. An ally of General Henry Halleck and an opponent to General Ulysses S. Grant and William Tecumseh Sherman, Thomas also sparred with Secretary of War Edwin M. Stanton. He received orders to organize recruitment of black soldiers in the Mississippi Valley in 1863, which many in Washington viewed as an appropriate form of exile.
Library of Congress Prints and Photographs Division, Washington, D.C.

General John A Logan, a fiery division commander in the Department of the Mississippi, brooked no sentimentality when it came to militarizing liberated slaves as a weapon against their former masters. Instead he saw it as a practical way to win the war.
Library of Congress Prints and Photographs Division, Washington, D.C.

that, he would settle for "intelligent Yankee farmers and mechanics; next, intelligent Irishmen; next, intelligent Germans." He would then enlist blacks according to their mental aptitude.[14]

Butler had other recommendations. He opposed pressing blacks into service and suggested only accepting volunteers. Federal authorities would clothe, feed, and educate them in lieu of pay. These eager recruits should also serve with black officers. "If a man is fit enough to be a soldier and fight for his country, if he is intelligent, enough, he is fit to be an officer," Butler explained. They would willingly enter the army if they could follow officers of their own choosing. Otherwise, he predicted, raising—and keeping—black troops in the ranks would prove more difficult than imagined. It might come off as another form of slavery.[15]

Liberated slaves had peculiarities, Butler explained, that challenged their employment as soldiers. They would "do as they are told," he assured. However, should their regiments break in combat, they would not flee like normal U.S. troops. Instead, "they are gregarious in fright," Butler testified. They did not bolt but rather clumped up. "The negroes have been accustomed to stand in a body against master and overseer; they segregate—they run to each other." These wads of frightened men could neither surrender nor rally and instead might simply die in place.[16]

By the spring of 1863, General Banks was ready to do his part in ushering in this new era of U.S. history. Lincoln had personally admonished the Massachusetts politician to clean up Louisiana, to keep New Orleans in Union hands, and to maintain his domain safe and secure as a reconstruction laboratory. Banks had done that, much to Halleck's delight. "If the experience of General Banks near New Orleans should be satisfactory," he wrote, "a much larger force will be organized during the coming summer."[17]

The president had a favor to ask. At the end of March 1863, Lincoln wrote Banks: "Daniel Ullmann, with a commission of a Brigadier General, and two or three hundred other gentlemen as officers, goes to your department and reports to you, for the purpose of raising a colored brigade. To now avail ourselves of this element of force is very important, if not indispensable. I therefore will thank you to help Gen. Ullman forward with his undertaking, as much, and as rapidly as you can; and also to carry the general object beyond his particular organization, if you find it practicable." Lincoln maintained a personal interest in the success of this progressive social experiment.[18]

The president's suggestion had practical military merit. The Confederates in the region threatened to renew active operations against Union occupation. Banks brought a large army to Louisiana composed mostly of nine-month regiments drawn from New England militias, the only ready reserve the Union had at the time. Banks had since declared himself powerless against the Rebel strength at Port Hudson and the terms of enlistment for his New Englanders would expire in mid-summer. By whatever means, a military breakthrough must occur on the Mississippi before these men returned home.

Thousands of liberated slaves like this man would cast aside their ragged field hand clothing in favor of a Union uniform.
Library of Congress Prints and Photographs Division, Washington, D.C.

This Louisianan, photographed in New Orleans, was among the tens of thousands displaced by the war and headed for a future arranged and managed by the Federal government.
Library of Congress Prints and Photographs Division, Washington, D.C.

Black troops, Lincoln argued, might be the solution. "The necissity [sic] of this is palpable if, as I understand, you are now unable to effect anything with your present force," he wrote, "which . . . is soon to be greatly diminished by the expiration of terms of service, as well as by ordinary causes." Lincoln justified a critical political policy by implementing it in answer to military exigencies. "I shall be very glad," he wrote, "if you will take hold of the matter in earnest." Banks understood his orders.[19]

General Ullmann held a more radical vision of this experiment. He saw the creation of a black army of occupation as merely the next step in a long process of national rebirth. "Southern morals, manners, and ideas, must pass away before a real regeneration can be achieved," he observed. "This must be a work of time—based upon natural and socialistic forces, controlled by civil and political institutions." The armies and government of the United States must destroy Southern culture and recast it in Northern molds. Black troops would advance the process and inherit the gain.[20]

General Ullmann arrived to a confused jurisdiction in the Department of the Gulf and a frosty reception by its commander. Lincoln had sent him, with Vice-President Hannibal Hamlin's son in tow, as one of his future regimental commanders, as a way of keeping tabs on affairs in Louisiana. Ullmann, too, considered himself semi-independent under direct commission by the president. Banks made a show of embracing the help but clearly resented the White House's meddling. Ullmann's work threatened to disrupt the organization and recruitment of black labor for fieldwork—especially in the pacified Lafourche District. Besides, Banks had his own plans for arming blacks.[21]

The accumulation of freedmen from New Orleans, the Gulf Coast, the Lafourche District, and up the Mississippi to Baton Rouge, provided Banks with a head start on enlisting black soldiers. The Department of the Gulf already had nearly four thousand blacks in the ranks, whereas nearly eighty thousand black men of military age lay within his lines. Banks did not need Ullmann operating independently.[22]

New Orleans was the epicenter for raising black regiments. "There were several large contraband camps maintained at [Camp] Parapet, known as colonies 1, 2, 3, 4, and 5," a Union soldier wrote. Two other existed nearby—the Greenville colony and the Brickyard colony. "These camps received additional negroes brought from abandoned plantations by details of men sent up river to collect them," he continued. "A number of men . . . were detailed in various capacities to assist such officers as were in command of these negro camps, for they had to be governed and fed by the military authorities." Officers sketched the 1st Louisiana Engineers out of the people gathered at Camp Parapet. Others would be enlisted into one of three combat regiments, designated the 3rd through 5th Louisiana Native Guards to add to the first two regiments already in the field. When Ullmann and his officers arrived they would raise five additional regiments. Meanwhile, the ponderously named 1st Louisiana Regiment Heavy Artillery (African Descent) drilled with the cannon along the fortifications of Camp Parapet, which was a garrison role intended for most of the black troops raised along the Mississippi.[23]

Blacks in these camps served at the will of the government. "Opinions differ in regard to whether the negroes enlisted of their own free will," observed a Massachusetts soldier. Colonel Justin Hodge quickly mustered in twelve companies for his 1st Louisiana Engineers. "The men were drawn up in line, when a German speaking officer who spoke poor English, said something to them that [they] could not understand, though he stood near," wrote one witness. He then declared them "mustered into service." The men seemed confused. "These negroes afterwards asked what had been going on, and appeared ignorant of the nature of the ceremony." The new soldiers did not seem to mind, in the end. "At all events," the writer concluded, "none of them ever protested against enlistment, or mode of muster."[24]

Black soldiers would come from all over southern Louisiana. At Brashear City, Union troops habitually crossed Berwick Bay to raid farms and plantations for livestock and produce. Slave John Ogee, watching the national troops rolling across the cane fields near his home, joined the Union forces for practical reasons. "The Yankees comed 'bout a mile from us and they took every ear of corn, kilt every head of stock and 'bout thirteen beeves," he remembered. "When we think of all the good food the Yankees done got, we jus' up and jine up with them." He soon found himself in the army. "We figger we git lot to eat," he added, "the res' we just didn't figger." Processed into the army on Tiger Island, he soon found himself drilling with the 3rd Louisiana Native Guards.[25]

Some planters attempted to stay out of the path of the Union army and keep their slaves from being pressed into Federal service. In Louisiana this could be tricky. Dr. W. J. Lyle, at Smithfield Plantation, understood what the Emancipation Proclamation would mean for his more than one hundred enslaved people. He feared Federal authorities would take his property. Lyle's plantation, west of the Mississippi but just a few miles away from Union-held Baton Rouge, faced imminent destruction. His in-laws operated plantations near Bayou Sara, upstream from Rebel-held Port Hudson, and as long as the fortress remained in Southern hands he could preserve his slaves. Lyle gathered his cash and what few possessions he could and led his human property on an exodus north through Pointe Coupée Parish and across the Mississippi to Ira Smith's Estate Plantation and J. Seatt Smith's Island Plantation. Catherine Cornelius, one of Lyle's slaves, remembered the move: "Dey took us to Bayou Sara to hide us in tents on de plantation dere."[26]

The process of enlisting liberated slaves gathered momentum in northeast Louisiana as well. Notwithstanding Halleck's concerns, Grant perfectly understood what the government expected of him and he emulated the labors of his colleagues downriver. From Lake Providence, Louisiana, to Helena, Arkansas, and Memphis, Tennessee, Grant organized his crowds of liberated slaves into companies and regiments. Adjutants scribed into being a half-dozen black Louisiana infantry units, but recruiting proceeded slowly. Mustering officers established, at least on paper, the 7th through 12th regiments of Louisiana Infantry (African Descent). Similarly, officers culled through the crowds of liberated slaves elsewhere to cobble together the 1st Mississippi Infantry (African Descent); those from southern Arkansas became the 1st Arkansas Infantry (African Descent). Grant's staff lumped the collection into the exotically named "African Brigade" and ordered them to garrison and protect his bases at Lake Providence, Milliken's Bend, and Young's Point on the west bank.[27]

This great wave of recruitment changed the timbre and tone of the war along the Mississippi. A New England officer in Baton Rouge was ready for liberated slaves to lend a hand in this effort. "I have seen enough here to convince me that the best course the Government can pursue is to make soldiers of the emancipated slaves," he agreed. "I have seen negro regiments at drill, on dress parade, and at work on entrenchments. I have been through their camps and conversed with officers and men. There are no troops in this department that appear better." Their years in bondage made them a quicker study on the manual of arms than whites, he contended. "This is due to their universal faculty of imitation." He was convinced that they would fight well when the day came. They would also suffer fewer casualties from disease. "They are acclimated and can work here in the South," adding "they are ready to enter the service and regiments can be raised just as fast as the Government can arm and equip them. This is the way to raise an army for this country, and to solve the question: What is to be done with the liberated slaves?"[28]

Many of the soldiers believed that returning liberated slaves to plantation labor wasted their potential. "The negro now is in a transition state; just free from the shackles, he has crude notions of freedom, which make him uncertain as a hired servant. He 'recokons' he can 'quit' at pleasure if he is not suited with his place or work. He wants discipline till his notions are worked out of him and he finds his true level as a free man." Therefore, the officer argued, "the army is the place to learn this; and into the army 300,000 of them ought to go, officered by whites at present, to hold this country and help clean it out."[29]

Besides, argued another Northerner, arming and equipping the freed slaves would rub salt into the wounded Confederacy and serve as poetic, if not actual, justice. "There is one class of people who do object to negro soldiers—these are the lordlings of the South—the devotees of King Cotton, and the fiery blooded chivalry of the rebel kingdom," he wrote. "Their talk . . . is malignant and venomous against the negro soldier. It humbles their ancient pride to have their slaves successful in arms against them. They feel no greater insult can be offered to their ragged and tattered pride than to be taken prisoners and placed under a negro guard. Such is sometimes among the chances of war, and it is a sort of retributive justice, I must confess, I am not sorry to see."[30]

With this process underway and the calendar advancing, both Grant's Army of the Mississippi and Banks's Army of the Gulf restarted their campaigns. In mid-April 1863, General Banks launched his army on a massive raid deep into Confederate Louisiana, west of the Mississippi. His Bayou Teche campaign would accomplish two main objectives: he would pull more of Louisiana into the Union orbit, allowing its products, livestock, and slaves to serve the Federal cause, and he would move his army closer to Grant's.

Instead of making a direct assault on the fortress at Port Hudson, he intended to destroy the revitalized Confederate army under Major General Richard Taylor. Veteran Texas cavalry regiments fresh from their victory at Galveston reinforced this army—the same force General Godfrey Weitzel had driven from the Lafourche Country six months before. Smashing these Rebels would solve two problems bedeviling Banks. The Army of the Gulf intended to sweep the Rebels farther away from the Lafourche District during its delicate transition to free labor, and it would cut the supply line from West Louisiana and Texas sustaining Port Hudson and Vicksburg.

Banks succeeded. In mid-April, after hammering the Rebels hard in three days of savage combat around Franklin, Louisiana, Banks dislodged the Confederate army holding the region, mauled it, and pursued it north as far as Natchitoches on the Red River. Only the rearguard actions by Colonel Tom Green and his predominantly Texan cavalry prevented a complete rout.

This cartoon, first published on March 7, 1863 in Frank Leslie's Illustrated Newspaper *encapsulated the Northern* schadenfreude *of militarizing liberated slaves.*

"Our army is rolling like a ball of fire through the finest portions of Louisiana," a Yankee newspaperman crowed. "When the rebels are thoroughly driven out . . . the backbone of the rebellion will be very much broken, so as the State is concerned." Yet, the Confederate army was just out of reach. The Union troops had been marching nearly two dozen miles a day, chasing "a great distant dust, showing how close we were to the Rebel flight," wrote Captain John William De Forest of the 12th Connecticut. "It is a solemn and menacing phenomenon, the dust of a marching enemy."[31]

The arrival of the Union army toppled the lives of white and black Louisianans caught in its path. Harry Mahoney, a slave near New Iberia, remembered, "the day they came was a beautiful day and the whole country was in bloom. The next day came the terrible contrast. The whole plantation was devastated. Overnight the countryside had been swept clean." U.S. troops ransacked his home, Belmont Plantation, and others in the region. The days of white privilege and extravagance ended. "These people had hundreds of slaves to wait on them and keep everything in shape, and all the luxuries and improvements money could buy," he recalled. "The next day their slaves were all gone. The barns and the houses had been burned. Vegetation had been trampled down. Chickens, mules, cattle—all had been driven off."[32]

Some planters remained on their land, hoping to weather the Union storm. William T. and Cornelia Gates Palfrey were among the most prosperous families in St. Mary Parish and worked nearly two hundred people in their cane fields. Their plantation on Bayou Teche became engulfed in the fighting. Ellen Betts, an enslaved woman living there, remembered those terrifying days. "De war met right dere, and dem Yanks and [Confederates] fit for twenty-four hours straight runnin'," she said. "When de bullets starts rainin' down, Marse [Palfrey] calls us and slip us way back into de woods, where it so black and deep." After the Union army passed, Palfrey returned his hands to their cabins. "Sech a sight I never seen," Betts wrote. "Lawd, de things I can tell. Dem Yanks have kilt men and women. I seed babies pick up from the road with dere brains bust right out. M'Lasses run in the bayou and blood run in de ditches." Palfrey's orchard had been picked clean, and his cane trampled and shredded. His home, far removed from the public road, emerged undamaged. "Dey's awful, awful times after dat," Betts recalled.[33]

Valmer Cormier, a young mixed-race boy whose father was a local Creole and his mother, Celeste, a slave, lived near Vermilionville and had watched his master Duplissant Dugas leave for war. "I remember de day my marster go to de war," Cormier said. He missed his father. "He used to like to play de fiddle and make me dance when I was li'l, but he went to the war and got kilt." Unlike Palfrey, Dugas had been a man of modest means whose two adult and two enslaved children helped him work the farm. "Marster was jes a poor man and have jes' a ordinary house," Cormier said. The war had already brought privation. "Us drink French coffee befo' de war, but endurin' the war us couldn't git de good kind," he remembered. When Federal troops marched past the plantation, the sight frightened the young Cormier. "I seed de sojers and I run under de house, I was so scared" he recalled. "De Yankees come take de cattle and went 'way with dem."[34]

Taylor and his battered army of Texans and Louisianans fled in the face of this Yankee juggernaut. The Union army outnumbered them twice over and scattered most of the Rebel regiments besides sending hundreds of butternut-and-gray-clad prisoners toward New Orleans and captivity. The Rebel remnant remained uncertain where the chase would end. "The fairest portion of Louisiana is in possession of the Yankees," Sergeant Thomas R. Rootes of the 4th Texas Cavalry lamented. "They outnumbered us too heavy; had to run. Where we will stop at there is no telling." John W. Watkins in the 5th Texas Cavalry believed he knew. "Banks is said to have been reinforced," he wrote. "His officers have their baggage marked 'San Antonio, Texas'—and they bid fair to reach there unless troops are sent to check their onward move."[35]

Despite skedaddling, Confederate morale remained high. Even though the fighting along Bayou Teche had battered and bruised his regiment, Texas Sergeant

Colonel Tom Green arrived in Louisiana at the head of the 5th Texas Cavalry in March 1863. His leadership and aggressive style in the Teche Campaign earned him the admiration of his superiors, including General Richard Taylor, and promotion to brigadier general.
Author's Collection.

Rootes and most of his comrades in Taylor's army remained committed; he informed his sister back in Virginia, "The Louisianans don't like Texans but prayed for a few more when they found the Yankees coming. I am well and doing first rate, except the running part—don't like that part much."[36]

Taylor's infantry, although diminished, escaped along with his wagons and artillery, saved by the delaying tactics of Green's cavalry. Private Watkins reported Green "has fought the enemy nearly every day and fell back at night. General Taylor asked Green to let him take command so that he might rest, but the brave old Colonel replied 'no, I can stand it as long as the enemy can.'"[37]

Worn out in part by these rear-guard skirmishes, Banks ended the pursuit at Opelousas. Instead of trying to run down the Rebels and finish them off, the Union army moved on to their other chores. Liberated Louisiana could sustain the Union war effort in the region. The New Yorkers, Midwesterners, and New Englanders of Banks's army would put the region's produce and commodities to use in the cause and feed the armies. "Opelousas is just on the border of the vast cotton country of the west," one Northerner wrote. "Our army will . . . glean the country of all the cotton, sugar, cattle, &c., and leaving a good force there; try to most effectually cut off their supplies from the west to the Mississippi." Severing this supply line would hasten the Confederate collapse. "Their Texas cattle and corn no more coming," the Federal added, and "Louisiana sugar turned Yankeewards—these must nearly drive the rebels to starvation."[38]

Thomas H. and Mary Lewis understood that to save what they could from the Federal grasp, they had to leave. The couple owned more than thirty slaves at their sizable cotton plantation near Opelousas and they led their family—and slaves—to Texas. Virginia Bell, a slave girl in her early teens at the time, remembered the day the war came. "It sho' changed things," she recalled. "We heard this and that, but we didn't know much about what it was about." One morning the slaves emerged from their cabins and saw the family loading wagons with food, clothing, and furniture. "I heard him saying we was moving to Polk County, way over in Texas," Bell continued. "I know it took us a long time to get there, and when we did, I never see so much woods. It sho' was diff'rent from the plantation." In Louisiana, Bell had been a vivacious young woman favored as a social messenger by her mistress. In Texas, she worked the fields, "same as the res'," she continued. "We stayed . . . and made three crops of cotton, but not so much as on our old place, 'cause there wasn't so much clearin'."[39]

Convinced that Confederates troops west of the Mississippi no longer posed a creditable military threat, Banks gathered western Louisiana blacks into the service with impunity and without reservation. "It is not established upon any dogma of equality or other theory, but as a practical and sensible matter of business," he directed his officers, lest they harbor doubts. "The Government makes use of mules, horses, uneducated and educated white men, in the defense of its institutions. Why should not the negro contribute whatever is in his power for the cause in which he is as deeply interested as other men? We may properly demand from him whatever service he can render."[40]

He also planned to implement his vision of a black army. Clearly there would be blacks in combat within months, if not weeks, somewhere in the United States. The commander of the Army of the Gulf proposed to put his stamp on a grand vision for their effective training and employment in his department: he announced "the organization of a *Corps d'Armee* of colored troops, to be designated as the *Corps d'Afrique*." Banks issued General Orders No. 40 on May 1, 1863, announcing the creation of this new command. The thousands of freed slaves being collected by his army would become auxiliaries of the XIX Army Corps and potentially a model for Union armies on every field. The Louisiana Native Guard regiments already raised would simply keep their regimental numbers as they folded into this new regime.[41]

In the absence of national policies and procedures for militarizing blacks and placing them into the army, Banks's exotically named organization would address the inefficiencies and challenges encountered thus far. "The chief defect in organizations of this character has arisen from incorrect ideas of the officers in command," he wrote. "Their discipline has been lax, and in some cases the conduct of their regiments unsatisfactory and discreditable." Banks no doubt remembered General Weitzel's objections to arming blacks. "Controversies unnecessary and injurious to the service have arisen between them and other troops," Banks conceded, "but," he predicted, "the *Corps d'Afrique* would reconcile and avoid many of these troubles."[42]

He envisioned smaller regiments than their white counterparts—half the enlisted men—giving the officers fewer men to manage. The organization of the *Corps d'Afrique* otherwise mirrored a regular army corps. It would have a total of eighteen regiments including infantry, artillery, and cavalry, along with engineers and "flying hospitals." These units would serve in two-regiment brigades, three of which would form a division. The entire *Corps d'Afrique* would boast three divisions. Banks knew that his army was too small to simultaneously conquer *and* garrison all of Louisiana and the lower Mississippi valley. He needed his white army to destroy the Rebels. The *Corps d'Afrique* would hold conquered Louisiana while his white troops conducted the *real* war.

Union troops gathered black recruits but uprooted their families in the process. Among others, soldiers pressed the liberated slaves of former Louisiana Governor Alexandre Mouton near Vermilionville. Officers destined twenty-three-year-old Lewis Rede for service in the 9th Regiment, *Corps d'Afrique*. He left behind a wife and three young boys who moved to a nearby camp before a later relocation to Brashear City and the Lafourche District beyond. "After the sojers taken my pa to war," remembered Henry Reed, who was ten years old at the time, "we wuz sat free. I never is seen my father any more."[43]

Not every slave in the region proved eager to join the Yankee columns; not every slave owner lamented those that left. Confederate ordnance officer Lieutenant John Marsh Avery reported that "the Negroes behaved splendidly, refusing to go." Meanwhile, his uncle Ashbel Burnham Henshaw reported that New Iberia had settled down after the Union troops passed through. The Federals had relieved the town of a bothersome element, in his opinion. "We are living quietly and peacefully, as usual," he wrote. "Nearly all the rascally Negroes having run away."[44]

Mostly women and children, these liberated slaves, in a contraband camp in Baton Rouge, faced an uncertain future as wards of the United States.
State Library of Louisiana, Baton Rouge.

Banks urged Ullmann to move his recruiting efforts away from New Orleans and the "pacified" parishes on the Mississippi and Bayou Lafourche and instead build his brigade at Brashear City from slaves taken along Bayou Teche. Banks would send enough slaves to fill out the regiments. "I believe I have the men at hand, part of them already . . . organized, for his entire brigade," Banks reported to General Halleck. "My belief is that Brashear City, on Berwick Bay, is in all respects the best position for the organization of his troops. He can organize his regiments in one week after establishing his headquarters from the men I have collected."[45]

Banks and Ullmann recruited capable and experienced white officers to command these units. "With their aid," he wrote, "the corps will render important service to the army." Talented leaders should step forward, look past their bigotries, and think instead of their nation. "Officers and soldiers will consider the exigencies of the service in this department and the absolute necessity of appropriating every element of power to the support of the Government," he wrote. "The prejudices or opinions of men are in nowise involved." As incentive, commanders of black regiments were promised a rise of several grades in ranks for men volunteering for line duty.[46]

By May 1863, with the program of raising black regiments well underway, the great military climax of the Mississippi Valley campaign approached. Banks advanced from Opelousas and captured Alexandria, placing his army in the Red River Valley. With river communications largely unimpeded, he could now coordinate his efforts with Grant.

As the army moved up Bayou Beouf toward the Red River, Captain John Burrud of the 160th New York understood the ground he and his men conquered. He had read *Twelve Years a Slave*. New Yorker Solomon Northrup, a free man of color, wrote this harrowing account of being kidnapped and sold into slavery in Louisiana; it had become a literary weapon in the abolitionists' arsenal. Burrud recognized the neighborhood of the Edwin Epps Plantation, penciling into his diary that this agricultural heartland was "the most beautiful country I ever saw." He also realized where he was: "I think this is the place that Solomon Northrup operated."[47]

The captain investigated the house and buildings of the Epps Plantation and visited with some of the slaves who confirmed that Northrup—called Platt as a slave—had once toiled in that neighborhood. Burrud also examined the stocks, whipping post, straps and paddles used to intimidate and control the slaves. "Solomon's book is true to the letter only it does not portray the system as bad as it is," Burrud concluded. "It is not in the power of man to do it."[48]

Burrud, influenced by Northrup's seminal book, hated slavery, calling it "the most damnable man degrading, soul killing, God dishonoring institution that ever was permitted to exist on the face of the earth." He rejoiced that fate landed him and his regiment at this place—at this time. Slavery was dying, and he and his men were helping to slaughter it. "I think I can see its Death struggle and heare its Death Groans," he scribbled into his diary, "and Oh How I rejoice to see it writhe in agony!"[49]

After capturing Alexandria against negligible opposition, Banks convinced himself that he had effectively conquered Louisiana. He could now cooperate with Grant without fear of Confederates operating in his rear. To Banks's surprise, he learned that Grant's army at Vicksburg had already moved against

This image from Harper's Weekly *captures the challenges posed by the Louisiana terrain opposite Vicksburg.*

the Confederates in Mississippi, crossing the mighty river south of the Rebel fortress to gain a better position for cooperation with Banks. The Confederates unexpectedly gave way. Grant pursued, following up his successful crossing with an aggressive plunge deep into the state of Mississippi. "Meeting the enemy, as I did, south of Port Gibson, I followed him to the Big Black [River]," he wrote to Banks. "Many days cannot elapse before the battle will begin which is to decide the fate of Vicksburg."[50]

This unexpected twist to Union grand strategy left Banks in a quandary. Grant's bold stroke forced Confederate commander, General Pemberton, to draw off half of the Port Hudson garrison to meet the emergency in the north. Banks, bereft of the opportunity to participate in this grand action, believed cooperation between the Union armies might now be impossible. Grant would need all of his troops, boats, and supplies concentrated on Vicksburg. There would be none to lend to Banks. Nor could the Army of the Gulf relocate to Vicksburg without uncovering New Orleans and southern Louisiana to a counteroffensive from Taylor and his command. Banks and his army now idled deep in enemy country without means of advancing.

As commander of the Department of Mississippi and East Louisiana, Confederate Lieutenant General John C. Pemberton commanded both Vicksburg and Port Hudson. His attempts to manage both of these critical positions against mounting Federal pressure eventually overwhelmed him.
Library of Congress Prints and Photographs Division, Washington, D.C.

The isolation of Vicksburg also presented an opportunity. Banks abandoned his invasion of Louisiana and fell back from Alexandria following the path of the Red River to its mouth at Simmesport. With Grant engaging Pemberton, Banks decided to finish off the weakened Port Hudson garrison, secure the lower Mississippi, and then head north to help Grant. Halleck's plans for a grand cooperation between the armies fell apart in the face of unfolding events, and the net effect was that Union forces would simultaneously attack both Confederate citadels, which was the much riskier venture Halleck had hoped to avoid.[51]

Banks abandoned his ambitions west of the Father of Waters as he moved toward the Mississippi and his next project. The principal elements of the Army of the Gulf energetically plowed through Point Coupée Parish and crossed the Mississippi at Bayou Sara. On Thursday, May 21, the XIX Army Corps, nearly twenty thousand strong, surrounded the Confederate works at Port Hudson. Two days later, Banks arrived to take command of the reduction of the Rebel citadel. As Banks and his army settled in around Port Hudson, the U.S. War Department issued General Orders No. 143. This move signaled and enshrined the project to mobilize the slave population against the Southern Confederacy. The Bureau of Colored Troops now coordinated the national efforts then underway. The long awaited comprehensive national policy, and its governing agency, took shape.[52]

The crossing of the Union army at Bayou Sara ended Dr. Lyle's attempt to retain his slaves. He believed he had moved them to safety; instead he had relocated into the exact path of the Union army. "De Yankees found us," Cornelius remembered.

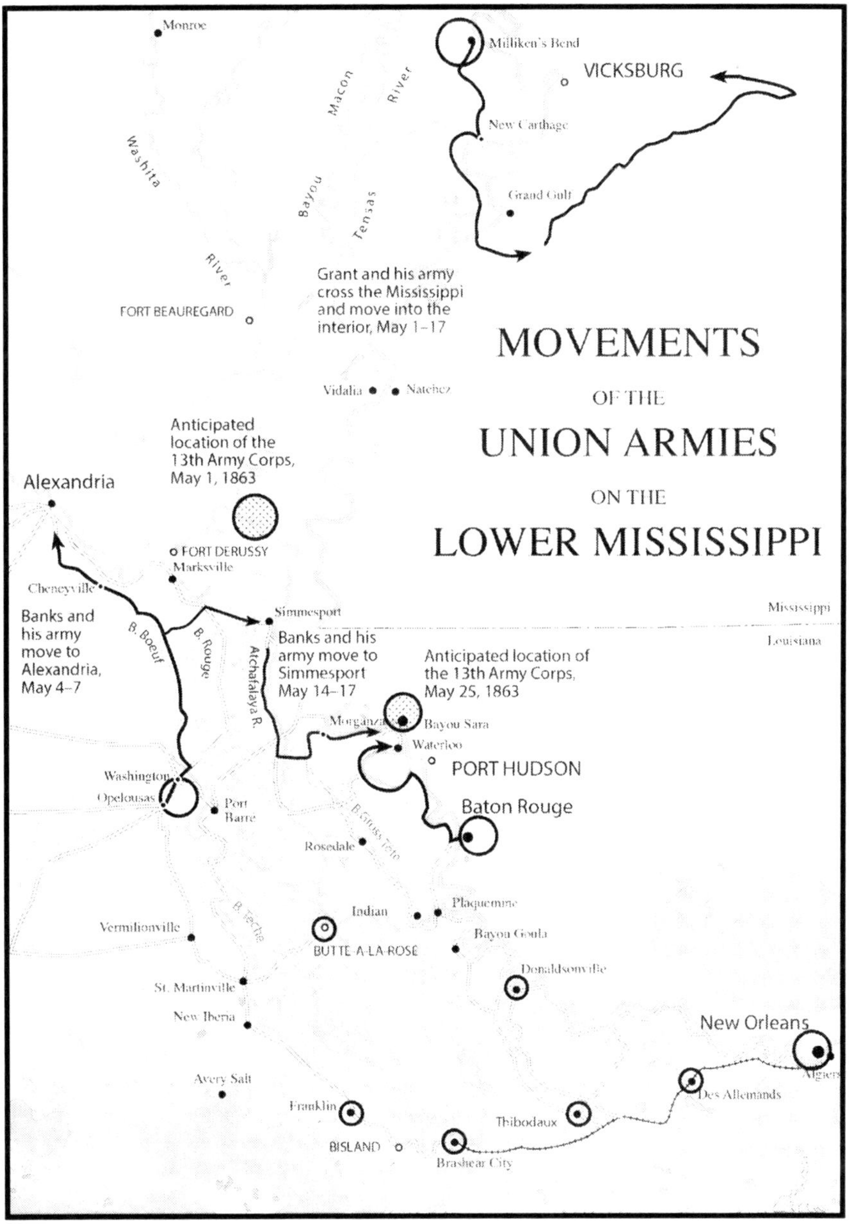

One of Dr. Lyle's employees, driving a buggy with a team of fleet black horses, tried to flee with two strongboxes full of the family gold and cash. In his haste, the driver fell from the carriage, hit the ground hard, and died. The Federals swooped

This 1840s' view of Bayou Sara clearly shows the river town on the bank of the Mississippi River, with the upper settlement of St. Francisville in the background. A ferry connected this town to Pointe Coupée Parish until the late twentieth century. General Nathaniel P. Banks crossed his army at this point on his way to besiege Port Hudson. Henry Lewis, German, (1819–1904) artist; Arnz and Company, Lithographer. Published in *Das illustrirte Mississippithal*, (published 1854-1857), opposite p. 400.

in. "De Yankees took loads of money dat missus and master had," Cornelius said. "It was carried in iron safes. De Yankees took all dere money to Port Hudson."[53]

General Halleck had hoped for more methodical cooperation between Grant and Banks. A setback at either Vicksburg or Port Hudson could cascade into a Union disaster. Halleck responded to the news that his generals had besieged *both* Confederate fortresses with shock and anger. Why had Banks not gone on to Vicksburg? "The newspapers state that your forces are moving on Port Hudson, instead of cooperating with General Grant!" Halleck gasped. "As this is so contrary to all your instructions, and so opposed to military principals, I can hardly believe it true."[54]

Banks ignored Halleck's hand wringing. Port Hudson could not resist for long. He risked everything on this gamble and ordered his Trans-Mississippi garrisons—a brigade at Opelousas, detachments in New Iberia and Franklin—to concentrate at Brashear City. He had neutralized Taylor's army, but these parties needed to tuck in behind the wide water barrier of Berwick Bay just to be sure. Banks trusted that his proposed army of African descent, the *Corps d'Afrique*, could organize rapidly and defend the Lafourche District. With a little time, tens of thousands of Louisiana's slaves would be wearing Union blue, and they would keep Taylor's Confederates at a distance.

Banks miscalculated. No longer pressured, the Confederates west of the Mississippi mended and prepared for another round with the Yankees. Green led his cavalry brigade to the Rebel depot at Niblett's Bluff on the Sabine River to resupply, rest, and recover. Battered, but healing quickly, the soldiers congratulated themselves on a job well done. "People may say what they please . . . but when we come to take into consideration the overwhelming odds our little army fought, we cannot compare it to anything better that the 300 Spartans under Leonidas, at the pass of Thermopylae," one Lone Star Rebel boasted. "Had we one half the force to oppose the invaders they had against us, we should have driven them back to New Orleans." The men believed they had hurt the enemy. "Our men seem conscious of having made the best fight of the war," another Texan wrote, "and claim to have killed four to one."[55]

Clearly the Rebels remained undefeated—a fact Banks would soon discover.

3

Vicksburg and Port Hudson

If you can do anything to succor Port Hudson, I beg you to do it.
—Lieutenant General Joseph E. Johnston

The Union Mississippi Valley campaigns of April and May 1863 and the simultaneous moves against Vicksburg and Port Hudson confounded Rebel strategists as much as they had Union General-in-Chief Henry Halleck. The Teche Campaign had knocked General Richard Taylor's army in west Louisiana to flinders just weeks after the arrival of General Edmund Kirby Smith, who had been tasked with creating and managing the Department of the Trans-Mississippi. Kirby Smith, too, had stampeded ahead of Banks's army, evacuating his Alexandria headquarters in favor of the more remote, and safer, Shreveport. Convinced that the Federal offensive aimed at conquering Louisiana, Texas, and Arkansas (and still unaware that Banks had turned toward Port Hudson), Kirby Smith and Taylor remained jumpy, begging for troops from General John C. Pemberton. The Confederate defender of the Mississippi, with his own problems multiplying in the shifting strategic scene, scoffed at the notion. He, instead, demanded reinforcements from *them*.[1]

Union planners had no interest in capturing Shreveport; Vicksburg was the key to victory. General Ulysses S. Grant, exceeding even his own expectations, penned thirty thousand Confederates with an army of forty-four thousand U.S. troops. He failed to break Pemberton's lines with a frontal assault on May 19, but Grant kept him trapped. This sudden reversal of Rebel fortunes rippled across the South. By late May 1863, the secessionists' cause in the Mississippi Valley, which had seemed ascendant in April, tottered on the tip of destruction. Between them, Banks and Grant had loosed an avalanche of Federal troops that now entombed some forty thousand Rebel soldiers. The forts at Port Hudson and Vicksburg had gone from bastions of defiance to earthwork prisons.

In Richmond, Confederate officials scrambled to make sense of the confusing situation on the Mississippi. General Robert E. Lee, anticipating a coming

Lieutenant General Edmund Kirby Smith arrived in Louisiana in March 1863 only to find his new command nearly overrun by Union troops led by Nathaniel P. Banks. He directed the Confederate armies of the Department of the Trans-Mississippi from his headquarters at Shreveport, but he faced many challenges.
Goelet and Buncombe Family Papers, #01112, Southern Historical Collection, Wilson Library, University of North Carolina at Chapel Hill.

calamity, suggested that he take his Army of Northern Virginia north toward Maryland and Pennsylvania to distract the Federals by threatening the interior of their country. At the same time, the Confederate government dispatched General Joseph E. Johnston to create a Rebel relief force in Mississippi of around seven thousand men, promising him eight thousand more. Johnston, en route, urged Pemberton to abandon Vicksburg while he still could. Perhaps the combined Rebel armies could turn and destroy Grant or perhaps pen him against the Mississippi. Despite this admonition, the garrison at Vicksburg hunkered down. Pemberton instead sent additional dispatches, more urgently framed, requesting reinforcements from the Confederate Department of the Trans-Mississippi.

Grant clearly understood his precarious position. He needed to maintain the strategic initiative. The Rebels might, in time, regain their senses and concentrate against him. Abandoning any pretense of helping Banks at Port Hudson, Grant called for an additional thirty thousand reinforcements from Federal commands in Arkansas, Missouri, and Tennessee, aiming to counter any move by Johnston. Whichever army—Union or Confederate—won its race for reinforcements outside Vicksburg might carry the day and win control of the Mississippi.

After reaching Meridian, Mississippi, and assessing the strategic situation facing the Confederate armies, General Johnston decided that rescuing Pemberton

Lieutenant General John C. Pemberton sent Major General Franklin Gardner to Port Hudson with orders to improve the works and put the post in the best possible condition. A New Yorker and veteran soldier, his mother hailed from Louisiana. Gardner married the daughter of Louisiana Governor Alexandre Mouton, making Gardner the brother-in-law to Confederate Brigadier General Alfred Mouton. In addition, Gardner's sister later married Governor Mouton, blurring family lines but cementing his ties to Louisiana.
State Library of Louisiana.

After Union forces laid siege to both Vicksburg and Port Hudson, Confederate President Jefferson Davis sent one of his most senior commanders, Joseph Eggleston Johnston, to retrieve the situation.
Library of Congress Prints and Photographs Division, Washington, D.C.

must be his priority. General Franklin Gardner at Port Hudson would have to find help from west of the river. "I am preparing to aid Vicksburg, but cannot march to Port Hudson without exposing my little army to destruction," he explained to General Kirby Smith. "If you can do anything to succor Port Hudson, I beg you to do it." General Taylor, reading this dispatch, searched for a solution.[2]

While Rebel armies at Vicksburg and Port Hudson faced starvation, the Union military policy of arming slaves simultaneously increased the Yankee strength. The logical center of this recruiting and training effort lay among the plantations and depots of the Laforuche District and along the banks of the Mississippi within Union lines.

A Confederate loss of the Mississippi would unlock additional regions to Union recruiters. Taylor, frustrated that his army remained badly strewn from Shreveport to the Sabine realized, that gathering it would rob him of precious time while Pemberton and Gardner's men grew hungry and black regiments gained confidence. Taylor needed a man of action. He summoned Colonel Tom Green and his cavalry from the Sabine River. These men and their energetic leader, Taylor believed, were the best troops he had at hand. "Col. Green," wrote one adoring subordinate, "has doubly proved himself a hero from the firing of the first shell." Another Texan echoed the sentiment: "Had it not been for the gallantry of Green's regiment and Waller's Battalion, who covered the retreat, our army would have been entirely cut to pieces." A fellow soldier bragged, "Green and his men have won laurels. The muse of the historian will point once again at them." In the middle of May 1863, Colonel Green led his refreshed cavalry brigade from Niblett's Bluff back into the heart of Louisiana, the Mississippi Valley campaign roaring to a crescendo. The Texan and his men had no idea how Taylor would put them to use. Neither did Taylor.[3]

The 2nd Louisiana Cavalry led the sortie out of Niblett's Bluff, heading east. They were to scout the enemy near Opelousas, determine the whereabouts of any remaining Federal forces, and scoop up Southern deserters, conscripts, and the timid and restore them to their Louisiana regiments. These steady troopers straddled their saddles and spurred their horses eastward, the vanguard of a gray torrent that would flood back into the region.

The Texans followed. "The battles of Texas will be fought in Louisiana," trumpeted one Lone Star Rebel in a letter to the Houston newspaper. "There it behooves us to strike for our homes." Major General John Bankhead Magruder agreed and ordered all the troops he could spare to cross the Sabine. At Natchitoches, Taylor watched the calendar nervously. If he could concentrate his current army and promised reinforcements in the next few weeks, he might save Port Hudson.[4]

Taylor rebuilt his army, and men, bolstered with reinforcements pouring in from Arkansas, Indian Territory, and Texas, might cause some havoc in favor of the garrison at Port Hudson. Taylor trusted Green and promoted him to brigadier general. "To me he was a tried and devoted friend," Taylor wrote. Green turned fifty years of age that month—twelve years older than the thirty-seven-year-old commander of the Confederate District of West Louisiana—but they shared a similar temperament. Others echoed Taylor's praises of this scrappy Texan. Lieutenant Colonel Ed Waller served alongside Green in the rearguard fights and compared him to Napoleon Bonaparte's most heroic marshal and described him as cool, sagacious, brave, and heroic. "If there was a 'Ney' in General Taylor's army," Waller wrote, "that man was . . . Tom Green."[5]

Taylor's efforts required deft planning and delicate execution. The longer Gardner held out at Port Hudson—and the more Yankees he killed—the more likely it became that Taylor could assemble a larger, more dangerous army than the Confederacy had ever seen in Louisiana and tip the strategic balance in the region. Pemberton, of course, had to also hold on at Vicksburg. With Banks and Grant locked in sieges at Port Hudson and Vicksburg, swift columns of Confederates could surge out of the Attakapas Prairies and the Red River Valley to sweep away Union garrisons and dismantle Federal efforts in protected areas like the Lafourche District. Confederates could then gain the west bank of the Mississippi and interdict supplies heading upstream from New Orleans.

Taylor gambled that this distraction would force Federals to give up their efforts at one or both of the Mississippi forts to confront his reanimated Rebel army. Taylor urged Lieutenant General Kirby Smith to embrace this strategic vision and aid the effort by mobilizing Confederates in Arkansas to use similar tactics there. A string of Union disasters on the Mississippi's west bank would certainly alarm Northern citizens and politicians. If Rebel cannon could interdict supplies heading to each army, they might lift the sieges.

Taylor ordered his forces to rally at Opelousas. First he would rid the region of any remaining Federal outposts. He hoped to deliver a string of Union defeats starting with the capture of Banks's baggage and plunder train, thousands of liberated slaves, and a brigade of white troops reportedly heading into Union lines across Berwick Bay. General Green, and his immediate superior, Brigadier General Alfred Mouton, agreed.

Hearing from slaves and deserters that the Rebel cavalry would soon be upon them, the few Yankees in the region knew they had to withdraw—and soon. On May 21, the same day Banks and the Army of the Gulf encircled Port Hudson,

The son of a wealthy Boston piano maker, Thomas Chickering came to Louisiana at the head of the 41st Massachusetts Infantry. General Nathaniel P. Banks mounted the regiment, later designating it the 3rd Massachusetts Cavalry.
Author's collection.

Colonel Thomas Edward Chickering evacuated Opelousas with all of the booty from Banks's Bayou Teche raid. "The long train . . . stretched for eight miles over the prairies, with a motley band of 5,000 negroes, 2,000 horses, and 1,500 beeves for a cumbrous accompaniment . . . the most curious column ever put in motion since that which defiled after Noah into the ark," remembered an officer. A brigade of around 2,500 men guarded this exodus. Chickering faced a footrace to Brashear City. With luck, he would arrive at the Union base before the Confederates.[6]

Harry Mahoney, a slave still living amid the ruins of the Belmont Plantation near New Iberia, watched as the Yankees column left the area. "All the negroes had followed it to get free grub, and there were hordes of them," he remembered. "Nothing that could be eaten or sold was safe for a minute."[7]

This assortment of liberated slaves headed for the service and mercy of the United States, outnumbering their protectors at least twice over. "It was a sight perhaps never witnessed before, and may never be again," Major Elias Pellet of the 114th New York wrote. "The carts were those used to transport cane and cotton from the field, and would hold as much as a small canal boat. They were covered with awnings made of all kinds of material. Carpeting, clothing, reed mattings, dried cow hides, boards, and everything else which would serve to protect from the sun." The animals pulling these strange conveyances appeared unorthodox as well. "Some of the carts were drawn by oxen, some by horses,

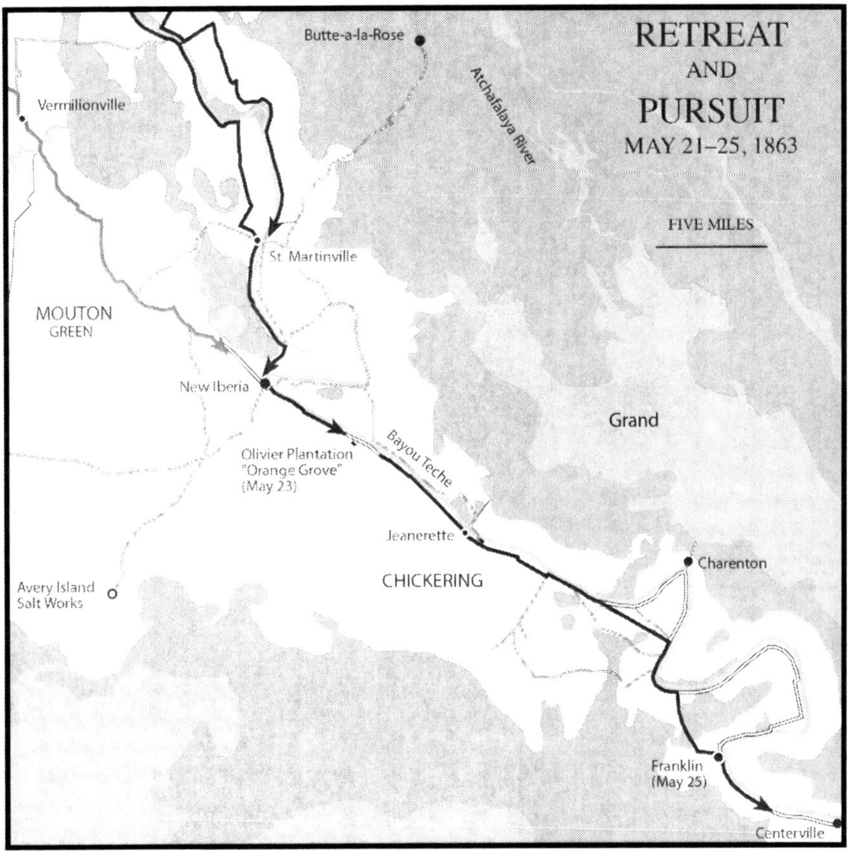

some by mules; and ox and a mule drawing at the same cart were not infrequent, and in one case a cow and a mule were harnessed together. The cooking utensils, clothing, bedding, and in fact all the traps of a negro cabin were loaded on, and the aged and the young were piled in promiscuously together."[8]

As Chickering feared, General Green and his cavalry overtook him. Early on Monday, May 25, the Confederates arrived at New Iberia, where "the ladies seem much rejoiced at our return," wrote Private William Randolph Howell of the 5th Texas Cavalry. Green was now within a single-day's march of the enemy, and he ordered his men to spur their mounts. He wanted to be in Franklin—and slicing into the Federal column—by dusk.[9]

Chickering and his command surged through Franklin at midday. Union soldiers from the 175th New York had just evacuated the supply depot and

Union forces in Louisiana removed thousands of slaves from their homes west of the Atchafalaya and concentrated them in more defensible areas along Bayou Lafourche and the Mississippi River.
Library of Congress Prints and Photographs Division, Washington, D.C.

departed on the bullet-scarred steamer *Louisiana Belle*, heading for Brashear City. As the last of Chickering's caravan left the town, the end of Green's column had just left New Iberia. Now the Rebels were only six hours behind Chickering.[10]

That evening, Green's advance entered Franklin, nabbing a Federal major and four lieutenants from the 175th New York, who remained behind to tidy up government paperwork. His appetite whetted, Green ordered his soldiers to pause, check their gear, and prepare for a fight. "Our column arrives . . . at 8 P.M., ready and anxious for a dash into the trains," reported Howell. Within minutes the sounds of pistols, carbines, shotguns, and rifles crackled in the streets of town as the Confederates ran afoul of some of Chickering's mounted rearguards.[11]

Toward the end of the retreating Union column, the infantry of the 114th New York Infantry watched as their cavalry scampered out of Franklin like so many rabbits. "The day was beautiful, and just as the sun was setting we were marching leisurely along, hoping soon to halt for the night, when in our rear we heard shouting, and soon a mass, a mob, came dashing headlong, crying 'get out of the way, the Rebels are coming,'" wrote a newspaper correspondent. "At first we thought the mounted negroes and soldiers were running a race, but soon a cavalryman, dust-covered and bare-headed came dashing down, and said the rear-guard had been attacked and some killed." Panic rippled along the column.[12]

The scuffle at the edge of Franklin alerted Chickering's command to their imminent danger. At the far end of the Union column, the 26th Maine had gone into camp near Centerville for the evening. They had completed a twenty-one mile march that day and planned to lead the exodus to its conclusion the next. The Confederates spoiled their timetable. "Just as we had got our coffee prepared," remembered Private Eldon D. Maddocks, "the bugle sounded and the Twenty-Sixth at once came into line and double quick, back four miles to assist our rear guard." Nearby the soldiers of the 52nd Massachusetts rolled out as well. "Silently, but with inward grumblings, we fall into line," wrote Sergeant Major Henry M. Whitney, "our silence broken only by an occasional expletive from one who does not see the fun of this all."[13]

Colonel Chickering sent couriers to Brashear City to alert the troops there and ordered the rest of his mounted infantry and the two guns of Captain Orlando Nims's Massachusetts battery to rush to the rear of the column. Masses of wagons, livestock, and freedmen passed south as Union soldiers pushed north. Three miles south of Franklin, a short Union battle line formed perpendicular to the road. It was the same ground where, only a month before, Green had fought the first of a series of successful rearguard actions. Now road-weary Union soldiers nervously peered into the darkness, and Federal skirmishers advanced, probing up the road toward town, searching for the Rebels.[14]

Officers interrogating a Confederate prisoner discovered that this was no ordinary dustup. "Colonel Chickering had learned somewhat of the plans of his pursuers," Ewer wrote. "The Confederate General Mouton . . . with Brigadier General Green, were preparing to attack the expedition and smash things generally." Part of the mounted forces would attack the rear of the Yankee train while the rest of the raiders would move around the flank of the retreating flood of humanity. Then they would cut across the column's midsection and raise havoc among the wagons, drivers, cattle herds, refugees, and freed slave families.[15]

Grasping the threat, Chickering sprang into action. He ordered his strengthened rearguard—which now included the 114th New York, the 26th Maine, and two cannon—to resist the Confederates as long as they could while he hurried the rest of the command to safety. The 3rd Massachusetts Cavalry fanned out toward

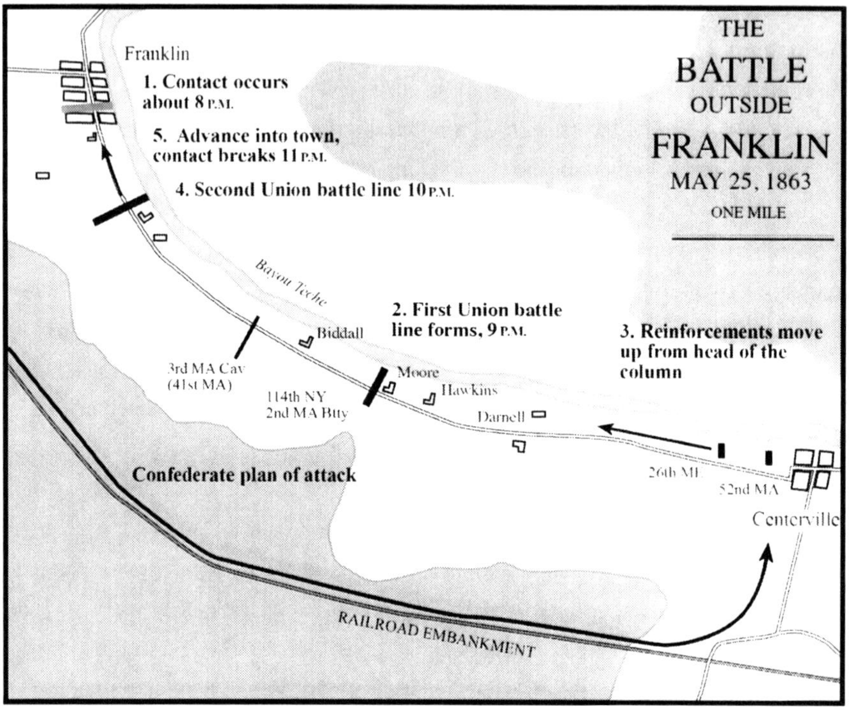

Franklin, trotting ahead to find the enemy. Chickering ordered the caravan back into motion down the Bayou Teche road. "The train pushed forward with surprising rapidity," Ewer noted. "The crack of the whip could be heard on the backs of the horses and mules. The negroes were terribly excited . . . . That night was a long one to be remembered. No one slept," he added. "Eyes, ears, feet, and hands were in constant demand."[16]

Lieutenant Colonel Samuel R. Per Lee took command of the Union defensive line. He ordered his 114th New York into a column to advance toward Franklin, hoping to buy time for the Union mass by pushing back against the Confederates. After two miles he ordered his troops to form a line of battle as clusters of mounted Federals from the 3rd Massachusetts retreated back from the streets of the town just ahead. "We had hardly completed our formation, when several cavalrymen came rapidly down," Major Pellet remembered, "and one of them gave his opinion as to the number and position of the enemy." Lieutenant Colonel Per Lee ordered the horsemen to fall in with his command. When the soldier who had delivered the report did not respond, the officer grew impatient.

"My boy, are you not going?" Per Lee inquired.

"I would go, Colonel, only for this," the rider responded, revealing a bullet wound to his side.[17]

The mixed command of Federal infantry and cavalry moved steadily back toward Franklin, gathering in stragglers, skirmishers, and soldiers wandering lost in the confusion, swelling their numbers. The growing gloom, combined with the dust of the maneuvering armies, impaired visibility. When the Federals reached the edge of town, about one hundred Confederates opened fire, killing a New York lieutenant and wounding several soldiers. The Federals halted, dressed their lines, and volleyed into town. Then, silence.

Lieutenant Colonel Per Lee ordered his command into Franklin. Observing how the buildings and fences of town broke up his formations, he reconsidered, ordering his troops back out again lest they fall into an ambush. The Yankees fell back a half-mile and reformed in the open. Per Lee ordered his command to dress ranks, and he rode to the front. "Boys, there are a lot of those devils in there, and I am for going back and cleaning that town out!" he bellowed amid the cheering of his troops, their bloodlust high. Couriers ran down the road and returned with two additional companies of the 3rd Massachusetts Cavalry and the two cannon. As a bright moon rose, Per Lee advanced some five hundred men back into Franklin, determined to drive the Rebels out.[18]

A night battle erupted. As the Federals came into range, firing again rippled through the streets and houses of Franklin. Bullets cut the air and whizzed overhead as the Yankees continued their approach. Methodically dressing their ranks, they returned a volley into the town. Officers ordered their men to reload, evoking the rhythms of an infantry regiment at war. Behind the riflemen, two 3-inch ordnance rifles began booming in cadence, blindly spinning shells among the houses of the town.

Then, again, all was calm. The Federals ceased firing, but nothing moved in town. The Confederates had once again faded away. Federal soldiers asked if they could pursue and take vengeance on the place. "We all hoped that the town might be burned," wrote Major Pellet. "Yet this treacherous town was spared." Lieutenant Colonel Per Lee wisely decided against plunging deeper into Franklin.

The scrap had already cost him about thirty men killed, wounded, and missing. A bushwhacking in the streets might cost him his regiment. The New Yorkers and their allies once again fell back, confident that they had discouraged any renewed attacks.[19]

They were correct; General Mouton had lost his nerve. The aggressive countermove by Lieutenant Colonel Per Lee had shaken Confederate confidence. "General Mouton deems it unsafe to go beyond Franklin to attack them," Private Howell wrote. "Consequently at 11 P.M. we are countermarched and greatly disappointed." In fact, Green and his troopers were fuming, ready to overrun the Yankees in the dark. "After a forced march of about 150 miles, [Mouton] came up," wrote Private John Watkins of the 5th Texas Cavalry. "After dilly dallying some time, [he] ordered a retreat from some cause I know not what. Green insisted on attacking them but was ordered to fall back by his superior officer and was bound to obey him, letting the Yankees off with over two hundred million dollars worth of property."[20]

New Iberia planter Ashbel Burnham Henshaw fumed when he learned that the Yankees had escaped unchastened. "Mouton made his appearance with about 3,000 cavalry," he wrote, "but as usual was just in time to be too late." After all they had been through in the last few weeks, Green's soldiers could not believe that Mouton would deny them their chance to punish the invaders. "Thus ended this part of the campaign," Watkins groused, "and I am afraid everyone will end likewise if we don't get more efficient Generals than we have."[21]

That night, Chickering marched his troops and the thousands of followers toward safety. At first light on May 26, the transport *Kepper* arrived at the mouth of Bayou Teche. It chaperoned the column on the last few miles of the retreat with two field pieces on its deck, keeping Confederates scouts and skirmishers still hovering off the rear and flanks at a distance. "There appeared around the bend of the bayou one of the grandest sights that any body of troops ever looked upon," gushed Private Maddocks of the 26th Maine, "one of Uncle Sam's gunboats with that grand old flag flying." Chickering brought his command into Brashear City at 11:00 A.M. "He had marched 110 miles in five days, and had made no mistake," wrote Pellet. "The authorities at Washington should have made him a brigadier." The tired and bedraggled column showed the rigors of the march. "A more dirty, dusty, ragged, and fatigued party of men never lived," Private Ewer concluded.

"Thus ended the Teche Campaign. It began in hope; it ended in fruition. It began with bright anticipation; it ended in victory."[22]

The influx of vast numbers freed people overwhelmed the Federal capacity to relocate and care for them. Lieutenant George H. Hanks, Superintendent of Negro Labor for the Department of the Gulf, did his best to find them new homes. More than twelve thousand men, women, and children flooded in. "One day 6,000 came in via Brashear City and for several days I had from 15 to 30 carloads sent me daily," he wrote from his New Orleans office to City Treasurer B. F. Flanders. He sent all he could to abandoned warehouses and cotton presses in New Orleans. With these spaces filled to capacity, Hanks ordered the homeless loaded onto flatboats and floated along Bayou Lafourche among the Union-controlled plantations, "whereever shelter could be obtained."[23]

On May 27, the day after Chickering arrived at Brashear City, Banks ordered an assault at Port Hudson, hoping to collapse the Rebel stronghold in one bold stroke. Grant had already failed twice in assaults on Vicksburg and his campaign appeared on the verge of faltering. He might soon need Banks's army. In addition, news of Taylor's efforts west of the Mississippi also caused concern. Banks wanted to complete this chore at Port Hudson; he failed. As the day's attack unraveled, Banks ordered in the 1st and 3rd *Corps d'Afrique*. The move only added to the list of fallen heroes that day and made no impression on the Confederate defenders.

John Ogee, a soldier in the 3rd *Corps d'Afrique* liberated from a plantation near Berwick Bay, faced combat for the first time at Port Hudson. He had not considered that he might have to actually *fight* the Confederates. "I thinks it great to be with the Yankees," he recounted, "but I wishes I hadn't after I got there. When you see 1,000 guns point at you I knows you wishes you'd stayed in the woods."[24]

Banks, headquartered among the flowering vines and garden hedges of A. McDonald Riley's plantation, learned that the fight of May 27 had cost his army more than two thousand casualties. Nevertheless, he believed his troops had fought ably and his black troops had breasted the fire as well as the whites. Would black regiments fight? Clearly, yes. That settled, Banks would cover his losses by accelerating the deployment of the *Corps d'Afrique*. He had likened Southern slaves to livestock pressed into the service of the nation. Now these black men would provide the fresh meat he needed to bring about the end of the rebellion.[25]

On May 27, Nathaniel P. Banks attacked Port Hudson (including the use of two black reigments) but failed to carry the Confederate works. Proponents of enlisting liberated slaves as soldiers used this occasion to trumpet their value as men of war. Harper's Weekly.

Across the Mississippi and north of Berwick Bay, the passage of the armies along the Teche left the citizens in a quandary. "We are occupying a curious position being neither Confederates nor Federals, that is, in point of law," wrote William Frederick Weeks of New Iberia. "We are not willing to be ruled by the Yankee rule, and dare not take our original position because we are likely at any time to have a Yankee force sent among us."[26]

The region's white population also distrusted the remaining blacks. When slave owners returned to the area north of New Iberia, they rounded up the men and locked them in jail. Mahoney was outraged. "I didn't think that was right, because we had been faithful." He organized a jailbreak that night, and the slaves returned to their homes. At Belmont Plantation, Mahoney and others sent word to the owner, Confederate officer Jim Wyche, to meet with them in the barn to discuss the matter. He refused. Impatient, Mahoney went to the house to see the nervous planter. "He told me," Mahoney continued, "he was afraid the negroes would murder him." Mahoney argued against this logic. "He need't be afraid of

This drawing by an artist in the field shows the house and grounds of Riley's Plantation. General Nathaniel P. Banks managed the Union efforts to reduce the Confederate stronghold at Port Hudson, Louisiana, from this location. Notice that the image has been gridded so that engravers could copy the sketch for publication.

John R. Hamilton, American, active 1863-1867; Headquarters of Major-Gen. Banks at Riley's Plantation, Near Port Hudson, La., 1863. Graphite, squared for reproduction, on paper; Catalogue Raisonné: Karolik (Civil War) 0958; Sheet: 17.8 x 25.1 cm (7 x 9 7/8 in); Musuem of Fine Arts, Boston. Gift of Maxim Karolik for the M. and M. Karolik Collection of American Watercolors and Drawings, 1800-1875; Photograph © Museum of Fine Arts, Boston

that because all the bad niggers had gone off with the Yankees, and those that stayed were faithful." Convinced, Wyche allowed the slaves to remain on the land. Mahoney accompanied the Rebel officer back to the army as his valet.[27]

Some of the remaining slaves fell prey to Rebel retribution. Calyle Stewart, a ten-year-old enslaved girl on a plantation near Jeanerette, watched the Yankees come and go, taking the able-bodied men with them. Her master forced her mother, a house servant, into the crops to make up for the lost field hands. She remembered a day when horsemen arrived on the farm during those chaotic days. "They liked to have scared me to death with their swords clanking," she recalled. One of the black slave drivers, Uncle Ned, approached the soldiers to ask them their business. "Dey axed him where was the Rebs," Stewart said, "and he pointed and said, 'that way.'" The cavalrymen—Confederates—beat the slave and tossed him in the Teche. "He shoulda stayed in an left his mouth shut," Stewart concluded. "We wuz al posted to stay in and be quiet . . . he was so smart, he went out and they fixed him."[28]

Believing that the Confederacy would soon collapse, Unionists living in remote farmsteads in Louisiana and Texas grew bold. News remained scarce and details sketchy, but the Federals seemed ready to crush the rebellion. Some Texas Unionists even took the risk and traveled to Louisiana, hoping to join Banks and find sanctuary once again under the Union flag. Otherwise, they feared, Confederate conscription officers would force them into the ranks of the Rebel armies.

Dennis Haynes, a forty-three-year-old resident of Hardin County, Texas, and native of Dublin, Ireland, figured the time was right to restate his allegiance to the United States and be free of secessionist tyranny. His home in the "Big Thicket," a densely wooded and swampy region in East Texas, had allowed him to remain a distant and unmolested spectator of the great national calamity. "When General Banks whipped Dick Taylor on the Teche," he observed, "the Confederates broke, helter-skelter, in every direction; Taylor's army was demoralized." Haynes hoped the storm had passed.[29]

He had cause to be optimistic. When Texas units from the Gulf Coast answered Taylor's call and moved toward Louisiana, not everyone in the ranks obeyed orders. Haynes soon found himself at the head of a growing squad of Confederate deserters who hid in the Big Thicket. "Spaight's Battalion was ordered from Houston, Texas . . . to reinforce Taylor," Haynes continued. "This battalion was chiefly composed of Texians from the southeastern counties. Many deserted for their homes intending to remain with their families at all hazards." Called to a meeting at a secluded pond, Haynes agreed to help the fifty or so men in attendance to organize and lead a resistance to Confederate authority in the region.[30]

The discontented soldiers complained that they had been duped by local planters and state officials into believing they had grievances against the Federal government. Once they threw their support to secession, Confederate promises to provide for their families vanished; instead Rebel commissary agents had seized corn, cattle, and hogs while offering vouchers in return. "Thus those cowardly

Not every Southerner supported the Confederacy. As the fortunes of war turned against the secessionists, the Rebel government turned to draconian measures to ensure compliance with their laws, including nearly universal conscription. This drove many into hiding and other into outright opposition.
Harpers Weekly, August 4, 1866.

vampires were fattening on the fat of the land," Haynes hissed, "and enriching themselves on the misfortune of their country and miseries of the poor." The assembled men declared themselves determined to resist Confederate conscription officers and to ignore Rebel authority. They outlined their grievances in writing. Their resolution affirmed "the injustice of the rebellion and the incompetency of the Confederacy to gain its independence," Haynes reported, and "that the rebellion was uncalled for by any act of the United States Congress, and much less by the election of Abraham Lincoln."[31]

The group intended to promote Confederate desertions and to offer armed resistance to authorities trying to enforce conscription laws. Texas Brigadier General George W. Van Vleck of Woodville, commander of the local brigade of state militia, responded by ordering a general roundup of the deserters and malcontents. Haynes and some of his companions dashed toward Louisiana, hoping that Federal forces rumored to be near Opelousas might come to their aid. "Before we quite got out of Texas," Haynes wrote, "we learned, to our

The U.S. navy added their heavy cannon to the bombardment of Port Hudson.
Author's collection.

great mortification, that Banks had evacuated." The roads into Louisiana turned dangerous for these dissenters, as thousands of Confederates rattled down these same wooded lanes answering Taylor's call for reinforcements. Haynes and his followers scattered.[32]

Marooned in the piney woods west of Alexandria, Haynes heard the Union army and navy shelling the Confederates on the Mississippi. "We could distinctly hear the Federal cannon battering at Port Hudson," he remembered. Clearly Banks had commenced the great battle for the Mississippi. Haynes and other Unionists would have to wait a while longer to rally to the old flag; they faded deeper into the wilderness of western Louisiana to bide their time.[33]

General Taylor, at Natchitoches, could not hear the Union guns, but he felt their cadences like the steady swinging of a clock pendulum. He had staked his personal fortunes on victory and remained determined to prevail. He had already sacrificed much by the summer of 1863. Union soldiers had wrecked his St. Charles Parish home, Fashion, the year before, and carried away his possessions, shipping many of his belongings—and those of his father, former President Zachary Taylor—north as trophies. Vicious Vermont soldiers, just out of meanness, even killed and skinned his son's pony. Government contractors now operated his plantation. His family currently lived as refugees; scarlet fever had taken both of his boys just a few weeks before. They died aboard a steamer carrying them from Alexandria to Shreveport surrounded by panicked soldiers and frightened civilians fleeing U.S. forces. Amid this crowd and tumult, Taylor's wife Margaret had to grieve without the support of her spouse.[34]

Perhaps energized by these personal tragedies, Taylor remained fixated on reversing Union gains in Louisiana. Only an aggressive and imaginative campaign—like those he had participated in under General Thomas J. "Stonewall" Jackson in the Shenandoah Valley—would bring victory. He had served in the army that whipped Banks a year ago. When the Yankees took New Orleans, Confederate officials sent Taylor home to Louisiana to push back the Federal juggernaut. When he arrived west of the Mississippi in the fall of 1862, he had discovered Rebel leadership disjointed, reactionary, and inert—a far cry from Lee's Army of Northern Virginia. The commander of Confederate troops in the Trans-Mississippi at that time, General Theophilus Holmes, had largely written off Louisiana and Texas from his perch in Little Rock, Arkansas. Taylor, peeved, had taken the initiative to arrange affairs in Louisiana to his own design, bypassing Holmes. Then, in March 1863, General Kirby Smith arrived to take command of the Department of the Trans-Mississippi. Under his more broadly conceived command, Louisiana and Texas now enjoyed new consideration.

The benefits of this change in command now became apparent. Facing a crisis in Louisiana, Taylor could now count on help. Under Kirby Smith's leadership,

Major General Richard Taylor sacrificed much by supporting the Confederacy.
Goelet and Buncombe Family Papers, #01112, Southern Historical Collection, University of North Carolina.

Confederate planners in Louisiana believed that Major General John G. Walker's Texas Division might be the most important unit at their disposal.
Edward Clifton Wharton Family Papers, Louisiana and Lower Mississippi Valley Collections, LSU Libraries, Baton Rouge, Louisiana.

commanders across his Department of the Trans-Mississippi shook loose any troops they could and ordered them to reinforce Taylor. A 1,600-man brigade of Texas infantry and dismounted cavalry under the command of Colonel Joseph Warren Speight marched out of the Indian Territory to Jefferson, Texas, and then boarded a steamer to Shreveport to join Taylor's command at Alexandria. Five cavalry regiments came in piecemeal as well, as did some infantry battalions from the Texas coast. The four thousand well-drilled soldiers of General John G. Walker's Texas Division, coming from Pine Bluff, Arkansas, remained the most anticipated reinforcements. These troops, along with Mouton's Louisiana infantry and Green's Texas cavalry brigades, would give Taylor a sizable command of some twenty infantry regiments, ten cavalry regiments, and eight artillery batteries. All told, Taylor believed he could shortly field more than ten thousand men and three-dozen cannon.[35]

Taylor, a Yale educated student of military history, plotted how best to employ this potent army. He believed that Banks might have blundered. Having given up a war of movement, the Federals had stupidly committed to the drudgery of siegecraft at Port Hudson. General Gardner, with just seven thousand men, commanded the attention of nearly three times that many Federals. The longer Banks stayed at Port Hudson, the weaker he would become from attrition and disease—especially if he tried more foolhardy assaults. Gardner would too, of course, but the Confederate commanders on both sides of the Mississippi River in Louisiana had been diligent about stocking Port Hudson with rations and ammunition. Even without resupply, Gardner might last six weeks, maybe even two months. That might allow time for Taylor to completely shift the momentum of the war in the Mississippi Valley.[36]

He assumed the offensive. "The value of the 'initiative' in war cannot be overstated," he lectured. "Holding it, a commander lays his plans deliberately and executes them at his own appointed time and in his own way." The Federal armies at Vicksburg and Port Hudson, committed to a war of pick and spade could do little to frustrate his plans. Taylor, a committed disciple of aggressive war, remained convinced that bold action would mitigate his lack of troops, supplies, and transportation. By falling back inside the fortresses, Pemberton had foolishly placed his command, and that of Gardner, into a potentially fatal position. "The 'defensive' is weak," Taylor declared, "lowering the *morale* of the army reduced to it . . . and keeping commander and troops in a state of anxious tension." He would not commit the same error.[37]

Other Confederates failed to appreciate Taylor's conviction. By threatening the sixty-mile-long Union supply lines on the Louisiana side of the Mississippi, Pemberton believed that the Confederate troops rushing toward Louisiana might compose a sufficient force to make a difference against Grant. "You can contribute materially to the defense of Vicksburg," he wrote Kirby Smith, "by a movement upon the line of communications of the enemy on the western side of the river. He derives his supplies and re-enforcements for the most part by a route which leads from Milliken's Bend." Then, Taylor's army might be crossed over to reinforce Vicksburg.[38]

When Taylor heard Pemberton's proposal, he scoffed. The Louisianan knew the fort was certainly doomed and that such a move would be useless. Certainly, by now, Grant had moved his supply lines to the east side of the Mississippi. Pemberton needed rescue. "The problem was to withdraw the garrison, not reinforce it," observed Taylor.[39]

He hatched a more daring plan, approximating the bold generalship of his mentor, Jackson, who had recently fallen at the Battle of Chancellorsville. By gathering as many troops as he could in Louisiana, Taylor planned to overrun Union positions in the Lafourche District and threaten New Orleans. He planned to make Banks choose between Port Hudson and the largest city in the South. The Confederates would enjoy favorable odds. Only a few thousand Union troops protected the Crescent City and spies attested that its citizens only awaited the return of Confederate authorities to throw off the Union yoke. "Its population of two-hundred-thousand was bitterly hostile to Federal rule," Taylor explained, "and the appearance of a Confederate force on the opposite bank of the river would raise such a storm as to bring General Banks from Port Hudson."[40]

With Banks thus unhinged, strategic elements east of the river would fall into place. General Gardner, freed from the siege, would abandon his works, join Johnston in Mississippi and, with a reinforced army of more than twenty thousand, seize the initiative, threaten Grant's lines, and possibly even extract Pemberton's garrison. Once freed from the shackles of Vicksburg and Port Hudson, the combined Confederates in Mississippi would form a formidable force of more than fifty thousand men. Although troops from the Trans-Mississippi might not be able to cross the river and help directly in this effort, they might generate enough noise to set into motion a complex chain of events leading to Rebel victory. At least the Confederacy would maintain an army in the field and remain a threat to Union control of the region.[41]

Taylor recognized that the Confederacy had already lost control of the Mississippi River. Union gunboats controlled the gap between Vicksburg and Port Hudson and blockaded the mouth of the Red River. The citadels themselves had ceased to be useful or relevant. Losing their garrisons, Taylor believed, would only compound the disaster. Time was short. Now, the best Confederates could hope for was to contest Union *control* of the Mississippi.

Taylor plotted his Jackson-style counteroffensive. His battered Louisiana infantry brigade marched south toward New Iberia to support operations in that region. Green with his Texas and Louisiana cavalry prowled near Brashear City. Taylor relied on General Mouton, senior commander of Confederate forces south of the Red River, to assess and report on the situation. Other reinforcements would gather at Washington and Simmesport to operate across the Atchafalaya and move along the Mississippi opposite Port Hudson or to reinforce Mouton on the lower Teche. Taylor counted just four brigades with which to launch this auspicious campaign. He needed more men.

On May 27, the same day Banks assaulted Port Hudson, Walker's Division arrived at Alexandria after more than a month moving from Pine Bluff, Arkansas. "The town is beautifully located in the midst of a cotton and sugar-cane country," wrote Private J. P. Blessington of the 16th Texas Infantry. "It is unrivaled, in the state of Louisiana, for its healthy and pleasant situation, and the grandeur of the surrounding scenery." Not every soldier in Walker's Division proved eager for the fight. "I just wish this confederacy was tore all to smash and turned bottom upward," wrote Private William Stoker, 18th Texas Infantry, to his wife Elizabeth, "or this war never will close until the men just quit." These troops—ready and reluctant alike—effectively doubled the size of Taylor's army and provided it with the heft to make a difference. Taylor took a steamer from Natchitoches to Alexandria to launch his campaign.[42]

The newly arrived Texans steeled themselves for the fight ahead, and some of Walker's Division traveled aboard transports to near the dismantled works at Fort DeRussy to make sure the Federals had gone. "They heard of us and skedaddled," Private Stoker boasted. "They taken all the negros they could hold of and destroyed all the crops of corn as they left Red River." The column of boats and soldiers turned back and concentrated at Alexandria. Stoker remained unclear as to his final destination: "I think . . . Vicksburg or some other place on the Mississippi. I don't know where we will go."[43]

Scouting the enemy at Brashear City, one of Green's troopers, Sergeant Alfred Petticolas of the 4th Texas Cavalry rode past a war-shocked citizenry, still reeling from the passage of armies. "We . . . were warily welcomed by the citizens," he wrote. "No complaints now of our men committing depredations—no outcry about our having pressed horses when afoot to mount ourselves." The residents offered up flowers and even waved small Rebel flags as the Confederates passed. As Petticolas continued south, closer to Union lines, the condition of the country worsened. "Almost all the negroes are gone off with the Federals," he noted, "and anything that the Feds desired to eat they took, and as a Yankee letter I saw expressed it, all they had to do was kill and eat."[44]

Petticolas remained baffled by the behavior of the Louisiana planters. Many hoped to weather the war by claiming sympathy with whatever army was at hand. Others sympathized with the soldier's bewidlerment. Parson Lucius Jones, a thirty-five-year-old Episcopal cleric in the 4th Texas, harangued against these lukewarm Rebels. "He is very much disgusted with the way the people of St. Mary's Parish have acted in the late raid," Petticolas recalled. "The greater portion of the rich slave owners have taken the oath of allegiance to the U.S. Government to save their property." The act apparently did not avail them much because marauding soldiers still ransacked their estates. "By sacrificing their principles," Petticolas chided, "they have lost both character and property."

For this introspective soldier from Victoria, Texas, the behavior of these Louisianans presented a dilemma. Why, he wondered, had he left his home on the Guadalupe River to put himself in danger on behalf of such slack-fibered poltroons? Was this a war about political principles, as he believed when he joined? If not, was he simply fighting so that people in Louisiana could keep their slaves—their property? Perhaps, Peticolas mused, he had erred when he joined the Confederate army.

He sought the counsel of Parson Jones. "He says that if this is a war for the salvation of property, we will fail," Petticolas scribbled. Because that seemed to be the view of most of the gentry of Louisiana, the soldier believed, it did little to justify his personal sacrifice. Petticolas wavered, not sure he wanted to die defending the property of slave owners.

Sensing the conundrum facing Petticolas, Parson Jones continued: "If it is a war for the right of self-government, we will succeed."

This buoyed the skeptical sergeant's spirits. Federal power must be checked, and state sovereignty protected. "I am satisfied," Petticolas penned in his dairy, "that it is a war for freedom."[45]

4

The Milliken's Bend Campaign

They were miserable looking wretches.
—Rear Admiral David Dixon Porter
U.S. Navy

General Edmund Kirby Smith had little faith in General Richard Taylor's plan. He had supported efforts to concentrate a force to oppose General Nathaniel P. Banks. Now that the Federals surrounded Port Hudson and had quit the Mississippi's west bank, Kirby Smith made other plans. The Confederates would target General Ulysses S. Grant, not Banks. "I was informed," Taylor recalled, "that all Confederate authorities in the east were urgent for some effort on our part in behalf of Vicksburg, and that public opinion would condemn us if we did not *try to do something*." Taylor, who had directed campaigns in his district unimpeded for nearly a year, chafed at Kirby Smith's intrusion. He also disliked his superior's patronizing tone. Kirby Smith wrote, "I know your desire is naturally great to recover what you have lost in Lower Louisiana, and to push on toward New Orleans but the stake contended for near Vicksburg is the Valley of the Mississippi and the Trans-Mississippi Department; the defeat of General Grant is the *terminus ad quem* [limit to which] of all operations in the west this summer." He concluded by insinuating that Taylor's bold and imaginative plans would yield only "minor advantages."[1]

Kirby Smith embraced General John C. Pemberton's plan aiming at Grant's supply lines. For the previous six months, Federal forces occupied extensive camps along the west bank of the Mississippi stretching from opposite Vicksburg for seventy miles upriver to Lake Providence. Dry ground proved hard to find and Grant's forty thousand Union troops spread out in narrow bivouacs between the Mississippi levee and the margins of various bayous and streams to their west. Commissary, quartermaster, and ordnance officers spent the spring stockpiling rations, ammunition, and gear in great magazines for the day when Grant and his army moved against Vicksburg.

Pemberton assumed that Grant's army, although now east of the river, would still draw supplies from these long-established depots. The Confederates believed they had an opportunity to pounce because only newly raised black regiments and convalescents guarded these key points. Kirby Smith agreed to destroy these caches before the Federals could relocate them to the east bank of the Mississippi. "The amount of stores, munitions, and rations exposed to capture is great," he explained to Taylor. Should Confederates manage to cut this supply line for ten days, Grant would have to abandon the siege of Vicksburg. If Pemberton and Lieutenant General Joseph E. Johnston defeated the Federals in the meantime, it would "insure his destruction." Combined, all these Rebel armies could then save General Franklin Gardner at Port Hudson.[2]

Taylor could not believe what he read. "Remonstrances were to no avail," Taylor grumbled, furious at Kirby Smith's sabotage. Dutifully, Taylor issued new orders for General John G. Walker's Texas Division. It would head back northeast in a great circle toward Monroe, a town they had passed through just ten days before. Kirby Smith ordered Taylor to personally lead these Texans into battle. Brigadier General Alfred Mouton had to handle operations in south Louisiana.[3]

Taylor had no heart for this fight for Vicksburg and wanted to finish it quickly. He diligently rolled out maps of northeastern Louisiana and noted its latticework of streams draining north to south across the flat terrain. The most important of these, the Ouachita, began deep in southern Arkansas. It coursed largely parallel to the Mississippi, forming a fertile "V" some seventy-five miles wide on a line stretching from Monroe to Vicksburg. This wedge of farmland narrowed to a point where it joined its principal tributaries, the Tensas and Little Rivers, at the aptly named village of Trinity. These comingled streams formed the Black River here, some twenty-five miles west of Natchez, Mississippi, and flowed into the Red River some forty road miles downstream.

Each of these streams was a potential Rebel line of supply and communications—or obstacle—in the coming campaign. The Little River, flowing roughly northwest to southeast, came to within fifteen miles of Alexandria. The Tensas River, an ancient channel of the Mississippi, flowed southwesterly from its origins near an oxbow of the Mississippi at Lake Providence, Louisiana, until joining a large parallel stream to the west, Bayou Maçon, whose origins were at Lake Chicot in southeastern Arkansas. Both of these twisting streams passed within thirty to

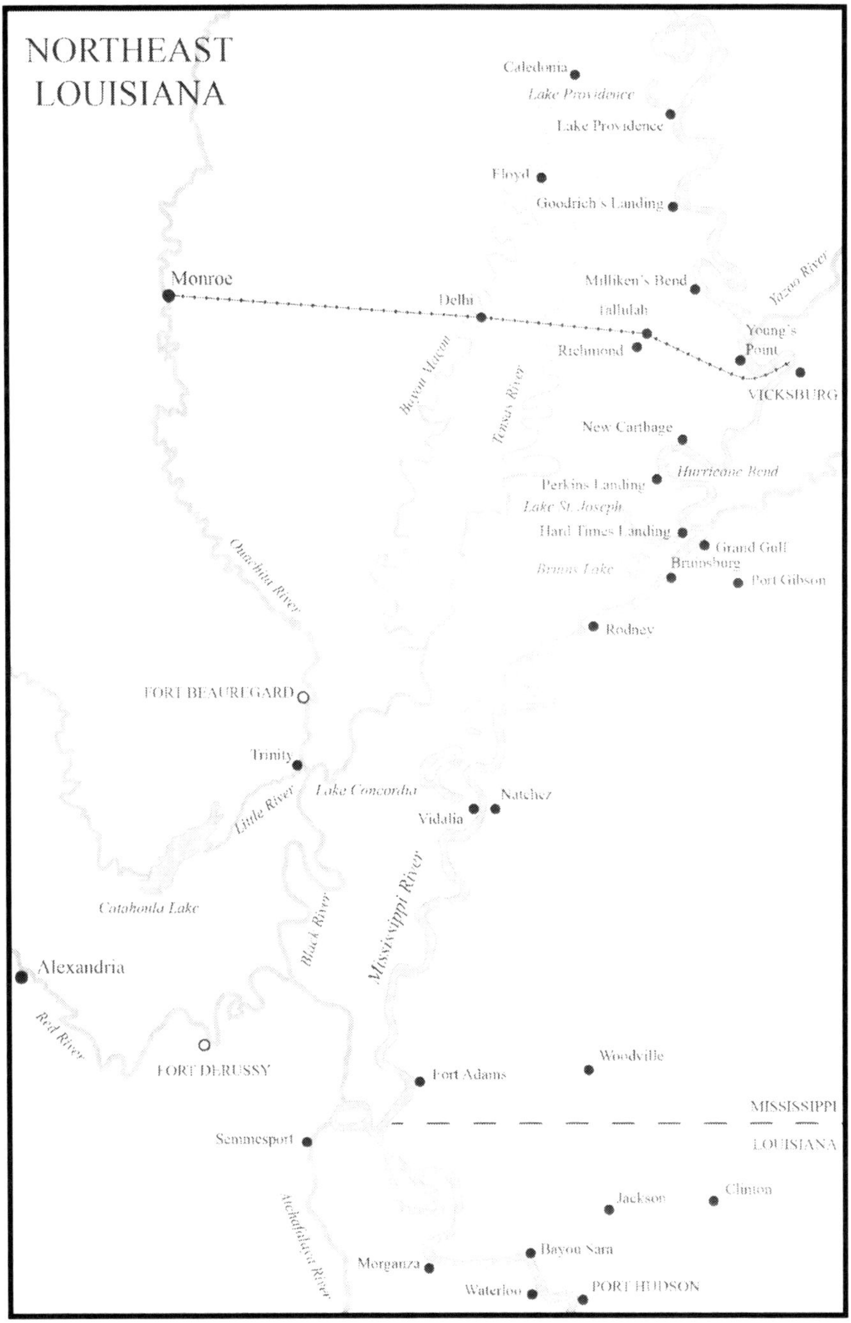
NORTHEAST LOUISIANA
Caledonia
Lake Providence
Lake Providence
Floyd
Goodrich's Landing
Monroe
Milliken's Bend
Yazoo River
Delhi
Tallulah
Young's Point
Richmond
VICKSBURG
Bayou Macon
Tensas River
New Carthage
Hurricane Bend
Perkins Landing
Lake St. Joseph
Hard Times Landing
Grand Gulf
Bruinsburg
Bruins Lake
Port Gibson
Ouachita River
Rodney
FORT BEAUREGARD
Trinity
Lake Concordia
Natchez
Little River
Vidalia
Mississippi River
Catahoula Lake
Black River
Alexandria
Red River
FORT DERUSSY
Woodville
Fort Adams
MISSISSIPPI
LOUISIANA
Semmesport
Jackson
Clinton
Atchafalaya River
Bayou Sara
Morganza
Waterloo
PORT HUDSON

thirty-five miles of the Mississippi at Vicksburg. Could steamers still navigate these streams? If so, how far?

In the antebellum period, planters had an economic incentive for understanding these watercourses. The ability to ship crops from northeastern Louisiana, to the Red River, and on to markets in New Orleans in turn attracted riverboat and railroad men. By 1860, the Vicksburg, Shreveport, and Texas Railroad stretched from Monroe, on the Ouachita, crossed the Maçon at Delhi, Louisiana, passed across the Tensas near the villages of Talullah and Richmond, and continued to the river hamlet of De Soto on the bank opposite Vicksburg. Cotton and corn cultivation by large populations of slaves dominated this agricultural Eldorado and planters enjoyed easy access to distant markets.

The eastern margins of this fertile "V" remained prone to flooding and presented complicated terrain for moving armies. Several Mississippi River oxbows and overflow streams looped and meandered across the lands between the west bank and the Tensas. One of the deepest, Walnut Bayou, left the Mississippi at Milliken's Bend and snaked to the south, then west, until it joined Roundaway Bayou near the market town of Richmond, Louisiana. This stream continued south again before rejoining the Mississippi at New Carthage. A second channel, Bayou Vidal, broke away just before this confluence and arced around to the south before entering the river near Perkin's Landing. Below this junction, an oxbow loop—Lake St. Joseph—started below Perkin's Landing and approached the Mississippi again at Hard Times Landing. Another body of water—Bruin's Lake—lay west of the river and the town of Bruinsburg, Mississippi, on the opposite bank.

Grant's army had already navigated the levees of these water features on its way to crossing the Mississippi. As the army passed, commissary officers established camps and supply caches along the route. Pemberton and Kirby Smith believed they remained in place even after Grant's army had passed over the river.

Taylor, unconvinced, followed Kirby Smith's directive and led Walker's Division in a swift strike against Grant's putative supply lines. East of Alexandria, Confederates loaded onto steamboats on the Little River, and proceeding to Trinity, moved up the Tensas. This route might to be prove perilous should Union gunboats prowl these navigable streams. "Time was so important," Taylor wrote, "I decided to run the risk."[4]

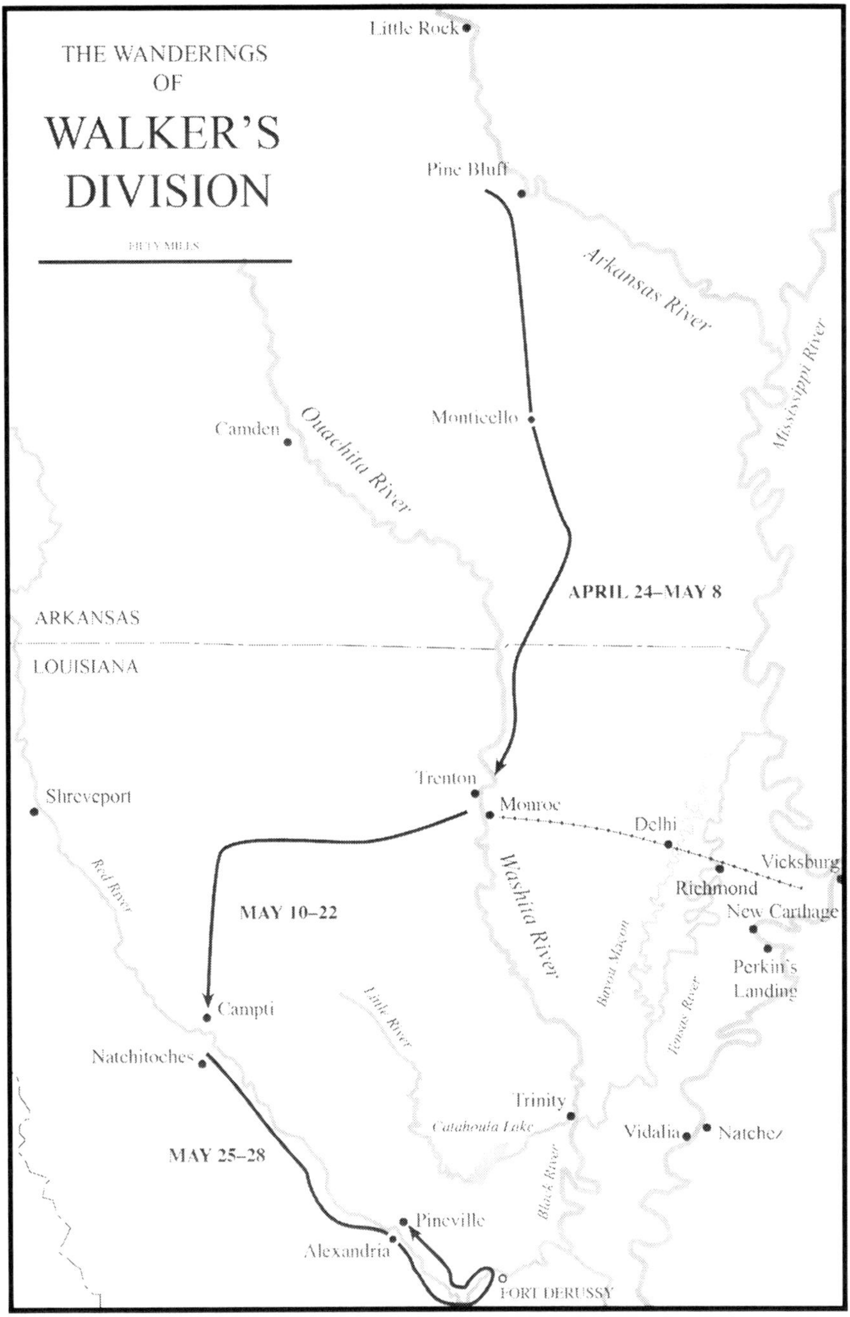
THE WANDERINGS
OF
WALKER'S
DIVISION
Little Rock
Pine Bluff
Arkansas River
Mississippi River
Monticello
Camden
Ouachita River
APRIL 24–MAY 8
ARKANSAS
LOUISIANA
Trenton
Shreveport
Monroe
Delhi
Vicksburg
Richmond
New Carthage
Red River
MAY 10–22
Washita River
Bayou Macon
Perkin's
Landing
Tensas River
Campti
Little River
Natchitoches
Trinity
Catahoula Lake
Vidalia
Natchez
MAY 25–28
Black River
Pineville
Alexandria
FORT DERUSSY

On May 30, Walker's Division traveled more than two hundred miles via Louisiana's interior rivers, lakes, and bayous. In the late afternoon, two brigades disembarked about twenty-five miles southwest of Vicksburg; a third brigade landed a day behind. One of Walker's regiments, the 13th Texas Cavalry (Dismounted), passed up the Ouachita to Monroe to escort supplies destined for Taylor's command. A small mounted force from the 15th Louisiana Cavalry Battalion—local men—waited to meet the Texans and guide them toward the enemy.

The Louisianans were late. A disgruntled Taylor rousted a neighborhood doctor to show the way. "That was a night that tried men's souls," remembered Private J. P. Blessington: "The route . . . was through a cane-brake, dark and dismal, and as desolate and dreary as the imagination could picture, and highly musical with the croaking of frogs." The Texans expected to blunder into Union pickets at any moment. Yet, the Texans moved through the night, undetected, "like a band of dark spirits, over the hard and uneven road, accompanied by the dull rumbling of the artillery carriages."[5]

At first light on May 31, the Confederates arrived outside the Union camps at Perkins Landing on the Mississippi River. A few miles upstream lay New Carthage, a potential target, and a few miles south lay Hard Times Landing, where Grant had crossed his army. Charts named this Mississippi curve "Hurricane Bend"; others called it Davis Bend after Jefferson Davis and his brother's plantations on the east bank. The wreck of the USS *Indianola* lay on the far shore as well. None of this mattered to Taylor; he aimed his army at three hundred Union soldiers of the 60th Indiana garrisoning Perkins Landing along with a like number of black laborers and recruits. At daybreak, these Federals milled unconcerned about their camps, the smoke of their cooking fires clearly visible to the Texans.[6]

Union pickets detected the Texans forming on the skirt of timber to the west and dashed into camp to spread the alarm. They were nearly too late. At 9:00 A.M., the four regiments of General Henry McCulloch's brigade had already formed into line and stepped toward the attack. Colonel Horace Randal's Brigade followed close behind McCulloch while Captain William Edgar's Texas Battery shelled the camp with four 6-pounders. "The enemy . . . left precipitately, leaving behind their provisions and cooking utensils," Blessington remembered. "Our troops helped themselves to the enemy's hardtack and coffee." After looting the camp, the Texans pressed after the fleeing Federals. The Hoosiers reformed behind an improvised a cotton bale breastwork in a wood along the Mississippi levee. After exchanging shots with Texan skirmishers, the Yankees fell back to the edge of the river.[7]

A veteran of the Texas Revolution and a well-respected Texas Ranger, Henry Eustace McCulloch followed his more famous brother, Ben, into the Confederate army and helped secure the surrender of Federal troops in Texas at the outbreak of the war. He later took command of the Texas Division, but, superseded by John G. Walker, he returned to brigade command. This image, from the mid-1850s, shows him at age thirty-nine.
McCulloch Family Papers, San Jacinto Museum of History. Author's collection.

Believing their enemy trapped, the Confederates advanced. As they crested the levee, however, they encountered a terrible war machine. The booming of heavy guns from the river and heavy rounds whirring overhead brushed the Texans back. Sailors aboard the USS *Carondelet*, having arrived early that morning to investigate the loss of telegraph communications with the west bank, fired blindly toward the Rebels hoping the harassing fire would drive them away. The men of the 60th Indiana and their black auxiliaries used the respite to destroy the supplies stacked at the landing before loading onto the tinclad *Forest Rose* to make their escape. The Rebel infantry, inert against the ironclad, took cover.[8]

Flummoxed, McCulloch turned to his artillery. Captain Edgar's "Alamo City Guards" battery gamely played on the Union vessel, but its 6-pound rounds barely scuffed the *Carondelet*'s armor. Over the next ninety minutes, the Texans exchanged fire with the Federal gunboat, to no effect. By noon, the Texans had fallen back. The attack at Perkins Landing had killed nearly a dozen Federal soldiers, whereas the Texans lost one killed—Captain Gallatin Smith of General McCulloch's staff—knocked dead from his saddle by a spinning shell fragment.[9]

The ironclad USS Carondolet *was one of the most active gunboats on the Mississippi and compiled an impressive service record.*
Naval Historical Center.

Smith was the first combat casualty for this Confederate division in whom so many placed so much faith; this minor dustup was its first real combat in more than a year of service. Some mistook this minor affair as real war. Captain Elijah Petty had finally seen action and stood it well, he thought. "Not a nerve twitched or muscle trembled—not a palpitation of the heart, not a misgiving," he wrote home. "I was as cool, quiet, and self possessed as you ever saw me. I thought no more of it than going to a frolic." He had passed the test. "If this is all the fear, I don't mind a battle."[10]

The Texans backed away from the river seeking new victims. Walker ordered his troops to fall back the way they had come, then north toward the Vicksburg, Shreveport, and Texas Railroad and the crossing of Bayou Maçon at Delhi. The day after the fight at Perkin's Landing, Walker's Division crossed the Tensas River, then turned right and angled toward the east bank of Bayou Maçon, "a deep, dirty, sluggish stream," observed Blessington, "stocked with a variety of fish and alligators." Meanwhile, the tardy Louisiana cavalry fanned out to locate other enemy outposts and reconnoiter the roads and avenues of approach.[11]

Rebel success depended on the railroad and its bridges over the various streams. The Louisiana cavalry reported the crossing over Roundaway Bayou, closest to

Tinclad Number 9, USS Forest Rose, *served in a variety of utility roles on the Mississippi, including transport, gunboat, and dispatch vessel.*
Naval Historical Center.

the enemy, intact, but the Federals destroyed the bridge over the Tensas. Taylor crossed a detachment of the Texan infantry over the Tensas on a barge to reinforce the Louisiana cavalry at Richmond and to hold the Roundaway Bayou crossing. Confederate engineers rebuilt the Tensas bridge, reconnecting Taylor's advance guard with the rest of the army. The tracks at the town of Delhi at the crossing of Bayou Maçon remained operative and the 13th Texas Cavalry (Dismounted) waited there with rations and ammunition brought in from Monroe.[12]

Major Isaac F. Harrison, commander of the 15th Louisiana Cavalry Battalion, arrived at Taylor's headquarters at Richmond confirming his assumptions. To the south, at Lake St. Joseph, a Louisiana cavalry company jumped a collection of black troops in a camp of instruction, killing its captain and twelve soldiers and capturing around seventy recruits along with sixty women and children. The Louisianans scoured abandoned Union camps from that point to New Carthage, discovering the enemy long gone. Harrison concluded that Grant had abandoned the supply line from the railroad south, at least. Taylor appreciated the news. "I cannot speak too highly of Major Harrison as a cavalry officer," the general reported. "I do not think he has a superior in the service."[13]

The Louisiana cavalryman had a murkier picture of what lay along the west bank of the Mississippi north of the rail line. Harrison believed the Federals maintained only a few depots and camps there. Fifty miles to the north, scouts reported that just a few companies held the Lake Providence positions. Only six hundred or so rear-echelon quartermaster and commissary troops and convalescents left behind when Grant crossed the river maintained the depot at Young's Point.[14]

Kirby Smith, Taylor concluded, had sent him on a fool's errand. Taylor still had to make the attempt and operated under the premise that four depleted Union supply dumps lay within striking distance of his army at Richmond. Besides, these lightly guarded outposts might prove easy pickings. With orders from Kirby Smith "to do something" on behalf of Vicksburg, Taylor ordered Walker's four thousand Texans to strike at these Federal leftovers. Taylor decided to hit three—Young's Point, Milliken's Bend, and Lake Providence—simultaneously, and then pick off Goodrich's Landing afterward.[15]

Major Harrison's Louisiana scouts missed a few important details that would influence the outcome of the Confederate campaign. Although noting the various enemy strengths and positions, the Louisianans could not gauge the ability of U.S. troops to pass freely along the Mississippi to reinforce threatened points. In addition, Harrison's men had been wrong about Young's Point. Grant's officers had not abandoned it but instead transformed Young's Point into an important transportation hub. Laborers hacked out a new road from Young's Point to Bower's Landing below the city. This route, a west bank supply workaround, allowed Grant to pass ammunition, food, and equipment from his northern lines, across the Mississippi, down the west bank, and then back across to the troops investing the Rebel defenses south of the Baldwin's Ferry Road.[16]

Grant considered Young's Point vital and designated this supply pivot as the headquarters of the Union District of Northeast Louisiana. He dispatched an energetic officer, Brigadier General Elias S. Dennis, to take command of the district and to defend it from Taylor's army. He also sent a brigade of troops to hold this ground.[17]

Major Harrison had guessed correctly about the camps north of Young's Point being occupied, but no longer of vital strategic importance. Grant had shifted his supply lines to Haynes Bluff on the Yazoo River, east of the Mississippi and out of Rebel reach. Milliken's Bend, Goodrich's Landing, and Lake Providence no longer held much importance to the logistics of Grant's army and the conduct of his siege of Vicksburg.[18]

Although no longer supply depots, these camps still held strategic and symbolic value. Recruiters for black regiments continued to bring in freedmen from area plantations for service in the army throughout the fifty miles of Louisiana recently vacated by the Union army. Several camps of instruction for Grant's African Brigade existed at points along the river. Black wage-labor supervised by government contractors also operated dozens of plantations in the area.[19]

An Illinois Democrat, Congress appointed Elias Dennis as Marshall of the Leavenworth District in Kansas Territory in 1857. A political casualty of "Bleeding Kansas," Dennis returned home. At the outbreak of the Civil War, he took command of the 30th Illinois and led that regiment as part of the Army of the Tennessee and later earned promotion to brigadier general. He crossed the Mississippi with Ulysses S. Grant's army and fought well at Port Gibson and Raymond before assuming command of forces in the District of Northeast Louisiana. Author's collection.

Protecting this sprawling dominion proved a daunting task. General Dennis's garrisons lay scattered and isolated. Young's Point, the most critical transit point for beans and bullets heading to the siege lines south of Vicksburg, lay nearly opposite the Mississippi Squadron's anchorage at the mouth of the Yazoo River. Dennis knew he must hold this place and so maintained a strong garrison, relying on the veteran 108th, 120th, and 131st Illinois Infantry and the equally seasoned 23rd Iowa. About fifteen miles up the river road lay Milliken's Bend and its garrison of four partially organized black regiments, the 9th, 11th, and 13th Louisiana Infantry (African Descent), and the 1st Mississippi Infantry (African Descent) along with four companies of the 10th Illinois Cavalry. This brigade remained poorly trained, understrength, and ill-equipped.[20]

Other Union outposts lay upstream. About fifteen miles upriver from Milliken's Bend lay Goodrich's Landing and the camps of the 1st Arkansas and 10th Louisiana

A Swiss immigrant, Herman Lieb moved to Illinois in 1856 to practice law. From 1861 to 1863, he served as a line officer in the 8th Illinois infantry before assuming command of the 9th Louisiana Infantry (African Descent) and the post at Milliken's Bend. Author's collection.

infantries (African Descent), which were also new to soldiering. Another dozen miles beyond, the veteran 1st Kansas Mounted Infantry and the 16th Wisconsin Infantry served as provost guards for the government plantations around Lake Providence. These regiments presented a significantly beefier force than the few companies Harrison had reported. Besides these military enclaves, there remained scattered pockets of hospitals and refugee camps where mostly displaced black patients, ill from a variety of diseases including smallpox, lay unprotected and at the mercy of the microbes and the enemy. Altogether Dennis commanded a fifty-mile line of targets vulnerable to Confederate attack.[21]

If Dennis could locate the main body of Taylor's army, he might discern Rebel intentions. In the small hours of June 5, the general ordered a reconnaissance from Milliken's Bend. At 2 A.M., two companies of the 10th Illinois Cavalry headed toward Richmond, supported by infantry from the 9th Louisiana (African Descent). The road toward Richmond led southward along the Mississippi until it branched off the river road at Oak Grove Plantation near Duckport. The one hundred Union horsemen under Captain Christopher Anderson continued along the Mississippi toward Young's Point instead, planning to drop in behind any Rebels scouting in that vicinity. Colonel Hermann Lieb continued to Richmond at the head of several hundred foot soldiers, crossing the Walnut Bayou bridge.[22]

Lieb's early morning reconnaissance yielded mixed results. The 9th Louisiana (African Descent) arrived near Richmond, but, failing to uncover any Rebel troops, continued north of that town heading for the Tensas. Three miles from the river, Lieb's scouts scurried back reporting Rebel pickets in force holding the road. The colonel, convinced that the enemy must occupy Richmond as suspected, could not gauge the Confederate strength. The enemy's main body appeared to be west of the Tensas. Unwilling to neither probe for answers nor risk his command, Lieb ordered his troops back to Oak Grove.[23]

Captain Anderson and his cavalry found plenty of Rebels. Confederate cavalry had been snooping around Young's Point but doubled back before sunrise. Louisiana pickets discovered Anderson's Illinois troopers heading south down the road and reported their presence in time for the Rebels to lay an ambush. After an initial volley, the Confederates overran the Federals, killing and capturing one-third of them. The surviving bluecoats scattered, reaching the safety of Lieb's infantry heading toward Oak Grove. The Confederate cavalry, outgunned by the men of the 9th Louisiana (African Descent), checked their pursuit and took a byway to Richmond with their prisoners, allowing the Union force to fall back to Milliken's Bend.[24]

After the fight, Dennis teased out Confederate intentions. Lieb's and Anderson's scouting expeditions accomplished little beyond alerting the Federals to potential danger. Confederate cavalry clearly hovered nearby, and the fight at Perkin's Landing suggested that enemy forces in the region included infantry and artillery. Dennis alerted the garrisons at Young's Point and Milliken's Bend to the danger and ordered the 23rd Iowa onto two transports to form a mobile reserve. Signalmen wigwagged a request for a gunboat to escort the steamboats upstream where they could come to Colonel Lieb's aid should the blow land there. Lieb, understanding the danger, ordered his outposts strengthened; the raw and largely untrained black regiments were to remain vigilant and man the Milliken's Bend defenses by 3 A.M.[25]

The Confederates, though, did not strike. Taylor intended to initiate his chain of attacks several miles north at Lake Providence. On the evening of June 5, the 13th Texas Cavalry (Dismounted) traveled north to the town of Floyd, Louisiana, joining with Colonel Frank Bartlett's 13th Louisiana Cavalry Battalion. These nine hundred troops would move to Lake Providence, rough up the garrison there, and perhaps draw off Union reserves. The swift Rebel column would then move along the Mississippi and gobble up the troops at Goodrich's Landing before joining Walker's Division in the vicinity of Milliken's Bend.[26]

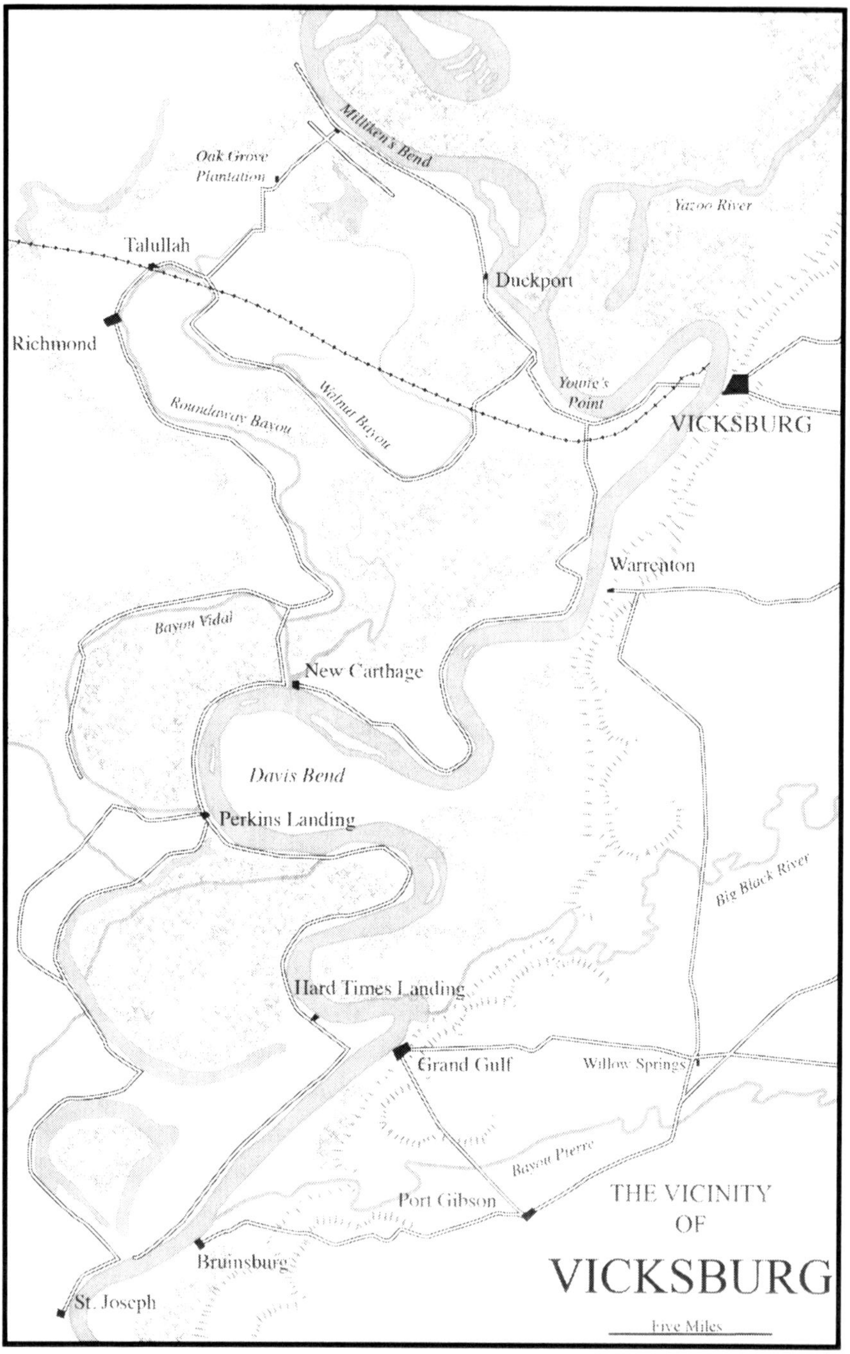
Milliken's Bend
Oak Grove Plantation
Yazoo River
Talullah
Duckport
Richmond
Young's Point
Walnut Bayou
Roundaway Bayou
VICKSBURG
Warrenton
Bayou Vidal
New Carthage
Davis Bend
Perkins Landing
Big Black River
Hard Times Landing
Grand Gulf
Willow Springs
Bayou Pierre
Port Gibson
Bruinsburg
St. Joseph
THE VICINITY OF VICKSBURG
Five Miles

Lieb's reconnaissance had been a day premature. While his Federal troops had approached the Tensas, Taylor was moving his command from Delhi to Richmond. The black soldiers had been within hours of seeing most of Walker's Division coming up the road, but instead, they had turned back. Taylor, with his operational secrets intact, coiled his army to strike at the center of Grant's assumed supply line, Milliken's Bend and Young's Point, theoretically benefiting from the strategic confusion caused by Rebel operations at Lake Providence.[27]

The next morning, June 6, dawned quietly at Milliken's Bend. Lieb's garrison lay in line of battle for hours before the sun made its appearance. Yet, no Rebels appeared. As the day wore on, the ironclad USS *Choctaw* hove into view, as did the transports carrying the men of the 23rd Iowa. Lieb, reinforced and relaxing a bit as the hours passed uneventfully, ordered the white infantry, who had arrived without camp equipment, to stay aboard their boats that night. The Hawkeyes might be more comfortable, and Lieb anticipated sending them back to Young's Point the following day anyway. The danger—if there had ever been any—had passed. The crew of the *Choctaw* banked its fires and allowed the pressure to drop in their engines, believing that conserving fuel was more important than remaining under power to meet an emergency.[28]

Lieb spread the African Brigade across various sections of his line. His best-drilled unit, the 9th Louisiana Infantry (African Descent) held the left closest to the road, which was the most likely line of attack. With a little more than one-month's service, this regiment was his oldest and best. The semi-formed 1st Mississippi, 13th Louisiana, and 11th Louisiana filled in to the right. Just days removed from slavery, the majority of these troops were raw recruits in ill-fitting uniforms and armed with inferior muskets.[29]

Colonel Lieb had his men fortify Milliken's Bend. In general, the position resembled a long narrow rectangle redoubt with the short ends on the northern and southern flanks. Behind—to the east—lay the Mississippi levee and river. A lower levee covered the front, which troops had modified into a breastwork with the addition of logs and cotton bales. Cross levees bordering sloughs to the north and south finished the fortification. The road from Richmond and the village of Milliken's Bend lay to the south, beyond the Federal left. To the immediate front was a farm with three fields edged in a thick hedge of Bois d'Arc trees. Federals filled the space between the hedge and western levee with felled trees and other

A big ironclad with a crew of more than one hundred men, USS Choctaw *mounted one 100-pounder rifle, three IX-inch smoothbores, and two 30-pounder rifles. Photographic History of the Civil War.*

obstacles. Inside these fortifications lay the African Brigade's regimental camps and residual supplies from Grant's army.[30]

Lieb miscalculated the Confederate timetable and let his guard down. Just five miles away, Taylor assembled his army. The various regiments of General Walker's Division had arrived at Richmond from Delhi around 10:00 A.M. and Rebel officers received their orders. The command would march to Oak Grove and divide. One brigade would turn right and continue to attack Young's Point, some five miles distant, whereas a second would veer left and move against Milliken's Bend twelve miles to the north. A third Texas brigade and the three batteries of artillery would remain at the intersection as a strategic reserve. Taylor, convinced he would be raiding lightly held outposts with little strategic value, had no intention of committing the whole division to what now amounted to a reconnaissance in force. The Texans were to rest that day but be ready to make a night march by 6:00 P.M. to avoid the Louisiana heat. The attacks would follow in the dark hours of the next morning, June 7.[31]

Taylor knew that the events of the next few hours would prove beyond doubt if Grant still had supply lines west of the Mississippi, which had been Kirby Smith's justification for the entire expedition. If the Federal positions revealed Major Harrison's recent assessment to be correct, Taylor's command would be striking at thin air. At any rate, Taylor believed he still held an element of surprise, and he sent a signal officer, Lieutenant S. M. Routh, to wigwag a message to the defenders at Vicksburg that an effort "to do something" had been made. After the Texans carried and plundered both points, Walker's Division would reassemble on the reserve and await developments. Taylor, with his project in southern Louisiana still fresh in his mind, did not anticipate tarrying long in the region after these easy fights proved Pemberton and Kirby Smith wrong. Either way, he wanted credit for following orders—misguided as he believed they were.[32]

The Confederates started an hour late, wasting precious daylight. After tramping down the road to beyond Walnut Bayou, General McCulloch turned his column to the left and headed toward Milliken's Bend with 1,500 men of the 16th Texas Cavalry (Dismounted) and the 16th, 17th, and 19th Texas infantries. Brigadier General James Hawe's brigade, 1,400 strong, headed toward Young's Point, the soldiers of 12th, 18th, and 22nd Texas Infantry facing their first combat. Colonel Horace Randal's Brigade—the 11th and 14th Texas infantry, the 28th Texas Cavalry (Dismounted), and R. S. Gould's 6th Texas Cavalry Battalion (Dismounted)—and the three batteries of divisional artillery stayed at Oak Grove ready to support either effort.[33]

McCulloch's Brigade traveled all evening and past midnight to get into position. In the darkness, the Texans had no idea what they faced, although they could hear the chuffing and stamping of horses and mules from the farm to their front, and the voices and coughs of men far to the rear nearer the Mississippi. In the gloom, officers formed the brigade into assault columns of divisions, one half of each regiment in battle line forward, and the balance in line behind. Three units—the 16th Texas Cavalry (Dismounted), 17th and 19th Texas infantry—took position north of the Richmond road, facing roughly the southwest corner of the Union position several hundred yards ahead. The 16th Texas Infantry remained in reserve. The men in all four regiments fixed bayonets.[34]

McCulloch ordered his detachment of Louisiana cavalry to scout ahead, followed by a heavy line of infantry skirmishers. He wanted to map the battlefield before sunrise. The Louisiana troopers picked their way through the fields in the humid night air. Federal pickets, perhaps thinking the horses were the government

West Point graduate and Tennessee-native Horace Randal served in the 1st U.S. Dragoons on the Texas frontier before the war but resigned to serve in a number of staff positions for Confederate leaders including Braxton Bragg and Joseph E. Johnston. Randal returned to Texas to raise and lead the 28th Texas Cavalry. He eventually took charge of a brigade in Walker's Texas Division.
Huntington Library, San Mateo, California.

A West Point trained Kentuckian, James Morrison Hawes served with General Winfield Scott in Mexico before returning to his alma mater as an instructor. In the early 1850s, Hawes studied cavalry tactics in France before receiving an assignment to serve on the Texas frontier. He resigned at the outbreak of the Civil War and served in a Kentucky regiment before assuming command of all of the Confederate cavalry west of the Appalachians. He left this position to take command of mounted troops in Arkansas, before moving again, this time to command an infantry brigade in Walker's Texas Division.
Library of Congress Prints and Photographs Division, Washington, D.C.

animals held in the fields edged with Bois d'Arc, allowed the horsemen to come in close, before discovering their error. The raw recruits fired once and then fled. The Texan skirmishers, seeing the flashes in the night, instinctively fired back, striking a few of their allies' horses in the exchange. The Louisianans prudently fell back as the infantry moved in position for the coming assault.[35]

Convinced he had learned all he could of the Union defenses, McCulloch wasted no time. He bellowed to his command, "McCulloch's Brigade, advance!" The Texans stepped out in the darkness in neat formations. Although the skirmishers advanced nimbly toward the Union line, the main body only covered several hundred yards before becoming tangled in the first of the thick Bois d'Arc hedges. The trim lines of the well-drilled brigade fragmented, and men searched in the dark for openings through which to pass. The Texans, now broken into squads and clumps, nevertheless pushed ahead.[36]

The Battle of Milliken's Bend began in darkness and confusion. Union drummers beat the long roll as the men of the 9th Louisiana (African Descent), hearing the movement of troops to their front, assembled into position to face their baptism of fire. A volley from the Union breastworks flashed in the night and the Texas skirmishers—having uncovered the enemy line—fell back. Amid the confusion and push of men through the hedges and around the farm buildings, Texans spooked a herd of mules that bolted for the Union lines; the animals unnerved many of the raw Union recruits who fled into the night.[37]

Lieb needed help. He dispatched some of his staff to the river to signal the navy to land the 23rd Iowa. Sailors on night watch aboard USS *Choctaw* saw the torches and lanterns on shore a little after 3 A.M.; an officer rowed out and reported a heavy Confederate attack in the making. Clearing for action, the navy gunners aimed their 100-pounder Parrott and the IX-inch Dahlgren in the general direction of the enemy, holding their fire for the time being, unable to get a clear shot because of the darkness and the intervening levee.[38]

With their formations hashed and command and control compromised, the Texans faltered. They crossed the last few hundred yards to the back of the farm fields as a mob. Surprised that the Rebels had not already hit his line, Lieb ordered skirmishers to grope for the attackers and buy time for reinforcements to come ashore. His poorly trained black regiments crashed into the Texans amid the fields, but they proved no marksmen. The Federals fell back to the cover of farm buildings and hedges to snipe at the dark silhouettes once again, this time coming toward them. As the Confederates closed, the Federal skirmishers scurried back over the breastworks. One squad of a dozen or so Union troops, having taken shelter in one of the farm buildings to the Texan left, still held their ground, pestering the Confederate flank.

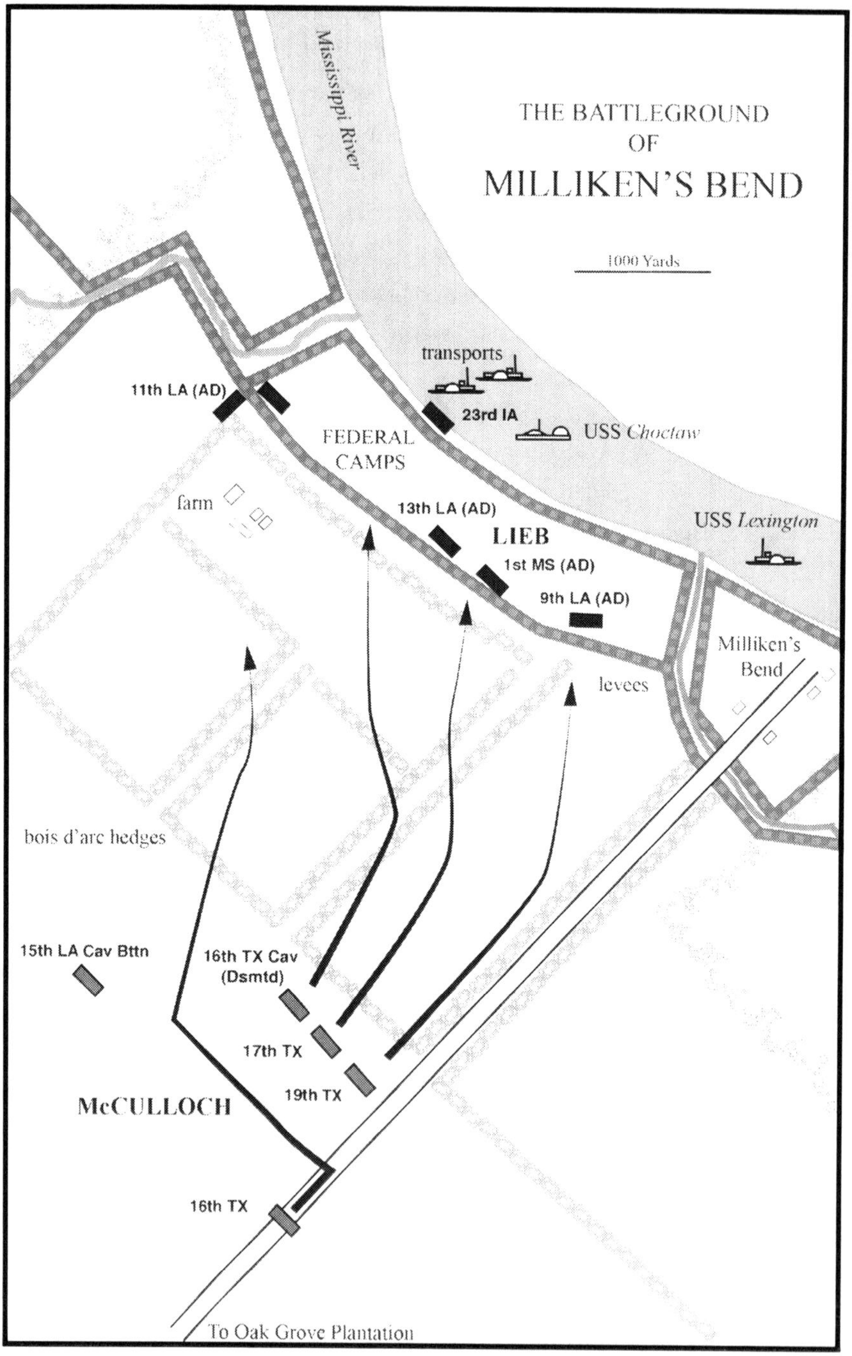
THE BATTLEGROUND
OF
MILLIKEN'S BEND
1000 Yards
Mississippi River
transports
11th LA (AD)
23rd IA
USS Choctaw
FEDERAL
CAMPS
farm
13th LA (AD)
LIEB
USS Lexington
1st MS (AD)
9th LA (AD)
Milliken's
Bend
levees
bois d'arc hedges
15th LA Cav Bttn
16th TX Cav
(Dsmtd)
17th TX
19th TX
McCULLOCH
16th TX
To Oak Grove Plantation

McCulloch's brigade had spent nearly two hours to cross a half-mile of ground, finally reforming just yards away from the African Brigade and their fortified levee. Confederate officers worked to get their men back into formation for a decisive drive. Meanwhile, the 16th Texas Infantry, moving up from reserve, headed behind and to the left of the Rebel line to clear out Union troops still firing from that direction. With the sky beginning to show signs of dawn, the Texans charged their bayonets and started through the final belt of obstacles and toward the Union breastworks.

Lieb hoped his men would hold. He took heart that the 23rd Iowa had unloaded from their steamers and were making their way methodically to his line. USS *Choctaw*, firing blindly, began throwing heavy shells over the levee in the general direction of the Texan advance, but too high for effect. When the Rebel line began to push into the obstacles to his front, Lieb ordered a volley into the Confederate ranks. Commands rang up and down the line as each regiment fired in turn into the mass of Texans. Momentarily stunned by the weight of this close range fire, several of the Confederates turned to the rear, and Lieb's troops let out a visceral cheer. At almost the same time, the 23rd Iowa marched steadily forward to stiffen the Union line.[39]

The fight was far from finished. Colonel Samuel L. Glasgow of the 23rd Iowa trotted ahead and climbed the Mississippi levee to see how the battle was progressing. He arrived just in time to see the Rebel line shake off its shock and surge forward. The Iowan reined his horse about and spurred back toward his regiment. "Double quick, for God's sake, they are right on us," he shouted. The Iowans crested the Mississippi levee to see the Texans clambering up and then over the ten-foot breastwork on the far side of the Union camps.[40]

Lieb's line wavered as the Texans closed in to kill at close range. "No quarter for the officers, kill the damned abolitionists, and spare the niggers," rang out from the Rebel ranks as they crested the levee. As the two lines crashed into each other, bayonets jabbed into bodies and clubbed muskets smashed sculls. One Federal officer urged his men to take steady aim and make every shot count. "Aim low, boys, and give them Hell, give them Hell, give them Hell," he bellowed. A nearby Texan sighted his musket on the man's chest, "two inches below and to the right of the second button, and sent a ball and three buckshot into him. He fell with the word Hell on his lips." Most of the 11th Louisiana, 13th Louisiana, and 1st Mississippi

The image that ran on July 4, 1863, in Harper's Weekly *captured some of the fear among the black troops, showed some in flight, and seemed to portray the Confederates with overwhelming numbers of troops.*

(African Descent) regiments dissolved, the men fleeing north toward the safety of a belt of timber or east and over the top of the Mississippi levee.[41]

The 23rd Iowa and 9th Louisiana (African Descent) held their ground. Lieutenant William A. Skillen, at the head of a black company, faced off against five Texans before falling beneath multiple bayonets, several bullets to the body, and a clubbed musket to his skull. The battle raged as close quarters. "We charged the levee and fought bayonet crossing bayonet for full one minute," a young Texan wrote. "My antagonist was a huge negro who fired and missed me, and then clubbed his gun and tried to strike me." The Rebel ran his bayonet into the man twice, before the wounded soldier struck back, hitting him "over the shoulder . . . darn near breaking the shoulder blade." The Texan recovered, drove his bayonet through the soldier a third time, then fired a load of buck and ball at point-blank range "which blew him all to pieces."[42]

The Federal line dissolved. Clearly outnumbered, the Hawkeye veterans of many a hard fight understood their peril and prudently retreated toward the river and the protective guns of the navy. The black Louisianans, too raw to know when to run, stayed put, alone. Friends clustered together to face their fate. In the brutal, bare-knuckle melee, the iron-muscled farm hands proved tough scrappers. Even so, they did not stand a chance against such odds. "We continued firing wherever we could see a way," admitted a Texan. Eventually overwhelmed, the remnant of the 9th Louisiana fled over the top of the Mississippi levee, taking Colonel Lieb, who had been wounded in the thigh, with them.[43]

The drawing in Frank Leslie's Illustrated Newspaper *from January 16, 1864, captured some of the brutal hand-to-hand combat of the Battle of Milliken's Bend and shows a transformation of the event into a more even encounter.*

The Texans were winded and scattered after the severe fight. With the enemy out of reach, squads of Rebels spread out among the camps, rounding up prisoners, gathering up useful supplies, and plundering what they wanted. Only the 19th Texas, having missed most of the close fighting along the west levee moved in good order to pursue the fleeing enemy over the Mississippi levee. When the Confederates crested this next berm, the gunners aboard USS *Choctaw* saw them clearly and opened on them, driving them back. The men of the 23rd Iowa and 9th Louisiana (African Descent) formed a new line at the water's edge, and waited, watching the top of the levee for a target. Texans who believed they might take a pot shot at the Union transports or ironclad would have to contend with hundreds of Yankee muskets as well.[44]

With no effective way of striking at the enemy, the Texans turned to mopping up pockets of resistance, seizing prisoners from among the scattered black soldiers. General McCulloch, riding among his troops, felt the "whizz" of a bullet from a Union soldier still in the fight. The former Texas Ranger pulled a carbine from its saddle boot and, with a single shot, coolly dropped his assailant. Captain George T. Marold of Company E, 16th Texas led some men in a rush against a squad of black soldiers holding out in a building far to the left, compelling nearly twenty men to surrender.[45]

The Texan attack slumped into stalemate in the full light of a hot and humid day. The temperature climbed toward ninety-five degrees and most of the men carried canteens now long empty. Shells from the USS *Choctaw* skimmed just over the top of the Mississippi levee, bursting in midair or tumbling end over end in unpredictable flight, keeping the Rebels on edge. Compounding their concern, the Confederates also misidentified the two transports that had carried the 23rd Iowa as gunboats. Most of the soldiers fell back to better shelter. The western levee—the first line carried—now served as a backrest and breastwork against the whirring fragments of this harassing fire. Texans who still had a view of the Mississippi reported another gunboat, USS *Lexington* coming upstream at about 8:30 A.M., which convinced the Rebels that they faced four warships to their front.[46]

McCulloch needed some direction. His brigade's second battle had been decidedly more vicious than its first. He had no weapons capable of fighting gunboats. The best his men could do was to avoid presenting themselves as targets. Shells passed overhead at a rate of about one a minute. He dispatched a courier to Walker to bring up the reserve infantry and artillery to break the deadlock.[47]

After waiting for a few hours for a response from Walker, McCulloch decided instead to retreat. The *Lexington* added its guns to the steady bombardment and before long these heavy shells took their toll. When word arrived that the Texan wounded had been loaded onto ambulances or otherwise carried away, McCulloch withdrew his command. The soldiers received the news with enthusiasm and poured away from their sheltering berm, back through the Bois d'Arc hedges, and down the road toward Richmond. They slackened their pace a bit when they cleared the range of the big guns on USS *Choctaw*. No federal infantry appeared over the Mississippi levee to see them off.

The battle of Milliken's Bend simply sputtered out. McCulloch and his disorganized brigade encountered General Walker and Colonel Randal with his brigade and divisional artillery near Oak Grove. The Texans prepared, once again, to assail Milliken's Bend, but now with the addition of twelve field pieces, mostly 6- and 12-pounders. After Walker heard the details of the fight and the circumstances leading to the retreat, he ordered both of the infantry brigades and the three batteries to hold their ground and rest. Should the Yankees launch a counterattack these Texans would receive them, but Walker determined that no one would be returning to Milliken's Bend for a second round. Officers gathered

A timberclad gunboat, the USS Lexington *had four IX-inch Dahlgren cannon and two 32-pounder smoothbores.*
Library of Congress Prints and Photographs Division, Washington, D.C.

details from among the ranks to strip nearby Union-controlled plantations of their livestock and burn any sheds or facilities used to bring in a cotton or corn crop.[48]

Now bloodied in earnest, the men of McCulloch's Brigade lay in the shade. The fight killed 44 Texans and wounded another 131. The 17th Texas suffered half of these losses. Confederate officers simply could not account for ten of their men. Considering other battles on other fields, these Rebels had only lost one-in-ten of their number—a baptism of fire by sprinkling, not immersion.[49]

One question had been answered beyond doubt. Black regiments—even raw and recently organized—*would* fight. General Walker understood the implications. "The obstinacy with which they fought," he wrote, "opened the eyes of the Confederates to the consequences to be apprehended by the Federal employment of these auxiliaries."[50]

The Texans brought in prisoners. These included more than fifty black soldiers from the African Brigade. These men were former slaves. One soldier wrote home that he had collared two of these troops, both from Mississippi plantations. Confederate policy remained unclear regarding captured black troops, and no one involved in the fight knew what exactly to do with them. Before the war, these people would have been considered valuable property and preserved for labor in

Admiral David Dixon Porter's flagship, the tinclad USS Black Hawk *typically had an array of heavy guns including four 32-pounders, two 30-pounder rifles, a 3-inch rifled cannon, and a 12-pounder smoothbore.*
Naval Historical Center.

the fields. As a result, some Texan officers believed the captured blacks should be considered "contraband of war" and parceled out to worthy men as trophies, sold, or returned to their owners. General McCulloch suggested that Captain Marold keep two captives as his personal property—a reward for bravery shown during the fight. Others, especially among the Louisiana troops, believed them to have participated in servile insurrection and worthy of a speedy death. Black prisoners taken at Milliken's Bend, the first to fall into Rebel hands, raised important issues that would roil for the rest of the war.[51]

The two white officers from the African Brigade faced a more uncertain future. Captain Corydon Heath of the 9th Louisiana (African Descent) and Lieutenant George L. Conn of the 11th Louisiana (African Descent) headed toward the Monroe jail and close confinement in chains and handcuffs. A third, Lieutenant Elisha DeWitt of the 9th Louisiana (African Descent), still wore his Sergeant's chevrons from his old regiment while he waited for his commission. Rebels assumed he was a simple noncommissioned officer in a white regiment and paroled him.[52]

Back at Milliken's bend, Colonel Lieb and his officers took stock of their losses. The 1,100-man garrison lost more than 100 dead, 285 wounded, and 266 missing, which was more than a quarter of the men committed to the battle. The 9th Louisiana Infantry (African Descent), too raw to recognize when the battle turned against them, lost 165 of their number. Texan bullets and bayonets killed or wounded more than half of the 120 men in the 23rd Iowa engaged in the battle.[53]

David Dixon Porter, commanding the Mississippi Squadron, rushed to the scene of the Battle of Milliken's Bend.
Library of Congress Prints and Photographs Division, Washington, D.C.

Rear Admiral David Porter, aboard the USS *Black Hawk*, arrived late in the morning to see the battlefield for himself. "I . . . saw quite an ugly sight," he reported. "The dead negroes lined the ditch inside of the parapet, or levee, and were mostly shot on the top of the head. In front of them, close to the levee, lay an equal number of rebels, stinking in the sun. They were miserable looking wretches." He believed he counted some eighty dead Confederates. Porter also realized that no supply depots west of the Mississippi served any useful purpose and suggested that Union troops at least evacuate Milliken's Bend and join the garrison at Young's Point. The Confederates, he feared, would be back. "Those fellows will be scouting about here for some time," he added, "and it is no longer safe."[54]

A little past noon, while Porter surveyed the carnage at Milliken's Bend, a messenger arrived from the fleet anchorage with word of a Rebel attack on Young's Point. The dispatch reported that the tinclad USS *Romeo* (Gunboat Number 3), already on patrol, had headed down the Mississippi to support the garrison. Porter directed that the tinclad USS *Petrel* go as well, followed by the hospital steamboat *Red Rover*.[55]

While McCulloch had flailed at Milliken's Bend, General Hawes had finally arrived at his objective after wasting most of the night lost amid the tangle of bayous and roads in the region. His guides had become confused, Union patrols

The Red Rover *had been a Rebel barracks vessel at Island Number 10 before falling into Union hands. Designed as a floating hospital, USS* Red Rover *could handle dozens of casualties and included a medical staff of nearly fifty. More than 2,400 patients had been treated aboard ship by the end of the war.*
Photographic History of the Civil War.

had burned important bridges, and when he finally had his three regiments in position to attack the Union camps from their northern flank, it was already mid-morning. Around 10:30 A.M., about the time Walker called off any renewed attacks on Milliken's Bend, Hawe's skirmishers drove in the Union pickets about two miles away from Young's Point. The Confederates pressed on through a dense wood and across several bayous, picking up a few Federals along the way who, not expecting trouble, had gone fishing. When the Texans finally emerged from the trees and into an open field, the depot and camps lay just a quarter-mile away to their right front. The Texans had come in on the rear of the Union works. Hawes ordered the 12th and 22nd Texas Infantry to form a line of battle facing south with their left near the Mississippi levee, and the 18th Texas in reserve. To his front, the Yankees of the 108th, 120th, and 131st Illinois shifted their position and formed a line to face the Texans, ready for action.

Hawes hesitated. Scouts atop the levee reported two gunboats closing fast. The gunners aboard USS *Romeo*, seeing Confederates massing on the north end of the Union camps and preparing to sweep around the levee and overwhelm the position from the rear, opened up with 24-pounders. Hawes gauged the situation, then ordered his men back into the woods and away from the navy's guns. Comrades carried away one soldier who was wounded. Hawes would not attack Young's Point. The brigade spent the rest of that hot June day making its way back toward toward Oak Grove Plantation. After his scouts reported that the Rebels had truly gone, General Dennis ordered the 120th and 131st Illinois loaded into transports and shipped to Milliken's Bend.[56]

The remnants of the African Brigade would not need them. Taylor's little Confederate army fell back that night. McCulloch's Brigade along with General Taylor left the vicinity of Milliken's Bend and continued marching to Richmond. Walker, with Randal's Brigade and the artillery, waited for Hawes at Oak Grove; he did not arrive until 5:00 A.M. on the morning of June 8, having lost another two hundred of his command as heat casualties, stragglers, or men who had simply gotten lost. Walker, clearly irritated with the pitiful effort against Young's Point, ordered his men on to Richmond. Harrison's cavalry rounded up the Texan wanderers.[57]

The expedition against the Union garrison at Lake Providence also proved unlucky. Colonel Bartlett and his two unfortunately numbered units—the 13th Texas Cavalry (Dismounted) and the 13th Louisiana Cavalry Battalion—bridged Bayou Maçon at Floyd but commanders changed their minds and opted to move to a more secure location at Caledonia, some eighteen miles upstream, wasting valuable time in the process. About the time McCulloch's weary infantry tramped into Richmond after the Battle of Milliken's Bend, Colonel Bartlett's command had only just crossed Bayou Maçon at Caledonia, which was too late to have any bearing on Taylor's grand design. In the coming days, this force would continue to demonstrate against Lake Providence but eventually fell back to Floyd, having achieved nothing.[58]

General Taylor had grown tired of the whole expedition and the leadership of Walker's Division. On the evening of June 8, back at his headquarters in Richmond, he dashed off a report of the movements of his army to General Kirby Smith. The brigadiers of Walker's Division disappointed him. "General McCulloch appears to have shown great personal bravery," Taylor wrote, "but no capacity for handling masses." He could not even stand speaking to General Hawes. The Texan rank and file also came under Taylor's censure. "I discovered too late that the officers and men of this division were possessed of a dread of gunboats," he wrote. "To this circumstance, and the want of mobility in these troops, are to be attributed the meager results of the expedition."[59]

Taylor argued that he had done his best with the troops he had. "I beg the lieutenant general commanding to believe that I used every personal exertion in order to insure success," he wrote. He had personally built bridges and seen to the security of the operation, allowing him to bring his army to within a few miles of the enemy undetected. General Walker defended Taylor as well, writing, "Taylor, on the subject of relieving Vicksburg . . . always expressed the utmost anxiety . . . to strike a blow that would bear directly on the siege." This campaign, Walker argued, could never have accomplished this aim. Kirby Smith had launched it too late. Instead of marching from Monroe to Alexandria in late May, Walker's Division should have struck east toward Vicksburg. The Teche Campaign had stampeded Kirby Smith into making the wrong move. "A few weeks previous to our coming, the enemy's operations could have been seriously embarrassed by cutting his line of communication at Richmond," Walker pointed out, "but the golden opportunity had passed."[60]

Taylor would head back to Alexandria alone. "I leave this evening for Monroe and Alexandria, to look after affairs in the southern portion of the state, which are every day increasing in interest." He traveled by rail to Monroe and early on the morning of June 9, met with General Paul O. Hébert, commander of the Sub-District of Northeast Louisiana. Taylor directed Hébert to round up and drive a herd of beeves to the Mississippi, and by some miracle, cross them over into Vicksburg. Learning also that James Tappan's Arkansas Brigade was expected daily, Taylor left word for Hébert to send those troops to Richmond and forward Walker's Division to Alexandria. In the meantime, Taylor concluded, "if General Grant's position on the Yazoo is shaken or broken by General Johnston, and the enemy should have to retreat, a considerable force could be highly available along the west bank of the Mississippi."[61]

Taylor had no idea what to expect when he returned to his headquarters at Alexandria. His plan to relieve Port Hudson might not even be feasible. He was certain, though, he had wasted his time in northeast Louisiana. Incompetent subordinates bungled his elegantly crafted strategy. On June 10, he arrived in Alexandria determined to assess the opportunities presenting themselves farther south and perhaps strike a blow that would matter.[62]

5

Mouton's Army

There are so many bad people here that sometimes you fear for your life.
—Private H. F. Kopke, Gibson's Texas Battery

Before General Richard Taylor left for operations in northeast Louisiana, he had placed his senior subordinate, Brigadier General Alfred Mouton, in charge south of the Red River. Taylor expected his veteran officer to discover the enemy strength in southern Louisiana, especially that opposite Port Hudson and at Berwick Bay. Now he needed Mouton's reports to formulate the mechanics for the rescue of General Franklin Gardner and his garrison.

Feeling the weight of command, Mouton had faced a difficult task. Strategically, his jurisdiction resembled a draftsman's compass, or an inverted "V," with Alexandria at its apex. The longest side was the left—west—of this triangle, stretching nearly 150 miles to the Union base at Brashear City and roughly following the lines of Bayou Teche, Bayou Cortableu, and Bayou Boeuf. The other leg of this imagined caliper ran roughly 100 miles along the Red River and into the region between the Atchafalaya and the Mississippi Rivers—a "Creole Mesopotamia" as one historian termed it.[1] The massive Atchafalaya Basin, a tangle of trackless swamps, shallow bayous, and interminable logjams separated these two distinct zones of operations.

The area east of the Atchafalaya Basin—especially the position of Union forces in Pointe Coupée and West Baton Rouge parishes opposite the Union lines at Port Hudson—remained mysterious. While General Nathaniel P. Banks operated east of the Mississippi, the question remained: Where else were his troops positioned? Did Federal regiments seal the bank opposite Port Hudson as well? If not, could Confederates west of the river run in supplies? Union troops had captured the Rebel signal detachment at Hermitage Plantation a few weeks before, ending any cross-river communications. Mouton needed answers, and he ordered a newly arrived Texas infantry brigade of two regiments under command of Colonel Joseph Warren Speight down to Simmesport; Speight was accompanied by the 3rd Arizona Cavalry led by Colonel Joseph Phillips and a

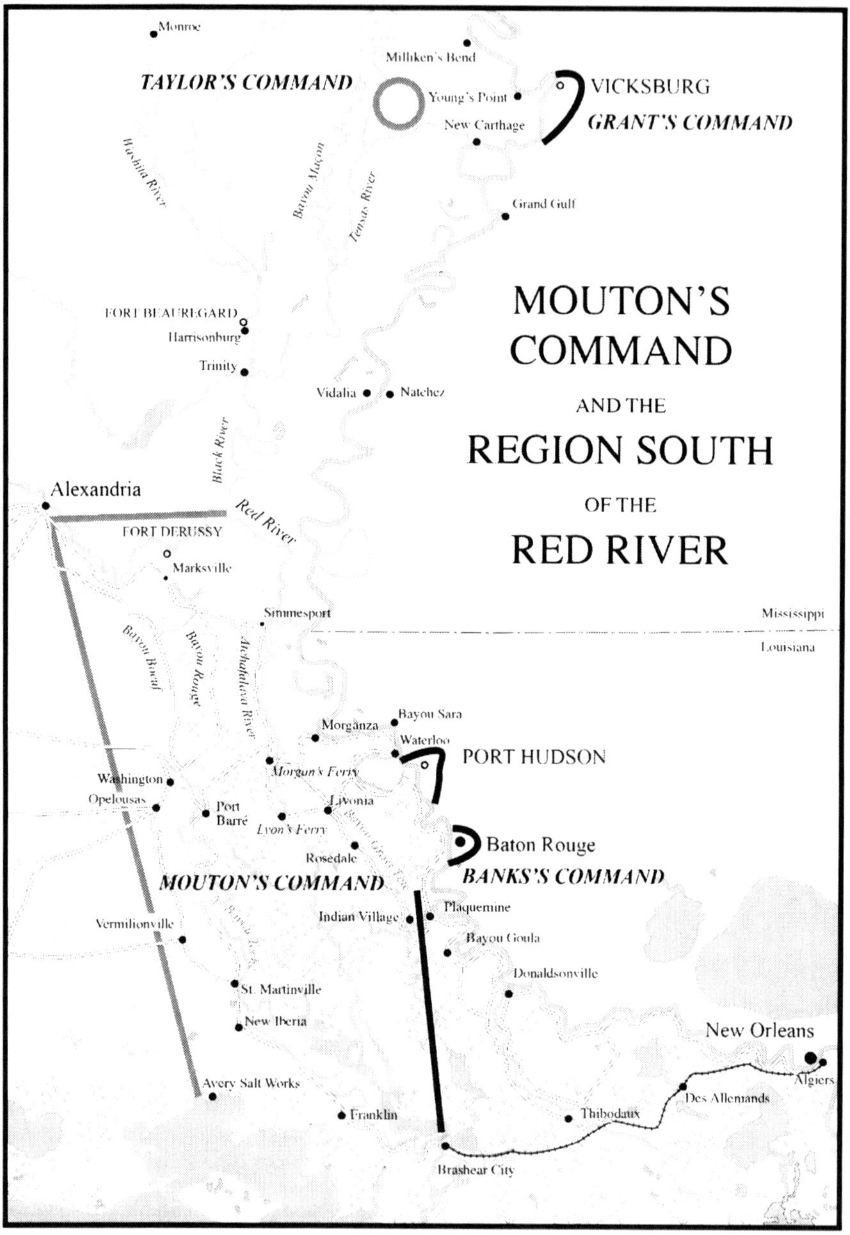
MOUTON'S COMMAND AND THE REGION SOUTH OF THE RED RIVER
Monroe
Milliken's Bend
TAYLOR'S COMMAND
Young's Point
VICKSBURG
GRANT'S COMMAND
New Carthage
Ouachita River
Bayou Macon
Tensas River
Grand Gulf
FORT BEAUREGARD
Harrisonburg
Trinity
Vidalia
Natchez
Black River
Alexandria
Red River
FORT DERUSSY
Marksville
Simmesport
Mississippi
Louisiana
Bayou Boeuf
Bayou Rouge
Atchafalaya River
Bayou Sara
Morganza
Waterloo
PORT HUDSON
Washington
Morgan's Ferry
Opelousas
Port Barré
Livonia
Lyon's Ferry
Baton Rouge
Rosedale
MOUTON'S COMMAND
BANKS'S COMMAND
Plaquemine
Indian Village
Vermilionville
Bayou Goula
Donaldsonville
St. Martinville
New Iberia
New Orleans
Algiers
Avery Salt Works
Des Allemands
Thibodaux
Franklin
Brashear City

Part of the United States Ram Fleet, USS Switzerland *became a useful, if fragile, reconnaissance vessel along the Mississippi during the Vicksburg and Port Hudson Campaigns.*
Naval Historical Center

battery of Louisiana artillery. The foot soldiers would secure the lower reaches of the Red River and the upper reaches of the Atchafalaya and keep the way open for the cavalry to come and go. Phillips and his horsemen would then scout the Mississippi's western bank to see where the enemy lay.[2]

The Federals remained curious about Rebel movements west of the river and responded swiftly to reports that the enemy had returned to the mouth of Red River and the Atchafalaya. On June 3, USS *Switzerland* went to investigate. A half-mile from Simmesport, the crew of this Union ram got their answer. The Confederates unleashed their field batteries, hitting the steamer seven times, wounding three sailors, cutting a steam pipe, and starting a fire. The soldiers of companies B and G of the 15th Texas Infantry and men from the 3rd Arizona "poured a perfect storm

Morgan Wolfe Merrick, a hospital steward with the 3rd Arizona Cavalry, sketched his command and some Louisiana field artillery hammering USS Switzerland *near Simmesport.* Daughters of the Republic of Texas Library, The Alamo, San Antonio, Texas.

of Minié balls upon us as we passed," reported Lieutenant Colonel John Ellet from aboard *Switzerland.* Staggered by this onslaught, he prudently withdrew to the cover of the ironclads USS *Pittsburgh* and USS *Lafayette*. "I thought it best," Ellet concluded, "not wishing unnecessarily to expose my men and my frail wooden boat single-handed to the heavy fire of the enemy."[3]

The three vessels returned the following day, but this time Captain Henry Walke of *Lafayette* led the way, easing over the bar on Red River and lumbering down the Atchafalaya. After shelling the Texans out of Simmesport, landing parties plundered the Rebel camps and set the town ablaze. The Federal flotilla left, reporting low water in the Atchafalaya, which would probably prevent a Union return before waters rose again in the spring. The bar at the mouth of the Red River would soon be out of the water. The raid yielded useful intelligence: letters brought back from the Southern camps revealed concerns about slave insurrections in Louisiana—which was a logical expectation given the new national policy—and plans for a Rebel ironclad to be built at Shreveport.[4]

The Texans returned to the wrecked town shortly after the gunboats left but prudently camped on Smith's Plantation, three miles farther inland from Simmesport. With the nosy gunboats gone, Speight launched Phillips to scout the interior of Pointe Coupée Parish opposite Port Hudson. The countryside bore plenty of evidence of Banks's army having been in the region on their way to the siege. "The Yankees have laid waste this whole country," Phillips wrote. "What a great pity. It is the most beautiful country I ever saw."[5]

A Virginian, Captain Henry Walke had served in the U.S. Navy since 1827. He tangled with the Confederate ironclad CSS Arkansas *in 1862 while commanding the USS* Carondolet *before taking charge of the newly outfitted USS* Lafayette.
Library of Congress Prints and Photographs Division, Washington, D.C.

Phillips, a thirty-one-year-old officer from Hampton, Virginia, and kinsman of Confederate cavalry beau ideal General J. E. B. Stuart, seemed out of place in Louisiana, especially at the head of an Arizona regiment. He owed it all to Major General John Bankhead Magruder, Confederate commander of the District of Texas, Arizona, and New Mexico and a friend of the family. Phillips had served as a junior officer in the 3rd Virginia Cavalry before joining Magruder's staff early in the war. Phillips fought in the 1862 campaigns near his home on the peninsula of Virginia; had been praised by luminaries, including General John Bell Hood, for his conduct at the Battle of Second Manassas, but followed his friend and chief into Texas exile later that year. Magruder rewarded his protégé's loyalty by giving him command of the 3rd Arizona Cavalry. Although this unit included some men recruited from the desert Southwest, most of its soldiers were Texas conscripts or those who had enlisted just ahead of being compelled. Magruder had only recently ordered this regiment and several others to be cobbled together from the various "independent" companies ranging along the Texas coast. Officials had intended them to reinforce Confederates in New Mexico and Arizona; when that effort collapsed, the mission changed but the regimental designations remained.[6]

Phillips, a slave-owning Virginia tidewater blue blood, found himself in alien circumstance but among familiar faces. "I have seen a great many of our old acquaintances . . . and several of our old Peninsula friends," he wrote Magruder from Smith's Plantation, "in the swamps of Louisiana a thousand miles from nowhere." He had but one request for his old friend: he wanted his enslaved valet forwarded to Louisiana. "Send my boy Billie," he requested. "For God's sake I am needing him badly."[7]

The Virginian found the 3rd Arizona a nettlesome command. His men favored a New Mexico veteran, George Madison, as their leader, but Magruder chose his favorite instead. "This act surprised us all, to give us . . . a total stranger, and not even of our state," Morgan Wolfe Merrick, a surgeon's assistant in the regiment wrote. Phillips was, though, "a gentleman of military education." The new leader apparently was short, as well.[8]

Merrick remembered an exchange with a comrade:

"Have you seen the new Kernal," asked Corporal James Fitzgerald.

"No, what does he look like?" Merrick responded.

Fitzgerald joshed back. "Don't know, he is so small I can't make him out well. He h'aint no bigger ner a bar of soap after a hard day's rubbin'."

"He may be bigger than you think he is! Valuable goods come in small packages, don't you know?" Merrick rejoindered. "He may make you think he is immense before we get through this biz we are in."[9]

Naturally Phillips encountered discipline issues with his new command. Several officers in the Texas "coast guard" commands resented being shoved into his regiment and led their companies close to mutiny when they approached the Sabine River. "Dissatisfaction I deem the fault of the officers," Phillips wrote. He believed the rank and file to be reliable. "The men," he wrote, "are an orderly, quiet set of soldiers." Phillips reported that, although bothersome, the conflict had passed, and that despite missing two companies left behind in Texas to round up additional conscripts, in general, the understrength regiment remained in fine spirits since arriving in Louisiana. He had good reason for not arresting the troublemakers. "I thought I should soon put my regiment in action," he wrote, "and need the services of all."[10]

In the fullness of time, the men grew to like the Virginian. When the regiment left Texas, some miscreants had shaved the tale and mane of Phillips's horse. "The Colonel took no notice whatever," Merrick noted. "By this time we had found out what a fine man [he was] and every day he grew in popularity. The little colonel had created a favorable impression—nothing overbearing or haughty about him."[11]

The Virginian dutifully spent several days scouting the Mississippi's west bank near Port Hudson and searched for ways to cross cattle or other supplies to the Confederate garrison. After crossing the Atchafalaya at Morgan's Ferry, he pushed on to Morganza and followed the river road south to within five miles of Port Hudson. His troops brushed against Union outposts near Waterloo and captured two prisoners. From them he learned that Federal troops from the 110th New York along with a company of cavalry held a fortified position at Point Maunoir, the former Rebel signals station, which the Northerners called Fausse Pointe. Union gunboats and warships including *Arizona*, *Albatross*, *Estrella*, *Hartford*, *Lafayette*, *Marmora*, *Pittsburgh*, *Signal* and *Price* prowled the river upstream of Port Hudson. As Phillips's command gathered more information about the enemy positions, one of his soldiers—an Irishman—went missing. The colonel, perhaps fearing he had deserted to the enemy and revealed their location, ordered his regiment back to Morgan's Ferry and safety beyond the Atchafalaya.

Phillips reported his discoveries. "I believe it is likely something will be done to relieve Port Hudson from this side," he wrote to Colonel Speight at Simmesport. "In my opinion it can be done with 1,000 cavalry." The Confederates now knew the lay of this once-unfamiliar land. Pointe Coupée Parish had several decent roads, but terrain cut up the countryside into few avenues of approach. Framed by the Atchafalaya River to the west, the Red River to the north, and the twisting Mississippi River to the east, Pointe Coupée Parish had several predictable, but widely separated routes allowing infiltration toward Port Hudson. Defenders would have to guess correctly or the Rebels might slip by. To the south, the road along Bayou Grosse Tête offered a route through Rosedale and into the Union-controlled Lafourche District via the town of Plaquemine.[12]

Three crossings of the Atchafalaya dictated future strategy. Simmesport, on the west bank of the upper Atchafalaya at its junction with Bayou des Glaises and near its junction with the Red River, four miles away, was the northern gateway. A

A big ironclad with eight big cannon, USS Lafayette *helped suppress the Confederate batteries at Grand Gulf, Mississippi, before moving to guard the mouth of the Red River.*
Naval Historical Center.

With most of the Union troops in the Mississippi Valley involved in the sieges of Port Hudson and Vicksburg, it fell to the crews of the Union gunboats to keep the banks clear of Confederates. These Yankee tars aboard USS Lafayette *include grizzled veterans and young boys.*
Library of Congress Prints and Photographs Division, Washington, D.C.

A veteran gunboat, the slab-sided USS Pittsburgh *patrolled the Mississippi above the mouth of the Red River and could bring an impressive battery of fourteen guns to bear on targets ashore.*
Naval Historical Center

Union blockaders snatched up USS Estrella *early in the war and put it to Federal use, the shallow draft vessel being especially useful in the shallow coastal waters of the Gulf of Mexico and the bayous of Louisiana.*
Marshall Dunham Photograph Album, Mss. 3241, Louisiana and Lower Mississippi Valley Collections, LSU Libraries, Baton Rouge, Louisiana.

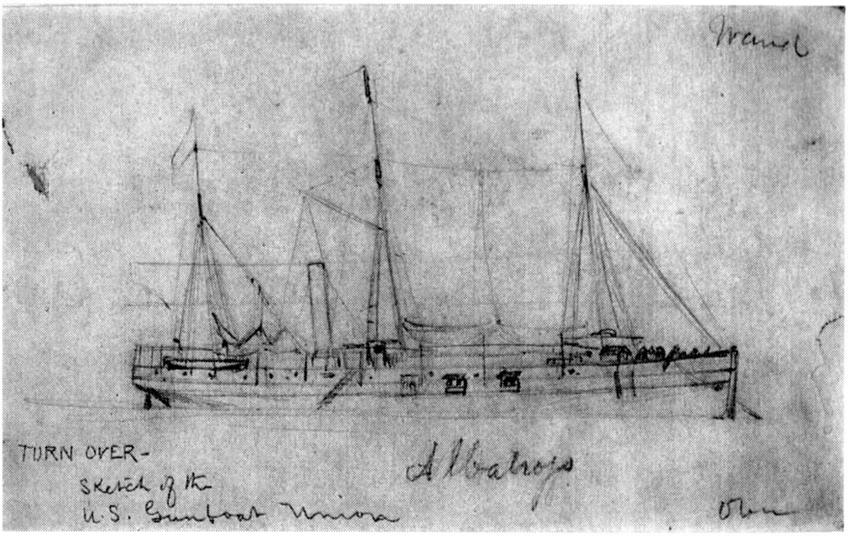

USS Albatross *ran the guns of Port Hudson and sparred with Confederate defenses at Fort DeRussy before assuming its station off Bayou Sara, Louisiana.*
Library of Congress Prints and Photographs Division, Washington, D.C.

Captured from the Confederates at Memphis, USS General Price *served the Union navy as a patrol vessel on the Mississippi.*
Naval Historical Center.

Intended for duty on the high seas, USS Hartford *instead shelled Port Hudson during the siege.*
Library of Congress Prints and Photographs Division, Washington, D.C.

USS Marmora, *tinclad #2, one of more than seventy such gunboats commissioned by the U.S. Navy, was simply a Mississippi sternwheel steamboat with the addition of iron plating and a dozen medium weight cannon.*
Naval Historical Center.

USS Signal, *tinclad #9, patrolled the Mississippi River between Vicksburg and Port Hudson. The 190-ton vessel drew less than two feet of water making it useful as a dispatch boat.*
Library of Congress Prints and Photographs Division, Washington, D.C.

ferry led to roads cutting east to the Mississippi River following the Atchafalaya to the southern, or lower, mouth of the Red and followed it six miles farther to the Mississippi at Red River Landing. Swampy terrain and an oxbow lake, "Old River," formed a cypress tangle called Raccourci Island, which isolated these northern stretches from the rest of the parish. This tangled country below the Red River's mouth might be useful for ambushing vessels on the Mississippi.

Morgan's Ferry, where Phillips had crossed, served as a true postern to Pointe Coupée Parish. About a dozen miles south of Simmesport, it led to two roads headed east toward the Mississippi, which was about ten miles away. The "state road," a route favored by cattle drovers in the antebellum period, led directly to New Texas Landing. The "Opelousas Road" went to Morganza. A month before, the Federal army now at Port Hudson had used this route to get to the Mississippi and followed the road to the river, then along the levee for several miles to their eventual crossing to Bayou Sara. Lyon's Ferry lay several miles south down the Atchafalaya and provided a third route into the region by less-traveled roads and emerged at the tiny settlement of Livonia.

Once across the Atchfalaya River at Morgan's Ferry, Confederate troops would have essentially two routes to move north and south. About halfway to the Mississippi at Morganza via the Opelousas Road, the Grosse Tête Road branched off just past the crossing of stagnant Bayou Fordoche. The sizable Norwood and Sterling sugar plantations marked this intersection. The Grosse Tête route headed south through the woods along this fetid ditch for a dozen miles until it picked up the course of Bayou Grosse Tête and intersected the Lyon's Ferry Road at nearby Livonia. At this junction, travelers could continue in three directions: south along the bayou toward Rosedale on a route roughly parallel to the Mississippi River, west toward Lyon's Ferry, or northeast to False River and the agricultural heart of Pointe Coupée Parish.

Phillips optimistically reported that a brigade of well-handled cavalry could sweep the Federal outposts in Pointe Coupée and raid the poorly guarded stations farther south. The Grosse Tête Road provided the gateway. The twelve-mile-wide Greves Swamp intervened between this route and the river road, which provided security from Federal patrols. The road ended near a Chitimacha Indian village at the junction of Bayou Grosse Tête and Bayou Plaquemine. Just six miles down that stream, where it mingled with the Mississippi, lay the Federal depot at Plaquemine. From here, all roads led toward the Lafourche District. Donaldsonville's Fort Butler would be the only obstacle, but clever Rebels could bypass that post.

Phillips outlined two tempting possibilities. In a conventional approach, Confederates could occupy the west bank of the Mississippi opposite Port Hudson and perhaps cross over cattle or reinforcements. Or, more daring, they could create havoc and a larger disruption by pushing deeper behind enemy lines. Either way, Phillips believed his untested command of Arizonans would do its duty. "Should we ever get into a fight," he wrote his friend Magruder, "I believe the Bloody Third will give a good account of itself." By the time Phillips returned, and his report made its way to the desk of General Mouton, General Taylor was retreating from Milliken's Bend. In his absence, Mouton, headquartered at home near Vermilionville, did nothing with this newly acquired intelligence.[13]

Morgan Wolfe Merrick sketched his peaceful camp on the banks of the Atchafalaya at Morgan's Ferry. Notice the haunch of beef hanging in the tree, the supply wagon marked "US," the men fishing or swimming in the river, and the pile of clothing on the riverbank shed by the bathers.
Daughters of the Republic of Texas Library, The Alamo, San Antonio, Texas.

Taylor, now back in Alexandria after his distraction in northeastern Louisiana, sifted through his reports to get an idea of the strategic situation in southern Louisiana. He read Colonel Phillips's account of his reconnaissance of Point Coupée Parish and believed that route held promise for the relief of Port Hudson. Taylor scribbled dispatches and called for couriers, ordering all reinforcements arriving at Washington to congregate at Simmesport, and sent word for the Louisiana Infantry Brigade to go there as well. Down south, the general had no idea what he was facing at Brashear City. "From Mouton's reports I am quite in the dark as to the condition of affairs on the Lower Teche, and as to the presence or absence of the enemy's troops on this side of Berwick Bay." Taylor needed answers—and quickly. He would go and see for himself. With part of his army now in motion toward the Atchafalaya, the general took an ambulance and relays

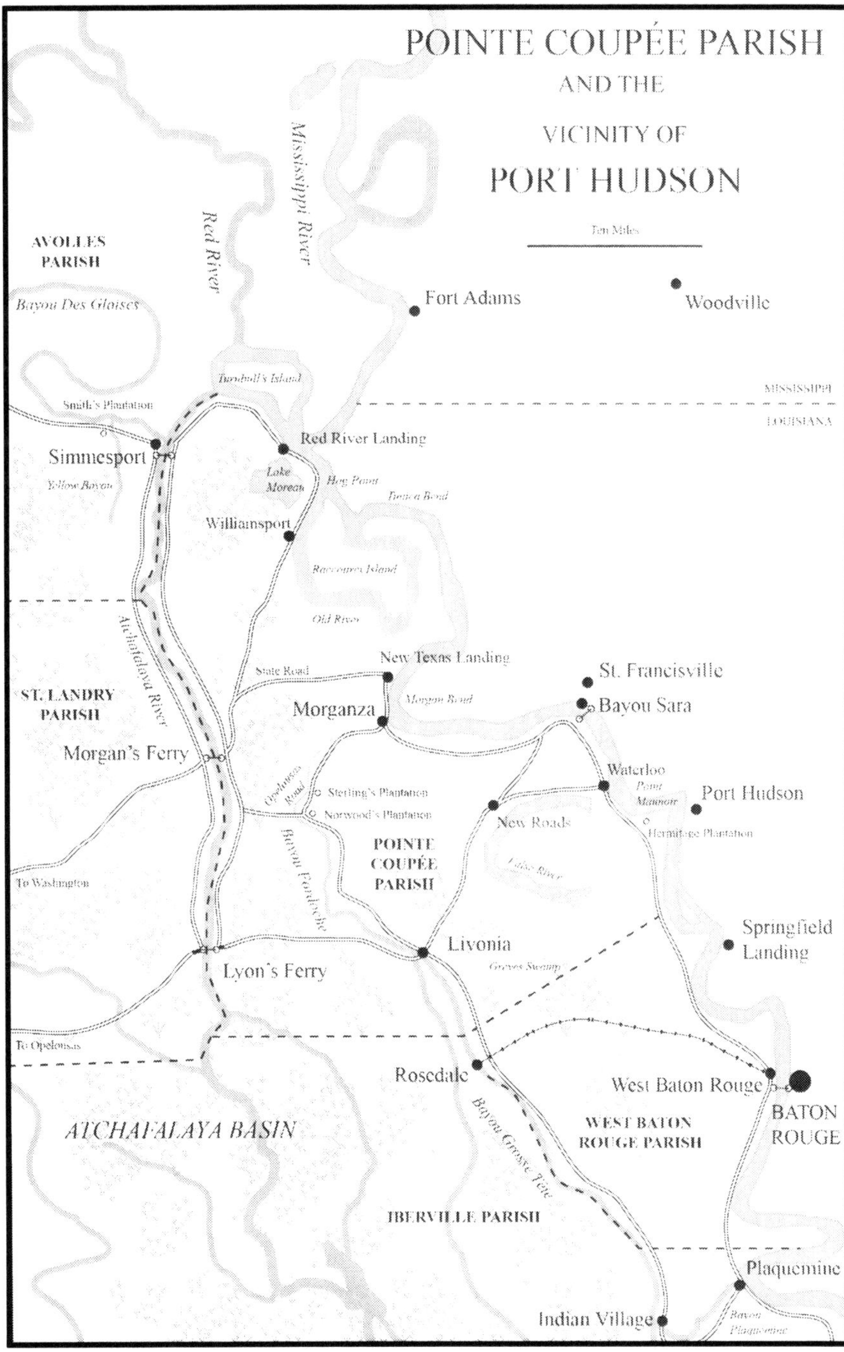
POINTE COUPÉE PARISH
AND THE
VICINITY OF
PORT HUDSON
Ten Miles
AVOLLES PARISH
Red River
Mississippi River
Fort Adams
Woodville
Bayou Des Glaises
Turnbull's Island
MISSISSIPPI
LOUISIANA
Smith's Plantation
Simmesport
Yellow Bayou
Red River Landing
Lake Moreau
Hog Point
Williamsport
Raccourci Island
Old River
Atchafalaya River
ST. LANDRY PARISH
State Road
New Texas Landing
Morganza
Morgan Bend
St. Francisville
Bayou Sara
Morgan's Ferry
Waterloo
Point Manoir
Port Hudson
Sterling's Plantation
Norwood's Plantation
Opelousas Road
New Roads
Hermitage Plantation
Bayou Fordoche
POINTE COUPÉE PARISH
To Washington
False River
Springfield Landing
Livonia
Lyon's Ferry
Grosses Swamp
To Opelousas
Rosedale
West Baton Rouge
BATON ROUGE
ATCHAFALAYA BASIN
WEST BATON ROUGE PARISH
Bayou Grosse Tete
IBERVILLE PARISH
Plaquemine
Indian Village
Bayou Plaquemine

of mules toward Franklin to learn what he could. Taylor admired the thirty-four-year-old Mouton and respected his soldierly bearing but did not believe him a great thinker—or doer.[14]

Taylor, disappointed by his recent experience with the officers of General John G. Walker's Texas Division, wanted—needed—a man of action in southern Louisiana to not only implement his plans, but also to initiate the next move. Strategic initiative, Taylor often lectured, trumped everything else and enabled small commands to best larger commands.

He feared that his senior subordinate in Louisiana might not possess these aggressive qualities. Mouton, with around two thousand effectives on hand and more coming in daily, had done little over the last two weeks to prepare for offensive operations. What was more, Mouton had wasted five days after Phillips returned from his scouting expedition, neglecting even to prepare for a movement to aid Port Hudson. "On my arrival here I received several reports from Brigadier General Alfred Mouton . . . which are exceedingly unsatisfactory," he fumed to General Edmund Kirby Smith, "and indicate that no movements commensurate with the forces under his command have been made, and that little activity has been displayed by that officer." Taylor, having finished Kirby Smith's ill-conceived errand opposite Vicksburg, wanted to launch an offensive to succor Port Hudson immediately. Instead, he found troops idling in various outposts, short of intelligence on the location and strength of the enemy, and without a strategy.[15]

He liked Mouton personally and believed him gallant and brave but found him a dismal strategist. "While an excellent officer on the field," Taylor wrote, "he is, I fear, unequal to the task of handling and disposing of any large body of troops." Mouton did well at the head of his brigade, but larger responsibilities seemed to overwhelm him. He "ever proved faithful to duty," Taylor noted, and was "modest, unselfish, and patriotic," but his talents lay in combat and tactical maneuvers. "He showed best in action," Taylor concluded, "leading his men." Mouton simply thought too small. Taylor would have to handle the big picture and command in person when it mattered.[16]

Others in Louisiana distrusted Mouton as well and believed he had been promoted beyond his abilities. "At Shiloh Mouton proved himself to be a splendid Colonel, but on the Lafourche and the Teche his failures and management have

Private John W. Watkins, Company B, 5th Texas Cavalry, came to Louisiana in March 1863, fought in the Teche Campaign, and then participated in the struggle to relieve the Rebel army at Port Hudson.
Courtesy Martha Hartzog, Austin, Texas.

been such that public opinion, both in the army and out of it, pronounce him to be no General," read an editorial in the Franklin *Planters' Banner*. "If the interests of the country are to be consulted, a stronger man than General Mouton will be sent to command the Confederate army of the Teche."[17]

Mouton did not warrant all of this censure. He had not sent word about Federals operating west of Berwick Bay because there was nothing to report. Newly promoted Brigadier General Tom Green and his Texans camped in that region and reported no signs of the Federals closer than Berwick Bay. The Union army had, however, stripped the region of its livestock, slaves, and groceries. Banks had no reason to return; the main Union effort at Port Hudson required all the men he could get. Confederates watched Berwick Bay closely from a safe distance but did not fear a renewed Federal offensive.

Taylor, frustrated by Mouton's apparent lethargy, arrived at the Confederate camps between Franklin and Berwick Bay in the late hours of June 9 to bring some imagination to his subordinates. Taylor believed that fast-moving columns might make a difference in this far-flung region. If he advanced into Pointe Coupée, might the Yankees launch a counteroffensive on the Teche front?

Based on his experience, Taylor relied on the large number of mounted regiments in the region. Mouton dutifully issued orders organizing his growing cavalry corps. Brigadier General Green, Taylor's reliable warhorse from the Teche Campaign, would lead the First Brigade, including the 4th, 5th, and 7th Texas cavalries, Lieutenant Colonel Ed Waller's 13th Texas Cavalry Battalion, and the 2nd Louisiana Cavalry. The Val Verde and Nichols's batteries provided the artillery.

The man pictured here is taken from a detail of a group picture of Trans-Mississippi Confederate officers. He is believed to be Colonel James P. Major, a recent addition to Major General Richard Taylor's army and commander of the 2nd Cavalry Brigade. McIlhenny Company Archives, McIlhenny Company, Avery Island, Louisiana.

The Texans that Green commanded frustrated Taylor. "The men—hardy frontiersmen, excellent riders, and skilled riflemen—were fearless and self-reliant," he observed, "but discharged their duty as they liked and when they liked." They did not follow the military conventions that Taylor had so admired in the Army of Northern Virginia. On the march, the men tended to wander; in camp, they often left to find a comfortable bed, a pretty girl, or a warm dinner. Only the promise of an impending fight persuaded the men to assemble—and stay assembled. Ordnance officers, too, chafed at their habit of discarding worn or dirty weapons, expecting to draw new ones. "Yet with these faults, they were admirable fighters," Taylor conceded, "and in the end I become so much attached to them as to be incapable of punishing them." Green and his veterans remained near Berwick Bay to counter any Yankee moves there.[18]

Taylor created another brigade of mounted Texans and assigned newcomer Colonel James P. Major to command the Second Cavalry Brigade. These troops included the 1st and 2nd Texas Partisan Rangers, the 2nd and 3rd Arizona Cavalry, Lieutenant Colonel Ashley W. Spaight's Texas Cavalry Squadron, and Captain Oliver J. Semme's 1st Confederate Regular Artillery Battery. Major's brigade looked tidy on paper but in reality lay scattered from Beaumont, Texas, to Simmesport and would be days in gathering. Taylor intended these newcomers to operate along the Atchafalaya River and spearhead the raid into Pointe Coupée.

Colonel Major, a Missourian, might be new to Taylor's district, but he was not new to the Trans-Mississippi. He had served on the Texas frontier as a cavalry officer in the Old Army and had resigned to join Confederate forces when Texas seceded. Early in the war, General David Twiggs appointed him to his staff but had released him to take command of a mounted regiment in General Sterling Price's Missouri State Guard. In August 1861, Major led these troops at the Battle of Wilson's Creek. He had stayed with that army throughout its vicissitudes and passed over the Mississippi with it in April 1862. Major received promotion to lieutenant colonel and left field command to serve as a staff officer for General Earl Van Dorn in Mississippi. After a jealous husband assassinated that officer, Major found himself without a staff position. Shortly after General Kirby Smith received his assignment to command the Department of the Trans-Mississippi, Major headed west as well, "for such duty as [Kirby Smith] may assign him."[19]

Confederate officials believed Major quite capable. "He is a man of thorough business habits, earnest, energetic, and industrious," wrote one admirer. Major had a clean reputation. "Amid the almost universal free living of our officers, he is invariably, at all times & at all occasions," the writer emphasized, "a perfectly sober man. No one stands higher for integrity, character, and courage." Besides, the author argued, "he knows the country and the troops [in the] west, and with his spirit, enterprise, and capacity I believe he would be imminently useful." Colonel Major established his headquarters at Washington, Louisiana.[20]

Major harbored ambitions and sent dispatches to Richmond requesting a promotion to brigadier. Adjutant General Samuel Cooper had promised Major that if he went to Louisiana, promotion would follow. Trusting that pledge, Major reported himself ready for action. "I am now commanding, as you will see, a cavalry brigade and hope soon to do good work with it in the vicinity of Port Hudson," Major predicted, "hoping and trusting that I may be enabled so to act with my brigade as to cause you not to regret your kindness toward me."[21]

The men composing Major's brigade, though, lacked polish. Taylor particularly lamented their lack of military bearing. "Their experience in war was limited to hunting down Comanches and Lipans, and, as in all new societies, distinctions of rank were unknown," he observed. "Officer and men addressed each other

Colonel George Wythe Baylor commanded the 2nd Arizona Cavalry. He had served on General Albert Sidney Johnston's staff, but he returned to Texas looking for a regiment of his own. He arrived in Louisiana looking for a fight.
Edward Clifton Wharton Family Papers, Louisiana and Lower Mississippi Valley Collections, LSU Libraries, Baton Rouge, Louisiana.

as Tom, Dick, or Harry and had no more conception of military gradation than that of *The Celestial Hierachy.*" Clearly these new Texans were no angels.[22]

One episode drove his point. Taylor approached the camp of one of these newly arrived regiments to evaluate the kind of men that had come to fight in Louisiana. "The profound silence in the camp seemed evidence of good order," the general observed. He was mistaken; it was evidence of an intense card game. "Drawing near, I found the colonel seated in the center, with a blanket spread before him, dealing . . . *monte*." The Texan, seeing Taylor approach, offered to let him play next round. "Learning that I would not join the sport, this worthy officer abandoned his amusement with some displeasure."[23]

Like it or not, these men would compose Taylor's army, and the roads between Texas and Louisiana remained busy with the passage of reinforcements. Colonel George Wythe Baylor led the 2nd Arizona Cavalry toward Franklin, having missed the orders to head to Washington. One of the newcomers, Marshall McIlhenny, a thirty-six-year-old quartermaster clerk from Bell County, Texas, had friends and also family in southern Louisiana. His brother, Edmund, had married Mary Eliza Avery whose family operated the salt mines at Petite Anse Island near New Iberia. "I have been intending to visit the Island but have had no opportunity as yet," he wrote his kinsman. "I . . . have learned that while they have destroyed all they could about the salt works they have taken only those negroes who would go with them and would not remain behind."[24]

As he rode toward Berwick Bay, McIlhenny viewed a countryside scarred by war. Most farms he passed were vacant. "The crops are not planted, and in others the crops are being destroyed by weeds," he wrote. "Nowhere do we see the plow or the hoe at work in the field." The slaves that had made this land prosperous had vanished. "But very few of the negroes," he noted, "are left on any of the plantations."[25]

Another cluster of troops gravitated toward Washington. Colonel Charles L. Pyron brought the 2nd Texas Cavalry, only partially mounted. These men, like Green's Brigade, had served in New Mexico and at Galveston. They had garrisoned that island city before Magruder tapped them for service in Louisiana. The men of Colonel Joseph Bates's 13th Texas Volunteers, which were divided between four mounted companies, six infantry companies, and Captain William E. Gibson's artillery battery, came from the mouth of the Brazos River. Now they, too, marched through scenes of desolation. The Federals "have rummaged through the houses and burned fences and took all the Negroes with them," wrote German-speaking Private H. F. Kopke of Gibson's Battery to his family back in San Felipe, Texas. "The people have hardly no crops, all of the corn is burned." A handful of infantry companies from the 11th Texas Volunteers also tramped in.[26]

Officers held the 2nd Texas in town so it could join Major's Brigade, but they decided to send Colonel Bates and the 13th Texas menagerie along with the 11th Texas Battalion's infantry toward Green and Mouton at Berwick Bay. As Private Kopke and his comrades headed south, they passed sinister people. The neighborhood around Opelousas harbored threatening ruffians that appeared to be hostile to Confederates in particular. The young German wrote his mother that his biggest need was a sidearm. "Tell father," Kopke wrote, "I would like to have his pistol. It is worth more to me than a bag of money." Hard men clearly lurked just out of reach of the Rebel authorities. "There are so many bad people here," he added, "that sometimes you fear for your life."[27]

After organizing his army and studying the strategic situation, Taylor harangued his commanders. Rebel troops must find a way to cross Berwick Bay and capture Brashear City to pose any creditable threat to New Orleans. An attack there would form a splendid double-envelopment of the Lafourche District in concert with operations in Pointe Coupée. Without steamboats or other vessels, crossing Berwick Bay seemed an intractable problem. Taylor proposed an innovative solution: "Mouton and Green were directed to collect small boats,

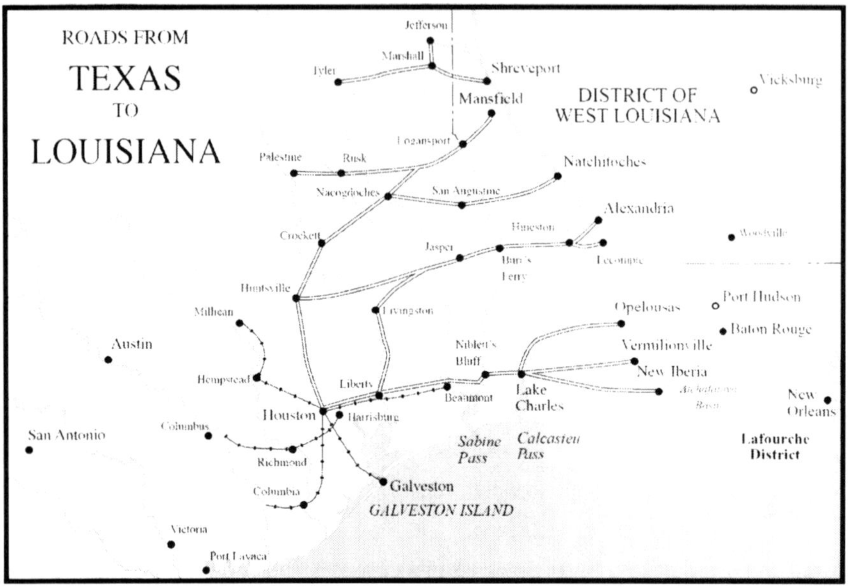

skiffs, flats, and even sugar coolers, in the Teche." Taylor urged his officers to be stealthy. A robust line of Rebel pickets had to keep the operation undiscovered.[28]

Once gathered, this ratty collection of swamp and bayou boats became the means for carrying the Rebel assault force into and along the margins of Grand Lake and around the right flank of the Brashear defenses. The marauders intended to drop in behind the Union works and create havoc while Rebel artillery covered them from the west bank of Berwick Bay. After capturing the Union defenses from behind, the rest of Mouton's and Green's men planned to cross by employing skiffs and pirogues and reinforcing the fight. Taylor would send word when—and if—the attack should take place.[29]

Clearly the forces Taylor had scraped together constituted the leavings of the Army of the Trans-Mississippi. The muscle of Confederate power west of the river lay opposite Vicksburg or in Arkansas. On June 11, Taylor crawled back into his ambulance and headed toward his headquarters at Alexandria to catch up on the mail from headquarters in Shreveport. He also wanted to secure more troops for his operations to save Port Hudson.

General Kirby Smith, Taylor learned, remained characteristically inflexible. Despite the poor showing of Walker's Division at Milliken's Bend and the irrelevance of those Mississippi River depots to General Ulysses S. Grant's siege, Kirby Smith sent assurances to Lieutenant General Joseph E. Johnston that Vicksburg remained his area of focus. "That is the most important point," he wrote. "The stake there contended for is both the Valley of the Mississippi and the Trans-Mississippi Department." Kirby Smith kept Walker's Texas Division hovering near Richmond, Louisiana, awaiting reinforcements from Arkansas. There had been some minor skirmishing with Union forays from Young's Point but little else to report. Taylor, Kirby Smith urged, was to return to Richmond and "spare no exertions." Confederate authorities concurred. Vicksburg mattered most. This was the point where the Rebel leadership must shine. "If [Johnston] allows Vicksburg to fall," observed Major Josiah Gorgas, Confederate Chief of Ordnance, "his reputation will be gone past all redemption."[30]

Kirby Smith dismissed Taylor's emerging southern Louisiana plan, telling him instead to rely on "Mouton, with his cavalry command and such infantry as could be collected" to do what they could down south. Not much, he believed. "I have but little hopes," Kirby Smith confided, "of affording any assistance to the garrison at Port Hudson."[31]

Taylor disagreed. He believed that Kirby Smith had already wasted two critical weeks butting his head against Grant that could have been used to threaten New Orleans, relieve Port Hudson, save its garrison, and turn the tables at Vicksburg. Taylor needed to make up this lost time. Because he could not be in northeastern and in southern Louisiana at the same time, Generals Walker and Kirby Smith would have to see to affairs near Vicksburg without him. Besides, Mouton could not handle the chore Taylor had in mind. "My experience in the past two weeks satisfies me that it is necessary that I should rely upon myself not only to devise the plans," he grumbled, "but also to execute them, in order to insure their being carried out vigorously."[32]

Taylor instead tasked Mouton for a different mission that was better suited to his talents. When Federal troops occupied Opelousas in May, they had aided local bandits, Unionists, and other allies to resist Confederate oppression. This often included supplying them with weapons and ammunition. After Banks departed, a sizable band of "jayhawkers" led by Ozémé Carrière formed in St. Landry Parish in a heavily wooded region along Bayou Mallet. Louisiana officials and soldiers identified most of the perpetrators as draft dodgers, deserters, or blacks

This collection of Confederate officers included men from General Alfred Mouton's staff as well as soldiers associated with Colonel James P. Major (center, second row) and the 2nd Cavalry Brigade. John Marsh Avery, an aide-de-camp to Colonel Major, is seated at the left of the first row, whereas his brother Dudley Avery, aide to General Mouton, is third from the right on the first row. The other officers are not yet identified but seem to be civilians, captains, majors, and colonels. Notice the two slaves peering from behind the Confederate officers.
McIlhenny Company Archives, McIlhenny Company, Avery Island, Louisiana.

mixed with a heavy leavening of local bandits that had plagued the region for years. Mouton had experience hunting these outlaws as part of the Lafayette Parish militia. Estimated at upward of one thousand men, locals called these scattered bands of raiders "the clan" and lumped them all together as pro-Union jayhawkers. In reality, their motives varied even if their tactics did not. Louisiana civil authorities asked Taylor and his soldiers to clean them out and to restore order to the region. Mouton, who hailed from that part of Louisiana, seemed perfectly suited for the chore.

The Acadian general had a battalion of troops he could not rely on in a stand-up battle against Yankees but might make perfect partisans. He mounted and dispatched the 11th Louisiana "Yellow Jacket" Battalion—itself wracked by rampant desertion—into the region northwest of Opelousas to recover deserters,

John Marsh Avery (on the right), *son of a distinguished Southern Louisiana family that included, among its holdings, the salt mines at Avery Island near New Iberia. He joined the militia early in the war, serving under Captain Frank Kloppenburg who may be the officer pictured here.*
McIlhenny Company Archives, McIlhenny Company, Avery Island, Louisiana.

As the war progressed, Lieutenant John Marsh Avery served west of the Mississippi and near his New Iberia home. He held staff positions, ending the war as the ordnance officer for the First Division, Confederate Army of the Trans-Mississippi.
McIlhenny Company Archives, McIlhenny Company, Avery Island, Louisiana.

patrol the road, and keep open communications with Texas. Major Gabriel Fournet established his headquarters at Hineston, Louisiana, some twenty miles southwest of Alexandria. Mouton was clear: This small band of Confederates moved into the piney woods, under orders to "scour the whole country . . . in search of these outlaws, highwaymen, and traitors. These bands, beyond the pale of society, must be exterminated, especially the leaders." Every man found with arms, especially those resisting Confederate laws, "must be executed on the spot. No prisoners should be taken."[33]

Texas Unionist Dennis Haynes found himself in a predicament. He had hoped to remain unnoticed until the Union army returned. The war now sought him out. "We were between two fires," he realized. Trying to maintain a low

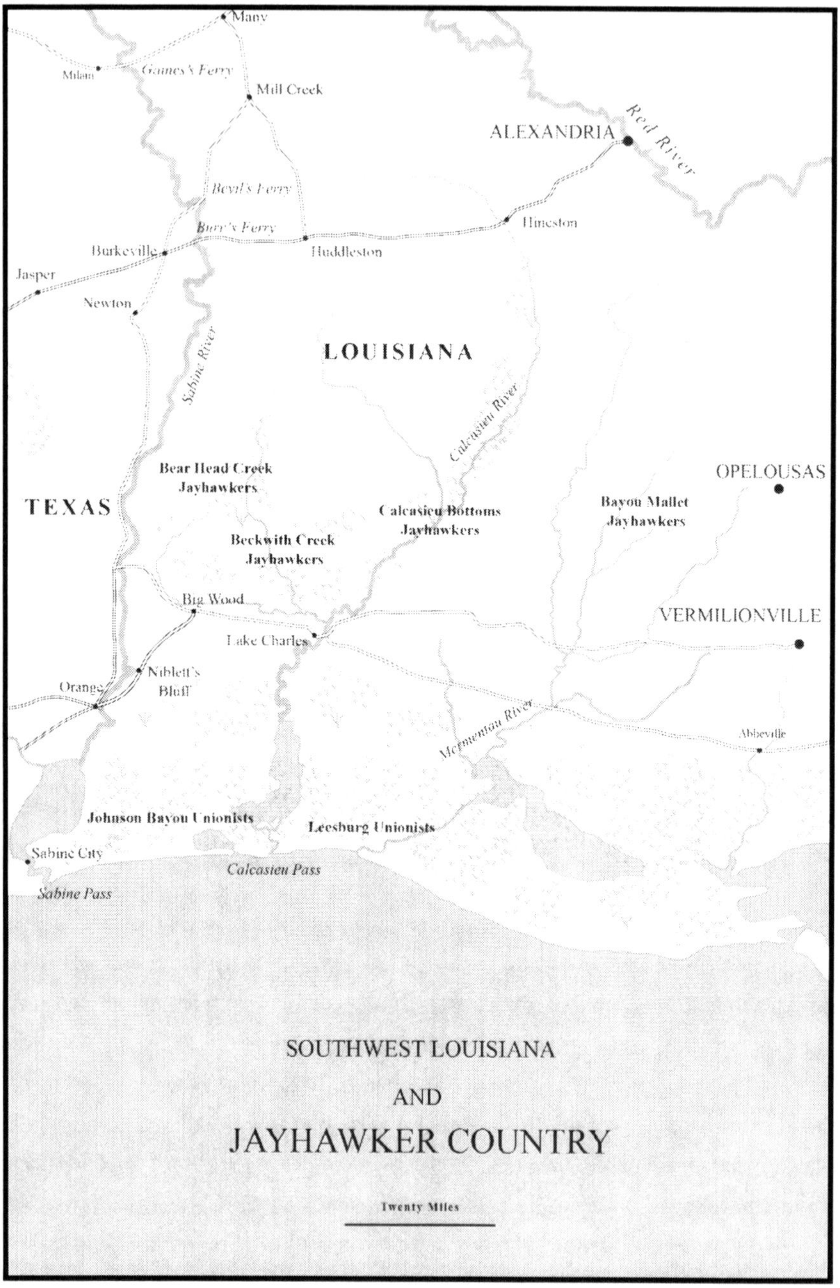
Many
Milam
Gaines's Ferry
Mill Creek
ALEXANDRIA
Red River
Bevil's Ferry
Burr's Ferry
Hineston
Burkeville
Huddleston
Jasper
Newton
LOUISIANA
Sabine River
Calcasieu River
Bear Head Creek Jayhawkers
OPELOUSAS
TEXAS
Calcasieu Bottoms Jayhawkers
Bayou Mallet Jayhawkers
Beckwith Creek Jayhawkers
Big Wood
VERMILIONVILLE
Lake Charles
Niblett's Bluff
Orange
Mermentau River
Abbeville
Johnson Bayou Unionists
Leesburg Unionists
Sabine City
Calcasieu Pass
Sabine Pass
SOUTHWEST LOUISIANA
AND
JAYHAWKER COUNTRY
Twenty Miles

profile, he aquired a farm in the piney wilderness of western Rapides Parish and tilled its acres.[34]

The Confederates arrived in the neighborhood and Haynes and his like-minded neighbors suffered the Yellow Jackets's sting. The soldiers of the 11th Louisiana Battalion plundered Unionists in the region. "They robbed . . . everything they could get their hands on," Haynes remembered. "Horses, mules, oxen and cattle, wagons and harness, bed-clothes, plow-gear, horse bells, even the women's shoes and little trinkets of jewelry." The Confederates shot down any Unionists who did not flee beyond the range of their shotguns and pistols. "It is a fact worthy of note that the first robberies committed in this section of Louisiana were committed by the Rebels," Haynes claimed, "which led to retaliation by some of the Union men, who in return, robbed some of the Rebels." When jayhawkers attacked a family of refugees heading from Alexandria to Texas, Haynes warned his neighbors that this lawlessness would soon engulf them all. "Evil would come of it," Haynes predicted. "The innocent would suffer for the sins of the wicked."[35]

6

The Lafourche

I have a mob, officered by fools.
—Lieutenant Colonel Albert Stickney
47th Massachusetts Infantry

Union commanders, fixated as they were with events at Port Hudson and with transforming the Sugar Parishes from slave labor to free, paid little attention to Rebel movements west of the Atchafalaya Basin. The country on the Union side of Berwick Bay and along the Lafourche lay serene and the liberated slaves unmolested by what had become a distant war. The fortifications at Brashear City protected this Federal enclave, and it settled into a new routine focused on free labor and the extermination of slavery.

The U.S. government promised to transform this part of Louisiana into an agricultural paradise based on wage labor. Union outposts protected this liberty laboratory, but General Nathaniel P. Banks continued to draw on its dwindling garrisons to feed the fight at Port Hudson. As a result, Union infantry companies and detachments lay isolated and scattered from Plaquemine, Bayou Goula, and Donaldsonville on the Mississippi River to Thibodaux, a distance of seventy miles, running generally north to south. Overtaxed and understrength units also guarded the entire length of the railroad from Brashear City to Algiers opposite New Orleans—its depots, bridges, and culverts—which was another seventy-mile stretch.

Only two Union regiments protected the line. Men from the 23rd Connecticut guarded Jefferson Depot, Boutte Depot, the bridge crossing Bayou des Allemands, the tracks at Raceland, and the crossing at Lafourche. Troops from the 176th New York covered the sidings at Terrebonne, Chacahoula, and Tigerville. General William H. Emory, in charge of defending New Orleans, maintained a keen interest in all the Lafourche District approaches to the city but especially positions up the railroad. He commanded elements of another four regiments he could send in that direction should the Confederates find a way into the Lafourche.[1]

The New Orleans, Opelousas, and Great Western Railroad bridge over Bayou Boeuf connected Tiger Island with the rest of the Lafourche District.
David Hunter Strother, Drawings and Sketches, The West Virginia and Regional History Holdings, West Virginia University Libraries, Acc. No. p.95.30.142.

There had been no combat in the area for more than seven months. "All was quiet at these various posts," wrote Private Charles P. Bosson of the 42nd Massachusetts Infantry, "the detachments on duty having what soldiers call 'a soft thing.'"[2] The country proved prosperous and comfortable. "In peace times, Bayou Lafourche was gay," an officer noted, "with pleasure steamers and watering houses."[3] Thibodaux, the seat of government in Lafourche Parish remained "a *distingué* town," a Northerner observed, "holding its head up among rural districts. Its wealthy creole residents and planters hereabouts . . . sip their *café* and claret like *grands seigneurs*."[4]

Life for these sugarcane aristocrats had certainly changed under Federal control. Labor contracts replaced slavery; government contractors working for the Treasury Department now ran plantations that had been declared "abandoned" by Federal law. Agents of the freshly organized Internal Revenue Service collected income taxes from the wealthier citizens. Union soldiers imposed the new rules. Lieutenant Colonel Augustine Joseph Hickey Duganne of the 176th New York

The waters of Bayou Lafourche flowed past an agricultural empire with few peers in the world. Sugar plantations lay alongside Creole homesteads, and prosperity had turned the region into a Louisiana paradise.
Harper's Weekly, January 19, 1867.

Infantry was one of the enforcers. A man of letters, this Boston-born writer, labor activist, social theorist, and political operator welcomed the transformation the war would make on—by his standards—a benighted part of the United States. "This war has played the mischief with all your luxurious security," he lectured some locals, "but you have yourselves to thank for the change, and must . . . make the best of it."[5]

He, like most Union officers in the region, employed eager blacks who, seeking security, worked for scant wages, food, and shelter in the garrisons. "My cook George," reflected Duganne, "yellow in epidermis and African in descent, who has lately emancipated himself from some Lafourche owner . . . is quite satisfied with his portion of the war changes."[6]

Despite Duganne's Yankee optimism, these changes had bewildered most of the black population. Many became homeless refugees in their own country. Some of the former slaves lingered at abandoned plantations, even though their owners had fled the Union advance. At one great estate of a Confederate officer, Duganne saw "those few poor negroes—driftwood—who have survived their

Union soldiers often hired liberated slaves to handle domestic chores for them, including serving as cooks. Yankees often commented on their servants, and found them nearly inexhaustible sources of fascination.
Homer, Winslow, 1836–1910, artist. Boston, Mass.: Lith. & pub. by L. Prang & Co., [1863]. Library of Congress Prints and Photographs Division, Washington, D.C.

Lieutenant Colonel Augustine Joseph Hinkley Duganne of the 176th New York was an up-and-coming poet, novelist, essayist, and labor advocate before the war.
Duganne, Augustine Joseph Hickey. *Camps and Prisons: Twenty Months in the Department of the Gulf.* New York: J. P. Robens, Publisher, 1865.

master's awful shipwreck." There was yet no policy for dealing with the needs of the displaced. "They are left, these victims of the Past and the Present," he reflected. "God help them! What shall be their Future?"[7]

To implement the new regime, Federal military officials employed the position of provost marshal to police and administer the region. Headquartered at parish seats, these squads of U.S. troops oversaw the implementation of wage labor, enforced contracts, and kept the peace. Planters, who had signed statements declaring their loyalty to the United States, would bring disputes for military arbitration. Provosts, mostly lieutenants and captains detailed for the job, became minor potentates in the process. If a freedman violated the terms of his contract, Union troops forced him to return to work. Officers might detail individual soldiers, or perhaps a squad, to calm especially troubled plantations.

Duganne believed this a misuse of Yankee volunteers. "A company of brave men who enlisted for the battlefield, are quartered here and there upon plantations, to awe the blacks and hold them closely to the labor-contract," he complained, "to protect the planters interest by hunting straggling recusants, and generally to act as overseers in pay of the Federal treasury."[8]

The provost marshals in the Lafourche District made themselves comfortable. A large mansion in Thibodaux served as the headquarters for Federal authority in that town. "No simple tent of line-officer, fronting his company street, but a gentleman's costly mansion, shaded by fragrant trees, with lawn and garden shrubbery, and grounds and outbuildings and stables for the 'stud' which must be kept at call for provost-captain's service," grumbled Duganne. Black attendants held the bridle and stirrup for arriving visitors as they dismounted, which was a similar duty performed by slaves on area plantations. On entering the house, Duganne observed, "one mild lieutenant" lolled about "on silk-cushioned sofa, [while] and another thrums the piano-forte. Their orderly mixes claret-punch in cut glass goblets." The new regime in Union-occupied Louisiana had developed a taste for the old order's luxury.[9]

The labor contract system had its flaws. Although former slaves could negotiate their wages, they still tilled other people's dirt. Many blacks preferred going it alone. Duganne asked a worker on one plantation if he could return the farm to production without white supervision. "I think, sah," the man answered encouragingly, "that a hundred men might do as much as a hundred slaves."[10]

Clearly, white Louisianans resented these reforms. The Emancipation Proclamation had exempted the parishes occupied by Union forces, but more often than not, the slaves simply left their masters, liberating themselves anyway. Plantation owners turned to the provost marshal and his heavies to help them recover their human property. They met with passive-aggressive tactics from the Federal officers. At the swamp- and bayou hemmed-hamlet of Tigerville, an irate planter approached Lieutenant George Quien of the 23rd Connecticut Infantry for help. The Union officer brushed the Southerner off, saying he would file a report. This stunned the slave owner. "In a rather ruffled tone," he asked, "is this all the help we can get from the Government?" The New Englander shot back with a rhetorical flourish. "Who is to blame that your slaves have left you? Nobody but yourselves."[11]

Many observers, upon seeing the extensive slave quarters on the massive Louisiana sugar plantations, referred to them as "towns" or "villages." In this sketch from the Lafourche District, the master's large home can be seen in the background.
David Hunter Strother, Drawings and Sketches, The West Virginia and Regional History Holdings, West Virginia University Libraries, Acc. No. p.95.30.127.

Lieutenant Quien refused to abide haughty slave owners. "All the planters in this parish signed the Government's document, but one by the name of Hopkins kept misusing his slaves as before the war," he remembered. In one instance, a black woman fled to the provost marshal's headquarters to escape her former owner. She "opened our door and fell flat on the floor," Quien wrote. Soldiers raised her to her feet to have a look. She had clearly been beaten and bled from a wound on her head. A captain, serving as provost marshal, ordered out a six-man squad to arrest the attacker.

When they brought him in, the captain asked, "Did you beat up this woman?"

"Yes, I did; she belongs to me," Hopkins, the attacker, confessed.

"You beat her up again, I will lock you up in the guard house," the Captain responded. With the warning delivered, the troops escorted the man away.

"I will beat her up again because she belongs to me," Hopkins mumbled as he left. Hopkins terrorized his slaves, exposing the excesses and nuances of the South's "peculiar institution," whereas Catherine Cornelius of the Smithfield Plantation and subject of the WPA interview seventy years later, praised her kind master.[12]

In this sunset of slavery, provosts became unwitting instruments in returning freedmen to a status approaching chattel. Oath-taking, loyal planters, or government contractors new to the area, were eager to make a crop and sell it for max-

Many Louisiana planters chose to take the oath allegiance to the United States in hopes that they could continue to operate their businesses without fear of seizure by the Federal government. Here well-heeled ladies and gentlemen take their turns to sign their pledges. Brigadier General James Bowen served as the Provost Marshall General of the Department of the Gulf and oversaw all such operations from his headquarters in New Orleans. Harper's Weekly, June 6, 1863.

imum yield. They required stable and reliable labor. These entrepreneurs understood that favors, bribes, and other gifts to the local Federal authorities might advance their ambitions. Profit trumped social justice. Military officials looked the other way as long as the region remained peaceful and food from plantations filled the bellies of laborers and soldiers. Sugar provided the money that greased the wheels of graft.

These conditions reduced freedmen to simply another commodity. "That great black human Force," wrote Duganne, "is reckoned in the labor contracts only as the 'stock' whose service is to multiply the gains of capital." A longtime champion of labor over property in the great socialist debates of the mid-nineteenth century, he loathed what he saw emerging in Louisiana. Once the war ended, what would happen to these quasi-free people? Would they would become wage slaves—free only in name?[13]

A railroad executive before the Civil War, James Bowen raised several regiments for the Union cause and led them, temporarily, in Louisiana. With his genius for organization, General Nathaniel P. Banks tapped Bowen for service as the Provost Marshall General of the Department of the Gulf. As the top Union military policeman in Louisiana, he was responsible for everything from gathering black troops and labor, confiscating Rebel property, and maintaining law and order in the occupied sugar parishes.
Library of Congress Prints and Photographs Division, Washington, D.C.

The U.S. government struggled to balance the social and economic implications of radical emancipation. Informed by the great economic and political thinkers of the day, many in Washington studied the issue in theoretical terms. Yet, Duganne noted, the freedmen had "never heard of Adam Smith, [Thomas] Malthus, or [David] Ricardo." U.S. policies in the occupied parishes was "well intended, [but] neither satisfies the planter nor protects the negro." The only winners would be capitalists and middlemen in position to exploit the situation. The solution imposed on the emancipated labor of Louisiana "can never end in aught but profit to the speculating hordes that swarm about this Gulf Department," lamented Duganne, "like voracious sharks upon the track of fever-ships."[14]

This New York champion of labor believed loftier work remained. As long as the government allowed Northern and Southern opportunists to exploit black labor, the newly emancipated people would never reach the full promises of their blood-bought liberation. Duganne explained that the government remained short-sighted, providing, "no sound, humanitarian plan for lifting up this 'stock' to manhood, no provisions for a future self-respecting peasantry, whose souls and bodies now are in our hands, as clay, to mold them as we will; no statesmanlike attempt to solve the mighty labor-problem of our nation's future." The labor-contract system and

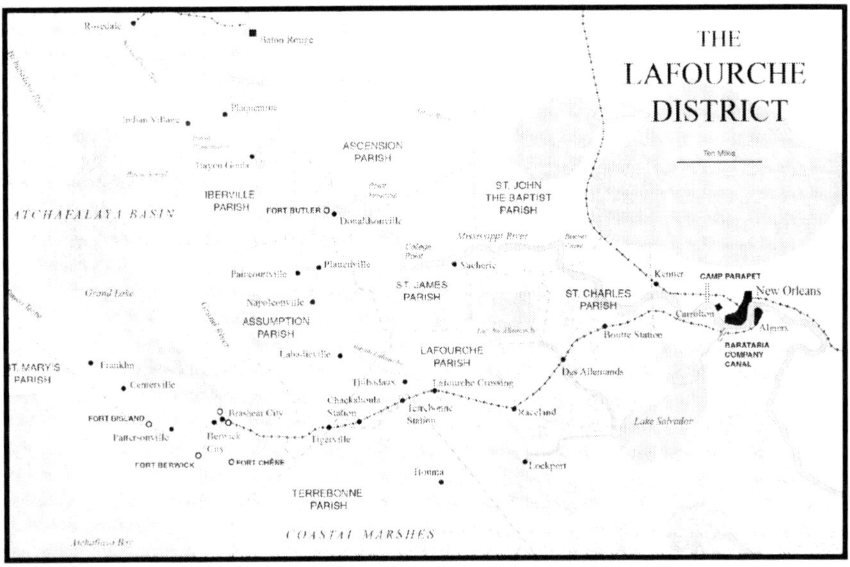

plantation leases handled the immediate requirements, but they would not bring this black population into full citizenship. “This is the day of provost marshals and omnipotent staff-officers,” he groaned. “God help our country.”[15]

Once the soldiers left, Duganne feared, the future might work itself out—violently. “Here,” Duganne continued, “have accumulated teeming folios full of questions for the future, between capital and labor, bond and free. I have more faith in war-guns than law-canons for the ultimate adjudication of these knotty problems.” Enlisting blacks into the U.S. army, too, might lead to raised awareness and expectations among the former slaves. “Black diplomacy, supported by black courage, and enlightened by contact with bayonets that have learned to think,” Duganne mused, “might settle all labor contracts on a sounder basis.”[16]

Duganne hoped for a general rising of the black population. “I see a grand militia armed and drilled upon these green savannahs, no longer chattel souls, but conscious of their strength and numbers,” he wrote. He believed these black men should be a labor-militia, “marching to the cane and cotton fields by the tap of drum, and guarding bridge or railway line with ready rifles.” In short, these armed agricultural workers would assert their new rights with weapons while the rest of the Union army defeated the Confederates. “Who,” he mused, “will drill these negroes into semi-military laborers on their old plantations, and make them an 'army of occupation' for the soil?"[17]

General Banks had already factored this "grand militia" into his plans for defending the region. As Confederates scrounged for more troops, the Union army was busy creating its own from the secessionists' former slaves. From Brashear City to Baton Rouge and New Orleans, Union officers culled the military-aged males that had come into the sprawling camps of freedmen and trained them as soldiers. "They do first rate," wrote Union soldier Sam White of Company D, 4th Massachusetts Infantry, observing the black troops drilling near Brashear City. "They make tip top soldiers, better than white ones ever dared to be." This New Englander, having enlisted for nine months, believed these black soldiers would be the salvation of the nation. His enlistment nearly up, he was ready to go home. "They can well spare us since they got them, all right, because they will fight like the devil."[18]

Moreover, Banks had no intentions of ever leading another campaign up Bayou Teche. He had pulled all Union forces west of the Atchafalaya Basin back to Brashear City—a place he considered virtually impregnable. When his assault on Port Hudson failed on May 27, Banks turned to the Lafourche District for the last of its surplus troops. Most of the forces defending the area marched toward the meat grinder on the Mississippi, leaving but a scant garrison of white soldiers, while their black comrades learned the soldiers' trade. Officers brought in from New York with General Daniel Ullmann would surely raise a new garrison of *Corps d'Afrique* regiments to guard Brashear City.[19]

The obstinacy of General Franklin Gardner's Confederates derailed this plan. Banks's need for more troops at Port Hudson cut Ullmann's efforts short. "General Ullman[n] will forward to Port Hudson immediately all the colored troops which he has raised, whether armed or unarmed," Banks ordered, and "report the number of each class and regiments to which they belong." Ullmann needed to hurry. "Press forward the organization of [these] troops," Banks urged from Port Hudson, "as they are much needed here." They would be fed into the battle as quickly as they could be sent. In New Orleans, some twelve hundred men, mostly liberated field hands from plantations in the Sugar Parishes with little training, no weapons, and few uniforms, crowded aboard the steamboat *Fulton* to begin their service to new masters.[20]

For Northerners enthusiastic about enlisting black troops, the idea of thousands of eager volunteers coming from the ranks of liberated slaves seemed like common sense. This series of cards shows the progression of an imagined slave from his days in the cotton fields, his courtship and marriage, his separation from his family, his abuse at the hands of a cruel master, his revenge, and his escape into the Union lines. Ultimately, this mythology has the liberated slave sacrificing his life in battle for his new found liberty. Library of Congress Prints and Photographs Division, Washington, D.C.

A steady stream of black soldiers also left Brashear City; white officers had to constantly start over as they attempted to raise new commands. Brashear City became the hub for transforming the liberated slaves into enlisted men. Captain Albert Allen trained black sergeants and corporals, who in turned drilled awkward squads and platoons destined for the 6th and 7th *Corps d'Afrique*. Lieutenant Charles E. Page, assigned to Company F, 9th *Corps d'Afrique*, sorted the gathered freedmen into labor details and identified those most likely for military duty. Surgeon David Hershey of the same regiment tended to the ill and performed medical inspections on the recruits.[21]

Other black soldiers assembled at Brashear City. Companies D and F of the 1st Engineers, *Corps d'Afrique* arrived from Camp Parapet in New Orleans. They had come to assist with breaking up the raft—a logjam—that clogged Bayou Sorrel deep in the Atchafalaya swamp. Once cleared, steamers could navigate between Brashear City and Plaquemine via Grand Lake and Lake Chicot to Bayou Sorrel and gain the junction of Bayous Grosse Tête and Plaquemine at Indian Village. The Mississippi River lay just a few miles beyond. This engineering project, if successful, would cut days off the travel time between Berwick Bay and the Mississippi. Once accomplished, smaller gunboats, transports, and supply vessels could shuttle between Union depots, adding security to the region. After a few weeks at Brashear, the engineers and a platoon of thirty lumbermen from the 12th Maine headed deep into the great Atchafalaya Basin aboard the tugboats *Sykes* and *Anglo American* towing two large barges.[22]

Union planners, fixated on Port Hudson, did not fear a Rebel attack at Brashear City, and the terrain there fed Bank's sense of security. To assault that position, Brigadier General Alfred Mouton's listless and disorganized Confederates to the west of the town had a six hundred-yard water crossing of Berwick Bay ahead of them in the face of cannon and small arms. Such an amphibious assault would be suicidal. Banks believed his raid up Bayou Teche had destroyed every Rebel steamer in southern Louisiana. The enemy had no boats with which to make a crossing. Banks gambled that Mouton dared not attempt it.

The Rebels could not bypass the Union positions either. To the north of Brashear City, a dense swamp bordered Lake Palourde and its outlet, Flat Lake. Even if the Confederates located some transports (perhaps moved in from the Red River by way of the Atchafalaya River) no steamers could

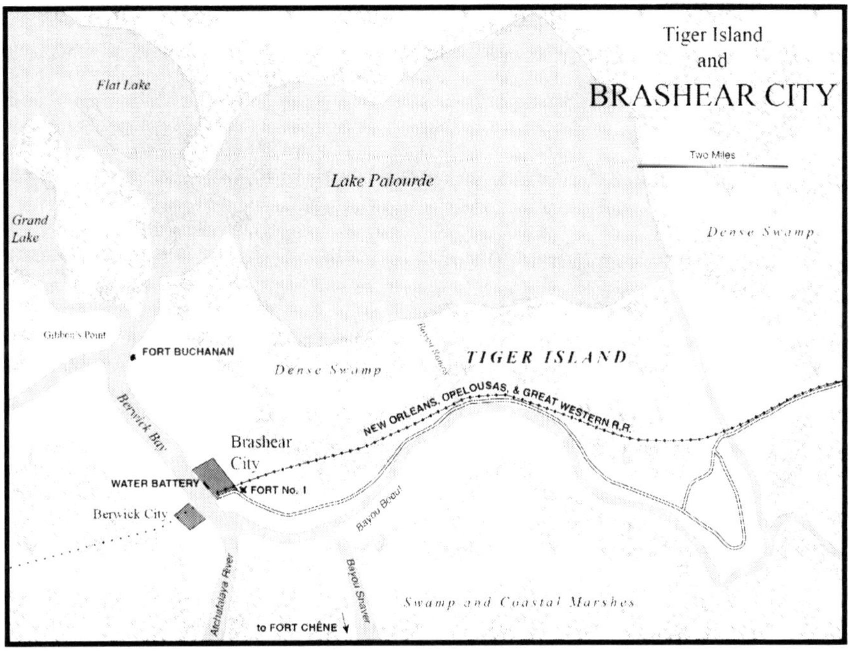

navigate these shallow waters. Bayou Boeuf also protected the base at Brashear City, connecting Berwick Bay and Lake Palourde. Deep enough to navigate, the Boeuf was too wide to cross without boats. Plantations lined its southern shore but sea marshes stretched for miles at the back of those properties. Thus guarded by a natural moat, Brashear City simultaneously enjoyed communication with the Gulf by water and New Orleans by rail. The locals called the seven-mile length of flat dry ground bracketed by swamps and bayous "Tiger Island."

The location of this Union power hub, however, concealed many drawbacks. Ideal for sugarcane with its flat fields and bottomless topsoil, its sod and roads were constantly churned into a morass by large bodies of troops. Frequent rains made the place miserable for men in tents. A New York sergeant could not believe the conditions near Bayou Boeuf on the east side of Tiger Island:

> Mud! Mud!! Mud!!! Such mud as has existed nowhere else since the ark stuck on Ararat. Mud in our boots, mud in our tents, mud in the water,

> mud in our food. We eat, sleep, and drink mud, and believe that if we die in this mud hole we will become mud—slimy, oozy mud, the favorite resort of catfish and alligators.[23]

Despite the men's wretchedness, most Union officers in Louisiana shared Banks's confidence in the defensibility of Brashear City. During the fall and winter of 1862, Brigadier General Godfrey Weitzel had used it as his depot for operations into the interior of Louisiana. In April 1863, the Army of the Gulf had staged the invasion of the Teche Country from there. Since then, supplies and weapons to equip the regiments of the *Corps d'Afrique* had poured in by rail from New Orleans and lay crated in mountains stowed in buildings near the tracks at Brashear City. Defensive works safeguarded this stockpile. The guns of Fort Buchanan faced the northern end of Berwick Bay and commanded the Atchafalaya as it came in and mingled with the waters of Grand Lake. A water battery that the Confederates had originally excavated in 1861 and left open in the back lay midway down the west shore of Berwick Bay and covered the hamlet of Berwick across the water. A four-bastioned, star-shaped earthwork, with the unglamorous name of Fort Number 1, guarded the rail line as it entered the Union camp and covered the southern end of Berwick Bay. A few heavy cannon, mostly 24-pounders, pointed southwest from this position.

Union earthworks also guarded other approaches. A small garrison occupied the muddy and wretched bastion, Fort Chêne, in the swamps six miles south of Tiger Island; its two 24-pounders covered two deep-water bayous that Confederates might employ to work around the strong works at Brashear. Seven miles east, at the other end of Tiger Island, a small garrison minded the railroad bridge crossing Bayou Boeuf and the critical connection with the Lafourche District. Just across this stream, the extra baggage for General Cuvier Grover's and Weitzel's divisions, dumped at the start of the Teche Campaign and now in storage while these units fought at Port Hudson, lay neatly stacked in a massive sugar house.[24]

Brashear City had mushroomed in other ways. Commissary, medical, and provost detachments crowded the village, camps, and fields with the tools of war, the sick of the army, and an array of clerks. Trains continued running regularly and the steamer *Kepper* provided water transportation around Berwick Bay.

The economic heart of every prosperous sugar plantation was its refinery complex, or sugarhouse.
David Hunter Strother, Drawings and Sketches, The West Virginia and Regional History Holdings, West Virginia University Libraries, Acc. No. p.95.30.145.

The Union depot and encampment at Brashear City was the hub of Federal activity in the Lafourche District. This position commanded Berwick Bay, enjoyed communications with New Orleans by rail and by sea, and had served as the staging area for General Nathaniel P. Banks's Teche Campaign and recruiting center for the Corps d'Afrique. *In the summer of 1863, it also proved unhealthy. The catamaran-hulled steamboat Kepper is at the docks.*
David Hunter Strother, Drawings and Sketches, The West Virginia and Regional History Holdings, West Virginia University Libraries, Acc. No. p.95.30.68.

Federal officers had laid out a sprawling cantonment. The nerve center was the depot, and its spine the railroad. Sizable wharves lined the waterfront at Berwick Bay. A five-hundred-yard-long train of more than fifty cars and two locomotives stretched eastward. Beyond lay a smaller train, fewer than ten cars, that the troops used as ready mobility to transport men and supplies to the depots down the railroad. A massive quartermaster tent and associated canvas awnings spread out about two hundred yards down from the depot and along the north side of the tracks. Employees of the New Orleans, Opelousas, and Great Western Railroad lived in homes and barracks south of the tracks near Fort Number 1.

To most eyes, the post seemed vast. A wide, white, belt of tents spread out along the waterfront of Berwick Bay north of the tracks and stretched toward Fort Buchanan in a canvas city nearly a mile long and some one hundred yards wide. This bright field of cloth housed the able-bodied garrison, including seven companies from the 176th New York—A, B, C, D, E, F, and H. The camps of the five companies from the 23rd Connecticut, C, F, G, I, and K, lay just behind. Small cavalry detachments—with horses picketed in lines—camped nearby. The men of Company F, 21st Indiana Heavy Artillery under the command of Captain Francis W. Noblette, bivouacked near their guns at Fort Buchanan. A fragrant orange grove backed by marshy woods a half-mile to the east of the shores of Berwick Bay provided a leafy backdrop to the sprawling encampment.[25]

The harsh climate, bad water, and omnipresent Louisiana bugs steadily whittled away at the Union army. Officials warehoused many suffering soldiers at Brashear City. A hospital complex stretched out north of the garrison bivouac and made use of the house, sugarhouse, and buildings of Thomas and Robert Brashear's Tiger Island Plantation. Malaria and other maladies ravaged many a New York and New England soldier, and the tents of the one thousand shivering and fatigued convalescents lay in the fields behind and to the east of the hospital.[26]

Union commanders believed they might summon these ailing troops to defend Brashear City. Most of these sickly soldiers from Banks's army left behind during the Teche Campaign could at least shoulder a musket. Lieutenant Colonel Duganne remained less hopeful. No one had deigned to organize this mob into an army. "In round numbers, there were probably a thousand privates, more or less able to do duty," he noted, "who, under nominal supervision of some surgeons

This sketch of the encampment of the 176th New York Infantry shows a typical regimental bivouac. Company "streets" are arranged in the same order in which the men will muster in line of battle. Line officer share tents at one end of the street, and latrines occupy the opposite. The levee in the background partially hides plantation buildings where the field grade officers lived.
William V. Shaw, "Camp of the 176th Regt. N.Y.S. Vol's. Bonnet Carre. La." no date. Courtesy of the Becker Collection, Boston, Massachusetts.

or sergeants, pass their days in lounging and card-playing, without organization, drill, or duty."[27]

The longer men lingered at Brashear City, the weaker they became. Banks and his officers did not realize that Tiger Island harbored a secret that festered under the Louisiana summer sun. The hot, humid, weather grew unbearable, and the water supply slimy and tainted. "A platoon of soldiers were kept busy all day and every day burying the dead," remembered Lieutenant Quien. "The weather was hot enough to boil a teakettle in the sun. We had quit drilling . . . on account of the heat." Troops that had dribbled in from the army now fighting at Port Hudson faced long odds in the grip of a Louisiana coastal summer.

The 38th Massachusetts, for example, had been pulled from the defenses of Baltimore in January, fought in the Teche Campaign in April, and now served in the trenches at Port Hudson. In the wake of this advance, the regiment lost eleven men to the slow attrition of wounds, weather, and disease. On April 13, three of these dead men had been hit at the Battle of Bisland, evacuated to Brashear City, and lingered between two and six weeks as their infected wounds robbed them of life. The others had come to Brashear City ill only to die from maladies lumped together as "chronic diarrhea." The 38th Massachusetts was typical of Banks's army. This sea of the sick, dying, and malingering included the castoffs from more than forty Union regiments and batteries that had marched in the Teche Campaign.[28]

Malaria and maladies including typhus and typhoid sapped the strength of the garrison. Mosquitos injected plasmodia into the men, who in turn developed chills, coughing, delirium, high fever, headaches, and sore joints and muscles. Flies feeding at latrines spread bowel diseases. Nearly half of the newcomers reported sick within ten days of arriving. Corporal Andrew Sherman of Company F, 23rd Connecticut, feared for his life after arriving at Brashear City, preferring to face the Rebels on the Mississippi. "It is still a question in my mind," he recalled, "which of Lincoln's boys in blue faced the greater peril, those at Port Hudson and Vicksburg or those doing duty in the lowlands of Louisiana . . . with its malarial atmosphere, its unwholesome water and its disease-imparting mosquitoes."[29]

Illness and climate did not respect rank either. Officers remained scarce. The post commander during the Teche Campaign, Colonel Henry Walker of the 4th Massachusetts fell ill and left for New Orleans. After proper care and hygiene, he recovered and reported to his regiment at Port Hudson. The next in rank, Colonel Charles C. Nott of the 176th New York was already ill. His replacement as post commander, Colonel Charles E. L. Holmes of the 23rd Connecticut, reported to the hospital soon after assuming command. The control of this important, but forgotten, depot fell to his second-in-command, Lieutenant Colonel Charles W. Worden. Disgusted with this backwater pesthole, he refused the job and offered it to the next in rank, Lieutenant Colonel Duganne of the 176th New York. This idealistic officer also declined, reporting that he was already ill. Any ailing officer that could usually arranged to go to New Orleans to recover from the shakes and trots.[30]

Lieutenant George Hepworth, a New England preacher, came to Louisiana as chaplain of the 47th Massachusetts. He soon turned his attention to the plight of liberated slaves and helped their transition into free citizens.
The Whip, Hoe, and Sword.

Liberated slaves shared this island of misery. Blacks outnumbered whites at Tiger Island by almost five to one. Camps housing enrollees for the *Corps d'Afrique* regiments lined the railroad tracks from the edge of the village for several hundred yards. While waiting to become soldiers, they provided labor. Some three thousand came from the Teche parishes; officers shipped perhaps two thousand more from New Orleans where they had accumulated after leaving their homes along the Mississippi and Bayou Lafourche. Wives and families followed many of these men to Tiger Island. Several colonies of liberated blacks lived among the cabins and buildings of seven different plantations along the southern rim of Tiger Island. Although the Federals had removed many of these people from the Teche region the month before, intending them to work government-leased plantations under the new wage-labor system, the military's transportation priorities marooned most of them. They now faced an uncertain future, subsisting on government rations.[31]

The liberated slaves congregating at Tiger Island suffered as badly as the Yankees. "The negroes are in a most deplorable condition," wrote George Hepworth, an official tasked with helping implement wage labor in Louisiana. "Six thousand came from the plantations between [Berwick] bay and Alexandria and are living in such a way, that the mortality during the summer will be most terrible." The useful, military-age men lived in camps of instruction with some semblance of order and discipline. All others had to

Union soldiers occupying the Lafourche District had, many for the first time in their lives, close and daily contact with blacks.
Frank Leslie's Illustrated Newspaper.

fend for themselves. "They are free; but alas! Freedom only means the power to die."[32]

Tiger Island's squalor convinced this Union officer of the value of the new wage-labor arrangements. "The old, the young, and the women are living in little huts," Hepworth continued, "with more than a fair prospect of a speedy death before them. Their proper place, indeed the only place where they can learn the meaning and the privileges of freedom, is on the plantation, as hired hands." Barring that, he argued, officials should ship these free people to New Orleans. "They ought to have perfect liberty," he concluded, "to try their pluck and their luck in the city."[33]

Most Union plans for liberated slaves regarded them in general terms—in aggregate—as a resource to advance the Union war effort. Government planners had not carefully considered the logistics of caring for them during the transition. "How was the slave to be transformed into a freeman?" was a common question challenging abolitionist thinkers. Conditions at Brashear City posed more pressing questions. One official asked, "How was he to be fed and clad and sheltered?" Who would feed him and tend him—and his family—if they were sick? At Brashear

City, at least, the U.S. government failed to appreciate that dying people would never transform into freedmen.[34]

The suffering souls on Tiger Island weighed heavily on General Emory, who was tasked with defending the Lafourche District. He watched helplessly as Banks stripped the region of soldiers. He also received a steady drip of bad news about conditions on Berwick Bay, and he found himself hard-pressed to find someone who would actually command at Brashear City. Since the colonels there refused to serve, he searched the rolls of able-bodied officers in New Orleans and found few of suitable rank. He settled on Lieutenant Colonel Albert Stickney of the 47th Massachusetts, who was described as a "very intelligent and spirited young officer." Emory sighed: "Well, let Stickney go." The twenty-three-year-old attorney from Cambridge, Massachusetts, served as a militia officer in Boston's "Merchant's Guard Regiment" of nine-month's volunteers. Since arriving in the Department of the Gulf, he served at civic and political functions in the comforts of New Orleans. He had no field experience. "So Lieutenant Colonel Stickney [was] relieved from duty of attending public school festivals, in full dress, with the band of his regiment," mocked Duganne, adding that, "a new military broom begins to sweep" at Brashear City.[35]

The assignment overwhelmed the young, inexperienced officer. The Rebels across Berwick Bay also intimidated the new commander. If they attacked, his post would not be ready for defense. "I have a mob, officered by fools," wrote Stickney.[36]

He tried to anticipate *how* the Rebels would attack. The Confederates might manage to pass around to the south side of Tiger Island with a steamer brought in from somewhere along the coast, but that seemed unlikely. Besides, he had Fort Chêne covering that approach. The swamps to his north, engineers assured him, were impassible for anything but a canoe. With no Union positions guarding the far shore of Berwick Bay, the Rebels might still attempt a crossing. A concentration of Confederate cannon might play freely on his garrison to cover such a landing.

If they made it across, the fight might be closer that Stickney cared to admit. Union planners relied too heavily on the sick soldiers at Brashear City. The troops Stickney found at the hospital and camps struck him as little more than a loafing rabble. "The convalescents I cannot depend on," he fumed, complaining that these men seemed accountable to no one, never answered a roll call, and had no particular military routine. "They were in utter confusion."[37]

To demonstrate to the Confederates that he remained vigilant, and to boost his own confidence, Stickney allowed his cannon to shell the western shore and the village of Berwick on the slightest provocation. "Bombardment of that tenantless town and the lonely shore above it goes on incessantly," reported Duganne. "A bunch of pendant moss can hardly stir in the breeze, on that Berwick side, but straightaway Fort Buchanan launches its thunders, and our shore batteries pound at it."[38]

On the other side of Berwick Bay, Confederates fell back to Camp Bisland above Pattersonville on Bayou Teche, several miles away. Pickets, though, watched the Union base. Few expected a serious probe by the Federals—or a renewed invasion. Junius Harris, a soldier in the 4th Texas Cavalry, dared them to try. "If they do come over they will meet a different reception this time, for we are better prepared for them." The April campaign had already devastated the region. "The Yankees have almost ruined this country," he lamented. "Large and beautiful plantations entirely deserted, some few negroes remain true to their masters." The enemy could not return to that tortured region. "I believe old General Banks wants to get out of here," he wrote. "I do not know his exact whereabouts myself, but I expect our leaders do." Harris figured the greater part of the enemy to be either at Port Hudson or operating east of the Atchafalaya in Pointe Coupée Parish.[39]

At the same time, few of the Texans on picket duty believed they would attack such a formidable bulwark as Brashear City. Private John Adam Lorenz of Company D, 5th Texas Cavalry, contemplated the Federals across Berwick Bay from a mile away, which he considered a safe distance. As he and a comrade rode up to relieve another pair of pickets, Lorenz loped a little way past his friend, Lieutenant Jacob "Jack" Marshall, to take a better look at Fort Buchanan in the distance.

"You'd better come back," Marshall yelled.

"For what?" Lorenz shot back, intent on watching the fort.

"They will shoot at you from the fort," said Marshall.

"Not at one man," Lorenz reasoned, turning to his friend. Lorenz was a twenty-three-year-old veteran who believed he knew about such things. He had fought alongside the lieutenant in New Mexico. On that brutal campaign, his horse had drowned beneath him as he forded the Rio Grande. The Yankees had taken him prisoner at Apache Canyon, New Mexico, and paroled him six months later. For this grizzled warrior, picket duty in the face of the enemy was no novelty.

Marshall assured him, "They done it yesterday . . ."

The words still hung in the air when one of Fort Buchanan's embrasures flashed fire. "I looked toward the fort and seen a cloud of smoke," Lorenz remembered. "I taken the hint and moved toward Jack." The solid shot whizzed past the two Texans, kicking up mud and grass as it impacted beyond.

"Didn't I tell you," Marshall lectured smugly.

The two soldiers let the moment pass, and then debated how their army would even attempt to strike at Brashear City protected as it was by Berwick Bay and the big guns.

"I'll [bet] you more, our officers are going to try and capture the fort and we will have to swim to get it," Marshall grumbled. "The Yankees will kill us all before we get across."

Lorenz told him not to worry. Certainly generals like Green and Mouton had better sense than that.

Marshall disagreed, "Yes, but I know better." The generals—Taylor and Green at least—favored bold action and he wanted no part of it. "They will try it," Lieutenant Marshall declared, "and I am not going."[40]

Union General Emory, like Stickney, also believed that Taylor, Mouton, and Green might try something, and fretted over his lack of troops. Taylor certainly would try something to aid Port Hudson. Even if the Rebels did not butt up against Brashear City, he believed they would eventually infiltrate the Lafourche region—and raise hell. Early in June an escaped Union officer traveled to New Orleans with tales of Rebel plots for attacking Brashear City. His suspicions aroused, Emory telegraphed Baton Rouge requesting a gunboat for service on Berwick Bay. Surely, the navy could spare *one* from the lower fleet then shelling Port Hudson. Or, perhaps, a vessel undergoing repairs in New Orleans would do. The boat could slip down the Mississippi and into the Gulf, then around through Atchafalaya Bay to Brashear City. The naval commander upriver ignored the inquiry. "I am quite sure that the answer will be that he has none to send," Emory complained.[41]

Still, the general persisted. "Cannot one be detached, if only for a day or two? It would, in my opinion, if done promptly, save the place and divert attack." Eventually naval officers relented, settling on the USS *Hollyhock*, a Mississippi River tug turned into a light gunboat, and sent it on its circuitous journey to Brashear City. Emory still needed reinforcements—he asked Banks for at least a brigade. Something, he believed, was afoot. "The city was never

A veteran of the Army of the Potomac, General William H. Emory had been famous before the war for surveying the U.S.–Canadian border as well as the border between the United States and Mexico. He accompanied General Nathaniel P. Banks to Louisiana and commanded the garrison at New Orleans as well as the troops guarding the approaches to the city.
Library of Congress Prints and Photographs Division, Washington, D.C.

more quiet," he admitted, "but I learn the rebel sympathizers are confidently anticipating a move."[42]

New Orleans itself lay lightly guarded. Only one regiment of infantry and fragments of two more lay at hand, while part of a newly raised regiment of Unionists Texas cavalry and a handful of foot and mounted detachments patrolled its streets. Several batteries manned the line of works at Carrolton, but all together provost and guard details into the surrounding regions actually left it with fewer than four hundred men reporting for duty inside the city limits.

When pressed for reinforcements, Banks argued that he needed every man he had to see to New Orleans's security. His army must keep General Gardner's Rebel forces trapped inside their works at Port Hudson. "The vigor and strength of the enemy," he argued, "show that with the aid of the garrison at Port Hudson, New Orleans could not be defended." Banks, with circular logic, claimed he had weakened his forces in southern Louisiana to trap Gardner so that the Confederates could not threaten the weakened forces in southern Louisiana. Obviously the garrisons in the Lafourche and at New Orleans must hang on until Gardner surrendered. Taylor would not attack, Banks assured his subordinate. Unsatisfied, General Emory informed the leadership in Washington of his concerns.[43]

Affairs in the Department of the Gulf concerned Major General Henry Halleck, General-in-Chief. Banks assured him that a little more time and more liberated slaves were all he needed to see everything secure in the Lafourche

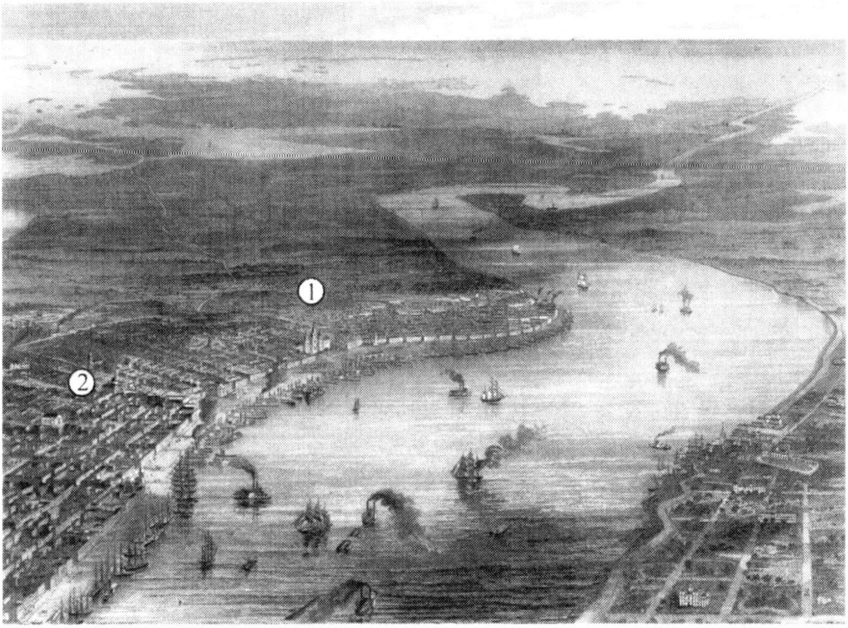

This 1863 bird's-eye view of New Orleans looking south toward the Gulf of Mexico shows a levee crowded with boats, the spires of St. Louis Cathedral near the center of the image (1), and to the left near Canal Street the large, domed edifice of the St. Charles Hotel, the nerve center of Union occupation (2).
Library of Congress Prints and Photographs Division, Washington, D.C.

District. New Orleans faced no credible threat. When inquiries from Washington, D.C., questioned his management of the department, Banks answered that his employment of black troops fed by the toil of black hands would secure Louisiana. "The organization of the colored troops is progressing steadily," he boasted to Halleck. "Every negro within the present lines of this department, or within reach of them, without distinction of age, sex, or condition, is in the service of the Government, either in the army or in producing food for the army and its dependents." In Banks's view, Emory possessed all he needed, save guts.[44]

Banks took the opportunity to showcase his successes. He hoped to emerge from the War of the Rebellion a statesman, soldier, and prophet of the new order, which was a potent combination for any ambitious politician. The laurels gained in Louisiana would blot the stains from his failures in Virginia. Once he lifted himself from the mud of Port Hudson and populated the state's outposts with black occupation forces, he could declare his mission accomplished and handle more important—and higher profile—chores for his nation.

Meanwhile, Emory scavenged the defenses of New Orleans for troops he could send to Brashear to calm Stickney's nerves. The 42nd Massachusetts, less three companies lost at the Battle of Galveston, camped nearby. Officers cannibalized the regiment to bring Company B up to full strength by pulling troops from companies A and E. At 5:00 P.M. on June 9, this consolidated command left the depot at Algiers, heading up the tracks to Brashear.[45]

The Massachusetts troops arrived to find the post in disarray. The mosaic of commands, functions, and facilities had simply overwhelmed the officers in charge. There seemed to be no system of command or control and no plan for defense. "Food was plenty, but there was no system for delivering rations," noted Private Bosson. "There did not seem to be a head to anything." First Sergeant George Ballow, seeing to the needs of his Massachusetts men, spent much of his day trying to convince quartermasters to release rations. "It appeared . . . as though the 42nd were visitors who had remained too long," remarked Bosson, "but did not leave because there was no one to tell them to go."[46]

Stickney inspired little confidence in the Bay State men. "He had a habit of riding around, often alone, to give verbal orders for all sorts of petty things, and to find fault with trifles," complained Bosson. "As to perfecting the organization of what troops he had, or establishing any system out of the chaos that existed, there seems to be but one verdict from those on duty under him. He did nothing."[47]

Bosson was perhaps too harsh. Stickney *did* order his men out into formation several times a day, under a broiling sun. "Drilling gets chronic under a midsummer sun," Duganne carped. Soon tiring of Brashear, its climate, its commander, and its chaos, the captain and a lieutenant from Company B, 42nd Massachusetts, reported at sick call. They received orders to recuperate at the hospital in New Orleans. They invited the remaining company officer, Lieutenant Benjamin C. Tinkham, to be sick along with them, but, resigned to his fate, the dutiful soldier refused.[48]

The morale of the men at Brashear City, already low, plummeted under Stickney's command. "I think Emory, before experimenting with an important outpost through a post commandant who wears out the energies of our few organized companies by extra duty," grumbled Duganne, "should have come here and examined matters for himself." Eventually Stickney arrested the carping New York officer for insubordination. Duganne responded by reporting himself ill once again. He would rather stay in bed than in a guardhouse.[49]

At the same time, signs pointed to a stirring among the Rebels. Unionists refugees coming in from west of Berwick Bay reported Texans gathering by the thousands. "They feared the rough riders from the prairies, and told many tales of their lawless cruelty," wrote Colonel Nott, "and of the reckless fierceness of those Wild Texans." Union lookouts in Brashear reported Rebel cavalry occupying the village of Berwick just over the bay. "They came down in little scouting parties, hiding behind houses and bushes," Nott recounted. "They never fired, but flitted silently about, always observing us."[50]

Stickney needed to know what the Confederates had in mind, but he feared to patrol west of Berwick Bay. When USS *Hollyhock* arrived a week later, he believed that its two 12-pound howitzers would do to cover a crossing and reconnaissance. "The enemy was active in an annoying sort of way across the river," noted Private Bosson. He received orders to gather a squad from his company. The gunboat, along with the transport *Kepper* steamed to the opposite bank with a company of the 176th New York, part of the 42nd Massachusetts, and some cavalry on board. After poking around in the village of Berwick, the Federals headed up the bayou toward Pattersonville. Rebel horsemen kept just out of reach but seemed ready to make a stand about a mile ahead of the mouth of Bayou Teche.

Not curious about what the Texans might be hiding, the Northerners fell back, gathering about one hundred cattle, mules, and horses as they retired. After a long day, the Yankees returned to Brashear with their plunder, only to discover that they had forgotten about twenty of their command on the other side. The *Kepper* returned and brought them all to safety. The expedition lost two men to duty—one Massachusetts soldier had leapt a fence and landed in a beehive, and a New Yorker had dropped his loaded musket and shot himself in the head.[51]

Stickney's foray learned nothing new about Confederate intentions.

7

The Raid

Six hundred rebel horsemen, riding and yelling like Cumanches, pursue our flying provost-marshals.

—Lieutenant Colonel Augustine Joseph Hickey Duganne
176th New York Infantry

General William H. Emory might have worried more had he known Confederate General Richard Taylor's intentions. The Rebel war chief continued searching for a way to save Port Hudson. Based on the scouting reports, General Nathaniel P. Banks and his army might remain vulnerable to some sort of disruption coming from west of the Mississippi. How, and where, remained the question. Taylor moved his army toward Simmesport to consider his options. On June 13, 1863, Rebel horsemen crossed the Atchafalaya heading east, Colonel James P. Major and his Second Cavalry Brigade in the van.

Taylor and his men invaded Pointe Coupee Parish. At the crossing of Bayou Fordoche near Sterling's Plantation, the 2nd Texas Partisan Rangers turned left and rode toward Morganza; these Texans scouted down the river road to the shore opposite Port Hudson. Colonel Joseph Phillips and the 3rd Arizona turned south down the Bayou Grosse Tête Road and traveled another twenty miles. From the road junction near Livonia, he headed toward False River and rode north and east toward New Roads and rendezvoused with the column coming from Morganza. Together these commands swept most of the parish, disrupting any efforts to recruit men for the *Corps d'Afrique*, gathering horses, mules, and cattle, and threatening to envelope the Union outpost at Point Maunoir.

Behind them, the rest of the scattered commands arrived in parcels and assembled at Morgan's Ferry. Taylor, now commanding a combined Confederate force of more than three thousand men and twelve cannon, rode at the head of this reconnaissance-in-force across the Atchafalaya and into Point Coupée Parish. He intended to establish his next headquarters at Livonia.[1]

On the early morning of June 14, as the Confederates invaded Point Coupée, a crescendo of violence rolled across the river at Port Hudson. Banks, having shelled General Franklin Gardner's position the previous day, again demanded his surrender. Rebuffed, Banks ordered a night assault. The attack rolled forward around 3:00 A.M., but fell apart by daybreak, adding another eighteen hundred casualties to the tally. Fewer than fifty Confederates fell in the defense. Captain Dyer D. Bullock of the 114th New York could not believe the slaughter. "Our dead remained on the field four days," he wrote. "They became so offensive to [the Rebels], as they were under their breastworks, they sent to us a flag of truce, requesting us to come and bury them. Decomposition had taken place, and they could not be recognized by the regiments to which they belonged." Catherine Cornelius, like the rest of the liberated slaves that once worked at Smithfield Plantation, could hear the roar of the guns that day at Port Hudson: "Ah was right in the middle of de war. Ah hyar de guns and de bullets. Dey went like dis, 'pop, pop, pop, pop.'"[2]

This fresh disaster came at the same time that Banks received worrisome news of Rebels prowling about Pointe Coupée. Freedmen fled toward the Union positions near Waterloo and reported that Confederate cavalry were gathering laborers to build a bridge across Bayou Grosse Tête. When navy lookouts observed Texans riding along the river from Morganza toward New Roads, the commander of USS *Arizona* landed a squad of his sailors and marines to investigate. The Rebel cavalry quickly overwhelmed the bluejackets, killing a few and capturing the rest near the western end of the Bayou Sara ferry. Meanwhile, Union cavalry patrols brought in two of Colonel Barton W. Stone's 2nd Texas Partisan Rangers from False River. Colonel C. H. Sage learned that up to three thousand Rebels were heading his way and prudently ordered the 110th New York to abandon their works at Point Maunoir. On June 15, these troops scurried south along the Mississippi to the safety of the flotilla bombarding Port Hudson from downstream. The Confederates, unfettered by interference from Union troops, spent the next four days gathering supplies, news, and livestock from the citizens of Pointe Coupée. The bank opposite Port Hudson now lay open.[3]

Taylor intended to make contact with Gardner's army. That same day, Taylor received dispatches from Colonel John L. Logan operating with his fifteen hundred-man cavalry brigade beyond the Federal siege lines at Port Hudson advising him of the situation on the opposite shore. In response, Taylor revealed his plan. He intended to swim cattle across to the garrison and then crimp the Union supply lines with field batteries. He also contemplated sending over his

The June 14, 1863 Union attack on Port Hudson failed and left the approaches to the Rebel works strewn with Yankee corpses. The Confederates refused to allow the enemy to collect their dead until the odor of decomposing bodies became unbearable.
Harper's Weekly, July 18, 1863.

cavalry. "If any means can be devised to cross the river," Taylor assured Logan, "I would be glad to throw one or two cavalry brigades to operate on the east bank of the Mississippi."[4]

Taylor grew bolder. His opposition in Pointe Coupée had been light and gave way easily so he concentrated his Confederate forces at the junction of Bayous Fordoche and Grosse Tête and gathered supplies for two days, trying to learn what he could about events across the river, the dull booming of cannon constantly rumbling in the distance. Taylor and an escort employed the time to ride to the house of an acquaintance on False River to learn about conditions along the Mississippi and in the Union-occupied parishes below. "Two ladies of the family, recently from New Orleans, told me that the Federal force left in the city would not exceed a thousand men," Taylor wrote. The women also told what they knew about Union troops along Bayou LaFourche. Taylor plotted his next move, sensing an opportunity.[5]

The Confederate troops in Pointe Coupée and their potential for mischief vexed Union commanders. The naval officers with the fleet above Port Hudson received daily reports of Rebel activity on the west bank. Some rumors placed General Edmund Kirby Smith or Brigadier General Alfred Mouton on the scene. Then, lookouts reported that all the Rebels had simply disappeared. "The enemy are evidently mustering in force for some purpose," wrote Captain James S. Palmer aboard USS *Hartford*, "whether to drive our friend Colonel Sage into the Mississippi and then run supplies into Port Hudson, or go down to Donaldsonville, I am uncertain, but one of the two is evidently their object." The overall Rebel goal, Palmer believed, was to "intercept Banks's supplies from New Orleans."[6]

As the Federal skipper penned those lines, officers in the Confederate army honed in on the same conclusion. General Taylor could move his entire command against the four hundred Federal infantry fleeing Point Maunoir, communicate with Gardner, and throw across some men and supplies as he had promised Colonel Logan. Or, the Confederates could push below Port Hudson toward Donaldsonville and the Lafourche District. If Taylor threatened Union positions farther south, Banks would have to react, weakening his forces at Port Hudson and perhaps drawing reserves away from Brashear City and New Orleans. Satisfied with his choice, Taylor believed more good would come of aggressive operations west of the Mississippi than attempting to move men and supplies across it.

For his Trans-Mississippi army to have any influence on the siege of Port Hudson, though, Taylor would have to coordinate the movements of both wings of his widely separated forces. Mouton must carry Brashear City while Major and his mounted forces penetrated the Lafourche District with his invading column backed by the Louisiana and Texas infantry brigades. If the two forces, nearly equal in strength, turned both positions, he could combine them into an army of more than five thousand to threaten the one thousand Federals in New Orleans. Then he could unleash Major General John G. Walker's Texas Division to deliver the coup de grâce.

This plan contained several strategic flaws. By putting his whole command along the Atchafalaya into the effort, Taylor would leave the Red River uncovered, and a Federal gunboat raid toward Alexandria, or even up the Black River to Trinity, and up the Ouachita to Monroe might be devastating for operations in northeastern Louisiana. They might pin Walker's Texans against the Mississippi.

Or the enemy might drop down the Atchafalaya and cut off his line of retreat and pin *him* against the Mississippi. Mouton, he feared, might not move with the requisite alacrity against Brashear City to make the gamble worthwhile.

After studying the issue, Taylor concluded that Gardner, perhaps refreshed by beeves driven across the Mississippi, was holding his own. In addition, Confederate cavalry operating east of the river in the vicinity appeared capable of harassing Union outposts there and perhaps could cooperate with intended operations downriver as well. The Port Hudson garrison did not appear to need immediate rescue, Taylor concluded. Instead, they seemed to have locked Banks and his command in place.

After this realization, Taylor mulled a second, bolder option. He might closely coordinate the efforts of his army along the Atchafalaya with that on the lower Teche, giving Mouton a better chance at capturing Brashear City by allowing Major to come in from behind. If he split his command in Point Coupée, Taylor could send his fast-moving cavalry on a wide, looping raid that would disrupt Union operations in the Lafourche District and culminate in cutting railroad communication with Brashear City. Colonel Major's Second Cavalry Brigade would have to ride more than 170 miles through enemy territory. The Federals at Brashear City, isolated from reinforcements by Major, could then be flanked by a surprise pirogue attack from Grand Lake. Taylor believed the enemy would fold up. Taylor would send the balance of his troops in Pointe Coupée, Colonel Joseph Speight's Texas Brigade and the Louisiana Brigade, back to Simmesport for a feint toward Trinity and up the Ouachita as though marching to the relief of Vicksburg. Having distracted the Federals from their true intentions, the infantry could double back toward Berwick Bay to reinforce a successful crossing.

Taylor made up his mind. He trusted Major more than Mouton. His new cavalry officer would slash his way through the Lafourche District and sever Union rail links with Brashear City, isolating that post. He had but one week to get there. When he arrived, Mouton and Colonel Tom Green would carry that Union base by assault as planned, using their fleet of little boats while Major attacked from the rear. "Minute instructions and guides were given to Major," the general added. "He was expected to reach the Boeuf on the morning of [June] 23rd. The necessity of punctuality was impressed upon him and his officers. Their cooperation was required to secure success." If Major failed, he might trap himself and his brigade in enemy territory. "Their own safety depended on promptness." Similarly, if Mouton failed, Major's brigade was certainly doomed. Taylor would supervise the attack on Brasher City personally to avoid that calamity.[7]

On June 17, General Taylor divided his army. Major's cavalry drew a few days' rations before the infantry and the supply wagons returned to Simmesport. Taylor continued on to Washington, and from there, the Teche. General Kirby Smith received a dispatch telling him that Taylor believed he could do little directly opposite Port Hudson, but that movements farther south held promise.[8]

Colonel Major, leading the 1st and 2nd Texas Partisan Rangers, the 2nd Texas Cavalry—only partially mounted—the 3rd Arizona, and a section of the 1st Regular Battery, continued south along Bayou Grosse Tête before stopping at Rosedale to feed men and animals. He did not tarry; he drove his men all that day and into the night. Just after midnight on June 18, Major arrived at Indian Village at the junction of Bayous Grosse Tête and Plaquemine. His first target, the Union depot at the town of Plaquemine, lay six miles to the east on the banks of the Mississippi. With most of his men and mounts jaded from the long ride, Major dispatched Colonel Joseph Phillips's 3rd Arizona with a local guide to ride east along the south bank of Bayou Plaquemine to strike the Union depot. These men were as exhausted as the rest, but Major considered Phillip's his best officer and relied on his experience and ability.[9]

About daybreak, the Arizonans surprised the small garrison. Lieutenant Charles H. Witham of Company E, 28th Maine was in town recovering from buckshot wounds in the head, neck, and shoulder received two months before. Believing the town safe, medical personnel had sent him to Plaquemine to heal. He had just returned from having a light breakfast and a cup of tea when the Rebels swarmed the town.[10]

A Union soldier burst into the building, yelling, "Confederates are riding into town on every street."[11]

Witham reacted quickly. "I told the men that were there to get on their equipment," he remembered, "but before I could turn around the bullets were coming through the windows and doors. One soldier fired back, knocking one of the Texans from the saddle." Realizing that he and his men could not put up much of a fight, Witham ordered his solders to surrender. "We were all invalids," the Lieutenant explained, "it was useless to stand out against so large a force."[12]

Captain Albert Stearns of the 131st New York, serving as Plaquemine's provost marshal, knew he was in trouble. "Before I could dress myself two or three volleys followed in quick succession." He dumped his Union uniform and dressed in civilian clothing to make his getaway. "Running to the front door, I saw a dozen Rebel cavalrymen," remembered Sterns. "A look out a side window showed another squad on the side street, and soon a hundred rode by with a yell." He dashed out and dove into a chicken coop. "I was the biggest one of them all," he admitted, "only I did not carry my feathers quite as high just then."[13]

Texan Morgan Wolfe Merrick sketched the looting of the waterfront stores at Plaquemine, Louisiana, as well as the destruction of cotton and three steamboats on the wharves. Soldiers from the 3rd Arizona are helping themselves to clothing and food.

Daughters of the Republic of Texas Library, The Alamo, San Antonio, Texas.

The Rebels rounded up the Union garrison, and then began plundering the depot. Eighty-seven prisoners now burdened the Confederate command. "We were soon formed into line and started on the march out of town," Lieutenant Witham recalled. Confederates torched eighty bales of confiscated cotton, the steamers *Anglo-American*, *Sykes*, and *Belfast* at the landing, and two steam-powered barges up the bayou. The Texans enjoyed their rampage through town. "We . . . sacked the stores of Union sympathizers," wrote Morgan Wolfe Merrick of the 3rd Arizona, and "emptied hogsheads of sugar and pounds of molasses into the river, too many to mention." The raiders then turned to looting commissary and quartermaster stores.[14]

Bad luck plagued other Union troops at Plaquemine. Just the day before, two companies—D and F—of the 1st Engineers, *Corps d'Afrique*, and thirty men of the 12th Maine had ended three weeks of sawing, hacking, and yanking their way through the logjam on Bayou Sorrel deep in the Atchafalaya Swamp. They had emerged into Bayou Plaquemine sunburned, exhausted, and malarial aboard the *Sykes* and *Anglo American*. Having beaten their way through the logjam in tropical heat and mosquito swarms, commanders ordered the expedition disbanded. Some of the troops were bound for Port Hudson; the ill—including most of the Maine men, half of the black troops, and five of the eight officers—would go to New Orleans. Yet, before they could leave, *Sykes* had run on a piling at the Plaquemine wharves and sank to the main deck. The 130 weary black soldiers, their officers, and their thirty New England comrades transferred their gear to their remaining vessel and went into camp on the east bank of the Mississippi opposite Plaquemine until carpenters could repair their vessel or they could find another ride.[15]

They awoke the next morning in time to witness the Texans ransacking the commercial district across the river and their boats burning along the wharves. The veterans of the logjam-clearing expedition moved discreetly down the levee on the east bank of the Mississippi, looking for help. The small Union sternwheeler *Southerner* came up packed with 350 unarmed soldiers en route from the hospital in New Orleans returning to their regiments around Port Hudson. From shore, the marooned laborers flagged down the boat. Alerted to the danger just upriver, and seeing columns of smoke rising from Plaquemine to prove the point, the vessel rescued the troops, crammed them aboard, turned about, and headed downriver to Donaldsonville. From the safety of Fort Butler, a Union officer telegraphed, "Negros report all our men are either shot or taken prisoner. What shall we do?"[16]

News of the disaster spread rapidly. USS *Winona* arrived within two hours and disrupted the Texan looting by lobbing ninety rounds into and around the town. Following the barrage, a Federal shore party found the ruins deserted and rescued the provost marshal, Captain Stearns, along with thirteen of his men who had eluded capture. The Confederates faded into the interior with their prisoners and spoils, out of range, and rejoined the balance of Major's Brigade at Indian Village that afternoon. The Rebels spent the rest of the day crossing the bayou before pushing deeper into enemy territory. While the Federals shelled and scouted the banks of the Mississippi above and below Plaquemine, searching for raiders, the Texans disappeared into the dusk, galloping south.[17]

In the middle of the Rebel column, Union Lieutenant Witham struggled to keep up, attracting the sympathy of one of his escorts in the 2nd Texas Cavalry.

"Aren't you unwell?" the Texan asked. Witham responded that he was. The Rebel reigned in his horse and dismounted, offering it to the Federal.

"Here, take my horse, I am better able to walk than you." The thankful Yankee continued on, mounted, while the Texan doubled up on a horse behind a comrade.

Major could not accommodate prisoners. His officers paroled the Union enlisted men. The furor surrounding the Federal enlistment of black troops, though, doomed Witham; the Confederate government had issued orders to hold all captured officers for investigation of inciting servile insurrection—a war crime. Witham, the only officer, remained in Rebel hands. "So they took me along with them," he lamented, "and my case began to look pretty dark."[18]

The attack on Plaquemine had caused a stir. Admiral David G. Farragut, above Port Hudson, decided to see for himself what was occurring downstream. It also provided him an excuse to travel to New Orleans and away from the tedium of Banks's siege. He landed opposite Bayou Sara, then spent the day riding across Pointe Coupeé Parish to opposite the lower siege lines where he boarded the USS *Monongahela* and continued downriver. He arrived at Plaquemine at 8:00 P.M., by which time the Confederates had been gone for hours.[19]

The admiral assessed the situation. "I read a lecture to the mayor, who assured us that they knew nothing of the raid, and that they were all strangers to them," Farragut reported. "There is no doubt in my mind that these cavalry raids are to distract General Banks," Farragut concluded. "They have no cannon." Convinced that only about one hundred Texans had been involved, he ordered *Monongahela* to leave its station and carry him to Donaldsonville to check on conditions there. The gunboats USS *Winona* and USS *Kineo* already sat anchored near Fort Butler. "I found," wrote Farragut, "everything very safe, and very confident of their ability to hold it against a large force." Farragut and his officers congratulated themselves on their quick thinking. "The moral effect of our force gathering about them so quickly," he added, "was very good both against the enemy and in favor of the soldiers and ourselves."[20]

Not everyone shared Farragut's sunny outlook, and the explosion of activity west of the Mississippi shook the already fading Federal confidence. One navy officer above Port Hudson imagined that the tide of war had turned against them. "Affairs are going on badly here, I imagine," wrote Captain Palmer of USS *Hartford* to Admiral David Dixon Porter operating up the Mississippi with General

Ulysses S. Grant's army. "All we know is that Banks has been severely repulsed in two successive assaults, both of which I hear were badly managed." Palmer also reported the nerve-racking affairs on shore, writing, "we are surrounded by the enemy's cavalry and guerillas innumerable." If affairs had deteriorated this badly against Port Hudson against only seven thousand Confederates, he reasoned, the news from upriver against General John C. Pemberton's thirty thousand must be worse. "We have heard nothing from Vicksburg for a long while," Palmer continued, "so we conclude it is not going on better with you."[21]

That night, Major led his Texans along the road behind the Mississippi levee toward a lesser Union depot at Bayou Goula. While his men rode along in the darkness, the silhouettes of three prowling Union warships glided past. "I allowed them to pass unmolested," Major wrote smugly.[22] At dawn on June 19, some of Major's Texans dashed into Bayou Goula and looted that Federal supply cache while the rest scoured the surrounding area. Confederates ransacked dozens of Union-operated plantations and rounded up nearly one thousand liberated slaves who had been carried away from around Opelousas and Alexandria during the Teche raid. Federal officials had settled them into camps where Major found them "starving and in great destitution." The Confederates segregated the males of military age. "We kept the men," Major reported, "and left the women and children." Major, in essence, *pre-captured* a regiment of black conscripts bound for the Union army while leaving their families to remain a drain on the Federal commissary. His Texans spent the better part of the day burning, looting, eating or resting, and bringing in enough horses to completely remount the 2nd Texas Cavalry.[23]

The Union forces at Fort Butler braced for an attack. Located at the confluence of Bayou LaFourche and the Mississippi River at Donaldsonville, the well-constructed earthwork mounted six heavy guns and housed two companies of the 28th Maine—around a hundred men. The numbers had swollen to more than five times that number with the addition of the men aboard the *Southern* and a eighty-man detachment from the New Orleans hospitals that General Emory rushed upriver aboard USS *Kineo*. With the fort thus reinforced and three warships on station, Emory felt as though the reinforced garrison could hold the post. Major agreed, deciding the cost would not be worth the gain. "If I took the place it would be at a great sacrifice of life," he wrote. Besides, the gunboats would just shell him until he abandoned it. The Texans, thus blocked, searched for a way forward into the heart of the Lafourche District.[24]

Colonel Major clearly faced a dilemma. Two roads stretched from Bayou Goula to the vicinity of Donaldsonville. One ran along the Mississippi levee and under the guns of Fort Butler into town. The other, a more primitive track known as the "cut-off" or Sacramento Road, passed through low countryside and skirted the swampy margins of the Atchafalaya Basin before emerging at Bayou Laforche near Palo Alto Plantation, six miles south and down the Lafourche from the fort. Union troops had blocked this alternate route weeks earlier and Major would have to spend time clearing obstacles and repairing the road to get his artillery and wagons through. This would waste momentum and open him to attack. To follow the river and assault Fort Butler, under the guns of the navy, though, would be folly. A third route, the Ricard Cut-Off, led through the swamp along Bayou Sigur and emerged at Belle Rose Plantation above Paincourtville but would be unsuitable for his wagons and artillery. This path had its own hazards: Federals might trap him in that green tunnel with no chance of escape if they blocked the route from above and below.[25]

Bypassing the fort, encumbered as he was, posed the greatest challenge. He would be leaving an easily reinforced and potentially dangerous enemy in his rear. If the Federals learned of his presence, they could hem Major and his command into the LaFourche region with no way out. If the Second Cavalry Brigade continued past Fort Butler, only a rendezvous with Mouton's forces at Tiger Island would save them.

Major's choices appeared to be abandoning the raid and passing back up to Point Coupée—or bluffing his way past Fort Butler. Major boldly ordered his command forward, deeper into enemy territory.

On June 19, Major divided his forces into three parts to accomplish this ticklish task. He ordered portions of Colonel Walter P. Lane's 1st Texas Partisan Rangers along with Phillips's 3rd Arizona to leave the slower elements behind and move as rapidly as possible on a sixteen-mile looping route down the Ricard Cut-Off along Grand Bayou and back to the Lafourche Road near Paincourtville. They would then race toward Thibodaux, capture that town, seize the railroad, and cut the telegraph lines at Terrebonne Station three miles beyond. The troopers with Lane and Phillips mounted up and rode out. Next, he ordered a detachment from the

The 3rd Arizona, in company with the 1st Texas Partisan Rangers, took the Ricard Cut-Off road as they approached Thibodaux. The route passed through swamps and tangles, ably captured in this pencil sketch by Morgan Wolfe Merrick. Note the snake and alligator. Daughters of the Republic of Texas Library, The Alamo, San Antonio, Texas.

2nd Texas Partisan Rangers and the 2nd Texas Cavalry to feint against the Union defenses at Donaldsonville and to draw attention along the Mississippi road. While these Texans made noise, he would put the captured freedmen acquired at Bayou Goula to work clearing the cut-off and moving his artillery through. He now faced the most dangerous part of the raid thus far. If the Federals got wind of his maneuvers and hit him now, he would lose his guns, his plunder—possibly his entire command.[26]

The Federals, however, remained cautious. The Texans hovering near Fort Butler drove General Emory into a frenzy at his headquarters in New Orleans. The Union officer reacted defensively. He correctly sensed from the demonstrations against Fort Butler that Major was leading his Confederates into the Lafourche Country but believed he could do little to counter them. He might, though, slow their progress. If the Texans reached the railroad, they could effectively isolate

Brashear City. To avoid this outcome, Emory ordered the various scattered railroad guard detachments concentrated near Thibodaux, ready to resist a Confederate attack and keep the line open. Union authorities also commandeered a loaded steamer bound for New York, put ashore its passengers, and diverted it to Pensacola, Florida, to bring up the 15th Maine Infantry as reinforcements, the only troops close enough to lend a hand that weren't already tied down at Port Hudson.[27]

Emory informed the overwhelmed Lieutenant Colonel Albert Stickney at Brashear City that he was now in charge of an even larger operation that would probably culminate in combat. The young officer, considering his options, telegraphed for Captain Charles Blober and his Company G, 1st Louisiana Cavalry (Union) positioned at Thibodaux to scout up Bayou Lafourche to provide ample warning against a Rebel descent along that route. If the Texans were coming, Stickney wanted to know in plenty of time to rush reinforcements down the railroad to the threatened point. The German cavalry captain complied and led his horsemen two miles beyond Labadieville—ten miles above Thibodaux—before turning back, reporting no signs of Rebel horsemen.[28]

He had blundered. The lackluster reconnaissance had simply not gone far enough down the road. The Federals had turned around just miles ahead of the two oncoming Rebel regiments under Phillips and Lane. Blober's dispatches made their way first to Brashear City, then via telegraph to New Orleans. Stickney and Emory remained puzzled. Had the Rebels retreated to Pointe Coupée?[29]

Stickney remained alert to the Rebel threat and bolstered his Brashear City defenses. He sent the USS *Hollyhock* and *Kepper*, along with a work detail from the 42nd Massachusetts, down to Fort Chêne and dismantled that swamp battery, moving its garrison and guns to the railroad crossing of Bayou Boeuf. If the Confederates attacked Brashear, Stickney believed, they would more likely be coming up the railroad from the east than from the swampy islands to the south.[30]

Emory continued to fear the Rebels, despite Captain Blober's report. The Confederates could not have simply vanished. On June 20, as Major's main column slipped around Donaldsonville in the stormy morning hours around 4:00 A.M., the telegraph at Brashear City clattered away, tapping out an order for Lieutenant Colonel Stickney to send as many men as prudent from the various defenses in the region to the Lafourche crossing of the railroad. He would create a blocking force there to react to whatever the Rebels had in mind, and from whichever direction they might come. Emory could not have known he had ordered these men into the teeth of Texas cavalrymen under Phillips and Lane riding hard for Thibodaux. If the raiders intercepted the train as it passed near that town, they might trap the few hundred Yankees on a narrow track surrounded by swamps.[31]

The Union rally point, Lafourche Crossing, already served as one of the key garrisons on the tracks. A village had grown up around the New Orleans, Opelousas and Great Western Railroad train depot there and sprawled to the south. The homes, barns, and sugarhouses of local planters served as hospitals, quarters, and storage for the men posted there. "Near the railroad tracks are clumps of negro huts," observed one Union officer, "here by the station are dilapidated warehouses, a tenantless hotel—once fashionable—and a half score straggling domiciles fronting the bayou bank." Before the war Lafourche Crossing had been a minor resort just a few miles from Thibodaux. "This dull 'Crossing' was a famous summering-place," the officer continued, "where sporting gentry came to eat Buffalo-fish and drink Burgundy." Algiers, the eastern terminus, lay about sixty track miles east and Brashear City about twenty-five track miles west.[32]

Stickney roused his troops and started them on their mission. "I awoke . . . and heard the men assembling and the ammunition wagons rolling past," recalled Colonel Charles C. Nott, lying in his hospital bed. "I watched from habit, expecting the rattling of small arms of an attack, but the night wore away in unusual silence." Three companies of the 176th New York and one of the 23rd Connecticut boarded a train that had come in from Lafourche Crossing to fetch them. The men of the 42nd Massachusetts remaining at the post did not move. Lieutenant Colonel Stickney lost his patience. He hurried to their camp and, "wanted to know why the men . . . were not ready to board the train." As usual, no one had issued them an order. Stickney told their only officer, Lieutenant Benjamin C.Tinkham, to get his men rounded up and on the cars. He was missing many of his men; nearly half served on fatigue detail aboard the *Hollyhock* and *Kepper* with First Sergeant George Ballow, while another detachment guarded the base water supply. Tinkham loaded the remainder—around fifty—aboard the train.[33]

Stickney determined to lead the expedition in person. He searched for a suitable subordinate to command at Brasher City. The field officers remained ill, or in the case of Lieutenant Colonel Augustine Joseph Hickey Duganne, under arrest and *feigning* illness. A recent arrival, Major Robert C. Anthony of the 2nd Rhode

Island Cavalry, who was in charge of the mounted detachments on Tiger Island, proved the only viable candidate. The hapless horse soldier, who did not know the post, the plan, and who had orders to escort recruits for his regiment to Port Hudson, found himself in command. "Major Anthony did not possess the qualities to make a successful soldier," Private Charles P. Bosson noted. Quartermaster Sergeant George Haven Putnam of the 176th New York, however, disagreed. "The Major is a good fellow, and we have great confidence in him."[34]

At nearly the same moment that Stickney loaded the cars at Brashear City, Phillips and Lane arrived at Thibodaux. The two Confederate regiments took precautions to surprise the enemy, fearing the Federals might strongly defend the town. Texan officers ordered each command to designate three hundred of the best mounted men as a shock force to overrun the garrison. On June 20, the Rebels surrounded Thibodaux and, at about 4:00 A.M. swooped out of the rainy shadows yelling wildly to create confusion, pouncing on a surprisingly small Union detachment and several score of convalescents.[35]

"Six hundred rebel horsemen, riding and yelling like Cumanches, pursue our flying provost-marshals," one Federal described. The one hundred unsuspecting Union troops there—mostly malaria victims Stickney had moved there from the pestilent Brashear City—found themselves mobbed by hundreds of wet, tired, and hungry Texans spoiling for a fight. Texan Private Frank Price, astride his warhorse "Rowdy," rode in the charge. "I never saw a better cavalry horse," Price boasted. "I can assure you Rowdy stood the fire of the enemies guns as well or better than the rider."[36]

Achieving an easy victory, the Rebels fanned out into the surrounding countryside, rounding up Federal troops serving as plantation guards. A Northerner lamented the Rebels' return to the region, claiming their "scouts and patrols whipped in reluctant darkies to new masters." The exhausted raiders, the tension broken, ransacked the commissary stockpiles—the biggest catch thus far—and inventoried their prisoners. By many accounts, they also became riotously intoxicated.[37]

The early morning commotion roused the town. "The sidewalks were lined with ladies waving us welcome," wrote Merrick. "Beside them stood their servants bearing vessels and baskets containing all kinds of drinks and eatables—Yea a royal reception with a feast. And at what an hour, standing in the rain as

The weary soldiers of Colonel James P. Major's brigade captured a Union stockpile at Thibodaux. Morgan Wolfe Merrick sketched the piles of commissary stores, including crates marked "hard tack," "crackers," and others with labels displaying canned tomatoes and fish. A pile of hams lays to the right of the image, while soldiers rummage through quartermaster stores on the left searching for boots and clothing.
Daughters of the Republic of Texas Library, The Alamo, San Antonio, Texas.

heedless of it as if it were a pleasant night. Such actions causes a man to feel he is a host within himself and ready to challenge hell with all its legions." Their bellies full, and after so many hours in the saddle, most of the troops disappeared to find a dry place to sleep. Just three miles to the south, Stickney and his emergency force passed unmolested along the railroad tracks toward Lafourche Crossing, unmindful of the nearby danger as their locomotive chuffed along. Lane and Phillips had missed their chance.[38]

Later that morning, as the sun climbed above the trees, Stickney arrived at the railroad crossing of Bayou LaFourche, still unaware that the Confederates held Thibodaux. The Federals collected fewer than two hundred men in a makeshift battalion commanded by Major Morgan Morgans, Jr., of the 176th New York "Ironsides" Infantry. This medley included three companies from that regiment, two companies of the 23rd Connecticut, and the rump company from the 42nd

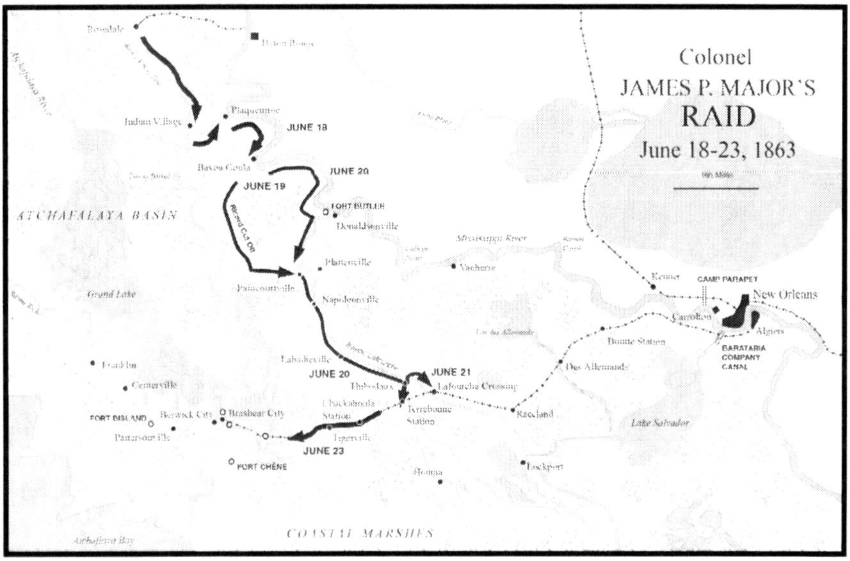

Massachusetts, as well as a 6-pounder cannon and a 12-pounder howitzer. As the troops detrained, the Connecticut troops stationed there appeared surprised. An officer approached, seeking news. "When informed that the post was threatened by the enemy, he laughed heartily," reported one soldier, "and told Stickney no enemy had been seen around there for six months." Hadn't he heard? Captain Blober's cavalry had not found any.[39]

Even so, line officers dutifully deployed their commands into positions to face an attack. The tracks east of the bayou sat atop a high embankment bordered by heavy timber, forcing Stickney to deploy his battle line two hundred yards to the north in the angle of the bayou and railroad, his left anchored on the bayou levee, and his right flank refused and resting on the raised track bed. Fields of high grass stretched out to his front, providing cover to an advancing enemy. He ordered it cut or stamped down.[40]

Far up Bayou Lafourche that same morning, Major's main column passed its greatest point of danger. The Rebels emerged from the cut-off road six miles below Donaldsonville and thirty miles from Thibodaux. The Federals on the Mississippi had done nothing to stop him. The garrison at Fort Butler had not even scouted his command. The enemy had been content to let him slip past—and disappear.

Colonel Major ordered another feint against Fort Butler by his rearguard as he turned the rest of the brigade south down the bayou and toward Lane and Phillips at Thibodaux. The immediate danger now in his wake, he could relax—at least for a moment. Other dangers still lay ahead.[41]

Prisoner Lieutenant Witham of the 28th Maine had traveled with the Texans for twenty-five miles. The road was rough, the country broken, and the rain fell heavily. The wounded Federal, soaked, had handed back his borrowed horse and now traveled in a forage wagon, suffering from every bump and jolt. His guards did what little they could to ease his situation. "The men were very kind to me," he wrote, and "seemed very sorry that they had not a better conveyance and something better to eat. I did not look for any such feeling and I felt very thankful."[42]

At midday on June 20, the Confederates halted at a plantation, probably Charles Kock's St. Emma, to eat and to let another heavy thunderstorm pass over. "The overseer put the negroes to preparing grub for us," remembered Merrick. "No one had a better dinner or breakfast. They had fired up the immense sugar kettles into which they had dumped barrels of potatoes, meat of different kinds, making a huge Irish stew, and it was a royal treat for the wet, hungry, and tired men." The raiders fed their horses from the planation's supplies of fodder before finding shelter from the rain beneath the roofs of the sugarhouse and work sheds.[43]

Secessionists along the Lafourche, surprised by the sudden appearance of these Texans, believed they had been liberated from Union occupation. "The Confederates came within a mile of this place," wrote French-speaking Heléne Dupuy, a sixteen-year-old girl living on the P. O. Ayraud and Company Sleepy Hollow Plantation. "I dare not believe in so much happiness! We shall see again our friends." She trusted the Rebels were here to stay. "I hope they will take their same position again and will maintain it," she wrote in her diary. "After waiting eight months they have at last returned." The teenager also understood what was afoot. "They will intercept the retreat of the enemy, while others will attack them," she predicted. Then, perhaps, they would double back and attack Donaldsonville. "Both troops combined will certainly take the fort from the Yankees, which they caused our negroes to build."[44]

As the Confederates rested at St. Emma, Lieutenant Witham—still the only Union prisoner—dismounted from his forage wagon and helped himself to a drink from the cistern. Lieutenant Colonel James W. Walker of the 2nd Texas Cavalry approached him.

"Why lieutenant, I did not know you was still with my regiment," said the Texan while extending a friendly handshake to the Yankee. These people could not have been more different and still been Americans. The Texan, a resident of the coastal prairie town of Hallettsville, and Witham, a native of the rock-bound fishing town of Surry, Maine, had lived 1,863 miles from each other. For all their differences and the hostility of war, their humanity remained intact.

The two officers retired to the porch where Walker ordered lunch as well as pen and paper. After scribbling a few lines, the Texan handed the document to the New Englander. Witham read a statement releasing him from custody.

"You can remain here as long as you wish and no Confederate force will trouble you, unless you are found with arms in your hands," Walker explained.

"One cannot imagine my surprise," Witham remembered. The Texan, who had enlisted two years before and had served in New Mexico and fought at Galveston, told the New Englander that he regretted the war and hoped it would soon be over.

Walker rose to go. "Well, I will have to leave you as my regiment is already falling in." The Texan shook Witham's hand again, turned, and left. The New Englander watched with a full heart as the Texan column departed.

Witham had nothing but admiration for his enemy. "I . . . returned his kind salute as he rode by at the head of his regiment," he remembered. When the last Rebel faded from sight, the bedraggled Yankee rested for the balance of the day, then headed for Plaquemine and Baton Rouge, eager to avoid the coming battle.[45]

8 Lafourche Crossing

I'll see you damned first . . . go get it yourself!
—Lieutenant Benjamin C. Tinkham
Company B, 42nd Massachusetts Infantry

At midday on June 20, 1863, at the exact moment that Lieutenant Colonel James W. Walker and Lieutenant Charles H. Witham parted ways, the troops in Donaldsonville telegraphed to New Orleans announcing that the Confederates had that morning reappeared—then vanished. Major General William H. Emory and his officers in New Orleans correctly guessed that Colonel James P. Major was heading directly toward the Union depot at Berwick Bay. Lieutenant Colonel Albert Stickney, at Lafourche Crossing, concurred. His soldiers, though, remained unconcerned, lounging about convinced that the crisis, if, indeed, there ever had been one, had passed. Complacent, they were nonetheless tired and hungry. Stickney, originally thinking this Rebel foray little more than a scout, had brought his men out in light marching order, without rations. He telegraphed to Brashear for some food to be brought forward. "The men lay around carelessly until afternoon," a soldier wrote, "as it was extremely hot and nothing could be had to eat." A telegram from New Orleans arrived at Stickney's headquarters later that morning directing him to return two of his companies to Brashear City to beef up its defenses; Emory would send reinforcements from New Orleans to take their place at Lafourche Crossing.[1]

Receiving these instructions, Stickney hesitated. He hated to weaken his position in the face of a potential fight. Before complying with Emory's orders, Stickney ordered Captain Charles Blober and his Company G, 1st Louisiana Cavalry (Union) back out on the hunt early that afternoon to ensure all was well. In the meantime, he sent word to his officers to ready the two 23rd Connecticut companies to head to Brashear. He, too, would go, and resume command of the post. Thunderclouds on the horizon boded for another Louisiana drenching, and if

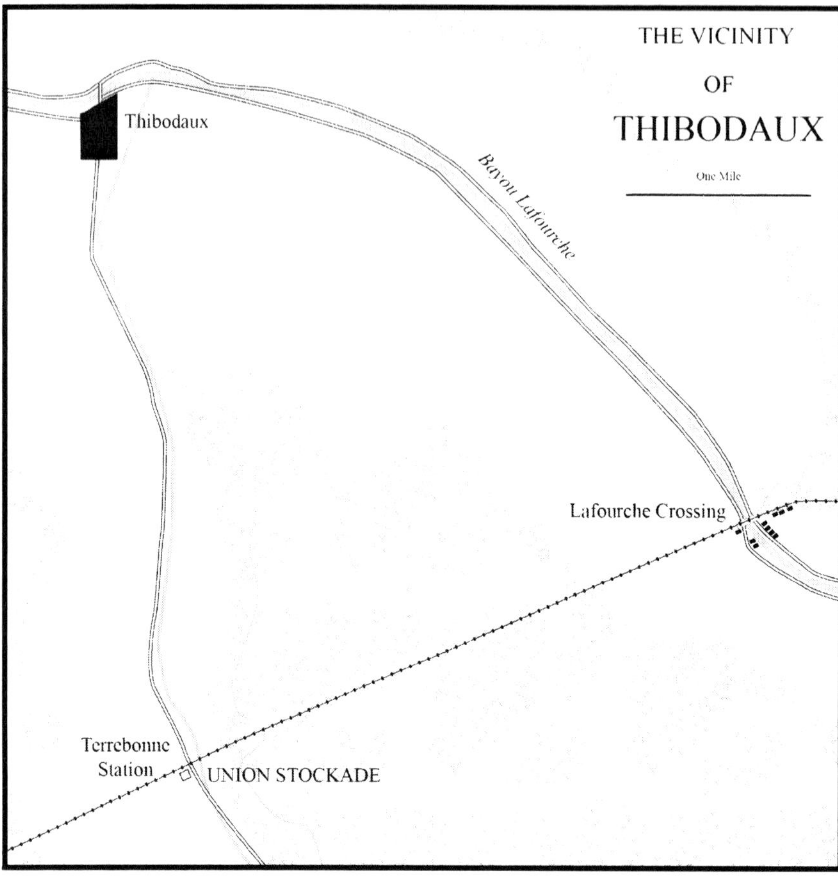

he hurried, he might have his men dry inside boxcars before the storm struck. To defend Lafourche Crossing, Stickney would leave behind three companies of the 176th New York and the men from the 42nd Massachusetts.[2]

As the men awoke from their naps and formed into companies, hoof beats thundered in from the north. This time the Louisiana Unionists had made contact with the enemy as evidenced by two riderless horses. A soldier remembered, "up rode a cavalryman in hot haste, with bare breath enough to say 'The rebs are coming.'" The Texans at Thibodaux had surprised and routed the fifty Union troopers and pursued them at a gallop down the course of the Lafourche, knocking two from their saddles. Other refugees streamed in as well. "When the rebs came down," Lieutenant George Quien of the 23rd Connecticut recalled, "all the provost marshals and soldiers that were kept on the plantations to keep the darkies straight . . . ran into our camp with their baggage and flung it in a pile."[3]

Alarmed by Blober's encounter and this exodus of troops from the countryside, Stickney surmised that Thibodaux must already be in enemy hands. One of the men reporting was Captain Charles H. Barber of Company K, 176th New York, stationed down at Terrebonne Station three-and-a-half miles down the track. This officer had ridden to Thibodaux about midday to investigate rumors that the town had fallen, and then became swept up in Blober's rout. His men down the tracks, he reported, probably remained unaware of their danger. Stickney hastily telegraphed them to come to Lafourche Crossing; he would send a train. He shuttled the locomotive and cars that had brought him from Brashear to fetch them, a single artillery piece on a flatcar serving as its only armament. Having received Stickney's telegram, the twenty-five men of Company K, 176th New York manning the stockade at Terrebonne Station destroyed what they could not carry. Soldiers kindled fires to burn boxcars loaded with provisions. Nervously, they waited for the train to extract them, watching down the tracks for any sign. Instead, the threatening thunderstorm broke overhead.[4]

Amid the crash of thunder and flashes of lightening, Texans from the 3rd Arizona arrived and opened fire on the New Yorkers, their bullets smacking into the log stockade in an increasing patter. The Texans fired blindly. "The rain, mist, and smoke prevented us from discerning their movements," one of them recalled. Unable to get at the New Yorkers, some of the Texans stepped forward with white flags to suggest a parley with the trapped troops. Lieutenant Phoebus W. Lyon stepped out of the fort to hear their demands. Moments later, the rescue train arrived. "We heard the rumble of cars, and thought perhaps they were reinforcing," Morgan Wolfe Merrick recalled. The Texans took the Union officer into custody, fell back into cover, then renewed firing into the haze; the return fire from the Federals slackened, then ceased.

The Texans had been mistaken. "We made a dash for the place," Merrick added, "and found they had retreated." Abandoned freight cars filled with provisions, torched by the Federals, sputtered and burned in the storm. "The rain being in our favor, this time," he continued, "we reached them in time to save all." Inside one freight car were barrels of eggs, "which," the Texan added, "furnished us an

An understrength company from the 176th New York occupied a fortified stockade at Terrebonne Station on the New Orleans, Opelousas, and Great Western Railroad in present-day Schriever, Louisiana. Troops from the 3rd Arizona tried unsuccessfully to force the men out.
Daughters of the Republic of Texas Library, The Alamo, San Antonio, Texas.

unusual opportunity to display our feeding qualities which would have struck an onlooker as rather strange." After cutting the telegraph lines, scouts from the 3rd Arizona rode east along the tracks toward Lafourche Crossing to size up the enemy. The rest of the Texans gathered their plunder.[5]

The rainy day passed peacefully at Brashear City. A hospital steward mentioned to Colonel Charles C. Nott that half of the garrison had gone during the night. "The sick men whispered to each other that we were defenseless, and it was well that we had the telegraph and railroad," the ailing colonel remembered, "and could call our troops back in case of an attack from across the river." Then, the usual tapping and clatter of the receiver in the train depot fell silent. "The telegraph suddenly ceased its ticking," Nott noted with dread. "The railroad was cut and the enemy was between us and our forces at La Fourche."[6]

Major Robert C. Anthony, unclear what to do, ordered rations and reinforcements loaded for Stickney's troops. He ordered USS *Hollyhock* to shell

Berwick, setting the town on fire and denying its cover to any lurking Rebels. "Berwick City is on fire," remarked Lieutenant Colonel Augustine Joseph Hickey Duganne. "From wall to roof, from garden fence to outbuilding, from hedgerow to orchard trees, a devastating flame sweeps along the shore road . . . leaving the lower portion of Berwick City a blackened waste." Soldiers loaded into half of the fifty boxcars and packed rations and ammunition into the others. A locomotive painted with the name "Lafourche" in jaunty lettering heaved out of the station at 4:00 P.M., dragging its passengers and freight behind.[7]

Thirty minutes later, the train slowed to a crawl and then chugged to a stop, just short of the bridge over Bayou Boeuf. Agitated soldiers there reported rumors that Stickney and his men had met with disaster, and nothing lay between the Rebels and New Orleans—or Brashear. Unconvinced, the engineers throttled forward, and the locomotive lurched back into motion, passing through Tigerville, eight miles east, unimpeded. Three miles further, Federals at Chacahoula, waved signal flags and lanterns to stop the train. No one there had heard from Stickney. The Confederates, though, were definitely at Terrebonne Station, a little more than eight miles down the track, the entire road between bordered by dense swamp. There would be no escaping an ambush. Anthony recalled the detachments on the railroad and the train reversed to Tiger Island.[8]

During his foray, Major Anthony had learned much. At Tigerville, Lieutenant John P. Robin and a few of his provost guards climbed aboard with interesting news. The freedmen at his post wanted weapons. "They will fight to the death," he claimed, "rather than return to bondage" In addition, a black woman had begged Robin for protection, claiming her master had said "his friends would soon drive the Yankees from Terrebonne [Parish], when he should be able to take the 'airs out of his niggers once more.'" Another officer reported Rebels had taken Houma as well; the Confederates had isolated Brashear City.[9]

At Lafourche Crossing, Stickney also realized the enemy was between him and Brashear City. As the muggy daylight of June 20 drained away, the nearly five hundred men he had assembled at Lafourche Crossing, suffering in the showery weather, faced an uncertain future. Stickney made the most of what he had. Reinforcements from the other railroad outposts had dribbled in all day, and Stickney now had three companies of the 23rd Connecticut—B, E, and K—totaling around 200 men under Major David H. Miller. The 176th New

York under Major Morgan Morgans, Jr., counted more than 150 men between companies B, E, and K. The 46 men from the 42nd Massachusetts stood ready. Another similar-sized command composed largely of men from 26th Maine but including squads—plantation guards, quartermasters, hospital stewards, provost guards—from four other regiments formed a reserve.[10]

Would this mélange from so many different detachments hold their ground? They were strangers to their commanders and to each other. None had been in combat before. Lieutenant Colonel Stickney rode up to Lieutenant Benjamin C. Tinkham and asked him to predict the behavior of his 42nd Massachusetts men under fire. The officer hesitated, saying "he did not know . . . but thought they would fight."[11]

Stickney deployed his unseasoned troops. He held Captain Blober's cavalry to his right and rear where he could command them quickly. The lieutenant colonel distributed his various infantry commands along the line but ordered Major Miller to take a company from the 23rd Connecticut and push down the bayou road about 450 yards and to lay quiet in the tall grass, providing early warning should the Texans come all at once. Pickets spaced every few yards spread out to their right. With his lines set, Stickney ordered Blober to find the enemy. "He was a plucky little German," noted one Yankee, "boiling over for a fight."[12]

Lacking unit cohesion, Stickney enjoyed plenty of artillery for so small a front. Two-dozen gunners from the 21st Indiana Heavy Artillery manned four cannon. Stickney put one gun, a 12-pound Napoleon, on the tracks near the east edge of the bridge where it commanded an elevated view of the field. His detachment of Maine provost guards stood nearby. He placed a 12-pound howitzer at the angle on the far right and a second a few yards to its left. A 6-pounder remained to cover the left center.[13]

The Texans arrived later that afternoon. Captain Blober's cavalry fell back, passing down the soupy bayou road and through the Union pickets. "As our cavalry filed by us," observed Lieutenant Quien, "the men and horses were covered with mud, some of the bridles hanging and dragging in the mud, men and horses completely tired out." The Texans from Colonel Walter P. Lane's 1st Texas Partisan Rangers followed "close behind on a dead walk" in a column of fours. A shot from the 12-pounder on the bridge screamed overhead, causing them to reign in. The Texans sheltered behind a cluster of buildings half a mile in front of the Union positions, dismounted, and shook out skirmishers to probe the Union

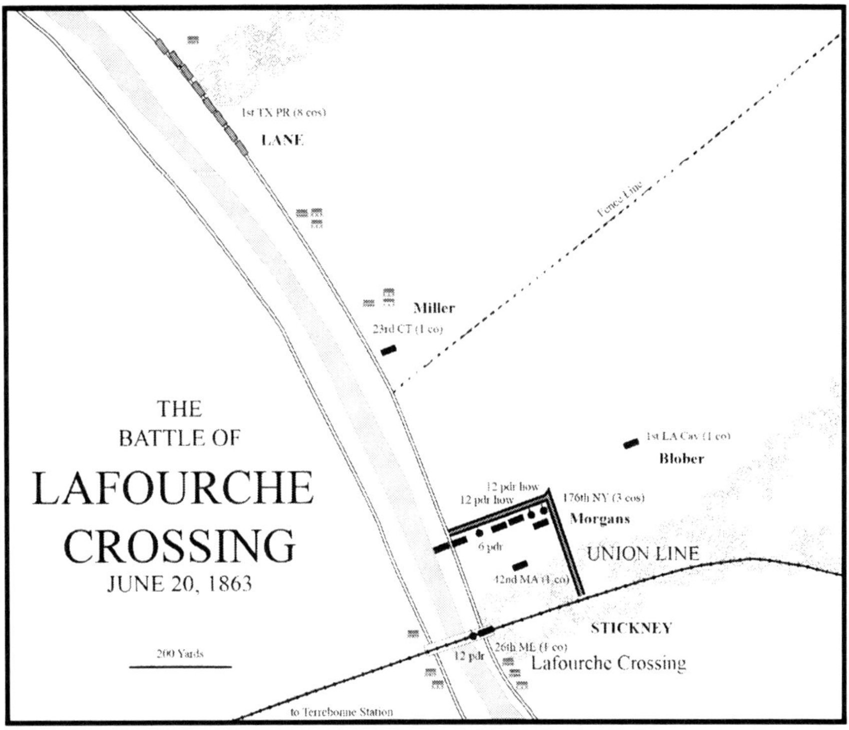

picket lines. The Yankees fired their warnings and then gave way. The Texans, encouraged, pressed on, only to fall afoul of the Connecticut troops hiding in the grass along the bayou road.[14]

After a brief firefight, Union Major Miller fled, abandoning his men; they quickly followed, withdrawing to their main battle line and then filing away to a new position on the right and away from the incoming bullets. The Rebels, encouraged that the Yankees had given way so easily, probed ahead, searching for the meat of the Union line. As they approached closer, the four Union guns fired shell and solid shot at the Texan skirmishers. Their blasts, coupled with musket fire, shrouded the damp battlefield in clinging gossamers of smoke and haze. The Texans disappeared into the gloom, educated.[15]

Lieutenant Quien held his troops between the levee and Bayou Lafourche during the skirmish. Some of the Texans had crossed over the berm, hoping to flank the Union pickets from that direction. Quien's ad hoc command brushed

Colonel Walter P. Lane led the 1st Texas Partisan Rangers but lived an extraordinary life of danger and daring-do. An Irishman, he was born in County Cork in 1817, before moving to Ohio as a toddler. His family relocated to Kentucky, but in 1836, the nineteen-year-old Lane went to Texas to fight in its war for independence from Mexico. Wounded at San Jacinto, the tough youngster recovered to serve in the Army of the Republic of Texas and was nearly killed in combat with Indians. He tried to settle down in San Augustine, Texas, but adventure called, and he fought with Colonel John Coffee Hays in Mexico. Lane tried his luck in the California gold fields, but returned to Marshall, Texas, his youth and his energy spent. When the Civil War erupted, Lane served as lieutenant colonel of the 3rd Texas Cavalry and saw action in Indian Territory, Missouri, Arkansas, and Mississippi. He left that regiment to raise the 1st Texas Partisan Rangers, leading it at the Battle of Prairie Grove, Arkansas. He came to Louisiana with years of combat experience, battle scars, and the memory of more than ten horses shot from under him.
The Adventures and Recollections of Walter P. Lane.

them back with loads of buck and ball from their smoothbore Springfields. When the Texans disappeared, Quien dashed ahead to make sure they had gone. "The rebs left one horse," the lieutenant recalled. "I got on him and rode into camp with a bridle cut out of a cowhide, hair on, not a stitch on it."[16]

Stickney readjusted his position. He realized that buildings to his front had shielded the Confederates. They also served as a Union hospital. Finding the Texans had withdrawn toward Thibodaux, Stickney ordered the medicines and the patients brought into his lines, his men burning the structures as they left to open the field of fire. He also hoped the dancing flames might reveal enemy silhouettes if they came again that night. A squad burned a building on the west side of Bayou Lafouche for the same purpose in case the Confederates tried to rush the bridge. Stickney ordered out patrols as well. Just before midnight, the chuffing of a locomotive and cheers from men on flatcars announced the arrival of welcomed reinforcements from New Orleans. Lieutenant Colonel Josiah A. Sawtell brought 306 men of his 26th Massachusetts along with a cannon, nearly doubling the number of defenders. They also brought rations. Stickney offered to turn over the command to the higher-ranking newcomer. Sawtell refused, happy for Stickney to finish what he started. The five fresh companies deployed, two on the main line, two on the right, and the last on the bridge. That night the Union troops lay in their line of battle, a light rain pattering on their kepis.[17]

The next morning, General Emory grew apoplectic at his New Orleans headquarters. Stickney remained in place, but no one had heard from Berwick Bay for several hours. Messages tapped out for Brashear City brought no response. Emory feared for the safety of that post. Only one way remained to communicate with Brashear. Summoning a courier, the general scribbled a note addressed to "Commanding Officer at Brashear City," whomever that might be by the time the message arrived. "I send round to you by sea, to direct you to hold on till the last extremity," he wrote. The courier galloped to the docks at New Orleans and boarded the steamer *St. Mary's* for a circuitous passage out of the mouth of the of the Mississippi, into the Gulf, and then up the Atchafalaya. With luck, he would arrive at Brashear in three days, four at the outside.[18]

Emory also dashed off messages to Stickney and Banks. "Hold on bravely," he tapped to Stickney. A force of two regiments with additional artillery would be coming up from New Orleans to help. "As soon as it does, if strong enough, attack and disperse the enemy," Emory directed, adding, "but, before doing anything, secure your communications." Stickney, reading this message, believed Emory had given him permission to proceed both forward *and* backward. He telegraphed back for clarity. "You must use your own discretion," came the reply from Emory. "That must be decided on the ground. Whatever you decide, telegraph me." Meanwhile Emory gave General Nathaniel P. Banks a less hopeful picture. "I fear . . . nothing can effectively relieve them but a strong force landed at Donaldsonville and marching on the enemy's rear," he wrote. "Without aid from you, the force here cannot reoccupy Brashear."[19]

Confederate Colonel Major, still moving down Bayou Lafourche with his main column, understood that time was growing short. In the small hours of July 21, he reassembled his army at Thibodaux as the rest of his brigade along with artillery, wagons, captured freedmen, and livestock arrived. The raiders, facing a nearby enemy force of unknown size but well supplied with artillery, would have to proceed prudently. Observers reported that a train had come into the Federal position during the night probably bringing reinforcements. The weather, too, remained miserable—muggy, hot, and rainy. As dawn broke, pickets reported Federal scouts heading in toward Thibodaux; the Confederate commander responded by dispatching his most seasoned troops, the New Mexico veterans of Colonel Charles L. Pyron's 2nd Texas Cavalry across the bayou to the east bank, along with his section of Captain Oliver Semme's artillery and two companies from Colonel Barton W. Stone's 2nd Texas Partisan Rangers. Colonel Pyron would probe toward the enemy, brush back their scouts, and get a sense of what the Federals now had at Lafourche Crossing. The balance of the brigade gathered at Terrebonne Station to block the railroad and isolate Stickney from Brashear City and to advance on the Yankee left. Once Pyron reported the enemy strength, Major would decide how to proceed.[20]

The Confederate cavalry moved out in the wet morning but soon struggled amid the onset of "one of the heaviest rains I ever saw," Major wrote. By noon, the Rebel advance slowed to a crawl. Late that afternoon, Pyron's Texans sniped at the Union pickets but did not come into range of the Union guns, which were now reinforced by a section of the 25th New York Battery that had arrived that morning. Powder smoke, haze, and fog clung to the ground and obscured the field in the wet air. The downpour, falling on Rebels with few cartridge boxes among them, ruined most of their ammunition, leaving each man with perhaps three rounds of dry ammunition. Pyron fell back, and the Union pickets once again advanced.[21]

Major knew his strategic position was deteriorating with each passing hour, but his command seemed sluggish, even mushy, from all the rain. He told Pyron that if the weather ever broke, he could test the enemy's strength but to use his judgment. At 6:30 P.M., the rain stopped. Captain John W. Lane received orders to take two companies of Colonel Stone's 2nd Texas Partisan Rangers to support the probe from the west bank of Bayou Lafourche. Major gave Pyron "some discretion in the matter," and the Texas veteran ordered his command to dismount on the edge of some woods fronting the Union line and to cross the open field a half-mile in their front. Two supporting guns moved to the Rebel left and rear, struggling in the mud to get into position.[22]

The Federals had waited all day for the Confederates to return. They had used their time to make an attempt—with few picks and shovels—to dig in, but only accomplished a two-foot-high mud wall near the angle on the right of their line. When the rain let up, Stickney ordered Lieutenant Tinkham to bring up his Massachusetts boys along with a gang of black laborers to remove a fence a quarter-mile ahead of the Union line. Soldiers and hands stepped out and got to work. Then, they spotted the advancing Texans. While the unarmed blacks fled, Tinkham ordered his men to form up, and they delivered a volley. Their smoothbores failed to lob their bullets even half the distance to the enemy. Tinkham sent runners to report the news to Stickney.[23]

The Union commander signaled to Blober to ride out and provoke the Confederates. Perhaps the Rebels might be lured within range of his cannon. The German captain and his men, "wearing . . . regulation hats, made quite a large appearance," Lieutenant Quien observed. The troopers of the 1st Louisiana Cavalry (Union) rode toward the Confederate-occupied trees, then sheered off, trying to bait the enemy. They did not bite. After ninety minutes, Stickney ran short of ideas. He ordered one of the guns from the 25th New York battery brought forward and run out where the 42nd Massachusetts men held their ground. The cannon could then shell the enemy woods. Perhaps, Sickney thought, this would get a response.[24]

The men in the ranks believed something would happen soon enough. Lieutenant Quien, leading strangers, wondered how they would handle their, and his, first combat. He tried to buck them up. "Boys, here we are, close to the work we came here to do. Now show yourselves men." He feared they might skedaddle. "If you are going to run we had better have stayed home," he barked. "The Government would have been better off without us." He would let them know when it was time to quit. "When you see me run," Quien paused, "then you all have a right to run."[25]

He also appealed to their patriotism. "The rebs are on the wrong side," he reasoned. "They are trying to overthrow the best government God and man has in this world; where all oppressed people longing for liberty can come; which God gave to our forefathers who fought and bled for it and handed it down to us to preserve for future generations." According to the lieutenant, it now fell to this band of untried provost guards, plantation minders, and military clerks to preserve that legacy. "So," he reiterated, "let us show ourselves men."[26]

Stickney determined to brush the Rebels back in the fading daylight. The New Yorkers deployed their smoothbore cannon where the Massachusetts men watched the far tree line. The artillerymen raked the woods with canister. They reloaded and fired again. On their third blast, the provoked Texans boiled out of the woods in an extended line, heading across the field toward the Yankees. The Federals panicked. The Confederates halted, and bullets from Texan rifles zipped through the ranks of the 42nd Massachusetts. One private clutched his belly in shock and horror, imploring, "what have I done that they should hit me?" as he dropped to his knees and crumpled. Another bullet carried away a soldier's right thumb before passing through his chest. He fell, gasping for air. The men began to waver; some broke and ran. The artillerymen, fearing their supports were about to quit, dashed to their limber, desperate to haul their gun out of action; the draft horses bolted, hurrying back toward the tracks and safety, leaving the gun behind. The crewmen followed on a run. The remaining Bay State soldiers turned about, marching toward their friends at the double-quick but losing all order. A third Massachusetts soldier fell, the bullet hitting him in the back of the neck, blasting through his mouth, and blowing out his front teeth.[27]

The Texans watched as the Union advance line evaporated. Sensing an easy kill, Pyron's troopers rashly pursued, blindly lunging forward in a grand bushwhack. A mile away, the Rebel artillery, struggling to keep up in the muddy fields, had barely taken position with a 12-pound howitzer. Losing control of his advance, Pyron surrendered to the momentum, encouraging this bold charge through the smoke, rain, and gloom to capture the abandoned Union gun. A squad of mounted Texans closed on the retreating Massachusetts men, masking them from Stickney's main line. The Yankees barely beat them to safety.[28]

Stickney watched the crisis unfold. "All this time our artillery had been constantly firing, using shell for the most part, but the infantry did not, as of yet, reply to the straggling bullets which came from the enemy. The moisture of the atmosphere held the smoke of the cannon so close to the ground," he observed, "that it was almost impossible to ascertain the distance or numbers of the enemy, or at what point he would mass his force." Around 7:00 P.M., the Union infantry opened up, blindly firing by ranks at the sounds of the Rebel Yell closing in on their front, while the gunners unleashed canister into the haze. The rain returned, lighter, but added to the chaos. A Union staff officer rode to where Lieutenant Tinkham had rallied his heaving and shaken men. He ordered the 42nd Massachusetts to charge into the surging Texans and retake the lost gun. "I'll see you damned first, Tinkham snapped, "you go get it yourself!"[29]

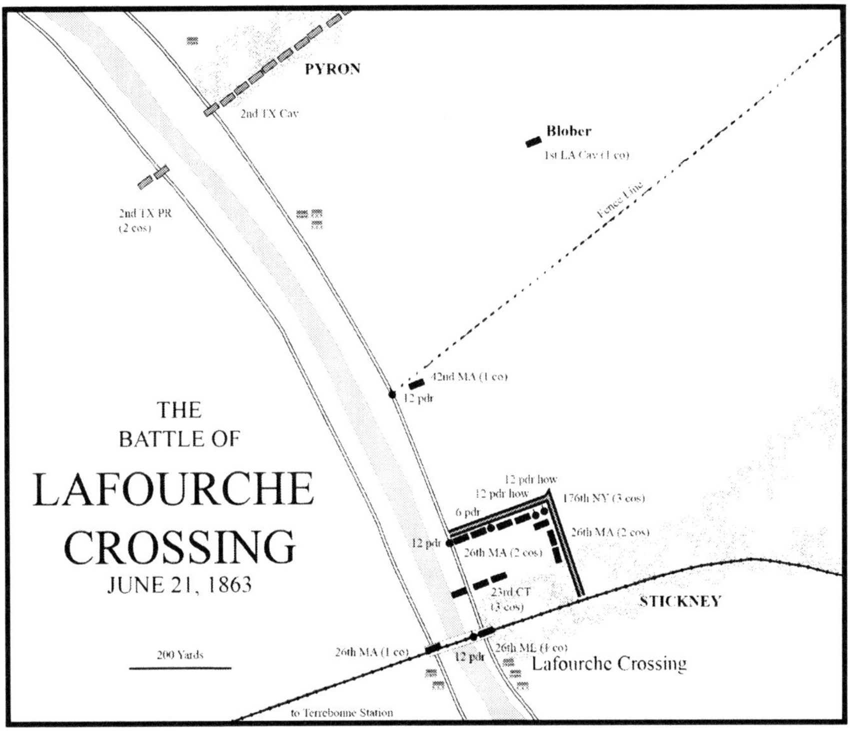

On horseback, Pyron trotted with his two hundred troops into what became a rain-streaked deathtrap. As his men surged toward the Yankee line, a canister round caught the Texas colonel, breaking his arm and thigh, and killing his horse. His second in command, Lieutenant Colonel Walker, astride an iron gray horse, took charge, riding well ahead of the 2nd Texas as it charged forward in an open ragged line. To Federal eyes, the Confederates appeared as whisps and shadows in the smoke and haze. Rebel officers lost control of their men; they now fought by instinct. The Federals, wavering, lost their discipline and simply fired at will in the general direction of the Texans. "The darkness rendered it impossible to see the enemy's movements," wrote Stickney, "and few of the troops were steady enough to trust . . . in the excitement of action."[30]

The Texans, "full of whiskey and gunpowder," according to one Connecticut soldier, closed with the Union line even though the Yankees outnumbered them more than two to one. Starting at the bayou road, the Rebels swept over the abandoned gun and rushed forward to crumble the Union left. Frightened men and horses plunged toward the Union rear, eager to reach the elevated railroad tracks and cover. In a nasty brawl on the far right, the Texans captured the two cannon at the angle. A Rebel lieutenant, placing his hand on the tube claimed the honor; he fell quickly, shot, bayonetted, and clubbed. Another Texan clutched a Union officer by the throat, demanding his surrender. The Connecticut soldier grabbed the Rebel's neck in turn while one of his comrades ran him through with a bayonet. Major Morgans and his Federals drove the enemy back. "Our major distinguished himself with gallantry and bravery," reported one New Yorker. "This was his first fight, yet his orders were delivered as coolly as if drilling the battalion. He fought as long as there was a rebel to be shot at." Texan Lieutenant Colonel Walker emerged from the darkness, clutching his left arm, and addressed a Union officer. "I am badly wounded. Will you be kind enough to take me to the rear?"[31]

The wild assault had rattled the Federals. Scores of panicked soldiers streamed toward the tracks, taking shelter behind the berm and buildings and climbing aboard the train parked at the depot. The color-bearer of the 26th Massachusetts, ordered to the rear by his colonel, heard the fleeing troops crying, "all is lost, the rebs are inside our lines and gobbled up the whole force." Intent on saving the honor of his regiment, the soldier removed the flag from the staff and hid it inside his blouse. The panicked mob clambered aboard boxcars and flatcars as the frightened train engineer pulled away from the fight, heading east to safety.[32]

The battle, though, had already turned against the Rebels, and more than half of the two hundred impetuous Texans fell dead or wounded in just a few minutes during the close-ranged free-for-all. Captain Lane's two companies from the 2nd Texas Partisan Rangers hovered nearby, but the attack of the 2nd Texas Cavalry had caught him off guard. "Instead of orders to support Pyron, he had *strict orders* not to bring on a fight, but to stand as pickets to mask our movements," explained Lieutenant James O. Crutchfield, adjutant of Stone's 2nd Texas Partisan Rangers. Captain Lane simply froze. "Certainly most officers placed in the situation," Crutchfield lamented, "would and should have disobeyed orders and gone into the fight." Crutchfield was, perhaps, overly harsh. The addition of sixty to eighty men would have done little, except create more Confederate casualties.[33]

The soldiers in the other regiments of the Second Cavalry Brigade could hear the Federals slaughtering their comrades but could do nothing to save them. In

Morgan Wolfe Merrick sketched this battle, fought in a heavy rain, as chaotic and bloody.
Daughters of the Republic of Texas Library, The Alamo, San Antonio, Texas.

the confusion, the sounds of the fleeing Union train convinced Major that enemy reinforcements had arrived; he would not add more men to this stupid assault. His regimental commanders begged to join the fight. "Colonel Phillips several times asked permission to go to their aid," Merrick lamented, "but to no avail." Major refused to let his officers goad him into compounding the blunder. "Colonel Pyron had no support," explained Lieutenant Crutchfield, "and in truth his attack was a surprise." Major had wanted to gauge the enemy strength so that he could plan an attack. Instead, Pyron rashly charged. Understanding the error, Major rode to the head of Stone's regiment and ordered him to cover the retreat of the survivors. "Of course," Crutchfield explained, "they arrived on the ground too late to be of service."[34]

By 8:00 P.M., the wrath of Pyron's attack had evaporated in the darkness. The Yankees continued shooting until "the Colonel ordered 'Cease firing!' Horses were tumbling and groaning in the weeds, men were calling for water by the scores," remembered Lieutenant Quien. "It was dark. It did not sound very friendly." Federal officers attempted to advance pickets across the battlefield to make sure the Rebels had gone. Their frightened soldiers refused.[35]

Instead, the stunned Federals held their ground and caught their breath. Stickney could not believe his luck. Federal casualties numbered only around fifty. "Had the enemy brought up their reserve, which was in line at no great distance," recalled the Union commander, "or had he made his attack on the right flank with equal force and with the same persistent energy as was displayed upon our front, perhaps the result might have been different."[36]

The Texan survivors slunk back into the night, the fight having lasted only thirty minutes. Major tried to shed a positive light on what had obviously been a disaster: "Pyron was forced to retire from a position won by daring assault unequaled, I think, in the War. Had I known his intention to assault the works I could have sent him such re-enforcements as would have insured success." Major lamented the outcome, but events east of the Lafourche had unfolded too quickly for him to react.[37]

Neither side claimed many prisoners. Some two dozen scared or wounded Texans fell into Union hands, still boasting about being "the oldest regiment in Confederate service," Stickney recalled, "and that they had never been beaten in action." Lieutenant Colonel Walker, politely led to the rear by his captors at the height of the battle, found himself unguarded in the Union camp. Passing into a tent, he emerged with a Union uniform, and simply walked away to freedom.[38]

Early in the morning of July 22, Confederate medical corps men approached the Union lines after an arranged truce. They had come to bear away the dead and to recover the wounded. Ambulances carried nearly sixty stricken Texans back to Thibodaux. Confederate medical steward Merrick approached the Union line, lantern in hand. "I came upon the body of one of my neighbor boys, Miguel Rodriguez of the Mission San José," the San Antonio soldier remembered. "He was lying beside the body of a Union soldier." The Confederate had grabbed his foe by the collar and had plunged a Bowie knife into the man's heart. Someone must have put a bullet through Rodriguez's head at nearly the same instant. Merrick had served with the young Tejano through the New Mexico Campaign the year before. "Poor Miguel," he lamented, "he was one of the bravest of the brave." The battle had ruined the regiment. The men had been too bold for their own good. "Colonel Pyron," Lieutenant Crutchfield acknowledged, "was a brave and impetuous officer and commanded a splendid set of men—men who would not falter when it came to hard fighting."[39]

Morgan Wolfe Merrick, a hospital steward serving with the 3rd Arizona, made this charcoal self-portrait.
Daughters of the Republic of Texas Library, The Alamo, San Antonio, Texas.

On June 22, as daylight broke on the battlefield, trains shuttling Federal forces from New Orleans rumbled into Lafourche Crossing. At midday, a train arrived bearing Colonel Thomas Cahill—the hero of the Battle of Baton Rouge—and five companies of the veteran 9th Connecticut "Irish" Infantry supported by a few more companies of the 26th Massachusetts and a section of artillery, swelling the Union force to eleven hundred men. Lieutenant Colonel Stickney, victorious in battle but now superseded in rank, transferred command of his motley army to the newcomer, who accepted. Later that afternoon, yet another train arrived, this time bearing the six hundred men of the 15th Maine, pulled from duty at Pensacola, Florida, just days before and hurried to meet the emergency facing the Lafourche District.[40]

At isolated Tiger Island, some twenty miles on the other side of the Confederate army, Major Anthony could not decide what to do. Troops with little direction or leadership prepared to defend the post, while others plotted to break through to Stickney. Facing an emergency, noncommissioned officers from the 42nd Massachusetts leant a hand in drilling squads of recruits for the *Corps d'Afrique*. Colonel Duganne, miraculously recovered from his "illness," and now beyond Stickney's wrath, believed someone should organize, arm, and drill the sick and loafers at the convalescent camp. "These men are nearly all veterans," he insisted. "We shall have a force of two thousand men. Add to these two thousand negroes

This sketch of Morgan Wolfe Merrick's Texas home stands in stark contrast to the opulent homes and plantations of Louisiana. His family is shown handling various chores—chopping wood, hunting, feeding chickens—while a servant hauls water. The jacal home and lumber addition would have barely passed as slave quarters along Bayou Lafourche. Daughters of the Republic of Texas Library, The Alamo, San Antonio, Texas.

who can be mustered in twenty-four hours to dig and fortify the approaches to this post," and Brashear would remain secure from all comers.[41]

Lieutenant Colonel Duganne—the highest-ranking officer still on his feet—left the implementation of this ambitious idea to Major Anthony, while he led a company from his regiment to Bayou Boeuf to reinforce the company from the 23rd Connecticut already there as well as the 176th New York men and guns Stickney had wisely relocated from Fort Chêne. Should the Confederates attempt to push their way across, he reasoned, they would find the passage guarded by his two hundred men and three heavy guns. This would buy time for Major Anthony to plan and organize his defenses.[42]

Some of the soldiers guarding the depot thought Duganne's move foolish. "They were thus strung seven miles out . . . without any food supply except what could be daily sent to them by cars, instead of concentrating at Brashear, where danger existed," Private Charles S. Bosson observed, "and all the necessary equipment was on hand to defend and subsist, if properly applied." Duganne might defend Bayou Boeuf, but who would counter the Rebels if they found their way across Berwick Bay?[43]

Major Anthony wilted under the pressure. On June 22, the inventory of troops at Brashear City seemed pitiful. Two companies of the 176th New York posted at Fort Buchanan along with gunners from the 21st Indiana, numbering in total just more than one hundred men. Other troops from the 176th, perhaps one hundred, served as crews among the guns on the water battery, guarded the depot, or defended the star fort south of the tracks. As many as three hundred black soldiers in various stages of training and discipline carried arms and, for the most part, knew how to use them. They, like every other formation in this dustbin army, lacked officers but might reliably defend a fortified position. Among the camps and hospital, few of the sick could be counted on, and few had organized themselves into combat formations. The quartermaster, commissary, provost guard, and ordnance details might be useful but remained disorganized. The half-company from the 42nd Massachusetts, under hard-working First Sergeant George Ballow, served as the only ready reserve.[44]

Anthony struggled to bring order to his ersatz army, but at least he had gunboats. The steamer *Kepper* remained a medium-weight workhorse, carried no guns, but could support some field pieces and troops. The USS *Hollyhock* patrolled from Berwick Bay up to the bridge on Bayou Boeuf, but the little tugboat only carried two 12-pound howitzers and no armor. It could throw shells no farther than Rebel field batteries could. Confederates with rifled artillery could shred the *Hollyhock* and *Kepper* with impunity. The vessels could scout, however, and Major Anthony ordered the *Hollyhock* and a squad of soldiers from the 176th New York to investigate down Berwick Bay and reconnoiter the Rebel shore. When lookouts spotted something suspicious along the wood's margins, the vessel hove to and sent ashore a boat. The handful of Yankee soldiers moved toward the trees but discovered nothing dangerous.

What they found on one abandoned plantation shocked them. "In the sugarhouse, a dilapidated old shed, a poor family had taken shelter when Berwick was first shelled, and had seen their home . . . burnt to ashes," recorded Sergeant George Haven Putnam. The family included a mother—sick with a raging fever—two teenaged daughters, four or five young children, and "a sickly looking father." The civilians claimed to be Unionists; the father had even been employed at odd jobs around at the Brashear City depot but had never received payment. The returning Confederates harassed the family for putting their faith in the U.S. government. Now Union shells had destroyed their home. "Persecuted and hunted like dogs by the Rebels, suspected, worried, and cheated by the Federals, and plundered by both sides and the darkeys," Putnam observed, "the fate of the Union men of the South is not to be envied."[45]

Major Anthony did not intend to be caught by surprise. He ordered the *Hollyhock* to patrol a circuit from Berwick Bay up to the bridge on Bayou Boeuf. He also ordered his troops to convert two railroad dirt cars into mobile forts. Gangs of laborers heaved 12-pound howitzers up ramps and into the cars. Pointing the guns forward, they fortified the edges with breastworks of railroad ties, creating a pair of blockhouses. Pushed ahead of a locomotive, these wood-armored cars might serve as a way of reconnoitering down the tracks toward Terrebonne Station. They might also allow Anthony's troops to clear the railroad of the Rebels at Terrebonne Station and cut their way through to Stickney.[46]

Duganne's position on Bayou Boeuf defended the vulnerable eastern edge of Tiger Island, and he also took precautions to avoid surprise. He ordered the levee modified into a parapet with firing steps for his men and redoubts for his guns. Around noon, a locomotive arrived from Brashear City pushing a fortified flat car with Lieutenant Lewis Stevenson and twenty men of the 176th New York aboard. At nearly the same time, USS *Hollyhock* paddled up the Boeuf. The skipper of the gunboat offered to help dismantle the bridge; instead, Duganne ordered the tugboat back to Berwick Bay while the train engine pushed Lieutenant Stevenson and his fortified dirt car down the tracks to locate the enemy.[47]

The reconnaissance down the railroad proceeded cautiously. When the train approached Tigerville, they encountered no signs of the Rebel advance. At Chacahoula, the engineer hesitated before moving forward. The next half-dozen miles of track traversed a dense cypress swamp where ambush seemed likely. Stevenson boldly ordered the train forward. As the engineer feared, the Confederates waited patiently ahead. Captain Henry H. Hall positioned the men of Company A, 3rd Arizona Cavalry at "a point midway of jungle that lines the railroad on either side . . . and had placed obstructions on the track," wrote a Texan. The train came into view but slowed to a stop short of the roadblock. A few of the Federals dismounted and walked cautiously toward the obstacles. As they approached the Rebel positions, Hall stepped out and ordered the men to surrender. "They very wisely did," a soldier observed, "as every one of the twenty men and the lieutenant was covered by a gun in the hands of good marksmen." The locomotive reversed, abandoning the hapless Union privates. Stevenson fired a shot from the howitzer as they left. Pleased with his ambush, Hall had one of his men tap the telegraph line, cleverly sending word toward Brashear: "So far all is well, enemy moving in direction of N.O."[48]

Stevenson reported the dustup back at Bayou Boeuf. Outposts down the tracks would be useful, he believed. Tigerville seemed to be the most appropriate picket post if Duganne wanted to place troops that far forward. Stevenson advised against a repeat of the scout down the tracks and through the swamp. Duganne could not afford the loss of a locomotive, cannon, and troops—or an officer. He ordered the train back to Brashear City. A little before 9:00 P.M., Duganne wrote out a report for Major Anthony, sending one of his lieutenants aboard the locomotive to carry it to headquaraters. He would conserve his force, and energy.[49]

Before he turned in, Duganne ordered a handful of soldiers and two sergeants out into the night pumping a handcart. First, they would organize the freedmen at Tigerville as scouts and pickets. From there, Sergeant Delwya P. Lewis would proceed alone with a message to Stickney—if he could find him. Duganne needed to know Rebel intentions. If the Confederate raiders had beaten Stickney and pursued him toward New Orleans, Brashear might still be evacuated by sea. Certainly Emory had already sent boats for that purpose.[50]

On the night of June 22, Duganne, Anthony, and the men on Tiger Island remained ignorant of the Confederate situation near Thibodaux, but Colonel Major felt it keenly. He faced hard choices. The intermittent rains returned, and his ammunition remained scarce, wet, and largely useless. The Federals had mauled the 2nd Texas Cavalry, a seasoned regiment. His wounded required attention and most could not travel. Major had rested his command that entire day at Thibodaux, hoping that the rain would stop, but it had not. Neither had he received word from the Confederates across Berwick Bay. Colonel Major, opposed by a reinforced enemy just a few miles distant, had to choose between forcing another fight at Lafourche Crossing or conserving his ammunition to cut his way through to Generals Alfred Mouton and Tom Green.[51]

He agonized over the decision. "The temptation was great to revenge the death of those gallant men who fell in Pyron's assault," Major claimed. Reluctantly, he decided prudence dictated an advance toward Tiger Island. He hoped that Connecticut Colonel Cahill would not pursue. This decision would require the Confederates to abandon their wounded at Thibodaux, probably to fall into enemy hands. Such were the fortunes of war. Major put his army into motion that night. Later that evening, his gunners shelled Cahill's camp and some of his troopers feigned a night attack on Lafourche Crossing, but he had done all he could with soggy ammunition and the resources at hand. As the sodden night closed around his road-weary brigade, Major and his men realized that the capture of Brashear City had truly become their only chance of escape.[52]

9

Brashear City

The post given us to hold is in the hands of the Rebels and the lone star of Texas floats over the road from Brashear almost to Algiers.

—Seargent George Haven Putnam

176th New York

The fate of Colonel James P. Major's Second Texas Cavalry Brigade lay balanced on the competency of two remarkably different men. One was a Louisiana blueblood; the other, a luckless Arizona adventurer.

Alfred Agricole Fusilier, the thirty-three-year-old son of privilege, had much at stake in this conflict. His way of life depended on Confederate success. His father, Gabriel LeClerc Fusilier, owned thousands of acres in sugarcane worked by hundreds of slaves on several plantations in southern Louisiana. In a flourish of patriotic zeal for the new Confederacy, the sixty-year-old LeClerc volunteered to serve as an aide-de-camp to General Richard Taylor. "Possessor of great estates, and of a hospitable, generous nature, this gentleman had great weight in his country," Taylor said of him. His son, Alfred, had answered the secessionists' call by serving in the ranks of an elite New Orleans militia unit where young men on the make could demonstrate their manly courage among their peers. Pride of membership bore a hard price on the terrible field of Shiloh. Wounded and abandoned by his friends, the younger Fusilier became a prisoner of the men he had come to kill. Exchanged, he limped home to St. Mary's Parish to recuperate, regaining his strength on the family estate just north of Franklin, Louisiana.

Once again fit, but still too fragile for rugged field service, Fusilier found a place as a civilian on the staff of Brigadier General Alfred Mouton, serving as an assistant engineer. Fusilier helped survey and design the Rebel works at Bisland. When Union General Nathaniel P. Banks and his army advanced up Bayou Teche, Fusilier retreated with the Louisiana Brigade to Natchitoches. The Yankees caught his father, who now languished in a New Orleans pen.[1]

Fusilier would get a chance to strike another blow. He attended the staff meetings when Taylor came to south Louisiana to unveil his grand design for saving Port Hudson. Most officers at these war councils believed the plan of attack on Brashear City impractical, if not impossible. To get across the expanse of Berwick Bay, the Confederates faced two immediate challenges. First, the Yankee gunboats needed to be neutralized. Next, Confederate gunners needed to locate, and smother, the Union artillery on the opposite shore. Failing these two events, a crossing attempt would be suicidal. Even with these conditions met, a successful amphibious assault faced long odds. The Rebels only had three small steamboats.

General Tom Green modified the plan. Perhaps, he argued, troops might land to the rear of the Union positions and attack from behind. A fast-moving strike force could neutralize the Union artillery positions, at least for a while, and buy time for the rest of the army to cross. There remained a catch. Once launched, coordination with this strike force—dubbed "the forlorn hope" by history buffs in the room—would be nearly impossible. Once away they would have to navigate the shallow waters of Grand Lake in the dark, land at a location of their choosing, and keep their force together and under control while maintaining the element of surprise.

They must succeed or die. Should the Federals compromise this effort, nearly every man involved would be doomed and beyond help from the rest of the army. Should the Confederates succeed in landing, they would have to keep quiet until Rebel guns west of Berwick Bay opened up, signaling the attack. The raiders would then have to instantaneously pounce on the unsuspecting Federals, capture their artillery, and open the way for the crossing. Leadership and initiative would be critical.

Fusilier listened as the generals debated this bold plan to attack Brashear City. Confederate commanders realized that any crossing required a swarm of pirogues and skiffs, at least for the forlorn hope and the first wave. The Confederates could not afford to risk their fragile steamboats in an opposed landing. Instead of concentrating their army, the Rebels favored infiltration by small craft, hoping that a swarm of targets stood a better chance against Yankee guns. Taylor agreed and directed his commanders to gather anything that could float. Mouton turned to Fusilier, his staff engineer, to see to it.

Fusilier succeeded. For two weeks—while Taylor raised commotion in Pointe Coupée and Major invaded the Lafourche District—Fusilier gathered boats. He scoured the haunts of his youth, the bayous, streams, and swamps of St. Mary's

Parish, and his efforts yielded much. On the afternoon of June 22, Taylor returned to Mouton's army at Pattersonville and discovered that Fusilier and his team had assembled fifty-three craft of all types including pirogues, canoes, and sailing skiffs for use by the forlorn hope and scores more for the passage of Berwick Bay. When supplies of traditional boats ran out, Fusilier set his men to gathering the stout wooden troughs used to cool sugar syrup. These large flat wooden trays, two feet by ten feet, lay abundant in the sugarhouses of the region and on calm water would easily bear the weight of a pair of men and their equipment. They could stand, Venetian gondola style, and pole their way across calm, shallow water, or kneel and paddle like Indians.

Near the mouth of Bayou Teche, Fusilier assembled the armada, the hundreds of small craft dubbed "the mosquito fleet." The boats assigned to the forlorn hope could carry 320 men between them, roughly equivalent to the number of men transported aboard a modest steamboat like the *Kepper*. The rest of the assembled craft formed a caravan that steamboats towed toward Berwick Bay. Mouton, proud of Fusilier's resourcefulness, praised his "indomitable energy and devotion to duty."[2]

General Mouton's man had found the boats, and General Green would fill them. He had needed a soldier of initiative, dash, and daring to lead the forlorn hope; he decided on Major Sherod Hunter of the 2nd Arizona Cavalry. A native of Tennessee, he had been an ambitious merchant, storeowner, and family man in the 1850s. He married the daughter of his business partner and had faced bright prospects, but in 1857, the birth of his son killed his wife; the infant died soon after. Grieving, Hunter sold out in Tennessee and vanished into the American West. The war found him homeless. Apaches had driven him from a hardscrabble ranch northwest of Mesilla, New Mexico Territory, and he had sheltered in the safety of the town.

When Texans invaded that region in 1861, twenty-seven-year-old Hunter joined them. He eventually led Company A, Arizona Rangers, a command of "picked men, inured to the hardships of frontier life." In early 1862, these fifty-three troopers took Tucson then scouted and skirmished nearly to California. Hunter and his men retreated to Texas as part of the Arizona Battalion when General Henry Hopkins Sibley's campaign collapsed. In September 1862, he joined Colonel George Wythe Baylor's 2nd Arizona as its major. Green knew Hunter's reputation and trusted this scrappy partisan.[3]

Major Hunter named Major James D. Blair of the 2nd Louisiana Cavalry as his second in command. These two officers called for volunteers from the cavalry regiments camped along Bayou Teche. More than three hundred stepped forward, including detachments from the 2nd Louisiana, 2nd Arizona, 5th Texas, the mounted companies of the 13th Texas Volunteers—now designated as Major Leonidas C. Rountree's 12th Texas Battalion—and Lieutenant Colonel Ed Waller's 13th Texas Cavalry Battalion.[4]

On the night of June 22, Hunter's men loaded onto Fusilier's assortment of mismatched watercraft and pushed off from the mouth of Bayou Teche amid cheers and waved hats. "Imagine if you can the novelty of the scene," wrote Private William Randolph Howell of the 5th Texas Cavalry. "Three hundred and twenty men with arms, ammunition, and well filled haversacks all crowded into fifty little boats, loading most of them down to the guards." The flotilla headed off into the growing darkness. "Truly it was a noble scene," Howell remembered. "Fifty-three skiffs . . . marching first by twos and then promiscuously down the beautiful Teche to the junction, and thence up the Atchafalaya into and across Grand Lake."[5]

Navigating the waterways at night, and landing behind a fortified enemy, was daunting. The mosquito fleet navigated twelve miles of river and bayou before finally breaking free into Flat Lake. By midnight, a good many of the boats had become lost and scattered in the cypress-studded lake and only about two hundred of the men remained together when they reached their landing site northeast of Brashear City. At a point where Lake Palourde and Flat Lake mingled together, the Texans and Louisians jumped into knee-deep water and waded to a swampy shore, about an hour behind schedule. "At daybreak," Howell continued, "we landed, dried gun tubes, loaded pieces, and set off for the scene of action by single file, through mud, water, and the tall palmetto." Others, lost in the darkness, continued on to the mouth of Bayou Boeuf, marooned on the far side of Tiger Island and out of the fight.[6]

While Hunter paddled toward his destiny, Green executed the final preparations for the assault across Berwick Bay. The balance of the army—1,500 rifles—moved into position opposite Brashear City. Three units, the 4th and 7th Texas and the remainder of the 2nd Arizona, crossed the Atchafalaya to Gibbon's Point where they could snipe at the gunners of Fort Buchanan. The flats, sugar

This Harper's Weekly *image of Brashear City shows the principal structures, docks, and signal tower of the Federal installation.*

coolers, and pirogues secreted nearby would carry them across Berwick Bay after Hunter had sprung his trap. The 2nd Louisiana, 5th Texas, and Waller's and Rountree's Cavalry Battalions would open fire on the Yankee camps from the ruins of Berwick. Armed with Enfields, they would pepper the Union defenders to keep them pinned in place. Once the fight had developed, these men would constitute the third wave.

Excellent marksmanship by the Rebel artillery was critical to suppress the Union cannon. Green moved two batteries into position. Crews rolled four 6-pounders and two 12-pound howitzers, a 12-pound Napoleon, and a pair of 10-pound rifles into the burned portion of Berwick City, their cannon wheels wrapped in moss, hides, and cloth to muffle their passage. A few hours after midnight, his men in position and, he trusted, Major Hunter's forlorn hope in place, Green took position atop an Indian mound and waited until dawn provided enough light for his gunners to select targets.

At 5:00 A.M., as the sky brightened, he gave the order to the Val Verde battery to bombard the enemy's camp. A ripple of fire and smoke erupted on the western shore of Berwick Bay. Captain William H. Nichols's battery opened next, its two rifles

A quartermaster sergeant at the time of the Battle of Brashear City, George Haven Putnam gave a literary and astute account of the campaign and aftermath.
From George Haven Putnam, *Memories of My Youth, 1844–1865* (New York: G. P. Putnam's Sons, 1914).

spinning solid shot through the Union tents and buildings of Brashear City.[7]

In the fading darkness, the first rounds fired traced a glowing arc toward the enormous cluster of canvas near the center of the waterfront. "I was roused from my comfortable quarters in the big quartermaster's tent by the sound of a round shot coming over from the Rebel side," wrote Sergeant George Haven Putnam of the 176th New York. The soldier rolled off of his cot, now wide awake. A second round came whistling in, ripping and tearing fabric, smashing the center pole. "The gunner got the range," Putnam recalled, "bringing down the canvas in a confused tangle. My . . . tent was a mark for the Rebel battery. It was probably mistaken for the headquarters." No doubt it was also easy to see. So was the depot. "A few solid shot crashed through the structure," Private Charles P. Bosson wrote. Others Rebel rounds splintered wood on the wharves or ricocheted through the camps.[8]

Sergeant Putnam, having crawled out from under his fallen tent, mused that the incident would blow over quickly once the Union guns answered. "It seemed quite possible that the little bombardment had been undertaken merely on the general principal of worrying the other fellow," he wrote. "It was evidently only a field battery with which we had to contend, the guns being probably 10-pounders." As the sun rose and sparkled off the waters of Berwick Bay, USS *Hollyhock* moved to investigate the Rebel positions but soon drew fire from the Val Verde Battery. Its skipper ordered the engines reversed, and the tugboat backed down Berwick Bay and into the cover of Bayou Boeuf, followed by *Kepper*. They would be spectators, positioning south of Fort Number 1. USS *Hollyhock* lobbed harassing fire toward the Confederates at a long, ineffective, range.[9]

"There was naturally considerable excitement," Putnam understated. The surprise pounding set people to flight, especially among the camps of liberated slaves. "Almost all our darkeys had fled on the mules when the first shot was fired." Meanwhile, soldiers took cover and shot at the Rebels across Berwick Bay. "Our men in camp," noted Putnam, "taking advantage of trees, little embankments, corners of houses, etc., for shelter, commenced using their muskets." A ragged firing line formed along the shore as the infantry tried to get at the Rebel gunners. "I fired two or three shots," the New York soldier added, "but am ignorant whether or not I am guilty of manslaughter."[10]

Fifteen miles to the east, the sounds of battle lightened the hearts of Colonel Major's weary troops as they arrived at Chacahoula Station on the New Orleans, Opelousas, and Great Western Railroad after a night march from Thibodaux. "At the same instant heard with no little pleasure," Major reported, "the cannonade at Brashear." Relieved that Green was attacking the enemy as scheduled, Major confidently ordered his men to rest themselves and their mounts. He could reach his objective, Bayou Boeuf, in just hours. Details had torn up the tracks at Terrebonne Station to prevent any unexpected arrival from New Orleans. Even so, he did not believe the Federals would press him.[11]

He was correct. The echo of cannon also reached Colonel Thomas Cahill at Lafourche Crossing. After listening carefully, he telegraphed General William H. Emory that he heard "continuous and heavy firing" toward *both* Brashear City and Donaldsonville. The enemy, he feared, had divided and simultaneously hit both positions. Or, there might be even more Confederates slipping into the Lafourche District from Pointe Coupée. Emory, convinced the main effort lay at Berwick Bay, telegraphed Cahill ordering him toward Brashear City to fall on the rear of Major and his Texans. With that dispatch sent, Emory also hedged his bets, telegraphing Banks to send cavalry to Fort Butler so they could scout down Bayou Lafourche.[12]

What Emory failed to realize was that Banks, facing troubles of his own at Port Hudson, had little interest in affairs west of the Mississippi. At just that moment, a telegram arrived from Banks. Emory could not believe what he read. "The commanding general does not regard it as important that we should run any great risk to save Brashear," read the message from Port Hudson. "Send orders to Brashear to get off everything of value." Banks refused to send help. He abandoned Emory—and the little commands under Cahill and Major Robert C. Anthony—to their fate. Emory and his regiments would fight alone. From the vantage point of the carnage at Port Hudson, Brashear City no longer mattered, and Banks refused to be distracted by outpost skirmishing in the Lafourche District. From the scantily defended city of New Orleans, this little battle erupting on Berwick Bay seemed pregnant with dire consequences.[13]

Emory had no way of communicating this cynical change of plan to the surrounded Union forces at Brashear City. Instead, a courier carrying completely contradictory orders sailed aboard the *St. Mary's*, already splashing along the shores of the Gulf of Mexico toward the mouth of the Atchafalaya. Even if Emory could recall these orders, evacuating the base with the vessels at hand would save little. Cannon, wagons, munitions, and commissary stores appeared destined to fall into Rebel hands.

Banks's verdict seemed especially cruel given the accumulation of liberated slaves at Tiger Island. Their freedom had been a national priority; their safety and security was not. These men, women, and children were now free—but also homeless, sick, hungry, and frightened. The able-bodied men now enlisted in the *Corps d'Afrique* at Tiger Island had yet to show their mettle. Most were not yet truly soldiers. Even so, they would now face the rifles, pistols, and shotguns of veteran Confederates offended by their mere existence. If Brashear City fell, those who survived the battle faced further torments.

Of course, none of the isolated Federals at Brashear City had any idea that Banks had forsaken them. They focused instead on the rude awakening they had received that morning. Yet, the shock wore off quickly. The now wide-awake camp turned out to see the excitement, careful to dodge the incoming projectiles. "It was great sport, as I distinctly recollect, for the boys," wrote Corporal Andrew Sherman of Company F, 23rd Connecticut. He watched from the convalescent camp. "Few . . . had ever witnessed such a sight," he noted, "to watch the shells in their encircling aerial flight across the bay and as they exploded in our rear." The Confederates unloaded each of their guns at least four times; the Federal cannon did not reply.[14]

Major Anthony ordered his outposts to remain vigilant but waited to see what the Confederates did next. He dispatched a locomotive to Bayou Boeuf to let

Lieutenant Colonel Augustine Joseph Hickey Duganne know—if he had not already realized—that some artillery action was occurring at Brashear.

Satisfied that this was a mere probe, Anthony ordered his gunners into action. Crews ran to the 24-pounders of the water battery and returned fire. The guns from Fort Buchanan joined in. "Our own batteries . . . made such a vigorous reply to our Texas friends that their fire gradually slackened," Putnam wrote, "no serious mischief being done on either side." The steady thumping from both shores continued for an hour—more annoying than deadly. General Green once again found himself outgunned and pounded by Union artillery. "The shot of the enemy was so well directed," he wrote, "that we found it necessary several times to shift the position of our guns and caissons." Green, dodging 24- and 32-pounder rounds on his side of the bay, wondered what had become of the forlorn hope. He could not sustain this escapade indefinitely.[15]

Far behind the Union camps, the Rebel raiders stealthily moved into position. As the artillery duel heated up, Major Hunter and his two hundred men traversed a narrow trail through four miles of swamp before reaching solid ground a few yards back from the edge of the woods. The roar of the cannon rolled over them, heightening the tension. The Rebel soldiers joked and joshed with each other but knew their hour was at hand. "Could you have heard the many remarks—droll, witty, and amusing—you could not possibly have repressed a smile at least," Private Howell reported, "although you knew you were fast approaching . . . Yankee bayonets, fortifications, [and] artillery . . . entirely separated from friends by water."[16]

Rebel scouts hustled back through the cover of an orange grove in the growing light, reporting row after row of tents spread in the fields before them and the Union works of Fort Buchanan eight hundred yards beyond. Hunter, Blair, and their troops emerged into a large field, and officers quietly brought the command into line. "Here we threw down blankets, provisions and every encumbrance," Howell remembered.[17]

The men of Hunter's detachment beheld the scope and enormity of the enemy camp—the complex at Brashear City seemed vast, its garrison probably numbering in the thousands. They were but two hundred but seemed to hold the element of surprise. Union soldiers sat near campfires just seventy-five yards away, their backs turned. "The forlorn hope," recalled Private Bill Davidson of the 5th Texas Cavalry, "could see and hear the enemy talking, yet they paid no attention to us." Hunter saw the shade of panic and the shadow of doubt spreading among his troops. Having cut off "all means of retreat," Major Hunter reported that "we could only fight and win." But would these men chance the attack against such insuperable odds? [18]

Major Hunter knew the time for his assault had come, but his men needed courage. He addressed his soldiers. "We may all be shot," he admitted. "Not many of us may get back to the brigade, but, gentlemen, we'd better just fall down [dead] in our tracks than go back disgraced." Although inelegant, the pep talk worked. The soldiers moved toward Fort Buchanan in a steady line.[19]

After moving forward for several hundred yards, Hunter halted his command. He reorganized the force into two columns. Hunter would lead men from the 2nd Arizona straight for Fort Buchanan and a large sugarhouse near the bank of Berwick Bay. Once he carried these positions, the way would be clear for Confederate reinforcements to come across. Major Blair, meanwhile, would take his Louisianans and drive south into the interior of the Union position, cross the tracks, and head for Fort Number 1 east of the depot, aided by Captain Phil Clough of the 5th Texas Cavalry and the men of the other detachments. Once they had captured that position, Blair's troops could use the fort and its cannon to cause havoc behind enemy lines. With these two positions carried, the Rebel war bands would converge on the depot and tracks to buy time for their compatriots to make the dangerous crossing of Berwick Bay. With the plan settled, the forlorn hope split and continued their separate advances.[20]

While Hunter finalized his plans, the first hour of the artillery duel passed into a second and neared a third, causing the Union commanders in Brashear City to wonder why the Confederates seemed so determined to use up their ammunition. Many feared the bombardment as the harbinger of a more serious contest. Would the Rebels cross their army today? If so, where? The Texan artillery fire concentrated on the depot and town. Perhaps they would come from Berwick City.

The Confederate fire slackened as the Federals turned up the heat, but enough shots continued to bounce through the camps to keep the Union soldiers on edge. At the first racket of the bombardment, First Sergeant George Ballow roused the men of the 42nd Massachusetts and formed the company under cover but remained without orders. Post commander Major Anthony rode to Fort Buchanan,

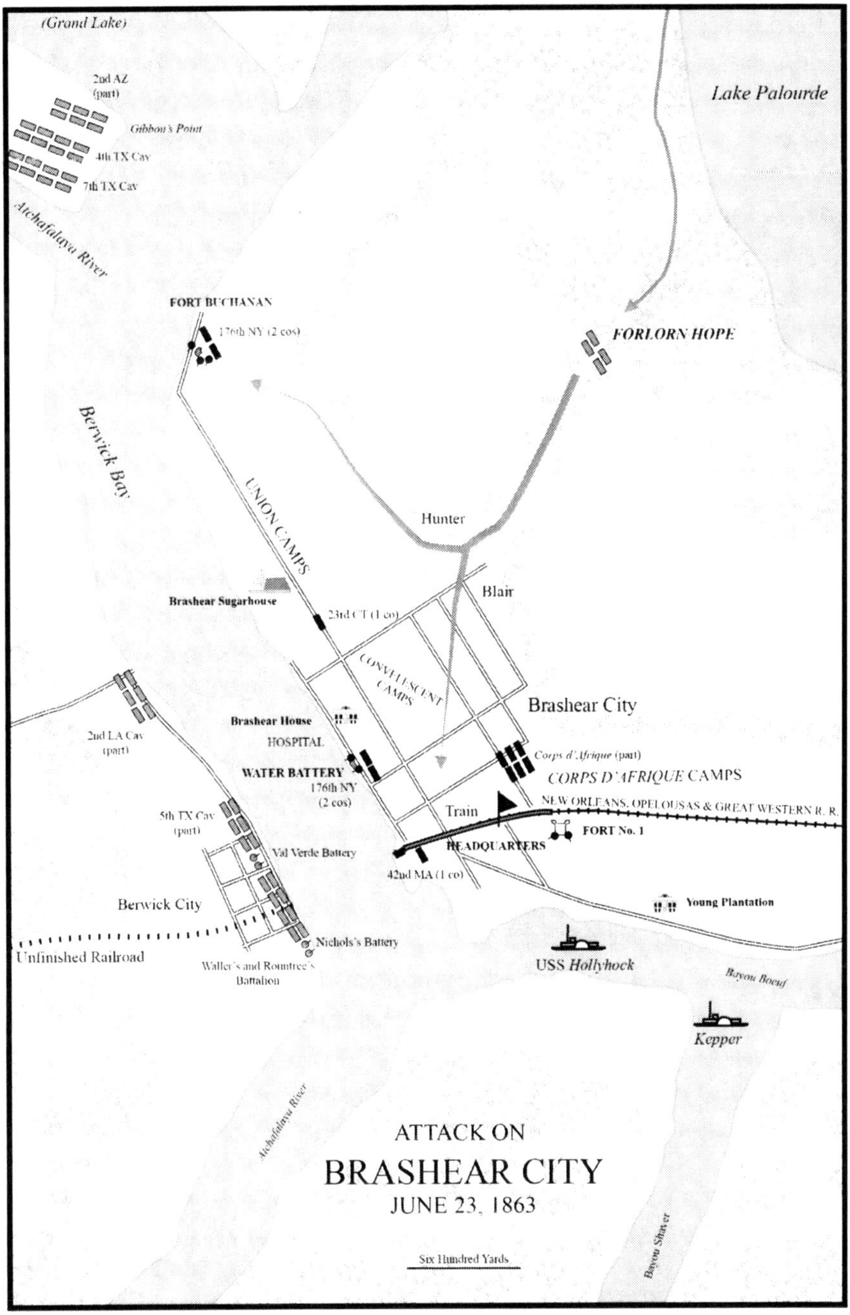
(Grand Lake)
2nd AZ (part)
Gibbon's Point
4th TX Cav
7th TX Cav
Atchafalaya River
Lake Palourde
FORT BUCHANAN
176th NY (2 cos)
FORLORN HOPE
Berwick Bay
UNION CAMPS
Hunter
Blair
Brashear Sugarhouse
23rd CT (1 co)
CONVALESCENT CAMPS
Brashear City
Brashear House
HOSPITAL
2nd LA Cav (part)
WATER BATTERY
176th NY (2 cos)
Corps d'Afrique (part)
CORPS D'AFRIQUE CAMPS
NEW ORLEANS, OPELOUSAS & GREAT WESTERN R. R.
Train
FORT No. 1
5th TX Cav (part)
HEADQUARTERS
Val Verde Battery
42nd MA (1 co)
Young Plantation
Berwick City
Nichols's Battery
Unfinished Railroad
Waller's and Rountree's Battalion
USS Hollyhock
Bayou Boeuf
Kepper
Atchafalaya River
ATTACK ON
BRASHEAR CITY
JUNE 23, 1863
Bayou Shaver
Six Hundred Yards

ordering Captain Francis W. Noblette of the 21st Indiana to get his gunners there to manhandle one of their heavier pieces down toward the Brashear sugarhouse where the range to the enemy batteries was shorter by half a mile. The weight of this heavy gun would also be useful against any boats or barges the Rebels might have hidden on the opposite shore. With his men hauling the gun to its new position, Captain Noblette wheeled his big black horse around and began the ride to the ordnance dump near the depot to bring up some ammunition.[21]

The garrison at Brashear City, agitated after nearly two hours of artillery fire, noticed a new development across Berwick Bay that confirmed their suspicions. A line of Confederates marched out of the ruins of the town and moved to the shore. A ripple of small arms' fire erupted at the water's edge, and bullets whirred across the six hundred yards of water. "To our surprise, a couple of long rows of butternut uniforms came down to the edge of the bayou and began peppering across with their rifles," Sergeant Putnam wrote. "Our surprise was due chiefly to the fact that the rifle shots barely carried over the intervening water and the balls that did reach our tent lines were for the most part spent." The Union gunners shifted their focus to the Rebel infantry. Perhaps they would attempt a crossing after all.[22]

The Massachusetts men near the depot acted independently and moved smartly to the wharves, glad to finally add their muskets to the fight. They delivered a volley—their 1842 Springfield smoothbores bucked and roared—but their bullets skipped harmlessly over the water. The Confederates returned fire. "Sergeant Turner . . . had a bullet go through his blouse sleeve at the elbow," Private Bosson wrote. Because the Rebels could hit them with their Enfields, and they could not strike back with their inferior weapons, the company turned about and took cover; their role ended after this pathetic showing. First Sergeant Ballow searched for an officer to provide him with instructions. No one seemed to be in charge. A mob of confused soldiers, though, gathered around the depot to gawk, ask questions, and speculate.[23]

Then, a cry from above rang out. In the depot's rooftop cupola, men with spyglasses spotted movement from the north. At about 7:00 A.M., lookouts caught a glimpse of two distinct lines of infantry moving forward in a ragged, open line, *behind* the Union positions. One line had already passed between the convalescent camp and closed to just four hundred yards from Fort Buchanan, heading directly for the undefended rear of that work. A second line headed south through the orange groves heading for Fort Number 1.[24]

Unaware of this development, Captain Noblette, having started his ride from Fort Buchanan toward the depot, rode unsuspectingly into the middle of this advance. The Indiana artilleryman believed these scruffy men were railroad workers coming from their camps toward the depot to lend a hand. The mistaken Indiana officer planned on using a few of them to help him bring up ammunition. He waved his hat at the unrecognized Rebels and ordered them to come on and help him find a wagon to load up with powder and shell. "Phil Clough . . . turned his double-barreled shotgun loose on him," Private Davidson of the 5th Texas Cavalry recalled. "Horse and man went down, and the ball opened."[25]

Crawling out from beneath his slain mount, Noblette ran toward the cover of the nearby hospital, firing three shots from his pistol over his shoulder as he ran. The Indiana artilleryman made it to the building and ducked inside. Colonel Charles C. Nott, rising from his sick bed amid the commotion, saw the Hoosier tumble in. "The captain was full of wrath, and vowed he would put the two or three charges still in his revolver, in places where . . . the murdering villains would feel them."[26]

The surprise announced, the Confederate lines paused, and then blossomed into a roll of smoke and fire. "Suddenly there was a volley from our rear," Sergeant Putnam wrote, "and we realized that the firing in front had been carried on only to engage our attention." He moved to where he could see what was happening: "A couple of long lines of butternuts . . . in open formation came across the cane fields at a double quick pace firing half volleys as they ran." Bullets whizzed through the Federal camps. The Rebels across Berwick Bay, seeing Hunter's attack, increased their volume of fire. "Our men, thus hemmed in between three fires," Putnam reported, "naturally broke and fell into disorder." The Texans and Louisianans raised a Rebel Yell and charged forward.[27]

The artillery crews at Fort Buchanan, once fixated on targets across the water, now had bullets spinning in from behind. With only a low parapet to the rear of the battery, the crews lay exposed. Its guns, mounted on clumsy siege carriages, would be hard to turn that direction. Instead, a sergeant in the 176th ordered the men there to forget the cannon and form a musket firing line facing their assailants.[28]

Major Anthony rode forward and overruled the infantryman, ordering the confused soldiers to manhandle one of the heavy siege guns out of its tracks and into position to fire at the oncoming Rebels instead. The infantrymen obliged, knowing this clumsy task was not easily undertaken. By the time they had it turned, the Confederates had passed into the convalescent camps, mingling friend with foe. Major Hunter boldly emerged from a line of tents about one hundred yards behind Fort Buchanan and called out for Anthony to surrender. The New Yorkers stopped wrestling with their cannon to see a line of Texans advancing, rifles leveled, prepared to unleash death. Anthony ordered his men to give up. With little struggle, Fort Buchanan fell.[29]

Hunter's assault force had achieved its first objective and turned south toward the Brashear Plantation, its sugarhouse, and the hospital, sweeping through the convalescent camps along the way. The crew handling the heavy cannon at the sugarhouse dragged it about and fired a few shots over the heads of the Texans coming from Fort Buchanan but did not slow Hunter or his men. They abandoned their ordnance and fled toward the depot. Across Berwick Bay, Rebel officers celebrated. Watching from Gibbons Point, Captain Willis L. Robards thought it "delightful sport to see the Yankees stampeding in every direction." He ordered the Texans there to commence their crossing.[30]

An awkward swarm of pirogues, sugar coolers, and rafts pushed across the north end of Berwick Bay, carrying reinforcements from the 4th and 7th Texas cavalries. As the boats reached the eastern shore, enthusiastic soldiers—with little experience with such craft—leapt onto dry land, often causing the now back-heavy boats to upend, dumping the rear occupants into the water. "In this way," Private Davidson snickered, "a good many of the boys got 'ducked.'"[31]

Hunter and his Texans, now joined by a steady trickle of troops from across Berwick Bay, swept toward the hospital. Convalescents crawled from their tents; many were shot down in the smoke and confusion. One of the ill, New York Captain John S. Cutter, responded to racket outside his tent by leaving his bed to rally a squad of fleeing soldiers; the Rebels were on them in an instant. Cutter ordered his scattered New Yorkers to fall back to the cover of the train, firing as they went. As he gestured to his men, an onrushing Texan demanded Cutter give up his sword, covering him with his rifle. The Yankee turned defiantly. "I never surrender!" The Rebel cooly shot him through the head and continued the fight. "He was one of our best men among our officers, a gentleman, a scholar, and a soldier," a stunned New Yorker lamented. "His loss is much deplored by all who knew him."[32]

Colonel Nott, still weak from the effects of his prolonged illness, left the hospital to rally his regiment. He mounted his horse and called for his soldiers to fall back on the depot, but before he had gone far, he swooned and fell to the ground. Picking himself up, he returned to the building. As the shooting outside intensified, he worried about the men inside, who, like himself, were too weak to resist. "The red flag of our hospital was not understood by the assaulting party," he feared, "and for a little while it looked as if no quarter would be given by the wild Texans to our sick and wounded."[33]

He was wrong. "A wild looking squad, with broad hats and jangling spurs rushed, revolver in hand, upon the building." Nott stepped out and told the men that this position was off limits. He turned to a Confederate nearby. "Sergeant, put two men on guard at the door, and don't let any but the wounded pass in." The Texans did as they were told. "It was the first and the last order I ever gave a Confederate soldier."[34]

Hunter's and Blair's advance roared through the town toward the Federal troops at the depot and tracks in a crescendo of yells and gunfire. Shouts of hundreds of men, at first incoherent, became clear: "The Rebs are coming!" Men too ill to serve found the energy to scramble away from the Confederates that were even then shooting their way through the camps. Panic ensued. Texans and Louisianans shot anything that moved, ill or sound, as they swept through. Corporal Sherman, among these light duty troops, took to his heels. "When I first saw the Confederates they were rushing in squads of fifteen or twenty through the streets of the village, yelling and firing as they came."[35]

Sherman scurried toward the depot with a cluster of frightened soldiers. "For the first time in my army life, I saw a Union soldier wounded," he recalled. "I shall never forget the scene. This soldier . . . was hit somewhere in the lower part of the body; with a shriek . . . he clapped both his hands over his abdomen, bending nearly double as he did so." Civilian railroad employees stampeded, flocking to the two locomotives. Engineers built their steam, uncoupled them from the heavy freight of the fifty-car train, and chugged away toward Bayou Boeuf, unencumbered.[36]

Small clumps of Union soldiers attempted to make a stand. Captain Samuel E. Thomason formed a line of battle in the space between the camps of the 176th New York and 23rd Connecticut. His men fired a volley against the Rebel skirmishers flitting about to their front. The Rebels simply swarmed past his left, threatening to engulf him and his men. The captain ordered his soldiers to fall back toward the tracks and depot to make a second stand there. Another squad of New Yorkers, led by a corporal, fell back in a clump, firing in two directions at both groups of attacking Rebels. "All these isolated attempts to fight showed great pluck and courage," wrote Bosson, watching from the depot. "A sure sign that if handled properly . . . it would not have been a holiday affair for the enemy."[37]

The Union troops facing Berwick Bay, now flanked on their right and rear by a growing number of Texans and Louisianans, turned to face their closest tormentors. "We tumbled back from the shore line and got into such formation as was possible under the circumstances," continued Sergeant Putnam. Major Blair's troops had already passed beyond their position. "The Rebel line overlapped us . . . at both ends while our groups were scattered and spread in such fashion that it did not prove practicable to bring them together into any effective fighting line."[38]

These Union troops also prudently scattered for safety. Putnam, trotting down a road toward the depot, saw that the Confederates had already cut him off. The Federals who found cover, shooting at these Rebels, sent bullets flying past Putnam as well. He realized his double danger of being killed by unfriendly—and *friendly*—fire. "I turned into the camp," he wrote, "and surrendered myself to the first half-dozen ragged rascals who ran up."[39]

Blair's Confederates closed in on the town, its depot, and the five hundred yard-long train still sitting on the tracks. Union line officers and their detached commands all across Brashear City fought their own battles but instinctively gravitated toward the cover of the rolling stock and the railroad embankment. The raw soldiers of the *Corps d'Afrique* moved there in good order. One company mounted the two fortified dirt cars and began firing at the Confederates as they moved through the camps and streets north of the tracks. The gunners aboard USS *Hollyhock* south of town raised their guns to maximum elevation to lob shots at Blair's men, but extreme range and poor visibility coupled to make the fire ineffective—and irresponsible given the presence of so many friendly troops mingled with the Rebels.[40]

After thirty minutes of sweeping the Federal camps north of the tracks with near impunity, the Confederate attacking force now faced stiffening resistance. Union Lieutenant Lewis Stevens gathered together his provost squad and put their shoulders to a cannon on the water battery to turn it "against the 'surprise party' at our rear," quipped one Yankee. The men fired the piece at the Rebels several times. Their action, described by one soldier as "the most gallant stand of the day," seemed to slow the enemy advance. Captain Clough's Confederates, taking cover, systematically picked off these makeshift gunners. Stevens had his legs knocked out from under him when a bullet tore through his boot, instep, and ankle. Private Nikolas Newlan, a seventeen-year old German immigrant, stooped to carry the lieutenant to safety only to take a round through his arm, another through his body, and a blast of buckshot to the head. Two others at the gun fell in quick succession.[41]

These individual gun battles and dramatic stands bought time for the Federals along the tracks to organize a defense. Fleeing Union troops rallied around the men of the *Corps d'Afrique*. Corporal Sherman crawled onto a flatcar with some black soldiers. He realized, though, that the Confederates had begun to concentrate their fire at that point. "I concluded it was the better part of valor to change base." He abandoned his comrades and slipped off the back of the car. He could see the men of the 42nd Massachusetts hurrying up from the depot in a column of fours, arms at right shoulder, led by a sergeant—"a large fine looking fellow"—so he took position to help. The Bay State soldiers trotted forward, dropping into the ditch behind the train, to fire from behind the berm and beneath the cars. As First Sergeant Ballow energetically directed his men, a bullet zipped through, catching him in the left forearm, gouging a nasty wound. For the next half-hour, the two sides blazed away. Two more Massachusetts men fell, one shot through the body and killed outright, and another nursing a wound to the calf.[42]

Union troops held their ground and now it became the Rebels' turn to fall. A sergeant from the 2nd Louisiana fell dead with a bullet through the head while another limped back, clutching a bloody hip. Another Louisianan nearby tumbled backward, a shot having glanced off his ribs, exiting his back. A fourth lay propped up under cover, a bullet having passed through both thighs. The Texans took several hits as well. Two men in Clough's company had serious wounds that, more than likely, would cost each a limb. Five others nursed bloody but less dangerous wounds. Private Howell of the 5th Texas Cavalry also recoiled, grazed in the hand and shoulder.[43]

As the Federals did their best from the cover of the train, the Confederates simply worked their way around both ends and then charged, "with a genuine Texas yell," Howell remembered, "driving them before us." A Connecticut soldier turned to face the enemy and bucked backward, shot through the forehead. "The bullets were flying all about me," Sherman remembered. "They seemed to be coming from two or three directions . . . with their 'zip, zip,'" Bosson recalled, realizing his danger. "A few men had fallen previous to this, [but] under this crossfire they commenced to drop quick." The men of the *Corps d'Afrique*, at the right of the Union line, now took fire from the front, flank, and rear from only thirty yards away.[44]

A soldier in the 176th watched as Rebel bullets cut down the black soldiers. "A colored company of the [7th *Corps d'Afrique*] made a good stand, but were cut to pieces," he wrote, "and, I understand, all killed—the last seen of them, their commander stood with a few men about him, fighting desperately." The rest of the black soldiers broke and fled for the tree line to the east.[45]

Sergeant Ballow, clutching his useless left arm, knew the time to leave had arrived. Raising up to address his men, he shouted, "Boys, take care of yourselves!" The men obeyed, scattering. Some of the white soldiers followed the black troops bolting toward the trees and swamp east of town; others fell back in a rough skirmish line toward a sawmill to the southwest where Bayou Boeuf met Berwick Bay. Corporal Sherman headed south, too. A friend dodged behind a tree to shoot at their pursuers but spun back in pain as a bullet shattered his right arm. Sherman, horrified, gave up, throwing his weapon and cartridge box into a water-filled ditch.[46]

By 9:00 A.M., the combined Confederate forces swept the area south of the tracks for any remaining Federals. Some Yankees sheltered in Fort Number 1, but they were too few to make a convincing stand. The USS *Hollyhock* and the transport *Kepper*, with the guns of Fort Number 1 now in Rebel hands, paddled down Bayou Shaver, running for the Gulf. A group from the 176th New York and 42nd Massachusetts took up positions behind the walls and tombs of a small cemetery to the southeast of the fort, but Confederate rifles pinned them down. Others ran down the tracks toward Colonel Duganne's outpost at Bayou Boeuf, seven miles away. Seven fugitives clambered aboard a rowboat south of town and pulled hard for Fort Chêne following the smoke from the funnels of the retreating *Hollyhock*. Franklin Borden, the fourteen-year-old fifer of Company B, 42nd Massachusetts, found a small sailing skiff and glided into Berwick Bay, drawing fire from Confederates in town as he passed out of range. Later, sailors aboard the

USS *Hollyhock* rescued these eight soldiers. By noon on June 23, the last Federal holdouts had given up.[47]

Blair and Hunter herded their Federal prisoners into Fort Number 1. "Our captors were the most ragged, dirty-looking set of rascals I had ever seen," Sergeant Putnam observed. "There was plenty of pluck and spirit among them, but a great want of order and discipline. The only thing uniform about them was dirt—shirts, pants, and skin being all of a fine mud color." Officers seemed indistiguishable from the men," Putnam continued, although "sometimes a suit of gray made its appearance." The Rebels carried a variety of weapons, from knives and pistols to carbines, shotguns, and Enfields. "They were on the whole, a good-natured, jolly set of country boys," Putnam wrote home, "and they treated us with considerable kindness and humanity." The Federals had no idea how the enemy had gained their rear. Putnam lamented that "the swamps had been pronounced by our engineers to be impassible, and so I believe they would be by any but Texans."[48]

The rest of the Confederate troops began surging across Berwick Bay. Barges tied up dockside in Brashear City now proved useful to ferry across the occupying army. Generals Green and Taylor shared a pirogue and arrived to discover a state of utter pandemonium. "A Texan came upon a telegraphic instrument, clicking in response to one down the line," he wrote. The Texan, fearing the device might be a booby trap, destroyed it with his boots. "Boys! They is trying to blow us up," Taylor reported the man saying. "I seen the triggers a-working, but I busted them." Other soldiers resented Taylor's astonished reaction. The general implied that "we were so infernal ignorant that we did not know a telegraph battery from a can of dynamite," a ruffle-feathered Texan later wrote.[49]

Colonel Nott watched the Rebels from his hosptial window at the Brashear House. "We could see the Confederate forces crossing the river," he recalled, "in flat boats and dugouts. A little steamer dropped out of one of the narrow bayous, and worked ceaselessly, bringing over artillery. Ere sunset, we estimated that five thousand men and four batteries had crossed."[50]

The Confederate victory yielded a bountiful harvest. At the Union camp, officers discovered a scene beyond their greatest hopes. Stacks of musket crates and piles of scavenged weapons yielded more than 2,500 firearms. Uniforms, food, equipment, and ammunition—everything the Confederates needed to make war—

lay as spoils, as did a dozen heavy cannon. The Texans also found the liquor stores and commissary and were busy wolfing down whiskey and rations. Guards herded the thousand Union prisoners—ill and healthy, alike—toward Fort Buchanan, the designated holding area. The capture had come at small cost. Hunter lost three killed and twenty-one wounded. Union artillery killed or wounded fifteen Rebels west of Berwick Bay.[51]

A few hours later, news of the disaster at Brashear City washed over Lieutenant Colonel Duganne at his camps on Bayou Boeuf at the far end of Tiger Island. A wave of fleeing locomotive crews arrived mid-morning with two engines but no cars. Later, a handcar arrived from Tigerville with news that the Rebels were only eight miles out that direction. Duganne realized that he now lay between two Rebel armies. As the minutes ticked by, a steady tide of fleeing black families, civilian railroad employees, and a smattering of white and black troops followed. By midday, the flow of refugees was pouring in from both directions.

The surrounded New York officer and his men faced a terrible dilemma. Groceries and cartridges had been aboard the boxcars abandoned back at Brashear City. Duganne had no rations and barely enough ammunition at hand to make a fight. He might rush down the tracks toward Terrebonne Station but feared he would only trade being captured by one group of Rebels for another. His only option remained to improve his fortifications and fields of fire and make the best stand he could. Then, he would hope for the best and possible rescue by the Federals coming from Lafourche Crossing. Some of those gathered refused to stay. Duganne ordered the railroad engineers to disable the locomotives. They did so, knowing that if the Confederates caught them, they might face an ugly vengeance for having collaborated with the Yankees. Their task complete, they and several civilians, including government plantation managers, located a skiff and pushed off down Bayou Boeuf, less fearful of the surrounding swamps than of the onrushing Rebels.[52]

Deciding to stand, Duganne attempted to improve his odds. Across Bayou Boeuf stood an enormous sugarhouse that served as a storage facility for the XIXth Army Corps. It contained all of the spare baggage, private effects, and personal plunder of the two divisions of Banks's army that had advanced up the Teche two months before. Letters from home, diaries, books, Bibles, blankets, coats, and the like lay in large stacks and bundles, each marked with a man's name

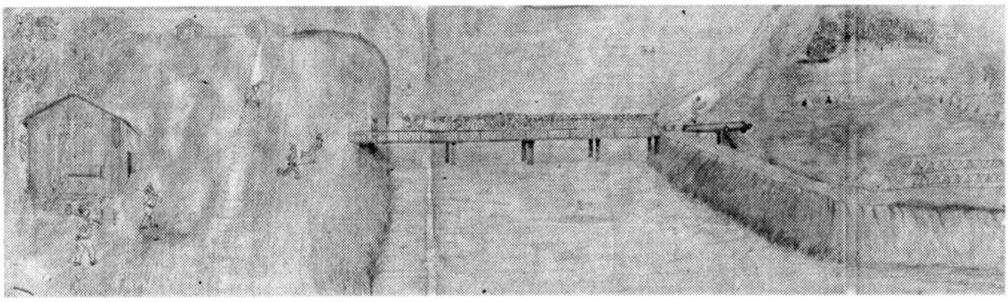

This sketch from Morgan Wolfe Merrick shows the bridge that remained intact over Bayou Boeuf as well as the Federal camp and artillery positions.
Daughters of the Republic of Texas Library, The Alamo, San Antonio, Texas.

and regiment. Duganne regretted it, but he ordered the sugarhouse and its contents burned, reasoning that the structure would only provide cover for the enemy and its contents spoils of war. Better to burn it than let it become booty. "With a sigh over the necessary sacrifice, I . . . devoted the baggage of brother officers," he wrote, "to the flame of a Federal bonfire." Secondly, he ordered Captain Dwight Hopkins to lead his Company K, 23rd Connecticut to Bayou Ramos, a little more than a mile to the west, to burn the railroad and wagon bridges there, and to hold on as long as possible against whatever came.[53]

Lastly, Duganne called for men from the *Corps d'Afrique* to step forward from the mob of people gathering and milling at the Bayou Boeuf camps. He would put these one hundred or so soldiers to work. Supply officers issued weapons and equipment. "Several . . . of the *Corps d'Afrique* have come in among the fugitives from Brashear," he wrote. "In making a stand, the blacks can be serviceable."[54]

He pinned his hopes on the Union troops at Lafourche Crossing. Certainly they could sweep aside the Confederates down the tracks and rescue his remnant. "I am sure," he reasoned, "they . . . lost no time in bringing a few regiments from New Orleans, by rail, to hang upon the rear of Major and his mustangs." He had no way of knowing that Colonel Cahill had not moved further than the wrecked tracks at Terrebonne Station where he waited for a repair crew from New Orleans.[55]

Green understood that the fight remained unfinished. Two locomotives had gotten away, and he had yet to see Major or his men. Late that afternoon, Green organized his command for pursuit and gave chase. At Bayou Ramos, two miles west of the last Union strongpoint on Tiger Island, he caught the Federals as they torched both the railroad and the public bridge. With daylight fading, Green's

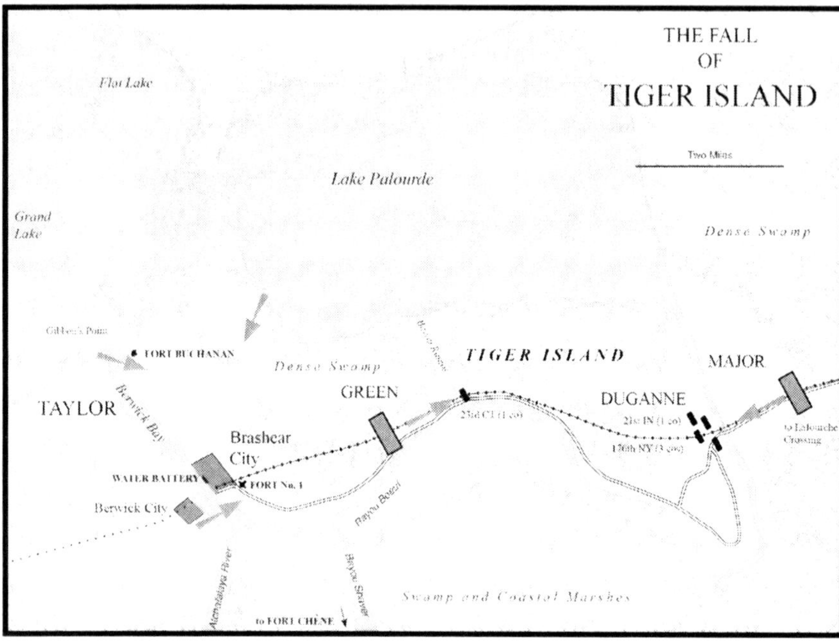

troops neared the stream but were met by scattered gunfire from the opposite bank. "I had quite an animated skirmish . . . at the Ramos," Green reported. This holding action and the burning spans delayed the Texan pursuit for several hours. That evening, the Confederates swam men across the stream and around the right flank of the Connecticut troops making the stand, and the Federals fell back. That night, General Green made his headquarters in a house on the Brashear side of Bayou Ramos. Having dislodged the Connecticut troops, he believed the coming hours would witness his Texans gobbling up the last intact Union garrison just a few miles away. He sent a trusted scout, Leander McNelly, to see what he could learn about the enemy position.[56]

At the same time Major closed the trap. Late in the afternoon, he ordered his men to mount up and ride toward Bayou Boeuf. Arriving on its banks just before dark, he ordered his men to find a way across the bayou to flank Duganne's fort. "We were in a dilemma," remembered Colonel Walter P. Lane of the 1st Texas Partisan Rangers. "We could not go back, as we expected every hour troops from New Orleans in pursuit of us while in front there was a wide river to cross, and a strongly fortified fort facing us." Lane made a makeshift pontoon footbridge by tying sugar coolers end to end. By midnight he had his, Phillips's, and Stone's regiments across. At first light, Major intended his cannon to open fire, signaling Lane to launch his assault.[57]

In the hot darkness of the Louisiana night, one of Duganne's captains rushed into the lieutenant colonel's tent with troubling news. The Confederates had arrived in the woods just a half-mile to the west. Duganne ordered his men to their positions but had second thoughts about using men from the *Corps d'Afrique*. He ordered them into formation, to stack arms, and then to retire. He feared a massacre, he claimed; better to be re-enslaved than have vengeful Rebels slaughter them. These men, shed of their U.S. uniforms, would blend in with the majority of the people huddled in the last Union stronghold on Tiger Island. "As the dark, slow night hours wane gradually," he wrote, "I think of the thousand unhappy negro men, women, and children, who have sought refuge in this camp. Hard is their fate, to be returned to slavery after having tasted freedom." He called for his three black employees and told them to save themselves. He gave two of them his pistols, entrusting his cook George with a letter to his wife.[58]

Federal morale plummeted. Sergeant Delwya P. Lewis returned that night from his deep scouting mission and reported that he had failed to get through with his message to the Union troops near Thibodaux. Clearly, they were not coming. Duganne called his officers together, and they voted to surrender. As the sky lightened on the eastern horizon, Duganne approached the first Rebel he encountered to the west, a "dirty and dilapidated" youth. The Texan was Green's scout, McNelly, and he recived Duganne's surrender. "The post given us to hold," groaned a New Yorker, "is in the hands of the Rebels and the lone star of Texas floats over the road from Brashear almost to Algiers."[59]

Confederates soon converged from every direction to secure their prisoners. Colonel Major stepped gingerly across the railroad bridge spanning Bayou Boeuf to discover who had stolen his prize. Duganne, when questioned, seemed puzzled. He thought all the Confederates came from the same command. He had no idea where the scruffy scout fit in. "The surrender was in fact to my force," Major declared. "The gallant General Green waived the honor of the capture to me." Duganne didn't care. At least Colonel Major looked like an officer and bore the manners of a gentleman.[60]

The New Yorker asked the Confederate where he was off to next.

"New Orleans," Major replied.

"You think you will get there this time, Colonel?" Duganne jibed.

"We shall be in New Orleans by Saturday night, sir," Major assured him. It was Wednesday morning. "Nothing can stop us. We've driven your troops below Lafourche, and shall follow them to Algiers."

Duganne and Major finished their professional conversation and worked out details about protecting the private property of the officers. The Rebel turned to leave. Major allowed Duganne to keep his sword. "We shall meet in New Orleans, Colonel," Major said with a laugh as he walked away.

"So opens our intercourse with Texans," Duganne noted, "of whom we conceive quite a favorable first impression."

Colonel Joseph Phillips of the 3rd Arizona, a Virginian, came up soon after. He demanded—and received—Duganne's sword. The time for gallantry had passed.[61]

10

Retaking the Lafourche

His name was General Green, sir! Not to be trifled with.
—Captain Augustine Thompson
28th Maine Infantry

"I predicted that young Stonewall, General Dick Taylor, would . . . astonish the entire Confederacy by his acts," crowed a correspondent for the Houston *Tri-Weekly Telegraph.* The Confederate hammer and anvil had met, and General Richard Taylor's audacious plan had worked. Colonel James P. Major addressed his men. "Starting badly armed and clothed and partially mounted, you . . . in a word, [freed] from the tyranny of the vandal hordes of Yankeedom the finest and richest portion of Louisiana." Their campaign had also been about protecting the folks back home. "The gallant officers and soldiers from Texas of this brigade," he added, "while they are suffering and fighting in Louisiana, they are defending the homes and firesides of the loved one in our own state."[1]

The operation to capture Brashear City had been daring and complex. Colonel Major's Brigade had traveled 176 miles in four days, averaging 44 miles a day, and passed through enemy territory to arrive at the rendezvous with General Tom Green. Majors Sherod Hunter, James Blair, and their 320 men paddled more than 12 miles at night across unfamiliar waterways to arrive at their point of attack. Green's bombardment, Major's raid, and Hunter's forlorn hope, organized far from each other over the course of a week, had all come together at nearly the precise moment to bring about success against daunting odds. "General Taylor . . . told Texans what he wanted done, and when he wanted it done, and then left them free, as a committee of ways and means, to execute," bragged Private William Lott Davidson of the 5th Texas Cavalry. A writer for the newspaper in Houston believed Taylor could not have done it without soldiers from the Lone Star State. "He had many of our Texas jewels with him," his story read, "and where they go they win fresh laurels."[2]

Colonel Thomas Cahill took command of the Union forces in the Lafourche District but quickly lost his nerve and retreated to New Orleans, his army routed.
Center for Military History.

To many, operations on Berwick Bay and along the Lafourche indicated military genius. "General Taylor has given promise of a great General," the editorial in the Houston *Tri-Weekly Telegraph* continued. "This brilliant achievement stamps him as no common man." The Confederates, reunited on Tiger Island, spent little time basking in their fame, but plunged back into the Lafourche District. Green and Major headed toward Thibodaux and Taylor busied himself with securing the captured material at Brashear City. He ordered General Alfred Mouton to follow the push to Thibodaux with his Texas and Louisiana infantry.[3]

Green, Major, and their onrushing Texans spooked Union Colonel Thomas Cahill. Troops from the 15th Maine and the remnant of the 176th New York covered by the four guns of the 25th New York Battery occupied Thibodaux shortly after Major had left. Now, he had no way of knowing where the enemy lurked. On the morning of June 24, while Confederates mopped up the last of the Federal troops at the Boeuf, Cahill dispatched five companies of the 9th Connecticut from LaFourche Crossing to guard a railroad repair crew heading toward the break in the tracks at Terrebonne Station. Having finished that task, they pressed on cautiously toward Brashear City, seeing smoke from a burning bridge near Chacahoula Station. They also spotted Confederate pickets.[4]

"As we came in sight of the rebels they opened a brisk fire," reported Captain John G. Healy of the 9th Connecticut. "The rebels had the advantage of us, as they were fighting from behind the cover of houses, while our men were on the railroad track." The New Englanders took casualties. One soldier, shot through the body, loaded and fired twice more before collapsing. Another Yankee fell back, his arm shattered. A third writhed in pain, a bullet passing through his left arm and into his ribs. Two other skirmishers surrendered. The Union forces could advance no further without provoking a serious dustup. Brashear City had obviously fallen. The men of the 9th Connecticut retreated, fearing that Rebel cavalry might bypass them as they rode for Thibodaux.[5]

This move proved prescient. That same afternoon, June 24, the warning of Green's approach came as thousands of white and black refugees poured into Thibodaux like rabbits before a grassfire. Panic spread to the Union ranks as rumors arrived in rapid succession placing the Texans at a dozen different points. The Federals in town fell back across the bayou and covered the bridge. Cahill telegraphed for more cars to carry his sizable command to safety. "Matters began to look ominous," reported Captain John Grow of the 25th New York Battery. Cahill ordered cannon fired to recall the 9th Connecticut—still somewhere down the tracks. Those Federals returned, less five of their men, and also reported Texans coming their way. Cahill sent out Captain Charles Blober and his Louisiana cavalry to make contact and keep him advised.[6]

By 8:00 P.M., no trains had arrived and panic nipped at the heels of Federal officers near Thibodaux and spread as far as New Orleans. None of the Union commanders had actually seen the Rebels in any numbers but remained certain they were near. Cahill telegraphed General William H. Emory. "The enemy is advancing on both sides of Bayou Lafourche in large force, four miles above," adding, "my trains have not arrived." Emory's reply only stoked the panic. "Why do you wait for the train? Destroy the artillery, if necessary," he wrote. Cahill ordered his entire command back to Lafourche Crossing, fearing an attack that night. Federals burned the Thibodaux bridge and fell back.[7]

About the same time, Emory received word of the fall of Brashear City, sparking a false epiphany. As Cahill reported, the troops that captured Brashear must be *different* than those that had attacked Lafourche Crossing three days before. The Rebels now had twice as many men as he previously thought, with reports of perhaps ten thousand more coming. He telegraphed Cahill to get out—quickly. "If you cannot bring your horses, kill every one on the spot," Emory tapped. "Kill them with a knife, so the enemy will not hear your guns." Union officers executed these orders. "Up to this time not a soul of our own forces had seen or heard of an enemy," grumbled Grow. Some of the troops, impatient to be off, marched overland to Raceland Station, twelve miles away.[8]

Eventually trains arrived at Lafourche Crossing to carry away the balance of Cahill's shaken command. By midnight, reason had evaporated when the cars arrived at Raceland Station. "The colonel's aides seemed to be possessed with the besom of destruction," Captain Grow howled. Cahill's army disintegrated. On orders, gunners spiked all four of the 25th New York's cannon, dumped ammunition in the bayou, and turned out battery horses to make room on the cars for soldiers. The victors of Lafourche Crossing returned to New Orleans a rabble. "There was no necessity of a retreat," Grow protested from the safety of the Metarie Racecourse outside the city. "We were strong enough to hold our position," the red leg captain admonished. "Two thousand men, with one battery can with the aid of a good gunboat, retake Brashear City. I am satisfied the enemy are not 2,000 strong." On the morning of June 25, as he watched his demoralized men come in, Emory disagreed, estimating instead that he faced upward of twelve thousand.[9]

The Texans kept up the pressure, adding to Union jitters. Confederate cavalry units—the 13th Texas Cavalry Battalion and the 2nd Texas Cavalry—under the command of Lieutenant Colonel Hannibal H. Boone attacked Bayou des Allemandes and shoved aside a small Union garrison, then continued on past Boutte Station. With these posts cleared, Boone continued toward New Orleans and the Union works on the far bank of the Barataria Company Canal, just eight miles down the tracks from Algiers and three miles below the imposing works at Camp Parapet across the river. Wishing to avoid another frontal assault, Taylor ordered Boone to gather boats at Lake Salvador to flank the Union works on the west side of the river in a *coup de main* as he had done at Brashear City. Taylor also believed that a "nest of smugglers" located at Barataria might help as well, as in the days of Jean Lafitte and Andrew Jackson. Union officers, afraid of this rapid advance, advised the garrisons at Forts St. Philip and Jackson to be on guard lest the Confederates "surprise and capture you, as Brashear City had been, and by the same party."[10]

Emory inflated the danger by more than double. Besides the nearly 2,300 cavalry under Brigadier General Green and Colonel Major, General Mouton marched Colonels Joseph Warren Speight and Henry Gray with about 2,000 Texas and Louisiana infantry to Thibodaux. A makeshift mounted brigade composed of the cavalry squadron of the 11th Texas Volunteer Battalion, the 2nd Louisiana, two companies of the 5th Texas, and the 2nd Arizona—about 1,000 additional mounted troops—served as a reserve. Taylor had few other troops at hand. The artillery and infantry of the 13th Texas Volunteers crossed over at Brashear City with Lieutenant Colonel Ashley W. Spaight's infantry of the 11th Texas Volunteer Battalion—in all about seven hundred men—to serve as a garrison. Although not as many as Emory feared, the Confederates did outnumber the Union troops in the Lafourche District and defenses of New Orleans by nearly three-to-one.

From Brashear City, General Taylor extolled his triumphs. "The quantity of quartermaster's and commissary and ordnance stores captured at this place exceeds belief," he wrote to General Edmund Kirby Smith. He also enjoyed some personal satisfaction. Two of the captured 24-pounders had come from his own works at Bisland the previous June; Confederates fished a 12-pounder lost in that battle from the bayou at Raceland as well. Taylor mounted four of his new heavy guns at Fort Berwick on the Atchafalaya below that village, and another two at Fort Chêne. Should the Federals attack from the Gulf, he would at least cause them trouble.[11]

Tools of war abounded. Besides the food, clothing, and ammunition, he counted five thousand Enfield rifles and Burnside carbines, several 30-pounder Parrot Rifles, $3 million worth of food, $1.5 million in clothing, 250,000 rounds of ammunition, $100,000 in medicines, one thousand tents, and two thousand horses and mules. Confederates who entered the battle wearing butternut and gray jean cloth now advanced wearing Union uniforms—ironically from the stockpiles intended for the new black regiments. The flags from the 176th New York, 23rd Connecticut, 42nd Massachusetts, and 21st Indiana also became trophies. "Every courier . . . brings official intelligence of the increased value and quantity of the capture," one Texan gushed. Having informed General Kirby Smith that all was well in south Louisiana—and that Colonel Major should be promoted to brigadier general—Taylor pushed on to Thibodaux to command the next phase of his campaign to relieve Port Hudson.[12]

Other Confederates tended to the more than one thousand Union prisoners. Captured officers headed to Camp Ford in Tyler, Texas, to await exchange. The Federal enlisted men received paroles and the 2nd Arizona Cavalry escorted them to New Orleans. Both armies considered breaches of such accords to be serious, potentially deadly. One Texan officer saw U.S. troops with emblems of the 42nd Massachusetts Infantry on their gear and assumed they had violated their parole from a battle in Texas the previous January. "It was hard work to make the fool understand that only three companies of the regiment were made prisoner at Galveston," Private Charles P. Bosson wrote, "and not the entire regiment."[13]

Troops from the 2nd Louisiana Cavalry remained in Brashear City, as did the men of the 11th and 13th Texas volunteers, and to them fell the majority of the spoils. "Our boys have been helping themselves pretty freely, as the whole town was lined with Yankee plunder," reported Sergeant John Sibley of the 2nd Louisiana Cavalry. The soldier from near Many, Louisiana, in Caddo Parish, packed a number of mementos including pocket Bibles, coats, letters, newspapers, and novelties for shipment home. "Tell ma that I could not find anything that I thought would suit her but a little glass lamp," he wrote. "I sent a sundial, I reckon you never saw one before. It is placed in the sun to tell the time of day." He also had his photograph taken in a captured Yankee suit—he pilfered it and a letter from the personal effects of Private Albert Lapham, a soldier in the 4th Massachusetts. Sibley lamented that he arrived too late to send something nice for his wife. "I was very anxious to get you some calico, muslin domestic, etc., of which there was an abundance here," he explained. "As I was not an officer I could not get into the government stores before all the fancy goods were all disposed of."[14]

Some of the Federals bemoaned the loss of their possessions. One had papers that belonged to a famous Rebel. "In my knapsack I had several letters which I had found in the garret of General Dick Taylor's house near the Mississippi River," wrote Connecticut Corporal Andrew Sherman. He also had seashells collected at Ship Island. "I have often wondered, what became of these articles."[15]

When soldiers from Brashear City trickled into New Orleans, word of its sacking spread throughout General Nathaniel P. Banks's army. Officers learned that private possessions left behind in storage had either burned or carried away as loot. Captain Dyer D. Bullock, Company H, 114th New York lamented his losses, writing, "I am sorry to say that my trunk, with all my choice clothing, and all my military paraphernalia and company books, was captured, the value of which is over three hundred dollars of my own private property. We were ordered to leave all behind when we marched to Port Hudson." The captain now owned only a spare set of drawers besides the uniform on his back.[16]

Among the spoils of war taken at Brashear City was this suit, possibly once owned by Albert Lapham of Duxbury, Massachusetts, a soldier in the 4th Massachusetts Infantry whose personal effects Sibley pilfered. Sibley sent his wife one of the Yankee's letters from home as a trophy, as well as this photo taken in his new clothes.
John Coleman Sibley Collection, Cammie G. Henry Research Center, Northwestern State University of Louisiana, Natchitoches, LA.

Sergeant John Coleman Sibley of the 2nd Louisiana Cavalry poses with a Federal frock coat, carbine, and other uniform trapping taken at Brashear City.
Courtesy of Donald Parker, Indianapolis, Indiana.

The sheer abundance of Union stockpiles stupefied the Confederates who walked the streets of Brashear City, picking through its camps, and examining their prizes. Banks—"Commissary Banks" to General Thomas "Stonewall" Jackson's Army—served a similar role in Louisiana. "Banks's provisions and supplies will [feed] about forty thousand men," Private H. F. Kopke wrote. "We got two thousand barrels flour and one hundred fifty thousand pounds of coffee. The Yanks live like kings." The German personally stuffed bacon, flour, potatoes, dried peas, apples, and pickles into his haversack. He also donned a new uniform of Union blue and sky-blue kersey. "We have new clothes, boots, shoes, and everything a person can wear," he marveled. "We got Yankee clothing, it is beautiful woolens, ten times better than our gray material."[17]

The once orderly camp turned into a dishevled sty. "Brashear looks dreary enough at present," wrote Quartermaster Sergeant George Haven Putnam of the 176th New York. "Our long line of deserted and pillaged encampments, the closed and empty houses, the vacant railroad depot . . . the desolation and disorder everywhere . . . contrasts most painfully with the animation, busy life, and neatness of the scene a fortnight ago."[18]

Texas Colonel Joseph Bates, described as "an officer with long white hair and of imposing appearance," now commanded the post. He made a point to meet the captured Union officers. "Nothing could have been more elegant, chivalric, and delightful," remembered Colonel Charles C. Nott of the 176th New York. "He could not have been more courteous and respectful." The two talked about the differences between New Yorkers and Texans. Bates "spoke highly of the Texan character, which, he said, excelled in bravery and simplicity."[19]

Nott agreed with this assessment. He had an escort from Spaight's Battalion that challenged his previously held notions of Texans as scapegraces. "They . . . completed our confusion as to what Wild Texans are," he observed. "They did not drink; they did not swear; they did not gamble. They were watchful of us, but did everything kindly and with a willingness that greatly lessened our feeling of dependence." Nott admired the look of these Lone Star soldiers. One corporal he described "was mounted on a compact little bay, called in Texas a pony; a long revolver was stuck in his belt; a lariat rope loosely coiled hung on the saddle bow; his bright Springfield was balanced across the pommel, and with his broad hat and heavy, jangling Spanish spurs, he formed a brilliant picture of a Wild Texan."[20]

Most of these captured Federals had never seen a Confederate soldier before, and certainly not a Texan. Yankee and Rebel found common cause. The men of the Lone Star State, like the New Englanders and New Yorkers in their care, grumbled about service in Louisiana. "Dog gone the Lousanny climate, and the bayous, and the beef, and dog gone the Lousanyans," one Texan groused to a captured New York officer. "They're the meanest set of people ever I see. I'd just as soon shoot one of 'em as a Yank." Sergeant Putnam reported similar findings. "They don't consort readily with the Louisianians, whom they call 'lazy, cowardly Creoles,' and by whom they are cordially hated and termed 'Comanches and thieves,'" he wrote home. "Both charges have, I expect, some foundation."[21]

The Texans and the Yankees got along. "One of the Rebel captains appeared to take quite a fancy to me, and wanted me to go home with him to Texas," Sergeant Putnam wrote his mother, "where he said he would direct my energies and my spunk into better courses than the defence of abolitionism." The literate New Yorkers and New Englanders tried to swap books with their captors but found few takers. Sergeant Putnam, the son of one of the nation's most important publishers, George Palmer Putnam, seemed astounded. "One Texas captain to whom I offered some books told me there was not a man in his company could read," Putnam reported. If these soldiers could not read, then how could they understand and study the issues of the day? Why did they fight? When he asked the Texans, their answers bewildered him. Some said they fought to oppose the Emancipation Proclaimation, only recently passed. "Many of the privates have very confused notions of what they are fighting for," he concluded. "When caught off their guard . . . many of the privates say openly they would give much if some accomodation could be made, in order to bring the war to an end, and give them a chance to see their homes again."[22]

Beyond the lines of prisoners and the officials taking inventory of the war booty, Union and Confederate surgeons cleaned up the battle's human wreckage. The hot, steamy weather made conditions unbearable. Sergeant Putnam volunteered to help with nursing duties, missing his chance at parole and removal to New Orleans with the rest of the enlisted men, and instead found himself surrounded by misery. "The old plantation house," he remembered, "became a very uncomfortable center of suffering. Fortunately perhaps for the doctor, the men died pretty fast, and those who died first had the easiest time." Maggots crawled in most wounds. Amputees died within days, if not hours. Putnam believed nearly three hundred battlefield casualties passed through the door, suffering from "the heat, the stench from the wounds, and the dirt of the building which . . . was impossible to keep clean."[23]

First Sergeant George Ballow of the 42nd Massachusetts faced the surgeon's saw. The Rebel bullet that caught him while he defended the train had gouged out more than two inches of the long ulna bone in his forearm and broken the radius. He refused to lose the limb. The New York surgeon packed the wound, set his remaining bone, and promised to do his best. "Sergeant Ballow saved his arm and hand," Private Bosson recalled, "but the hand has never been of use to him since."[24]

Re-enslaved laborers carried away the dead. Some they hauled off prematurely. A Rebel surgeon saw two laborers bringing a blanket-wrapped body back from the cemetery. "The Texan surgeon," observed Putnam, "asked pretty roughly what the men were doing with that thing."

"Why massa! We done seen him kick," came the response.

"Well put him down where you stand," the Southerner demanded. "He'll be ready for you before night."[25]

The newcomers also discovered horrors behind the Union camps. The Louisiana thunderstorms over the previous days had washed the dirt from graves near the town and across Tiger Island. "We have very much rain here," Kopke wrote to his father in German. "When the Yankees buried the dead, they dug a hole and dumped everybody in it, whether it was deep enough or not," he noted. "I have seen hands not buried . . . flesh and parts not under the dirt; I have seen boots away from the body with someone's foot and part of the leg still in the boot." Days after he penned this letter, Kopke caught the common malady of Brashear City and died, his corpse tossed into one of graves he found so revolting.[26]

As it had the Yankees before them, disease ravaged the Texan garrison. Sergeant Putnam saw Rebels passing through the hospital in a steady stream. "This Louisiana climate . . . seems to sicken Texans as fast or faster than it acts upon Northern troops, and loud and deep are the curses of the 'Lone Star' men upon this 'God forsaken land,'" he wrote. "Then the exposure to the heavy showers of this month, their utter want of cleaniness, and often of a change of clothing, and their poorly cooked food, must have damaging effects upon their constitutions."[27]

Some of the Federal captives wondered what had become of the men of the *Corps d'Afrique*. "A curious feature in regard to prisoners taken at Brashear is that no negro soldiers were among them," Bosson noted. "As no one saw or heard of any cut-throat actions towards colored Federal soldiers, the supposition would seem well founded that they all escaped capture in some way through the wooded swamps." Lieutenant Colonel Augustine Joseph Hickey Duganne believed the Rebels had simply not taken black prisoners. "We hear that many blacks were murdered by the rebels during the attack on Brashear City," he wrote. This same officer, though, admitted to having the black soldiers strip off their Union uniforms to blend in with the civilians. The four *Corps d'Afrique* officers taken in the fight would face weeks in chains and solitary confinement—and an uncertain fate.[28]

While Cahill and his Federal forces evacuated the Lafourche District, Taylor continued his great effort to relieve Port Hudson. On the evening of June 24, he gathered his commanders at Thibodaux and ordered them to fan out across the Lafourche District. Boone and his Texas cavalry would attempt a move to the Mississippi below New Orleans. Green and Major would head toward Donaldsonville and hazard the Mississippi above the Crescent City. Mouton's infantry moved to Napoleonville and took position to support either effort while detachments from these, and mounted troops, gathered useful plunder.

Confederate reports noted between four and seven thousand liberated slaves recaptured. Given the stockpile of weapons, uniforms, medicines, and rations they had taken at Brashear, these estimates may have only counted those likely to be pressed as soldiers. The total might have been higher if observers had tallied women, children, and the elderly. Confederate officials returned captured blacks to their owners if possible, sold those with unclear titles, and put others to work for the Confederacy. Notwithstanding Duganne's fears, the recaptured slaves were simply too valuable to slaughter.[29]

Colonel Nott overhead two Texans discussing the fate of the captured blacks: "The niggers don't look as if they wanted to see us," he heard one Confederate soldier say to another.

"No," said the other, "but you'll see a herd of fat planters here after them. *They* don't fight any, but they are always on hand for their niggers."[30]

Indeed, Louisiana planters did shadow the army hoping to recover their slave property. Instead of the well-toned and obedient chattel that had worked their farms before the war, they discovered insolent, broken, and bewildered people suffering from nightmarish conditions and rampant disease. East of Bayou Ramos, in a thicket of undergrowth and briars, "were encamped—without shelter—a wretched, death stricken crowd of human beings who, but a few short weeks before, had been driven from their homes," wrote one observer. Decomposing corpses littered the woods nearby. The stench was overpowering.[31]

Henry T. Sanders's sugarhouse, near Bayou Ramos and in between the rail and wagon road, harbored additional horrors. "Soon the door was approached," a witness recounted, "but most recoiled at the first view." Hundreds of newly freed people suffered inside of what had been an attempt at a hospital. Dr. George Hill of Opelousas ventured in. "On the right hand female corpses in a state of nudity, and also in a far advanced stage of decomposition," he noted. "Many others were lying all over the floor, many speechless and . . . dying." Feces, mucus, vomit, and blood from rampant dysentery slicked the floor. "All appeared to have died of the same disease," the physician concluded. "Bloody flux."[32]

The doomed suffered horribly. Most had forgone clothing from the waist down because of the frequency and violence of their intestinal distress. "Every time an involuntary discharge of blood and feces, combined with air, would pass, making a slight noise," Doctor Hill observed, "clouds of flies, such as I never saw before, would immediately rise and settle down again on all the exposed parts of the dying." He could not bear it. "In passing through," he wrote, "a cold chill shook my frame."[33]

Captain Silas Grisamore, quartermaster of the 18th Louisiana Infantry, passed that way sometime later, en route to the Lafourche. He had reached Bayou Ramos near midnight, threw down a blanket, and slept until sunrise only to discover he had rested amid a sea of graves. Shaking off his revulsion, the soldier pressed on to Sanders's sugarhouse searching for items of use for the army. Instead, he "saw one of the most horrible sights ever witnessed. There were about 50 Negro men and women lying around, some of them dead, others dying, some of them being eaten by worms before life was extinct." He described it as a "panorama of filth, destitution, and misery." He hurried his wagons past and on toward Tigerville, but the horrors continued. "The roads," he wrote, "were lined with Negroes half starved, almost destitute of clothing, sick and unable to help themselves . . . who had been two months experiencing Federal sympathy and charity."[34]

Colonel Bates sent the foot soldiers of Lieutenant Colonel Spaight's 11th Texas Volunteers to Bayou Boeuf to guard the railroad bridge. They also hunted for fugitive blacks. "There we saw Negro freedom and Yankee cruelty in its prime," wrote Sergeant H. N. Connor. "We found them dead and dying, in the outhouses, fields, swamps, and by the road side. And those who had died . . . were found buried in slight ditches, and the rain had washed off the dirt and left them exposed." The dreadfulness of Sanders's sugarhouse repeated itself at nearly every plantation in the area. "The sugar houses were filled with them, dead, dying, and rotting, until the stench was such as to be nearly impossible to be borne, [even] for a few seconds," recorded Conner. When asked, the black refugees claimed that Banks had simply abandoned them on Tiger Island, which, of course, he had. "Disease and starvation was what they had found in place of freedom," concluded Conner. These benighted people, glad to be fed, looked for a way out of their predicament. "After we caught them, they . . . wanted to go to their homes," the Texan noted, "or ours if we chose to take them."[35]

Louisiana slave owners from the Teche country scoured Tiger Island and the Lafourche District near Thibodaux looking for people that were once their property. "[In] the cabins of every government plantation were found some of the living, while the adjacent fields were marked by the graves of many of the dead." When they did find their former slaves, many had been separated from their loved ones by the Federal labor system. "Dismembered fragments of families were found recklessly scattered, without regard to affinities of family ties," claimed one Confederate official. Children had lost parents to the army or to government plantations; parents had lost children to disease or exposure. "Every planter who lost slaves has . . . tales to tell," observed a Louisianan.[36]

The Confederates took measures to save those they could. Colonel Bates ordered sick and unclaimed blacks rounded up and relocated across Berwick Bay where they could be nursed—and returned to distant owners if possible. "Had this not been promptly done," an observer wrote, "it is the opinion of the medical men present that every soul, amounting to many hundreds, would have perished." Even so, an estimated two thousand of the ten thousand emancipated slaves that had come from the Teche Country died between April and July.[37]

Duganne witnessed the exodus of blacks from Tiger Island back up the Teche, driven like livestock. "Rebel steamboats are constantly conveying plunder away," he noted. "Trains of captured negroes, mules, horses, are daily crossed to Berwick, and thence to be convoyed to upper Louisiana and Texas." Crowds of slave owners collected them and headed home. "For days, planter after planter appeared, and party after party of men, women, and children, laden with their beds and baggage, tramped sorrowfully past our quarters," Colonel Nott remembered.[38] Re-enslaved blacks from the Lafourche District also passed by. "It is bitter to see them look half-reproachingly, half imploringly, to us as they are driven off like sheep to the slaughter," Putnam wrote, "as if to say, 'How could you betray us, promising us liberty and safety, and now abandoning us to slavery and misery worse than death.'"[39]

Yet, some liberated slaves managed escape. New Orleans experienced a wave of black refugees fleeing the Confederate advance. Private Rufus Kinsley of the 8th Vermont, recuperating at the hospital there, expected an attack on the city; the harbinger was the crowds of blacks streaming in from the Lafourche District.

This view up Canal Street portrays a deceptively peaceful New Orleans.
Marshal Dunham Photograph Album, Mss. 3241, Louisiana and Lower Mississippi Valley Collection, Louisiana State University Libraries, Baton Rouge.

"These guerilla raids have frightened several thousand negroes that General Banks has hired out to slaveholders," he noted, "and they are flocking to New Orleans in droves."[40]

As Taylor gathered his Rebel army at Thibodaux, dispatches arrived from Lieutenant General Joseph E. Johnston regarding Vicksburg that demanded Taylor's attention. He immediately departed for Alexandria. With luck, he would be returning with General John G. Walker's Division from east of Monroe to lend their muscle to the next phase of operations. In addition, the weapons captured at Brashear would do much to equip two Texas infantry regiments training at Shreveport. They could also come to Brashear. Taylor left Mouton, the ranking officer in Thibodaux, in charge of securing the Lafourche—the same region he had surrendered nine months before.[41]

While Taylor headed north, Mouton dawdled. Most of Green's Texas cavalry spent two days gathering at Thibodaux and scouting the roads, having spent time moving their horses from west of Berwick Bay. On June 26, Union cavalry pickets

The news of Federal disasters in the Lafourche District caused many a worried glance upstream beyond the extensive wharves of New Orleans.
Marshal Dunham Photograph Album, Mss. 3241, Louisiana and Lower Mississippi Valley Collection, Louisiana State University Libraries, Baton Rouge.

at the Kesslar Plantation tangled with the Texans, but the Federals scampered away to Donaldsonville, alerting the garrison at Fort Butler. After whiling away the better part of two days, Mouton decided that Green had better take Donaldsonville to keep the Federals from pushing reinforcements into the Lafourche District from the Mississippi. The Texan obeyed, leading his and Major's brigade out of Thibodaux that evening. Four cannon and the red-shirted gunners of Oliver Semmes's Louisiana Battery accompanied Green's small army.[42]

The few Federals left in the Lafourche District, first alerted by the raid at Plaquemine, and now fully aware of the fall of Brashear City, realized that a crashing wave of Rebels was about to break upon them. Admiral David G. Farragut directed three ships to take positions along the Mississippi approaches to Donaldsonville and directed others to stand by in case they were needed. When Major had slipped by a few days before, Union regimental officers at Fort Butler had prepared to defend their position. Major Joseph D. Bullen, with two

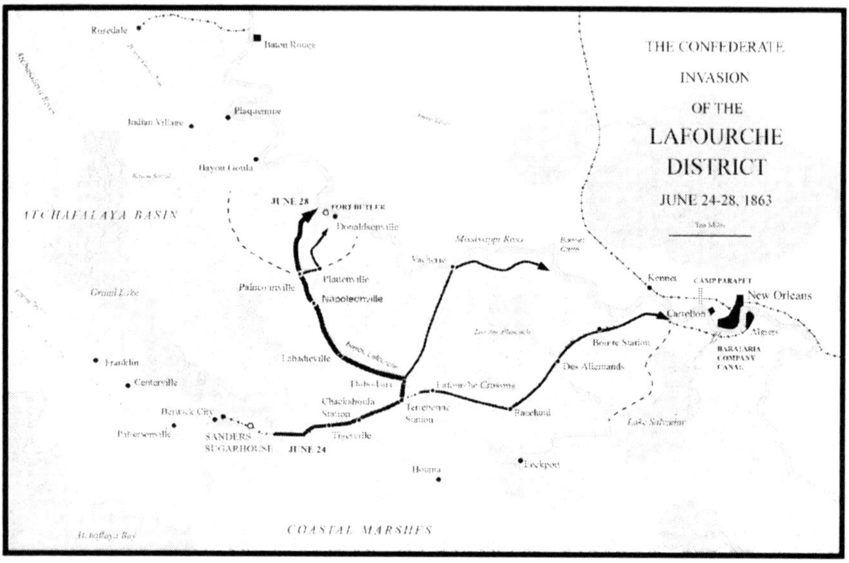

companies of the 28th Maine and a few dozen convalescents, knew he must have more troops if he was to hold Fort Butler and end the string of Union disasters.[43]

Bullen held many advantages. An impressive design, Fort Butler featured three landward facing bastions each mounting a 32-pound howitzer. From above, it resembled a fractured six-pointed star with the missing piece on the Mississippi side. Bayou Lafourche protected it from the south, and the Mississippi, potentially alive with Union gunboats, guarded its rear. Engineers had incorporated the Mississippi and Bayou Lafourche levees into the rear rampart of the fort. Stockades made from eight-foot tall upright logs defended its flanks by serving as extensions of the northern and western walls and intersecting the waterways at right angles. A sixteen-foot wide and twelve-foot deep brick-lined moat protected the western walls.[44]

Ever since the report of the Rebel attack at Plaquemine, Bullen worked to upgrade his defenses. The imposing fort had served well as a symbol of Federal authority and as a headquarters for local provosts since the previous November. The Confederates, however, had never challenged its defenses. Warehouses, quarters, and other buildings radiated out to the west. These would have to go, Bullen decided, lest they cover an enemy advance while blocking the sweep of his guns. Troops with torches trotted out to see it done. The moat, although impressive, could be bridged with ladders and planks. Bullen wanted to slow down any enemy assaults and keep them under fire as long as possible. He ordered his men to create an extensive *abatis*—a French military term literally meaning a "pile of tossed down things." Axe men downed trees to create the obstacle belt beyond the moat that also cleared a nine hundred-foot wide field of fire that his cannon could sweep with abandon. If the Texans attacked from the west, they would be tangled up in tree branches, blocked by ditches, and raked with canister.

The fort's Mississippi face challenged Bullen and his officers. No moat protected the opposite side of the levee. The fluctuations of water levels in the river made one impractical—and if connected to the moat on the other side, it might cause a massive crevasse during the spring rise. During the summer, though, the water remained low. Bullen apparently ordered his men to dig a ditch anyway. Should the Confederates get past the northern stockade and sweep across the space known as the *batture* (French for foreground) between the river and levee they would still have to negotiate this additional obstacle. There would be little time to dig it as deep as those in front of the fort, or line it with bricks, but anything to slow an attack might help.

His tiny garrison had additional laborers to assist with these projects. A week prior, companies D and F, 1st Engineers, *Corps d'Afrique*, had washed up at Fort Butler, carried there aboard the steamboat *Southerner* after their close call at Plaquemine. These 120 men served as pick, spade, and axe men for the improvements before rejoining their regiment at Port Hudson.[45]

Other reinforcements replaced them. Soldiers assigned as superintendents and provosts on the region's government-leased plantations brought their field hands into the fort. Drilled in the rudiments of the manual of arms, they became a black militia. Bullen doubled the size of his garrison, the four-hundred-man force a blended collection of white volunteers and black levies.[46]

The next morning, General Green arrived at a road junction near Paincourtville (French for "breadless town") having covered about twenty-four miles. His command now rested but nine miles from their objective, Green's headquarters strategically located at the Ford and Davenport Plantation astride a semi-circle of roads that could take troops to the Mississippi above or below Fort Butler. To his left, the Ricard Cut-Off road went via the Grand Bruly to twenty miles above Donaldsonville and three miles below Bayou Goula. A week before, Colonels

Walter P. Lane and Joseph Phillips had traversed this road during Major's raid. South of Bayou Lafourche and down a ways to Green's right lay the village of Plattenville and its landmark Church of the Assumption of the Blessed Virgin Mary, easily visible with binoculars from the steeple of the Church of St. Elizabeth near the Texan camps, two miles away. From Plattenville, an irregular network of farm roads stretched to the Mississippi ten miles away, hitting the levee eight river-miles below Donaldsonville. Green sent scouts ahead, to the left and to the right, to learn what he could about Fort Butler and the lay of the land. He also ordered his men to construct a makeshift footbridge from sugar coolers and planking to give access to both sides of the bayou.[47]

Secessionists in the region rejoiced at the return of the Confederate forces. As the Texan scouts rode past Sleepy Hollow Plantation, teenager Heléne Dupuy hoped to recognize friends and family among them. She did not. "The Confederates passed before our house on June 27, at 2 P.M.," she scribbled in her diary. "Our joy was great, but it would have been much greater if the Confederates had been Louisianians." A distant kinsman, thirty-eight-year-old Charles Oscar Dupuy of Plaquemine, remained optimistic. "It is reported and credited hereabout, that we have a considerable army marching on New Orleans," he wrote, "and should New Orleans be retaken, farewell to the army of Mr. Banks. The Federal endeavors to take Port Hudson have so far proved a failure, with great disasters to their troops. There is still a fair prospect of its standing their shocks yet a while."[48]

The Texans discovered a region in turmoil. The restoration of the old order placed many freedmen in a quandry. Slaves returned to their former masters hoping for refuge amid the storm of war. "The blacks are running away from the Yanks and returning to their owners," Charles Oscar Dupuy noted. "Father had eighty five negroes gone for awhile, but about twenty have returned since." Louisianans who had taken the oath of allegience to the United States now had cause for regret as Confederates plundered their farms. "Among them are some of our nearest relatives and most intimate friends, but as it is imprudent, and dangerous, I will not mention their names," cautioned one plantation owner. One of his friends, this Louisianan noted, "has swallowed [the oath], but wishes now he could throw it up again."[49]

Despite this secessionist optimism, daunting news greeted the Texan scouts. Union engineers had rendered Fort Butler formidable. It mounted six heavy guns

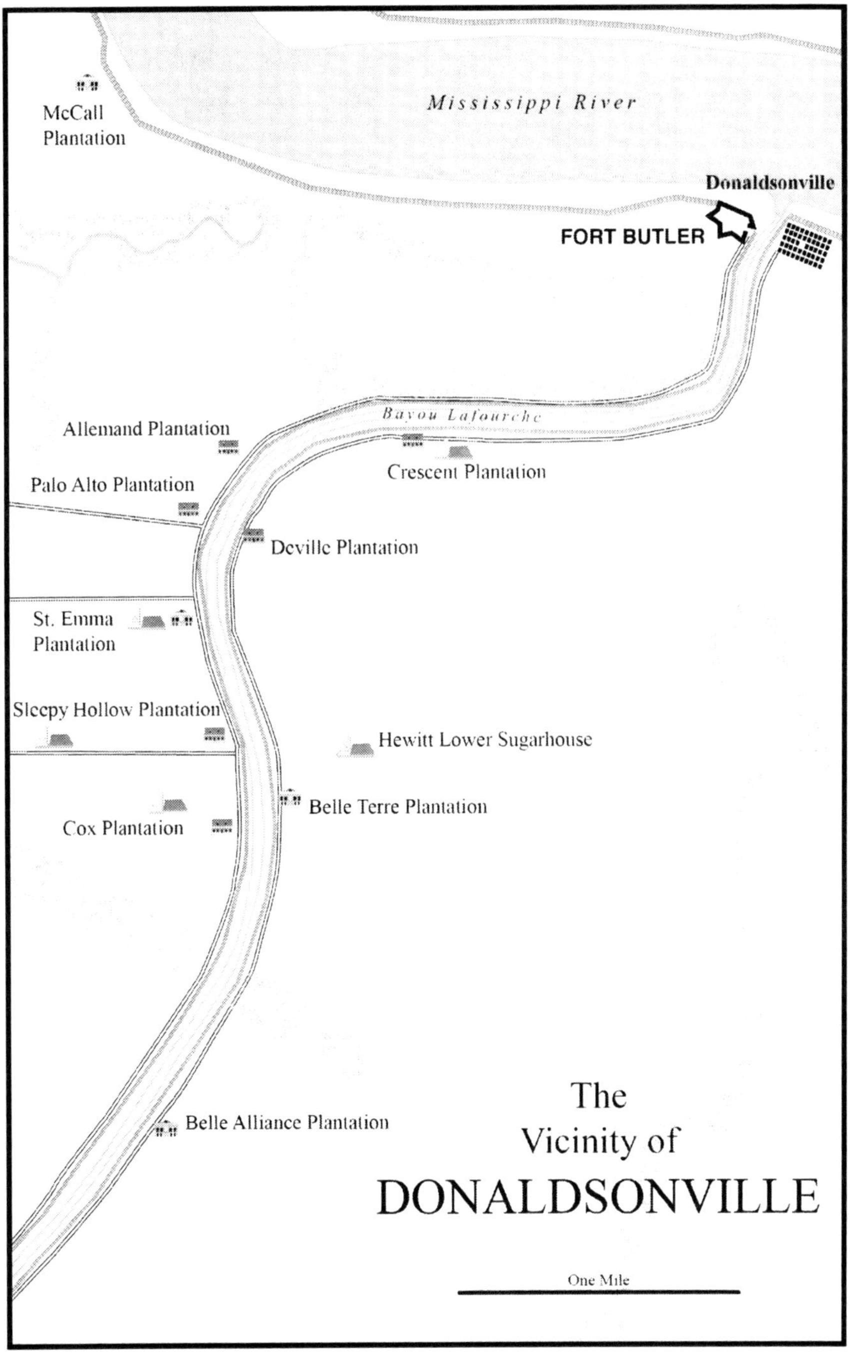
Mississippi River
McCall Plantation
Donaldsonville
FORT BUTLER
Bayou Lafourche
Allemand Plantation
Crescent Plantation
Palo Alto Plantation
Deville Plantation
St. Emma Plantation
Sleepy Hollow Plantation
Hewitt Lower Sugarhouse
Belle Terre Plantation
Cox Plantation
Belle Alliance Plantation
The Vicinity of DONALDSONVILLE
One Mile

in five bastions and fronted a wide, flat plain. One angle pointed southwest with one cannon, one due west with another gun, and one northwest bearing two. An additional gun poked out where the parapet met the Mississippi levee. A brick-lined moat protected this outer wall, as did the abatis. The main gate faced south, toward Donaldsonville. An outwork mounting one gun, just ahead of the southwest bastion, covered the approach down the Lafourche road. Green rode up to scan the fort himself and "expressed doubts as to the final result of the assault," reported Lieutenant Colonel Hugh McPhail of the 5th Texas Cavalry. The general, burdened by written orders to attack, prepared a dispatch to Mouton asking for latitude on his instructions. "Until I came down here I had no idea of the position, strength, or feasibility of taking the fort," Green reported "or the value when taken."[50]

Scouts did report weaknesses. Determined troops might breach the stout palisade bridging the batture. Then simply scaling the levee—the fort's back wall—would put them inside. A similar palisade closed the interval between the outwork and Lafourche to the south. The batture, fenced in, often served as camping grounds for troops passing through, black labor gangs, livestock, and a convenient location to stack supplies. A semi-permanent pontoon bridge connected Fort Butler with the wrecked town of Donaldsonville. None of the locals reported any obstacles beyond the palisade, although a gunboat, *Princess Royal*, had remained on station for the past week.[51]

Pierre Barre Rougeau, a long-time resident and constable of Donaldsonville, offered to guide the Rebels. A book binder and store owner before the war, this Parisian-born father of thirteen had taken the oath of allegiance to the U.S. government but now reneged. He offered to show the Texans the best avenues of approach and to serve as a guide in the fight. Two of his sons served with the Confederate army in Virginia, and he would strike a blow, for their sake, in their hometown.[52]

The Texan officers gathered to discuss the best way of cracking this Union nut. Short of a ladder assault, few had confidence they could carry the fort. A night attack might negate the Union naval strength, and once the Rebels penetrated the palisade, the heavy cannon aboard the gunboats would be inert for fear of killing the men inside the fort. Even so, the planning and execution of an assault would be tricky and many miscarriages loomed. Green concurred with his officers and reported "an attempt to storm will be attended with great loss and no adequate benefit, even if successful."[53]

Green needed a decision that he could not make alone. He believed he remained bound by Mouton's orders to carry Fort Butler but did not want to disregard the views of his officers or the reports of his scouts. If Mouton truly believed it critical to reduce the fort, he should see to it himself. "Come down and take command," Green urged. "I want you badly as I do not know fully what your views are, and would not like to take any steps in conflict with them."[54]

It was Mouton's decision, not Green's, to make.

11

Fort Butler

If we ever meet them again, we have made up our minds to leave none of them unscalped.
—Anonymous Private, 3rd Arizona Cavalry

As General Tom Green awaited clarification, his officers persisted in arguing against the attack and urged him to ignore General Alfred Mouton's order. Veterans of many a battle—from Val Verde to Galveston, from Glorieta to Irish Bend—believed an assault foolhardy. Colonel William Polk "Gotch" Hardeman of the 4th Texas Cavalry—Green's old friend, a former ranger, and a Texas hero—approached with counsel. "If the fort were taken," he advised, "the gunboats would shell the Confederates out as soon as the sun shone on them." An attack on Fort Butler would fail or end poorly.[1]

Perhaps isolating the post and blockading the river would be enough. His officers believed Green would do better scouting the river north and south of Fort Butler, harassing the warships on the Mississippi, and mounting field artillery to the south to interdict river traffic. Colonel Barton W. Stone, Jr., an alcoholic veteran of the earliest days of the war, would take his motley 2nd Texas Partisan Rangers across Bayou Lafourche and threaten Donaldsonville with all of its regimental depots and camps and report back his assessment of the Union position. Stone ordered most of his troops to dismount and cross over the bobbing bridge; others swam the horses across.[2]

Green believed that, failing a release from Mouton, he was still honor bound to attack. That morning, June 27, his courier galloped toward Thibodaux, more than twenty miles away. As he waited for Mouton's reply, Green realized that precious time was slipping away and that Union troops and gunboats must certainly be en route to bolster Fort Butler's defense. If they stood any chance for success, they must act soon. That afternoon, his chief scout, Leander McNelly, some mounted pickets, and local sympathizers investigated the Union works confirming some five hundred Federals inside.[3]

Behind Fort Butler's massive walls, Union Major Joseph D. Bullen also feared the outcome of an attack. He had done his best to ready his command but he also knew that most of his soldiers were strangers to combat, and he doubtlessly realized that his nine-month volunteers from companies C and F of the 28th Maine would struggle to fend off the assault of Green's veterans. Bullen's convalescents also remained questionable. Still, sick and wounded soldiers were better than no soldiers.

When his pickets came in from their fight at the Kesslar Plantation, Bullen dispatched a frantic note to New Orleans begging for additional support. General William H. Emory, himself in a panic over the security of the Crescent City after Colonel Thomas Cahill's stampede back into the city, had released few troops north. "Make a good fight," Emory advised, writing off Bullen as lost. That day, June 27, only Company G of the 28th Maine and a scattering of convalescing soldiers, stragglers, and volunteers swept up from the rump encampments of a half-dozen regiments within the lines at New Orleans, came to Fort Butler's aid. Another one hundred men swelled Bullen's force. The newcomers also brought word that more gunboats were approaching.[4]

By mid-afternoon on June 27, the Texans hovering near the fort chased the Union pickets into their works. Later that day, Bullen received a flag of truce from Green, offering to receive the fort's immediate surrender to avoid a battle that neither wanted. "A sense of responsibility dawned upon the little squad of . . . men detailed to keep open 135 miles of communications with our base and Port Hudson," wrote Captain Augustine Thompson. The officer knew his enemy. "His name was General Green, sir! Not to be trifled with . . . the name begat a thrilling sensation down my spine."[5]

Major Bullen, suffering from malaria, called together his ad hoc garrison and, while they were standing around the flag staff, asked for the feelings of his troops, most of whom were strangers. A newly arrived convalescent private from the 16th New Hampshire sang out, "Never pull [the flag] down; let it hang!" The Major answered defiantly, "It shall hang there as long as there is a man of you left to defend it!" He sent his reply to the Confederates.[6]

Disappointed, Green contemplated his next move. At about 6:00 P.M., a courier from Mouton's staff galloped into his camp; the dispatch he carried depressed Green further. The missive contained no mention of his request and instead directed the Texans on what to do with captured cannon and supplies when Fort Butler fell. Mouton was not coming but clearly anticipated that the Texans would carry the Union position. It fell to Green to decide.[7]

The moment became a Gethsemane for the Texans. Green wanted to avoid the violent assault he faced. Perhaps, he reasoned, the Federals might still give up. He sent a second message to Fort Butler, an additional warning that he and his men were in earnest. The Texan general instructed his Federal opponents that they should evacuate women and children within a radius of three miles. In reply, Bullen calmly agreed to notify the civilians. Refusing to be bluffed into surrender, the Maine Yankee instead ordered his drummers to beat the long roll as his troops grabbed their traps, straps, and equipment, and fell into line to defend against the blow that must soon fall.[8]

As dusk fell, Green ordered his officers together. "General Green laid his orders before them," wrote Colonel Hugh McPhail. The soldiers all agreed that Mouton's directive left little to interpret. There would be blood before dawn. "He was bound to make the attack," McPhail lamented, "as he had no discretion."[9]

On the night of June 27, darkness shrouded the woods, fields, and river near Fort Butler. The whitewashed and battle-beaten buildings of Donaldsonville stood eerie and deserted in the gloomy, cloudy, Louisiana night. Union pickets kept a careful watch for the approach of the Rebels, but none came. The hour had not yet arrived.

A few miles away, General Green reviewed scouting reports and concluded that Fort Butler would only fall by a bold, coordinated stroke by every regiment at hand. His Texans needed to get behind the fort on the Mississippi side and gain that entrance while others forced the main gate. A sudden, coordinated, rush might overwhelm the garrison with minimum losses. The dark night would prove an ally, hiding the assaulting troops from the gunboat lurking in the river.[10]

Green explained his plan to his colonels. He crafted a simple double envelopment. Green's senior regiments, the 4th and 5th, would launch simultaneous attacks on two sides of the fort and carry the position. The 4th would storm the sally port near Bayou Lafourche, whereas the seven companies present from the 5th would pass behind the Mississippi levee, breach the stockade between that feature and the river, and rush into the fort from behind. With luck, the two Texan units would meet in the middle of Fort Butler. To draw off fire, three other regiments would keep up a steady, close-range fusillade on the fort to keep the defenders off balance and pinned down. Colonel Stone's men should clear out Donaldsonville and keep up a steady fire on the southern face of the fort—although he had no

Twenty-seven-year-old Denman William Shannon, son of an Irish father and English mother, was orphaned at an early age and raised by his relative, William Bissel Shannon, twice-governor of Ohio. The young man moved South, eventually living in Mississippi where he met and married his wife, Belle. The couple moved to Washington County, Texas, then to Anderson. He enlisted in the 5th Texas Cavalry as captain of Company C from Grimes County at the beginning of the war and served throughout the New Mexico Campaign before receiving promotion to major of his regiment. Captured during the retreat, officials exchanged him and sent him back to Texas. He often led the 5th Texas Cavalry in Louisiana after Colonel Tom Green's promotion, eventually commanding the assault on Fort Butler on June 28, 1863. Courtesy of Manning Brady Shannon, Dallas, Texas.

specific orders to do so. Green hoped he would just *know* to throw in. Upriver, Captain Oliver Semmes's battery would duel with any gunboats. The signal for the assault would be the sound of Major Denman Shannon's attack from the Mississippi side. All seven regiments would hammer Fort Butler at the same time. To succeed, the affair must end quickly.[11]

In the hours before midnight, Green's cavalry left their positions around Paincourtville and headed up the road toward Fort Butler. As he moved his command forward to their jumping-off points, Green issued appropriate orders to Colonel James P. Major and all of the regimental officers committed to the attack. Within two miles of Fort Butler, they dismounted. Colonel Hardeman, the wise Texas Ranger, gathered his 4th Texas Cavalry and inched along the Bayou Lafourche road with orders to await a guide to show him the way to Fort Butler's gate. At the same time, Major Shannon, the ranking officer of the 5th Texas Cavalry, led his men wide to the north before angling right toward the Mississippi levee and his starting point nearly two miles above Fort Butler.[12]

While these assault troops moved into position, Colonel Major ordered his three regiments guided to the left to follow the 5th Texas away from the Bayou Lafourche road. After a brief march, these troops halted and faced right, fronting the

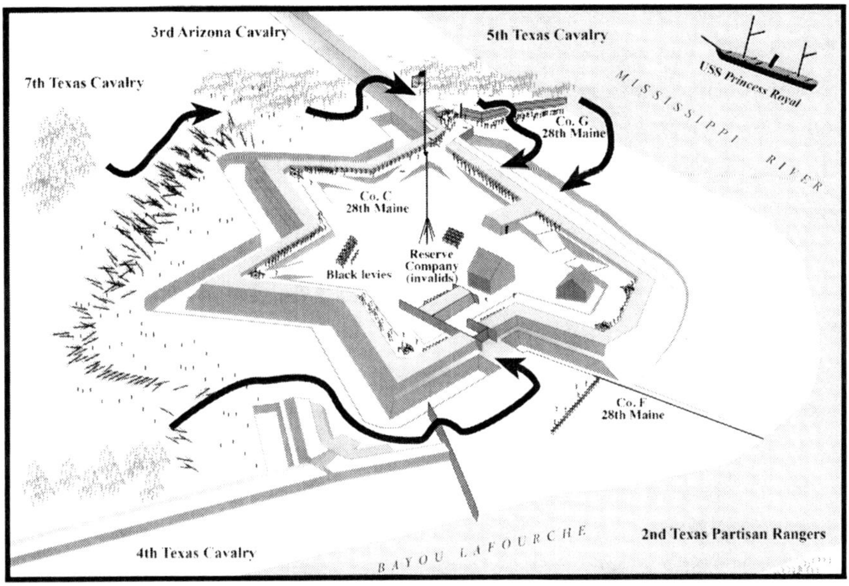

fort across its nine hundred-yard open field. When the signal came, Major's troops would charge from the woods, across the open plain, through the obstacles, to the edge of the moat, and there keep up a steady fire on Fort Butler's ramparts from nearly point-blank range. Colonel Philemon Herbert, a short-tempered Southern fanatic from Tucson, moved his 7th Texas troops to the field's edge, followed by Colonel Joseph Philips—the short Virginian—and his 3rd Arizona. One regiment, though, was missing. In the darkness, the fiery Irishman, Colonel Walter P. Lane, remained behind in the road, unaware that his companion regiments had moved on and supposing that a guide would come and fetch him as well. Major, busy with his own preparations, failed to miss them.[13]

Inside the fort, Bullen could hear the Texans moving into position and organized his Yankee volunteers and liberated slaves to make best use of their limited numbers. "When the facts noised about in our little hospital, sick and well put on cartridge boxes and seized the old Enfield for a chance in the glory to come," remembered a Federal captain. "The sickest man was to pull the lanyard. The convalescents were to pass the ammunition, if not able to back a bayonet." Those troops not manning cannon formed into two squads to cover each side of the fort.[14]

Bullen reserved the critical assignments for men he knew and trusted from the 28th Maine. Company G, under command of Captain Thompson, a twenty-seven-year-old blacksmith from Rockland, Maine, had just arrived from New Orleans; Bullen ordered them to hold the northeastern, or right, entrance closest to the Mississippi. "What shall I say of my men," remarked Captain Thompson of his soldiers defending the northeastern palisade. "Sailors and granite cutters . . . my sixty-six said they were good for their part of that crowd. I proudly patted their ambition, knowing that two thirds of them were more than my equal. Ah—what a citizen soldiery was that!" A second squad, Company F, under Captain Edward B. Neal of Wiscasset, Maine, covered the southern or left entrance. Bullen formed Company C into a mobile reserve with orders to stand fast until needed, supported by an ad hoc squad of convalescents under the command of lieutenants from his regiment, ready to strengthen any threatened point. In front of the fort, Union detachments set fire to the remaining buildings that would block a clear shot at the Rebels while also providing illumination. Signal corps soldiers ignited flares and placed lanterns to mark the edges of the fort so that overeager navy gunners would know where to aim. They also flashed red Coston lights, signaling the approach of danger. In the river, marines beat the general quarters, and sailors aboard the USS *Princess Royal* cleared its decks for battle while the engine room coal heavers stoked the fires for the long night's work.[15]

In the first minutes of June 28, the three hundred men of the 2nd Texas Partisan Rangers slipped into deserted Donaldsonville, a lurid glow pulsating from burning buildings a half-mile to their left. Riding past the ghostly shapes of the white clapboard houses, the Rebels cautiously searched street to street for any sign of Federal troops. In no time, shots rang out as pickets from Company F, 28th Maine, fired at the horsemen and retreated to a pontoon bridge near the mouth of Bayou Lafourche and clattered across to their fort. Immediately, a red signal rocket soared skyward from Fort Butler, announcing the arrival of the Rebels to the crew of the *Princess Royal*. Colonel Stone's Confederates retreated a short distance, dismounted, and moved toward their deadly assignment. Climbing onto the roofs of the deserted town, ambitious sharpshooters began sniping at the Yankees from 150 yards out, but with little chance of hitting anything specific in the darkness.[16]

The guns of *Princess Royal* flashed in a blossom of fire and smoke and sent grapeshot and shell into the stricken town. Unfazed, Stone ordered his troops to

This Scottish-built blockade runner fell into Union hands in early 1863 off of Charleston. Reconfigured as a gunboat, the Princess Royal *arrived on station just days before seeing combat at Fort Butler and used its two 30-pounder Parrot Rifles, its IX-inch Dahlgren, and its four 24-pounder howitzers to good effect. The postwar fate of* Princess Royal *remains murky. One story has it involved in a bloody incident in the Taedong River near the Korean city of Pyongyang in a clumsy attempt to open trade with that reclusive nation in the early 1870s. Another ending has the ship lost off Cape Fear, North Carolina, about the same time.* *American Neptune* XXI, no. 4 (1961).

take cover in positions behind the Lafourche levee to maintain a harassing fire into the fort. As his men shot away their ammunition, Stone anxiously awaited any sign of a more substantial Rebel attack. Nothing happened. The Texans hunkered down and waited; in the river, *Princess Royal* glided upstream and away from the uninteresting shooting in town, its crew sponging and reloading its guns after the ship's initial, but harmless, broadside.[17]

Occasional Texan buck and ball zipped and popped among the wood and mud of the fort, eventually forcing the few score men of Company F, 28th Maine, to take cover among the outworks. The Yankees returned fire. Meanwhile the 24-pounder on the parapet sprayed canister into the night, directing it at the flash of the Rebel guns. "[Captain Neal] and his men endured the fire without wavering and replied with vigor," read a report. Before long, reinforcing reserves and two more of the fort's cannon joined in with Neal's soldiers to overwhelm Stone's Rebels with a heavy storm of lead and iron. The troops of the 2nd Texas Partisan Rangers began drifting out of their sniper's perches, no doubt wondering what had become of Green's anticipated attack.

From that point onward, one Union observer noted, Stone's part in the fight "was confined to yells."[18]

Upstream from the fort, the commander of the trolling *Princess Royal* feared a greater threat than Stone's trifle and ordered his gunners to train their pieces on the levee. He brought his ship around and ran the guns out on the starboard side. "At 1:25 A.M.," Commander Melancthon Brooks Woolsey reported, "this ship commenced . . . shelling the woods to the right of the fort in the direction of the enemy." Without fully knowing it, he was firing at Shannon's Texans and Semmes's gunners as they moved into position. Because of the low water in the river, his crews elevated the pieces 4 1/2 degrees to barely skim the embankment. Raising the tubes a bit more, the ship then hurled "a few IX-inch and 30-pounder shot over the fort up the Bayou, for the purpose of dislodging troops that might be in the rear." Hardeman, too, was getting some attention. Although unable to pinpoint the enemy in the darkness, the Union sailors knew where they were likely to be.[19]

Princess Royal was hungry for targets. Blue jacket officers barked orders at gun crews to keep up their steady and deadly rhythms. As he turned his ship about and moved in close to the shore, Woolsey spoke new instructions down the tube into his engine room. "I sheered close in and kept up a fire from all guns with shrapnel and IX-inch 5-second fuses until about 2 A.M."[20]

While enduring this Yankee gunboat's blind probing, Major Shannon moved his Texans to within four hundred yards of the northern side of Fort Butler under cover of a dense wood. After the harassing gunboat passed downstream, Shannon ordered his troops to mount their assault. Captain "Grif" Killough of Company I and ten men armed with axes moved into the open several yards in advance and trotted toward the fort, aiming to hack through the palisade. Shannon directed the rest of the regiment, now breaking into the open as well, over the levee and to the water's edge along the forty-yard batture to have a clear approach to the fort. Dead ahead, looming in the darkness, was the saw-toothed stockade wall. Without a shot, the surging Rebels overwhelmed the first few Federal pickets. Those further back, however, fired their rifles, turned, and ran for the gate, Captain Killough's axe-wielding Texans in close pursuit. The 5th Texas surged forward, the orderly advance turning into a dash as the Rebels scurried to achieve their objective, parading in full view of the *Princess Royal* a few hundred yards away to their left front. The Yankees could barely see them in the darkness. "The moon had just set and left the night dark," Captain Thompson wrote. *Princess Royal* glided on the river, a ghostly silhouette amid a low-lying nighttime river mist, steady blasts of fire flashing through the haze. The rolling smoke from its guns further masked the Rebels. "The thick smoke enveloped the outer defenses," Thompson remembered, "I could not see 10 feet from the stockade."[21]

"Despite a deadly hail from front and flank," Private James H. McLeary remembered, Shannon's Texans closed the distance to their target and the combat became extremely close and vicious at the stockade. Behind the cypress posts, the Maine men fired their rifles through loopholes; when the Texans reached the wooden wall, some passed their weapons through the same holes to fire blindly at the defenders on the other side. Killough's squad attacked the cypress logs with axes or boosted their comrades over the jagged top. Others discovered a way around by wading into the river and passing the end of the wall. After a terrible few minutes, the men of the 5th Texas carried this outwork. "Dropping a number with our rifles, we then considered it best to retreat behind the earthworks of the fort," Captain Thompson wrote. "I ordered my men to fall back . . . and fix bayonets." The heavily outnumbered Yankees of Company G, 28th Maine, streamed backward into the fort's inner defenses. All appeared to be going well for the 5th Texas Cavalry as more Rebels surged through and around the stockade.[22]

Responding to the pressure, Major Bullen reorganized his defenders. With his line of defense contracting on his right, Bullen ordered the reserve squad under Lieutenant Isaac Murch to support Thompson's men who were at that point redistributing themselves along the inner works of the fort.

As more and more rifles topped the parapet, Shannon's attack disintegrated. Shrapnel and fragments from the guns of *Princess Royal* churned the water and clattered among the cypress posts as the Texans dove for cover. Major Shannon crumpled into a heap, seriously wounded by a bullet from the fort's defenders who clustered in ever-greater numbers along its ramparts. Swept by fire from the fort and the river, the now leaderless Texans pushed forward for a desperate dash up the muddy, grassy slopes of the fort. Many, though, turned back and sought the safety of darkness and distance. There would be no dramatic lunge over the fortress walls. The Texans that continued the assault unexpectedly faced a substantial ditch at the base of the levee that protected the eastern face of the fort. This

This 2014 piece by renowned military artist Gary Zaboly portrays the attempt by the 5th Texas Cavalry, supported by the 3rd Arizona, to take the rear wall of Fort Butler. The ditch, noted in some accounts, is clearly portrayed, as is the palisade in the background. USS Princess Royal *lends its weight to the fight from the Mississippi River. Note the employment of liberated slaves in the defense of the work, fighting alongside the white soldiers of the 28th Maine and squads from other regiments. Signal lanterns marked the walls of the fort so that the gunboats did not fire on their own men.*
Author's collection.

unanticipated development threw the men into confusion; hemmed in by the gunboat in the river and fort to their front, the men of the 5th Texas leapt into the ditch to find cover, trapped between two fires. "Not one officer or man knew which way to turn," McLeary wrote.[23]

Captain Killough tried to organize a cluster of men to climb up the slope, as did Captain Dan Ragsdale. Taking command of a tattered platoon, he ordered his men to scale the slippery wall as best they could and top the fort's ramparts. Scores of his troops attempted this perilous climb, many slipping back into the ditch because they lost their footing on the slick mud and grass of the levee wall. Yankees shot down those who did reach the summit. "Each man," Captain Thompson recalled, "caught his man with a bullet and then caught another on his bayonet and pushed him and all behind him down the bank." Captain Ragsdale, his fingers finally gripping the edge of the parapet, heaved himself upward only to be shot at point-blank range through the head. As his lifeless corpse tumbled back into the ditch, the men of the 5th Texas abandoned their climbing and crouched for safety. "They seemed to be astonished," Thompson noted. Where were General Green and the rest of the regiments?[24]

On board *Princess Royal*, Woolsey asked the same question. His gunners ceased firing at the 5th Texas simply because they could no longer tell friend from foe amid the smoke. "I could not see the lights showing the position of the fort," Woolsey reported. He ordered his ship to turn about. He suspected that Confederates still infested the same woods that had sheltered Shannon. "I . . . stood upstream about 200 yards, continuing the fire on the Rebel troops who were in the woods north of and at a distance of 400 yards of the fort. Their position was indicated by their constant yelling, as I could not see their fire for the smoke."[25]

The Confederate plan unraveled. Colonel Hardeman and his 4th Texas Cavalry, critical to the scheme, had still not come up. Because their guide had not arrived, they remained at their staging point. Hardeman, hearing the violence down the road, used his own initiative and groped his way along the Lafourche through the night to try and make up lost time. Miles away, Lane, with a more difficult path to travel, simply waited, the flash and sounds of battle echoing from the eastern horizon.[26]

A private in Lane's 1st Texas Partisan Rangers believed his regiment's confusion had been deliberate. "We were under orders to take [Fort Butler] at all hazards," wrote Private Frank Price of San Augustine, Texas. "Colonel Lane, knowing the utter impossibility of taking the place, would not carry his men into the slaughter pen." The veteran ranger sat this fight out.[27]

Inside the fort, the whistle and buzz of bullets overhead kept the defenders in a low crouch. Captain Thompson and Lieutenant Murch held their two commands near the back wall of the fort, trying for a shot at the Rebels pinned below. "Some of our men were wounded at the stockade, but they were still fighting," Thompson recalled. "A big wound was [but] a scratch, [as long as] their hands were untouched." Captain Neal and Company F kept close to the Lafourche-side wall of the fort and its stockade, keeping a harassing fire on Donaldsonville.[28]

Green knew that his friends and neighbors in the 5th Texas were getting massacred behind the fort and galloped forward to retrieve the situation. "Hearing the firing from Shannon's rifles amid the roar of the artillery," McLeary reported, "General Green ordered an advance of the whole line."[29] Private Samuel K. Savage, Company H, 53rd Massachusetts, and one of forty ailing soldiers recently sent up from New Orleans as reinforcements, heard the Rebels coming. "They came with a yell of 1,000 Indians," he wrote. As they surged forward, the fort's 32-pounders sprayed canister and grapeshot "which mowed them down like grass," Savage effused. Colonel Major veered his two regiments to the left in an attempt to carry

Morgan Wolfe Merrick, with the 3rd Arizona, drew this primitive and wildly inaccurate sketch of the attack on Fort Butler. He got the date of the battle wrong, the perspective is reversed and confused, and the type of gunboats is incorrect, but he generally captures the nature of the fight. Texans are seen scaling the walls after being stuck in a ditch, all the while under fire from the river.
Daughters of the Republic of Texas Library, The Alamo, San Antonio, Texas.

the fort at a point where it jutted out from the Mississippi levee but came under an increasingly bothersome fire from *Princess Royal*. Charging at the head of the 3rd Arizona, Major fell to his knees with a painful wound to his left arm.[30]

Colonel Philips carried the charge forward in a diagonal across the fort's field of fire before passing over the levee to reach the relative safety of the stockade. Passing around the end, the 112 men of the 3rd Arizona took the same route as the 5th Texas Cavalry. They also committed the same mistake. Dozens of Yankee rifles fired into this mob of attackers. Phillips disappeared in this hail of gunfire. "His voice was heard no more," a witness recalled. "He was called for in vain." Unknown to his men, he lay near the palisade, a grievous head wound slowly draining him of life. Lieutenant Colonel George T. Madison took command and

This detail of a larger drawing—the only known image of the battle crafted by a contemporary—shows the confused and desperate nature of the night battle.
Daughters of the Republic of Texas Library, The Alamo, San Antonio, Texas.

led the regiment toward the fort; these troops confronted the same damnable ditch, but even amid the noise and confusion, somehow bypassed it and took their chances to scale the levee wall.[31]

Madison, a thirty-three-year-old New Yorker, was a veteran filibuster in Mexico before the war and a gambler and merchant in New Mexico Territory at the outbreak. He had been in many tight places. He recognized the ditch as a death trap; his men must keep moving forward or lose all in the effort. Urging his men ahead, the Arizonan crawled up the fortress wall, dozens of his troopers alongside. "We had to climb," wrote a soldier in the 3rd Arizona, "and would get perhaps half way up when down would come a volley from the top and our poor boys would roll down like sheep." Captain Henry Kennedy of Arizona spun backward, half his left hand shot away. The regimental adjutant, Lieutenant W. K. Walker, was the first to gain the top of the wall until he, too, lurched backward, stone dead.[32]

Some of the 3rd Arizona managed to enter the fort. Captain Henry H. Hall and Lieutenant William Mitchell of Company E, along with a cluster of their men, made it in following Major Alonzo Ridley. Almost immediately they found themselves surrounded and disarmed. Lieutenant Colonel Madison made it in as well but retreated out almost as quickly as he had come, tumbling down the slope and nursing a slight arm wound. The attack of the 3rd Arizona had failed. The survivors of Madison's charge, like their 5th Texas comrades cringing in the ditch, sought shelter from the whirring storm of flying bullets.[33]

Alonzo Ridley, son of New England parents, was a thirty-four-year-old Indian agent in Central California at the outbreak of the Civil War. He made his way back to the South in company with Colonel Albert Sidney Johnston of the regular army and George Wythe Baylor, who was then serving with the Confederates in New Mexico. Ridley and Baylor joined Johnston's staff in Kentucky but after his death at the Battle of Shiloh, went to Texas and joined the Arizona Brigade. Baylor led the 2nd Arizona, while Ridley received appointment as the major of the 3rd Arizona Cavalry. Lieutenant Frank Mullen of San Antonio, pictured on Ridley's left, was the Assistant Quartermaster for the 2nd Arizona.
Edward Clifton Wharton Family Papers, Louisiana and Lower Mississippi Valley Collections, LSU Libraries, Baton Rouge, Louisiana.

The 7th Texas followed the 3rd Arizona forward but jammed up and scattered outside the fort amid the abatis, obstructions, and palisade. Felix Collard, a private in Company G, entered the maelstrom but instead of charging wildly into the doom ahead took cover and reviewed his situation. He scanned the parapet of Fort Butler to gauge his chances. "Four deep, negroes and whites with bayonets fixed, gave the Confederates a volley, shooting [many] in the head who rolled down the levee." Collard began firing into the fort, rolling onto his back and reloading a number of times before receiving an injury. "One of [my] comrades jumped down off the levee and onto the back of [my] hand," he wrote, "and the end of the [ram] rod pierced through the hand."[34]

Fort Butler's defenders had not escaped unharmed. Several Yankees fell to Rebel bullets. Lieutenant Murch, pistol in hand, led eight of his reserves to aid Thompson's men in repelling the charge of the 3rd Arizona before taking a fatal bullet through the neck. The first sergeant of Company G also fell. These men were "brave and fearless," wrote Thompson, "but the living could not stop to remove the dead." Sergeant George Cotton of the 16th New Hampshire, taking command of the invalids, also found himself stunned and knocked to the floor of the fort. As he gasped for air, he felt for the wound that had killed him. Although shot in the chest, he was not doomed after all. His company roll book had slowed the bullet.[35]

Commander Woolsey aboard *Princess Royal* now had plenty of targets because, through the clearing smoke, he saw hundreds more Confederates milling about north of the fort. Presenting his port broadside through a break in the levee, he ordered his crews to fire at will. "Having reduced the range to point blank, I fired shrapnel from the 30 and 24-pounders and grape from the IX inch enfilading the levee," he wrote.

Without clear targets on Fort Butler's walls, the men of the 7th Texas Cavalry and Semmes's Rebel artillery turned on the gunboat. Bullets whipped through the rigging, and one sailor fell, shot through the head. Commander Woolsey ordered his gun crews to lie down while moving the vessel out of range. Rebel canister rattled against the ship as well, splintering wood, piercing the hull, and knocking holes through the whaleboats on deck. Coming about, *Princess Royal* presented its starboard side guns to the enemy, firing as it passed downstream.

Woolsey knew he had to keep *Princess Royal* moving or dead and wounded sailors would soon litter his deck. After dueling with the Texans north of the fort, the ship steamed below and pulled up even with the town. "Fired a broadside up the main street," Woolsey reported, "and another up the south bank of the bayou." Colonel Stone's men sniped back at the vessel, bullets singing across the deck of *Princess Royal*; another crewman fell, shot through both thighs. The commander of the forecastle, too, reported to the ship's surgeon with a painful wrist wound. Woolsey ordered his ship back to midstream, then turned about to have another go at the 7th Texas with his heavy guns. He even ordered his marines and spare blue jackets to open fire with rifles. "At about 3:45 A.M. the yelling of the rebels discontinued and the fire materially slackened. Shortly after we heard three cheers from the fort."[36]

Fort Butler's defenders could not believe their luck. The garrison found more to cheer about when USS *Winona* hove into view from upstream, passing the fort and unloading its starboard broadside of grapeshot into the streets and buildings of Donaldsonville. This vessel steamed past the town, bullets smacking into its hull, then moved out of range of small arms, turned around, and made its way against the current to take position near the mouth of Bayou Lafourche. Although the battle had turned in their favor, the Yankees in the fort's interior still stooped as they moved from wall to wall. Bullets continued buzzing over the ramparts, and the fragments of naval grapeshot rounds and exploding shells whizzed and spun overhead.[37]

The attack on Fort Butler appeared to be finished. The dreaded Texans had attacked piecemeal, ideal for Major Bullen's plan of defense, and those Rebels who could drifted away from the fight. Private Collard, his palm skewered and bleeding, took the opportunity to depart. He followed the levee away from the fort until he reached timber and turned left to safety. On emerging from the backside of this wood, Collard discovered twelve men from his company who had also abandoned the battle. "Among them were Jim King, a grape shot opening the shoulder joint, and Tom Jones, shot in the face, breaking the lower jaw." Colonel Stone's Texans in Donaldsonville faded out of town and out of the battle.[38]

The situation in Fort Butler's ditches and parapet remained stalemated. Two tangled Texas regiments filled the gory ditch. In the 5th Texas, Major Shannon was bleeding badly and Captain Ragsdale, his second in command, lay dead. The Yankees had crippled the 3rd Arizona: Philips was missing, Lieutenant Colonel Madison was wounded, and Major Ridley, the dashing and colorful Californian, was missing. Only a few line officers in either regiment remained unscathed. The stranded Texans could do little to strike at their opponents, but every Yankee that leaned over the ramparts received the full attention of multiple Rebel muskets and rifles. Both sides quickly learned that exposure meant death and turned to indirect weapons—including bricks and debris—to strike their enemies. Captain Killough, one of the most conspicuous of the Texan officers, huddled among his men while clutching a bloody contusion atop his head, the victim of a hurled brick.[39]

Outside the fort, the Texans continued shooting, but Green had no idea how to save his beleaguered regiments. "We kept the big guns playing on those outside to keep them back," Private Savage of the 53rd Massachusetts, described. "Those behind the levee were obliged to keep their heads down to prevent being shot." Stone, across the Lafourche, provided no assistance. The 7th Texas, having mostly avoided the trap that had swallowed the 5th Texas and 3rd Arizona, backed away from the fort. Lane and the 1st Texas Partisan Rangers had vanished, and the 4th Texas Cavalry, who might have prevented this wretched situation had they coordinated their attack, was also missing. A look to the horizon revealed the first graying of dawn and most of the Confederates knew, before too much longer, daylight would reveal the tragedy of the night's attack. Green's command could then be cornered and destroyed. The battle had evolved into a disaster.[40]

Despite his regiment's tardiness, Colonel Hardeman resolved not to miss the fight. Just as Green was losing faith in this veteran officer, the 4th Texas surged up the Bayou Lafourche road and slammed against the south sally port in one last effort to gain the fort. In an instant, the Texans carried the outwork of the fort protecting its main entrance, and, shielded by its embankment, poured in a heavy fire of .69-caliber bullets. "Although Hardeman arrived too late," McLeary stated, "that veteran regiment stood its ground."[41]

Bullen's men, swallowing their previous cheers, scrambled for cover from this onslaught, and went back to work. The major, disease ravaged and weak, left his cot and urged on his defenders, eager that his men see him. Most of his troops had already shot away the full forty-round loads in their cartridge boxes and had been using the lull to gather more ammunition. The soldiers of Company F, 28th Maine, dropping the cartridges not yet in their boxes, gripping hot and fouled rifles, braced themselves against the southern stockade wall. The New Englanders kept the gate shut by brute force as Texans, just six inches of cypress away, strained as hard to open it. Federal Lieutenant John Perry, realizing the new danger, rushed his squad away from the doomed Rebels in the back ditch and across the fort to do its part in repulsing this new threat. As they rumbled into the fight, Perry's head snapped back and he rolled to the ground. A large slug had shattered his face and severed his tongue. Disregarding their lieutenant's fall, the reserve troops closed ranks with the men of Company F, 28th Maine, and a close-range, bare knuckle shoving match with Hardeman's Texans ensued.[42]

The trapped Texans in the ditch and along the river side stockade knew that something was happening in their favor on the other side of the fort. Besides the shooting and screaming coming from that direction, the Rebels noticed Federals leaving their post above. Bullets flew past with decreased regularity. Several took this opportunity to make good their escape, prudently using the distraction caused by Hardeman's attack.[43]

The U.S. Navy moved in to create an iron hell for Hardeman. *Winona*, having completed its turn, fired round after round of shell and grapeshot down Bayou Lafourche. Rattled soldiers of the 4th Texas fled for safety, leaving many of their comrades stranded and pinned down near the southern stockade of Fort Butler. "Our fire was delivered with such fatality they withdrew in confusion," reported

Lieutenant Commander A. W. Weaver of *Winona*. "At 4:30 the enemy's fire had ceased entirely." At the first blush of dawn, clusters of exhausted Texans held their positions in front and back of Fort Butler, hoping that General Green might somehow save them.[44]

Rewarding their faith, their general presented a bluff to extract the survivors. Green ordered staff officers forward under a flag of truce to negotiate a cease-fire to gather the wounded. The general believed that Bullen would certainly refuse the offer but hoped—via the truce party—to communicate with the men trapped among the fort's outer works. Green's scout, McNelly, his Adjutant J. B. Wilkins, and a sergeant, rode across the field toward Fort Butler while the Federals held their fire and waited. The soldiers' mounts picked their way through the battlefield debris and angled toward the fortress wall; as the Rebel officers encountered survivors, hunkered down behind cover, they told them to scamper away as quickly as possible. When the truce-bearers arrived at the Union position, a steady stream of bruised and bleeding Rebel soldiers were surreptitiously scuttling toward freedom. Bullen, in a rage, refused the flag of truce. Nevertheless, the ruse worked. On inspection, the Federals discovered that most of Hardeman's trapped Texans had employed the distraction to escape.[45]

Yet, Fort Butler's defenders harvested plenty of prisoners. To hasten the Rebel retreat, the two gunboats shelled the woods, and just after daybreak, the Union garrison moved atop the parapet and signaled to the remaining Texans in the trench below to surrender. "There was a memory of Yankee muscle and bayonet," Captain Thompson wrote. "I called upon the Rebs to throw down their arms and surrender. They did." After their night in hell, most offered no argument. Some one hundred soldiers rose up from their positions behind the fort, while two dozen more surrendered near the main gate.[46]

The Rebel soldiers emerging from the shadows amazed Fort Butler's New England defenders. "Fine, gallant, stalwart fellows, and such fighters," Thompson wrote. "I looked upon them with such admiration—and then I was afraid they would overpower us without arms." Besides the thirty-one men left standing in Company G, 28th Maine, reinforcements arrived from across the fort to help him with his captives. "The Confederate prisoners were driven into a back corner of the earthwork and compelled to lie down and not speak to each other. A strong guard, with cocked rifles, covered them every minute."[47]

As the Yankees corralled their prisoners, additional reinforcements arrived. Around 6:00 A.M., the USS *Kineo* hove to, followed by the transport *St. Mary's* on its way from New Orleans to Port Hudson loaded with troops returning to their regiments. They continued on after a short halt, convinced the fighting had ended. A short while later, a tugboat reached Fort Butler, bearing ammunition. By noon, USS *Monongahela* came on the scene, followed two hours later by USS *Genesee*. With five powerful ships on hand and plenty of ammunition, Union veterans of the Battle of Fort Butler could now rest easy. Soldiers and sailors put single irons on the captured Texans, broke them into small squads, and put them aboard the warships.[48]

Free from the threat of a renewed Texan attack, the defenders set about clearing away the carnage. The Texans suffered nearly one hundred casualties, dead and wounded. Among others, Union soldiers located and dragged in Colonel Phillips. Samuel Hancock Smith, a corporal in the 5th Texas Cavalry, lay in the ditch for six hours, suffering from a painful body wound. Lifted out of the mud and gore on a sailcloth sling, Union soldiers laid him out in the middle of the fort to die, surrounded by the contorted, lifeless bodies of his comrades. Union surgeons gave Smith no hope.[49]

After spending the day in torment, covered with flies, Smith finally convinced his captors to move him into a tent full of wounded, placing him next to the unconscious Colonel Phillips, who was gasping his final breaths. "While in his death agony," Smith remembered, "the poor boy twitched convulsively as if struggling to hold [his] noble spirit." Before he expired, Union soldiers arrived and looted the officer, cutting off his gold uniform buttons and the wedding ring from his hand. Sergeant Samuel Pollock of the 6th Michigan claimed his sword as a trophy. He—or his squad of black field hands from the government plantation he supervised—had fired the mortal shot. A captured Texan later confirmed the deed in a letter to a newspaper back home, stating that the highly respected Phillips had fallen "to a negro's bullet." The sword may have been the one Phillips took from Lieutenant Colonel Augustine Joseph Hickey Duganne of the 176th New York just four days before on Bayou Boeuf.[50]

Stinging from their repulse, the Confederates withdrew five miles and halted. Green collected his men, noting that he had lost almost half the troops committed. The assault cost him nearly three hundred men. Green reported his reverse, well knowing he should have obeyed his initial instinct and ignored Mouton's order to assault the fort. He ordered his men to picket the river while keeping at least one regiment near the fort in case the garrison attempted to pursue.

As the day brightened and the bloodied regiments shuffled back to Paincourtville, a courier arrived from Thibodaux. "General Green received another dispatch from General Mouton *revoking the order to attack*," wrote an officer in the 5th Texas Cavalry. "It came too late, the work had been done."[51]

A smaller Union force inside a stout fort backed by gunboats had whipped Green's Texans. "There never was more desperate courage displayed than by the assailants in this assault," McLeary claimed. "The failure of the attack has been attributed to the existence of [the] ditch within the stockade . . . on the river side of the fort, but this would not have prevented the Fourth and Fifth from capturing the fort if they had arrived simultaneously." A fellow soldier in the 5th Texas Cavalry echoed his sentiment. "The failure to take the place was simply attributable to a want of concert of action, and to nothing else." Confusion, darkness, and an overly complicated plan had doomed the attack.[52]

The Confederates wanted to recover the bodies of their slain. Green forwarded yet another flag of truce to Fort Butler, "accompanied by an apology for his failure," wrote an incredulous Yankee. Green explained that his assault miscarried on account of his "not getting his men into the skirmish owing to the rashness of his commanders." Bullen, duped by the Texan once before and surprised by this *mea culpa*, refused the request.[53]

Green's command had received a drubbing. Although the missing rejoined their commands in the coming days, initial casualty numbers for his old brigade looked grim. Green's regiment, the 5th Texas, had lost more than one hundred men—nearly half the number carried into the fight—but only nine killed. The rest were wounded, missing, wandering, or confirmed as prisoners. Entire companies had simply disappeared. The 7th Texas, the Union gunboats' favorite target, had lost six men killed and more than ninety wounded, including its major, Gustav Hoffman, hit badly in the neck. The 4th Texas arrived late to the battle but still lost forty men from its nine companies.

The battle had also bloodied Major's Second Texas Cavalry Brigade. The chaos on the wall and in the ditch had gutted the 3rd Arizona. One Texan noted that a lieutenant now commanded the unit. "The field officers and captains are all killed or wounded." Fort Butler's defenders killed twelve men in that regiment, and wounded nineteen more. More than thirty surrendered. Companies E and F had essentially ceased to exist. "There are less than eighty men . . . fit for duty," recorded one of the survivors. By contrast, the only other regiment from Major's Brigade engaged in the battle, the 2nd Texas Partisan Rangers, lost seven men—two deserted to the enemy by flagging down a gunboat the following morning. "Stone's regiment has proved itself brave, daring, and unflinching in the hour of battle," a Dallas editor claimed. Their record suggested otherwise.[54]

General Green tried to ease their loss by congratulating them on a well-fought battle. "You did everything that gallantry and daring could do," he insisted. "You have shown to our enemies an example of daring which will terrify them when we meet again in the open field." A 3rd Arizona private looked forward to that vengeance day. "If we ever meet them again, we have made up our minds to leave none of them unscalped."[55]

As the sun set on June 28, 1863, Union cannon aboard four of the gunboats boomed from the Mississippi, blindly probing for any Rebels lingering nearby. As details buried the Federal dead, these shots became an accidental salute. The huge rounds passed just thirty feet above the fort, with Union soldiers, liberated slaves, burial details, and Rebel prisoners flinching reflexively. "It was a wild, magnificent scene I shall never forget," remembered Captain Thompson. "The deafening roar of the heavy guns, . . . the shrieking, hissing shells above us, the solemn voice of the chaplain as he gave our heroes back to God . . . it was such a service as the soldier's ambition craves." Rebel bullets had killed eight men among the three companies of the 28th Maine and the convalescent troops, and had wounded another thirteen. Union officers at the fort never reported the number of casualties among the black conscripts or even their role in the fight. Lieutenant George H. Hanks, Superintendent of Negro Labor for the Department of the Gulf made sure to chronicle their contributions. He telegraphed Banks that several dozen "plantation negroes . . . fought bravely and sustained their share of the casualties."[56]

For most of the men in the 28th Maine, this had been their first engagement. Even so, "there were no cowards there," Captain Thompson remembered. "They had fought the best troops the Confederacy had ever put into the field. . . . and preserved the road to the sea."[57]

Firing blindly into the distance to keep the Texans on edge, the mighty naval guns periodically sent shells arcing down the Lafourche. They also terrified civilians. The women at Sleepy Hollow Plantation fled as heavy rounds landed near their home. "Two bombs exploded in the meadow while we were running away," Heléne Dupuy wrote. The shells had traveled more than three miles.[58]

For the fallen of Green's and Major's brigade, the cause and outcome for the disaster were now unimportant. With little ceremony, freedmen dug a mass grave on the Mississippi batture and laid the dead Texans between levee and river. Local planters could not bear to see the officers treated without ceremony and many donated coffins to contain their remains. When the Mississippi rose that following winter, the graves of the Texans were inundated and erased. Local tradition at Donaldsonville relates that the bodies of the officers—including Ragsdale and Phillips—sealed in airtight "torpedo" caskets, bobbed to the surface and floated, along with the rest of the river debris, unvexed to the sea.

12 Time

The enemy will do us some harm in the Lafourche and cause us considerable annoyance on the river.

—Major General Nathaniel P. Banks
Department of the Gulf

As he headed toward his headquarters at Alexandria, ignorant of recent events in the Lafourche District, General Richard Taylor believed conditions for his attempt "to succor Port Hudson" looked promising.[1] Viewing the strategic situation across the Mississippi with a clarity that came from distance, he had suggested that Lieutenant General Joseph E. Johnston, instead of trying to relieve Vicksburg, might instead finish off the Union army under Nathaniel P. Banks. Johnston, with more than twenty thousand men, might deal a mortal blow to the disease-ravaged Army of the Gulf while also saving the Rebels trapped at Port Hudson. Major General Franklin Gardner told his garrison as much. Johnston scoffed at the idea. So, Taylor devised his own solution.[2]

Arriving at Alexandria, Taylor listened as his aide, C. LeDoux Elgee reported back from a meeting with Johnston. Even with twenty-five thousand troops, Johnston had given up on Vicksburg, too. Major General Ulysses S. Grant's army had grown significantly larger and more powerful. "This, added to the strength of position," Johnston claimed, "renders the condition of Vicksburg . . . almost hopeless." He wanted to coordinate efforts with General John C. Pemberton so the trapped Confederates could perhaps fight their way out, but could not get word to him. Perhaps Taylor could facilitate that effort by putting a semaphore team on the western shore. Johnston implied that there was nothing left for General John G. Walker to do west of the Mississippi. "He suggests no other mode of rendering him assistance," Elgee added. Puzzled, Taylor needed clarification from Lieutenant General Edmund Kirby Smith. Could Walker and his division finally come south?[3]

Gallopers arrived at Shreveport, but the commander of the Confederate Department of the Trans-Mississippi had gone to Monroe. Since Taylor would not take command of operations opposite Vicksburg, Kirby Smith had. What Taylor did learn though was that Walker's men were ill, and his position ineffective. Even with Kirby Smith's presence, the campaign in northeastern Louisiana accomplished little. Confederate reinforcements arrived—some Texas cavalry under command of Colonel William H. Parsons and Brigadier General James C. Tappan's Arkansas infantry brigade—but they still had no effect on Grant's siege of Vicksburg.

The Federals had reinforced and reorganized the Mississippi west bank outposts and pushed a division as far west as the Tensas River near Richmond, Louisiana. On June 15, the Yankees happened on the Texas infantry. "I don't think General Walker intended to fight then at that place," admitted Private William Stoker. Both forces squared up for a battle, exchanging artillery and small-arms fire among the skirmishers that killed or wounded several dozen men. Eventually the Confederates gave way and fell back to Delhi, burning the bridge over the Tensas behind them but losing some of their number that "couldn't keep up, men that was puny and with sore feet." The Texans had been lucky. "General Walker," Private Stoker explained, "said we done well to come out with any men at all." Reinforced, Walker prepared his men for a showdown but abandoned the region east of the Tensas. The Yankees rounded up prisoners and returned to the Mississippi.[4]

Mostly, the Confederate troops in northeast Louisiana prowled the country toward the Mississippi trying to cause mischief, the booming of artillery from Vicksburg a constant drumbeat from the east. "The Feds have been through here and destroyed everything," Stoker lamented. "There isn't any farms in cultivation so far as have been on the Mississippi. I have seen thousands upon thousands of acres of the best land in the world just turned out and the negroes all run off to keep the Feds from getting them. The big negro quarters that look like towns are all desolate." The only farms in production were federally leased plantations. Confederates raided these operations and rounded up more than two thousand of their contract black laborers and returned them to slavery. Besides these symbolic measures, Walker's only other option was to place his artillery on the Mississippi River near the Louisiana and Arkansas line and shell supply vessels heading toward Grant's army.[5]

The Texas Division became a shadow of the well-drilled, if inexperienced, force Taylor had led just weeks before. "So large a number of sick men had, perhaps, never belonged to so small a force," Walker reported to Kirby Smith. "Excessive heat of the weather, the deadly malaria of the swamps, the stagnant and unwholesome water, are the causes to which are attributable these sad results. My division looked like a vast, moving hospital." Taylor sent couriers to bring the sickly Texas Division to Berwick Bay. Diminished though they were, the two thousand healthy soldiers remaining might make a difference against Banks and his link to New Orleans.[6]

Taylor also hedged his bets. If Vicksburg fell, he reasoned, his army needed to concentrate and prepare for what might come next. Taylor harbored few illusions that he could hold the Lafourche District if Confederate forces could not keep the Mississippi River. In anticipation of that event, he planned a future line of defense in Louisiana from Vermilionville to Niblett's Bluff on the Sabine, and the line of the Atchafalaya River to the east. Nearly all of the sugar parishes would be given up to the enemy. Meanwhile, duty required Taylor make a heroic effort to save the Confederate army at Port Hudson. After issuing his orders calling Walker to south Louisiana, Taylor turned around and headed back for the Lafourche.[7]

On June 29, 1863, couriers intercepted him as he traveled between Franklin and Brashear City, delivering a blast of bad news. The unpleasant report that Federals had whipped General Tom Green at Donaldsonville surprised him. "General Green dispatched . . . to Mouton," Taylor wrote, "that an examination of the enemy's fort induced him to withhold an attack." Brigadier General Alfred Mouton had agreed and called off the assault, Taylor believed. "General Mouton cannot account for the change of purpose shown in attacking."[8]

General Taylor believed the attack had been rash and that Green should have known better. "Although the attack may have been in some respects an unwise one, I am not disposed to attach the slightest censure to so gallant a soldier," he explained. Taylor credited the cause to his Texas general's aggressiveness. Taylor excused him, considering him a fighter of his own stripe. "Like the Irishman at Donnybrook, Green's rule was to strike an enemy wherever he saw him," Taylor remembered. "A most commendable rule in war, and covering a multitude of such small errors as the attack on Fort Butler."[9]

The battle at Donaldsonville had roughed up his best troops, but Taylor received promising news relating to his plot to come at New Orleans from above and below. Rebels controlled the west bank of the Mississippi and, except for the environs of Fort Butler, remained uncontested. Colonel James P. Major's Brigade patrolled a span from the Barteau Road connecting Green's headquarters at Paincourtville to the Mississippi at Buena Vista Plantation, past the great bend at College Point, and down to the Vacherie Road connecting Thibodaux to the Mississippi. Some of his troops had even traveled to St. Charles Courthouse—past Taylor's wrecked home, Fashion—without encountering Union pickets. Armed with this news, Taylor planned to squeeze the Mississippi supply artery sustaining the Federal army at Port Hudson. He rode hard to find General Green and discuss details.[10]

The Union troops surrounding Port Hudson consumed a staggering amount of supplies. Every day, soldiers gobbled up about twenty tons of food packed into about one thousand barrels, bags, and crates. These supplies, as everything else that could be chewed, shot, or hauled in Banks's army, depended on the backs of horses and mules. They, too, were hungry. An estimated five thousand animals kept the army and its six hundred wagons, limbers, and caissons moving, serving the various artillery, cavalry, and infantry units as well as the ordnance and quartermaster departments. Daily, these creatures consumed nearly fifty tons of food in hay and grain. For every day this army of around twenty thousand men and animals remained at Port Hudson, they chewed through seventy tons of food.

The journey for these rations began at slaughterhouses, packing plants, mills, and bakeries more than one thousand miles away. Civilian contractors packaged their products—hardtack, salt pork, salt beef, desiccated vegetables, sugar, coffee, salt, flour, oats, corn—in crates, sacks, and barrels then hauled them to shipping centers at the east coast ports of New York, Boston, and Philadelphia. From there, ocean-going vessels carried these rations to New Orleans. Stevedores loaded them onto steamboats for shipment to Port Hudson, where laborers unloaded them at Springfield Landing. Under the best of circumstances, the journey from New York to New Orleans took two weeks, and from New Orleans to Springfield Landing about a day.

The Federals outside Port Hudson also burned away ammunition. Every one of Banks's dozen or so brigades required about ten wagonloads of cartridges to fight a battle. His artillery needed full limber and caisson chests, as well as two wagonloads of rounds in reserve. Every assault Banks ordered consumed nearly two hundred tons of munitions. The daily sniping and cannonades constituted a continuous drip on the logistics pipeline.

This sketch captures the Union supply chain in microcosm. The oceangoing steamer North Star, *chartered by the U.S. Quartermaster Department, is tied alongside the riverboat* Iberville. *Laborers carry goods from the hold of the largest vessel, across the decks of the paddle wheeler, and onto shore. These vessels and others like them kept the Union army at Port Hudson supplied.*
Francis H. Schell, "Scene on the levee at Baton Rouge, La. Contrabands discharge the ammunition from the U.S. Transport *North Star* [?], Capt. S____ over the Mississippi steamer '*Iberville*.' Courtesy of the Becker Collection, Boston, Massachusetts.

The navy also proved voracious. Its heavy guns hurled tons of iron toward Gardner's Confederates daily and Federal ordnance systems had to replace this powder and shot. Other teams kept gunboats fueled with coal. A steady parade of steamboats hauled pyramids of heavy rounds, piles of anthracite, and kegs of gunpowder upriver.

A crowd of efficient officers and bookkeepers presided over the logistics of the army. In depots at Baton Rouge, Brashear City, and New Orleans, they had stockpiled many of the beans, bullets, and shells Banks relied on. Even so, a steady drumbeat of ships and boats refreshed this critical supply chain. Ocean-going steamers and sailing vessels handled the heavy lifting from the East Coast to the

Gulf Coast, carrying about a week's worth of rations per vessel. Each steamboat splashing upriver only carried a load that might feed the army for a day, leading to a steady shuttle of paddle wheelers of every make and size passing to and from New Orleans and Springfield Landing. For Taylor and his Confederates, every one of these vessels seemed an easy target; every delay in the feeding schedule for the Federal monster increased its discomfort and clouded its thinking.[11]

In contrast, Banks had to maintain focus on Port Hudson while Taylor tried to break his concentration. To do so, the Confederates needed to continue to appear threatening and sinister. Like a fighting rooster, they needed to ruffle their feathers and flash their spurs. They needed to frighten the Federals. Above all, Taylor knew his army must remain relevant and impossible to ignore.

Union commanders in New Orleans took the Rebel bait. Spooked by events at Brashear City, they believed the next blow would fall on them. Confederate prisoners locked up in the ironworks at Algiers caused a riot when captives from the Battle of Lafourche Crossing arrived spreading the news that the Texans had come. "One continuous and prolonged shouting might have been heard even across the river," wrote Private Theophilus Noel, a prisoner from the 4th Texas Cavalry taken in the Teche Campaign. "We became so boisterous and noisy that the 26th Massachusetts, who were guarding us, was compelled to call for reinforcements." Fearing that the Texans might soon enter Algiers and spring these rowdy Rebels, Federals ushered the prisoners onto the steamer *Catawba* for a trip to City Point, Virginia, and exchange. Federal details also evacuated ammunition, rations, and other supplies from the west bank.[12]

Spies and scouts brought Taylor news of the pandemonium near New Orleans. "The city is greatly excited," he gloated to Kirby Smith. "The enemy have worked night and day to remove Negroes and stores from Algiers to the other side."[13]

A jittery General William H. Emory could not convince Banks of the looming peril, so he sent dispatches to Washington listing his worries and raising the alarm in higher circles. "The land force in this city, and in the extensive line of defenses contiguous to it, is less than a brigade," Emory lamented. With the Confederates astride his line of communications with Baton Rouge, reinforcements for New Orleans might have to come from someplace other than Banks and his army. "*If* they can be gotten here in time," Emory warned. Banks had derailed efforts at raising black troops to defend New Orleans against such a threat by siphoning them off to the trenches upriver. Instead of fighting, they had been swinging picks and pushing shovels. Brigadier General Daniel Ullmann could do little to alter these conditions, writing, "as soon as my officers can be relieved from this duty I will proceed as rapidly as possible with the raising and organizing of my command." Fearing no help would come from any quarter, Emory called for his staff to form a body of troops from the city's "unconditional Union men."[14]

The Federals in New Orleans feared being overrun. The upriver defenses of New Orleans needed tending. The 26th Massachusetts, relieved of guarding unruly prisoners, deployed near Fort Banks on the western shore opposite Camp Parapet. Cavalry pickets from the 1st Texas Cavalry (Union) led by Georgia-born, Austin refugee Lieutenant Colonel Jesse Stancel posted well ahead to watch for snooping Rebels. Colonel Thomas Cahill and the 9th Connecticut, the 15th Maine, and the remnants of three regiments—the 23rd Connecticut, 176th New York, and 42nd Massachusetts—manned the breastworks bordering the Barataria Company Canal.[15]

The Confederates, Emory believed, would cross the Mississippi some eighteen miles above New Orleans with an estimated eight thousand men while sending four thousand to cross four miles below. If they got across, he would be powerless to stop them. He sent a dispatch to Admiral David G. Farragut asking him to "have all the schooners, sloops, and barges of every sort between here and Donaldsonville, and also for several miles below town, brought to this side of the river." No sense in leaving them as gifts to the Rebels, Emory thought.[16]

Fort Butler also required reinforcements. Banks released one regiment, the 1st Louisiana Infantry (Union) from the siege lines at Port Hudson and they arrived at dawn on June 29, tramping down gangplanks to sights and smells of death and suffering. "New graves were seen along the levee," observed Sergeant George Smith of Company C. "The slope of the parapet towards the river was completely covered with a gore of blood."[17]

Other help also came. Emory ordered Lieutenant Colonel Josiah A. Sawtell to send two companies of his 26th Massachusetts Infantry aboard the tugboat *Zephyr* from the already thin defenses of New Orleans toward Donaldsonville. The gunboat USS *Tennessee* also headed upstream with Admiral Farragut aboard. With these reinforcements, Major Joseph D. Bullen would have six gunboats and about one thousand men on hand if Green wished to try again. Some of these

The only known photograph of Fort Butler shows the mouth of Bayou Lafourche, the pontoon bridge into Donaldsonville, and the batture *behind the levee wall. Stacks of supplies litter the space, and the ditch reported by the Rebels during the attack on the post appears at the bottom of the wall. Notice the sluice gate to the left that regulated drainage and the sod-covered wall with pathways worn through the grass. The stockade wall appears in the background.*
Courtesy of Andrew Capone, Napoleonville, Louisiana.

troops entered the town of Donaldsonville and torched buildings near the bayou to provide clearer fields of fire.[18]

On June 29, Emory still remained on edge. He ordered Colonel Cahill on a reconnaissance down the tracks from Algiers toward Lafourche Crossing. They got no closer than Boutte Station before tangling with Texan pickets. That same day, a small body of Confederate cavalry moved in on the Union outpost east of the Mississippi at Bonnet Carré. "Make a brave stand," Emory advised. He had been expecting a crossing—and believed this might be it because Confederates appeared on both banks. The USS *Kineo* headed upstream to investigate. Emory pulled the 15th Maine from its position on the Barataria Canal to man the works at Camp Parapet, fearing the coming battle. "Keep your pickets on the *qui vive*, and all your forces in hand," he advised. He also ordered Stancel and his Texas Unionists to "fall back slowly" toward Fort Banks on the west bank when the Rebels came, as surely they must.[19]

Commander of the West Coast Blockading Squadron, Admiral David G. Farragut chafed under the tedium of siege craft. His blue-water warships hammered away at the defenses of Port Hudson and covered Union garrisons ashore, but he longed to return to operations in the Gulf of Mexico.
Library of Congress Prints and Photographs Division, Washington, D.C.

Union uncertainty rippled up the Mississippi. From Vicksburg, Grant feared for Port Hudson almost as much as Emory feared for New Orleans. These Union officers dreaded that Banks might be in trouble, and both said as much to General-in-Chief Henry Halleck. Banks asked for troops from Vicksburg, but Grant demurred, sending a staff officer instead to gauge the situation at Port Hudson. "Should it be my good fortune to get into Vicksburg while you are still investing Port Hudson," Grant wrote, "I will commence shipping troops to you." Meanwhile, Emory also urgently needed men. "The time has come," he wrote Banks. "I do not think you have one moment to lose in sending reinforcements." Despite the hand wringing, Banks kept his focus. The Confederates, he believed, had far fewer numbers than Emory believed and could not gain much in the region. Banks gambled. "I do not think . . . the city is in peril. Some inconveniences and annoyances must necessarily ensue from the operations of the enemy while the bulk of our forces are engaged at this point." Besides, he told Emory, the end was near. "We shall," Banks assured, "be released in a few days."[20]

Not every Federal surrounding Port Hudson shared their commander's optimism. The army, Captain Dyer D. Bullock of the 114th New York wrote home, lay spent. Rumors swirled that Banks planned another assault to break Gardner's lines. "If we are not successful," the captain wrote, "the enterprise will

USS Kineo *stands at the head of the column to resupply at the Baton Rouge coaling yard. Mountains of anthracite, seen in the foreground, fueled the Union navy as it patrolled the Mississippi.*
Library of Congress Prints and Photographs Division, Washington, D.C.

be abandoned. Our army is being very fast reduced. The bombardment and picket fighting continue night and day, and the number killed and wounded daily, and becoming sick, depletes our army very much." Bullock also knew about the plight of New Orleans but feared there would be too few left in the Army of the Gulf to make a difference. "And then we want our forces for the defense of the city," he scoffed. For the Federals, the coming days would be long and trying.[21]

The Confederates tried to gauge how well they had frightened their enemy. On the morning of June 30, Green's troops pushed hard against the pickets at Fort Butler to learn what they could about the reinforcements coming in and perhaps capture some prisoners. Officers aboard the USS *Princess Royal* ordered the men beat to their stations and barricades of awnings and hammocks erected to protect the crew from bullets. The Texans fell back, having learned nothing. When the USS *Genesee* arrived late that afternoon, it shelled the woods just to assure the Rebels stayed away.[22]

General Ulysses S. Grant, portrayed here in heroic pose, wore down the Confederate garrison at Vicksburg.
Library of Congress Prints and Photographs Division, Washington, D.C.

Once again Yankee shells whined for miles down Bayou Lafourche. The incoming artillery terrified the residents of Sleepy Hollow Plantation. The sound of firing from the two 30-pounder Parrots aboard *Genesee* took two seconds from flash to rumble from that far away. Then, for an agonizing twenty-five seconds, its 29-pound shell hurtled through space toward its unseen target. When it finally struck earth, its percussion fuse detonated the round, scattering jagged hunks of iron for yards around. "Today," Heléne Dupuy wrote in her diary, "we came near being killed at the sugarhouse by the explosion of a bomb." The civilians fled to the woods, the young girl writing, "during our flight from the sugarhouse we threw ourselves on the ground three times to avoid the bombs."[23]

The family decided to shelter in a makeshift cabin hidden in the tangle of trees south of Sleepy Hollow. They soon regretted that decision. "We passed a bad night and were much tormented by insects," Dupuy wrote. "This morning we are covered with stings." The random shelling continued. "I believe that here we are protected from the bombs," she speculated. She could easier tolerate the mosquitoes and ants.[24]

These civilians weighed the hardships and dangers of war. When rain fell, the flimsy roof of their hideaway leaked badly making sleep difficult. The bugs, though, finally drove them home. "We are back in our house. Glad I am!" Dupuy wrote a few days later. "We passed the whole morning cleaning up the house and putting back in the armoires the clothes, which we had taken out . . . when we thought our house was going to burn." Dupuy and her family wagered that the Rebels had come to stay. "Now I am no longer afraid, for I am sure that the

Battery A, 1st U.S. Artillery, pictured here, occupied a position northeast of Port Hudson, using cotton bales and sandbags for fortifications.
Library of Congress Prints and Photographs Division, Washington, D.C

The 21st Indiana Infantry came to Louisiana with General Benjamin Butler in 1862. By the siege of Port Hudson, the Hoosiers had been converted to the 1st Indiana Heavy Artillery and in that capacity hammered away at Rebel defenses at Port Hudson. These men, fighting from improvised works, toiled under the relentless heat during the summer of 1863 against the stubborn defenders at Port Hudson.
Library of Congress Prints and Photographs Division, Washington, D.C.

These gunners of the 1st Indiana Heavy Artillery served amid the shredded cotton bales of their makeshift fortifications.
National Park Service photo.

Another Union warship on the Mississippi, USS Genesee *could bring the weight of its heavy battery against targets miles away from the banks of the Mississippi.*
Library of Congress Prints and Photographs Division, Washington, D.C.

Confederates will not go away," she wrote, "and if they stay here they will prevent the Yankees from coming."[25]

Taylor and Green had potential allies in their efforts to crimp the Union supply line. Colonel John L. Logan's cavalry forces on the east bank of the Mississippi also caused mischief. On July 2, these riders dashed in on Banks's principal depot at Springfield Landing south of his Port Hudson lines and burned quartermaster and commissary stores. The soldiers of the 2nd Rhode Island Cavalry fled, as did many of the white officers of Ullmann's Brigade; the black rank and file rallied. "The black soldiers of that command, on being supplied with muskets and ammunition by my ordnance officer, were easily formed into line, and did not," reported Brigadier General William Dwight, "yield to the panic about them." After destroying what they could, the Confederates retreated from the stiffening resistance, troopers from the 1st Louisiana Cavalry (Union) in pursuit. They had killed or wounded more than 140 of the Federals, losing about 20 of their own in the process.[26]

A correspondent from the New York *Times* believed that the poorly trained and disorganized men of Ullmann's Brigade had saved the army's principal depot. "Perhaps some of your Northern negro-haters will begin to acknowledge the value to the nation of our black friends down here." The same soldiers had dug most of the Union trenches as well. "I can only tell you that without their aid in this department," he added, "from the handling of a spade to the shouldering of a musket . . . we might long ago all have packed up and gone home."[27]

The Federals would have to replace the supplies Logan's troopers had destroyed. Anticipating this, Taylor, Green, and their Confederates inaugurated the next phase of the war on the lower Mississippi. A few days after the battle of Fort Butler, Green ordered Rebel gunners to build three emplacements for field batteries below Donaldsonville. They located the first near the late Judge Benjamin Winchester's Buena Vista Plantation about nine miles downstream. A steamer coming from Fort Butler would reach that point in less than an hour. The second Confederate gun position lay opposite College Point, nine miles further on. Officers located the last battery about six miles further down still, where the Vacherie Road intersected the Mississippi River Road. Union vessels going downstream would endure a twenty-five-mile, two-hour-long gauntlet of fire. Steamers bucking the current upstream with supplies for Banks would be in the kill zone longer. A dozen cannon belonging to four batteries—Captain Oliver Semme's 1st Regulars, the St. Mary's Cannoneers, the Pelican Artillery, and Nichols's Texas Battery—took turns providing the firepower.[28]

Hospital steward Morgan Wolfe Merrick of the 3rd Arizona set up shop in the outbuildings of the Winchester Plantation. "The residence at this plantation was one of the most elegantly furnished houses I was ever in," he wrote. "It belonged to a widow lady who had two sons in the Virginia army and the place had been left in charge of two old servants, an old negro man and woman." The house bore battle scars. "The Yankees seemed to take pleasure in throwing a shell or two through this house when passing with their gunboat," Merrick continued. "In one of the elegant bed rooms a shell had dropped through the roof and canopy of the bed and exploded . . . the feathers extinguished the fire, otherwise the place would have burned."[29]

On July 3, the large side-wheeler *Iberville*, laden with 450 tons of supplies heading upstream from New Orleans bound for Springfield Landing, became the first victim of the Rebel ambush. Just after midnight, a flash of fire rippled along the west bank as troopers from the 4th Texas Cavalry and the gunners of the 1st Regular Battery and Nichols's Texas Battery fired on the vessel from the Winchester Plantation. Shot, shells, and bullets crippled the vessel, holing the *Iberville* seven times, cutting up its machinery, and scalding some of the crew. The boat drifted downstream before beaching on the east bank of the Mississippi, two dead and six injured aboard.[30]

Only keen lookouts prevented a Union disaster. The tugboat *Ida*, passing downstream from Springfield Landing bound for New Orleans, saw the *Iberville*'s distress rockets and turned about, intercepting the side-wheeler *Sallie Robinson* along the way and saving it from entering the trap. The steamers tied up at Donaldsonville, alerted the nearby USS *Winona*, and all three vessels headed downstream, wary of lurking Rebels.

At 3:30 A.M., Texan riflemen opened on *Winona*. Drummers beat the crew to quarters and crews answered with a few blasts of their heavy guns. The convoy proceeded, rescued the *Iberville*, and cast a line to its crew. The *Sallie Robinson* and *Ida* escorted it on to New Orleans, while *Winona* returned to Donaldsonville, throwing a few more shells at the Winchester Plantation as it churned by. The gunboat soon passed the small steamer *Zephyr*, heading downriver after it

USS Winona *and other similar "90-day gunboats," had to be clearly marked to establish their identity. Note the number "2" on USS* Winona's *funnel.*
Library of Congress Prints and Photographs Division, Washington, D.C.

landed reinforcements at Fort Butler. As it returned to New Orleans, the vessel took two hits.[31]

Men from *Sallie Robinson*, *Ida*, and *Iberville* alerted the crew of the USS *Monongahela*, on station near Bonnet Carré, and the powerful warship headed upstream to investigate the trouble at Winchester Plantation. Around 11:00 A.M. the next morning, someone from shore (most likely a local slave or freedman) told the officer on watch that the Rebels could be found behind the house, resting in the outbuildings and sugarhouse. The Union warship fired in that direction with its smallest gun, a 3-inch rifled cannon, to elicit a response.[32]

The round stirred the lounging Texans but did not drive them off. "The gunboat knocked me out of a good Irish stew," Merrick remembered. "When we arrived at the plantation, I had gone direct to the old woman and told her to get me up a dinner, as she had on one occasion before; and when it was ready[,] to bring out the pot and place it on the table under the little shed at the end of the negro quarters." While the elderly slave cooked, other Confederates gathered for the meal. The hungry soldiers paid little attention when the masts of *Monongahela* appeared above the levee. "We were approaching the table when she opened up and a twelve pound shot came whizzing along," Merrick complained, "knocking my Irish stew into a blot. This shot passed through the long line of negro quarters and in the last house it roused a soldier who was sleeping."[33]

Fully alerted to their danger, the Texans roiled out of the buildings; as the *Monongahela* opened with the rest of her broadside, eight shots from its largest gun, a 200-pounder rifle, pummeled the grounds of Buena Vista. Merrick watched as a soldier headed toward the levee to take a shot at the Federal warship. One of the big rounds hit the levee, ricocheted up, then bounded beyond, unexploded. "When it struck, [it] rolled along the ground slowly and directly in his path," Merrick recalled. "It was coming so slow that he put his foot out thinking it would stop it, but he did not. It broke his ankle short off and kept on."[34]

Despite the fracases on the river, the tension slackened in New Orleans. The Rebels still had not attacked the city, substituting instead these pinprick exchanges along the Mississippi. Even Emory's officers in the field began to have their doubts about the danger facing New Orleans. Colonel Sawtell, from his advance position on the West Bank above the Crescent City, believed only 2,500 Rebels operated in the region, a lower estimate than Emory's by 10,000 men. Sawtell suggested that he might sweep the Mississippi's western bank of these pesky Rebel batteries by starting around Bonnet Carré and rolling toward Donaldsonville. Emory's staff remained incredulous. His aide, Lieutenant Colonel W. D. Smith, believed Sawtell had mistaken Taylor's vanguard for his entire army. "If the enemy had only 2,500, I have no objection to fighting 40 or 50 miles above," he snorted. "I take this force to be [only] the advance."[35]

Emory and his staff believed a battle for New Orleans would begin in a few days, and the garrison remained weak. Efforts to raise emergency troops from among the population failed spectacularly. Emory's recruiting officers uncovered an ugly mood among the residents. He believed that as soon as the Rebels appeared, these surly people would rise up and challenge the Union occupation.

A popular uprising would indeed aid the Rebels. "There are at least 10,000 fighting men in this city (citizens)," Emory explained, "and I do not doubt, from what I see, that these men will, at the first approach of the enemy within view of the city, be against us to a man." The paroled Union prisoners taken at Brashear City arrived as well, relating horror stories of impending doom. "The estimate I made of the strength of the enemy . . . is fully confirmed," Emory declared, still believing them to number more than thirteen thousand. "They are slowly but steadily advancing on this place." He even suspected that some in the city plotted to seize steamers to come to the assistance of the Confederate army looming upriver. Officials placed a curfew on the city and forbade public assemblies by either whites or blacks. Owners had to shutter bars, coffee houses, and gambling dens at 9:00 P.M. Emory reiterated his need for troops. "It is a choice between Port Hudson and New Orleans."[36]

In the city, Private Rufus Kinsley of the 8th Vermont agreed. He saw fellow soldiers celebrating Independence Day but took no part. "Celebrated the 'Glorious Fourth' by . . . wondering how men could be so jubilant," he wrote. "Things in this department have never looked so dark as now."[37]

From his headquarters at Brashear City, Taylor hoped for a miracle. What he needed most of all was time. Although the Confederate campaign had spooked Emory, Banks remained clamped down on Port Hudson. For Taylor's blockade to succeed, he needed time. Even if Vicksburg fell, as he believed it must, he might still save the garrison at Port Hudson. Given sufficient time, Walker might arrive and Taylor would attack New Orleans and deliver a defeat that would make Brashear City seem a trifle.

The Rebel general also understood that time was running short. The crisis required boldness and speed. "If any opportunity, however slight, offers," Taylor wrote to Kirby Smith, "I will throw myself into New Orleans, and make every effort to hold it, leaving my communications to take care of themselves." The inventory of successes so far in the campaign justified his confidence. "At all events," he wrote on July 4, "I have used every exertion to relieve Port Hudson, and shall continue to the last."[38]

Taylor awaited Walker but in vain. Later that day, news arrived from northern Louisiana that vexed Taylor, sending him into a rage and souring relations with his superiors. While he had been plotting against New Orleans, Johnston—and Kirby Smith—plodded around Vicksburg. Johnston, who had no advice for Taylor, had plenty of suggestions for Kirby Smith. Johnston wanted to break Pemberton out of Grant's prison, but he could not do it alone. "Our only hope of saving Vicksburg now depends on the operations of your troops on the other side of the river," Johnston lectured Kirby Smith. "Your troops up to this time have done nothing."[39]

Stinging from this rebuke, Kirby Smith took the field to lead Walker's Texas Division and the other troops in northeastern Louisiana to do what he could to save Vicksburg. Pleased, Johnston believed Kirby Smith should now attempt three tasks: plant batteries on the river to challenge Union communications; drive cattle into Vicksburg; and bring Walker and Tappan's infantry across to join the garrison in preparation for a breakout. One thousand beeves could sustain Pemberton's thirty thousand troops for more than two weeks. Johnston claimed that an officer fresh from Pemberton's headquarters agreed with this scheme. "If your troops could send an abundance of cattle, and themselves (8,000) to join the garrison, the place would be saved."[40]

Taylor could not fathom the sanguine nature of these letters. Not only was Walker not coming, but Johnston also advocated throwing his division into the Vicksburg abyss to share the fate of Pemberton's garrison. The Confederate hero of First Manassas also implied that Taylor had personally failed to act with any energy. "I am pained at its contents," he wrote to Kirby Smith—a clear understatement of his anger. Johnston had complained about efforts west of the Mississippi, Taylor reasoned, but failed to explain exactly what *he* had accomplished with three times as many men east of the Mississippi.[41]

Johnston had neither come to aid Port Hudson, as Taylor had suggested, nor had he done anything at Vicksburg. He had no Mississippi River between him and either fortress as an excuse. "A tone of complaint seems to prevail that nothing has been accomplished on this side of the river," Taylor groused. "It is to be presumed that the difficulty of communication prevents us from hearing what efforts the army under General Johnston has made to relieve Vicksburg."[42]

Taylor applauded Kirby Smith's decision to leave his headquarters in Shreveport and take the field in northeastern Louisiana. Only a mathematician—like Kirby Smith—or magician could make the numbers work. "I certainly accord most heartily with the suggestion," Taylor conceded to Kirby Smith with a touch of bitterness. "In the present critical state of the campaign, [your] presence would be of great utility." Taylor also wondered what Confederate troops in Arkansas had been doing to save Vicksburg. They, too, could interdict supplies on the Mississippi. Why, Taylor wondered, had Johnston put the burden almost exclusively on him and his troops in Louisiana?[43]

From his reading of these week-old dispatches, Taylor now knew that Vicksburg would fall—and soon. Johnston had thrown in the towel. To save Port Hudson, Taylor rethought his campaign. "The plan I had arranged for an attack on New Orleans fell through as soon as I was advised that Walker's Division would not join me," he conceded. He simply did not have enough men to accomplish that outcome. "That the plan referred to would have succeeded . . . I do not entertain the slightest doubt. Whether the city could have been held is another question." When Vicksburg fell, Taylor knew, Port Hudson would naturally follow. If he could have taken New Orleans, he might have broken the siege and rescued Gardner's men. Yet, Kirby Smith had dashed all Taylor's hopes—save one.[44]

Time was up for General Pemberton. Upstream from Vicksburg, Captain William A. Smith, Walker's Assistant Adjutant General, and a few other Confederates snuck through the woods along the bank of the Mississippi. In his pocket was a glass bottle, weighted with a pistol bullet, and containing a slip of paper wound tight and tied with sewing thread. On it was a message written in cypher: "Gen'l Pemberton: You can expect no help from this side of the river. Let Gen'l Johnston know, if possible, when you can attack the same point on the enemy's lines. Inform me also and I will endeavor to make a diversion. I have sent some [percussion] caps. I subjoin a dispatch from General Johnston." The Confederates loaded a skiff and prepared to risk a crossing of the Mississippi into Vicksburg. With luck, Smith would deliver the munitions, and his coded message, to Pemberton that night. If intercepted Smith would sling the bottle as far as he could into the current before capture; it would either sink, or perhaps arrive on a friendly shore. Either way, Smith faced a perilous mission. In the afternoon light, he scanned the opposite bank. Then, he saw it—the Stars and Stripes floated above the Vicksburg courthouse. He forgot about the two-inch bottle in his pocket and instead headed back toward Monroe with the bad news.[45]

That same evening, July 4, 1863, Taylor had no way of knowing of Pemberton's surrender but clearly realized that his time in the Lafourche District was fleeting. Instead of taking New Orleans, he now shifted his focus to removing the region's slaves, produce, and livestock across Berwick Bay. He sent word for steamers to come down to the Atchafalaya via Grand Lake to Brashear City and assist with removing plunder. His military operations now amounted to merely buying time for looting because the river forts seemed destined for ruin. Taylor concentrated

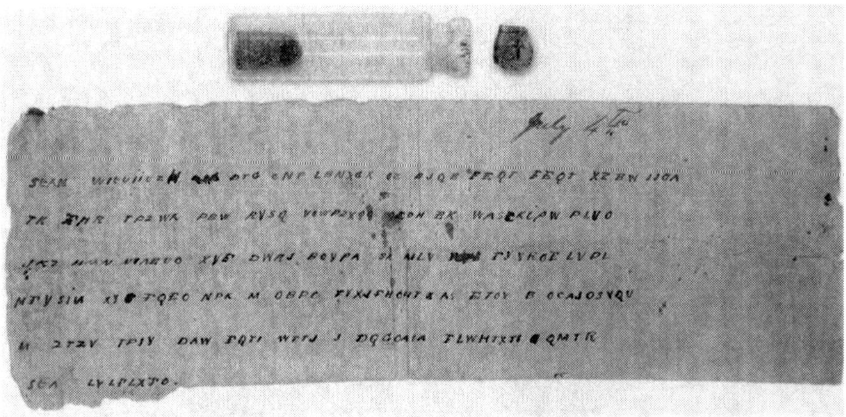

This artifact from the Museum of the Confederacy is a small but tangible reminder of the failure of Confederate forces to coordinate their efforts in the Mississippi Valley.
Museum of the Confederacy.

his army to make the most of his time remaining. Mouton had his Louisiana infantry brigade and the 2nd Louisiana Cavalry around Thibodaux recruiting new soldiers, breaking up government plantation operations, confiscating freed slaves, and gathering up livestock.[46]

In the capital of the Confederacy, Major Josiah Gorgas assumed that Taylor had already made his move against New Orleans. "The news yesterday was that Taylor and [John B.] Magruder were on this side of the Mississippi at [Kenner], ten miles out of New Orleans," he wrote. "An attempt would be made to surprise Fort Jackson, which, it is said, is held by a small force of negro troops." This rumor proved a Confederate fantasy.[47]

Grant had taken Vicksburg at 10:00 A.M. on July 4, and the news already flowed downstream toward Port Hudson. After notifying his immediate commanders, the victorious general sent a note to Banks. General William Tecumseh Sherman wasted no time in starting out against Johnston's Confederates north of Jackson, Mississippi. "This move will have the effect of keeping Johnston from detaching a portion of his force for the relief of Port Hudson," Grant explained. He reasoned, though, that Banks probably did not need the help. "I hope, general," Grant added, "this [dispatch] probably will find you in possession of Port Hudson."[48]

He was overly optimistic. The Union troops in Louisiana still remained entrenched outside the defiant fortress and Taylor—operating in ignorance of

This sketch shows elements of the Union navy above and below Port Hudson, adding the weight of their guns to the siege.
Frank Leslie, *Famous Leaders and Battle Scenes of the Civil War* (New York: Mrs. Frank Leslie, 1896).

events upriver—still believed that he might still have one last chance to save Gardner. Hope flickered. Taylor bypassed Mouton and headed directly to Paincourtville to meet with Green and plan the next stage of his operations. First, communications between New Orleans and Baton Rouge needed to be cut. Emory, kept ignorant of Union progress, might scare himself into surrendering. A squad of Texans galloped toward Plaquemine to cut the telegraph link between Baton Rouge and Fort Butler.

Someone also needed to handle that chore east of the river. Green understood Taylor's plans and scribbled out a dispatch addressed "To any Confederate Officer commanding on the east of the Mississippi." The missive assured the recipient that the Rebels west of the river would hold their own against all Yankee comers. What Green needed was additional cooperation from the mounted troops on the far side—the dustups at Bonnet Carré and Springfield Landing had been a good start. If Colonel Logan's Arkansas, Tennessee, and Mississippi troops mirrored what he intended to do with his Texans, the river supply line would be crimped shut. "We can stop the supplies to Banks' army, and force him to raise the siege of Port Hudson," Green assured. The Federals, forced by starvation out of their trenches, would be no match for the Confederates. "We will, I am confident, be able to whip his army in the open field should he move on this side," Green crowed. The Texan had just the man for the hazardous crossing of the Mississippi. He handed the note to Leander McNelly. The young scout headed toward another adventure.[49]

The bad news from Vicksburg had yet to reach Taylor's command and the mood of the Rebel army in the Lafourche District remained buoyant. This invasion had been a homecoming for many of the Louisiana troops. "Entering into Thibodaux," remembered Captain Silas Grisamore of the 18th Louisiana Infantry, "I met with a quantity of friends who literally pulled me off my horse and carried me about a square and made me eat, as near as I can remember, some six or seven dinners before I could get away." Locals furnished the troops with libations and delicacies to mark the occasion. "Well," Grisamore reflected, "we had not met for a long spell, and we could not resist the temptation for a little glory over our return and we had a good time."[50]

At Sleepy Hollow Plantation, Dupuy anticipated a family reunion. Her kin were among the Louisiana infantry. "We expect to see Oscar, Ninique and Charles in a few days," she wrote. It also reminded her of relatives in other Confederate armies. "Ah! If we had also the good fortune to see our other cousins who had departed two years ago," she scribbled, "but we do not even know what has become of them. We have not had a single word from any of them for the last ten months."[51]

At the same time, Green's Texans maintained a tight watch on Fort Butler. A belt of timber nearly a mile-and-a-half-wide east to west, and a one-third mile north to south on the west bank of Bayou Lafourche provided a perfect vantage point. The public road along the bayou bordered the trees on the southern margin; a local road bordered it on the east and north. Numerous logging roads also cut into the trees where area residents went for fuel. East of the bayou, fields of cane and corn made for good cover.

Almost daily picket skirmishes occurred near Donaldsonville. In one fight, Captain John J. Scott of Company B, 5th Texas Cavalry, learned the limits of personal courage. His troops, hidden in the trees one night, watched him head into the darkness toward Fort Butler. "The Captain took it in his head to go inside of the Yankee lines to find out how many . . . there were," wrote Private John W. Watkins. "He was drunk and all of us tried to keep him from going, but he was determined to try it. He never came back." The Texan officer stumbled on a pair of Union pickets who demanded his surrender. He refused. The two soldiers fired their weapons and fell back to the fort. "The next morning they came back and found his horse and saddle with a canteen partly filled with whiskey," Watkins continued. They also found a blood trail and followed it four hundred yards into the woods where they discovered the stricken Texan, shot through the left hand and the torso. The Federals carried him to Fort Butler where he died. "He was a brave man," concluded Watkins, "and if he had not been under the influence of whiskey would not have gone."[52]

On the Mississippi nearby, Confederate gunners and sharpshooters continued to pepper Union shipping. On July 5, *Sallie Robinson*, headed back upriver carrying two hundred tons of supplies, took several hits before picking up the gunboat *Kineo* as an escort near College Point. The pair arrived safely at Donaldsonville but only after the warship tossed a dozen rounds at Confederates near the Winchester Plantation. "From this time forward," noted Lieutenant Colonel Richard Irwin on General Banks's staff, "no transport passed up, except under convoy."[53]

Taylor's final option appeared to be vexing the Federals. His gunners might yet stop the flow of supplies to the Yankees besieging Port Hudson—given sufficient time.

13

Vexation

There are but little hopes of any of the transports coming up unless they are compelled.

—Admiral David G. Farragut
West Gulf Blockading Squadron

Later the morning of July 5, the USS *Winona* headed downstream from Donaldsonville and through Rebel waters to pick up the next supply boat, the small steamer *Cornie*. As the gunboat neared Buena Vista Plantation, small arms whacked into the hull and zipped through the rigging. Officers gave orders and drummers scrambled crews to their guns, which blasted back at the annoying Texans. *Winona* continued downstream and, around 2:30 P.M., preemptively shelled suspected Confederate gun positions opposite College Point. A half-hour later, the *Cornie* arrived at the rendezvous, loaded with about fifty tons of supplies. The duo headed upstream, coming under small arms and cannon fire again at Buena Vista, which prompted the *Winona* to unleash another broadside. The warship anchored off Fort Butler and the little steamer continued upstream. The day had been long and trying.[1]

That evening, other vessels faced the Texan and Louisianan guns. The steamer *North American* arrived at Fort Butler from Port Hudson with the balance of the 28th Maine Infantry as reinforcements. Lieutenant Colonel William E. Hadlock took command of the post from the ill—and failing—Major Joseph D. Bullen. This chore complete, USS *Monongahela* escorted the empty *North American* downriver to pick up another load of supplies at New Orleans. Just fifteen minutes out of Donaldsonville, Commander Abner Read called all hands to stations. The Rebels did not disappoint and fired at the steamers from Buena Vista and College Point. The sloop-of-war launched more than fifty rounds at its assailants, and by 8:30 P.M., the pair successfully completed their three-hour journey to Bonnet Carré. Ship carpenters noted bullet holes in the hull and spars but no significant damage. Shooting its way past the Confederates that evening, USS *Kineo* headed downstream to anchor near College Point.[2]

The next day, the harassment continued. Around noon, with no vessels to escort upstream, the *Kineo* went Rebel hunting. This time, however, the snipers followed the vessel, unleashing a running rifle fire against the ship. The Yankee gunners responded with their heavy guns—more sound than fury. The crew resorted to shooting back with small arms to save their heavy shot for enemy artillery. After hours of this scuffle, *Kineo* made port at the mouth of Bayou Lafourche alongside the *Princess Royal*.[3]

Meanwhile, tragedy roiled the Fort Butler garrison. The day before, Francis R. Scott of the 1st Louisiana Infantry (Union) had argued with an increasingly ill and unstable Major Bullen during an inspection. Malarial and delirious, the major excoriated the tired and irritable Scott, finally laying hands on the enlisted man. In the ensuing scuffle, Scott, in defending himself from his commander's irrational, physical assault, reflexively pushed his loaded rifle into Bullen's ribs and squeezed the trigger, the bullet angling upward through his torso, mortally wounding him. The unintentional assailant now lay in the hold of *Princess Royal* in double irons. Two accused Confederate spies, Frank Alema and Emile Brun, joined him. Bullen expired on the morning of July 6, and troops loaded his body aboard the steamboat *Cornie*.[4]

While the Yankees murdered each other, the Confederate gunners had accomplished little and fears of an attack on New Orleans faded. Federals' nerves uncoiled in the Crescent City. Admiral David G. Farragut, always cool under fire, assured General William H. Emory that all would end well. "I understand the play of the Rebels and think we can foil them." The admiral distributed his gunboats and warships up and down the river and had great confidence that his skippers could best any challenge. Farragut also believed the Navy had plenty of muscle at New Orleans, with "two sloops of war and three or four other vessels whose guns are as good as ever." If the citizens of New Orleans rebelled, he told Emory, his ships could simply shell the city into submission. Emory, assuaged, lifted his curfew. The coffee houses, billiard halls, and restaurants reopened.[5]

Although the Confederates had rattled Emory, General Nathaniel P. Banks still refused to be distracted and continued strangling Port Hudson. "As matters stand, the enemy will do us some harm in the Lafourche and cause us considerable annoyance on the river," he admitted to General-in-Chief Henry Halleck in the nation's capital, "but I consider it certain that Port Hudson will fall before New

Orleans is seriously endangered." After he crushed General Franklin Gardner and his army, Banks would deal with General Richard Taylor. The Union general felt vindicated in his conduct of the campaign. Halleck had wanted Banks and General Ulysses S. Grant to cooperate against Vicksburg. Had he done so, Banks pointed out, Gardner and Taylor would have combined against Emory and his tiny garrison. "New Orleans could not have been defended," Banks concluded with some satisfaction. He had gambled correctly, despite Halleck's angst.[6]

Communications between New Orleans and Baton Rouge remained sporadic, and the Confederate batteries along the west bank of the Mississippi, annoying. On July 7, the Rebels rotated in fresh troops, including the Louisiana Pelican Battery under the command of Captain Thomas A. Faries and a section of the Gonzales Texas Battery under Lieutenant Henry Angel. Faries dug in two rifled guns at the Gaudet Plantation, just downstream from the oft-punished Buena Vista, and waited. These newcomers soon took their turn against the Federal vessels.[7]

That morning, the Union navy made another run through the Rebel blockade. Downriver, USS *New London* escorted the tugboat *Ida* and its load of ammunition and powder for the fleet. They hove to at Bonnet Carré, joining USS *Monongahela*. About nine o'clock, these three vessels, bound for Port Hudson in line astern, came into view of Rebel lookouts. The Confederates opened fire, and the largest of the three, *Monongahela*, glided to a stop in front of the new Gaudet position to smother these Rebels with iron, covering the passage of *Ida* and *New London*. Faries's gunners aimed for the bridge of the now nearly stationary ship, sending a 10-pound bolt flying through a cluster of men there, mangling one seaman, crippling two others, and eviscerating the ship's skipper, Commander Read, which spattered Lieutenant George Dewey with gore. The same shell splintered a naval cutlass, driving the flat of the blade hard against another officer's thigh, knocking him to the deck. Bullets buzzing across the vessel hit another sailor in the shoulder. *Monongahela*'s guns answered. After this brief exchange, the three vessels passed on to Donaldsonville, bruised but undaunted. The Rebels had drawn blood but could not stop the passage of Union supplies.[8]

Admiral Farragut lamented the loss of this veteran officer. As skipper of *New London*, Read had taken thirty prizes. The previous April, he had lost an eye to Rebel gunfire at the Sabine Pass lighthouse. Still, he had remained on duty. His gruesome wound while commanding *Monongahela*, though, took five days to kill

Lieutenant George Dewey saw some of the fiercest naval fighting of the Civil War and seemed destined to live a charmed life. As an officer of the USS Mississippi, *he helmed that vessel in the passage of the forts below New Orleans. Months later, Dewey was among the last to leave the doomed ship as it lay grounded and burning under the guns of Port Hudson. He eventually found reassignment aboard USS* Monongahela. *After his conspicuous service on the Mississippi, he went on to serve as executive officer of USS* Colorado *and played a signal role in the capture of Fort Fisher, North Carolina. He ended the war with the rank of lieutenant commander. More than three decades later, aboard his flagship USS* Olympia, *Dewey would inaugurate the Spanish-American War at the 1898 Battle of Manila Bay.*
Photographic History of the Civil War.

him. "No navy can boast a better officer," Farragut opined, "and I deem him a great loss both to the navy and to his country." After the slaying of his friend, Farragut decided to personally investigate these Confederate batteries. "I am going down the river," he wrote aboard USS *Tennessee* at Baton Rouge, "to see what are the obstructions." He would probably need to see to New Orleans, as well, because "they appear to have such a stampede on them."[9]

The official news of Vicksburg's surrender arrived at Banks's headquarters later that day. He dispatched Grant a congratulatory note. "It is the most important event of the war," Banks wrote. "The freedom of the Mississippi puts an end to the rebellion, as far as an independent Confederacy is concerned." At noon that day, Union batteries at Port Hudson opened a celebratory barrage all across the line as a salute. Banks also sent a note to Emory with the news. He could rest easy about New Orleans.[10]

The news of this Confederate disaster trickled slowly into the region, and Taylor's campaign along the lower Mississippi continued in ignorance. Rebel cannon forced Union skippers to pilot their vessels at night from Fort Butler to Bonnet Carré to reduce their visibility. In the early hours of July 8, the steamer *St. Mary's*, carrying news of General John C. Pemberton's surrender to New Orleans and

The steam sloop-of-war USS Monongahela *was a new ship, launched in Philadelphia early in 1862. It joined the West Gulf Blockading Squadron in time to make the run past Port Hudson on the night of March 14–15, 1863. The vessel took serious punishment and failed to run past the Rebel fort, suffering six dead and twenty-one wounded in the attempt. The warship spent the next few months shelling Port Hudson or patrolling the lower Mississippi. Later, USS* Monongahela *operated off the coast of Texas and Alabama.* Naval Historical Center.

protected by gunboats *Kineo* and *New London*, ran a gauntlet of fire from west-bank batteries. Faries's and Angel's guns opened up on the steamboat eight miles below Donaldsonville near the Winchester and Gaudet Plantations, scored hits, but inflicted no casualties or even significant damage.

Having escorted *St. Mary's* past the point of greatest danger, the warships turned about while the steamboat continued paddling downstream with its glad tidings. At 4:00 A.M., the Pelican Artillery opened fire on the gunboats as they headed upstream. Faries claimed fifteen hits out of seventeen shots fired, whereas the Federals claimed to have swept the Rebels from the levee and embrasures. The gunboats anchored off Donaldsonville and repair parties aboard the *New London* reported that Rebel shot and shell had cut up rigging on the foremast, ripped up the main deck's canvas awning, and scuffed up the woodwork but accomplished little else.

Artillery boomed downstream as well. The *St. Mary's*, now running alone, faced a single gun and small arms at College Point, while farther downstream a section of rifled cannon blazed away near the Vacherie road. Five rounds struck the vessel but injured no one and did not stop its mission. The news of the Union victory at Vicksburg reached New Orleans a little after sunrise.[11]

Even in possession of this glorious intelligence, Emory remained wary of the nearby Rebels. He still believed a force of three thousand "watermen, fishermen, and irregular forces from the lagoons and bayous of Southern Texas and Louisiana" would wind their way through the lakes and swamps and drop in below New Orleans to cut its links to the Gulf of Mexico and signal an insurrection in the city. "I have expressed . . . my determination," Emory wrote on July 8, "to hold the city to the last extremity, even if it involves its destruction."[12]

Civilian pilots feared the Rebel blockade, even if the U.S. Navy did not. Clustered at Bonnet Carré and afraid to buck the current under the Rebel guns, steamers bound upstream waited for the cover of darkness. The captain of the *North American*, his boat loaded with tons of ammunition, decided to take a chance and headed upstream; he turned back after Rebel cannon rounds passed nearby. Clearly, the fall of Vicksburg had not opened the Mississippi. This vessel, and two others, waited all day for a navy escort. None came. Frustrated, the skippers turned the boats around, returning to New Orleans loaded with "2,000 negroes who had fled thither from the '*Government*' plantations on the approach of the guerillas," wrote Private Rufus Kinsley, a soldier in the 8th Vermont. After a long stay in a New Orleans hospital, he had boarded a vessel with orders to return to his regiment. At Midnight on July 9, he found himself back at the wharves of the Crescent City, the captain of his paddle wheeler afraid to brave the Rebel guns unprotected by an escorting warship.[13]

The Confederate blockade started to show promise. To improve it, General Tom Green remained hopeful that Colonel John L. Logan might bring his troopers east of the Mississippi into action on the opposite bank. After a three-day, one hundred-mile hunt, Texan scout Leander McNelly located Colonel Logan near Jackson, Louisiana. The Arkansas cavalry commander read Green's dispatch with interest, and forwarded it to General Joseph E. Johnston. He sent McNelly back with a reply. "I . . . urged General Green to hold his present position and cut off the enemy's supplies," Logan wrote, "and at the same time open communication with General Gardner, and provision the garrison at Port Hudson by swimming beeves across the river."[14]

Logan was not coming to help. Even if he had come, it would have been too late. The Federals grew tired of the mischief between Donaldsonville and Bonnet Carré, and Admiral Farragut headed downriver to take command in person. Rumors circulating at Fort Butler predicted that the Rebels would soon have in place heavy guns taken at Brashear City and thirteen thousand riflemen to back them. These cannon would dismantle any unprotected steamboats heading upstream. "There are but little hopes of any of the transports coming up," Farragut conceded, unless they are compelled." The navy needed more grit in this fight. He wrote to Admiral David Dixon Porter at Vicksburg asking to borrow some of his ironclads "until we can get clear of these Texans." In the meantime, he organized a convoy at Fort Butler including the ungainly ironclad USS *Essex*, brought down from Port Hudson. *Kineo*, *Monongahela*, and *Tennessee* gathered, along with the steamboat *Sallie Robinson* towing a schooner and a bark. The flotilla started down at 8:00 P.M. on July 9 into a stormy night, flashes of lightning illuminating the flotilla.[15]

Meanwhile, Louisiana gunners from the Pelican Artillery and the St. Mary's Cannoneers continued to improve their positions along the river. When the squadron of seven Federal vessels hove into view, the Confederates fired as fast as possible at this rich cluster of targets, each gun firing about six rounds before the ships passed out of range. The U.S. Navy responded with a broadside from their four warships that passed harmlessly over the Rebels' heads but did disrupt their accuracy. After the exchange, Captain Faries checked with his gunners and was convinced nine enemy ships had passed the point in the darkness. He assessed the damage to the Federals by sound, reporting to Green that "the heavy firing from this fleet prevented the effect of the shots . . . being accurately observed." Even so, it *sounded* like they had done fearsome execution.[16]

Faries's confident ears notwithstanding, the Union armada continued downstream, unruffled. The flotilla also took fire from the College Point and Vacherie batteries but again with little effect. The dark night and Rebel fire, however, did *disorganize* the column of vessels. Just out of danger from Confederate guns, *Tennessee* collided with *Kineo*, wrecking its railing and

Launched in 1853, the steamboat Tennessee *served routinely as a passenger vessel before becoming stranded in New Orleans at the beginning of the Civil War. Federal authorities captured* Tennessee *before Confederates could use it as a blockade runner, and Admiral David G. Farragut instead made the swift and elegant vessel his flagship. After the Battle of Mobile Bay, authorities renamed the steamer USS* Mobile *after the capture of the Confederate ironclad CSS* Tennessee. *Later that year, a hurricane off of Texas heavily damaged the ship, and it limped to New York for an overhaul. Navy officers decommissioned* Mobile *instead, and private interests bought the ship, renaming it S.S.* Republic. *In that guise, it plied the New York to New Orleans route, but it sank in a storm off of Georgia in October 1865, carrying $400,000 in gold coins 1,700 feet down. This treasure became a sensational find a century later.*
Photo by Odyssey Marine Exploration.

smashing the ship's boat. A little after 11:00 P.M., the flotilla reached Bonnet Carré. All of the Rebel smoke and fury had produced but one casualty, a single soldier slain by rifle fire.[17]

At that same moment in Donaldsonville, *New London* arrived from Baton Rouge with long-awaited news. Earlier that morning, the Confederate army under General Gardner had grounded its arms and surrendered Port Hudson. The forty-eight-day siege had ended. At 1:00 A.M. on July 10, 1863, *New London,* trailed by USS *Winona,* dashed down the Mississippi from Donaldsonville, bearing dispatches to General Emory that announced the fall of Port Hudson. When the ships arrived opposite Buena Vista, the Rebel batteries kept silent; *Winona* turned about, heading upstream on an errand to Baton Rouge. *New London* remained bound for New Orleans with its cargo of good news.[18]

Drowsy Rebel lookouts had simply not spotted the Federal ships, and their late alert sent gun crews scrambling to their guns to do what they could before the enemy vessels moved beyond range. When the artillerymen sighted down their tubes, only one Federal warship was in sight across the black water, barely visible in the inky darkness. The tardy attack began with flashes of fire and billows of smoke from the levee at the Winchester and Gaudet Plantations.[19]

General Franklin Gardner finally surrendered the garrison at Port Hudson after learning of fall of Vicksburg.
Louisiana State Museum.

Remarkably, the Rebels found their mark on the first volley. "The third shot struck the *New London*'s boiler, and exploding, made seven holes on a line with the upper flues," reported Lieutenant Commander George H. Perkins. "The steam rushed out with great force." Six men, severely scalded in the engine room, writhed in pain as the engines slowly cranked to a stop. *New London*, dead in the water, drifted with the current, bullets pattering against the hull, masts, and rigging or skipping across the water with a trail of white flashes. The helmsman, suffocating in the steam, turned the wheel hard to starboard before abandoning the hellish pilothouse. The stricken *New London*, turning a lazy half-circle, ran stern aground on the eastern bank of the Mississippi. Crewmen fired a signal rocket to announce their distress. Yet, *Winona*'s crew did not notice it as they headed upstream.[20]

The Confederates, now in a frenzy, did all they could to complete *New London*'s destruction. Lieutenant B. F. Winchester ran his two rifled guns over the levee and onto the *batture* to get a better angle on the gunboat. Quick-thinking Yankee crewmen lowered a ships boat, and, by kedging the anchor, got *New London* afloat and back into the current where it turned and drifted, stern first, out of range and

This blurry image may show a portion of the surrendered Confederate army at Port Hudson.
Marshall Dunham Photograph Album (Mss. 3241), Louisiana and Lower Mississippi Valley Collections, LSU Libraries, Baton Rouge, Louisiana, United States.

This image from Harper's Weekly *portrays triumphant U.S. troops taking possession of the Rebel fortifications of Port Hudson. The column of men, animals, and wagons stretches to the horizon.*
Library of Congress Prints and Photographs Division, Washington, D.C.

around a bend. Stranded between two known Rebel batteries, Perkins ordered the ship hauled to the eastern shore and secured to the bank until rescue arrived.[21]

But no help came. At Fort Butler, lookouts aboard *Princess Royal* sighted *New London*'s skyrocket. They also saw *Winona* glide by, bound upstream, seemingly

The famous engraving firm of Currier and Ives crafted this fanciful and celebratory image of the surrender of Port Hudson.
Library of Congress Prints and Photographs Division, Washington, D.C.

unalarmed. The commander of *Princess Royal* faced a dilemma. His gunboat protected Fort Butler, and he could not leave, but his crew believed something had gone wrong downstream. Who had launched the rocket, and why had *Winona* not responded?[22]

While the crew of *Princess Royal* pondered their conundrum, Commander Perkins, on the deck of *New London*, faced a genuine crisis. His ship listed to starboard on the Mississippi's east bank—helpless—its guns pointing skyward. Perkins ordered his crew off of the crippled ship and the sailors and marines grabbed rifled-muskets and took cover behind the Mississippi levee with orders to protect the ship should Rebels appear and try to seize it. He knew that Confederate cavalry had been active on this shore and might be in position to capture the ship. Perkins sent squads upstream and down to find help before all was lost.[23]

The Confederates on the western shore remained determined not to let this Yankee gunboat survive. Captain Faries ordered all six pieces to limber up and move to a point opposite *New London* and finish it off. As his teams pulled cannon down the road, however, Lieutenant Colonel Isham Chisum of the 2nd Texas Partisan Rangers galloped up with urgent news interrupting this deadly mission. The

Portrayed here with the prewar rank of midshipman, George H. Perkins earned promotion to lieutenant at the outbreak of the Civil War, commanding USS Cayuga *in the Gulf of Mexico and the Mississippi River. Promoted to lieutenant commander, Perkins served as executive officer of USS* Pensacola *before taking command of USS* New London. Naval Historical Center.

Yankees were coming down from Port Hudson—lookouts above Bayou Goula reported troops loading onto steamers near Springfield Landing. Until the situation clarified, Chisum ordered Faries to haul his guns four miles back down the Barteau Road toward the Lafourche. His coup de grâce on *New London* would have to wait. Denied his kill, Captain Faries sat out the rest of the night in the cover of the swampy woods, fuming.[24]

Chisum had been correct. The Federals were coming, just not yet. At daybreak, after ascertaining that the threat—although real—was not imminent, Faries ordered his guns back to the west bank. By 9:00 A.M., his artillery had moved to the levee opposite Godberry's Plantation where *New London* had tied up. His gunners feverishly cut embrasures for the rifled pieces and the heaviest of the smoothbores. If Confederate luck held, within the hour *New London* would lay a burning wreck.[25]

Characteristically, Rebel luck failed. Before Faries's men could finish sighting their guns, spotters reported the arrival of *Monongahela* and the metal leviathan, *Essex*, advancing upstream. The wooden warship lashed onto *New London*, dragging it downstream while the lumbering ironclad, sluggish in the Mississippi current, protected the operation. *Essex* sidled toward Faries and his guns, firing slowly from its massive XI- and XV-inch cannon. The Louisiana artillery, outmatched, prudently fell back. Faries reported: "I considered it useless to waste my light projectiles on the iron sides of the *Essex*."[26]

The foolhardy Texan cavalry tried their luck anyway. Sharpshooters attempted to pick off *Essex*'s crew by firing through its gun ports. The men competed with

Originally the steamboat New Era, *Federal authorities purchased the vessel and converted it into a timberclad gunboat for service on the Cumberland River. Eventually, the wooden armor gave way to iron and the steamboat underwent a complete metamorphosis. Emerging from the process as ungainly, inelegant, but deadly, USS* Essex *carried huge cannon and thick armor; the new creation proved hard for its engine to push against the current of the Mississippi River. It failed to destroy the ironclad CSS* Arkansas *in the summer of 1862, but it proved useful in defending Baton Rouge from the Confederates. Rebels on shore soon learned not to take on this clumsy heavyweight if they could help it.*
Naval Historical Center.

each other to see who made the best shot. Yankee sailors were not amused and unloaded on the Texans. "I was on the levee, encouraging my men," wrote Colonel Walter P. Lane of the 1st Texas Partisan Rangers. "A . . . shell struck the bank below me and exploded, turning over the planks I was laying on, and piling about eight wagon loads of earth on me. I thought I was murdered." Stunned, Lane's men pulled him out of the wreckage and withdrew, their colonel bleeding from a deep cut to the head but otherwise unharmed.[27]

Their retreat proved fortuitous. Riders arrived about that time with news that Federal troops in eight transports had landed at Donaldsonville. Lane and Faries headed for Plattenville and safety. "Our flank was now really threatened,"

Faries reported. "I then limbered up, and retired to the cut-off road leading to Assumption Church."[28]

The Confederate blockade of the Mississippi had failed. Taylor and Green had tried their best to strangle Banks's army. They simply could not beard the beast.

Now, it came for them.

14

Donaldsonville

We trembled at each cannon shot.

—Heléne Dupuy

Sleepy Hollow Plantation

Union reinforcements, lumbering down the gangplanks of a dozen steamers, quickly transformed Donaldsonville into a hive of Union activity. These, though, were not the bright and energetic warriors that had launched the Teche Campaign months ago. Instead, they were thousands of weary, sick, and tattered troops recently extracted from the grubby trenches at Port Hudson. First ashore were the men, cannon, and animals of Brigadier General Godfrey Weitzel's First Division, XIX Corps. Colonel Charles J. Paine led the way into town with the First Brigade including the 48th and 49th Massachusetts, the 116th New York, the 2nd Louisiana (Union), and the guns of the 1st Maine Battery. The new arrivals bivouacked in the fields beyond, driving away Texan pickets. Captain Orton S. Clark of Company H, 116th New York, had his men search the buildings inside the ruined town to ensure the Rebels had evacuated. "Before the desolation of war," he wrote, "it . . . had been a beautiful city, the abode of elegance and refinement. Now, however, it had a deserted look."[1]

Other troops also came ashore. Colonel Stephen Thomas led the Second Brigade, which included the 8th Vermont, 12th Connecticut, and 75th, 114th, and 160th New York. Colonel Nathan A. M. Dudley came ashore next, commanding the Third Brigade comprised of the 30th Massachusetts and the 161st and 174th New York, supported by four guns from the 6th Massachusetts Battery, and the skilled cavalrymen of Captain Richard Barrett's Company B, 1st Louisiana Cavalry (Union). By noon, these Federals also spread out around Fort Butler. General Weitzel, in command of these three brigades, had more men around Donaldsonville than General Richard Taylor commanded in the entire Lafourche District. These Yankees, too, laid out their camps around the town that, Major Elias Pellet of the 114th New York noted, had been "reduced to a heap of rubbish by shells from our gunboats."[2]

Brigadier General Godfrey Weitzel led an exhausted and ill army away from Port Hudson; he hoped to rehabilitate his troops by moving them to the agriculturally rich Lafourche Country where they could also check Rebel ambitions.
United States Archives and Records Administraiton.

The campaigns of April, May, and June had withered the strength of these Union regiments. In April, many of them had accompanied Major General Nathaniel P. Banks during his dramatic march up Bayou Teche. They had fought at Bisland and Irish Bend and endured the grueling march to Alexandria. In May and June, they had passed down the Red River and conducted the siege of Port Hudson, punctuated by two failed frontal assaults. As the campaign wore on, the weather had grown hotter and the work deadlier. "The labor of the siege," remembered Lieutenant Colonel Richard Irwin of Banks's staff, "pressed so severely upon the numbers of the besieging army . . . that the men were almost incessantly on duty." Clean water for the army had also become scarce, leading to a spate of camp diseases. "As the summer days drew out and the heat grew more intense, the brooks dried up; the creek lost itself in the pestilential swamp; the wells and springs gave out, the river fell," Irwin described, "exposing to the almost tropical sun a wide margin of festering ooze."[3]

Weather and terrain conspired against the Federal army on the lower Mississippi. By the time the Confederates surrendered, the Union army of twenty thousand that had hemmed it in had dwindled to merely eight thousand effectives. "Even of this small number," Irwin concluded, "every officer and man might well have gone on the sick-report." The wraith-like army stepping ashore at Donaldsonville fielded but shadow of the Army of the Gulf's original strength, and each regiment counted only between two hundred and three hundred men fit for duty. The rest were either dead, debilated, or exhausted by hard campaigning.

By the summer of 1863, the once-prosperous river town of Donaldsonville had become a wasteland of roofless buildings and burned out homes.
Courtesy Andrew Capone, Napoleonville, Louisiana.

Piles of fire blackened bricks lay strewn in the streets of the largely deserted town of Donaldsonville.
Courtesy of Andrew Capone, Napoleonville, Louisiana.

Hospitals from Baton Rouge to New Orleans teemed with convalescents from this army.[4]

Military discipline among the Union troops eroded. When paymasters arrived with eight-months' back pay, many soldiers—some recent immigrants to the United States—disappeared, their pockets bulging with more money than they had seen in their lives. "The camp guard wasn't very strict," remembered Private Joseph Klein, German swept into the 131st New York. "A good many of the regiment took a French leave and went to New Orleans to get rid of their cash. A number of them forgot to come back." After a fast spending spree, many of the troops found themselves broke, absent without leave, and in a strange city. They simply enlisted in other regiments to again draw a paycheck. "Some of them were brought back," Klein noted, "others we never heard from again." The problem became so acute that details left the Army of the Gulf encampments at Donaldsonville, Baton Rouge, and Port Hudson and headed to New Orleans, New York, and Boston to gather conscripts to fill out their regiments.[5]

This tattered force also faced a shortage of horses and transportation. During the siege, artillery teams sat idle too long while the mules and draft animals worked too hard. Fodder disappeared. Taylor's blockade of the Mississippi had slowed down the supply chain and had been hardest on the beasts of burden serving Banks and his army. "All the animals went upon half or quarter rations of grain, with little or no hay," Irwin continued. "The forage depots fairly gave out; the poor beasts were literally starving when the place fell."[6]

General Tom Green realized that this Union army, although winded and battered, might still fight. He ordered his troops back from the banks of the Mississippi to defend the region. Clearly, the arrival of these Union regiments carried one of two conclusions: either Taylor's army had succeeded in breaking the siege of Port Hudson, or General Franklin Gardner and his men had surrendered. Thousands of Confederates converged on Green's position at Paincourtville to await the answer. That night, July 10, news arrived by courier announcing the fall of Port Hudson, followed quickly by word that Vicksburg had fallen a week before. Taylor had failed. The Confederate commanders understood the implications. The Rebel army in the Lafourche District would be the Yankee's next target.[7]

General Taylor prepared for battle. He ordered his five Texas and Louisiana infantry regiments to prepare an ambush above Labadieville near Brigadier General

Alfred Mouton's old battleground of Georgia Landing. The narrowness of that field would negate, for a while, the Yankees' numerical superiority. These infantry rifles would provide Green a fallback position should the Federals come down the bayou in force. Like all of Taylor's troops, Lieutenant Colonel George Guess of the 31st Texas Cavalry (Dismounted) understood the Rebel predicament. He remained full of fight."There is trouble and danger up, but I can brook anything. Let it come," he declared. "Live or die, survive or perish." While preparing to make a stand, Taylor ordered General Mouton to have his quartermaster and commissary officers strip the region and send the loot up the Teche to safety. Taylor expected the U.S. Navy to return and shell Brashear City. If they did, Taylor's army might be trapped but at least the bounty of the region could be put to Rebel use. "An ironclad or two in Berwick's Bay, and the road at Plaquemine held by troops," he wrote, "would close all egress from the Lafourche, and the enemy could make arrangements to bag us at his leisure."[8]

Lieutenant Colonel George Guess, 31st Texas Cavalry (Dismounted), had been an import man in Dallas before the war. By the summer of 1863 he claimed he was ready to meet the Federal advance down Bayou Lafourche, come what may.
Guess (George W.) Letters (Mss. 793), Louisiana and Lower Mississippi Valley Collections, Special Collections, Louisiana State University Libraries, Baton Rouge.

Lieutenant General Edmund Kirby Smith, at his headquarters in faraway Shreveport, could also discern the danger. He ordered Taylor out of the Lafourche. "The fall of Vicksburg . . . has important bearing on your movements," he urged. The loss of Vicksburg meant the loss of Port Hudson, and with it, control of the Mississippi River. "Any occupation of New Orleans can now only be temporary." Taylor might make quite a haul in terms of supplies and munitions, but Kirby Smith believed it would be a doomed venture and merely result in the destruction of his tiny army. "Holding it would be placing your command in a *cul-de-sac* from which there could be no extraction." Taylor must retreat, and the Department of the Trans-Mississippi must contract. In the future, the Red River Valley, Monroe, Alexandria, and Shreveport would be the keys to holding Louisiana. Taylor had already arrived at the same conclusion and required little additional convincing.[9]

Flushed with victory, General Banks hoped to finally finish off Taylor's army. He still believed—as had General William H. Emory—that Taylor commanded up to fourteen thousand men. With the Army of the Gulf in rugged shape from four months' heavy service, he proceeded cautiously, fearing he might be outnumbered. After disarming Gardner's Rebels and packing them away to camps to await parole, he ordered Brigadier General Cuvier Grover to take his 4th Division, XIX Corps, to Donaldsonville to beef up Weitzel's forces. Together these troops would seal the Rebels into the Lafourche District and keep them away from the Mississippi. He believed Admiral David G. Farragut would plug Berwick Bay with gunboats and cut the Confederate line of retreat.[10]

Banks asked the navy to send light-draft gunboats down the Mississippi to seal the mouth of the Atchafalaya from the Gulf of Mexico. "Berwick Bay is now the all-important point," he explained. "This is the only possible way of their escape." He urged Farragut to move quickly. "I beg you will take immediate measures to send one or more of these boats to the bay, under the command of an energetic man," he pleaded. "Do not delay, as time is of the highest importance." Farragut had just the ships for this duty and ordered the USS *Estrella*, *Arizona*, and *Sachem* to head to New Orleans; the USS *Hollyhock* followed. The navy prepared to close the trap.[11]

With this operation underway, Banks placed General C. C. Andrews in control of Port Hudson. Banks threw the bulk of his veteran white troops against Taylor while the *Corps d'Afrique* garrisoned the captured Rebel fort. Andrews also had two white regiments and two white batteries to serve as caretakers of the place.[12] "It is fitting that black hands should hold Port Hudson," wrote Private Henry T. Johns of the 49th Massachusetts. "There, those hands signed the charter of the freedom of their race. In the future of the Africans . . . gifted orators will kindle a nation's patriotism with allusions to Port Hudson, even as *we* gather inspiration from the recollections of Bunker Hill." Recruiters began filling out these black regiments and mustered new black units at a steady pace.[13]

The men of the *Corps d'Afrique* spent the rest of the summer leveling the Union works—that they had helped dig—and filling the trenches and saps. They rebuilt the lines to face outward and cleared the surrounding forest to provide open fields of fire. Cotton bales, which both sides had used for cover, lay burst open and wads of fluffy fiber lay scattered and blowing across the battlefield. When these former field hands cleaned it up, quartermasters would sell it, using the proceeds to feed and clothe these new soldiers.[14]

Brigadier General Cuvier Grover had proven himself to be a steady and reliable officer during the Bayou Teche Campaign and the Siege of Port Hudson. Now he brought his battered command to Donaldsonville to face their next threat. Library of Congress Prints and Photographs Division, Washington, D.C.

The navy also had to untangle itself. Before its gunboats could help Banks bag Taylor, Farragut had to locate the vessels; they remained scattered all along the lower Mississippi. As a result, Farragut had trouble getting his shallow-draft armada assembled. *Arizona* had gone to Vicksburg with dispatches for General Ulysses S. Grant. Sending orders recalling that vessel would take time. *Estrella* remained somewhere north of Port Hudson and below the mouth of the Red River but had not reported lately. Naval officers spent another week locating this gunboat. Rumors claimed *Sachem* had fallen into the hands of the enemy. USS *Calhoun*, another light-draft boat, had been moving around Ship Island and recalling it would also require time. Workers continued to hammer and saw on the USS *Clifton*, which had been damaged in the fight at Butte La Rose back in early May; Farragut's officers ordered the repairs accelerated so this gunboat could bring its impressive firepower to bear. Every Union skipper knew it would take time to assemble this fleet. Farragut, wary of the haste Banks demanded, preferred being ready for whatever might lay in the swamps of the Atchafalaya—and move in with a powerful flotilla—than go piecemeal into a Confederate trap.[15]

The battle-scarred and chaotic landscape of Confederate Port Hudson gave way to orderly and tidy camps of Union troops as it blossomed into the headquarters of the Corps d'Afrique.

John Langdon Ward Lantern Slides (Mss. 4875), Louisiana and Lower Mississippi Valley Collections, Special Collections, Louisiana State University Libraries, Baton Rouge.

Regiments of liberated slaves leveled the old fortifications and rebuilt Port Hudson into a Union stronghold, depot, and training ground.

John Langdon Ward Lantern Slides (Mss. 4875), Louisiana and Lower Mississippi Valley Collections, Special Collections, Louisiana State University Libraries, Baton Rouge.

At Donaldsonville, General Weitzel wasted little time pushing back Rebel pickets. On July 11, soldiers from the 114th New York shook out into a skirmish line and cleared the Texans from the woods near Fort Butler. As the day wore on, Colonel Paine's brigade scouted north along the banks of the Mississippi for several miles toward Bayou Goula. The following day, Captain Richard Barrett's Company B, 1st Louisiana Cavalry (Union), backed by the 30th Massachusetts "Eastern Bay Regiment," pushed down Bayou Lafourche even farther, beating the bushes for Rebel scouts eyeing the Union concentrations at Donaldsonville.[16]

Having endured two weeks' worth of shelling and hiding in the woods, sixteen-year-old Heléne Dupuy began to fear a greater danger as news of the Federal approach reached Sleepy Hollow Plantation. "We heard from some Confederate soldiers that the enemy was at Donaldsonville," she wrote, "and we began to be troubled. Not that we doubted the courage and the skill of the Confederates! We knew that our soldiers were good Louisianians and Texans [and] are rarely beaten, but we lived so near Donaldsonville that we feared the two armies would again meet here." Her family grabbed some clothing and headed once again for the relative safety of their stout sugarhouse.[17]

Retreating Confederates streamed past Charles Kock's St. Emma Plantation on the west bank of Bayou Lafourche. One squad spotted Dupuy's group of civilians making for the safety of a sizable sugarhouse. "We had hardly arrived," she remembered, "when we saw that a body of Confederate cavalry was following us." The cluster of women—both black and white—spoke to the winded Rebels, but believed it imprudent to remain so close to the Texan cavalry lest they, too, become targets. "We retired a few arpents in the field, the negresses a little behind us," Dupuy remembered. "We wished to stay there until the enemy passed by." The Texans continued their retreat. The cluster of Louisiana women drew Yankee fire anyway. "We soon saw the smoke of a rifle shot, and the ball whizzed by our ears."[18]

One of the servants rose up and waved a handkerchief in the air at the Union skirmish line. "The Yankees then raised their caps and made us signs to advance," Dupuy wrote. "They told us we were more in safety in our house, for in the field we ran the risk of being killed. We reflected, and we thought that the advice our enemies had given us was the best we could take."[19]

When the women reentered their home, they discovered Federal cavalrymen ransacking their belongings. The civilians rushed in as a slave rushed out with an armload of pilfered clothes. Heavy footfalls upstairs revealed plunderers working over the bedrooms. The women clambered up the stairs. "When he heard us," Dupuy wrote, "he came out of the room with a large knife in his hand. Mamma was very much afraid." A second soldier emerged from Dupuy's bedroom carrying a drawer he had pulled from a nightstand; in it was her diary. "On seeing us," she wrote, "he laid the drawer on the bed without taking anything from it." In the kitchen, the Louisianans discovered a Union officer gulping down a bowl of milk. "He had long mustaches, from which the cream was dripping," observed Dupuy. Her aunt and mother scolded the soldier. "He answered with an air of bad humor that it was he who had prevented the men from stealing more."[20]

The Federal soldiers left the house and immediately came under fire from Texan skirmishers hovering nearby. The Union troops mounted, emptied their pistols at the Confederates, and trotted away. The women cowered inside their home, caught in the crossfire. "The balls were coming from both sides," Dupuy wrote. "We saw a Confederate aim at a Yankee; then fire and the man fell. I do not know whether he was killed or wounded." The men of Company B, 1st Louisiana Cavalry (Union) prudently retired toward Fort Butler, leaving the house once again in Rebel hands. "We had again the pleasure of seeing our friends, who were furious when they heard what the Yankees had done," Dupuy added. "They promised to avenge us."[21]

Both armies tried to learn about the other. The Federals successfully pushed the Confederate pickets back from Fort Butler, but the Rebels returned as soon as the Yankees retired. Weitzel remained ignorant of Confederate strength, yet Texans continued to scan his camps with impunity. He concluded that the Federals must control the woods near Fort Butler. His pickets reported that the Rebels rotated troops in and out of this cover daily.

Private Felix Collard of the 7th Texas Cavalry confirmed these reports. "The different brigades would send a regiment, or what was left of it . . . to this piece of woodland on picket duty." The Federals had routinely moved troops into these trees to scatter those pickets but never held the woods overnight. On July 12, Captain William Kirksey led the 7th Texas Cavalry to occupy these contested trees and resume monitoring the enemy at Donaldsonville.[22]

The Texans easily swept the woods and formed a cordon from the Mississippi to Bayou Lafourche, but their hold remained slippery. The Confederates watched as the Federal pickets reformed in the open fields around Fort Butler, reinforced by columns of blue-clad infantry. Unseen, another column of two Federal regiments passed north along the *batture* heading toward the McCall Plantation three miles upriver. The single Texas regiment faced an infantry brigade and the prospects of a flank attack under the guns of Fort Butler. When Federals on the Mississippi passed beyond the Confederate left, several of the officers and file closers foolishly climbed the levee to check on the progress of the outpost battle, alerting the enemy that their flank had been turned. This was the Texans' first inkling that the Federals had gotten around them. Rebel officers ordered their men to fall back—in a hurry.[23]

Texas Lieutenant Wiley Robin turned to Private Collard with urgent instructions. "Take word to Kirksey that we are being flanked by infantry, and GO!" The rider put spurs to his horse and headed back into the woods, bullets zipping past him, then turned left along the line of skirmishers and headed toward the bayou road. After reaching the right of the line, Collard turned and sped toward the regiment's commander. He never reached his destination—a culvert, unseen and collapsed, tripped his galloping steed. "The horse turned a complete somersault," Collard remembered. Thrown clear, he landed on his hands and knees. The horse crashed atop him, the saddle crushing the soldier's right arm between the shoulder and elbow. A nearby trooper came to his aid. "My arm is broken," Collard groaned, "but pay no attention to me, but run to Captain Kirksey and tell him we are flanked." The Texans retreated, reformed on the bayou road, and withdrew about a mile.[24]

With the Texans leaving, General Weitzel ordered a reconnaissance in force down Bayou Lafourche. Not only did he wish to keep the enemy at a distance, but he also planned to establish a new line four miles farther away from the Mississippi and bivouac his troops amid the cornfields of Palo Alto, St. Emma, and Sleepy Hollow Plantations. His new task was to hold Taylor's army in place until Farragut could bring his gunboats into Berwick Bay. "I think it was only our intention to camp at the place reached and wait until a force got in their rear," observed Captain Henry Howe of the 30th Massachusetts. Weitzel's Division controlled the west bank of Bayou Lafourche, General Cuvier Grover's division the east.[25]

Just after midday, Dudley's brigade spearheaded the advance. The few dozen troopers of the 1st Louisiana Cavalry (Union) led the way in a mounted screen, supported again by four companies of the 30th Massachusetts Infantry. The balance of this unit and two other regiments—the 161st and 174th New York—followed, as did four guns of the 6th Massachusetts Battery. A tattered four-regiment brigade under Colonel Joseph S. Morgan headed down the eastern bank of the Lafourche with orders to keep pace. Signalmen with semaphore flags maintained contact across the bayou that separated the brigades.[26]

Colonel Dudley's skirmishers rediscovered the 7th Texas waiting a mile down the road. "The enemy opened a brisk fire," Dudley reported, "driving in the cavalry to the infantry support." The Yankee artillery deployed and emptied their pieces toward the Texans before the advance resumed. Bullets whistled in from the left, across the bayou as well, indicating that Morgan's troops had not kept aligned, and Rebels sniped at Dudley's left flank. West of the bayou, Federals halted to let Morgan catch up.[27]

With gunfire creeping toward them, the residents of Sleepy Hollow again feared for their lives. "At 2:00 P.M. two cannon shots were heard announcing the approach of the Yankees," Dupuy remembered. The women watched as a section of Texan artillery under Lieutenant Henry Angel arrived and took a camouflaged position in a sycamore thicket near their house. Angel approached and warned the women to flee, fearing the coming battle might be waged across their lawn. Dupuy sighed, "we withdrew to our accustomed place of refuge, in the sugarhouse."[28]

The Texans fell back across the fields at St. Emma until, having reached Angel's ambush, they turned to face the enemy. When the Federal columns appeared on the bayou road, eight hundred yards away, the Confederate cannon opened up. "Such a destruction of men and good horses," Collard wrote. "The artillery cut lanes through them. Before they could get up and untangle," he added, "the artillery loaded up and let them have it again." The surprise halted the Federals in their tracks. Dudley ordered up his own guns and shelled the Texans. "We trembled at each cannon shot," wrote Dupuy, hiding behind the heavy steam-operated equipment of the sugarhouse. "It seemed to us as if they were firing upon us, and also we thought of our cousins and our friends who might be in the fight."[29]

As daylight faded, the fight sputtered out. The Texans took advantage of the Federal confusion to fall back toward Paincourtville, and Dudley advanced his

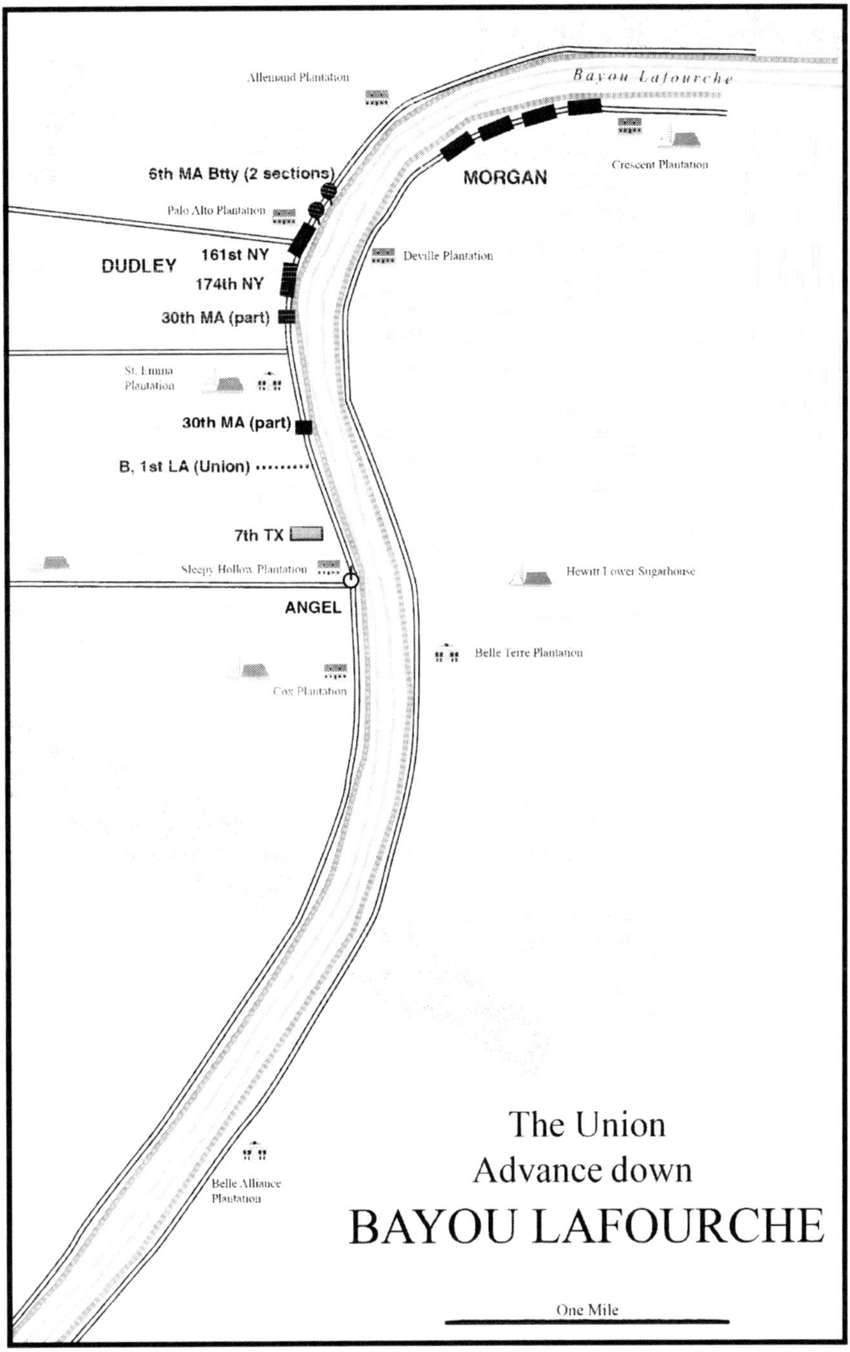

The Union Advance down BAYOU LAFOURCHE

troops past St. Emma and took positions near Sleepy Hollow. Along the road he placed two guns of the 6th Massachusetts—steel 6-pounder Sawyer Rifles—supported by two companies of infantry. The 161st and 174th New York extended a line of battle to their right, covering behind a rail fence, and facing a fallow field of a hundred yards width. Realizing that his right flank lay unanchored and exposed, Dudley ordered two companies of the 161st nearly a mile out to warn of any enemy approaches from that direction. The mounted troops from the 1st Louisiana Cavalry (Union) made a line of vedettes about three-quarters of a mile to his front in a strip of woods on the E. B. Cox Plantation. The 30th Massachusetts, in reserve, camped at St. Emma. Dudley also took the precaution of placing his second section of artillery, two more 6-pounder Sawyer Rifles, at the intersection of Charles Kock's Plantation road and the bayou road, facing to the right. Should the Confederates get behind his brigade, these gunners could cut them down.[30]

Dudley remained confident of his deployments, but his position suffered several flaws. His small command of around a thousand men lay scattered over more than a mile. Colonel Paine's brigade, his closest support, lay four miles farther back, still encamped at Fort Butler. A complex of long, narrow, cane and corn fields, nearly a mile square, lay behind these plantations obscuring visibility.

On the bayou's east bank, Colonel Morgan arranged his one thousand-man command to mirror Dudley's line. He positioned a tripwire of pickets opposite and a little downstream from Sleepy Hollow in the timber and cornfields around Belle Terre Plantation, and within a thousand yards of Kock's lower plantation, Belle Alliance. Morgan's regiments—the 90th, 91st, and 131st New York, and the 1st Louisiana (Union)—remained nearly two miles away on the grounds of the Deville Plantation and James Hewitt's lower plantation nearly opposite Palo Alto and across from St. Emma.

The Federals had not come looking for trouble. Instead, they simply hoped to feed their horses on the miles of corn on both sides of the bayou and keep Taylor's army cornered. "The enemy is evidently making preparations to escape if pursued by a strong force," General Grover reported to Banks, adding, "or to resist a small one." If the Yankees pressed hard, they might spook the Rebels into leaving before the navy arrived at Berwick Bay. Grover urged caution: "Our gunboats can hardly be expected at Breashear City for some days, and it is injudicious to press them until their retreat is cut off." If the Federals showed too little force, though, they invited attack.[31]

Colonel Dudley, nearest the enemy, told his men to forage for their dinners. "It was but a very short time before we were all living like fighting cocks," wrote Lieutenant T. S. DeWolfe of the 161st New York. "We were frequently greeted by a shell from the enemy's artillery, but the firing was so poor as to frighten no one. The firing did not last long, and we did not go hungry." One New York private gloried in the feast. "We fared sumptuously," he wrote, "on chickens, sweet potatoes, green corn, tomatoes, [and] melons."[32]

The women of Sleepy Hollow peered out from their sugarhouse citadel and saw their plantation swarming with soldiers. "The *savane* [back lawn] was covered," Dupuy lamented. She watched as Yankees annihilated her chickens. A lieutenant and four soldiers approached the sugarhouse "and asked us whether there were any rebels hidden in the cane," she recalled. "They pretended to look, but I am sure that they hid themselves instead of looking for the Confederates." Having satisfied his orders, the New York lieutenant offered to escort the women back to their home. They did not trust him. "We were much more secure without him so we refused, saying that we would remain a moment longer." As the Federals trekked back toward their line, Texans sheltered in the sugarhouse of the E. B. Cox Plantation a few hundred yards to the south tried their luck, sniping at the New Yorkers and sending them scurrying for cover. "In spite of our sad situation," Dupuy remembered, "we could not help laughing when we saw the terror of those scoundrels."[33]

As the sun set, the disparate cluster of women left refuge and walked the few hundred yards back to the big house. "And what did we see?" asked Dupuy. "More than 500 men were in the yard; they had taken all the provisions from the cellar, killed all the chickens, and devastated the garden." This time, though, the soldiers stayed out of the house. Colonel Dudley posted a guard to protect the women.[34]

The females were barely across the threshold when the Texans started firing at the Federals again. A rifleman from across the bayou picked off a Federal soldier rummaging among the slave cabins. "I heard that man utter piercing cries," Dupuy wrote. Dudley ordered his artillery to open up and brush back these annoying snipers as Yankee rifles fired back in reply. A Massachusetts officer dashed into the house and advised the women to take cover behind the home's stoutest walls. "All the time that the firing lasted there was a terrible noise. We all huddled together in a small corner," Dupuy wrote. Around 9:00 P.M., the skirmish finally flickered out.

Exhausted from their long, hot, hazardous, day, the women dragged mattresses onto the floor of the downstairs dining room and attempted to sleep. The next morning, they knew, promised even greater dangers. To Dupuy's dismay, the Yankees had returned to the Lafourche District. Surely, she believed, the Confederates would not let them remain unmolested.[35]

15 Kock's Plantation

Never were men better handled than were these rebels.
—Captain Orton S. Clark
Company H, 116th New York

On the night of July 12, generals Tom Green and Richard Taylor reviewed the day's news at Magnolia Plantation near Paincourtville. Both Rebel officers agreed that the general advance of the Union troops down both sides of Bayou Lafourche signaled an imminent fight and perhaps the beginning of a campaign to clear the Lafourche District. Taylor called for his infantry and artillery from near Labadieville toward Paincourtville. "The outlook was not cheerful, but it was necessary to make the best of it," Taylor wrote, "and at all hazards to save our plunder." Taylor crafted an infantry and artillery ambush; Green and his Texans were the bait. Taylor rode up to the Texan picket line that night and found the men ready and eager for the fight. "I joined Green, but did not interfere with his disposition," Taylor recalled, "which were excellent."[1]

Green laid out his battle. The two Rebel brigades would initially face two Union brigades. Colonel Walter P. Lane, with artillery, would square off with Colonel Joseph Morgan's four unsupported infantry regiments while Green would tackle Colonel Nathan A. M. Dudley's three infantry regiments and four guns. Green told Taylor that these Yankee commanders had blundered and left their brigades vulnerable, deploying too far from their reserves. The Yankees east of the bayou also had no artillery, giving the Rebels the advantage of range. Green would punish Dudley's and Morgan's mistakes by hammering their center, then outflanking, surrounding, and destroying them if he could. The terrain, a level sea of cornstalks and cane, masked Rebel plans.

The Texan crafted the mechanics of the fight. Captain Tom Gonzales and his Texas battery supported the 4th, 5th, and 7th Texas cavalry on the west bank of Bayou Lafourche with Green in command. Lane led the Rebel forces on the east bank, with Captain Thomas A. Faries's Louisiana Pelican Artillery supporting the 1st and 2nd Texas Partisan Rangers and the 2nd and 3rd Arizona. The gunners on each side of

At the beginning the Civil War, Nathan Augustus Monroe Dudley served as captain of Company E, 10th U.S. Infantry stationed at Washington, D.C., and served with the unit in the early days of the war. He earned promotion to colonel of the 30th Massachusetts Infantry in early 1862 and served in the campaign to capture New Orleans, the Battle of Baton Rouge, and the Siege of Port Hudson where Dudley led a brigade. After the Civil War, he went on to serve on the frontier and played a controversial role in the infamous 1878 Lincoln County War in New Mexico. Convicted twice by courts-martial for conduct unbecoming an officer and drunkenness, he nevertheless retired as a brigadier general in 1904.
National Archives and Records Administration.

the Lafourche would shell the enemy center—where their lines intersected the bayou—supporting an attack by the 5th and 7th Texas on the west bank, and the 1st Texas Partisan Rangers on the east. The other mounted regiments intended to sweep around either Yankee flank.

If the fortunes of war turned against him, Green explained, he and his small mounted force would fall back and lure the Yankees into Taylor's ambush near Paincourtville and into the waiting muzzles of the Confederate cannon and muskets—a fight of four Rebel brigades against six Federal. The weather was a factor. The coming midsummer Louisiana day would certainly be hot and humid, and the swift and mobile Texans could use the heat to their advantage. Green anticipated a running fight over several miles that would wear down his enemies; Taylor agreed.

The skillful use of artillery east of the bayou would be vital to this fight, and the Louisianans would open the show by pushing back the Federal picket line. Just before dawn, Captain Faries moved up from Charles Kock's lower plantation, Belle Alliance, deployed his guns along the eastern Bayou Lafourche road, and bombarded a wooded thicket on Belle Terre Plantation, flushing out a cluster of Union skirmishers posted in those

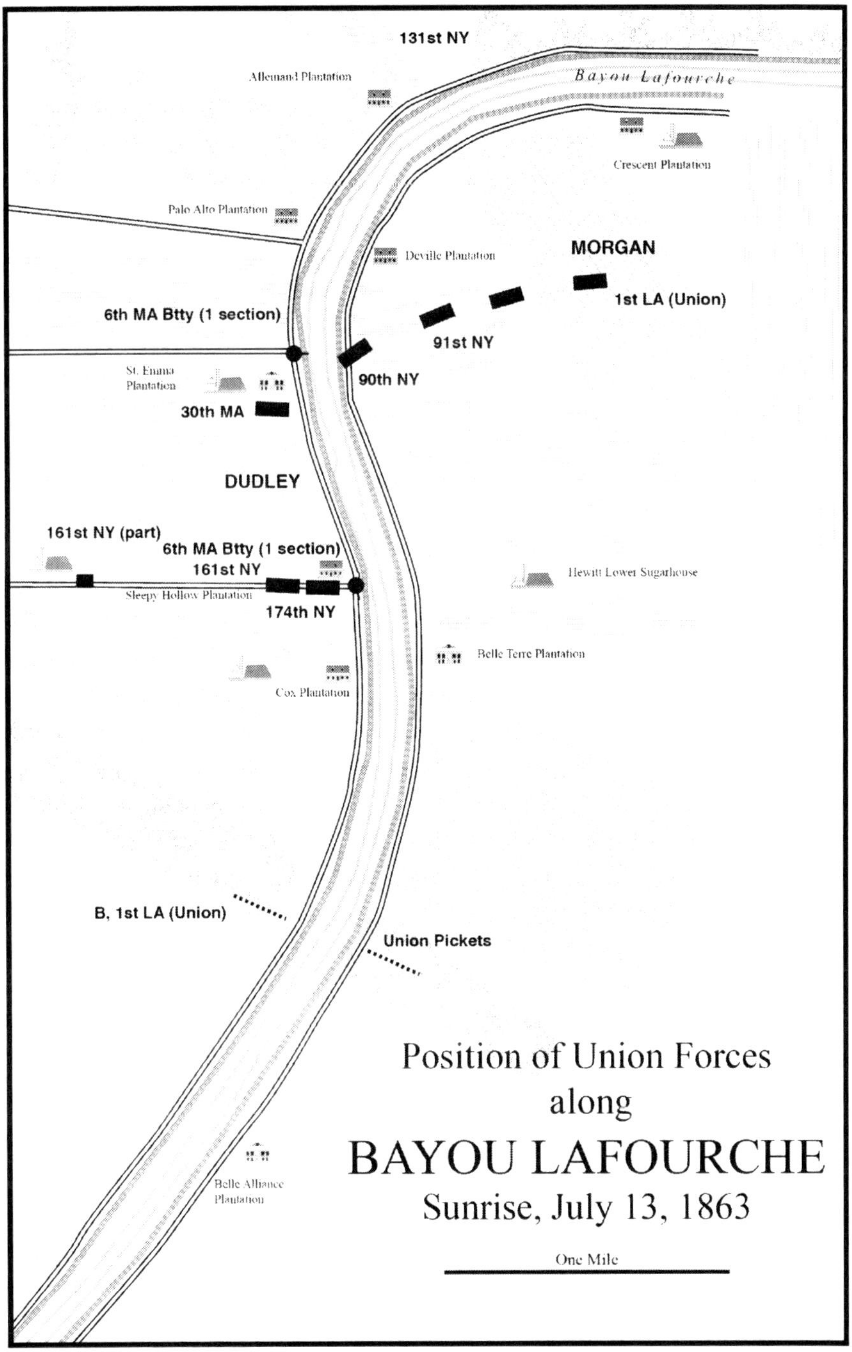
131st NY
Allemand Plantation
Bayou Lafourche
Crescent Plantation
Palo Alto Plantation
Deville Plantation
MORGAN
1st LA (Union)
6th MA Btty (1 section)
91st NY
St. Emma Plantation
90th NY
30th MA
DUDLEY
161st NY (part)
6th MA Btty (1 section)
161st NY
Hewitt Lower Sugarhouse
Sleepy Hollow Plantation
174th NY
Belle Terre Plantation
Cox Plantation
B, 1st LA (Union)
Union Pickets
Position of Union Forces
along
BAYOU LAFOURCHE
Sunrise, July 13, 1863
Belle Alliance Plantation
One Mile

trees. As the enemy soldiers scurried out, Faries and his gunners pursued them with shot and shell, the flashing guns and booming blasts shattering the stillness of the morning.[2]

Colonel Morgan's pickets on the east bank, thus hunted by the Rebel cannon, ran away, relocating to the cover of an immense sugarhouse, the second that served James Hewitt's massive Crescent Plantation. Captain Faries leapfrogged his guns up the bayou road, and his gunners began chipping away at the bricks and timbers of the Federal shelter. The rattled Union infantry fell back yet again. By the time the sun rose that morning, Faries had brushed the enemy pickets back more than half a mile. The Confederates next pivoted their guns across Bayou Lafourche, where the right of Dudley's line was now uncovered and exposed.[3]

While Faries had been driving in the Federal pickets east the bayou, General Green's skirmishers also drove in the enemy pickets west of the bayou, their scattered rifles adding to the early morning clamor. Lieutenant Henry Angel's section of Gonzales's Battery tossed shells up the road as well, hoping to unhinge the picket line from the bayou. The scattered *vedettes* of the 1st Louisiana Cavalry (Union) fell back across the grounds of Sleepy Hollow Plantation toward their reserves—the 30th Massachusetts—camped just beyond.[4]

The women inside Sleepy Hollow's house, awakened by the terrifying sounds of shooting and rushing men and horses just outside their door, knew the battle they had long feared was upon them. They would be injured or slain if they lingered. "When we saw it was no longer possible to remain there, we started, each one with his bundle on his back, to go to the woods," remembered young Heléne Dupuy. They scurried down the length of their fields in the early morning gloom and haze, bullets and shells hissing among them. "We had to pass between the two armies, the fire crossed above our heads, and more than ten times we came near being killed."[5]

The women feared they would not make the woods and sheltered once again among the heavy machinery of their sugar mill. "We placed ourselves behind *l'equipage*," Dupuy continued. As the women settled in, one of the enslaved girls that hid with them declared, nervously, that their sanctuary was "the best place that you may choose; it is as if you were in a fort." The fighting soon tested her theory. Minutes later, a shell crashed into a stack of cordwood nearby, scattering it in a dramatic clap of fire, splinters, and smoke. The group of refugees began to harbor doubts about the wisdom of their choice of refuge. "The logs flew in every direction," Dupuy noted, "and other bombs passed near the sugarhouse." The women were clearly trapped.[6]

Dudley's Yankees west of Bayou Lafourche, supported by artillery, did not give way as easily as had Morgan's pickets. Instead of retreating before Green's skirmishers and cannon, Dudley reacted to the firing in his front by stiffening his line. He called up the reserve section of the 6th Massachusetts Battery, and it rumbled into position next to the other guns, extending his artillery line down a plantation road perpendicular to the bayou road. The 174th New York held their position just behind. These four Sawyer Rifles returned the Texan fire.[7]

Green ordered his men to veer away from the enemy artillery concentration. The 4th Texas Cavalry galloped wide to the left. The 7th Texas Cavalry, dismounted, sidled that direction as well. The men of the 5th Texas Cavalry, their horses well to the rear, stayed closer to the bayou road to support Lieutenant Angel's guns.

Dudley began to worry when the Texans failed to advance. The Rebels to his front, he surmised, might by slipping around his right. At the same time, though, the Texans kept up a steady fire from the cornfields to his front, indicating a potential move against his artillery. To add to his troubles, Faries's Louisianans began to toss shells among his guns from the left, across Bayou Lafourche. Dudley needed more muscle and sent a courier to Donaldsonville requesting another brigade as well as the four guns of the 1st Maine Battery to come up. A section of artillery arrived first. Dudley placed these cannon on the bayou road on the left his line, positioning them to sweep both forward toward Green's Texans and across the stream to silence the Louisiana gunners on the east bank. Dudley now with a six-gun artillery line, felt more secure.[8]

This concentration of steel shut down the Confederate attack. The Texans to Dudley's front faded back. A second section of Sawyer Rifles arrived; these were commanded by Lieutenant E. D. Haley of the 1st Maine Battery. Dudley ordered a detachment of the 30th Massachusetts to escort these newcomers three hundred yards down the bayou road to smoke out enemy intentions. Positioning themselves near the house of Sleepy Hollow Plantation, the infantry and gunners could play on the Rebels east of the Lafourche while also brushing back Green's troops. The scheme seemed to work, and the battle slackened around 7:00 A.M. The Confederates faded away.[9]

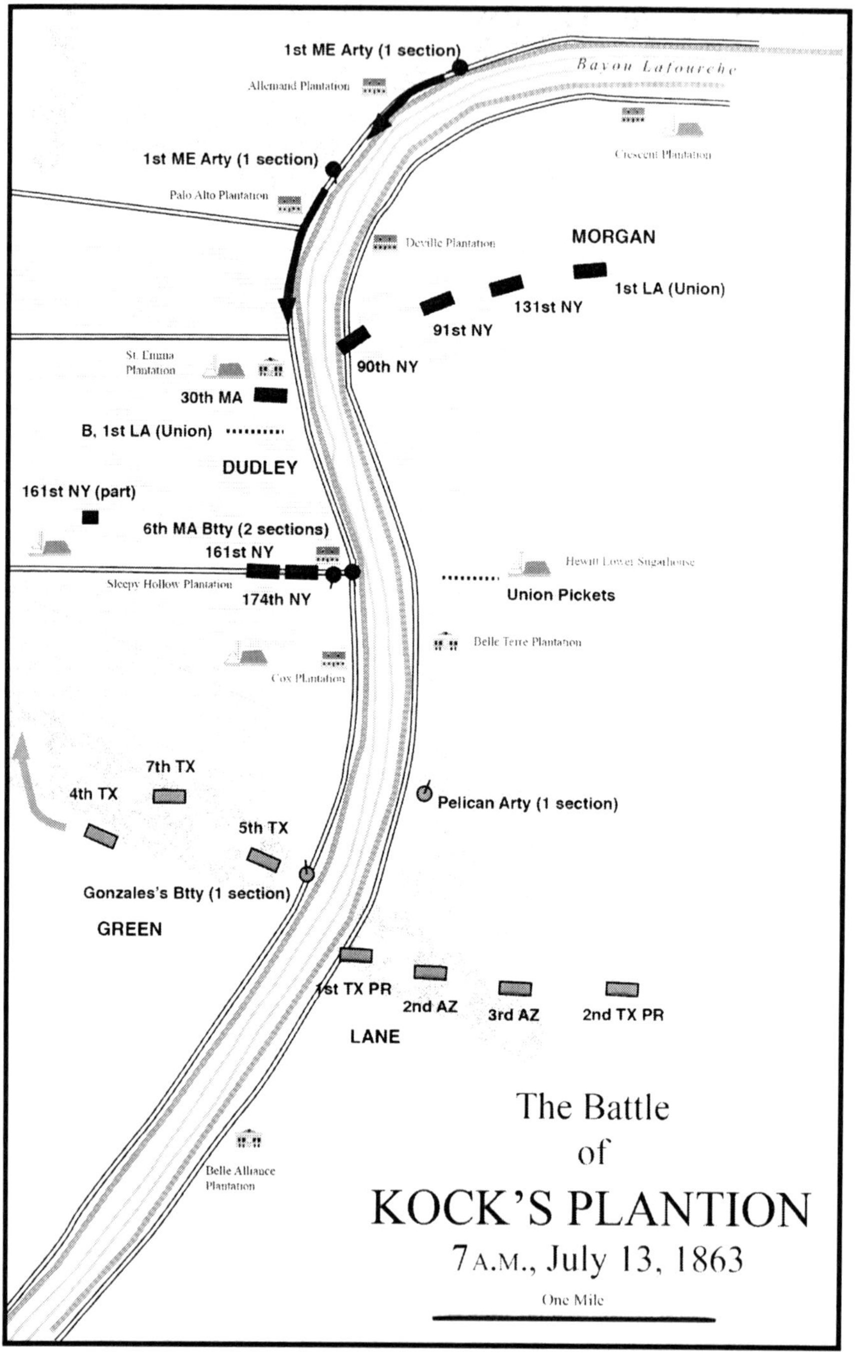
1st ME Arty (1 section)
Bayou Lafourche
Allemand Plantation
1st ME Arty (1 section)
Crescent Plantation
Palo Alto Plantation
Deville Plantation
MORGAN
1st LA (Union)
131st NY
91st NY
90th NY
St. Emma Plantation
30th MA
B, 1st LA (Union)
DUDLEY
161st NY (part)
6th MA Btty (2 sections)
161st NY
Hewitt Lower Sugarhouse
Sleepy Hollow Plantation
174th NY
Union Pickets
Belle Terre Plantation
Cox Plantation
7th TX
4th TX
Pelican Arty (1 section)
5th TX
Gonzales's Btty (1 section)
GREEN
1st TX PR
2nd AZ
3rd AZ
2nd TX PR
LANE
Belle Alliance Plantation
The Battle of KOCK'S PLANTION
7 A.M., July 13, 1863
One Mile

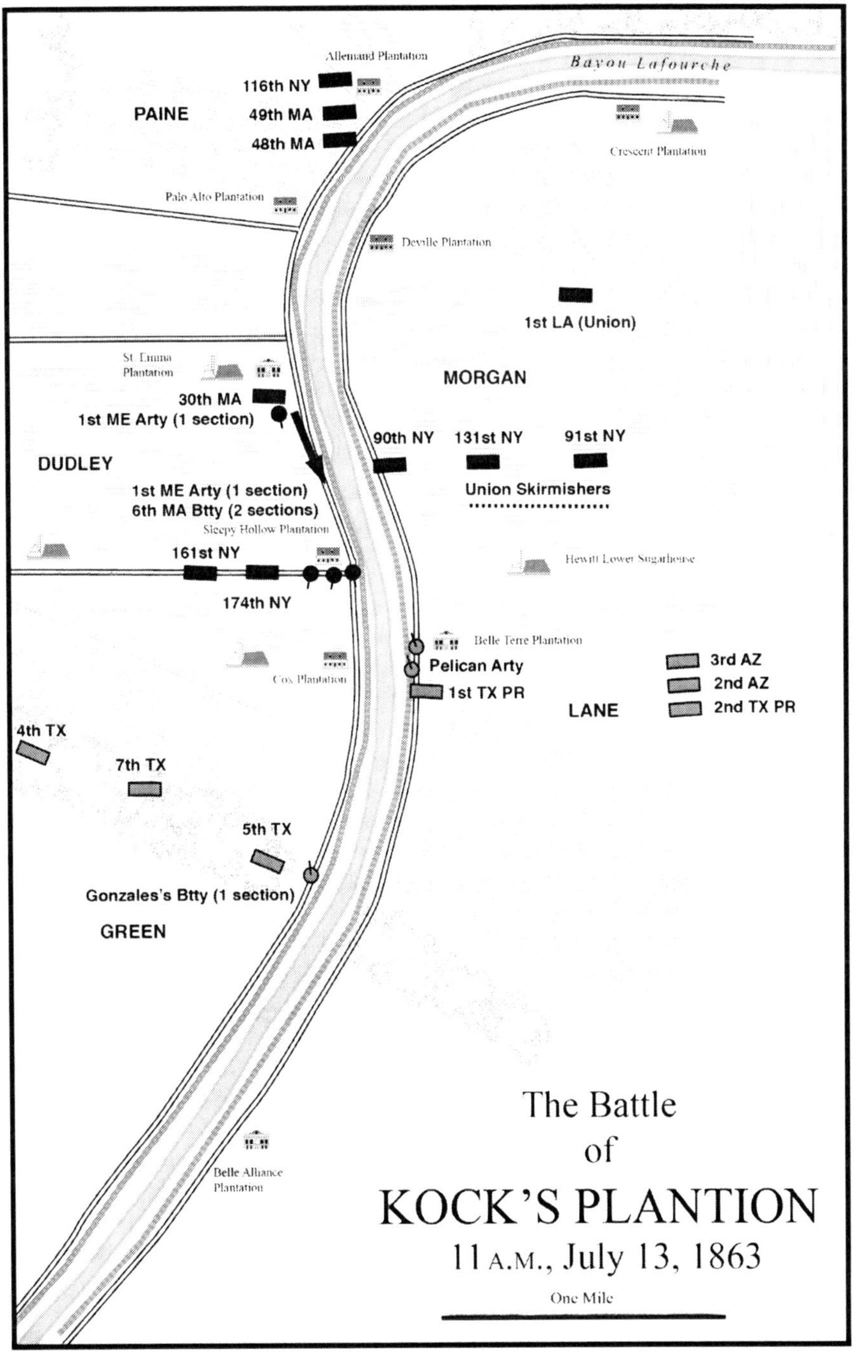
Allemand Plantation
Bayou Lafourche
116th NY
PAINE
49th MA
48th MA
Crescent Plantation
Palo Alto Plantation
Deville Plantation
1st LA (Union)
St. Emma Plantation
MORGAN
30th MA
1st ME Arty (1 section)
90th NY
131st NY
91st NY
DUDLEY
Union Skirmishers
1st ME Arty (1 section)
6th MA Btty (2 sections)
Sleepy Hollow Plantation
161st NY
Hewitt Lower Sugarhouse
174th NY
Belle Terre Plantation
Pelican Arty
3rd AZ
2nd AZ
Cox Plantation
1st TX PR
LANE
2nd TX PR
4th TX
7th TX
5th TX
Gonzales's Btty (1 section)
GREEN
Belle Alliance Plantation
The Battle of KOCK'S PLANTION
11 A.M., July 13, 1863
One Mile

Cowering in the sugarhouse, the women of Sleepy Hollow noticed a lull in the firing. They ventured a look outside. "Finally God permitted that there should be a moment of calm," Dupuy wrote. A slave hurried up a mule team and cart, and soon "twenty-five persons, whites and blacks" crowded in. The civilians fled toward the wooded swamps of the Brule Sacramento, three miles to the west. Union skirmishers filtered into the sugarhouse behind them.[10]

Dudley needed to know what the sunrise dustup had meant. By mid-morning, his Federal skirmish line on the west bank pushed south to discover what had become of the Texans. Green's men continued to fall back out of range. "The enemy pressed us with artillery and an unusually large force of skirmishers," Green reported. In this delicate dance of scouting and sniping, the Confederates, amid the cornfields, were as blind as the Federals.[11]

Green knew that the only way to learn Federal intentions was to push back. "I concluded to feel him a little more heavily, and," he added, "if a favorable opportunity offered, to make an assault on his advancing columns." He ordered his own skirmish lines reinforced and the probing Federals checked. East of the Lafourche, the levee masked the Louisiana gunners of the Pelican Artillery as they slipped two guns unseen past the 30th Massachusetts's left and shelled troops to their rear gathered in and around the St. Emma sugarhouse. As a barrage of 6-pounder shot and case scattered these Federals, Dudley's skirmishers stopped, stunned by this fire from their left rear. The Union lines fell back, Dudley fearing the worse. Was his left flank exposed? Where, Dudley wondered, was Morgan?[12]

Watching from several hundred yards away, Green noted the enemy's confusion. Under cover of Faries's bombardment, Green personally scouted the field and concluded that Dudley, his left exposed because Faries had driven in the pickets on the east side of the Lafourche, now lay too far forward and unsupported. Green sensed an opportunity and dashed over to the Bayou Lafourche levee to locate Colonel Lane, commander of the eight hundred Texans and Louisianans operating beyond the opposite bank.[13]

The former Texas Rangers discussed the next phase, shouting across the water "amidst a shower of bombs and minni balls," observed Private John W. Watkins of the 5th Texas Cavalry. That morning's artillery duel and skirmish had allowed the Confederates to size up the Union forces and the capabilities of their leaders. Clearly, the Federals had no intentions of a serious advance down the Lafourche.

Instead, Dudley and Morgan were there to keep the Texans at arm's length from the Union camps around Donaldsonville. Brigadier General Godfrey Weitzel had merely spread out his army to take in more fodder for his weary animals. Green could not be sure of the number of Federals at hand but believed that his Texans could deliver a telling blow. "Green determined, with his usual nerve to attack them," wrote Lieutenant John E. Hart, 4th Texas Cavalry, "though the enemy should outnumber him."[14]

The terrain favored the more mobile Confederates while confusing the Federals. Bayou Lafourche flowed nearly south after leaving the Mississippi. From there, it turned sharply west for nearly two miles before curving generally south again for an additional two miles. This stretch—where the water flowed north to south—was Green's battlefield. The terrain was completely flat and unremarkable but visibility would prove challenging. Tall crops stretched out for a mile from each bank until reaching the edges of the forests that marked the beginning of the swampy *marais* beyond. Neither the Federal nor the Confederate force could effectively cover a mile-long front in line of battle; their troops were too few. Green understood that and planned for his mounted cavalry, riding largely unimpeded across this flat cropland, to skirt the timber on either flank of the Union line and gain the enemy rear. A determined cavalry charge could then overrun the Yankee infantry pickets and skirmishers.

The east side of this bifurcated battlefield—Lane's domain—also held advantages for the Confederates. The curve of the bayou gave Lane's horsemen a direct approach to the Federal rear because the stream bent nearly ninety degrees to the right; by riding north, around Morgan's left, Confederate troops could strike the Lafourche two miles up between the Federals and their reserves at Donaldsonville. Vast cornfields would mask their movements and confuse the defenders. Willow thickets and stands of timber along the levee also provided natural cover. Morgan's entire command might be enveloped and cut off.

Lane, grasping this opportunity, planned to attack the enemy at two points. The wild riders of the 2nd and 3rd Arizona and the 2nd Texas Partisan Rangers would strike Morgan's center and left and gain his rear. Colonel Lane's own 1st Texas Partisan Rangers, rugged veterans, would work in concert with the Pelican artillery and, pressing up the bayou road, use the levee and willow thickets to harass the west bank, while also unhinging Morgan's right. The Federals had no artillery, and Lane believed that the Louisiana cannon would drive the enemy before them. Thus turned on either flank, Lane believed Morgan's brigade would collapse.

Green also liked what he saw west of Bayou Lafourche. If his men could push the Federals in the fields straight back—due north—they would eventually leave the cover of the Lafourche levee and hit the Mississippi River nearly three miles away but more than two miles west of Fort Butler. More importantly, their line would become unanchored at either end. Dudley and his men could be surrounded and gobbled up. Green decided to attack along three points. The mounted troopers of the 4th Texas Cavalry, led by Lieutenant Colonel George James Hampton, would ride around the enemy's right flank. Colonel Philemon Herbert would follow with his 7th Texas Cavalry. Captain Hugh McPhail would lead the 5th Texas Cavalry up the bayou road and distract Dudley's Yankees long enough for Hampton's troops to fall on their right flank. If Lane succeeded in disposing of Morgan as planned, Dudley would also be taking fire from his left flank.

Green believed he could destroy the enemy. His two brigades of Texas cavalry might achieve a nearly perfect envelopment on both sides of Bayou Lafourche, simultaneously. He would fix the Federals—Dudley and Morgan—in place long enough for the Confederate horsemen to encircle them.

While the Rebel officer plotted, Dudley, Morgan, and their Yankees believed the day's danger had passed. Responding to Dudley's previous request for reinforcements, Colonel Charles J. Paine's brigade moved up from Donaldsonville but halted on the grounds of the Francis Allemand Plantation after hearing the noise of battle fade to their front. He allowed his troops to fall out and find shade under the spreading oaks about a mile short of the sea of cane and cornstalks where Dudley's Union line lay. "It is a beautiful and rich country," wrote Private Henry T. Johns in the 49th Massachusetts as he marched down the bayou road. Even so, the sun was brutal. "It was the hottest, sultriest day we had experienced in Louisiana." The men of the 48th Massachusetts dined on hardtack, green corn, and coffee. Their comrades in the other regiments sought out heartier fare. "There being no indications of an engagement, preparations for our mid-day meal proceeded with more than the usual promise of a good dinner," wrote Captain Orton S. Clark of the 116th New York. They slaughtered any livestock and fowl they found. "Fresh pork and beef, chickens, and geese, . . . sweet potatoes and cabbages," Captain

A native Bostonian and descendent of a signer of the Declaration of Independence, Charles Jackson Paine made a fortune in railroads before the war. He entered the army as a captain in the 22nd Massachusetts Infantry before leaving the raise the 2nd Louisiana Infantry. Promoted to brigade command during the siege of Port Hudson, he led these weary troops in battle once again on the Lafourche.
National Archives and Records Administration.

Clark noted, "invited us to a meal fit . . . to set before a king."[15]

East of Bayou Lafourche, the soldiers of Morgan's brigade also took their ease. The Rebel shelling had ruffled them a bit that morning, but they feared no additional mischief. "The regiment, about noon, stacked their arms and all lay around resting, awaiting whatever might come up," remembered Sergeant Thomas H. McCann, Company C of the 90th New York. His regiment anchored the right of Morgan's line where it intersected the bayou road. Some of the troops, recently paid, used their time to divide into clumps to play cards. Along the plantation roads and cornfields, black cooks tended campfires, preparing a hot lunch for their Yankee employers. Despite that morning's cacophony, none of Morgan's men seemed concerned about a renewed Confederate attack.[16]

Yet they had not noticed that their picket line had steadily fallen back all morning and had not resumed its place far to the front. Dudley, west of the bayou, was first to notice this oversight. He ordered his signalmen to wigwag a warning to Morgan. The troops on the east bank must cover his left flank. Morgan reassured him that, although his battle line lay well to the rear of Dudley's Brigade, his skirmish line extended nearly even with the 30th Massachusetts's formation across the bayou at Sleepy Hollow. Morgan, with no artillery of his own, had prudently kept his men out of range of the Rebel cannon. The bulk of his regiments held positions along the lane separating Deville Plantation and Hewitt's

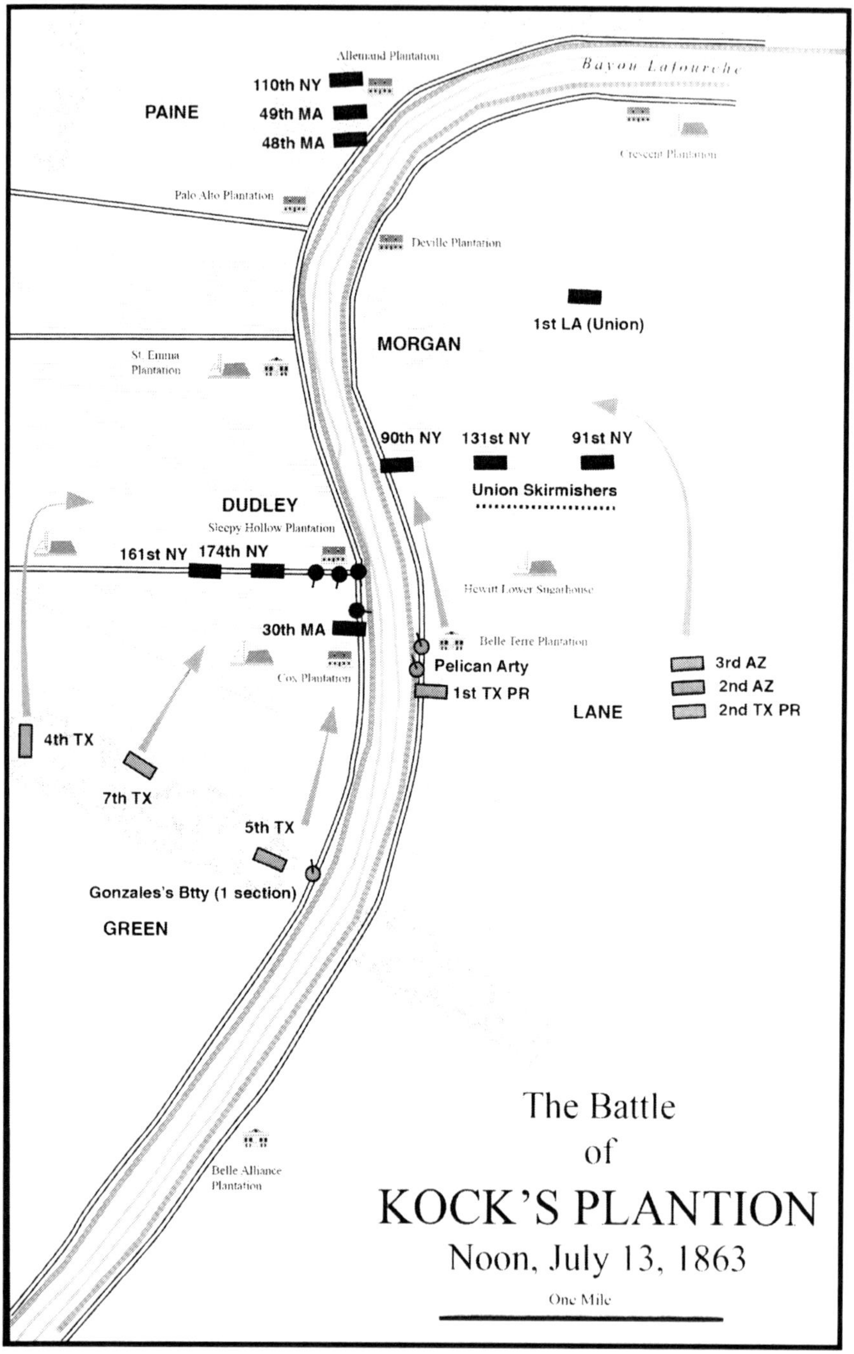
Allemand Plantation
Bayou Lafourche
110th NY
PAINE
49th MA
48th MA
Crescent Plantation
Palo Alto Plantation
Deville Plantation
1st LA (Union)
MORGAN
St. Emma
Plantation
90th NY
131st NY
91st NY
Union Skirmishers
DUDLEY
Sleepy Hollow Plantation
161st NY
174th NY
Hewitt Lower Sugarhouse
30th MA
Belle Terre Plantation
Pelican Arty
1st TX PR
Cox Plantation
3rd AZ
2nd AZ
2nd TX PR
LANE
4th TX
7th TX
5th TX
Gonzales's Btty (1 section)
GREEN
Belle Alliance
Plantation
The Battle
of
KOCK'S PLANTION
Noon, July 13, 1863
One Mile

lower plantation. His main line of battle therefore stood almost halfway between Dudley's and Paine's troops. Morgan assured his comrade that he had advanced a heavy line of skirmishers well to the front. If things turned ugly, he would advance the rest of his brigade.[17]

Dudley remained skeptical. If the Confederates returned and Morgan's screen gave way, his own left flank would be dangling, exposed. Indeed, it already was. Neither Dudley nor Morgan realized that the picket line east of the bayou had fallen back as far as it had and that officers had not reposted it, contrary to their instructions. The men eating lunch and playing cards along Morgan's battle line—instead of having several minutes' notice of a Rebel attack by the telltale firing of the pickets—would now have little advance warning. Dudley's troops, looking for action to their front, relied on Morgan's Brigade to cover their left. This faith would be betrayed.[18]

Around 1:30 P.M., Green launched his attack. Rebel gunners once again worked their way up the east bank and fired at the St. Emma sugarhouse, as well as up the road toward Morgan's main line. The surprise salvo by a section of the Pelican Artillery's 12-pounder howitzers simultaneously hit the left and rear of Dudley's line and the position of the 90th New York dead ahead.

Sergeant McCann had just walked over to join a card game when a shell burst directly over the huddle of gamblers. The concussion knocked him and a companion off their feet. The poker players, he believed, must have been massacred. "When the smoke and dust of the explosion cleared away, there were seen all five of the players stretched prone upon their stomachs, in every direction," he wrote. One player, the company musician, had clutched the "pot" tightly in his hand. "Curiously," McCann continued, "not a man had been hit, and when all got to their senses, there was a great laugh."[19]

The levity faded instantly. "The shells now came—fast and furious—they had got the aim right," McCann observed. The surprise shelling, followed by the thunder of hoof beats, rattled the Federals. The men could see cavalry far to their left. "The enemy . . . could be plainly seen fighting and capturing the whole picket line, half a mile away." Drummers beat the long roll and soldiers scurried after their weapons, belts, and cartridge boxes as they fell into line.[20]

The appearance of Rebel horsemen and the shock of the incoming shells stampeded the cooks in the rear of the regiment. They dumped their stews and loaded their mules with pots and kettles fresh from the fires, causing the balky animals to bite, buck and kick their way through the rear of Morgan's Brigade trying to shed the hot metal on their backs. "Coming from that perilous direction," McCann continued, "It caused all hands to turn, expecting to find the enemy." The 90th New York regained its composure, relieved to find no enemies behind them, but turned to see a real threat falling on them. Sergeant McCann and the rest of the regiment watched hundreds of Rebels galloping toward them. "Instantly the line was busy firing at the approaching Grays as they came charging over the fields," he wrote, "and through the willow thickets along the bayou road."[21]

The Texans had blown through the Yankee skirmishers, swept around Morgan's unsuspecting left flank, wheeled, and rolled up the 131st New York in the center of his line. "Our advance guard was out but a short distance," an observer wrote. "The time from their signal till the enemy was upon [them] was hardly sufficient to turn around." The Texas cavalry rode over and through the 131st New York, felling one in five. "Taken by surprise," a newspaper correspondent reported, "this regiment did not show . . . much coolness, and thereby caused quite a panic in the remainder of the brigade." The Federal center shattered. Jubilant Texans pursued, while others rounded up more than one hundred prisoners and the regiment's colors.[22]

While Lane's men sabered, shot, and trampled Morgan's Brigade, the roar of battle rolled toward them from the west bank of Bayou Lafourche. Green launched his attack as soon as he saw Lane's Brigade underway. The general dismounted, sent his horse to the rear, and then took his place at the head of his old regiment, the 5th Texas Cavalry, near the bayou road. "It is remarkable what energy and enthusiasm his presence instilled into the men," wrote C. D. Bigler of Company C. "General Green *led* . . . in person. Each [man] went in bent upon wiping out the stain of the 28th of June" [Fort Butler]. The Pelican artillery fired into the Union positions from across the bayou while Lieutenant Angel's section of guns fired up the road. "The enemy commenced a rapid cannonade at several points, followed up almost instantly by a warm musketry fire from cornfields in the front, down the bayou road, and from the left," Dudley reported.[23]

On the east bank, Colonel Morgan's command faced a crisis. The Texans had captured the skirmish line and routed the center. They now threatened to gain their rear and cut the Federal line of retreat. Morgan panicked. He ordered his regiments to change their facings from south to east, pivoting back on their right with their backs to the levee, "which was done on the rush," McCann wrote. The

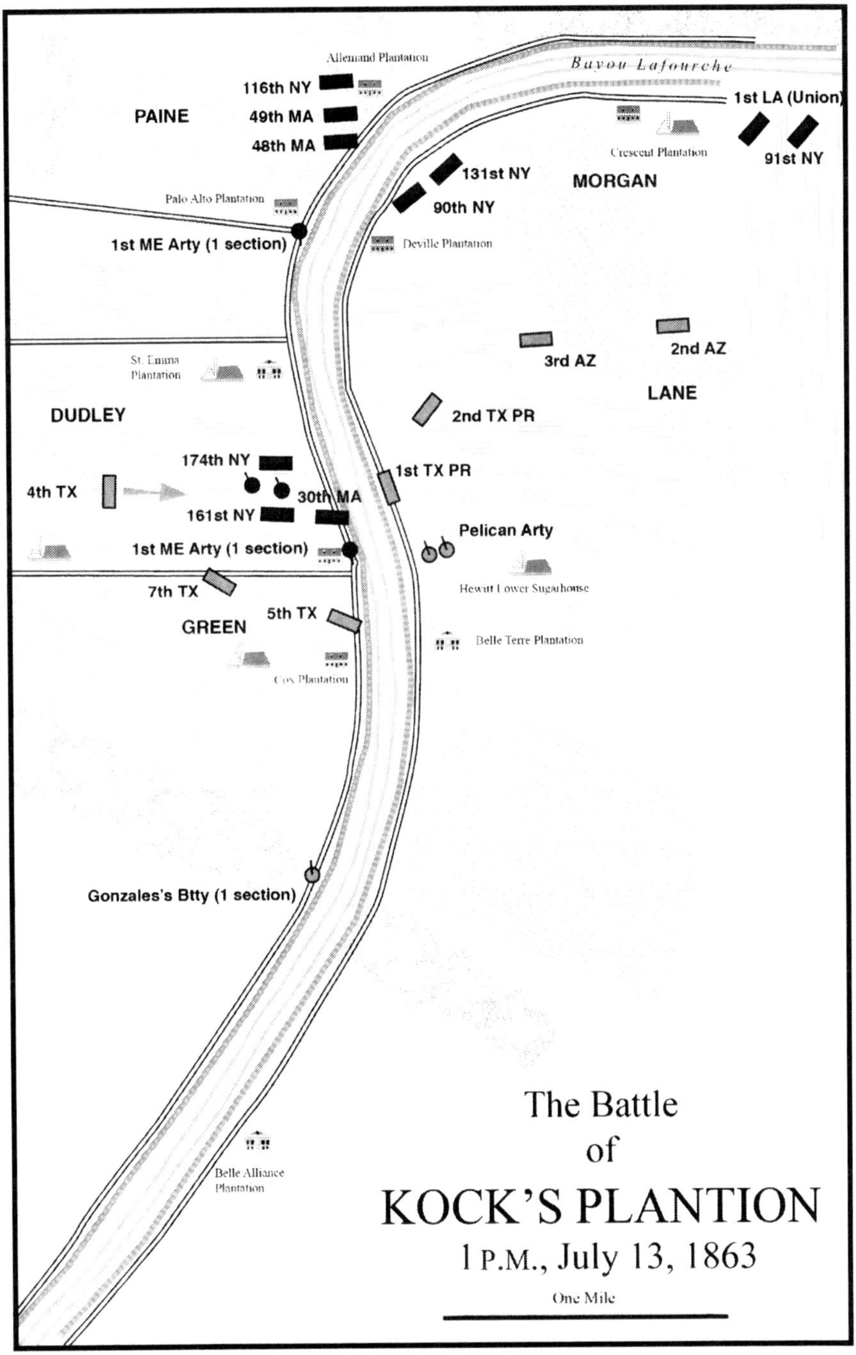
Allemand Plantation
Bayou Lafourche
116th NY
PAINE
49th MA
48th MA
1st LA (Union)
Crescent Plantation
91st NY
131st NY
MORGAN
90th NY
Palo Alto Plantation
1st ME Arty (1 section)
Deville Plantation
2nd AZ
3rd AZ
St. Emma Plantation
LANE
DUDLEY
2nd TX PR
174th NY
1st TX PR
4th TX
30th MA
161st NY
Pelican Arty
1st ME Arty (1 section)
Hewitt Lower Sugarhouse
7th TX
5th TX
GREEN
Belle Terre Plantation
Cox Plantation
Gonzales's Btty (1 section)
Belle Alliance Plantation
The Battle
of
KOCK'S PLANTION
1 P.M., July 13, 1863
One Mile

unorthodox maneuver, coupled with the shock and confusion all along the line, tangled the regiments. In addition, it exposed the new Federal right of the line—the 90th New York—to the flanking fire of the Pelican Artillery and the 1st Texas Partisan Rangers. The Confederates noticed the Union blunder and surged ahead. "Two or three of them dashed forward out of the thicket in the road at the exposed flank," McCann recalled, "not more than fifty yards distant." The Federals fired at these attackers, but mounted Texans in the cornfield fired into the left of the new Union line at nearly the same time. Clearly, the other Union regiments had fled and only the 90th New York remained. The Yankees realized the enemy had gained both of their flanks.[24]

"Suddenly there was heard a piercing yell from the rear, 'retreat, quick!'" McCann stood dazed. "Horror! The rest of the command had retreated and were off in the high cornfields out of sight." The sergeant broke for cover. "Did you ever have a nightmare . . . that you were being pursued by some savage animal and yet could not move a limb?" he asked. "That was the . . . sensation, only worse." Rushing blindly through the crops, he glimpsed the regimental colors heading away from him to his left. He chased after it, "through what seemed a hailstorm of screeching bullets which kept clipping the cornstalks." The regiment rallied a mile to the rear. Lane's attack had surprised and shattered Morgan's brigade as planned. "Pride had . . . a fall," McCann admitted. "Licked! Ran like cowards."[25]

The soldiers of Paine's Brigade noticed the crescendo of noise and violence erupting across the Lafourche and went to the levee to determine what was going on. "Horses, teams, ambulances, fugitives, passed by as rapidly as fear could move them," wrote Private Johns in the 49th Massachusetts. The skedaddling troops hollered, "the rebs! the rebs!" across the Lafourche as they passed. "Our friends across the bayou were evidently flanked, and retreating as best they could."[26]

On the west bank, Colonel Dudley realized he was now in serious trouble as the Rebels assailed his line in front and Morgan's command vaporized on his left. General Green swept up the road, "in the midst of shot, shell, grape, and canister," a Rebel remembered, determined to capture the two Union guns Dudley had thrown forward. Lieutenant Haley withdrew his cannon and continued past the main line of battle heading toward Palo Alto, assuming that Dudley would form a new line there. Haley and his men escaped unharmed. Dudley next ordered his other pieces out of danger and back to Palo Alto. The gunners of the 6th

Lieutenant Colonel William Baker Kinsey fought with the 161st New York at Kock's Plantation where his regiment performed admirably on an otherwise bad day for Federal forces. A Philadelphia pharmacist before the war, Kinsey joined the 23rd New York and served in Virginia before assisting with the creation of the 161st.
New York State Military Museum.

Massachusetts, out of ammunition, manhandled their guns through the corn until crews could safely limber them. Several mired in the muddy fields. The 161st New York, on the right, covered the retreat, dropping back steadily and periodically turning to fire. Two guns of the 1st Maine Battery remained to cover the retreat as well.[27]

Confederate rifles and artillery from three directions brutalized these stay-behind Union gunners, exposed in the open road near the house at Sleepy Hollow. Crewmen barely got one piece away. The other lay stranded, surrounded by horses lying dead in their traces, the limber immobilized. Union infantry swarmed the piece to try and haul it to safety. Rebel rifles cut them down. "Every effort was made on the part of the supports to save it," Dudley reported, "as the casualties in a space of 20 yards around the piece give sufficient proof." In just a few minutes, two understrength companies from the 30th Massachusetts lost more than half of their men before giving the gun up as lost.[28]

At this critical moment, the 4th Texas Cavalry fell on the Union right flank, "at just at the right time," Bigler noted. "The enemy wavered a moment, then fled." The soldiers of the 30th Massachusetts, near the bayou, broke when the rest of the brigade buckled. Sergeant Henry Warren Howe of Lowell, Massachusetts, remembered, "falling back and firing." He watched Corporal Martin Smith hurry down the road, the regimental colors in hand. Then, the regiment fell apart. Nearby, Lieutenant Orlando Smith of the 161st New York watched as the Bay State men bolted, writing, "The 30th Massachusetts, an old regiment, broke and run." Bullets coming in from rear and flank continued to claim victims, and each of Dudley's regiments dribbled dead and wounded soldiers in their wake. As

Howe neared the safety of Paine's Brigade, a spent round struck him in the ankle, causing him to limp the rest of the way to Fort Butler, bruised "something like a kicked shin," he remembered. The soldiers of the 174th New York tumbled back a half-mile to the rear toward the St. Emma sugarhouse and rallied, eager to be away from the murderous crossfire that had claimed nearly four dozen of their number. They made a brief stand before turning about and, marching in good order toward the rear, forming a line on the fence bordering the St. Emma Plantation road.[29]

The 161st New York joined them there, maintaining their formation even under the crossfire. "It was here that we suffered the heaviest loss," Lieutenant F. Scott DeWolfe observed. "I saw four men wounded out of my own company, within half a minute, and could hear upon all sides of me a succession of 'Oh's,' as the men were struck." The Yankees kept up a succession of steady volleys, keeping the Confederates from overrunning the artillery and the fleeing 30th Massachusetts. "Men could never stand up and fight better, and more obstinately than did the 161st Regiment," DeWolfe boasted. "I saw no officer in the regiment show any inclination to exhibit the white feather."[30]

Green, checked by these obstinate New Yorkers, reassembled his command to renew the attack. Hampton dismounted the 4th Texas cavalry and fell in on the Rebel left. "All the brigade, now shoulder to shoulder, led by their *favorite general*," wrote Hart, "rushed across the fields. Never did men dash upon their foes with more determination and vigor." The soldiers of the 161st New York tempered the Rebel advance. Seeing one of the guns of the 6th Massachusetts Battery abandoned in a drainage ditch, the regiment advanced and dragged the gun free, falling back in good order all the while.[31]

Dudley ordered his two intact regiments to fall back and the remaining artillery to deploy along the Sacramento Road at Palo Alto. He also sent a courier to hurry forward Paine's troops, telling them to form their line of battle on this plantation road to the left of the 1st Maine's guns, joined by the remaining pieces from the 6th Massachusetts. Dudley brought the remnant of his brigade back; Paine brought his forward.[32]

Paine understood the plan. "Our brigade was ordered to the front at 'double quick on the road parallel to the bayou,'" remembered Sergeant Albert Plummer of the 48th Massachusetts. In the lead, the 49th Massachusetts turned right and filed down the Sacramento Road just south of Palo Alto, faced left into line, and

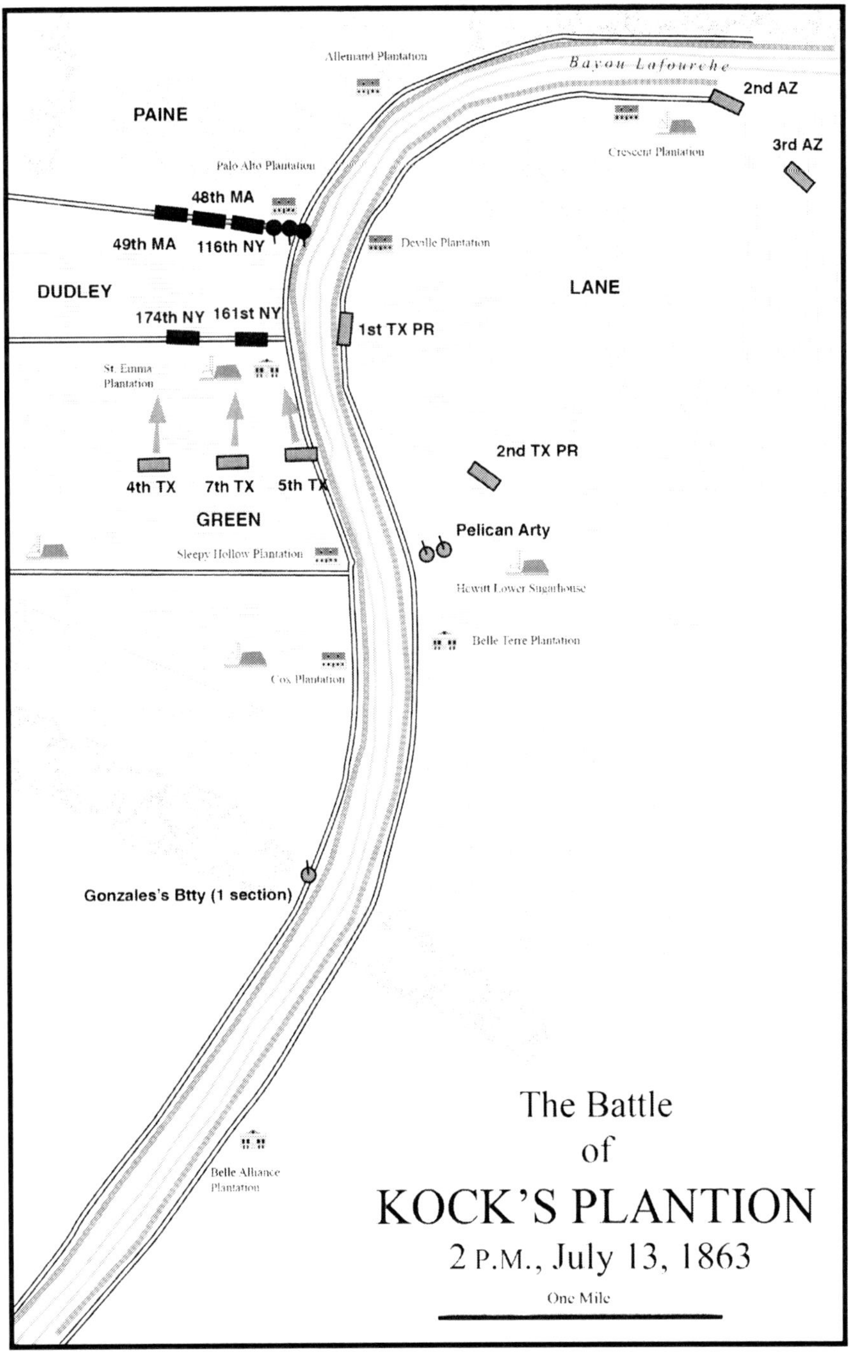
Allemand Plantation
Bayou Lafourche
2nd AZ
PAINE
Crescent Plantation
3rd AZ
Palo Alto Plantation
48th MA
49th MA
116th NY
Deville Plantation
DUDLEY
LANE
174th NY
161st NY
1st TX PR
St. Emma Plantation
2nd TX PR
4th TX
7th TX
5th TX
GREEN
Pelican Arty
Sleepy Hollow Plantation
Hewitt Lower Sugarhouse
Belle Terre Plantation
Cox Plantation
Gonzales's Btty (1 section)
Belle Alliance Plantation
The Battle
of
KOCK'S PLANTION
2 P.M., July 13, 1863
One Mile

prepared to meet the Texans. The 48th Massachusetts and 116th New York filed in behind, "meeting at almost every step wounded men from Dudley's Brigade," observed Captain Clark from his position near the bayou road.[33]

Dudley had chosen a strong position. This new battle line lay behind a rail fence, fronting a deep drainage ditch, and facing more than one hundred yards of open ground that gave way to cornfields. Eight hundred yards away Paine's men could see the roofs and upper stories of St. Emma, its slave quarters, its sugarhouse, and its outbuildings. Paine rode over to Lieutenant Colonel Eben P. Stanwood, holding the center of the line with his 48th Massachusetts, ordering him to cover their front and to also keep an eye to their right. He further "directed him to hold our ground at all hazards till his return," Plummer recalled. Paine advanced the 49th Massachusetts as skirmishers to locate Dudley's troops—and the Confederates.[34]

As Paine and the 49th Massachusetts advanced, the corn and cane swallowed them. Thrashing his way through the stalks, Private Johns "could hear the roar of artillery, the rushing tramp of many fugitives, while around us bullets were flying with much disregard of life and limb." As these Bay State men pushed forward, a sense of dread shrouded them. The Rebels now held the St. Emma sugarhouse and seemed all around them in the corn. Somehow they had missed Dudley's other two regiments as they fell back to Palo Alto, passing the 49th Massachusetts unseen in the corn. The 4th Texas Cavalry, though, continued working around the Federal right. "Through the rows of cane could be seen squads of enemies, how many we could not tell," Johns related. "Amid all the confusion, only one thing was certain, we were flanked on nearly every hand. There we were alone, and of our own regiment we could see but few at a time and it was impossible to keep a good line." The New Englanders halted and fired blindly into the corn at the enemies flitting about.[35]

While the 49th Massachusetts flailed away, what remained of Dudley's brigade fell back toward Paine's line of battle. Sergeant Plummer, in the 48th Massachusetts, saw them emerge from the crops. "By the waving of the corn tops we could trace the movements of Dudley's men and could see that they were slowly retreating and coming back gradually toward our line." The 174th stumbled out first and continued past Paine's men in a harried mob. The men of the 161st New York kept their formation, materializing from the corn and cane still in line

Along with Belle Alliance, St. Emma was one of two plantations owned by German Charles A. Kock. With three hundred slaves between them, these were large and lucrative sugar operations before the war. Confederate and Federal forces fought across the lawns and fields of both these plantations in July 1863.
Author's photo.

of battle, firing toward the Confederates with drill field precision. Turning smartly about, the regiment fell back across the open ground as they loaded, still covering the retreat, their ranks thinned by more than forty casualties. "A more soldierly appearance could not have been made than was made by that regiment," Plummer added. The New Yorkers passed through the ranks of the 48th Massachusetts and the 114th New York, reformed their lines behind them, and lay down as reserves.[36]

The soldiers of the 5th and 7th Texas cavalries followed, flowing from behind the buildings of St. Emma and thrashing toward Paine's Brigade. "Almost breathlessly we watched the advancing line," wrote Captain Clark. "It was, indeed, a beautiful sight, for never were men better handled than were these rebels." When the Texans debouched from the corn, the Federals, sheltered in a ditch and resting their arms on a fence, fired a volley at the Confederate ranks. "Their line melted as though it had been wax," Clark exclaimed. The rows of cane and corn reabsorbed the Texans as they retreated to the cover of the St. Emma Plantation buildings. The guns anchoring Paine's line shelled Rebels on both sides of Bayou Lafourche, shifting the momentum. The Confederate attack had stalled.[37]

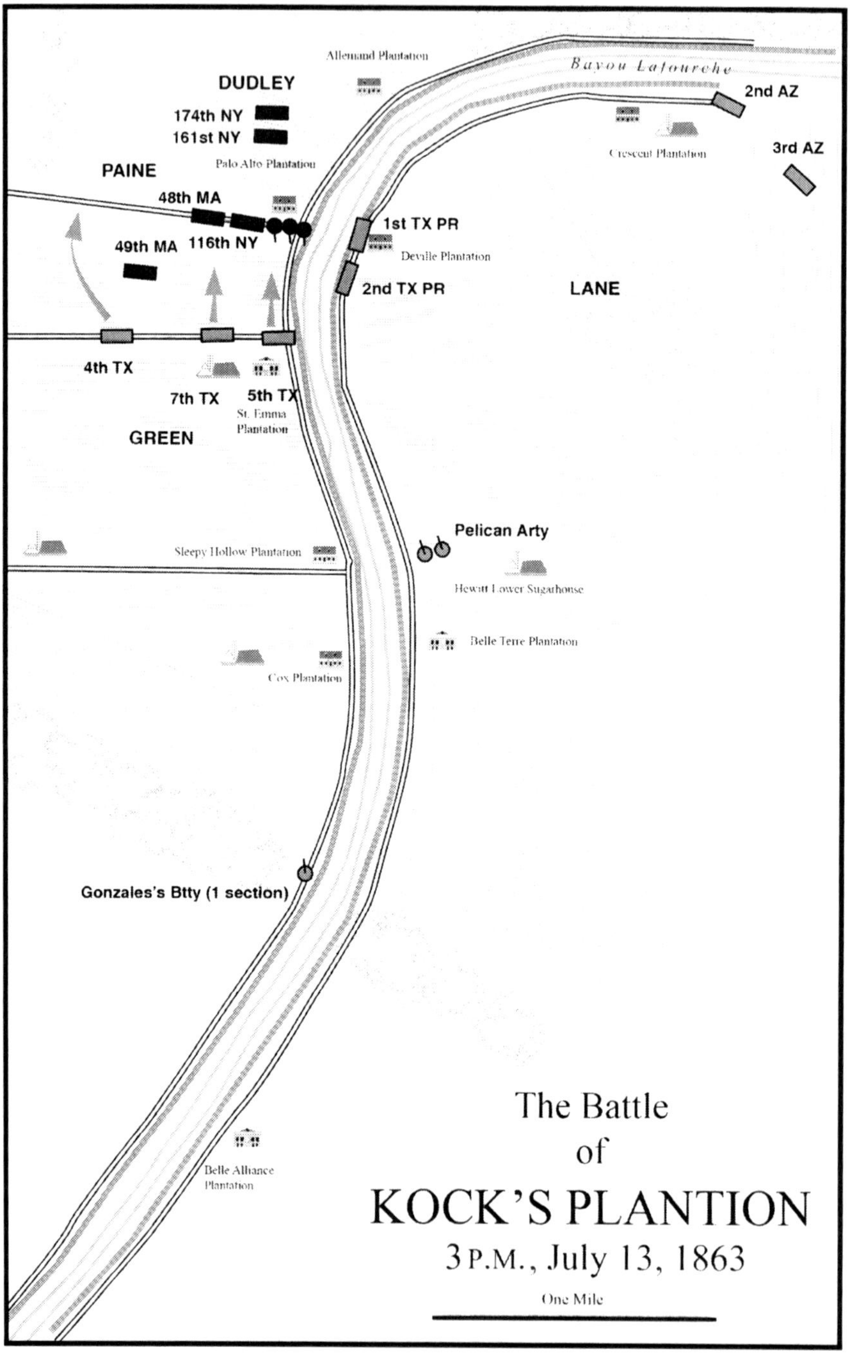
Allemand Plantation
Bayou Lafourche
DUDLEY
174th NY
161st NY
PAINE
Palo Alto Plantation
48th MA
49th MA
116th NY
1st TX PR
Deville Plantation
2nd TX PR
2nd AZ
Crescent Plantation
3rd AZ
LANE
4th TX
7th TX
5th TX
St. Emma Plantation
GREEN
Pelican Arty
Sleepy Hollow Plantation
Hewitt Lower Sugarhouse
Belle Terre Plantation
Cox Plantation
Gonzales's Btty (1 section)
Belle Alliance Plantation
The Battle of
KOCK'S PLANTION
3 P.M., July 13, 1863
One Mile

On the eastern bank, Lane's Texas and Arizona regiments lay scattered, some skirmishing with a handful of Federal cavalry, some harassing the remaining pieces of Morgan's Brigade still drifting toward Donaldsonville, and others moving up the levee to shoot at Paine's Brigade across the bayou. About 120 soldiers from the 2nd Texas Partisan Rangers dismounted at Hewitt's lower sugarhouse before rejoining the fight. "We ran . . . nearly a mile," reported Captain John W. Lane of Dallas, "all perfectly exhausted from the heat." The men caught their breath under cover of the levee, bullets zipping and buzzing in from several directions. The Union gunners on the west side of Bayou Lafourche turned their Sawyer Rifles on them, sending canister and shell whipping by at close range. Even so, the lieutenant and his men continued sneaking forward. "We moved slowly up, advancing under crossfire," Lane continued, "musket balls, grapeshot, and shell filling the air all around us."[38]

Having reached a point flanking Paine's position, these Texans popped over the levee and poured a steady and destructive fire into the Union gun crews on the left of the line. The Texans slaughtered the limber horses. Union gunners from both batteries once again left in a hurry. Yet, Lieutenant John F. Phelps and one of his 6th Massachusetts pieces lay stranded amid a pile of screaming, writhing horses. Nearby, Captain David W. Tuttle of Buffalo, New York, ordered his 116th New York soldiers to leap from the cover of their fence and ditch to help. "Amid a perfect hailstorm of bullets," Clark wrote, "they seized the piece and dragged it to safety in the rear." The gun escaped, but Captain Tuttle did not. He lay in the road behind them, shot through the head.[39]

The Union guns fled while General Green rallied his Texans at St. Emma but did not renew the advance. Instead, the Rebels kept up a long-range harassment of the entire Union line. The men of the 116th New York lay pinned under this steady patter of lead, which had already struck down more than two dozen from the regiment. "The increasing fire," Clark recalled, "made us long for either an order to advance or retire."[40]

When Colonel Dudley came upon Paine's men, he ordered those closest to the bayou to retire toward Fort Butler once his own battered brigade had safely withdrawn. The soldiers of the 116th New York rose up from their line and bounded through the crops behind Palo Alto toward safety, glad for the release. They left the dearly rescued cannon, and the corpse of the heroic Captain Tuttle,

This painting by Marie Adrien Persac from the late 1850s shows the tidy house and grounds of Palo Alto Plantation. The Sacramento Road and the fields on the left of this image saw the last round of fighting between Union and Confederate forces along Bayou Lafourche in 1863.
Private collection.

behind. "We entered a cornfield of immense growth, the stalks being between six and seven feet in height," Captain Clark remembered. "None would dispute that it was hot in that cornfield. Suffocating would be a better term, for it seemed as if the air was directly from the burning fiery furnace mentioned by the Prophet Daniel." Succumbing to the heat, soldiers began to drop.[41]

Far to their right, men of the 49th Massachusetts found themselves lost in a green maze. Paine, realizing his error in ordering this foolhardy advance, ordered the troops to fall back to the Sacramento Road where they had started; when the regiment emerged in squads and clumps, they discovered they were now alone. The Federals fell back behind cover of the fence, reformed their ranks, and waited for instructions.[42]

Word eventually arrived for them to retreat toward Fort Butler. They began in good formation. "This we did for some rods, when we again formed a line, and, for a short distance, fell back in tolerable order," wrote Private Johns. The 4th Texas Cavalry, still hovering on their flank, continued firing blindly toward them from the cane and corn. Few Yankees fell, but the shooting unnerved them. Under this bothersome fire, the regiment unraveled. "Every man started for the river," Johns admitted. "Confusion became worse confounded. We were convinced that we could do nothing but secure our own safety." The sun-stricken soldiers beat their way through crops and forest "four miles, measured by rods," remembered Johns, "forty, as computed by discomfort and fatigue." When the 49th Massachusetts reached the Mississippi, its men lay panting nearly two miles upstream from Fort Butler.[43]

Only one regiment remained south of Palo Alto Plantation. The 48th Massachusetts held its position, determined to keep the Rebels to their front at bay while following orders to stand firm until Colonel Paine returned. The men soon realized that their brigade commander had forgotten them. During the general withdrawal, a staff officer ordered the regiment to retire, but Lieutenant Colonel Stanwood refused until he had heard directly from Paine. "Soon on looking to the right and left not a blue-coated soldier could be seen," admitted Plummer, "and away to the right the rebels could be seen passing rapidly to the rear." The men could also hear firing across Bayou Lafourche, but well *behind* them. "From our front in the corn desultory shots came [in], viciously striking the fence rails above our head." Lieutenant Colonel Stanwood realized his predicament. He feared, with good reason, the Texans would swarm over his regiment. "He directed the men to pass the word quietly down the line without rising," Plummer wrote, "and retire from their position as best they could." Most of the regiment snuck away. Dawdlers—including two lieutenants—found themselves prisoners.[44]

Streams of wounded soldiers and panicked men and animals converged on Fort Butler and Donaldsonville. Drummers beat the long roll in the camps around town and thousands of troops fell into line, "to stem the tide of battle which was setting to the rear in a way that threatened disaster," remembered Captain Elias Pellet of the 114th New York, "with every prospect of an immediate and severe fight."[45]

Green, satisfied with his work, ordered his men to end their pursuit of the three broken Union brigades. The Battle of Kock's Plantation had already handed him a lopsided victory and he prudently recalled his victorious troops. Confederates counted two 6-pounder Sawyer Rifles, hundreds of muskets, and the camp equipment of a Federal brigade as battlefield plunder. They had also inflicted impressive casualties, killing or wounding nearly three hundred Federal troops and capturing another two hundred. The Confederates suffered ten dead and twenty wounded. "This great disparity of loss is most wonderful," Green crowed. "I have never before witnessed such determined valor as was displayed by our troops." He and Lane set out their pickets then fell back to the positions they had held that morning.[46]

At Donaldsonville, recriminations ricocheted among the Union leaders. General Weitzel placed Colonel Morgan under arrest on two charges. The first blamed him for complete tactical failure, including abandoning the ground to which he was assigned, exposing the flank of Union troops on the west bank of Bayou Lafourche to enemy fire, and also of forgetting to call in his skirmishers, forsaking them to the Confederates. The second accusation, "that he . . . in face of the enemy, did become so drunk as to be utterly unfit for duty, thereby exposing his command to disaster" echoed a similar claim made during the siege of Port Hudson. "Colonel Morgan behaved badly," his superior, General Cuvier Grover admitted.[47]

Lieutenant Colonel Richard Irwin, Banks's assistant adjutant general, analyzed the problem. "The result of this bad management," he wrote, "was that the whole command was in effect clubbed." Captain Clark agreed. The battle had been a severe drubbing. *His* regiment, though, did well. "The discredit . . . could not be attached to the One Hundred and Sixteenth, or Paine's Brigade," he asserted. "We had fought well . . . long after Colonel Morgan retreated."[48]

Sergeant Howe believed that Morgan's Brigade had done as well as one might reasonably expect. "They had no artillery on the other side of the bayou," he pointed out. "The enemy charged on them in large numbers, and they were obliged to fall back." Sergeant George Smith of the 1st Louisiana Infantry (Union), one of Morgan's regiments, believed the entire advance up the Lafourche had been ill advised and destined for disaster. "I never really understood the necessity of that movement," he later admitted.[49]

The Federal troops, flush with victory from Port Hudson, may have been simultaneously winded, yet overconfident. Disease, heat, and fatigue sapped their vitality. The Rebel blockade of the Mississippi had also deprived horses and mules of fodder and feed. The Union artillery lacked animals strong enough to pull its cannon. Consequently, Morgan advanced east of the Lafourche without the benefit of guns. Thinking the loss of the Mississippi forts had defeated and demoralized the Confederates, few Federals anticipated a serious battle in the Lafourche District. Green's Texans had disabused them of that notion.

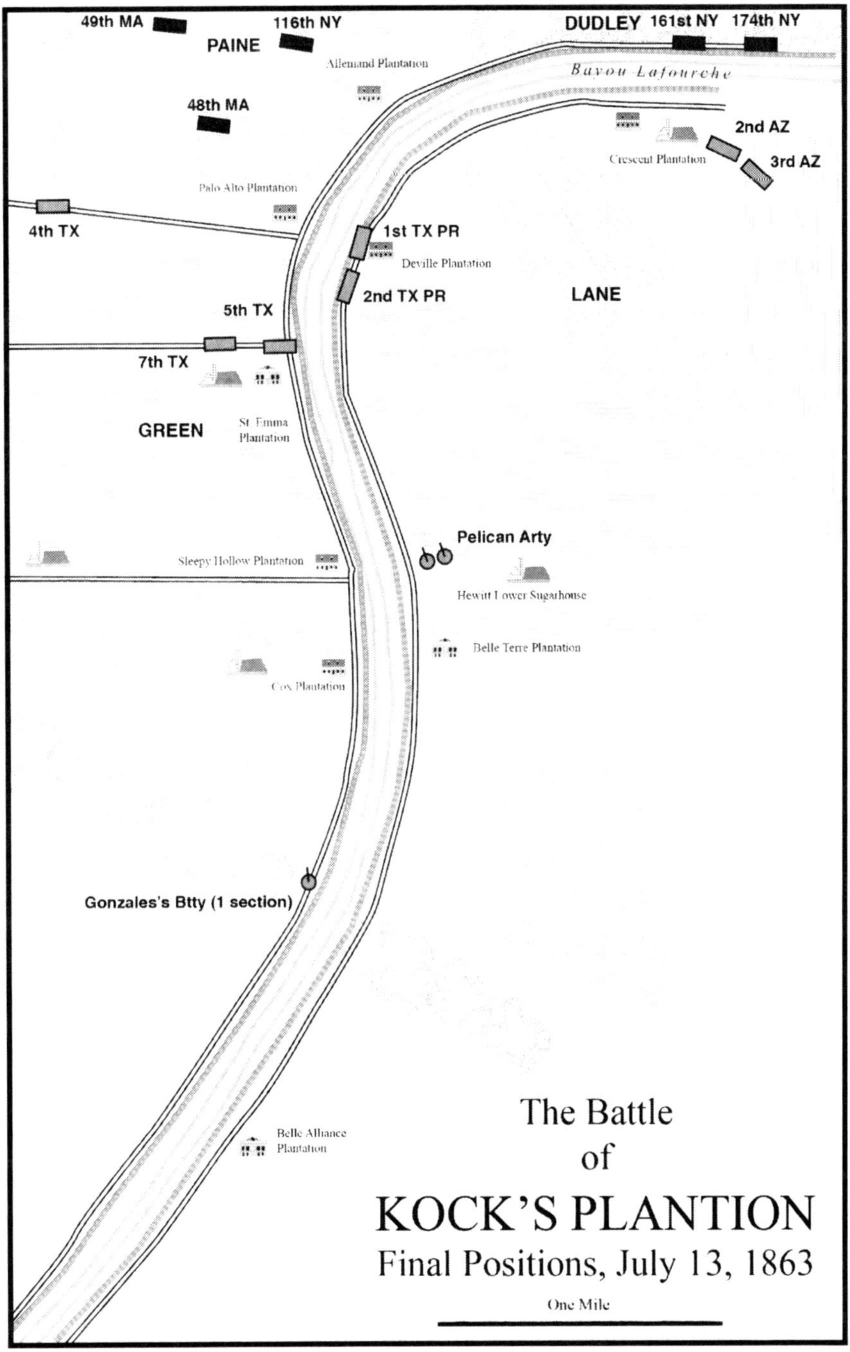
49th MA
116th NY
PAINE
DUDLEY
161st NY
174th NY
Allemand Plantation
Bayou Lafourche
48th MA
2nd AZ
Crescent Plantation
3rd AZ
Palo Alto Plantation
4th TX
1st TX PR
Deville Plantation
LANE
2nd TX PR
5th TX
7th TX
GREEN
St. Emma Plantation
Pelican Arty
Sleepy Hollow Plantation
Hewitt Lower Sugarhouse
Belle Terre Plantation
Cox Plantation
Gonzales's Btty (1 section)
Belle Alliance Plantation
The Battle of KOCK'S PLANTION
Final Positions, July 13, 1863
One Mile

Private Johns in the 49th Massachusetts credited the Rebels for the Union defeat. "It was a sad day," he lamented. "Surprised and flanked, we could do nothing but retreat. I do not know that anyone was to blame." General Dudley had made a prudent reconnaissance the day before and appeared to have the situation well in hand. "We have since learned the foe was a part of General Taylor's army, gathered in Western Louisiana and Texas, some 12,000 strong, for the relief of Port Hudson," Johns erroneously reported. Given what he believed were such incredible odds, Johns believed the 49th Massachusetts had done well. "For coolness, for obedience of orders, for forming again and again when left alone, they deserve much credit," he rationalized. "That officers got separated from their men, and that they nearly all returned in utter confusion, might be expected as the result of being flanked on all sides in a strange country, and was unavoidable when retreating through the luxuriant cane and corn fields of the Lafourche Country."[50]

The last to leave the field, the 48th Massachusetts lost a third of the two hundred men they brought into the fight—mostly captured. "The rebs had less than a thousand men on our side of the bayou," Plummer reported, "and our defeat was all owing to bad generalship on the part of our commanding officers." When prisoners filtered back into camp bearing letters of parole, they told a grim story, confirming what most men at Donaldsonville feared. The Rebels had a dangerous army nearby. Plummer talked with a Union soldier fresh from captivity. "He thinks there are from 10,000 to 20,000 rebels between Donaldsonville and Thibodaux, with considerable artillery." Taylor and Green frightened the veterans of Port Hudson, and the ferocious Battle of Kock's Plantation only contributed to the terror.[51]

For the women of Sleepy Hollow, the battle of Kock's Plantation only signaled the end of one nightmare and the beginning of another. One of their trusted slaves arrived at their hiding place in the woods to recover the women and take them back home. "The negro who had driven the cart . . . came back to The Brule [Sacremento] in the evening and announced the victory of the Confederates, and the complete pillage of our house by the Yankees," wrote Dupuy. "Our first emotion was joy, the second was the grief of thinking that in such hard times we were deprived of everything."

The next morning, the civilians made their way across the battlefield to see what they might salvage. They watched as squads of Yankees under flag of truce prowled the cane and cornfields looking for casualties. "When I passed," Dupuy continued, "the Yankees were taking away their dead. For the first time in my life I had the sad opportunity to see a field covered with bluecoats." Her sympathy for the fallen turned to anger when she arrived home. "One must have seen a place where the Yankees have come," she spat, "to imagine the condition in which was our house when we returned there."[52]

The victory had clearly wounded the Union command at Donaldsonville. Confederates still hovered nearby, observing the Union hospital stewards carry away their dead. "I passed over the battlefield, found Yankees lying in every direction," Private Watkins of the 5th Texas Cavalry wrote to his wife. "Such sights I never wish to see again. I saw all manner of wounds, but most of the Yankees were shot through the head." On the east bank, Sergeant McCann discovered the body of one of his friends from the 90th New York, "with two bullet holes, a deep sabre cut on the hand, and the cruel prints of a horse's hoof on the forehead." His regiment had lost more than seventy men, a third of the unit, and the highest number of any Union command in the fight.[53]

A Federal officer rode forward under a flag of truce bearing a note for General Green. The Texan read the letter, written by General Weitzel, which complimented the rebel's generalship and personal bravery. The Union commander also acknowledged that his forces had been "badly whipped," reported Confederate staff officer, Major Willis L. Robards.[54]

On July 14, no Federal troops besides these recovery teams dared make an appearance. "The enemy remained quietly in and around the fort, making no demonstrations toward us whatever," Green reported, "not even . . . with their pickets." Taylor trumpeted the good news to General Edmund Kirby Smith, giving credit to the Texans. "In the generalship and daring of the commander, and in the devotion of the troops," he wrote, "this action will compare favorably with any I have witnessed during the war." Taylor ordered Green to take his troops to Brashear City. Having checked the Federal pursuit at Kock's Plantation, he now needed to get across Berwick Bay before the U.S. Navy trapped him.[55]

The Union army that had won Port Hudson would not pursue. Green's battle at Kock's Plantation had seen to that. Taylor's month-long Lafourche Campaign was finished.

16

Rebel Retreat

The rebels seem to have retreated though I am afraid that we shall have trouble in that direction yet.
—Lieutenant William Fowler
173rd New York

Despite their convincing victory at the Battle of Kock's Plantation, the men of General Richard Taylor's army knew they faced long odds in escaping uncaptured. "I am afraid we are cut off," Private John W. Watkins wrote his wife, "and nothing but a miracle will save us. Reports are that Banks sent a large force to cut off our retreat and if he succeeds in getting gunboats in the bay, there will be no possible way for us to escape."[1]

The Confederate success stirred General Nathaniel P. Banks to leave his headquarters at Port Hudson and attend to affairs at Donaldsonville personally. Generals Cuvier Grover and Godfrey Weitzel provided details of the debacle. After discussing the issue, all three officers agreed that pursuing Taylor might be imprudent. Reading the reports coming from the Lafourche District, General Banks continued to believe that Taylor led a sizable, and dangerous, force. Besides, the siege of Port Hudson had ravaged the Army of the Gulf, and its commander did not believe he had the troops or wherewithal to tangle with these west bank marauders. With his nine-months' regiments heading home, Banks needed to wait for reinforcements to arrive from General Ulysses S. Grant's army before hunting down and, hopefully, finishing off Taylor. "The depleted ranks and wearied condition of the troops were perhaps taken into account," Lieutenant Colonel Richard Irwin of Banks's staff conceded. Sergeant Thomas H. McCann of the 90th New York thought as much. "Banks at first intended to follow them up," he wrote. "The weather getting hotter and hotter, he ordered his fagged-out command into summer quarters for rest and reorganization."[2]

There would, therefore, be no close pursuit of the Texans. Banks believed his army had fought enough that terrible, hot, summer. "There is an opinion . . . that our army is naturally sluggish; that its chief characteristics are fortitude and patience," acknowledged Union officer George Hepworth. The Confederates, although reckless, he believed, had a "certain genius for dash, which makes them a terrible foe. The rebels have done more to win respect for themselves by their cavalry raids than by all their infantry movements." Banks would let the Texas and Arizona horsemen alone.[3]

Many in the circle of command agreed with Banks, believing a campaign down Bayou Lafourche might prove premature. "It was inexpedient to press Taylor hard or hasten his movements in any way," Irwin wrote, "until time should have been allowed for the light-draught gunboats to re-enter Berwick Bay and thus gain control of Taylor's line of retreat."[4]

The plucky Rebels, having blunted Banks's ambitions, had already headed for the exit. Nearly as soon as the fight near Donaldsonville had ended, Taylor was on his way to Brashear City to supervise the retreat. He issued orders for the Confederate army in the Lafourche District to contract, falling back toward Berwick Bay from every direction. Quartermaster and commissary officers shepherded the last of the food and supplies from the region, while medical officers evacuated the sick, wounded, and injured.

This military exodus included many sufferers. While the Battle of Kock's Plantation raged, Private Felix Collard of the 7th Texas Cavalry, injured in a horse fall two days previously, arrived before Dr. T. B. Greenwood at the hospital in Paincourtville. Collard had dislocated his shoulder and, he believed, broken his right arm above the elbow. The army sawbones declared his case too complicated for him to handle in the field and sent him to Napoleonville in a mule cart in the care of another soldier, Private Vincent Faulkner. When they arrived at the next hospital, the soldiers saw stewards and stretcher-bearers frantically loading the sick and wounded from the various battles of the Lafourche Campaign onto barges for a journey to Lafourche Crossing. A train would meet them there and carry the casualties by rail to Berwick Bay. Amid this bustle, doctors merely outfitted the crippled Texan with a sling—and directions to head down the road to Thibodaux.

The news had already spread among secessionist sympathizers that the Confederates were leaving, and they did their best to get out while they could. "Vince and I took the road . . . which was filled with women and children in buggies, surreys, and two-horse wagons," Collard wrote, "and sometimes a balky team." One of these carriages carried a young lawyer, Felix Pierre Poché, his wife

Sélima, adolescent daughter Maggie, and several enslaved house servants. Originally from St. James Parish and a staunch secessionist, Poché had relatives and in-laws all over Louisiana and had taken his family to his sister-in-law's plantation near Morganza in Pointe Coupée Parish, hoping to dodge the war. Banks and his Federal troops had marched by their front door en route to Port Hudson. When the Rebels passed that way en route to retaking the Lafourche, he decided to follow, moving his family to a relative's plantation near Thibodaux.[5]

Felix Pierre Poché joined the Confederate Army at the beginning of the Civil War, but various issues related to raising regiments left him an officer without a command. He resigned, returned home to care for his family, but found himself on the run, trying to stay ahead of advancing Union armies. He moved his wife and daughter from Pointe Coupée Parish to Thibodaux, finally deciding they would be safer behind enemy lines. He bade them farewell and joined the retreating Confederates.
Diary of Felix Pierre Poché.

Poché arrived in Thibodaux in time to see the Louisiana infantry brigade file by, heading toward Berwick Bay. "This, and all other army movements strongly indicated a retreat or evacuation of this region of Louisiana," he recorded. Poché decided his family would be safer behind Union lines; he, however, as a known secessionist and former Confederate officer, would offer his services as a clerk on Brigadier General Alfred Mouton's staff.[6]

Behind Poché, Private Collard bobbed along on a torrent of refugees and retreating troops, injured, fatigued, and stressed, while his condition worsened. "My arm swelled as big as my leg, and turned . . . black," he wrote. The rough road jarred Collard's injured shoulder and he nearly fainted from the pain. After miles of torture, he directed Faulkner to turn off the main road and to take him to a nearby planter's house so he could rest overnight.

"The owner," Collard recalled, "replied that he could not take us in, that our army was retreating, and that if he was found aiding and abetting the Confederacy in any way, in any manner, that the enemy would burn his residence and all he possessed."[7]

"Can't you take care of a wounded man?" Collard implored.

The homeowner hesitated. "If one of you is wounded, alight. I don't think they will burn me out for taking care of a wounded man, but I can't take care of the other."

Collard bade his friend farewell and asked a favor. "Vince . . . take my horse to my mess mates, and write my father where you left me."[8]

The Louisiana planter, described by Collard as "a Frenchman," directed his slaves to bathe the young Texan, wash his clothes, and show him to a bedroom. The homeowner brought in a glass of wine. Collard passed out, probably helped along by a narcotic in his drink. The next morning, the Rebel ate a breakfast of hot coffee and fresh biscuits.

"How far is Thibodaux?" Collard asked the planter.

"Five miles," he responded.

"Can you take me there?"

"No. The negroes would report me as soon as the Federal Army got here."

Collard showed the Louisianan a five dollar gold coin. "He said he couldn't for five hundred," the soldier remembered. Instead, the planter recommend Collard see his nephew in Thibodaux who was Canadian—a British subject—who might help. After smuggling Collard along back roads to within sight of Thibodaux, the Louisianan dropped the injured Confederate off and quickly left. The Texan walked the rest of the way to town.

On July 14, Collard arrived only to discover the town deserted. There was no Frenchman's nephew. "All the citizens were gone and the buildings were locked up," Collard remarked. "Not a soul in town, white or black, except three old negroes who could not get away." A storm blew in, and soon Collard stood soaking wet, poorly sheltered under the eaves of a building. At 4:00 P.M., he heard the tramping of troops coming from the direction of Napoleonville. Two regiments of Texas infantry came marching through town heading toward Berwick Bay. "I knew my cousin was in that [brigade]," he wrote. When William E. Collard of the 15th Texas Infantry spied his injured kinsman, he hurriedly broke ranks to see him. "He came along . . . telling me where to go," Collard remembered. Officers ordered the infantryman back into line, hollering "fall in, fall in, no time to stop and talk."

"Write my father and tell him where you saw me," Collard yelled to his cousin as he disappeared back into the column of soldiers.

The wounded Texan walked along the bayou toward the train tracks at Lafourche Crossing, three miles away. He passed the barges of wounded he had seen loaded at Napoleonville. Upon reaching the tracks, Collard managed to climb aboard a crowded train headed for Brashear City that night.[9]

Collard, exhausted from pain and travel, awoke in darkness. The train bearing the wounded and sick had arrived at the depot on the shore of Berwick Bay. After everyone left the cars, he made a bed out of seat cushions and slept for a few hours in the aisle. After sunup on the morning of July 15, Collard stumbled out onto the platform and saw rows of dead and dying. Stepping around these corpses and sufferers, Collard passed into the depot and ran into a friend from school, Sergeant Asa Stratton, a soldier in Major Leonidas C. Rountree's Texas Cavalry Battalion then serving as a commissary clerk.

"Where did you drop in from?" asked the sergeant.

"From the front."

"It looks like it."

The sergeant gave Collard a quick breakfast of hardtack, pickled pork, and coffee. Refreshed, the injured private stumbled toward a building marked "hotel," entered, but discovered it vacant and bare. Collard claimed the only furniture left—a canvas cot on the porch. He patiently waited for someone to tell him what to do next.

Confederate doctors arrived later that morning and converted the structure into a hospital. When they examined the soldier's arm, they declared it dislocated, but not broken, much to Collard's relief. Soon, "my arm began to swivel and change its color from black to yellowish green, and was not as painful," he remembered. The doctors never set the shoulder, though. Four days later, the young Texan boarded a steamer with the rest of the Confederate wounded and headed across Berwick Bay and up the Teche to New Iberia. He emerged from the Lafourche District safe, but crippled, one passenger among many in a steady parade of small steamboats including *Indian No. 2* and *Anna Perret* shuttling Taylor's troops, cannon, supplies, clothing, plunder, wounded, sick, and prisoners to safety.[10]

At his headquarters in Brashear City, Taylor sought to keep his army relevant. His campaign to break the siege of Port Hudson had failed, and the enemy would certainly follow up with an invasion of Confederate-held Louisiana. Anticipating this move, Taylor identified Vermilionville and Niblett's Bluff as the new depots for his army and his next line of resistance. Meanwhile, he required knowledge of Union movements on the Mississippi. If the Federals landed troops in Pointe Coupée Parish during the next few days, they could march up the Red River Valley and cut the state in two, trapping his army in the southern parishes. He sent a staff officer to Morgan's Ferry to investigate. He also ordered his staff in Alexandria to keep him informed of any movements by Federals from Natchez, Mississippi. His efforts to save Port Hudson had exhausted him and left him short-handed for the work ahead. "I have no staff officer with me," he complained, "and am fatigued and jaded beyond description."[11]

Taylor also wrote to General John Bankhead Magruder in Houston, outlining the history of his campaign and detailing future plans. "I was most sanguine that my operations would so seriously embarrass the operations of General Banks as to force him to raise the siege of Port Hudson," he wrote. The fall of Vicksburg and Port Hudson, though, had now released large numbers of Federal troops. "My longer possession of this country depended upon the sufferance of the enemy," Taylor noted, "rather that upon my ability to prevent him from surrounding or cutting off my little army." He had landed a blow at Kock's Plantation. "This, having effectually checked his advance, I withdrew my forces."[12]

Yet, danger remained. "If the enemy means to overrun and occupy Louisiana, it is within his power to do so," Taylor admitted. If Grant or Banks invaded now, they would easily capture Opelousas, Washington, and Alexandria. They would also cut Taylor off from Lieutenant General Edmund Kirby Smith and the headquarters of the Trans-Mississippi at Shreveport. The Confederate resistance in the state would collapse. If that happened, Taylor and his army would retreat to Beaumont, Texas, and defend the line of the Sabine River. "The condition of affairs resulting from the fall of Vicksburg and Port Hudson indicates most strongly that an army of the Trans-Mississippi Department must concentrate in Texas."[13]

While Taylor sketched out his next move, General Tom Green ushered his cavalry out of the Lafourche District. Captain Keet McDade of the 13th Texas Cavalry Battalion had been waiting on the shores of Lake Salvador for the dash into New Orleans. Instead he now received orders to head for Berwick Bay. "What else could be expected when our two Confederate Sevastopols have fallen," he wrote, likening Vicksburg and Port Hudson to the famous Russian stronghold of

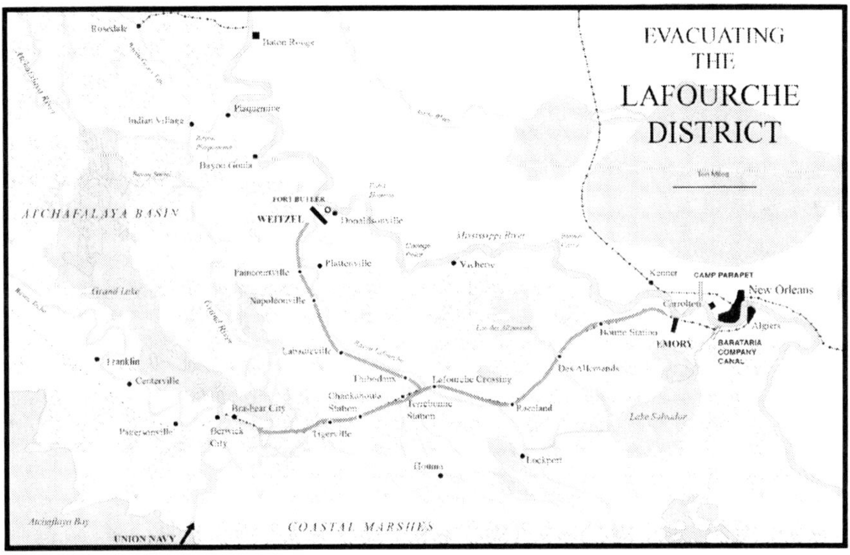

the Crimean War. As they retreated, the troops of this command, along with the 2nd Texas Cavalry, burned every span along the New Orleans, Opelousas, and Great Western Railroad from Lafourche Crossing to Bayou Boeuf.[14]

The Confederate infantry crossed first. The Louisianans especially hated to leave. "Our visit to Lafourche personally had been gratifying to members of our company, having afforded us all the opportunity to see our friends," remembered Captain Silas Grisamore of the 18th Louisiana Infantry, "and enabled most of the men to get a new outfit of clothing. We had lived well during our stay, having been fed principally by the commissary establishments of General Banks." With the foot soldiers safely across, Green's Brigade followed, camping in the ruins of Berwick City on the night of July 18 near the location where, nearly a month before, the Val Verde Battery had started the attack on Brashear City.[15]

Confederates carried off all the plunder they could. Captured weapons headed north to Grand Ecore to rearm two Texas regiments there serving with Brigadier General Camille Polignac. Federal uniforms now clothed many of the Rebel troops. The heavy cannon would be useful in Rebel forts on the Red River. Officers also bundled up trade items, civilian clothing, and general dry goods and sent them all to New Iberia to be auctioned for the benefit of the army. The Confederates attempted to take everything of value.[16]

Plunder also included people. Regulations allowed every officer in the army to keep a servant. Those who had none, picked from among the blacks taken during the campaign. Newly promoted Lieutenant John Sibley of the 2nd Louisiana Cavalry chose a young man named Green, but, having no way to keep him for the time being, sent him home to his wife. "He had been with the Yankees and says he belonged east of the Mississippi in the Yankee lines," Coleman instructed. "He is to remain on the place and work until I call for him."[17]

Sergeant George Haven Putnam of the 176th New York, a prisoner among the Confederates, watched the last of the Texans pass by. He wrote home to tell his parents about these strange men:

> A word before I close this epistle about the Texans, whose prisoners we had been for a month.
>
> I have called them half savages, and it is about true, but they have some of the noblest qualities of savages. They are brave to rashness, and will endure with patience any amount of exposure and suffering to accomplish their end. They are generous, good-natured, and treat their prisoners with much kindness. They are splendid horse-men, fine marksmen, and can go for days with but a morsel of uncooked food to eat. They are cheap troops to support, because they don't care for tents, will wear any kind of clothing, and will live on bacon and hoecake, or forage for themselves and their horses.
>
> But though brave, they are perfectly undisciplined and regardless of orders, and will fight every man on his own hook, breaking ranks as soon as they commence firing, so that, although they are excellent bushwhackers, they are often scattered and routed in the open field.
>
> They consider themselves the equals of their officers, and it is a risky matter to punish them for insubordination. When there is no fighting going on they soon tire of the restraints of camp-life, and often leave for home, coming back when it suits them. Then they will steal, even from their own officers; they will brag beyond all the bounds of truth, and they won't wash themselves or their shirts.

> To give you an example of the Texan way of doing things: Two or three days ago some of them broke into the stores of their post quartermaster, and came riding past our hospital decked out with their spoils of captured Federal clothing. One long, lank country boy had a hat *and* a cap on his head and another cap in his hand. One of our wounded men, looking over the balcony, called out: "I wish you would give me one of those caps; I haven't got any!" Not expecting, however, that his request would be granted. "All right," cried Texas, and chucked the cap up; it fortunately proved a good fit.
>
> On the whole, I don't know as we could have fallen into better hands.[18]

Sergeant Putnam believed the Confederates had cleaned out the Lafourche District "of all that is worth having. Negroes, cattle, wagons, tools, etc., and if they escape without punishment their raid may be termed a most successful one. They are occupied night and day in crossing over their ill-gotten plunder upon two or three antiquated-looking steamboats. Horses are carried over in barges or flat-boats, while the cattle are compelled to swim."[19]

Texas cowboys whipped and spurred droves of beeves into Berwick Bay. Men in boats worked the flanks and rear, driving the cattle toward the opposite shore. "The whole scene is accomplished by the shouts, yells, and war whoops," Putnam observed, "without which the true Texan can neither work nor fight." The lowing and bellowing of the animals, the whistles, the shouts, the cracking whips, and the splashing water created a huge commotion as the Texans drove the Lafourche beeves toward the Attakapas Prairies. "I have been told that this method was employed once or twice on dark nights to victual Port Hudson during the late siege," Putnam wrote home. "They must have made less noise about it."[20]

On July 19, Colonel James P. Major's Brigade and Lieutenant Colonel Ed Waller's Battalion evacuated Thibodaux, carrying with them the last of the pro-Confederate civilians. Poché saddled his horse, Parfait, kissed his wife and daughter good-bye, and departed hoping for a position as a civilian employee in the commissary department. He brought with him a young black servant who would attend to him during his time away from home.[21]

The small New York Sachem *entered Union service at the beginning of the war and served in New York Harbor before towing ironclad USS* Monitor *to Hampton Roads, Virginia, waiting out of range during the historic fight with ironclad CSS* Virginia. *USS* Sachem *next went to the mouth of the Mississippi to survey approaches to New Orleans. It served in a number of utility roles in the western Gulf of Mexico including operations near Fort Morgan and the Pearl River before moving to blockading duty off the Texas coast. Engaged in the vicinity of Corpus Christi, USS* Sachem *sustained some damage, causing it to call at the Union-occupied port of Galveston for repairs, arriving in time to participate in the battle there on January 1, 1863. The ship arrived in New Orleans battered and damaged, but after repairs returned to duty on the Mississippi. The light draft USS* Sachem *passed up the Atchafalaya River and served as a dispatch vessel keeping open communications between the Union armies besieging Vicksburg and Port Hudson. Farragut ordered the vessel toward Berwick Bay to try and trap the retreating Confederates.*
Daniel D. T. Nestell Papers, US Naval Academy.

Luck held for the fleeing Confederates—the Union trap failed to snap. During the week-long Confederate evacuation, Admiral David G. Farragut failed to assemble his shallow-draft armada for the capture of Berwick Bay. *Estrella* had come to New Orleans but required repairs. *Arizona* still remained somewhere up the Mississippi between Port Hudson and Vicksburg. Only *Sachem* arrived ready for action. Banks sent Farragut a nervous dispatch, warning him that the Confederates would escape if the navy did not hurry. The admiral believed otherwise. "He had better . . . find out that he can drive them," Farragut related to a friend, clearly referring to the debacle at Koch's Plantation. "It is always well to know that you can do what you attempt. The boats, [even] with all the delay,

A New York ferryboat, USS Clifton *proved useful in its role as a gunboat during the Civil War. After serving in the campaigns on the lower Mississippi River in 1862, the vessel prowled the coast of Texas, seeing action at Port Lavaca and Galveston. USS* Clifton *covered the advance of Union forces during the Teche Campaign, but Confederate gunners landed a lucky, debilitating shot on the vessel's machinery, sending it to New Orleans for repairs and keeping the gunboat out of action for weeks.*
Daniel D. T. Nestell Papers, US Naval Academy.

will be there before the army." True, but neither would arrive before the Rebels had gone.[22]

When the last Confederates moved through Brashear City, wrecking crews demolished the locomotives and rolling stock before burning the village. "The chances to travel from [Berwick] Bay to New Orleans are quite limited," McDade joked. "We would have destroyed the Bay if we could have." The army that General Taylor brought into the Lafourche a month before marched back up Bayou Teche in penny packets. They had failed to save Port Hudson but had disrupted—for a time—Union efforts to remake Louisiana. On July 21, the last of the Rebel garrison crossed over Berwick Bay. Sergeant H. N. Connor, riding with the cavalry battalion of the 11th Texas Volunteers, put the finishing touches on the destruction. "We are the last troops, the rear guard, to evacuate Brashear City," he wrote in his diary. "Crossed over after burning [the] railroad."[23]

With mixed emotions, New York Sergeant Putnam watched the Confederates leave: "The rebels completed their evacuation, and left us alone in our glory. The last able-bodied darkey was grabbed, the last straggling cattle swam over, the last crew of 'ragged riders' embarked." Long columns of troops, wagons, and animals snaked toward New Iberia. "By two P.M.," Putnam observed, "both shores were deserted."

A growing mass of civilians joined the evacuation as the Confederate army passed up the Teche. Sidney Harding, a twenty-two-year-old woman living at Old Brier Plantation between Berwick City and Pattersonville, believed it was time to go. This would be the third time she had abandoned her home, fleeing each time the Federals had passed the place in their various invasions. She had endured enough. "Oh, the sufferings of the people while the parish was in the hands of the enemy," she grieved. "The enemy destroyed a great deal." Then, Confederates had occupied her house, using it as a hospital and making it unlivable from the filth, blood, and stench. Harding and her mother decided to wait out the war in northwestern Louisiana at their old home at Keatchie, which was between Shreveport and Mansfield. Harding cut her hair short for ease of maintenance; "[I] look like an ugly bug," she lamented. Miss Harding supervised the loading of some of the family possessions into a wagon and left Old Brier to its fate.[24]

Now across Berwick Bay, most Confederates assumed that they were safe. Leaders, though, feared at least one danger remained. Might the Yankees send a column from the Mississippi to cut them off at Opelousas or Alexandria? "I thought affairs were looking much better and had hoped that this part of the country and all of Red River was safe for the summer," opined Lieutenant Sibley. "I learned this evening that none of our forces were safe on this side [of Berwick Bay]. I hope we will get out of this trap again without being cut off."[25]

That same day, as Taylor feared, one division of the XIII Army Corps under Brigadier General Francis J. Herron—some five thousand men—left Vicksburg heading for Port Hudson. They arrived within days. If these troops crossed the Mississippi and pushed into the interior by way of the Red River or Morgan's Ferry, they could march on Washington and Opleousas to cut off the Rebel retreat. Taylor believed he now faced a second race to safety.[26]

On July 22, other Federals returned to Berwick Bay. *Sachem* arrived and discovered the Confederates gone. "The Lone Star had been hauled down,"

Sergeant Putnam boasted. "The Stars and Stripes waved triumphantly over town." *Estrella*, *Clifton*, and *Hollyhock* arrived the following day. These warships scouted into Grand Lake and up Bayou Teche to the vicinity of the Rebel works at Bisland, but beyond shelling the elusive Texas cavalry, accomplished little. They did not push their luck and retreated to the safety of Berwick Bay. On July 25, Lieutenant Colonel Frank Peck and the 12th Connecticut arrived aboard transports with a detachment of infantry and reoccupied Brashear City. Soon afterward, the 6th Regiment *Corps d'Afrique* and the 114th New York also arrived.[27]

The Rebels had picked the one-time Federal depot clean. The Yankees investigated the forts Taylor resuscitated to cover water approaches from the south and only gleaned the battered tubes of five 24-pounders and two 32-pounders amid the cinders and ashes of their carriages. The trains and locomotives in town were total wrecks. Confederate pickets continued to patrol the opposite shore of Berwick Bay. The battle lines returned to the status quo of a month before.[28]

Many of the Army of the Gulf's soldiers rested easier knowing Taylor and his hard-riding army had gone. The Confederate escape from the Lafourche District signaled an end to active campaigning. Still, Taylor and his army remained threatening. "The rebels seem to have retreated," Lieutenant William Fowler of the 173rd New York wrote from the safety of an office at Port Hudson, "though I am afraid that we shall have trouble in that direction yet."[29]

Neither did Herron's Division, now encamped at Port Hudson, pursue Taylor. As both Grant and Banks tried to plot their next move, Herron remained without orders and all of his transportation had disappeared downriver carrying liberated slaves to New Orleans. Even if they had wanted to, the Union troops had no way to cross the Mississippi to intercept the Rebels. "I am in receipt of no orders or official communications from Major General Banks," Herron complained to Grant. In fact, the commander of the Department of the Gulf had passed by Port Hudson returning from a conference in Vicksburg and had not even stopped, leaving Herron to wonder why he was in Louisiana at all. He vented his frustrations to his former chief, writing, "left as I am in this department without orders of any kind, I find myself in a very unpleasant position." A veteran of Grant's victorious army, the hard-charging Herron longed to finish Taylor once and for all. An opportunity now presented itself to do so.[30]

Political, economic, and social considerations, however, intervened.

17 Confederate Collapse

We are now in the darkest hour of our political existence.
—President Jefferson Davis
Confederate States of America

As the Rebel columns passed along Bayou Teche, the battlefields of the previous April provided a macabre reminder of the horrors of war. Passing near Bisland, one Texan wrote, "I assure you it was far from a pleasant sight. The battlefield smells yet distinctly of the dead . . . nearly all of whom are Yankees." Troops had hastily covered their fallen comrades with earth and left them behind as the campaign progressed. Subsequent rains, however, uncovered the corpses. "All over the field," the horrified soldier continued, "can be seen an arm or leg projecting, or a whole skeleton." Some Louisianans found the casualties from the 7th Texas Cavalry. "Several . . . were found lying just as they fell on that day," recorded Captain Silas Grisamore. Friends buried the fallen and neglected remains, then moved on.[1]

As it straggled up Bayou Teche, gloom followed the Confederate army. Soldiers left the column and foraged freely, believing this region, too, would soon be under Union control. Commissary officers looted the salt mines on Petite Anse Island, near New Iberia. Their raiding did not stop with minerals. "Boats, wagons, carts, mules, horses and in fact everything that anyone has is taken without any sort of scruples," complained mine manager E. B. Cox to his boss, Edmund McIlhenny. "Query how long it will take us to whip ourselves by starving first the people and then the army." The soldiers, he reported, had no plans to stop until they reached Shreveport. In the meantime, "the people need salt very badly," Cox noted, "but [I] dare not attempt to transport it unless it is with a very poor miserable team not worth taking."[2]

Officials in Richmond feared that the compounded disasters on the Mississippi and the defeat of General Robert E. Lee's Rebel army at Gettysburg, Pennsylvania, had grievously, perhaps mortally, injured the Confederacy. President Jefferson

Davis admitted: "We are now in the darkest hour of our political existence." The army's Chief of Ordnance, Major Josiah Gorgas, agreed. "[The loss of the Mississippi] is indeed a terrible blow to our cause. It apparently sets us back indefinitely. It will enable the Yankees to recruit their armies, and will greatly depress our credit abroad." Davis blamed neither Generals Richard Taylor nor Edmund Kirby Smith for the disaster; he blamed Lieutenant General Joseph E. Johnston. "I saw the president the other day," Gorgas noted in his diary. "He is bitter against Johnston as I judge from a single remark. When I said that Vicksburg fell, apparently, from want of provisions inside, he remarked—'Yes, from want of provisions inside, and a general outside who would not fight.'"[3]

The Confederate Department of the Trans-Mississippi would have to continue the war in their region on its own. "By the fall of our fortified places," Davis wrote to General Kirby Smith, "your difficulties must be materially enhanced." Not only would Rebel commanders in Shreveport have to see to military matters, but political and economic affairs west of the river would fall into their purview as well. Confederate military officials would have to consult and assuage politicians in Texas, Louisiana, Arkansas, and Missouri. "Your department must needs be, to a great extent, self-sustaining," Davis warned. Kirby Smith needed to create bureaus, depots, and arsenals mirroring those east of the Mississippi that could collect and distribute weapons, clothing, food, and all the sinews of war.[4]

Davis reviewed the military situation out west and praised General Taylor's efforts alone. The Trans-Mississippi operations on behalf of the Confederate army trapped at Port Hudson had been the only good news Davis had received that summer. "I have rejoiced in the success which has attended the operations of your troops in Southern Louisiana," the president extolled, "and trust it is but the beginning of a career which will extend itself to every portion of your department." Perhaps, Davis wrote, Kirby Smith's Rebels could harass commercial shipping on the Mississippi much as Taylor had below Port Hudson. "Beyond that," Davis conceded, "I suppose your operations must be confined to the interior of the country."[5]

Felix Pierre Poché, now a commissary clerk on Brigadier General Alfred Mouton's division staff, worried about his family back in Thibodaux. Melancholy music played by the brass band of the 15th Texas infantry heightened his depression. "The soothing . . . music brought me in an instant to the side of my beloved ones," he wrote. "Thoughts of my dear wife and child whose fate is now in the hands of our enemies are always painful, and will I fear continue so until I can have encouraging news from them, and know that they are safely . . . gone through the crises."[6]

General Mouton pushed his infantry division to Vermilionville and camped them on the prairies north of town. Anxiety stalked the camps, and officers speculated that only foreign intervention would save the South. Others were more sanguine. Colonel Abel W. Bosworth of the 24th Louisiana Infantry believed that Confederate successes east of the Mississippi would draw the Yankees away, "and that we will enter New Orleans without firing a gun," Poché noted. Most, though, doubted that rosy prediction.[7]

A dress parade and inspection proved the antidote for military malaise. Mouton assembled his troops on August 1. Texas bands provided music as Colonel Leopold Armant, commanding the Louisiana Brigade, and Colonel Joseph Speight, head of the Texas Brigade—astride "the most beautiful bay horse in the whole army," noted Poché—aligned their troops on the crest of a rise in the middle of the prairie. Townspeople turned out to watch the spectacle. The Louisianans looked smart, well uniformed, and well disciplined, Poché believed, and beat the Texans in every category except martial music. The well-drilled artillery made the biggest impression. The men of Captain Oliver Semme's 1st Regular Battery drew the most attention, Poché believed, "especially with all the men dressed in red shirts."[8]

Officers barked orders for the review to commence. "General Mouton and his staff, Colonel Armant, Colonel Speight and their staffs dashed at a full gallop with drums beating, and bands playing," Poché continued. "The little army presented a pretty good view." A soldier in the 13th Texas Volunteers agreed. "The troops made a fine appearance," he wrote, "and the field presented a display highly creditable to our cause."[9]

At about the same time, a similar review occurred at Galveston. The troops in Texas, General John Bankhead Magruder believed, would soon face combat and they, too, needed encouragement. Sallie Patrick, a friend to Private William Randolph Howell of the 5th Texas Cavalry, wrote about her trip to the island: "We visited all the fortifications, saw the Yankee blockaders, rode on the beach, and had a fine time generally. The sight that pleased me most was a grand review of all the troops on the island by General Magruder. They were dressed in uniforms and presented quite a nice appearance." Patrick ended with a jab, "they have nothing else to do but look nice."[10]

Patrick wondered why General Tom Green's men were not brought home while these men took a turn in Louisiana. "Relieve them for awhile, anyway," she wrote. "These troops in Texas have never had a chance to display their worth." She also revealed a nagging fear. The Yankees, rumor had it, would soon invade Texas. "If that is the case the Lord only knows what will become of us," she continued. "I am certain I wish [Green's] Brigade would be here for I know they could whip out the Yankees for they have been . . . often tried, and have never failed yet."[11]

The Texas cavalry in Louisiana also wished to go home. One observer arriving in the camps of Colonel James P. Major's Brigade discovered plenty of men ready to leave, and believed this part of Taylor's army looked as lost as the secessionists' cause. Thomas Jefferson League, a Galveston lawyer, arrived in Louisiana as Deputy Confederate States Marshall to help handle legal chores related to the army and camped with what was left of the 3rd Arizona Cavalry. "Things look to me very blue," he wrote. "Our armies across the Mississippi are in retreat while this army is far from being . . . what I wished and expected to see. In fact, I have not much confidence in it." Regiments remained badly undermanned, with desertions common. The 2nd Texas Partisan Rangers alone had more than two hundred men under guard for attempting to desert.[12]

Poor discipline and a disregard for law and order among the troops disgusted League. "Common theft is passed off as a joke," the lawman wrote. "I do not believe the Yankees could behave . . . worse than our troops do. It is terrible to have an army of even one's friends near one's property." Officers attempted to check these excesses by establishing strong provost guards around the camps. "Poor Louisiana," he sighed, "she has and is suffering terribly." The brigade teetered on the edge of mutiny.[13]

Reliable information about the conduct of the war elsewhere remained scarce. "We hear no news here of any kind," League continued. "It seems to me we occupy some other planet besides earth." Speculation abounded. "The most authentic rumor we have is that France had landed one hundred thousand troops at Brownsville and has declared her intention to conquer and reclaim all of our country west of the Mississippi," he scoffed. "From this report you can judge of what the others consist."[14]

Indeed, General Kirby Smith faced an overwhelming new reality. He possessed limited access to his government in Richmond. His Department of the Trans-Mississippi remained chronically short of weapons, ammunition, and systems for reliable supply, and no money with which to wage war. The military policies of his command carried with them a concomitant political responsibility. Because they could not wrestle with Richmond, governors wrangled with him. His soldiers were few; his challenges many. To most observers, the dog days of 1863 promised to be the last Confederate summer, especially west of the Mississippi.

The reversal of Rebel fortunes in June and July 1863 had been breathtaking. At the beginning of the summer, Confederate officials believed the Mississippi Valley, although threatened, could be defended. News of Rebel triumphs in the region had arrived even at the height of the sieges of Vicksburg and Port Hudson. "Taylor had driven the enemy from the greater part of Louisiana and captured immense stores at Brashear," Major Gorgas had noted. Southern successes in Virginia had prompted an invasion of Pennsylvania. "All looked bright," Gorgas lamented. "Now the picture is just as somber as it was bright then." The loss of Vicksburg and Port Hudson coupled with General Robert E. Lee's reversal at Gettysburg appeared to signal the end of the South's bid for independence. "Yesterday we rode on the pinnacle of success—today absolute ruin seems to be our portion," Gorgas concluded. "The Confederacy totters to its destruction."[15]

There were other portents of collapse. A mass exodus of refugees headed west, away from Union armies. Since the early days of the war, planters had been moving tens of thousands of enslaved people from the broad fields of Louisiana into the Piney Woods and Grand Prairie of Texas. At first, owners intended these moves to keep their slaves from running into the lines of nearby Union armies. Now they moved their human property to keep them away from Federal armies coming to liberate them. Peaking in the spring and summer of 1863, Louisiana neighborhoods dissolved as people abandoned their fields and homes and searched for some stability in the sparsely settled counties west of the Sabine River. William Frederick Weeks fled New Iberia, believing that Texas remained the best option for maintaining control of his chattel. As he boasted from Houston, "Negro property will be safe here when not one is left a slave in Louisiana."[16]

That summer, Clarissa Grant Hewitt and her husband James quit Louisiana. Before the war they had been among the state's wealthiest people. He had made

James and Clarissa Hewitt abandoned their luxurious Crescent Plantation near Donaldsonville, Louisiana, to try their luck as refugees in Texas.
Diary of a Refugee

his first fortune in the 1820s producing salt in the Kanawha Valley of Virginia. He had married Clarissa Grant—a cousin of the Union hero of Vicksburg—in Mason County, Kentucky. The couple lived in Louisville and New York City before pursuing their second fortune, a sugar empire near Donaldsonville, Louisiana, in the 1850s. Their Crescent Plantation had included three miles of frontage along Bayou Lafourche and two huge sugarhouses, its fields worked by more than 170 slaves. The Hewitts owned two steamboats as well. Beside their Louisiana property, the couple also kept a townhouse in New York City. "Intending this to be the home of our old age, we had spared no expense in making it luxurious in all its appointments," Clarissa wrote, "we had been years in collection, old pictures, and rare manuscripts."[17]

The war had severely diminished their fortunes. The Hewitts sent three sons into the Confederate army. One, Richard M. Hewitt, was a captain in Miles's Louisiana Legion captured at Port Hudson; now he languished at the customs house in New Orleans. Another, James Hewitt, Jr., was a colonel, leading the 2nd Kentucky Infantry in the Army of Tennessee. The youngest, Louis, served as an officer in the "Irish Volunteers," Company F, 7th Louisiana Infantry in the Army of Northern Virginia. Union provost marshals had confiscated Crescent, and their two steamboats, *Mary T.* and *Lafourche* had both entered Confederate military service. Even their luxurious acres on Bayou Lafourche had served as a battlefield during General Green's triumph near Donaldsonville. By July 1863, the war had rendered the Hewitts refugees in Fairfield, Texas.[18]

They brought many of their slaves with them. In early April, James Hewitt returned to Crescent and offered his bondsmen a choice. "He called the negroes around him and told them that when the Federals took possession of the place they would be given their freedom," Clarissa wrote, "but if they wanted to go with him, he would take them to Texas where he would give them work and treat them as he had always done, but they would still be slaves." He had bought property in the Trinity River bottomlands and intended to safeguard his human property there until after the war. All but the young men agreed to go. He led a train of cane carts out of the Lafourche District, through Pointe Coupée Parish to the Red River Valley, beyond Alexandria and, turning west near Mansfield, crossed the Sabine River into Texas. Hewitt and his caravan were not alone on the roads of Louisiana. "It is a strange sight to see these trains of wagons and negroes going through the country often with only one member of their master's family," Clarissa noted, "and not infrequently there would be only a woman who most confidingly entrusted herself to the protection and care of her slaves."[19]

Another heading west was teenager Kate Stone. "The sword of Damocles in a hundred forms is suspended over us, and there is no escape," she had written when Federal troops arrived near her plantation, Brockenburn, across the river from Vicksburg. "The country seems possessed by demons, black and white." The slaves in the region became agitated and bewildered. Some left to join the Federals. One of them, "Charles . . . ran to the Yankees among the first," observed Stone, but "soon returned to stay at home. He said he had enough of Yankees." So had many of the families on the west bank of the Mississippi. That spring, one by one her neighbors fled. In April, she and her mother, sister, aunt, cousin, and two younger brothers joined the exodus, heading to Monroe to await the decision of the summer campaigns.[20]

Among the refugees who funneled in to town from the surrounding countryside, the dislocation of war created a grim camaraderie. Blacks, whites, horses, mules, wagons, dogs, children, baggage, and furniture crowded the streets, mingling with Confederate soldiers, "drunk and sober," Stone wrote. Everyone seemed to have a tale of hardship and narrow escape. Some fled Federal soldiers, and some feared vengeful slaves. "All have lost heavily," Stone observed. "Everyone was animated and excited. All were eager to tell their own stories . . . and everyone sympathized with everyone else. Nearly everyone," she added, "took his trials cheerfully, making a joke of them, and nearly all are bound for Texas."[21]

The journey west, taken by so many Louisianans, introduced them to new lands and people. "The country was not particularly interesting," Clarissa Hewitt wrote, although "some parts were made pretty . . . by the beautiful wild flowers." Stone longed for the trees, streams, and fields of her lost home. She also missed the fashionable girls and handsome boys of the elite society she once kept. "There must be something in the air of Texas fatal to beauty," she wrote. Dwellings were scarce, small, and the residents poor. Even so, "these country people are very simple and kind-hearted," Hewitt wrote. "Many of them have had very tragic lives coming to this state from all parts of the country. They welcome strangers, as in them they feel a link with the world they have left behind."[22]

The Louisiana families mourned their losses. "At night when we stopped," Stone wrote, "I had only spirit enough . . . to look up at the stars and think of all the dear friends that the waves of Fate are sweeping farther and farther away from us every day. I had such a longing for home and the dear life of the past that my very soul would grow sick."[23]

Clarissa Hewitt feared mostly for her sons. She learned that Richard was bound for captivity at Johnson's Island in northern Ohio. She tried to use her family connections to improve his situation and wrote to her cousin, Major General Ulysses S. Grant. "The great soldier will never be to me anything but the shy boy with a big, loving, generous heart, and a simple nature," she wrote. "I feel sure he will use his influence for Richard, his cousin." Yet, he did not. For more than a year and a half, Richard remained a captive in icy and inadequate conditions in a Northern prison camp.[24]

Once settled in northeastern Texas, near Paris, Stone loathed her new home. "This part of the land abounds in white-headed children and buttermilk, my two pet aversions," she groused. "It is a place where the people are just learning that there is a war going on, where Union feeling is rife, and where the principal amusement

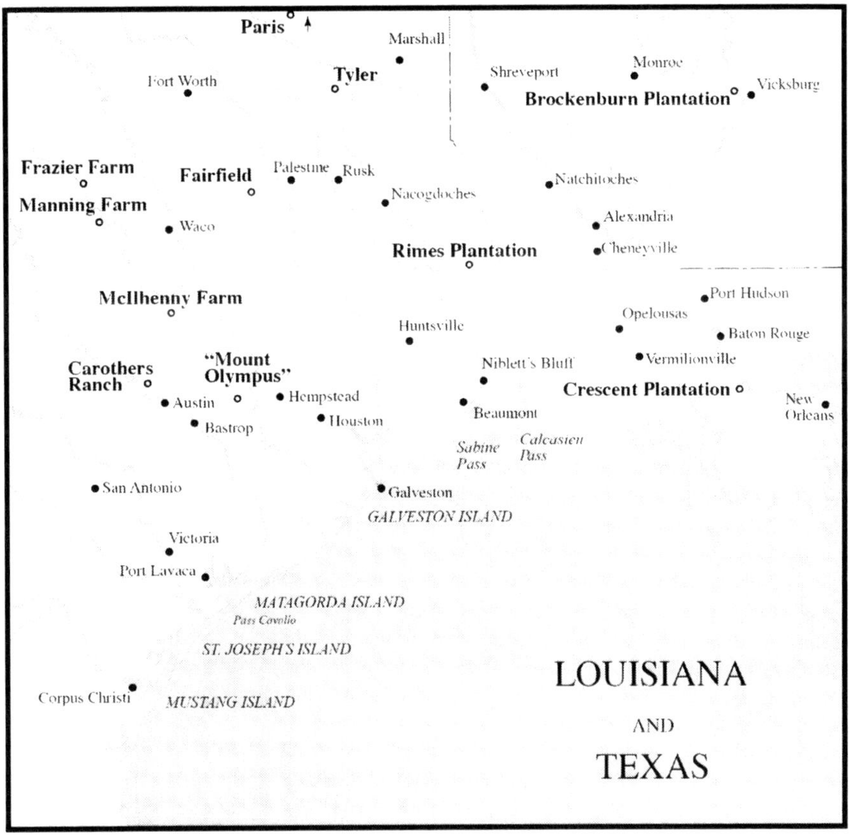

. . . is hanging suspected Jayhawkers." Cuisine lacked the usual variety the genteel Louisiana women expected. "The frying-pan was the one cooking utensil in which all their food was cooked," gasped Clarissa Hewitt. Even beefsteak was breaded and fried. This frontier state also seemed inhospitable to families. "Texas seems a hard land for women and children," observed Stone. "They fly around and work like troopers while the men loll on the galleries and seemingly have nothing to do."[25]

Begrudgingly, these refugees adjusted to altered circumstances. Most newcomers found housing among friends or acquaintances, eventually moving up in style and comfort as their means afforded. The Hewitts' spread along the Trinity River proved too rustic for Clarissa's refined tastes. "In spite of our efforts to make our wooden shanty even hospitable," she whined, "we find it impossible.

It is not a question of money, for we have plenty, but the necessary materials are not to be had for any price." She and her children moved to a rented home in Fairfield.[26] The Stones first lived with friends on Blue's Prairie, near Paris, Texas, in a "two room shanty." Kate and her family eventually moved to Tyler to live in a rented house with some of their fellow Louisiana refugees.[27]

Clothing proved as rustic as their dwellings. Stone believed the Texans to be several years behind on stylish trends. "We saw several nice-looking families but all were in the fashion of three years ago," she observed. By the beginning of the Civil War, hoop skirts had faded in popularity, but not in Northeast Texas. Shoes proved rare. "Nothing looks funnier," Stone laughed, "than a woman walking around with an immense hoop—barefooted. I wonder," she added, "shall we look as old-fashioned as they after a year or two of prairie life?"[28]

Some of the planters arriving in Texas had been running ahead of the war for months. William Manning, a sixty-three-year-old Baptist preacher and farmer, owned a sizable plantation near Quitman in eastern Mississippi. In the fall of 1862, he had crossed the great river at Baton Rouge and reestablished a cotton operation near Vermilionville, Louisiana. One of his hands, a thirteen-year-old enslaved boy named Allen, remembered his time in southern Louisiana. "All us Negroes thought this a mighty strange place," he recalled. "We would hear white folks talking and couldn't understand what they said, and lots of the Negroes talked the same way, too." The youth saw Rebel soldiers but never an army. "It was all full of French people . . . but they had all their menfolk in the Confederate army just the same," Allen continued. "I seen lots of men in butternut clothes coming and going . . . they was mostly coming home to see their folks."[29]

The Mississippi refugees found themselves on the run again that summer. "Everybody was scared all the time," Allen said. Rebel officials conscripted his master's adult son, thirty-four-year-old William D. Manning, into the 28th Louisiana Infantry. The rest of the family and their slaves headed toward Texas. "I think he left there partly because he didn't like the people at that place," Allen continued. "They wasn't no Baptists around anywhere, they was all Catholics." The caravan headed north through Opelousas and Cheneyville to the Red River Valley, then to Natchitoches before turning west toward Nacogdoches, Texas. "It looked like everybody in the world was going to Texas," Allen recalled. "When we would be going down the road we would have to walk along by the side all the

Some families displaced by the war resorted to makeshift homes like this dugout in the Red River Valley.
Library of Congress Prints and Photographs Division, Washington, D.C.

time to let the wagons go past." Just across the Sabine, Allen's mother gave birth to a baby girl. Manning "named her Texana, on account of where she was born."[30]

Even with their new addition, the Mississippians did not pause. They kept pushing west, putting as much of Texas between them and the war as possible. Eventually Manning settled his family and slaves on the frontier near the Bosque River in northeastern Coryell County. They had traveled more than five hundred miles from Quitman to escape the war. Manning put in a cotton crop and also planted corn. "He seem like he change a lot since we left Mississippi," Allen observed, "and seem like he paid more attention to us and looked after us better." Because his new neighbors proved hostile, he had no choice. "Most the people that already lived there . . . was mighty hard on their Negroes," Allen remembered. "They was mostly hard drinkers and hard talkers, and they work and fight jest as hard as they talk, too!"[31]

After reaching Texas, many of the refugees made the best of their predicament. Mary Eliza Avery McIlhenny, wife of Edmund McIlhenny, left their home and sugar plantations near New Iberia and finally settled in Galveston. "I am perfectly charmed," she wrote to her sister. "Its delicious sea breezes, splendid surf, delightful beach, [and] beautiful flowers would render a sojourn here very pleasant under any other circumstances. But ah! Refugees. Our pleasures here are almost pain."[32]

The fall of Vicksburg and Port Hudson and the threat of Federal invasion provided these displaced people with an uncertain future. Mary Eliza McIlhenny, having found sanctuary in Galveston with her husband and her parents, Daniel Dudley and Sarah Marsh Avery, once again worried about the family's future. "Papa does not consider the position safe from Yankee interference and Mama is terrified at the prospect of yellow fever in Houston, so that I fear we will soon again be wanderers." Her brother-in-law, Marshall McIlhenny, had a place in Bell County, Texas. Although far from the war, this home promised a harder, frontier life. "We have found the country so uncomfortable," she lamented. "Austin has been recommended, and if we can obtain accommodations we may go there."[33]

In Tyler, Stone also feared invasion. She and her mother might never be safe from the Union armies. "The fall of Vicksburg makes us tremble for Texas," she observed. "She can be invaded from so many points that Mamma knows not where to look for a place of greater safety."[34]

Conditions in Texas forever altered these refugees—black and white—but they also changed the Texans. The slave population blossomed and prices for human property plummeted. On the frontier, James Cason Frazier took advantage of this influx of exiles to realize a lifelong ambition. An aspiring slave owner, he traded some of his surplus acreage near Kimball's Bend on the Brazos River for a four-member enslaved family named Pollard, brought in by owners fleeing Georgia. Frazier, a soldier in the 19th Texas Cavalry, intended these laborers to work his rugged, but sizable, spread on behalf of his family, which included his wife, Emily, and three young children. "They were healthy, hearty Negroes, generally obedient and easily managed," Frazier's oldest son Jacob remembered. The newcomers included the parents, George and Minah, and adult children, Melinda, aged twenty, and brother John, eighteen. Whites and blacks worked together to construct a double-log cabin behind the Frazier home to shelter the slaves.[35]

Emily Frazier settled the Pollard family into their routines. "Father's delight was mother's embarrassment," noted Jacob. "In the trying days of the war, slaves often proved more of a liability than an asset. For a real Christian owner . . . the responsibility for the moral and physical welfare of the slaves was a matter not taken lightly." The parents and daughter were committed Baptists, which helped with discipline and morality. John's deportment proved more of an embarrassment for Emily. "Strongest among his vices was kleptomania," Jacob remembered, "not especially for profit, but just for the love of adventure and the exercise of superior cunning." He also tended to wander off the farm without a pass to visit enslaved women nearby, leading to brushes with the local slave patrol.[36]

New to slave ownership, Emily Frazier divided the chores between her family and the Pollards. Emily reared the children, tended the garden, and managed the blended households while Minah and Melinda cooked, did laundry, and manufactured homespun cloth. George and John farmed and worked the livestock. "During those dark days the negroes became, or were regarded, more as part of the family than slaves," Jacob recalled. "They were not the caricatures of *Uncle Tom's Cabin*." Instead, the young Frazier remembered sixty-five-year-old "Uncle George" as his version of another caricature, Uncle Remus.[37]

The absence of men on these remote Texas farmsteads led many enslaved people to test the limits of their bondage. William Stoker, in Louisiana serving with the 18th Texas Infantry, worried about his wife's ability to control the family slaves. His bondsman, Alf, used his master's absence to expand his personal freedom, coming and going as he pleased and riding the family horses to wander about at night. The Texan wrote home with specific instructions for his spouse. "Just take a stick and break his head," Stoker explained. "If you don't do that, send after the old man or Uncle Tommy and tie him down and whip him as long as he can bear it." Stoker insisted the woman land a few of the blows to establish her authority over the willful servant: "When you get him tied, whip him some your self. If I ever get home, I'll make him lift up."[38]

Abram Sells, an enslaved young man born and reared on the William A. Rimes's Plantation near the Sabine River in Newton County, Texas, escaped the immediate dangers of the war in Louisiana—but not its effects. He remembered many would-be Confederates hiding in the dense East Texas forests. "Some of them march off in their uniforms, lookin' so grand" he recalled, "and . . . some of them hide out in the wood to keep from lookin' so grand."[39]

Sells knew the war promised change. He remembered nights when gray-headed elders, roasting potatoes in dying campfires and smoking corncob pipes, lowered their voices and considered the future. "The oldes' niggers was settin' round the fire late in the night, stirrin' the ashes . . . whisperin' right low and quiet like [about] what they's [going to] do and whar they's [going to go] to when Mister Lincoln . . . turns them free." A youngster at the time, the thought of being on his own terrified Sells. Slavery provided him plenty to eat and place to live. Would that last? "The more they talk the more I git scared that the niggers is git sot free and wondering what I's gwine to do if they is," he said. "I sho seed lots of niggers not doin' so well . . . and not havin' nigh as much to eat."[40]

Texans, far removed from the fighting, still suffered from its upheaval. "The country is in the cruel grip of war," one observer wrote in his diary. The country around Bastrop, Texas, he observed, seemed populated by hungry women and children dressed in homespun. Although the Federals had not yet invaded, scarcity of imported goods, coupled with Confederate tax-in-kind and conscription, made life difficult. "Schools and churches are closed," he described. "All men between 18 and 45 are in the army. A tenth of the bacon, wheat, and corn goes to the government and half the horses and cattle. Everyone is crying 'when will this cruel war end?'"[41]

At more than seventy years of age, naturalist Gideon Lincecum could tell things were going badly. Writing from his farm, Mount Olympus, in Washington County, Texas, he lamented his sorry circumstances. "Until the war came, myself and my old lady were spending the evening of our protracted existence quite pleasantly," he wrote. "Our children settled all around us in good homes, and doing well. We had nothing to do but to go among them, receive their visits, and hear accounts of their successes." The conflict scattered his kin. Two grandsons fought with General Green in Louisiana. "Those that are left behind," he lamented, "are the helpless women and children."[42]

Lincecum spent long, lonely days on his farm. "Almost everybody has gone to the war now," he wrote to a friend in the army. "I stay here by myself, having no associates, until I have almost forgotten the language." His neighbors had to work diligently to get by, leaving little time for social calls. Spinning and weaving occurred in most homes in the state. "People here are struggling hard, trying to clothe themselves," he wrote. "I find [the] community well enveloped in homespun." Lincecum was a man of education and letters and spent many of his hours in correspondence with friends and family far afield. Even this activity would soon cease, he feared. "Paper nearly all gone," he scrawled to a correspondent, adding sarcastically "all's well."[43]

One Texan's wife insisted that her suffering was too much to bear and demanded her soldier come home. Officials had dragged thirty-seven-year old Private William N. Carothers into the war from his Hill Country cattle ranch northwest of Austin. While he served in the 2nd Arizona Cavalry, his wife Sarah and their three small children drifted into despair. "I think if they have nothing else to do they had better send the men home to their distressed families to make bread," she lamented. She did not trust the Confederate government and its management of the war. "If I was a man I would go to Mexico," she hissed. "I hope the Yanks will take the state. I would just as care [to] live under them as some we have to be under."[44]

Later that summer, sick and wounded Texas soldiers from the various Louisiana campaigns began to drift home, drawing pictures of the horrors of war. Private Felix Collard finally returned to Texas, his right arm shriveled and still in a sling. He had traveled by ambulance from New Iberia to Niblett's Bluff, where he boarded a steamboat for a journey down the Sabine River into Sabine Lake and then up the Neches River to Beaumont. There he boarded a train for Houston. "The [rail] road was in very bad condition" he remembered, "so bad that it took forty-eight hours to reach Houston." From here he switched trains and traveled to Navasota, Texas, and then by hack to Huntsville. A borrowed horse carried him the final twenty miles to his home.[45]

During the course of this Piney Woods odyssey, his injury remained untended. "My arm, still in the sling, had perished away and gave me no pain," Collard wrote. "I could run my left hand up in my armpit of my right arm and feel the head of the bone against my ribs." A local doctor examined the wound, declaring that scarring and adhesions had probably cut off circulation to the limb. Despite this gloomy prognosis, Collard was game for him to set it if he could—despite the warning that an internal tear of an artery might cause him to bleed to death. If left untreated, the arm might have to come off. If he could regain its use, Collard accepted the risk.

In one of his father's sheds, Collard faded under a chloroform haze. The physician—employing a block and tackle, several strong slaves, stout ropes, and iron rings fastened to the walls—successfully popped Collard's humerus back into the shoulder socket. In time, the wounded soldier regained the use of his arm but was never again truly whole. Collard, like the cause he served, emerged from the campaigns for the Mississippi Valley still alive—but permanently enfeebled.[46]

Epilogue

Federal Triumph, Confederate Despair

I want to go back to Texas and start fresh again.
—Private Joseph Ferdinand Boesel
Company G, 4th Texas Cavalry (CSA)
Company A, 1st New Orleans Infantry (Union)

In the face of cascading Confederate misfortunes, many Southern soldiers in the Trans-Mississippi struggled to remain true to their cause. Private Joseph Ferdinand Boesel, a twenty-six-year-old German immigrant from Hanover, had served in the 4th Texas Cavalry after enlisting in Washington County. Suffering a leg wound at the Battle of Irish Bend in April 1863, Boesel fell into Union hands. He arrived at a New Orleans military hospital a prisoner and at first had few complaints about his Yankee captors: "My treatment here could not be any better. They make no distinction between me and Federal soldiers. We lie in clean beds in a big room. We have good food and drink." He wrote his worried parents that he expected to be exchanged soon—perhaps to Port Hudson or Mobile.[1]

As the Confederate campaigns in the sugar parishes intensified and Rebels threatened New Orleans, Boesel observed the Federal attitude change. "Lame and on crutches, I was thrown into prison where I had to go hungry," he complained. "Had it not been for the southern citizens, especially the ladies, who brought us food as well as clothing, things could have been much worse. We prisoners of war were very little better off than common criminals." Close confinement under dark, dank, and inhumane conditions began to break the men. "For the last two months, I have not seen anything of the world except a little piece of sky," Boesel continued. "Hundreds took an oath to the government, the Union, just to escape this place of suffering. Some thought they were doomed to a slow death and they deserted the South." The stalwart German, though, remained loyal throughout the summer and into the fall.[2]

The New Orleans customs house became a prison for Confederate soldiers. Conditions convinced many incarcerated there to cooperate with Federal authorities in exchange for better treatment.
Library of Congress Prints and Photographs Division, Washington, D.C.

While Boesel suffered, President Abraham Lincoln, his government, and his generals prepared for the imminent end of the war. General-in-Chief Henry Halleck argued that General Nathaniel P. Banks could easily destroy the remaining Confederates in Louisiana and drive into Texas. "I suppose the first thing done by your army after the fall of Port Hudson," Halleck guessed, "was to clean out the Teche and Atchafalaya countries." He was wrong. Instead, Confederate General Tom Green had embarrassed Banks's war-weary and disease-ravaged army. Banks had done nothing but reoccupy Brashear City since.[3]

The government needed Rebel Louisiana finished. Political considerations added urgency to military operations there. Lincoln advised Secretary of War Edwin M. Stanton that he anticipated bringing the state back into the Union shortly under a new constitution that outlawed slavery. What good would it be to take the Mississippi, and defeat the Confederacy, only to have these Southern states revive the peculiar institution after the restoration of peace? To destroy slavery in Louisiana forever, Lincoln wanted Union forces to overrun as much of its territory as possible. Military governor General George Shepley could then register every Unionist in every parish, Lincoln explained, "after the people are relieved from the presence of the rebel troops and included within the lines occupied by the armies of the United States." With most of Louisiana retaken, Shepley could call a convention to reorganize the state government.[4]

A Harvard and Dartmouth trained lawyer from Bangor, Maine, Colonel George Shepley led the 12th Maine Infantry to Louisiana but left the regiment to become military mayor of New Orleans and quickly rose to governor of Louisiana after promotion to brigadier general. The critical job of getting the state politically reorganized and readmitted to the Union fell to him.
Library of Congress Prints and Photographs Division, Washington, D.C.

Yet, Banks needed to deliver the deathblow to Rebel resistance in the region so the politicians could get to work. Halleck wanted Banks to destroy Confederate General Richard Taylor's army, also understanding the vital role that Texas played in sustaining that force. "While your army is engaged in cleaning out Southwestern Louisiana, every preparation should be made for an expedition into Texas," Halleck directed. Banks had to conquer Louisiana—so it could rejoin the Union—but this also required that he conquer Texas.[5]

Beyond these directives, Banks also needed to finish the project begun in April and raise as many black regiments as Louisiana could supply. The systematic reconstruction of society would facilitate victory in the field. Charles Prosper Fauconnet, the *gérat* (office manager) of the French consulate in New Orleans and a veteran diplomat, believed he understood the Federal strategy. The *Corps d'Afrique* "seems to me to be in reality a coerced conscription of all blacks, slaves, and free men alike," he reported to the government of Emperor Napoleon III. "It is racial exploitation by the abolitionists but under a different name; it will mean the downfall of the South . . . for the benefit of Americans in the North."[6]

As the Frenchman surmised, the militarization of liberated slaves served a much larger scheme. President Lincoln anticipated that recruiters could raise one hundred thousand fighting men in the Mississippi Valley from among the freedmen. Banks was willing, but knew it would take a massive effort. He had run out of soldier material—his press-gangs had exhausted the supply of the military-aged black males within his lines. Rebels, understanding the new Federal tactic that shifted focus from slavery to slaves, moved tens of thousands into Texas to keep them out of reach. This tactic starved the *Corps d'Afrique* project of its human fuel in Louisiana. Invading other slave-rich zones, Banks urged, could rejuvenate the project. "It is necessary to possess ourselves of other portions of country within the control of the enemy to increase this strength." Still, to do so, he required reinforcements. He wanted more white men to take more of Louisiana, so that he could gather more black men and take Texas and satisfy the president.[7]

He intended black soldiers to usher in a new regime in Louisiana and ensure its survival. Fauconnet reported that to suppress the spirit of rebellion—forever—U.S. troops would have to garrison Louisiana for the foreseeable future, and especially until its citizens accepted a government that forbade secession and slavery. White soldiers would want to return to their homes at the end of the war. Locals, blacks under government control, could complete the processes of victory already underway. At the same time, service in the army would employ and educate these former slaves so they could become productive citizens. "The least costly method of achieving this result is clearly the government's policy," Fauconnet observed. "Louisiana will be guarded by these colored troops . . . . The *Corps d'Afrique* will remain under arms as long as the government has need of its services." Race relations would reverse, and whites in Louisiana would face a black army of occupation.[8]

This project largely succeeded. In 1860, Louisiana had nearly seventy-nine thousand military-aged black men, enslaved and free. Of these, nearly a third—more than twenty-four thousand—found their way into the ranks of the U.S. army. Officials tasked with raising the *Corps d'Afrique* organized these soldiers into twenty-two regiments of infantry, a cavalry regiment, a regiment of heavy

To fill the ranks of the Corps d'Afrique, *Union troops often dragooned vagrants and homeless black men from the streets of New Orleans. When these sources proved insufficient, Federal soldiers gathered men from businesses, wharves, and plantations in the region.*
Library of Congress Prints and Photographs Division, Washington, D.C.

The black troops gathering at Port Hudson, like these members of the 1st Field Battery, Corps d'Afrique, *entered a world of constant military drill as well as education in such fundamentals as reading and writing.*
State Library of Louisiana.

This image from Harper's Weekly *illustrates the basic military training the newly enlisted black soldiers at Port Hudson received. Marksmanship became important.*
Library of Congress Prints and Photographs Division, Washington, D.C.

artillery, five regiments of engineers, and two bands. These results, combined with General Ulysses S. Grant's efforts from the Red River to Memphis, accounted for a third of all blacks raised for Federal service nationwide. The Union capture of the Mississippi, more than any other event, advanced the cause of black

Liberated slaves like these, with little military value, instead found themselves bound for resettlement in areas safely behind Union lines. Very few Louisiana blacks, either liberated or still enslaved escaped the disruption and displacement of war.
Library of Congress Prints and Photographs Division, Washington, D.C.

enlistment. To achieve these results, officers transported large numbers of people, concentrated populations, disrupted families, and transformed lives.

The waves of these policies washed over thousands of liberated slaves. Near Bayou Sara, Catherine Cornelius faced an unknown future. Her brother, Beverly Brown, disappeared into the *Corps d'Afrique*. Federal officials organized the less useful men, women, and children for shipment to New Orleans where they could more efficiently house and feed them. Soldiers handed each person a wad of cash and hustled these people toward steamboats—and resettlement. "It was the first dat Ah had seen Yankee money," Cornelius confessed. "Ah didn't know what to do with dat Yankee money. Ah lef mines in the stomp of a tree, but Ah sho wish dat Ah had it now." Soldiers loaded her and the others onto transports bound for New Orleans and housing in the U.S. barracks near Chalmette.[9]

All of these changes marked a shift from a war footing to a posture of postwar national reconstruction. President Lincoln believed that success in the Mississippi Valley signaled the closing days of the war, and he wanted to secure as much from the peace as he could. On August 26, 1863, he outlined his views

The Unionist press and Federal authorities made much of the arrival of the steamboat Imperial *at New Orleans on July 16, 1863, down from St. Louis and Natchez, loaded with cattle. "She had a pleasant, unmolested trip all the way down, and reported the river perfectly quiet between this and St. Louis," read the article in the August 8, 1863 edition of* Harper's Weekly. *"The* IMPERIAL *is an immense, showy vessel, one of the first-class river steamers, which completely dwarfs the* LAUREL HILL, EMPIRE PARISH, *and others that we have been long accustomed to look upon as leviathans. But it was not her size nor fine equipments which impressed the eager multitudes who thronged to see her; it was the fact that she was the first freight boat which had ventured down the Mississippi since the fall of Vicksburg and Port Hudson; and every one who gazed upon her proud form saw in her the embodiment of reawakened commerce with the Mississippi Valley." The journey of this vessel reinforced President Abraham Lincoln's claim that the river flowed "unvexed to the sea."*
Harper's Weekly.

in a letter to an old Illinois friend, James C. Conkling, declining an invitation to speak at a political rally in Springfield due to scheduling constraints. Even so, the president president wanted to address these "unconditional Union men," sharing his thoughts on the status of the war at the end of that bloody summer.[10]

He knew Northerners craved peace. He recognized three ways to achieve it. The rebellion might end "by force of arms. This I am trying to do," Lincoln wrote. A second option for peace would be to accept disunion, which he considered

These soldiers from the Corps d'Afrique *bear the military posture of men-of-war. President Abraham Lincoln no doubt has troops such as these in mind when he wrote, "they have helped mankind."*
Library of Congress Prints and Photographs Division, Washington, D.C.

unthinkable and—with the fall of Vicksburg and Port Hudson—wholly unnecessary. He would never accede to the third option: "I do not believe any compromise, embracing the maintenance of the Union, is now possible." The war had continued too long, the changes it wrought, irreversible.

The Confederacy had proven too inflexible to change. "The strength of the rebellion is its military—its army," Lincoln wrote. He and his generals viewed the war-ravaged Confederacy as little more than a military dictatorship wrought by secessionists at the expense of citizens' liberty. Even if Rebel politicians and civilians tried to broker a deal, who could make it binding on their forces in the field? How could civilians reach a treaty unless the enemy's legions agreed to disband? Only the destruction of the Confederate armies would answer those questions.[11]

These hoped-for events might arrive soon. "The signs look better," Lincoln opined. "The Father of Waters again goes unvexed to the sea." Victories won by hard-fighting Union armies, he believed, had broken the back of the Southern military tyranny. The navy—"Uncle Sam's web-feet" as Lincoln called it—had also done its part. "Not only on the deep sea, the broad bay, and the rapid river," he wrote, "but also up the narrow muddy bayou, and wherever the ground was a little damp."

Lincoln anticipated the speedy restoration of peace—but not before completing the transformation of the country. Raising an army of liberated slaves would hasten victory and secure the defeated South. The Mississippi Valley would be the nation's greatest recruiting ground. Following the war, Lincoln opined, "there will be some black men who can remember that, with silent tongue, and clenched teeth, and steady eye, and well-poised bayonet, they have helped mankind on to this great consummation."[12]

Amid this Federal optimism, hope faded for Private Boesel of the 4th Texas Cavalry. He could not endure the increasingly harsh conditions of his New Orleans imprisonment and his fealty to the Confederacy slowly eroded. In the fall of 1863, Federal authorities ended locals' ability to feed and comfort the captured Rebels. Instead of the wine and home-cooked meals that had sustained them, the prisoners received "ship's biscuits, over-salted, putrid horse meat, mule flesh, and who knows what other kind of meat," Boesel grumbled. "They served us dishwater as gravy." The German Texan stayed in the steamy, damp, airless prison for months. "It was so crowded that not all of us could lie down," he lamented. "And in this condition our worries overcame us—the mosquitoes, oh, how sadly we viewed our mosquito-riddled bodies each morning. And on top of that, lice, bedbugs, rats, etc."[13]

Ever the Rebel, Boesel and another soldier attempted to escape this Federal nightmare. After watching others successfully get away from the New Orleans hellhole, Boesel decided to take his chances. He braided a rope out of smuggled twine and used a pilfered file to shave away the prison bars until he and his companion could make their break. Boesel reached the ground, forty feet below. His comrade lost the rope and landed hard. "All at once we were surrounded by bayonets, so I lost my courage," he admitted. Now marked as a troublemaker, Boesel faced the prospect of his captors shipping him north to a prison camp for the duration of the war.

The Yankees finally wore him down. Late in November, having endured six months of incarceration in New Orleans's Customs House prison, he asked for an audience with Union Major James H. Bradley of the newly raised 1st New Orleans Regiment. "I informed him of my circumstances and declared

I wanted to go into service for the United States," Boesel confessed. The Federals gave him an easy job clerking for a military court and serving as a translator for the many German-speakers that passed through the city's government offices.[14]

Boesel hoped to play his injured leg as an excuse for a discharge. He, along with another Texan who had entered Federal service, planned to take a boat for New York City to find work until the war ended. He resigned himself to this exile. "One has to wander around in the world, even though I could be so comfortable in Texas," he bemoaned. "That is my life's ambition. I have started to build a home there, and I would be enjoying it now, if the awful war had not broken out. I want to go back to Texas and start fresh again."[15]

Union authorities denied him the chance. They insisted he remain in the ranks. Boesel came to realize that service in the 1st New Orleans was only another form of parole. At least he lived under better circumstances than the unrepentant Rebels wasting away in the Customs House. He resigned himself to serving the U.S. army until the war ended.

Then fate intervened. In 1864, Boesel fell ill in the Louisiana summer heat. After a few days of suffering, medical stewards took him to University Hospital with a galloping case of dysentery. Yet, doctors there could not save him. Boesel died on June 18, far from his native land, never to return to his adopted Texas home.

He, along with seven hundred thousand other Americans, would never see the new nation the Federal government was seeking to engineer.[16]

NOTES

Introduction

1. DaNean Olene Pound, "Slave to the Ex-Slave Narratives," (M.A. Thesis, Northwestern State University, Natchitoches, Louisiana, 2005), 95–98; Hazel Breaux and Robert McKinney, "Interview with ex-slave Catherine Cornelius in the 1940s," WPA Collection, State Library of Louisiana, Baton Rouge, Louisiana.

Chapter 1

1. The latest and most sweeping scholarship on this topic is James Oakes, *Freedom National*.
2. Sutherland, "Abraham Lincoln, John Pope, and the Origins of Total War," 574, 580.
3. LeGrand, *The Diary of Julia LeGrand*, 88.
4. New Orleans *Delta*, November 3, 1860.
5. Barringer, *A House Dividing*, 236; Adams quoted in Foner, *Free Soil, Free Labor, Free Men*, 223. Trumbull would go on to coauthor the 13th Amendment.
6. Phelps to Davis, June 18, 1862, *The War of the Rebellion*, XV: 489, hereafter cited as *OR* will all references (unless otherwise noted) to Series I; Williams, *A History of the Negro Troops*, 97; Phelps to Davis, July 30, 1862, *OR*, XV: 535.
7. Parton, *General Butler in New Orleans*, 495–516; Butler, *Private and Official Correspondence*, 154.
8. Butler to Stanton, August 14, 1862, *OR*, XV: 548–549; Butler to Halleck, August 27, 1862, *OR*, XV: 556.
9. Hollandsworth, Jr., *The Louisiana Native Guards*, 12–22.
10. Butler, *Private and Official Correspondence*, 448–449; Oakes, *Freedom National*, 417–418.
11. Ullmann, *Organization of Colored Troops*, 2.
12. Peña, *Touched by War*, 198.
13. Weitzel to Strong, November 1, 1862, *OR*, XV: 170.
14. Ibid.
15. Weitzel to Strong, November 5, 1862, *OR*, XV: 171–172.
16. Stanyan, *A History of the Eighth Regiment of New Hampshire Volunteers*, 156.
17. Strong to Weitzel, November 6, 1862, *OR*, XV: 165.
18. Ibid., 166.
19. Ibid., 165.
20. Ibid.
21. Strong to Weitzel, November 2, 1862, *OR*, XV:162–163.
22. Ibid., 162.
23. Ripley, *Slaves and Freedmen*, 44–45.
24. Butler, *Private and Official Correspondence*, 450.

25. Strong to Weitzel, November 6, 1862, *OR*, XV: 165.
26. Smith, *Leaves from a Soldier's Diary*, 35–37.
27. Ripley, *Slaves and Freedmen*, 45.
28. As quoted from the New Orleans *Delta* in the New York *Times*, November 23, 1863.
29. Strong to Weitzel, November 6, 1862, *OR*, XV: 166.
30. Smith, *Leaves from a Soldier's Diary*, 34; Peña, *Touched by War*, 201.
31. Cotham, Jr., ed., *The Southern Journey of a Civil War Marine*, 114; *OR*, XV, 163.
32. Current, *Lincoln's Loyalists*, 97; Butler to Pierce, Jr., November 12, 1862, *OR*, XV, 591–592.
33. Butler to Halleck, October 24, 1862, *OR*, 15:158–159.
34. Butler, *Private and Official Correspondence*, 33–35.
35. "General Order No. 111," *OR*, ser. 2, V: 795–797.

Chapter 2

1. *The American Annual*, 320; Ullmann, *Organization of Colored Troops*, 4.
2. Ullmann, *Organization of Colored Troops*, 4.
3. Bauer, *Creole Genesis*, 99–100; Bauer, "The Last Effort," 67–68; Herrington, ed., "A Peace Mission of 1863," 82; see also Levine, *Confederate Emancipation*.
4. Simpson, ed., *The Civil War*, 105–106; Williams, *A History of the Negro Troops*, 107.
5. Simpson, ed., *The Civil War*, 106–108.
6. Halleck to Grant, March 31, 1863, *OR*, XXIV, pt. 3: 156–157.
7. Simpson, ed., *The Civil War*, 105–106; Williams, *A History of the Negro Troops*, 106–108.
8. Halleck to Grant, March 31, 1863, *OR*, XXIV, pt. 3: 156–157.
9. Williams, *A History of the Negro Troops*, 109.
10. Cincinnati (Ohio) *Daily Commercial*, April 17, 1863; General Order 143; Henry T. Johns, *Life with the Forty-Ninth Massachusetts Volunteers*, 187.
11. Williams, *A History of the Negro*, 111.
12. Howard, *History of the 124th Regiment Illinois Infantry Volunteers*, 66.
13. Wheeling [West Virginia] *Daily Intelligencer*, June 1, 1863.
14. Berlin, et al., eds. *Freedom*, 440–441.
15. Ibid., 442.
16. Ibid., 441.
17. Simpson, ed., *The Civil War*, 105–106;
18. Lincoln to Banks [Draft 1], March 29, 1863, Abraham Lincoln Papers.
19. Ibid.
20. Ullmann, *Organization of Colored*, 8.
21. New York *Times*, September 21, 1892; Lincoln to Banks [Draft 1], March 29, 1863, Abraham Lincoln Papers.
22. Cornish, *The Sable Arm*, 102–103.
23. Winters, *The Civil War in Louisiana*, 208–209; Bosson, *History of the Forty-Second Regiment Infantry*, 335.

24. Bosson, *History of the Forty-Second Regiment Infantry*, 344–350.
25. Botkin, ed., *Slave Narratives*, 154.
26. Pound, "Slave to the Ex-Slave Narratives," 95–98.
27. Dobak, *Freedom by the Sword*, 177–179.
28. An officer of the 48th Reg., Baton Rouge, La., April 22d, 1863, published in the Amesbury, Massachusetts *Villager*, May 16, 1863; pg. 3, col. 1.
29. Ibid.
30. Mattison, "To the Editor of the Boston Journal," New Orleans, April 28, 1863, published in the Boston *Morning Journal*, May 11, 1863; pg. 2, col. 4.
31. *Boston Herald*, p. 2, col. 1, April 28, 1863; De Forest, *A Volunteer's Adventures*, 92.
32. Mahoney, "The Passing of Harry Mahoney, A Negro Politician of Radical Days."
33. Botkin, ed., *Slave Narratives*, Texas Narratives, Volume XVI, pt. 1, 75–84.
34. Ibid., 252–253.
35. Thomas Reade Rootes, Natchitoches, Louisiana, to Sarah A. Rootes, Hickory Fork, Virginia, May 12, 1863, Sarah A. Rootes Correspondence; J. W. Watkins, Natchitoches, Louisiana to Irene Watkins, May 15, 1863, Watkins Letters.
36. Thomas Reade Rootes, Natchitoches, Louisiana, to Sarah A. Rootes, Hickory Fork, Virginia, May 12, 1863, Sarah A. Rootes Correspondence.
37. J. W. Watkins, Mansura, Louisiana to Irene Watkins, Aril 23, 1863, Watkins Letters.
38. H. M. P., New Orleans, April 26, 1863, "From our Special Correspondent," to Boston *Traveler*, May 6, 1863; pg. 2, col. 2.
39. Botkin, ed., *Slave Narratives*, Texas Narratives, XVI, pt. 1: 62-66.
40. Banks, "General Order No. 40," May 1, 1863, *OR*, vol. 15, 717.
41. Ibid., 716–717.
42. Ibid., 717.
43. Pound, "Slave to the Ex-Slave Narratives," 299. Lewis Reed (also written as Rede and Redo) received promotion to sergeant by 1864 in the redesignated 81st U.S. Colored Infantry, serving in the color guard. Enlisted in May 1863 for three years, he died of pneumonia in New Orleans on March 12, 1866 (compiled service records of Lewis Rede and Lewis Redo, National Archives and Records Administration). None of his military records indicate his place of burial, or that he had a family.
44. John Marsh Avery to Daniel Dudley Avery, May 29, 1863; Ashbel Burnham Henshaw to Daniel Dudley Avery, June 1, 1863, Sarah Avery McIlhenny Collection.
45. Banks to Halleck, May 1, 1863, *OR*, vol. 15, 716.
46. Banks, "General Order No. 40," May 1, 1863, *OR*, vol. 15, 717; Harding, *The Miscellaneous Writings of George C. Harding*, 329.
47. Rothman, "The Horrors '12 Years a Slave' couldn't tell."; Tsapina, "Where Solomon Northrup was a Slave."; Captain John Burrud's diary is part of the Papers of John B. Burrud.
48. Ibid.
49. Ibid.
50. Banks to Halleck, May 12, 1863, *OR*, vol. 15, 314–315.

51. Ibid.
52. Eventually, nearly one out of three black males of military age in Louisiana served in the Union army. Many volunteered; many were also pressed into service by Federal authorities. See Berlin, et al., eds., *Freedom's Soldiers*, 17–19.
53. Pound, "Slave to the Ex-Slave Narratives," 95–98.
54. Halleck to Banks, June 3, 1863, *OR*, XXVI, pt. 1, 534.
55. Sioux (W. P. Doran), "In Camp on Bank of Sabine River," May 11, 1863, in *Houston Tri-Weekly Telegraph*, May 18, 1863; A. W. McKee to W. R. Scurry, April 22, 24, 1863, *OR*, XXVI, pt. 1, 534.

Chapter 3

1. The campaign for Vicksburg has many chroniclers, including Bearss's three volume epic, *The Campaign for Vicksburg*, Ballard's *Vicksburg* , and Winschel's similar, and almost competing books, *Vicksburg* and *Triumph and Defeat*. The campaigns for Port Hudson are less well known. The most comprehensive work detailing the actions leading up to the actual siege is Frazier, *Thunder Across the Swamp*; Hewitt's *Port Hudson*, and Edmonds' even older, two-volume *The Guns of Port Hudson* remain the standard works.
2. Johnston to Kirby Smith, May 31, 1863 *OR*, XXVI, pt. 2: 26.
3. J. E. H. to the editor, April 30, 1863, in *Houston Tri-Weekly Telegraph*, May 1, 1863; 11 May 1863; J. E. H. to the editor, April 30, 1863, in *Houston Tri-Weekly Telegraph*, May 11, 1863; Sioux (W. P. Doran), "In Camp on Bank of Sabine River," May 11, 1863, in *Houston Tri-Weekly Telegraph*, May 18, 1863; Winters, *The Civil War in Louisiana*, 198–207.
4. J. E. H., Nibletts Bluff, April 30, 1863, to the editor, *Houston Tri-Weekly Telegraph*, May 11, 1863.
5. Taylor, *Destruction and Reconstruction*, 235; Bellville [Texas] *Countryman*, July 11, 1863, p. 1.
6. Irwin, *History of the 19th Army Corps*, 156–157.
7. Mahoney, "The Passing of Harry Mahoney."
8. Pellet, *History of the 114th Regiment*, 83.
9. Howell Diary, May 25, 1863; John Watkins to Irene Watkins, June 16, 1863, J. W. Watkins Letters.
10. Ewer, *Third Massachusetts Cavalry*, 85; *New York Irish American*, p. 1, col. 8, June 20, 1863.
11. Ewer, *Third Massachusetts Cavalry*, 85; *New York Irish American*, p. 1, col. 8, June 20, 1863.The soldiers were Major John Gray; Second Lieutenant Patrick E. Walsh, acting adjutant; Second Lieutenant Mathias Hayes, Company A; and First Lieutenant Richard Dunn, Company B.
12. Pellet, *History of the 114th Regiment*, 79–80.
13. Maddocks, *History of the Twenty-Sixth Maine Regiment*, 36–37; Moors, *History of the Fifty-Second Regiment*, 144.

14. Maddocks, *Twenty-Sixth Maine Regiment*, 36–37; Moors, *History of the Fifty-Second Regiment*, 144.
15. Ewer, *Third Massachusetts Cavalry*, 84; Maddocks, *Twenty-Sixth Maine Regiment*, 36–37.
16. Ewer, *Third Massachusetts Cavalry*, 85.
17. Pellet, *History of the 114th Regiment*, 80–81.
18. Ibid., 81.
19. Ibid., 81.
20. Howell Diary, May 25, 1863, W. Randolph Howell Papers; John Watkins, Bayou Teche, Louisiana, to Irene, June 16, 1863, Watkins letters.
21. Howell Diary, May 25, 1863, W. Randolph Howell Papers; John Watkins to Irene Watkins, June 16, 1863, Watkins Letters; Ashbel Burnham Henshaw to Daniel Dudley Avery, June 1, 1863, Sarah Avery McIlhenny Collection.
22. Maddocks, *Twenty-Sixth Maine Regiment*, 37; Ewer, *Third Massachusetts Cavalry*, 85–86; Pellet, *History of the 114th Regiment*, 82–83.
23. Berlin, et al., eds., *Freedom*, 459.
24. Botkin, ed.,*Slave Narratives*, Texas Narratives, Volume XVI, Part 3, 155–156; The excerpt from the Chattanooga *Rebel* was reprinted in the Houston [Texas] *Tri-Weekly Telegraph*, July 10, 1863, p. 1.
25. William H. Emory to Richard Irwin, June 3, 1863, *OR*, XXVI, pt. 1: 534.
26. William Frederick Weeks, New Iberia, Louisiana, to Judge John Moore, May 20, 1863, David Weeks and Family Papers.
27. Mahoney, "The Passing of Harry Mahoney."
28. Pound, "Slave to the Ex-Slave Narratives," 320-322.
29. Haynes, *A Thrilling Narrative*, 5.
30. Ibid., 5–6.
31. Ibid.
32. Ibid.
33. Ibid.; William Shelly Diary, May 28, 1863, Mss. 3604.
34. For a thorough recounting of the life of Richard Taylor, see Parish, *Richard Taylor*.
35. Barr, *Polignac's Texas Brigade*, 19–20; Blessington, *The Campaigns of Walker's Texas Division*, 79–84.
36. See Hewitt, *Port Hudson*.
37. Taylor, *Destruction and Reconstruction*, 15–16.
38. Pemberton to Kirby Smith, *OR*, XXIV, pt. 3, 846.
39. Taylor, *Destruction and Reconstruction*, 179; Prushankin, *A Crises in Confederate Command*, 31–32.
40. Ibid.
41. Ibid.
42. Blessington, *The Campaigns of Walker's Texas Division*, 84; William Elisha Stoker, near Nachitoches, Louisiana, to Elizabeth E. Stoker, Coffeeville, Texas, May 22, 1863, William E. Stoker Papers. The original letter read "I just wis this confederacy

was toar all to smash & turned bottom upward or with ware never will close until the men just quits." His poor spelling has been edited for readability. The originals may be found at http://hd.housedivided.dickinson.edu.

43. William Elisha Stoker, near Nachitoches, Louisiana, to Elizabeth E. Stoker, Coffeeville, Texas, May 22, 1863, William E. Stoker Papers.
44. Alfred Petticolas Diary, vol. 3, May 31, 1863.
45. Ibid.

Chapter 4

1. Kirby Smith to Taylor, May 20, 1863, *OR*, XXVI, pt. 2: 13. Regarding the secondary sources, the most important sources consulted for this chapter include, Barnickle, *Milliken's Bend*, Lowe, *Walker's Texas Division*, and Bearss, *The Vicksburg Campaign* with volume III, *Unvexed to the Sea*, being the most useful. Primary accounts of this campaign abound and are expertly used by Barnickle, Lowe, and Bearss, and I rely largely on them to deliver the best lines but throw in a few I found useful for advancing my thesis. Some may find the extensive use of the citation "Ibid." distracting. What can I say? I am giving credit where credit it due. These authors came first! I am merely surveying and supplementing their genius.
2. Kirby Smith to Richard Taylor, May 20, 1863, *OR*, XXVI, pt. 2: 13.
3. Taylor, *Destruction and Reconstruction*, 179.
4. Ibid.
5. Blessington, *The Campaigns of Walker's Texas Division*, 86.
6. Ibid., 86.
7. Ibid., 88–91; J. Murphy to Porter, June 1, 1863, *Official Records of the Union and Confederate Navies in the War of the Rebellion*, XXV: 147–148; hereafter cited as *ORN*.
8. Blessington, *The Campaigns of Walker's Texas Division*, 88–91; J. Murphy to Porter, June 1, 1863, *ORN*, XXV, 147–148; Bearss, *The Vicksburg Campaign*, 3: 1171.
9. Ibid.; Lowe, *Walker's Texas Division*, 85.
10. Lowe, *Walker's Texas Division*, 86; Barnickle, *Milliken's Bend*, 83.
11. Blessington, *The Campaigns of Walker's Texas Division*, 93; Bearss, *The Vicksburg Campaign*, 3: 1173–1174.
12. Bearss, *The Vicksburg Campaign*, 3: 1174; Taylor to Boggs, June 8, 1863, *OR*, XXIV, pt. 2: 457.
13. Taylor to Boggs, June 8, 1863, *OR*, XXIV, pt. 2: 457–458.
14. Taylor to Boggs, June 8, 1863, *OR*, XXIV, pt. 2: 457–458; Bearss, *The Vicksburg Campaign*, 3: 1174–1175.
15. Taylor to Boggs, June 8, 1863, *OR*, XXIV, pt. 2: 457–458; Bearss, *The Vicksburg Campaign*, 3: 1174–1175.
16. Taylor to Boggs, June 8, 1863, *OR*, XXIV, pt. 2: 457–458; Bearss, *The Vicksburg Campaign*, 3: 1174–1175.
17. Taylor to Boggs, June 8, 1863, *OR*, XXIV, pt. 2: 457–458; Bearss, *The Vicksburg Campaign*, 3: 1174–1175.

18. Taylor to Boggs, June 8, 1863, *OR*, XXIV, pt. 2: 457–458; Bearss, *The Vicksburg Campaign*, 3: 1174–1175.
19. Bearss, *The Vicksburg Campaign*, 3: 1174–1175; Taylor to Boggs, June 8, 1863, *OR*, XXIV, pt. 2: 458.
20. Bearss, *The Vicksburg Campaign*, 3: 1175.
21. Ibid.
22. Ibid.; Taylor to Boggs, June 8, 1863, *OR*, XXIV, pt. 2: 458.
23. Bearss, *The Vicksburg Campaign*, 3: 1176–1177.
24. Ibid.
25. Ibid.
26. Ibid., 3: 1186.
27. Ibid., 3: 1174; Taylor to Boggs, June 8, 1863, *OR*, XXIV, pt. 2: 457.
28. Ramsay to Porter, June 10, 1862, *ORN*, XXV: 163.
29. Bearss, *The Vicksburg Campaign*, 3: 1176–1178.
30. Ibid.
31. Taylor to Boggs, June 8, 1863, *OR*, XXIV, pt. 2: 458.
32. Ibid.
33. Ibid.; Captain William Edgar's "Alamo City Guards" artillery also bore the designation of 1st Texas Field Artillery Battery, Captain Horace Halderman's "Van Dorn Light Artillery" the 4th Texas Field Artillery, and Captain James M. Daniel's "Lamar Artillery" was also designated the 9th Texas Field Artillery Battery.
34. Bearss, *The Vicksburg Campaign*, 3: 1176–1178.
35. Ibid.
36. Ibid.
37. Ibid.
38. Ramsay to Porter, June 10, 1862, *ORN*, XXV: 163; Bearss, *The Vicksburg Campaign*, 3: 1180–1181
39. McCulloch to Maclay, June 8, 1863, *OR*, XXIV, pt. 2, 467–470; Barnickle, *Milliken's Bend*, 90.
40. Barnickle, *Milliken's Bend*, 92.
41. Ibid., 90; Unknown, Milliken's Bend, Louisiana, to My Dear Pa, June 8, 1863; hereafter cited as Milliken's Bend Letter. The original letter had been written on wallpaper.
42. Barnickle, *Milliken's Bend*, 90, 102; Milliken's Bend Letter.
43. Barnickle, *Milliken's Bend*, 90, 102; Milliken's Bend Letter.
44. McCulloch to Maclay, June 8, 1863, *OR*, XXIV, pt. 2, 467–470.
45. Bearss, *The Vicksburg Campaign*, 3: 1181–1182, McCulloch to Maclay, June 8, 1863, *OR*, XXIV, pt. 2, 468.
46. Ramsay to Porter, June 10, 1862, *ORN*, XXV: 163; Bearss, *The Vicksburg Campaign*, 3: 1182–1183.
47. Bearss, *The Vicksburg Campaign*, 3: 1182–1183.
48. Ibid.

49. Ibid.
50. Lowe, *Walker's Texas Division*, 99.
51. Barnickle, *Milliken's Bend*, 90; Milliken's Bend Letter.
52. Barnickle, *Milliken's Bend*, 130–131, 195–197.
53. Bearss, *The Vicksburg Campaign*, 3: 1183.
54. Porter to Grant, June 7, 1863, *ORN*, XXV: 164.
55. Johnston to Porter, June 7, 1862, *ORN*, XXV: 162.
56. Ibid.; Bearss, *The Vicksburg Campaign*,, 3: 1185.
57. Bearss, *The Vicksburg Campaign*, 3: 1185.
58. Ibid., 3: 1186–1187.
59. Taylor to Boggs, June 8, 1863, *OR*, XXIV, pt. 2: 460–461.
60. Ibid.; Blessington, *Walker's Texas Division*, 120, 122; Lowe, *Walker's Texas Division*, 101.
61. Taylor to Boggs, June 11, 1863, *OR*, XXIV, pt. 2: 461.
62. Ibid., 460–461.

Chapter 5

1. Brian J. Costello of Pointe Coupée, perhaps the greatest authority on this region, used this phrase at a May 2013 meeting. I thought it apt, and it has stuck with me since. [AUTHOR: Here, it will delete the second repetitive note when edits are accepted.]
2. Costello, *A History of Pointe Coupée Parish*, 117–118; Lew Benedict to Richard Irwin, May 24, 1863, in US War Department, *The War of the Rebellion*, Series I, XXVI, pt. 1: 502; Barr, *Polignac's Texas Brigade*, 19–20. The unusaully named Arizona Brigade had originally been slated to reinforce Confederate successes in the territories of New Mexico and Arizona. When forces under General Henry Hopkins Sibley abandoned those regions, the Arizona Brigade no longer had a mission. The component units, raised to regimental strength through conscription and the dragooning of independent "coast guard" commands in Texas, was broken up. Some of the Arizona Brigade units served in Louisiana, Indian Territory, and Texas.
3. Henry Walke to James Palmer, June 3, 1863 in US Naval War Records Office, *ORN*, XX: 220; Henry Walke to David D. Porter, June 4, 1863, *ORN*, XXV: 153–154; John Ellet to Henry Walke, June 3, 1863, *ORN*, XXV: 154–155; Thompson, ed., *From Desert to Bayou*, 43. Chester G. Hearn's excellent book *Ellet's Brigade: The Stragest Outfit of All* misses this action. The rest of the Mississippi Marine Brigade was garrisoning at Snyder's Bluff, Mississippi, or Marion, Arkansas. Of the ram fleet, only the USS *Switzerland* had made it below Vicksburg and apprently became useful as a reconaissance vessel to keep open communications between Banks's and Grant's armies. See Hern, *Ellet's Brigade*, 166–167.
4. Charles P. Stone to David G. Farragut, June 15, 1863, *ORN*, XX: 232; Farragut to Stone, June 15, 1863, *ORN*, XX: 232; Henry Walke to David Porter, June 4, 1863, *ORN*, XXV: 154–155; Field and Staff Muster Roll, May and June, 1863, Fifteenth Infantry, in Compiled Service Records of Confederate Soldiers Who Served in

Organizations from the State of Texas. RG 109. M 323. National Archives and Records Administration.

5. Joseph Phillips. Smith's Plantation three miles from Simmesport. Louisiana. to Captain E. P. Turner. Assistant Adjutant General. District of Texas. Arizona. and New Mexico. Houston. Texas. June 8. 1863. in Compiled Service Records of Joseph Phillips. National Archives and Record Administration. Record Group 109. Publication M331. Compiled Service Records of Confederate General and Staff Officers. and none regimental Enlisted Men. hereafter cited as CMSR Joseph Phillips.
6. Ibid.
7. Ibid.
8. Thompson. ed.. *From Desert to Bayou*. 41.
9. Ibid.
10. Joseph Phillips. Smith's Plantation three miles from Simmesport. Louisiana. to John B. Magruder. Houston. Texas. June 8. 1863. CMSR Joseph Phillips: Joseph Phillips to Edward Surget. June 10. 1863. *OR*. XXVI. Pt. 2: 45–47.
11. Thompson. ed.. *From Desert to Bayou*. 41–42.
12. Phillips to Magruder. June 8. 1863. Phillips to Turner. June 8. 1863. CMSR Joseph Phillips; James S. Palmer to David G. Farragut. June 17. 1863. *OR*. XXVI. pt. 1: 567.
13. Phillips to Magruder. June 8. 1863. Phillips to Turner. June 8. 1863. CMSR Joseph Phillips: James S. Palmer to David G. Farragut. June 17. 1863. *OR*. XXVI. pt. 1: 567.
14. Taylor to W. R. Boggs. June 8. 1863. *OR*. XXIV. pt. 2: 461–462; Taylor. *Destruction and Reconstruction*. 140.
15. Taylor to W. R. Boggs. June 8. 1863. *OR*. XXIV. pt. 2: 461–462.
16. Ibid.: Taylor. *Destruction and Reconstruction*. 216.
17. Daniel Denett. "The Fight on the Teche." January 24. 1863. Franklin [Louisiana] *Planters' Banner*.
18. Taylor. *Destruction and Reconstruction*. 235–236.
19. Compiled Service Record of James P. Major. National Archives and Record Administration. Record Group 109. Publication M331. Compiled Service Records of Confederate General and Staff Officers. and Nonregimental Enlisted Men. hereafter cited as CMSR James P. Major.
20. D. C. Glenn. Richmond. Virginia. to Jefferson Davis. February 15. 1863. CMSR James P. Major.
21. James P. Major. Washington. Louisiana. to Samuel Cooper. Richmond. Virginia. June 8. 1863. CMSR James P. Major.
22. Taylor. *Destruction and Reconstruction*. 162. *De Coelesti Hierarchia* (*On the Celestial Hierachy*) was a pseudo-Dionysian tretis from the fifth century that discussed the ranking of angels and had a profound influence on Christian thought.
23. Taylor. *Destruction and Reconstruction*. 162.
24. Marshall McIlhenny. Franklin. Louisiana. to Ned [Edmund] McIlhenny. June 8. 1863. Weeks Family Papers. Box 2. Folder 2. Tulane University.

25. Ibid.
26. H. F. Kopke, Washington, Louisiana, to Mrs. C. H. Kopke, San Felipe, Texas, June 14, 1863, manuscript in possession of Randy Mallory, Tyler, Texas.
27. Ibid.
28. Taylor, *Destruction and Reconstruction*, 181.
29. Ibid.
30. Ibid.; Edmund Kirby Smith to Joseph E. Johnston, June 10, 1863, *OR*, XXVI, pt. 2, 43; Vandiver, ed., *The Civil War Diary of General Josiah Gorgas*, 43.
31. Ibid.
32. Taylor to W. R. Boggs, June 11, 1863, *OR*, XXIV, pt. 2: 460–461.
33. Haynes, *A Thrilling Narrative*, 131–132; see also Richard Taylor to Edmund Kirby Smith, April 23, 1863, *OR*, XV: 393. Taylor reported that "nearly the whole of Lieutenant Colonel Fournet's Battalion, passing through the country in which they men had lived before joining the army, deserted with their arms, remaining at their homes."
34. Haynes, *A Thrilling Narrative*, 8–10.
35. Ibid.

Chapter 6

1. Duganne, *Camps and Prisons*, 37, 59; Quien, *Lieutenant George Quien*, 30.
2. Bosson, *History of the Forty-Second Regiment Infantry*, 253.
3. Duganne, *Camps and Prisons*, 31.
4. Ibid.
5. Duganne, *Camps and Prisons*, 31, 37; Quien, *Lieutenant George Quien*, 30.
6. Duganne, *Camps and Prisons*, 31, 37; Quien, *Lieutenant George Quien*, 30.
7. Duganne, *Camps and Prisons*, 42, 49.
8. Ibid., 51.
9. Ibid. 51.
10. Ibid., 36.
11. Quien, *Lieutenant George Quien*, 29.
12. Ibid., 30
13. Duganne, *Camps and Prisons*, 68
14. Ibid., 48, 50. Adam Smith (1723–1790) was a Scottish moral philosopher and pioneer of political economy. His book, *The Wealth of Nations*, is considered the first work of modern economics, and argues that self-interest drives most human activities and that a free market—guided by an invisible hand—would determine the rate of exchange for goods and services. A generation later, Thomas Robert Malthus (1766–1834) argued that populations would thrive or decline based on the availability of resources. Society, he argued, could not be perfected because scarcity of resources would limit its ability to improve. His contemporary, David Ricardo (1772–1823), introduced the concept of "comparative advantage" and argued that countries should develop specialized industries where they held an international advantage while developing a thriving trade that exchanged these commodities for goods in shorter supply.

15. Duganne, *Camps and Prisons*, 68.
16. Ibid., 52–53, 89.
17. Ibid., 37–38.
18. Sam White, Brashear City, Louisiana, to "Anise," May 22, 1863, Civil War Letters, 1863, MSS 3188, Misc: C, Louisiana and Lower Mississippi Valley Collection, Hill Memorial Library, Louisiana State University, Baton Rouge.
19. Bosson, *History of the Forty-Second Regiment Infantry*, 288.
20. William H. Emory to Richard Irwin, June 3, 1863, *OR*, XXVI, pt. 1: 534.
21. Banks to Emory, May 31, 1863, *OR*, XXVI, pt. 1: 524; Albert Allen, Charles E. Page, and David Hershey, Compiled Military Service Records of Volunteer Soldiers Who Served the United States Colored Troops, 56th–138th USCT Infantry, 1864–1866, Record Group 94, National Archives and Records Administration.
22. Bosson, *History of the Forty-Second Regiment Infantry*, 346–350.
23. Murray, ed., *Madison County Troops*, 51.
24. Bergeron, Jr., "Fort Berwick and Fort Chêne," 435–450.
25. Duganne, *Camps and Prisons*, 108; Sherman, *In the Lowlands of Louisiana*, 22; Bosson, *History of the Forty-Second Regiment Infantry*, 263–264; Malone, *Sweet Chariot*, 111.
26. Duganne, *Camps and Prisons*, 108; Sherman, *In the Lowlands of Louisiana*, 22; Bosson, *History of the Forty-Second Regiment Infantry*, 263–264; Malone, *Sweet Chariot*, 111; Bell's *Mosquito Soldiers*, demonstrates that nearly 75 percent of the hospital cases in Louisiana showed symptoms consistent with mosquito-borne illnesses.
27. Duganne, *Camps and Prisons*, 108.
28. Quien, *Lieutenant George Quien*, 46–47; Powers, *The Story of the Thirty-eighth Regiment*, 245–301; Duganne, *Camps and Prisons*, 108; Sherman, *In the Lowlands of Louisiana*, 22.
29. Sherman, *In the Lowlands of Louisiana*, 19.
30. Quien, *Lieutenant George Quien*, 46–47; Duganne, *Camps and Prisons*, 108; Sherman, *In the Lowlands of Louisiana*, 22.
31. Edmonds, ed., *The Conduct of Federal Troops*, 115–121.
32. Hepworth, *The Whip, Hoe, and Sword*, 30–31.
33. Ibid.
34. Downs, *Sick From Freedom*), 36; Eaton, *Grant, Lincoln, and the Freedmen*, 19–20.
35. Irwin, *History of the 19th Army Corps*, 238; Duganne, *Camps and Prisons*, 111; The Adjutant General of the Commonwealth of Massachusetts, comp., *Massachusetts Soldiers*, VI: 389.
36. Albert Stickney to W. D. Smith, June 9, 1863, *OR*, XXVI, pt. 1: 544–545.
37. Ibid.
38. Duganne, *Camps and Prisons*, 112.
39. Junius B. Harris, near Franklin, Louisiana, to Richard Orton, Nacogdoches, Texas, June 13, 1863, Aimer Collection, Folder 6, Watson Memorial Library, Cammie G. Watson Research Center, Northwestern State University, Natchitoches, Louisiana.

40. Lorenz, "History of John Adam Lorenz," 22; J. H. Marshall, in Compiled Service Records of Confederate Soldiers Who Served in Organizations from the State of Texas, RG 109, M323; J. A. Lorenz, in Compiled Service Records of Confederate Soldiers Who Served in Organizations from the State of Texas, RG 109, M323..
41. William H. Emory to Richard Irwin, June 9, 1863, *OR*, XXVI, pt. 1: 544; Emory to Irwin, June 15, 1863, *OR*, XXVI, pt. 1: 559–560.
42. William H. Emory to Richard Irwin, June 9, 1863, *OR*, XXVI, pt. 1: 544; Emory to Irwin, June 15, 1863, *OR*, XXVI, pt. 1: 559–560; Bosson, *History of the Forty-Second Regiment*, 252.
43. Nathaniel P. Banks to Edwin M. Stanton, April 6, 1865, *OR*, XXVI, part 1: 15.
44. Nathaniel P. Banks to Henry W. Halleck, June 20, 1863, *OR*, XXVI, pt. 1: 573.
45. William H. Emory to Richard Irwin, June 9, 1863, *OR*, XXVI, pt. 1: 544; Emory to Irwin, June 15, 1863, *OR*, XXVI, pt. 1: 559–560; Bosson, *History of the Forty-Second Regiment*, 252.
46. Bosson, *History of the Forty-Second Regiment Infantry*, 256–257
47. Ibid., 258.
48. Ibid., 258.
49. Duganne, *Camps and Prisons*, 112–113.
50. Nott, *Sketches in Prison Camps*, 38–39.
51. Bosson, *History of the Forty-Second Regiment*, 256, 258, 260; William Shelly Diary, June 17, 1863, Mss. 3604, Misc: S.

Chapter 7

1. C. H. Sage to Richard B. Irwin, June 16, 1863, *OR*, XXVI, part I: 562.
2. Murray, ed., *Madison County Troops*, 59; Pound, "Slave to the Ex-Slave Narratives," 95–98.
3. J. S. Palmer to Nathaniel P. Banks, June 16, 1863, *OR*, XXVI, pt. 1: 561–562; C. H. Sage to Richard B. Irwin, June 16, 1863, *OR*, XXVI, pt. 1: 569; A. P. Cooke to James S. Palmer, June 17, 1863, *ORN*, XX: 238.
4. Taylor to John L. Logan, June 15, 1863, *OR*, XXVI, pt. 2, 53.
5. Taylor, *Destruction and Reconstruction*, 140.
6. James S. Palmer to Nathaniel P. Banks, June 17, 1863, *ORN*, XX: 237–238.
7. Taylor, *Destruction and Reconstruction*, 181; James P. Major to Louis Bush, June 30, 1863, *OR*, XXVI, pt. 1: 218.
8. James P. Major to Louis Bush, June 30, 1863, *OR*, XXVI, pt. 1: 217; Edmund Kirby Smith to Samuel Cooper, June 29, 1863 *OR*, XXVI, pt. 1: 209-210.
9. James P. Major to Louis Bush, June 30, 1863, *OR*, XXVI, pt. 1: 217.
10. Charles H. Witham, San Francisco, California, to Selden Connor, Augusta, Maine, July 31, 1896, Civil War Correspondence, Regimental Correspondence, Box 65, Records of the Adjutant General, Pre-1940, Maine State Archives, Augusta, Maine; James P. Major to Louis Bush, June 30, 1863 *OR*, XXVI, pt. 1: 217.
11. Witham to Connor, July 31, 1896, Civil War Correspondence, Maine State Archives.

12. Ibid.
13. Stearns, *Reminiscences of the Late War*, 18.
14. Thompson, ed., *From Desert to Bayou*, 43–45; Nathaniel P. Banks to David G. Farragut, June 18, 1863, *ORN*, XX: 235–236; M. Clapp to William Emory, June 18, 1863, *ORN*, XX: 235–236; Albert Stearns to James Bowen, June 19, 1863, *OR*, XXVI, pt. 1: 191–192.
15. Bosson, *History of the Forty-Second Regiment Infantry*, 348–349; Stearns, *Reminiscences of the Late War*, 17.
16. Thompson, ed., *From Desert to Bayou*, 43–45; Nathaniel P. Banks to David G. Farragut, June 18, 1863, *ORN*, XX: 235–236; M. Clapp to William Emory, June 18, 1863, *ORN*, XX: 235–236; Albert Stearns to James Bowen, June 19, 1863 *OR*, XXVI, pt. 1: 191–192; Bosson, *History of the Forty-Second Regiment Infantry*, 347–348.
17. James P. Major to Louis Bush, June 30, 1863, *OR*, XXVI, pt. 1: 217; Farragut to Banks, *ORN*, XX: 304; Stearns, *Reminiscences of the Late War*, 19.
18. Witham to Connor, Civil War Correspondence, Maine State Archives.
19. Farragut to Banks, *ORN*, XX: 237, 304; Farragut to James Alden, June 19, 1863, *ORN*, XX: 239–240, Alden to Banks, June 20, 1863, *ORN*, XX: 241; James P. Major to Louis Bush, June 30, 1863 *OR*, XXVI, pt. 1: 217.
20. Farragut to Banks, *ORN*, XX: 237, 304; Farragut to James Alden, June 19, 1863, *ORN*, XX: 239–240, Alden to Banks, June 20, 1863, *ORN*, XX: 241; James P. Major to Louis Bush, June 30, 1863 *OR*, XXVI, pt. 1: 217.
21. J. S. Palmer to David Dixon Porter, June 20, 1863, *ORN*, XX: 240–241.
22. Probably the USS *Monongahela*, USS *Winona*, and USS *Kineo*. James P. Major to Louis Bush, June 30, 1863, *ORN*, XX: 363.
23. James P. Major to Louis Bush, June 30, 1863 *OR*, XXVI, pt. 1: 218; "Oscar" [Charles Oscar Dupuy], Bayou Plaquemine, to Gustave Lauve, June 26, 1863, Gustave Lauve Letter, Mss. 893, Louisiana and Lower Mississippi Valley; Berlin, et al., eds., *Freedom*, 459.
24. James P. Major to Louis Bush, June 30, 1863, *OR*, XXVI, pt. 1: 218.
25. The roads of 1863 are often not the same roads those today in this part of Louisiana. Federal maps show the cut-off road as Sacramento Road, a name it still bears today. These same documents indicate that the "Ricard Cut-Off" appromiximates modern Avon Road near the hamlet of Belle Rose.
26. James P. Major to Louis Bush, June 30, 1863, *OR*, XXVI, pt. 1: 218; the name Ricard Cut-Off comes from Bearrs, ed., *A Louisiana Confederate*, 3; this route roughly corresponds to Louisiana Highway 69 to its intersection with Louisiana Highway 996 and thence by various outlets to Bayou Lafourche.
27. Albert Stickney to W. D. Smith, July 9, 1863 *OR*, XXVI, pt. 1: 193.
28. Ibid.
29. Ibid.
30. William H. Emory, Special Order No. 21, June 12, 1863, Compiled Service Records of Volunteer Union Soldiers Who Served in Organizations from the State of

Louisiana. Charles Blober. Personal Papers. RG 94. M396. National Archives and Records Administration; Bosson. *History of the Forty-Second Regiment Infantry* 262.
31. Albert Stickney to W. D. Smith. July 9. 1863 *OR*. XXVI. pt. 1: 192–197.
32. Duganne. *Camps and Prisons*. 30. 40.
33. Nott. *Sketches in Prison Camps*. 41; Bosson, *History of the Forty-Second Regiment*. 260–261.
34. Albert Stickney to W. D. Smith. July 9. 1863 *OR*. XXVI. pt. 1: 192–197; Stone. *Rhode Island in the Rebellion*. 371; Bosson. *History of the Forty-Second Regiment*. 262; Moore. ed.. *The Rebellion record*. VII: 76.
35. James P. Major to Louis Bush. June 30. 1863 *OR*. XXVI. pt. 1: 218; Albert Stickney to W. D. Smith. July 9. 1863 *OR*. XXVI. pt. 1: 193; In Stickney's report. he lists specifically forty-seven men of the 12th Maine and ten men of Company D. 176th New York; Duganne. *Camps and Prisons*. 123–126.
36. James P. Major to Louis Bush. June 30. 1863 *OR*. XXVI. pt. 1: 218; Albert Stickney to W. D. Smith. July 9. 1863 *OR*. XXVI. pt. 1: 193; In Stickney's report. he lists specifically forty-seven men of the 12th Maine and ten men of Company D. 176th New York; Duganne. *Camps and Prisons*. 123–126; Bryan. ed.. "Whip Them Like the Mischief." 74.
37. James P. Major to Louis Bush. June 30. 1863 *OR*. XXVI. pt. 1: 218; Albert Stickney to W. D. Smith. July 9. 1863 *OR*. XXVI. pt. 1: 193; In Stickney's report. he lists specifically forty-seven men of the 12th Maine and ten men of Company D. 176th New York; Duganne. *Camps and Prisons*. 123–126; Bryan. ed.. "Whip Them Like the Mischief." 74.
38. Thompson. ed.. *From Desert to Bayou*. 50.
39. "T" to Editor. New York *Times*. "The Capture of Brashear City by the Rebels—The Ironsides." New York *Times*. August 9. 1863; Albert Stickney to W. D. Smith. July 9. 1863 *OR*. XXVI. pt. 1: 193.
40. "T" to Editor. New York *Times*. "The Capture of Brashear City by the Rebels—The Ironsides." New York *Times*. August 9. 1863; Albert Stickney to W. D. Smith. July 9. 1863 *OR*. XXVI. pt. 1: 193.
41. James P. Major to Louis Bush. June 30. 1863 *OR*. XXVI. pt. 1: 218.
42. Witham to Connor. Civil War Correspondence. Regimental Correspondence. Maine State Archives.
43. Thompson. ed.. *From Desert to Bayou*. 48–50; Fortier. *Memorable Days and Various Notable*. diary entry June 20. 1863; typescript in the possession of the author. Hereafter cited as Dupuy Diary.
44. Dupuy Diary. June 20. 1863.
45. Witham to Connor. Civil War Correspondence. Maine State Archives.

Chapter 8

1. Bosson. *History of the Forty-Second Regiment Infantry*. 288; Albert Stickney to W. D. Smith. July 9. 1863 *OR*. XXVI. pt. 1: 193.

2. Stickney to Smith, July 9, 1863 *OR*, XXVI, pt. 1: 193; Quien, *Lieutenant George Quien*, 64; Bosson, *History of the Forty-Second Regiment*, 288
3. Stickney to Smith, July 9, 1863 *OR*, XXVI, pt. 1: 193; Quien, *Lieutenant George Quien*, 64.
4. Stickney to Smith, July 9, 1863 *OR*, XXVI, pt. 1: 193; Bosson, *History of the Forty-Second Regiment*, 289.
5. James P. Major to Louis Bush, June 30, 1863 *OR*, XXVI, pt. 1: 218; Thompson, ed., *From Desert to Bayou*, 50; T" to Editor, New York *Times*, "The Capture of Brashear City by the Rebels—The Ironsides," New York *Times*, August 9, 1863.
6. Nott, *Sketches in Prison Camps*, 41.
7. Bosson, *History of the Forty-Second Regiment*, 263–264; Duganne, *Camps and Prisons*, 121.
8. Bosson, *History of the Forty-Second Regiment*, 263–264; Duganne, *Camps and Prisons*, 117.
9. Duganne, *Camps and Prisons*, 130–131.
10. Stickney to Smith, July 9, 1863 *OR*, XXVI, pt. 1: 194–195.
11. Bosson, *History of the Forty-Second Regiment*, 291–292.
12. Stickney to Smith, July 9, 1863 *OR*, XXVI, pt. 1: 194–195; Bosson, *History of the Forty-Second Regiment*, 291–292; Quien, *Lieutenant George Quien*, 59.
13. Stickney to Smith, July 9, 1863 *OR*, XXVI, pt. 1: 194–195.
14. Stickney to Smith, July 9, 1863 *OR*, XXVI, pt. 1: 194; Bosson, *History of the Forty-Second Regiment*, 292.
15. Stickney to Smith, July 9, 1863 *OR*, XXVI, pt. 1: 194; Bosson, *History of the Forty-Second Regiment*, 292.
16. Quien, *Lieutenant George Quien*, 59–62.
17. Stickney to Smith, July 9, 1863 *OR*, XXVI, pt. 1: 195; Quien, *Lieutenant George Quien*, 62; Bosson, *History of the Forty-Second Regiment*, 293–294.
18. W. D. Smith to Commanding Officer at Brashear City, June 21, 1863, *OR*, XXVI, Pt. 1: 581.
19. W. H. Emory to Abert Stickney, June 21, 1863, in Murray, *History of the Ninth Regiment*, 134; William Emory to Albert Stickney, June 21, 1863, *OR*, XXVI, Pt. 1: 580–581; Emory to Richard Irwin, June 21, 1863, *OR*, XXVI, Pt. 1:580–581.
20. James P. Major to Louis Bush, June 30, 1863, *OR*, XXVI, pt. 1: 218.
21. Stickney to Smith, July 9, 1863, *OR*, XXVI, pt. 1: 195.
22. Major to Bush, June 30, 1863, *OR*, XXVI, pt. 1: 218; Overston [Texas] *Sharp-Shooter*, August 9, 1888.
23. Bosson, *History of the Forty-Second Regiment*, 295–296.
24. Stickney to Smith, July 9, 1863 *OR*, XXVI, pt. 1: 197.
25. Quien, *Lieutenant George Quien*, 64–65.
26. Ibid., 65–66.
27. Bosson, *History of the Forty-Second Regiment*, 295–296, 302.
28. Major to Bush, June 30, 1863, *OR*, XXVI, pt. 1: 218.

29. Stickney to Smith, July 9, 1863, *OR*, XXVI, pt. 1: 197; Bosson, *History of the Forty-Second Regiment*, 297.
30. Thompson, ed., *From Desert to Bayou*, 53.
31. "T" to Editor, New York *Times*, "The Capture of Brashear City by the Rebels—The Ironsides," New York *Times*, August 9, 1863; John A. Grow to Richard Arnold, July 5, 1863, *OR*, XXVI, pt. 1: 198; Thompson, ed., *From Desert to Bayou*, 53; Bosson, *History of the Forty-Second Regiment*, 304–306; Sherman, *In the Lowlands of Louisiana*, 25.
32. "T" to Editor, New York *Times*, "The Capture of Brashear City by the Rebels—The Ironsides," New York *Times*, August 9, 1863; John A. Grow to Richard Arnold, July 5, 1863, *OR*, XXVI, pt. 1: 198; Thompson, ed., *From Desert to Bayou*, 53; Bosson, *History of the Forty-Second Regiment*, 304–306.
33. Thompson, ed., *From Desert to Bayou*, 50–53; Major to Bush, June 30, 1863, *OR*, XXVI, pt. 1: 218; Overston [Texas] *Sharp-Shooter*, August 9, 1888.
34. Overston [Texas] *Sharp-Shooter*, August 9, 1888; Thompson, ed., *From Desert to Bayou*, 50–53; Major to Bush, June 30, 1863, *OR*, XXVI, pt. 1: 218.
35. Quien, *Lieutenant George Quien*, 72.
36. Stickney to Smith, July 9, 1863, *OR*, XXVI, pt. 1: 197.
37. Major to Bush, June 30, 1863, *OR*, XXVI, pt. 1: 218.
38. Ibid.; Stickney to Smith, July 9, 1863, *OR*, XXVI, pt. 1: 197.
39. Thompson, ed., *From Desert to Bayou*, 53. Private Miguel Rodriguez, Company B, 2nd Texas Mounted Rifles, enlisted May 23, 1861, in San Antonio, Texas. National Archives and Records Administration, M323, Compiled Service Records if Confederate Soldiers Who Served in Organizations from the State of Texas; Overston [Texas] *Sharp-Shooter*, August 9, 1888.
40. William H. Emory to Richard Irwin, June 30, 1863, *OR*, XXVI, pt. 1, 188–190.
41. Bosson, *History of the Forty-Second Regiment*, 264–265; Duganne, 113, 117.
42. Bosson, *History of the Forty-Second Regiment*, 264–265; Duganne, 113, 117.
43. Bosson, *History of the Forty-Second Regiment*, 264–265.
44. Ibid., 265.
45. Moore, ed. *The Rebellion record* , VII: 76.
46. Bosson, *History of the Forty-Second Regiment*, 265.
47. Duganne, *Camps and Prisons*, 133.
48. Thompson, ed., *From Desert to Bayou*, 43–48; Bosson, *History of the Forty-Second Regiment*, 265–266.
49. Duganne, *Camps and Prisons*, 134–135; Bosson, *History of the Forty-Second Regiment*, 266.
50. Duganne, *Camps and Prisons*, 134–135; Bosson, *History of the Forty-Second Regiment*, 266.
51. James P. Major to Louis Bush, June 30, 1863 *OR*, XXVI, pt. 1: 218.
52. Ibid.

Chapter 9

1. Taylor, *Destruction and Reconstruction*, 183.
2. Ibid.
3. The leading expert on the life and service of Sherod Hunter is L. Boyd Finch. See his article "Surprise at Brashear City"; also see Finch, *Confederate Pathway to the Pacific*.
4. Finch, "Surprise at Brashear City," 414.
5. Noel, *A Campaign from Santa Fe to the Mississippi*, 51; William Randolph Howell to Editor, July 3, 1863, published in Houston [Texas] *Tri-Weekly Telegraph*, July 20, 1863, 1.
6. Noel, *A Campaign from Santa Fe to the Mississippi*, 51.
7. Lorenz, "History of John Adam Lorenz," 22; William Shelly Diary, June 23, 1863.
8. Putnam, *Memories of My Youth*, 267; Bosson, *History of the Forty-Second Regiment Infantry*, 266.
9. Tom Green to Alfred Mouton, June 30, 1863, *ORN*, XX: 833–834; Putnam, *Memories of My Youth*, 267–268.
10. Moore, ed. *The Rebellion Record*, VII: 77.
11. James P. Major to Louis Bush, June 30, 1863, *OR*, XXVI, pt. 1: 218.
12. William Emory to Richard Irwin, *OR*, XXVI, pt. 1, 187–189;
13. Richard Irwin to William Emory, June 21, 1863, 2 P.M., *OR*, XXVI, Pt. 1, 582.
14. Sherman, *In the Lowlands of Louisiana*, 26; Tom Green to Alfred Mouton, June 30, 1863, *ORN*, XX: 834.
15. Putnam, *Memories of My Youth*, 267–268; Green to Mouton, June 30, 1863, *OR*, XXVI, Pt. 1, 225–226; W. L. Davidson, C. C. Linn, and Phil Fulcrod, "Reminiscences of the Old Brigade—On the March—in the Tent—in the Field—as Witnessed by the Writers During the Rebellion," published in The Overton [Texas] *Sharp Shooter*, July 5, 1888.
16. Overton [Texas] *Sharp Shooter*, July 5, 1888.
17. Noel, *A Campaign from Santa Fe to the Mississippi*, 51.
18. Duganne, *Camps and Prisons*, 145; Finch, "Surprise at Brashear City," 417; Overton [Texas] *Sharp Shooter*, July 5, 1888.
19. Bosson, *History of the Forty-Second Regiment*, 268; Finch, "Surprise at Brashear City," 417; William Randolph Howell to Editor, July 3, 1863, published in Houston [Texas] *Tri-Weekly Telegraph*, July 20, 1863, 1.
20. Noel, *Campaign from Santa Fe to the Mississippi*, 51.
21. Putnam, *Memories of My Youth*, 267–268; Green to Mouton, June 30, 1863, *OR*, XXVI, Pt. 1: 225–226; Overton [Texas] *Sharp Shooter*, July 5, 1888.
22. Putnam, *Memories of My Youth*, 268.
23. Bosson, *History of the Forty-Second Regiment*, 266.
24. Ibid., 267.
25. Overton [Texas] *Sharp Shooter*, July 5, 1888; Duganne, *Camps and Prisons*, 150; Nott, *Sketches in Prison Camps*, 41.
26. Overton [Texas] *Sharp Shooter*, July 5, 1888; Duganne, *Camps and Prisons*, 150; Nott, *Sketches in Prison Camps*, 41.

27. Putnam, *Memories of My Youth*, 268; Moore, ed., *The Rebellion Record*, VII: 77–78.
28. Duganne, *Camps and Prisons*, 151, 153; Putnam, *Memories of My Youth*, 256.
29. Duganne, *Camps and Prisons*, 151, 153; Putnam, *Memories of My Youth*, 256.
30. W. L. Robards, camp near Washington, Louisiana, to editor, July 27, 1863, published Houston [Texas] *Tri-Weekly Telegraph*, August 10, 1863, 1; Sherod Hunter to Alfred Mouton, June 26, 1863, *OR*, XXVI, Pt. 1: 223–224; Bosson, *History of the Forty-Second Regiment*, 267; Sherman, *In the Lowlands of Louisiana*, 28.
31. Overton [Texas] *Sharp Shooter*, July 5, 1888.
32. Bosson, *History of the Forty-Second Regiment*, 267–269; Sherman, *In the Lowlands of Louisiana*, 28; Duganne, *Camps and Prisons*, 152; Nott, *Sketches in Prison Camps*, 41; Moore, ed., *The Rebellion Record*, VII: 81.
33. Bosson, *History of the Forty-Second Regiment*, 269; Duganne, *Camps and Prisons*, 152; Nott, *Sketches in Prison Camps*, 41.
34. Nott, *Sketches in Prison Camps*, 40–42.
35. W. L. Robards, camp near Washington, Louisiana, to editor, July 27, 1863, published Houston [Texas] *Tri-Weekly Telegraph*, August 10, 1863, 1; Sherod Hunter to Alfred Mouton, June 26, 1863, *OR*, XXVI, Pt. 1: 223–224; Bosson, *History of the Forty-Second Regiment*, 267; Sherman, *In the Lowlands of Louisiana*, 28
36. Bosson, *History of the Forty-Second Regiment*, 267; Sherman, *In the Lowlands of Louisiana*, 28.
37. Duganne, *Camps and Prisons*, 148–149; Bosson, *History of the Forty-Second Regiment*, 268; Moore, ed., *The Rebellion Record*, VII: 77.
38. Putnam, *Memories of My Youth*, 268.
39. Moore, ed., *The Rebellion Record*, VII: 78.
40. Bosson, *History of the Forty-Second Regiment*, 269; Duganne, *Camps and Prisons*, 152; Hunter to Mouton, June 26, 1863, *OR*, XXVI, Pt. 1: 223–224.
41. Duganne, *Camps and Prisons*, 152; Moore, ed., *The Rebellion Record*, VII: 76.
42. Sherman, *In the Lowlands of Louisiana*, 29; Bosson, *History of the Forty-Second Regiment*, 271–272.
43. John Coleman Sibley to "My Dear Wife" [Nancy Elizabeth Sibley], June 26, 1863, in Donald Ray Parker, ed., *Civil War Diary and Letters of 2nd Lieutenant John Coleman Sibley, 2nd Louisiana Cavalry, Company E, Confederate States of America*, unpublished manuscript in John Coleman Sibley Collection, Box 2.; William Randolph Howell to Editor, July 3, 1863, published in Houston [Texas] *Tri-Weekly Telegraph*, July 20, 1863, 1.
44. Bosson, *History of the Forty-Second Regiment*, 269; Sherman, *In the Lowlands of Louisiana*, 28.
45. "T." to Editor, New York *Times*, "The Capture of Brashear City by the Rebels: The Ironsides Regiment," New York *Times*, August 9, 1863.
46. Bosson, *History of the Forty-Second Regiment*, 270; Sherman, *In the Lowlands of Louisiana*, 27.

47. Putnam. *Memories of My Youth*. 269–270: Bosson. *History of the Forty-Second Regiment*. 270.
48. Moore. ed.. *The Rebellion Record*. VII: 78.
49. Taylor. *Destruction and Reconstruction*. 141–142: Overton [Texas] *Sharp Shooter*. July 5. 1888.
50. Nott. *Sketches in Prison Camps*. 45.
51. Moore. ed.. *Rebellion Record*. 77: Overton [Texas] *Sharp Shooter*. July 5. 1888: William Shelly Diary. June 23. 1863.
52. Duganne. *Camps and Prisons*. 156.162–163.
53. Ibid.. 153–154. 157.
54. Ibid.. 164.
55. Ibid.. 142–143.
56. Tom Green to Alfred Mouton. *OR*. XXVI. pt. 1. 225: Duganne. *Camps and Prisons*. 179–180.
57. Lane. *The Adventures and Recollections of General Walter P. Lane*. 106.
58. Duganne. *Camps and Prisons*. 169–170.
59. Ibid.. 171: Leander McNelly. Thibodaux. Louisiana. to [John] McNelly. Washington County. Texas. June 26. 1863. as published in Houston [Texas] *Tri-Weekly Telegraph*. August 5. 1863. 2. and Bellville [Texas] *Countryman*. August 8. 1863. 1: Moore. ed.. *The Rebellion Record*. VII: 77.
60. Major to Louis Bush. June 30. 1863. *OR*. XXVI pt. 1: 218.
61. Duganne. *Camps and Prisons*. 172–176.

Chapter 10

1. Houston [Texas] *Tri-Weekly Telegraph*. August 12. 1863. 1.
2. Houston [Texas] *Tri-Weekly Telegraph*. July 6. 1863. 2: W. L. Davidson. C. C. Linn. and Phil Fulcrod. "Reminiscences of the Old Brigade—On the March—in the Tent—in the Field—as Witnessed by the Writers During the Rebellion." published in The Overton [Texas] *Sharp Shooter*. July 5. 1888.
3. Houston [Texas] *Tri-Weekly Telegraph*. July 6. 1863. 1–2: Overton [Texas] *Sharp Shooter*. July 5. 1888.
4. Richard Fitz Gibbons to Horace J. Morse. June 27. 1863. *OR*. XXVI. pt. 1. 201–202. The troops sent on this errand were companies C. E. G. I. and K. 9th Connecticut Infantry.
5. Murray. *History of the Ninth Regiment Connecticut Volunteer Infantry*. 139.
6. Richard Fitz Gibbons to Horace J. Morse. June 27. 1863. *OR*. XXVI. pt. 1. 201–202: John A. Grow to Richard Arnold. July 5. 1863. *OR*. XXVI. pt.1. 197–201.
7. William Emory to Richard Irwin. June 30. 1863. *OR*. XXVI. pt. 1. 188–190: Grow to Arnold. July 5. 1863. *OR*. XXVI. pt.1. 197–201: William H. Emory to Colonel Cahill. June 24. 1863. *OR*. XXVI. pt. 1. 594.
8. Emory to Cahill. June 24. 1863. *OR*. XXVI. pt. 1. 594: Grow to Arnold. July 5. 1863. *OR*. XXVI. pt.1. 197–201.

9. Grow to Richard Arnold, July 5, 1863, *OR*, XXVI, pt.1, 197–201.
10. Richard Taylor to William R. Boggs, July 4, 1863, *OR*, XXVI, pt. 1, 213; Keet McDade to Ann Cochran, July 22, 1863, typescript courtesy of Vernon Williams, Abilene Christian University; W. H. Emory to David G. Farragut, June 25, 1863, *OR*, XXVI, pt. 1, 598; W. D. Smith to Commanding Officer at Forts Jackson and Saint Philip, June 25, 1863, *OR*, XXVI, pt. 1, 599. The Union works west of the river included a line along the west bank of the Company Canal, corresponding to Louisiana Street and Sala Street in present-day Westwego, Louisiana. The Parapet giving the name to Camp Parapet, followed a course along what is now Causeway Boulevard in Metarie and Jefferson, Louisiana, upriver from New Orleans. Louisiana Highway 611, now Metarie Road, was the main route linking these advanced works with the city proper. Union troops camped at the Metarie Racetrack, now Lake Lawn cemetery, and Congo Square, as well as present-day Audubon Park in the Carrollton neighborhood of modern New Orleans.
11. Taylor to Boggs, June 24, 1863, *OR*, XXVI, pt. 1, 210–211; Taylor to Boggs, June 27, 1863, *OR*, XXVI, pt. 1, 211–212.
12. Taylor to Boggs, June 27, 1863, *OR*, XXVI, pt. 1, 211–212; Taylor to Boggs, June 24, 1863, *OR*, XXVI, pt. 1, 210–211; Sherod Hunter to Alfred Mouton, June 26, 1863, *OR*, XXVI, pt. 1, 223–224; James P. Major to Luis Bush, June 30, 1863, *OR*, XXVI, pt. 1, 217–220; H. P. to Editor, Houston [Texas] *Tri-Weekly Telegraph*, July 6, 1863.
13. Bosson, *History of the Forty-Second Regiment Infantry*, 278; Sherman, *In the Lowlands of Louisiana*, 30.
14. John Coleman Sibley, Brashear City, Louisiana to "My Dear Wife" [Nancy Elizabeth Sibley], Many, Louisiana, June 26, 1863, and June 27, 1863, in Donald Ray Parker, ed., *Civil War Diary and Letters of 2nd Lieutenant John Coleman Sibley, 2nd Louisiana Cavalry, Company E, Confederate States of America*, unpublished manuscript in John Coleman Sibley Collection, Box 2; Bosson, *History of the Forty-Second Regiment Infantry*, 278; Sherman, *In the Lowlands of Louisiana* , 30. Albert Lapham had a letter from his sister in Duxbury, Massachusetts, in his coat pocket.
15. Ibid.
16. Murray, ed., *Madison County Troops*, 60.
17. H. F. Kopke, Berwicks Bay, Louisiana, to C. H. Kopke, San Felipe, Texas, June 27, 1863, manuscript in possession of Randy Mallory, Tyler, Texas.
18. Moore, ed. *The Rebellion Record*, VII: 81.
19. Nott, *Sketches in Prison Camps*, 51–52.
20. Ibid.
21. Ibid, 50; Moore, ed., *Rebellion Record*, VII: 81.
22. Moore, ed., *Rebellion Record*, VII: 81; George Haven Putnam was the son of George Palmer Putnam who, with John Wiley, established the publishing house of Wiley and Putnam. Sergeant Putnam would go on to author ten major works on history and literature including the hagiographic *Abraham Lincoln: The Leader in the Struggle for National Existence*, several children's books including the classic *The*

Little Gingerbread Man as well as numerous articles in major national publications including *Putnam's Magazine* and *Scribner's Magazine*. Putnam took over the family business with his brothers John and Irving, renaming it G. P. Putnam's Sons, which he in turn passed on to his son, George Palmer Putnam, husband of Amelia Earhart and an important American author in his own right.

23. Putnam, *Memories of My Youth*, 272–273; Bosson, *History of the Forty-Second Regiment*, 278.
24. Putnam, *Memories of My Youth*, 272–273; Bosson, *History of the Forty-Second Regiment*, 278.
25. Putnam, *Memories of My Youth*, 273–274.
26. H. F. Kopke, Berwicks Bay, Louisiana, to C. H. Kopke, San Felipe, Texas, June 27, 1863.
27. Moore, ed., *Rebellion Record*, VII: 82.
28. Bosson, *History of the Forty-Second Regiment*, 279; Duganne, *Camps and Prisons*, 189–192.
29. H. P. to Editor, Houston [Texas] *Tri-Weekly Telegraph*, July 6, 1863; James P. Major to Luis Bush, June 30, 1863, *OR*, XXVI, pt. 1, 217-220.
30. Nott, *Sketches in Prison Camps*, 47; Sherod Hunter to Amfred Mouton, June 26, 1863, *OR*, XXVI, pt. 1, 223-224; James P. Major to Luis Bush, June 30, 1863, *OR*, XXVI, pt. 1, 217–220.
31. Edmonds, ed., *The Conduct of Federal Troops* , 115–118.
32. Ibid.
33. Ibid.
34. Bergeron, Jr., ed., *The Civil War Reminiscences of Major Silas T. Grisamore*, 123.
35. W. T. Block, ed., "The Diary of 1st Sergeant H. N. Connor," http://www.wtblock.com/wtblockjr/diaryof.htm (accessed March 31, 2014); the diary is supposedly owned by Professor Haskell Monroe, College Station, Texas but when contacted, Dr. Monroe had no knowledge of the diary.
36. Edmonds, ed., *The Conduct of Federal Troops*, 120–121.
37. Edmonds, ed., *The Conduct of Federal Troops*, 120–121; For a pathbreaking study of the human toll caused by unprepapred emacipation, see Downs, *Sick from Freedom*. Remarkably, this fine work does not even have "Louisiana" or "Brashear City" in the index.
38. Duganne, *Camps and Prisons*, 92; Nott, *Sketches in Prison Camps*, 47.
39. Moore, ed., *Rebellion Record*, VII: 81.
40. Rankin, ed., *Diary of a Christian Soldier*, 132.
41. Taylor to Boggs, June 27, 1863, *OR*, XXVI, pt. 1: 211.
42. "Arizonian" to Editor, June 28, 1863, published in the Houston [Texas] *Tri-Weekly Telegraph*, July 10, 1863, 1; "The Diary of Robert Thomas Williams," entry for June 26, 1863. Kessler is an unincorporated community on the Louisiana 1 side of Bayou Lafourche, near the intersection with Louisiana 1002. It lies about seven miles below Donaldsonville; Tom Green, camp on Lafourche near Paincourtville, to Lewis Bush, July 3, 1863, *OR*, XXVI, part 1: 226–227.

43. Augustine Thompson, late Captain, Co. G, 28th Maine to Seldon Conner, Adjutant General, State of Maine, Janurary 1, 1896, Adjutant General Records, 1895 (hereafter cited as Thompson letter); Townsend, *History of the Sixteenth Regiment*, 255.
44. Green to Bush, July 3, 1863, *OR*, XXVI, part 1: 227; Samuel K. Savage to "Comrade Willis," The Fitchburg (Massachusetts) *Dailey Sentinel*, September 3, 1909, 4.
45. Taylor, *Destruction and Reconstruction*, 141; Emory to Irwin, June 28, 1863, *OR*, XXVI, pt. 1, 605; see also appendix in Banks, "Emancipated Labor in Louisiana."
46. Emory to Irwin, June 28, 1863, *OR*, XXVI, pt. 1, 605; Ira Berlin, et al., eds., *Freedom*, 459.
47. Thomas Green to Alfred Mouton, June 27, 1863, *OR*, XXVI, pt. 1: 226; Green favored the location of the Ford and Davenport Plantation, located near the modern intersection of Pierre Part Road (Louisiana 70) and Louisiana Highway 1 on the west bank of Bayou Lafourche. Across the river at Plattenville, roads leading to the Mississippi intersected the river near present-day Louisiana 70 and the crossing at the Sunshine Bridge; Fortier, , Dupuy Diary, entry June 27, 1863.
48. Fortier, Dupuy Diary, June 27, 1863; "Oscar" [Charles Oscar Dupuy], Bayou Plaquemine, to Gustave Lauve, June 26, 1863, Gustave Lauve Letter, Mss. 893. Charles Oscar Dupuy was the son of Balthazar Dupuy. Augusto Gustave Lauve was Oscar's brother in law. The only name he mentioned as taking the loaylty oath, and who wished to recant, was Bougru Dansereau.
49. Fortier, Dupuy Diary, June 27, 1863; "Oscar" [Charles Oscar Dupuy], Bayou Plaquemine, to Gustave Lauve, June 26, 1863, Gustave Lauve Letter, Mss. 893.
50. Tom Green to Alfred Mouton, June 27, 1863, *OR*, XXVI, pt. 1: 226; Hugh McPhail, Camp Near Washington, Louisiana, to Editor, August 3, 1863, published in Houston [Texas] *Tri-Weekly Telegraph*, August 19, 1863, 1.
51. Tom Green to Alfred Mouton, June 27, 1863, *OR*, XXVI, pt. 1: 226.
52. "Charges and Specifications preferred against Pierre Roujean," August 27, 1863, Union Provost Marshals' File of Paper relating to Individual Civilians, Record Group 109, M 345, National Archives and Records Administration; Marshall, *Gallant Creoles*, 11, 435–436; see also Durel, "Creole Civilization in Donaldsonville."
53. Tom Green to Alfred Mouton, June 27, 1863, *OR*, XXVI, pt. 1: 226.
54. Ibid.

Chapter 11

1. Wooten, ed., *A Comprehensive History of Texas*, II: 714–715; Tom Green, Ford and Davenport Plantation, to [Alfred] Mouton, June 27, 1863, *OR*, XXVI, part 1: 226; Hugh McPhail to Editor, August 3, 1863, Houston [Texas] *Tri-Weekly Telegraph*, August 19, 1863, 2.
2. Green to Mouton, June 27, 1863, *OR*, XXVI, pt. 1: 226; Hugh McPhail to Editor, August 3, 1863, Houston [Texas] *Tri-Weekly Telegraph*, August 19, 1863, 2; Stone was the son of a prominent Disciples of Christ Church leader.

3. Green to Mouton, June 27, 1863, *OR*, XXVI, part 1: 226; Hugh McPhail to Editor, August 3, 1863, Houston [Texas] *Tri-Weekly Telegraph*, August 19, 1863, 2.
4. W. D. Smith to Commanding Officer at Donaldsonville, June 27, 1863, *OR*, XXVI, pt. 1, 601; Thompson letter; Townsend, *History of the Sixteenth Regiment*, 255.
5. Thompson letter; Townsend, *History of the Sixteenth Regiment*, 255.
6. Thompson letter; Townsend, *History of the Sixteenth Regiment*, 255.
7. Hugh McPhail to Editor, August 3, 1863, Houston [Texas] *Tri-Weekly Telegraph*, August 19, 1863, 2.
8. M. B. Woolsey, Donaldsonville, Louisiana, to David G. Farragut, June 28, 1863, *ORN*, XX: 326–328; Hugh McPhail to Editor, August 3, 1863, Houston [Texas] *Tri-Weekly Telegraph*, August 19, 1863, 2.
9. Hugh McPhail to Editor, August 3, 1863, Houston [Texas] *Tri-Weekly Telegraph*, August 19, 1863, 2.
10. Hugh McPhail to Editor, August 3, 1863, Houston [Texas] *Tri-Weekly Telegraph*, August 19, 1863, 2; M. B. Woolsey to David G. Farragut, June 28, 1863, *ORN*, XX: 326–328.
11. Tom Green, camp on Lafourche near Paincourtville, to Lewis Bush, July 3, 1863, *OR*, XXVI, part 1: 227; Hugh McPhail to Editor, August 3, 1863, Houston [Texas] *Tri-Weekly Telegraph*, August 19, 1863, 2; Wooten, ed., *A Comprehensive History of Texas*, II: 714–715; Hugh McPhail to Editor, August 3, 1863, Houston [Texas] *Tri-Weekly Telegraph*, August 19, 1863, 2.
12. Green to Bush, July 3, 1863, *OR*, XXVI, part 1: 227.
13. Green to Bush, July 3, 1863, *OR*, XXVI, part 1: 227–228; Wooten, ed., *History of Texas*, II: 714–715.
14. W. H. Emory to Richard Irwin, June 28, 1863, *OR*, XXVI, pt. 1, 605; Woodman to Adjutant General, February 13, 1864, "Report from Colonel Ephraim W. Woodman, Colonel 2nd Cavalry Maine Volunteers, late Colonel, 28th Maine," Adjutant General Records, Regimental Correspondence, 28th Maine, (hereafter cited as Woodman report).
15. Woodman Report; Whitman and True, *War for the Union*, 544–546; Woolsey to Farragut, June 28, 1863, *ORN*, XX: 326; Abstract Log, USS *Princess Royal*, July 6, 1863, *ORN*, XX: 354. Coston lights were handheld flare guns used to send a sequence of colored lights to communicate simple messages.
16. Thompson letter ; Dallas [Texas] *Herald*, July 29, 1863.
17. Woolsey to Farragut, June 28, 1863, *ORN*, XX: 326–328.
18. Ibid.; Irwin, *History of the 19th Army Corps*, 245.
19. Woolsey to Farragut, June 28, 1863, *ORN*, XX: 326–328; Thompson letter.
20. Woolsey to Farragut, June 28, 1863, *ORN*, XX: 326.
21. Wooten, ed., *History of Texas*, II: 714–715; C. D. B., Camp near St. Martinville, La, July 22, 1863 to Editor, Houston [Texas] *Tri-Weekly Telegraph*, August 5, 1863, 4; Thompson letter; Bauer and Medford, "Eyewitness Report on the Battle of Fort Butler," 207.

22. Whitman, and True, *War for the Union*, 545.
23. Wooten, ed., *History of Texas*, II: 714–715; Bauer and Medford, "Eyewitness Report on the Battle of Fort Butler," 207.
24. Wooten, ed., *History of Texas*, II: 714–715; Bauer and Medford, "Eyewitness Report on the Battle of Fort Butler," 207; Thompson letter; C. D. B., near Donaldsonville, June 29, 1863 to editor, Houston [Texas] *Tri-Weekly Telegraph*, July 24, 1863, 2.
25. Woolsey to Farragut, June 28, 1863, *ORN*, XX: 326.
26. Green to Bush, July 3, 1863, *OR*, XXVI, part 1: 227.
27. Bryan, ed., "Whip Them Like the Mischief," 74.
28. Woodman report; Thompson letter; Townsend, *History of the Sixteenth Regiment*, 252–259.
29. Wooten, ed., *History of Texas*, II: 716.
30. Dallas [Texas] *Herald*, 22 July 1863; Samuel K. Savage to "Comrade Willis," The Fitchburg (Massachusetts) *Dailey Sentinel*, September 3, 1909, 4.
31. Henry A. Boyce to John B. Magruder, July 1, 1863, Compiled Service Record of Henry A. Boyce, Record Group 109, M 331.
32. From a young friend in Phillips regiment, Camp near Donaldsonville, July 2, 1863 to editor, Houston [Texas] *Tri-Weekly Telegraph* 15 July 1863, 2; Green to Bush, July 3, 1863, *OR*, XXVI, part 1: 227.
33. From a young friend in Phillips regiment, Camp near Donaldsonville, July 2, 1863 to editor, Houston [Texas] *Tri-Weekly Telegraph* 15 July 1863, 2; Green to Bush, July 3, 1863, *OR*, XXVI, part 1: 227.
34. Collard, "Reminiscences of a Private," 20–21.
35. Townsend, *History of the Sixteenth Regiment*, 256; Thompson letter.
36. Woolsey to Farragut, June 28, 1863, *ORN*, XX: 326.
37. A. M. Weaver, "Abstract log of the U.S.S. *Winona*," *ORN*, XXVI: 357; "The Gunboat *Winona*," New York *Times*, February 4, 1864.
38. Collard, "Reminiscences of a Private," 21; Dallas [Texas] *Herald*, July 29, 1863.
39. Green to Bush, July 3, 1863, *OR*, XXVI, part 1: 228.
40. Samuel K. Savage to "Comrade Willis," The Fitchburg (Massachusetts) *Dailey Sentinel*, September 3, 1909, 4.
41. Wooten, ed., *History of Texas*, II: 716.
42. Witman, and True, *War for the Union*, 545; Townsend, *History of the Sixteenth Regiment*, 252–257.
43. Green to Bush, July 3, 1863, *OR*, XXVI, part 1: 228.
44. Weaver, "Abstract log of the USS *Winona*," *ORN*, XX: 357.
45. Green to Bush, July 3, 1863, *OR*, XXVI, part 1: 227; Mathews, "A Time for Desperate Valor," 23–34.
46. Witman, and True, *War for the Union*, 546; Thompson letter; Townsend, *History of the Sixteenth Regiment*, 252–257.
47. Thompson letter.

48. Ibid.; Commander M. B. Woolsey, "Abstract log of the U.S.S. Princess Royal," *ORN*, XX: 354.
49. McKinnon, "Escape from New Orleans Prison," 19; Sioux to editor, August 14, 1863, Houston [Texas] *Tri-Weekly Telegraph*, August 28, 1863.
50. McKinnon, "Escape from New Orleans Prison," 19; Sioux to editor, August 14, 1863, Houston [Texas] *Tri-Weekly Telegraph*, August 28, 1863; New York *Daily Tribune*, July 11, 1863, 8; Duganne, *Camps and Prisons*, 175–176.
51. Hugh McPhail to Editor, August 3, 1863, Houston [Texas] *Tri-Weekly Telegraph*, August 19, 1863, 2.
52. Wooten, ed., *History of Texas*, II: 716; C. D. B., Camp near St. Martinville, La. July 22, 1863, to Editor, Houston [Texas] *Tri-Weekly Telegraph*, August 5, 1863, 4.
53. Nathaniel P. Banks to Henry Halleck, June 29, 1863, *OR*, XXVI, pt. 1, 47.
54. [author unknown], Houston [Texas] *Tri-Weekly Telegraph*, July 17, 1863, 2; From a young friend in Phillips regiment, Camp near Donaldsonville, July 2, 1863 to editor, Houston [Texas] *Tri-Weekly Telegraph* 15 July 1863, 2; Tom Green, Camp Lafourche, to C. J. Shepherd, June 30, 1863, printed in the Houston [Texas] *Tri-Weekly Telegraph*, August 12, 1863, 2; Dallas [Texas] *Herald*, July 29, 1863.
55. [author unknown], Houston [Texas] *Tri-Weekly Telegraph*, July 17, 1863, 2; From a young friend in Phillips regiment, Camp near Donaldsonville, July 2, 1863, to editor, Houston [Texas] *Tri-Weekly Telegraph*,15 July 1863, 2; Tom Green, Camp Lafourche, to C. J. Shepherd, June 30, 1863, printed in the Houston [Texas] *Tri-Weekly Telegraph*, August 12, 1863, 2; Dallas [Texas] *Herald*, July 29, 1863.
56. Thompson letter; Irwin, *History of the Nineteenth Army Corps*, 245; Berlin, et al., eds., *Freedom*, 459. The defenders from the state of Maine and handful from other New England States were justifiably proud of their defense of the fort. However, most Confederate forces report the presence of a sizable number of blacks that aided the New Englanders in the battle and might account for the relatively low number of casualties among the white troops. Amazingly, there is absolutely no mention of black troops in the Union military accounts. Major Bullen never filed his official report. An insubordinate Federal soldier assassinated Bullen two days later. The only Union accounts by army participants to surface to this point were written many months, or in some cases, years, after the battle.
57. Thompson letter.
58. Dupuy Diary, June 28, 1863.

Chapter 12

1. Joseph E. Johnston to Edmund Kirby Smith, May 31, 1863 *OR*, XXVI, pt. 2: 26.
2. David G. Farragut to Nathaniel P. Banks, May 31, 1863, *OR*, XXVI, pt. 1: 525.
3. C. LeD. Elgee to Richard Taylor, June 22, 1863, *OR*, XXVI, pt. 2: 74.
4. William Elisha Stoker, Delhi, Louisiana, to Elizabeth E. Stoker, Coffeeville, Texas, June 17, 1863, William E. Stoker Papers.
5. Ibid.; Blessington, *The Campaigns of Walker's Texas Division*, 123–124.

6. Blessington, *The Campaigns of Walker's Texas Division*, 125
7. Richard Taylor to W. R. Boggs, June 27, 1863, *OR*, XXVI, pt. 1: 211.
8. Richard Taylor to William Boggs, July 4, 1863, *OR*, XXVI, pt. 1: 213.
9. Ibid.; Taylor, *Destruction and Reconstruction*, 144.
10. Richard Taylor to William Boggs, July 4, 1863, *OR*, XXVI, pt. 1: 213; Thomas Green to Louis Bush, July 14, 1863, *OR*, XXVI, pt. 1: 230.
11. All of the calculations for the rate of ration and ammunition consumption are calculated based on Case, *The Quartermaster's Guide*, 18; U.S. War Department, *How to Feed and Army*. See also Lackey, "Notes on Civil War Logistics: Facts and Stories."
12. Noel, *A Campaign from Santa Fe to the Mississippi*, 51.
13. Richard Taylor to William Boggs, July 4, 1863, *OR*, XXVI, pt. 1: 213.
14. W. H. Emory to Henry Halleck, June 30, 1863, *OR*, XXVI, pt. 1, 609; Daniel Ullmann to Adjutant General, US Army, June 30, 1863, *OR*, XXVI, pt. 1: 609; Emory to Nathaniel P. Banks, *OR*, XXVI, pt. 1: 609; W. D. Smith, General Orders No. 16, June 28, 1863, *OR*, XXVI, pt. 1: 603.
15. W. D. Smith to Lieutenant Colonel Josiah Sawtell, June 28, 1863, *OR*, XXVI, pt. 1: 604–605; W. H. Emory to David G. Farragut, June 28, 1863, *OR*, XXVI, pt. 1: 604; Rein, *Trans-Mississippi Southerners in the Union Army*, 60.
16. W. H. Emory to David G. Farragut, June 28, 1863, *OR*, XXVI, pt. 1: 604. These crossing points would be just about at the New Orleans International Airport upstream and Chalmette National Battlefield downstream.
17. Smith, *Leaves from a Soldier's Diary*, 80.
18. Abstract Log of the USS *Winona*, June 29, *ORN*, XX: 357; Abstract Log of the USS *Princess Royal*, June 29, *ORN*, XX: 353; Abstract Log of the USS *Monongahela*, June 29, 1863, *ORN*, XX: 359; W. D. Smith to Lieutenant Colonel Josiah Sawtell, June 28, 1863, *OR*, XXVI, pt. 1: 604–605;
19. William H. Emory to Commanding Officer at Bonnet Carré, June 29, 1863, *OR*, XXVI, pt. 1: 606–607; Richard Taylor to William Boggs, July 4, 1863, *ORI*, XXVI, pt. 1: 213; W. D. Smith to Colonel Marsh, June 29, 1863, *OR*, XXVI, pt. 1: 607; William H. Emory to Colonel Josiah Sawtell, June 29, 1863, *OR*, XXVI, pt. 1: 607.
20. U. S. Grant to Nathaniel P. Banks, June 30, 1863, *OR*, XXVI, pt. 1: 49; William H. Emory to Nathaniel P. Banks, July 3, 1863, *OR*, XXVI, pt. 1: 49–50; Nathaniel P. Banks to William Emory, July 5, 1863, *OR*, XXVI, pt. 1: 50.
21. Murray, ed., *Madison County Troops in the Civil War*, 59–60.
22. Fortier, Dupuy Diary, June 30, 1863.
23. Ibid., June 30–July 2, 1863; Sleepy Hollow is about six thousand yards from the center of the Mississippi River and would be in range of shells from 30-pounder Parrott Rifles and above shooting over Fort Butler. The ships operating on the Mississippi at the time included USS *Monongahela*, which had a massive 200-pounder Parrot as part of its battery, the USS *Princess Royal* with two 30-pounder Parrots, and USS *Genesee* with a 100-pounder Parrot. On June 30, the

date of this incident, *Princess Royal* fired four 30-pounder shells at "the woods" and *Genesee* fired eleven rounds.

24. Ibid.
25. Ibid.
26. John L. Logan to Joseph E. Johnston, July 6, 1863, *OR*, XXVI, pt. 1: 182; New York *Times*, July 19, 1863, 1–2.
27. New York *Times*, July 19, 1863, 1–2.
28. Peña, *Scarred by War*, 329.
29. Thompson, ed., *From Desert to Bayou*, 45.
30. Rankin, ed., *Diary of a Christian Soldier*, 133.
31. Richard Taylor to William Boggs, July 4, 1863, *OR*, XXVI, pt. 1: 215–216; William H. Emory to Nathaniel P. Banks, July 3, 1863, *ORN*, XX: 332; William H. Emory to Commodore Morris, July 3, 1863, *ORN*, XX: 328–329; Abstract Log, USS *Princess Royal*, July 3, *ORN*, XX: 355; Abstract Log, USS *Monongahela*, July 3, 1863, *ORN*, XX: 359; Abstract Log, USS *Winona*, July 3, 1863, *ORN*, XX: 358.
32. Abstract Log, USS *Monongahela*, July 3, 1863, *ORN*, XX: 360.
33. Thompson, ed., *From Desert to Bayou*, 45.
34. Ibid.
35. W. D. Smith to Lieutenant Colonel Josiah Sawtell, June 30, 1863, *OR*, XXVI, pt. 1: 608.
36. William H. Emory to Commodore Morris, July 2, 1863, *OR*, XXVI, pt. 1, 612; W. H. Emory to David G. Farragut, July 4, 1863, *OR*, XXVI. pt. 1: 616; William Emory to Nathaniel P. Banks, July 4, 1863, *OR*, XXVI, pt. 1: 51; General Orders No. 18, July 3, 1863, *OR*, XXVI, pt. 1: 615.
37. Rankin, ed., *Diary of a Christian Soldier*, 133.
38. Richard Taylor to William Boggs, July 4, 1863, *OR*, XXVI, pt. 1: 214.
39. J. E. Johnston to Edmund Kirby Smith, June 26, 1863, *OR*, XXIV, pt. 3: 979.
40. J. E. Johnston to Edmund Kirby Smith, June 26, 1863, *OR*, XXIV, pt. 3: 979.
41. Richard Taylor to William Boggs, July 4, 1863, *OR*, XXVI, pt. 1: 214.
42. Richard Taylor to William Boggs, July 4, 1863, *OR*, XXVI, pt. 1: 214.
43. Richard Taylor to William Boggs, July 4, 1863, *OR*, XXVI, pt. 1: 214.
44. Richard Taylor to Edward Surget, July 14, 1863, *OR*, XXVI, pt. 2: 110–111.
45. Livius, "Civil War Message Decoded: Help is not on the Way," *The History Blog*, http://www.thehistoryblog.com/archives/9199, accessed May 29, 2014.
46. John Coleman Sibley to "My dearest wife," July 11, 1863, John Coleman Sibley, diary, July 1, 1863, John Coleman Sibley Collection, Box 2; Richard Taylor to Edward Surget, July 14, 1863, *OR*, XXVI, pt. 2: 110–111.
47. Vandiver, ed., *The Civil War Diary of General Josiah Gorgas*, 48.
48. U.S. Grant to Nathaniel P. Banks, July 4, 1863, *OR*, XXIV, pt. 3: 470–471.
49. Tom Green to "Any Confederate Officer commanding east of the Mississippi," July 5, 1863 *OR*, XXVI, pt. 1: 183.
50. Bergeron, ed., *Civil War Reminiscences of Major Silas T. Grisamore*, 124–125.

51. Fortier, Dupuy Diary, July 4, 1863.
52. J. W. Watkins, Bayou Lafourche, Louisiana, to Irene Watkins, Marlin, Texas, July 7, 1863, J. W. Watkins letters.
53. Peña, *Scarred by War*, 329–330; Irwin, *History of the Nineteenth Army Corps*, 247; Abstract Log, USS *Kineo*, July 5, 1863, *ORN*, XX: 349.

Chapter 13

1. Abstract Log, USS *Winona*, July 5, *ORN*, XX: 358.
2. Abstract Log, USS *Monongahela*, July 5, 1863, *ORN*, XX: 360; Peña, *Scarred by War*, 332–333.
3. USS *Kineo*, July 6, 1863, *ORN*, XX: 349; Abstract Log, USS *Princess Royal*, July 6, 1863, *ORN*, XX: 355.
4. USS *Kineo*, July 6, 1863, *ORN*, XX: 349; Abstract Log, USS *Princess Royal*, July 6, 1863, *ORN*, XX: 355.
5. D. G. Farragut to W. H. Emory, July 5, 1863, *OR*, XXVI, pt. 1: 617; W. D. Smith, Special Orders No. 21, July 6, 1863, *OR*, XXVI, pt. 1: 618.
6. Nathaniel P. Banks to Henry Halleck, July 6, 1863, *OR*, XXVI, pt. 1: 48–49.
7. T. A. Faries to H. T. Wade, July 10, *OR*, XXVI, pt. 1, 220–223.
8. Abstract Log, USS *Monongahela*, July 7, 1863, *ORN*, XX: 360; Abstract Log, USS *New London*, July 7, 1863, *ORN*, XX: 352.
9. David G. Farragut to Gideon Welles, July 10, 1863, in *Report of the Secretary of the Navy, December, 1863* (Washington: Government Printing Office, 1863), 382 : David G. Farragut to Commander Macomb, July 7, 1863, *OR*, XX: 333.
10. N. P. Banks to U.S. Grant, July 7, 1863, *OR*, XXVI, pt. 1: 619–620; Richard Irwin to W. H. Emory, July 7, 1863, *OR*, XXVI, pt. 1: 619; W. H. Emory to Commodore Morris, July 8, 1863, *OR*, XXVI pt. 1: 627–628; Nathaniel P. Banks to Henry Halleck, July 10, 1863, *OR*, XXVI, pt. 1: 55.
11. Charles Emerson to Richard Irwin, July 8, 1863, *OR*, XXVI, pt. 1: 203–204.
12. N. P. Banks to U.S. Grant, July 7, 1863, *OR*, XXVI, pt. 1: 619–620; Richard Irwin to W. H. Emory, July 7, 1863, *OR*, XXVI, pt. 1: 619; W. H. Emory to Commodore Morris, July 8, 1863, *OR*, XXVI, pt. 1: 627–628; Nathaniel P. Banks to henry Halleck, July 10, 1863, *OR*, XXVI, pt. 1: 55.
13. Rankin, ed., *Diary of a Christian Soldier*, 134.
14. John L. Logan to B. S. Ewell, July 8, 1863, *OR*, XXVI, pt. 1: 182.
15. David G. Farragut to Captain Jenkins, July 9, 1863, *ORN*, XX, 336; Peña, *Scarred by War*, 341; Abstract Log of USS Kineo, July 9, 1863, *ORN*, XX: 350.
16. T. A. Faries to H. F. Wade, Jr., July 10, 1863, *OR*, XXVI, pt. 1: 221; D. G. Farragut to Gideon Welles, July 10, 1863, *ORN*, XX: 340–341.
17. T. A. Faries to H. F. Wade, Jr., July 10, 1863, *OR*, XXVI, pt. 1: 221; D. G. Farragut to Gideon Welles, July 10, 1863, *ORN*, XX: 340–341.
18. G. H. Perkins to D. G. Farragut, July 13, 1863, *ORN*, XX: 341.
19. Ibid.

20. Ibid.
21. T. A. Faries to H. F. Wade, July 14, 1863, *OR*, XXVI, pt. 1: 220–222.
22. G. H. Perkins to D. G. Farragut, July 13, 1863, *ORN*, XX: 341–342; Abstract Log of the USS *New London*, July 10, 1863, *ORN*, XX: 352–353.
23. G. H. Perkins to D. G. Farragut, July 13, 1863, *ORN*, XX: 341–342; Abstract Log of the USS *New London*, July 10, 1863, *ORN*, XX: 352–353.
24. T. A. Faries to H. F. Wade, July 14, 1863, *OR*, XXVI, pt. 1, 220–222.
25. Ibid.
26. Ibid.
27. T. A. Faries to H. F. Wade, July 14, 1863, *OR*, XXVI, pt. 1, 220–222; Lane, *The Adventures and Recollections of General Walter P. Lane*, 106.
28. T. A. Faries to H. F. Wade, July 14, 1863, *OR*, XXVI, pt. 1, 220–222; Lane, *The Adventures and Recollections of General Walter P. Lane*, 106.

Chapter 14

1. Clark, *The One Hundred and Sixteenth Regiment*, 110.
2. Peña, *Scarred by War*, 346–347; Pellet, *History of the 114th Regiment*, 134–135
3. Irwin, *History of the 19th Army Corps*, 217–218.
4. Ibid.
5. Klein, "Civil War Memories."
6. Irwin, *History of the 19th Army Corps*, 218.
7. Taylor, *Destruction and Reconstruction*, 145
8. Barr, *Polignac's Texas Brigade*, 20–21; George Guess, Camp near Thibodaux, July 6, 1863, to S. H. Cockrell, Dallas, Texas, in Guess (George W.) Letters, Mss. 793, Louisiana and Lower Mississippi Valley Collections, hereafter cited as George Guess Letters; Taylor, *Destruction and Reconstruction*, 145.
9. Edmund Kirby Smith to Samuel Cooper, July 16, 1863, *OR*, XXVI, pt. 1: 212.
10. Richard Irwin, Special Orders No. 166, July 10, 1863, *OR*, XXVI, pt. 1: 632.
11. Nathaniel P. Banks to Captain Jenkins, July 10, 1863, *ORN*, XX, 374–375; Banks to Farragut, July 10, 1863, *ORN*, XX: 375; Farragut to James S. Palmer, July 11, 1863, *ORN*, XX: 376; Farragut to M. Jordan, July 18, 1863, *ORN*, XX: 379.
12. Bangs, "The Ullman Brigade," II: 296, 308.
13. Johns, *Life with the Forty-Ninth Massachusetts Volunteers*, 330.
14. Bangs, "The Ullman Brigade," 2: 296, 309; Thirty-Eighth Congress, Second Session, *Report of the Joint Committee on the Conduct of the War at the Thirty-Eighth Congress*, 346.
15. Farragut to George Wiggin, July 18, 1863, *ORN*, XX: 379.
16. Howe, *Passages from the Life of Henry Warren Howe*, 49–50, 139; Johns, *Life with the Forty-Ninth Massachusetts Volunteers*, 335.
17. Dupuy diary, August 22, 1863.
18. Ibid.
19. Ibid.

20. Ibid.
21. Ibid.
22. Collard, "Reminiscences of a Private," 22.
23. Ibid., 23.
24. Johns, *Life with the Forty-Ninth Massachusetts*, 335; Collard, "Reminiscences of a Private," 23.
25. Howe, *Passages*, 140.
26. Howe, *Passages*, 49–50, 139–140.
27. Nathan Dudley to W. W. Carruth, July 15, 1863, *OR*, XXVI, pt. 1: 207.
28. Dupuy Diary, August 22, 1863.
29. Ibid.; Collard, "Reminiscences of a Private," 2.
30. Dupuy Diary, August 22, 1863; Nathan Dudley to W. W. Carruth, July 15, 1863, *OR*, XXVI, pt. 1: 207.
31. Irwin, *Nineteenth Army Corps*, 252.
32. New York State Division of Military and Naval Affairs, "161st Regiment New York Volunteer Infantry."
33. Dupuy Diary, August 22, 1863.
34. Ibid.
35. Ibid.; Nathan Dudley to W. W. Carruth, July 15, 1863, *OR*, XXVI, pt. 1: 207.

Chapter 15

1. Taylor, *Destruction and Reconstruction*, 145.
2. Nathan Dudley to W. W. Carruth, July 15, 1863, *OR*, XXVI, pt. 1: 208; T. A. Faries to H. F. Wade, July 14, 1863, *OR*, XXVI, pt. 1: 222; Dupuy diary, August 22, 1863.
3. T. A. Faries to H. F. Wade, July 14, 1863, *OR*, XXVI, pt. 1: 222; Correspondent of the *Boston Traveller*, "The War in Louisiana: Particulars of the Disaster near Donaldsonville, Items from New Orleans, July 18, 1863," New York *Times*, August 2, 1863.
4. Nathan Dudley to W. W. Carruth, July 15, 1863, *OR*, XXVI, pt. 1: 208; T. A. Faries to H. F. Wade, July 14, 1863, *OR*, XXVI, pt. 1: 222; Dupuy diary, August 22, 1863.
5. Nathan Dudley to W. W. Carruth, July 15, 1863, *OR*, XXVI, pt. 1: 208; T. A. Faries to H. F. Wade, July 14, 1863, *OR*, XXVI, pt. 1: 222; Dupuy diary, August 22, 1863.
6. Dupuy diary, August 22, 1863.
7. Dudley to Carruth, July 15, 1863, *OR*, XXVI, pt. 1: 208; T. A. Faries to H. F. Wade, July 14, 1863, *OR*, XXVI, pt. 1: 222.
8. Dudley to Carruth, July 15, 1863, *OR*, XXVI, pt. 1, 208; T. A. Faries to H. F. Wade, July 14, 1863, *OR*, XXVI, pt. 1: 222.
9. T. A. Faries to H. F. Wade, July 14, 1863, *OR*, XXVI, pt. 1: 223; Dudley to Carruth, July 15, 1863, *OR*, XXVI, pt. 1: 208; Dupuy diary, August 22, 1863.
10. T. A. Faries to H. F. Wade, July 14, 1863, *OR*, XXVI, pt. 1: 223; Dudley to Carruth, July 15, 1863, *OR*, XXVI, pt. 1: 208; Dupuy diary, August 22, 1863.
11. Thomas Green to Louis Bush, July 14, 1863, *OR*, XXVI, pt. 1: 231.

12. Ibid.
13. Ibid.
14. Ibid.; Lane, *The Adventures and Recollections of General Walter P. Lane*, 108; John E. Hart, Thibodaux, Louisiana, July 16, 1863, to editor, Houston (Texas) *Tri-Weekly Telegraph*, July 31, 1863.
15. Johns, *Life with the Forty Ninth Massachusetts*, 335; Plummer, *History of the Forty-Eighth Regiment*, 52; Clark, *The One Hundred and Sixteenth Regiment* , 110.
16. McCann, *The Campaigns of the Civil War*, 97.
17. Dudley to Carruth, July 15, 1863, *OR*, XXVI, pt. 1, 208.
18. McCann, *The Campaigns of the Civil War*, 97.
19. Ibid.
20. Ibid.
21. Ibid.
22. Correspondent of the *Boston Traveller*, "The War in Louisiana: Particulars of the Disaster near Donaldsonville, Items from New Orleans, July 18, 1863," New York *Times*, August 2, 1863; McCann, *The Campaigns of the Civil War*, 97.
23. Thomas Green to Louis Bush, July 14, 1863, *OR*, XXVI, pt. 1, 231; T. A. Faries to H. F. Wade, July 14, 1863, *OR*, XXVI, pt. 1, 223; Dudley to Carruth, July 15, 1863, *OR*, XXVI, pt. 1, 208; C. D. B., 5 miles below Donaldsonville, July 14, 1863, to editor, Houston (Texas) *Tri-Weekly Telegraph*, August 10, 1863.
24. McCann, *The Campaigns of the Civil War*, 97–98.
25. Ibid., 98.
26. Johns, *Forty-Ninth Massachusetts*, 335.
27. Dudley to Carruth, July 15, 1863, *OR*, XXVI, pt. 1: 208; C. D. B., 5 miles below Donaldsonville, July 14, 1863, to editor, Houston (Texas) *Tri-Weekly Telegraph*, August 10, 1863.
28. Dudley to Carruth, July 15, 1863, *OR*, XXVI, pt. 1, 208.
29. Howe, *Passages from the Life of Henry Warren Howe*, 140; Cuvier Grover to Richard Irwin, July 14, 1863, *OR*, XXVI, pt. 1, 205; C. D. B., 5 miles below Donaldsonville, July 14, 1863, to editor, Houston (Texas) *Tri-Weekly Telegraph*, August 10, 1863; New York State Division of Military and Naval Affairs, "161st Regiment New York Volunteer Infantry Civil War News Paper Clippings."
30. New York State Division of Military and Naval Affairs, "161st Regiment New York Volunteer Infantry Civil War News Paper Clippings."
31. John E. Hart, Thibodaux, Louisiana, July 16, 1863, to editor, Houston (Texas) *Tri-Weekly Telegraph*, July 31, 1863; New York State Division of Military and Naval Affairs, "161st Regiment New York Volunteer Infantry Civil War News Paper Clippings."
32. Plummer, *History of the Forty-Eighth Regiment*, 52; Johns, *Forty-Ninth Massachusetts*, 335; Clark, *The One Hundred and Sixteenth Regiment*, 111.
33. Plummer, *History of the Forty-Eighth Regiment*, 52; Johns, *Forty-Ninth Massachusetts*, 335; Clark, *The One Hundred and Sixteenth Regiment*, 111.

34. Plummer, *History of the Forty-Eighth Regiment*, 52.
35. Johns, *Forty-Ninth Massachusetts*, 335.
36. Howe, *Passages from the Life of Henry Warren Howe*, 140; Plummer, *Forty-Eighth Regiment*, 52; Clark, *The One Hundred and Sixteenth Regiment*, 111; Cuvier Grover to Richard Irwin, July 14, 1863, *OR*, XXVI, pt. 1: 205.
37. Clark, *The One Hundred and Sixteenth Regiment*, 112.
38. John W. Lane, July 14, 1863, in Dallas (Texas) *Herald*, August 5, 1863.
39. Clark, *The One Hundred and Sixteenth Regiment*, 112; Irwin, *19th Army Corps*, 253.
40. Clark, *The One Hundred and Sixteenth Regiment*, 112; Irwin, *19th Army Corps*, 253.
41. Clark, *The One Hundred and Sixteenth Regiment*, 113.
42. Johns, *Forty-Ninth Massachusetts*, 335.
43. Ibid. A rod is a surveyor's tool and unit of length equal to 5½ yards, 16½ feet, or 1/320th of a statute mile and one-fourth of a surveyor's chain.
44. Plummer, *Forty-Eighth Regiment*, 54.
45. Pellet, *History of the 114th Regiment*, 135.
46. Green to Bush, July 14, 1863, *OR*, XXVI, pt. 1, 231; T. A. Faries to H. F. Wade, July 14, 1863, *OR*, XXVI, pt. 1, 223.
47. G. Norman Lieber, General Orders No. 67, September 10, 1863, *OR*, XXVI, pt. 1: 205–206; Cuvier Grover to Richard Irwin, July 14, 1863, *OR*, XXVI, pt. 1: 204.
48. Irwin, *19th Army Corps*, 252; Clark, *The One Hundred and Sixteenth Regiment*, 113.
49. Howe, *Passages from the Life of Henry Warren Howe*, 140; Smith, *Leaves from a Soldier's Diary*, 89-90.
50. Johns, *Forty-Ninth Massachusetts*, 337.
51. Plummer, *Forty-Eighth Regiment*, 55.
52. Dupuy diary, August 22, 1863.
53. J. W. Watkins, Bayou Lafourche, Louisiana, to Irene Watkins, Marlin, Texas, July 15, 1863, J. W. Watkins letters,; McCann, *The Campaigns of the Civil War*, 98.
54. W. L. Robards, Camp Near Washington, Louisiana, July 27, 1863, to editor, Houston (Texas) *Tri-Weekly Telegraph*, August 10, 1863.
55. Green to Bush, July 14, 1863, *OR*, XXVI, pt. 1, 232; Taylor to Boggs, July 13, 1863, *OR*, XXVI, pt. 1: 215.

Chapter 16

1. J. W. Watkins, Bayou Lafourche, Louisiana, to Irene Watkins, Marlin, Texas, July 15, 1863, J. W. Watkins letters.
2. McCann, *The Campaigns of the Civil War*, 98; Irwin, *History of the 19th Army Corps*, 254.
3. Hepworth, *The Whip, Hoe, and Sword*, 287–288.
4. Irwin, *History of the 19th Army Corps*, 254.
5. Collard, "The Courier's Story," 32; Bearss, ed., *A Louisiana Confederate*, 5–7.
6. Bearss, ed., *A Louisiana Confederate*, 5–7.
7. This may have been the modest sugar operation of Delonde & Brothers, nearly halfway between Napoleonville and Thibodaux.

8. Collard, "The Courier's Story," 32.
9. Ibid.; Howell Diary, July 18, 1863, W. Randolph Howell Papers.
10. Collard, "The Courier's Story," 32; Howell Diary, July 18, 1863, W. Randolph Howell Papers; Brasseaux and Fontenot, *Steamboats on Louisiana Bayous*, 161, 196.
11. Richard Taylor to Edward Surget, July 14, 1863, *OR*, XXVI, pt. 2: 110–111.
12. Taylor to John B. Magruder, July 17, 1863, *OR*, XXVI, pt. 2: 116–117.
13. Ibid.
14. Keet McDade, New Iberia, Louisiana, to Ann Cochran, July 22, 1863, McDade Letters,; Williams Diary, July 18, 1863.
15. Williams Diary, July 18, 1863; Bergeron, Jr., ed., *The Civil War Reminiscences of Major Silas T. Grisamore*, 126.
16. The auction occurred in New Iberia on July 24, 1863. See Bearss, ed., *A Louisiana Confederate*, 8.
17. John Coleman Sibley to wife, November 17, 1863, p. 136, in John Coleman Sibley Collection.
18. Moore, ed., *The Rebellion*, VII: 83–84.
19. Ibid., VII: 82.
20. Ibid.
21. Bearss, ed., *A Louisiana Confederate*, 6.
22. Farragut to T. A. Jenkins, July 15, 1863, *ORN*, XX: 391.
23. Keet McDade, New Iberia, Louisiana, to Ann Cochran, July 22, 1863, McDade Letters; H. N. Connor Diary, July 21, 1863, Block, ed., "The Diary of 1st Sergeant H. N. Connor."
24. Miss Sidney Harding Diaries, July 1863, U-230, Mss #721.
25. John Coleman Sibley to wife, July 21, 1863, John Coleman Sibley Collection.
26. Dungan, *History of the Nineteenth Regiment*, 81.
27. Abstract Log of the USS *Estrella*, July 23, 1863, *ORN*, XX: 380; Frank H. Peck to Richard Irwin, July 25, 1863, *OR*, XXVI, pt. 1: 653; Peck to Irwin, July 30, 1863, *OR*, XXVI, pt. 1: 662; Moore, ed. *The Rebellion Record*, VII: 83.
28. Abstract Log of the USS *Estrella*, July 23, 1863, *ORN*, XX: 380; Peck to Irwin, July 25, 1863, *OR*, XXVI, pt. 1: 653; Peck to Irwin, July 30, 1863, *OR*, XXVI, pt. 1: 662.
29. Fowler, *Memorial of William Fowler*, 55.
30. Francis J. Herron to Ulysses S. Grant, August 7, 1863, *OR*, XXIV, pt. 3: 581.

Chapter 17

1. Thomas Jefferson League, Camp Hunter, Louisiana, to Mary D. League, Galveston, Texas, August 8, 1863, Thomas Jefferson League Paperss; Bergeron, Jr., *The Civil War Reminiscences of Major Silas T. Grisamore*, 123.
2. E. B. Cox, Salt Works, [Petite Anse Island, La.] to E. McIlhenny, July 27, 1863, Sarah Avery McIlhenny Collection.
3. Jefferson Davis to Edmund Kirby Smith, July 14, 1863, *OR*, XXII, pt. 2: 925–927; Vandiver, ed., *Diary of General Josiah Gorgas*, 49–50.

4. Jefferson Davis to Edmund Kirby Smith, July 14, 1863, *OR*, XXII, pt. 2: 925–927.
5. Ibid.
6. Bearss, ed., *A Louisiana Confederate*, 8.
7. Ibid., 10.
8. Bearss, ed., *A Louisiana Confederate*, 12–13; O. M. A., in camp on Vermilion Bayou, August 1, 1863, to Editor, [Houston, Texas] *Tri-Weekly Telegraph*, published August 21, 1863.
9. Bearss, ed., *A Louisiana Confederate*, 12–13; O. M. A., in camp on Vermilion Bayou, August 1, 1863, to Editor, [Houston, Texas] *Tri-Weekly Telegraph*, published August 21, 1863.
10. Sallie Patrick, Anderson, Grimes County, Texas, to William Randolph Howell, July 27, 1863, W. Randolph Howell Papers.
11. Ibid.
12. Thomas Jefferson League, Camp Hunter, Louisiana, to Mary D. League, Galveston, Texas, August 8, 1863, Thomas Jefferson League Papers.
13. Thomas Jefferson League, Camp Hunter, Louisiana, to Mary D. League, Galveston, Texas, August 12, 1863, Thomas Jefferson League Papers.
14. Ibid.
15. Vandiver, ed., *Diary of General Josiah Gorgas*, 55.
16. William Frederick Weeks, New Iberia, Louisiana, to Judge John Moore, October 31, 1863, David Weeks and Family Papers.
17. Fern, ed., *Diary of a Refugee*, 44.
18. Ibid.
19. Ibid.
20. Anderson, ed., *Brokenburn*, 184–185; Fern, ed., *Diary of a Refugee*, 40.
21. Anderson, ed., *Brokenburn*, 191.
22. Fern, ed., *Diary of a Refugee*, 38; Anderson, ed., *Brokenburn*, 223–224.
23. Anderson, ed., *Brokenburn*, 223.
24. Fern, ed., *Diary of a Refugee*, 40.
25. Anderson, ed., *Brokenburn*, 224–227; Fern, ed., *Diary of a Refugee*, 38.
26. Fern, ed., *Diary of a Refugee*, 44.
27. Anderson, ed., *Brokenburn*, 225.
28. Ibid.
29. Manning in Botkin, ed., *Slave Narratives*, XIII: 215–223.
30. Ibid.
31. Ibid.
32. Mary Eliza Avery McIlhenny to Sister Anna, August 23, 1863, Sarah Avery McIlhenny Collection.
33. Anderson, ed., *Brokenburn*, 230; Mary Eliza Avery McIlhenny to Sister Anna, August 23, 1863, Sarah Avery McIlhenny Collection.
34. Anderson, ed., *Brokenburn*, 230; Mary Eliza Avery McIlhenny to Sister Anna, August 23, 1863, Sarah Avery McIlhenny Collection.

35. Muenster and Edwards, eds., *From Tallow Candle to Television*, 26–27.
36. Ibid., 27–30.
37. Ibid., 31.
38. William Elisha Stoker, Alexandria, Louisiana, to Elizabeth E. Stoker, Coffeeville, Texas, May 29, 1863, William E. Stoker Papers. Changes in spelling have been made from the original.
39. Sells in Botkin, ed., *Slave Narratives*, XVI, pt. 4: 44–46.
40. Ibid.
41. F. S. Wade, "Hog Eye Stories," 43.
42. Lincecum, Phillips, and. Redshaw, eds., *Gideon Lincecum's Sword*, 225.
43. Ibid., 242–243.
44. [Sarah Carothers] to William Carothers, n.d., Duncan C. Carothers Collection.
45. Collard, "Reminiscences of a Private, Co. G, 7th Texas Cavalry," 36–37.
46. Ibid.

Epilogue

1. Jordan-Bychov, Branum, and.Hood, eds., "The Boesel Letters," 474.
2. Ibid., 476.
3. H. W. Halleck to N. P. Banks, July 24, 1863, *OR*, XXVI, pt. 1.: 652–653.
4. Edwin M. Stanton to George Shepley, August 24, 1863, *OR*, Series III, III: 711.
5. Halleck to Banks, July 24, 1863, *OR*, XXVI, pt. 1: 652–653.
6. Brasseaux and Moody, eds., *Ruined by this Miserable War*, 12–13.
7. Nathaniel P. Banks to Abraham Lincoln, August 17, 1863, Abraham Lincoln Papers at the Library of Congress.
8. Brasseaux and Moody, eds., *Ruined by this Miserable War*, 12–13.
9. Pound, "Slave to the Ex-Slave Narratives," 95–98.
10. Lincoln, *Collected Works*, VI: 406–407.
11. Ibid., VI: 410.
12. Ibid.
13. Ibid., 478–479; Compiled Service Record for Joseph Ferdinand Boesel, Compiled Military Service Records of Confederate Soldiers, Record Group 109. He is described as 5'7", fair hair and light complexion with gray eyes.
14. Jordan-Bychov, Branum, and Hood, eds., "The Boesel Letters," 479–480.
15. Ibid., 480.
16. Compiled Service Record for Joseph Ferdinand Boesel.

Sources Consulted

Manuscript Collections

Dolph Briscoe Center for American History, University of Texas, Austin

Howell, Randolph W., Papers, 1861–1879.

Library of Congress, Washington, D.C.

Lincoln, Abraham, Papers, transcribed and annotated by the Lincoln Studies Center, Knox College, Galesburg, Illinois.

Louisiana and Lower Mississippi Valley Collection, LSU Libraries, Baton Rouge, Louisiana

Civil War Letters, 1863, MSS 3188, Misc.: C.

Guess, (George W.), Letters, Mss. 793.

Harding, Sidney, Diaries, July 1863, U-230, Mss. 721.

Lauve, Gustave, Letter, Mss. 893.

Shelly, William, Diary, Mss. 3604.

Weeks, David, and Family Papers.

Wharton, Edward Clifton, and Family Papers, Mss. 1553, 1575, 1594, 1610, 1613, 1663, 1714, 1736.

Maine State Archives, Augusta, Maine

Adjutant General Records, 1895, History Material.

Adjutant General Records, Regimental Correspondence, 28th Maine.

Civil War Correspondence, Regimental Correspondence, Records of the Adjutant General, Pre-1940.

McIlhenny Company Archives, McIlhenny Company, Avery Island, Louisiana

Avery, Sarah, McIlhenny Collection.

National Archives and Records Administration

Compiled Military Service Records of Volunteer Soldiers Who Served the United States, Record Group 94.

Orders and Circulars, 1797–1910, Records of the Adjutant General's Office, 1780s–1917, Record Group 94.

Compiled Military Service Records of Confederate Soldiers, Record Group 109.

National Civil War Museum, Harrisburg, Pennsylvania

Stoker, William E., Papers.

Huntington Library, San Marino, California.

Burrud, John B., Papers, 1862–1870, MssHm 75115–75334.

Private Collections

Petticolas, Alfred, Diary, Volume III, courtesy of Don Alberts, Rio Rancho, New Mexico.

Block, W. T., ed., "The Diary of 1st Sergeant H. N. Connor," available at http://www.wtblock.com/wtblockjr/diaryof.htm.

Collard, Felix Robert, "Reminiscences of a Private, Co. G, 7th Texas Cavalry, Sibley

Brigade, CSA." (typescript in possession of the author and used with permission of Dr. Felix Robert Collard, Silver City, New Mexico).

Collard, Felix Robert. "The Courier's Story." (typescript in possession of the author and used with permission of Dr. Felix Robert Collard, Silver City, New Mexico).

Fortier, Alcee trans., Heléne Dupuy, *Memorable Days and Various Notable Circumstances during the Civil War in the United States in the State of Louisiana from 1861 to 1865*, diary entry June 20, 1863, typescript in the possession of the author.

Klein, Joseph. "Civil War Memories," available at http://marilyndoyle.com/Klein/klein.html.

Kopke, H. F. Letters, manuscript in possession of Randy Mallory, Tyler, Texas.

Mahoney, Harry. "The Passing of Harry Mahoney, A Negro Politician of Radical Days." Unsourced newspaper clipping in possession of the author.

McDade, Keet, Letters. Typescript courtesy of Vernon Williams, Abilene Christian University.

Milliken's Bend, Louisiana, to My Dear Pa, June 8, 1863, original in possession of Mary Kay Lester Forbes, Salisbury, North Carolina.

Wade, F. S. "Hog Eye Stories," originally published in the Elgin (Texas) *Courier*.

Rosenberg Library, Galveston, Texas

Jefferson League, Thomas, Papers, 1855–1863.

Harold B. Simpson Confederate Research Center, Hillsboro, Texas

Watkins, John W. letters.

"The Diary of Robert Thomas Williams: arches, Skirmishes, and Battles of the Fourth Regiment, Texas Mounted Volunteers, October 1861 to November 1865."

State Library of Louisiana, Baton Rouge, Louisiana

Hazel Breaux and Robert McKinney, "Interview with ex-slave Catherine Cornelius in the 1940s," WPA Collection.

Archives and Information Division, Texas State Library and Archives Commission

Carothers Duncan C., family papers, diary, and correspondence.

Special Collections, University of Texas at Arlington

Hackney, Mary Martha, transcriptions of Price Family Papers.

Watson Memorial Library, Cammie G. Watson Research Center, Northwestern State University, Natchitoches, Louisiana

Aimer Collection.

Machen, Henry L., Collection.

Sibley, John Coleman, Collection.

Rubenstein Library, Duke University, Durham, North Carolina

Rootes, Sarah A., Correspondence, 1822–1884.

Young Sanders Center, Franklin, Louisiana

John Adam Lorenz, "History of John Adam Lorenz."

U.S. Government Documents

Naval Historical Center, Department of the Navy. *Dictionary of American Fighting Ships*. 8 vols. Washington, D.C.: Government Printing Office, 1975–81.

Thirty-Eighth Congress, Second Session, *Report of the Joint Committee on the Conduct of the War at the Thirty-Eighth Congress*. Washington, D.C.: Government Printing Office, 1865.

U.S. Department of the Navy. *Report of the Secretary of the Navy, December, 1863* Washington: Government Printing Office, 1863.

U.S. Naval War Records Office. *Official Records of the Union and Confederate Navies in the War of the Rebellion*. 27 vols. Washington, D.C.: Government Printing Office, 1894–1922.

U.S. War Department. *The War of the Rebellion: A Compilation of the Official Records of the Union and Confederate Armies*. 128 vols. Washington, D.C.: Government Printing Office, 1880–1901.

Newspapers

Amesbury [Massachusetts] *Villager*

Bellville [Texas] *Countryman*

Boston [Massachusetts] *Herald*

Boston [Massachusetts] *Morning Journal*

Boston [Massachusetts] *Traveler*

Chattanooga [Tennessee] *Rebel*

Cincinnati [Ohio] *Daily Commercial*

Dallas [Texas] *Herald*

Fitchburg [Massachusetts] *Dailey Sentinel*

Franklin [Louisiana] *Planters' Banner*

Houston [Texas] *Tri-Weekly Telegraph*

New Orleans [Louisiana] *Delta*

New York [New York] *Times*

New York [New York] *Irish American*

New York *Times* "Opinionator"

Overton [Texas] *Sharp Shooter*

Wheeling [West Virginia] *Daily Intelligencer*

Published Primary Sources

Anderson, John Q. ed., *Brokenburn: The Journal of Kate Stone, 1861–1868*. Baton Rouge: Louisiana State University Press, 1955.

Bangs, I. S. "The Ullman Brigade," *War Papers Read Before the Commandery of the State of Maine, Military Order of the Loyal Legion of the United States*. 4 volumes. Portland: Lefavor-Tower Company, 1898–1915.

Basler, Roy P. ed. *Collected Works of Abraham Lincoln*. Springfield, Ill.: The Abraham Lincoln Association, 1953.

Bauer, Craig, and Todd Mefford. "Eyewitness Report on the Battle of Fort Butler, Donaldsonville, Louisiana, June 27–28, 1863, and a Review of African-American Participation in the Fight." *Louisiana History*, 45, No. 2 (Spring, 2004), 201–208.

Bearrs, Edwin C. ed., *A Louisiana Confederate: The Diary of Felix Pierre Poché*, translated by Eugenie Watson Somdel. Natchitoches: Louisiana Studies Institute, Northwestern State University, 1972.

Beecher, Dr. Harris H. *Record of the 114th Regiment, N.Y.S.V.: Where It Went, What It Saw, and What It Did*. Norwich, N.Y.: J. F. Hubbard, Jr., 1866.

Bergeron, Arthur W., Jr., ed. *Civil War Reminiscences of Major Silas T. Grisamore, CSA*. Baton Rouge: Louisiana State University Press, 1993.

Berlin, Ira, Thavolia Glymph, Steven F. Miller, Joseph P. Reidy, Leslie S. Rowland, and Julie Saville, eds. *Freedom: A Documentary History of Emancipation, 1861–1867, Selected from the Holdings of the National Archives of the United States*. Series I, Volume III: *The Wartime Genesis of Free Labor: The Lower South*. New York: Cambridge University Press, 1990.

Berlin, Ira, Joseph P. Reidy, Leslie S. Rowland, eds. *Freedom's Soldiers: The Black Military Experience in the Civil War*. New York: Cambridge University Press, 1998.

Blessington, J. P. *The Campaigns of Walker's Texas Division*. Austin: State House Press, 1994.

Bosson, Charles F. *History of the Forty-Second Regiment Infantry, Massachusetts Volunteers, 1862, 1863, 1864*. Boston: Mills, Knight, and Company, 1886.

Botkin, Benjamin A. ed., *Slave Narratives: A Folk History of Slavery in the United States from Interviews with Former Slaves*. 17 volumes. Washington, D.C.: Library of Congress, 1941.

Brasseaux, Carl A., and Catherine Carmines Moody, eds. *Ruined by this Miserable War: The Dispatches of Charles Prosper Fauconnet, a French Diplomat in New Orleans, 1863–1868*. Knoxville: University of Tennessee Press, 2012.

Bryan, Jimmy L. ed., "Whip Them Like the Mischief: The Civil War Letters of Frank and Mintie Price." *East Texas Historical Journal*, 36, no. 2 (1998): 68–84.

Camouche, Annie Jeter. *The Life of Annie Jeter Carmouche*. New Roads, La.: Pointe Coupée Historical Society, n.d.

Clark, Orton S. *The One Hundred and Sixteenth Regiment of New York State Volunteers*. Buffalo: Mathews and Warren, 1868.

Cotham, Edward T., Jr., ed. *The Southern Journey of a Civil War Marine: The Illustrated Notebook of Henry O. Gusley*. Austin: University of Texas Press, 2006.

De Forest, John William. *A Volunteer's Adventures: A Union Captain's Record of the Civil War*. Baton Rouge: Louisiana State University Press, 1996.

Duganne, Augustine Joseph Hickey. *Camps and Prisons: Twenty Months in the Department of the Gulf*. New York: J. P. Robens, Publisher, 1865.

Dungan, J[ames] Irvine. *History of the Nineteenth Regiment, Iowa Volunteer Infantry*. Davenport, Iowa: Lush and Griggs, 1865.

Eaton, John. *Grant, Lincoln, and the Freedmen: Reminiscences of the Civil War with Special Reference to the Work for Contrabands and Freedmen of the Mississippi Valley*. New York: Longmans, Green and Company, 1907.

Edmonds, David S., ed. *The Conduct of Federal Troops in Louisiana during the*

Invasions of 1863 and 1864: Official Report Compiled from the Sworn Testimony under Direction of Governor Henry W. Allen, Shreveport, April 1865. Lafayette, La.: Acadiana Press, 1988.

Ewer, James K. *The Third Massachusetts Cavalry in the War for the Union.* Maplewood, Mass.: William G. J. Perry Press for the Historical Committee of the Regimental Association, 1903.

Fern, Frances ed., *Diary of a Refugee* [Clarissa Grant Hewitt, author]. New York: Moffat, Yard and Company, 1910.

Fowler, P. H. *Memorial of William Fowler.* New York: Anson D. F. Randolph & Company, 1875.

Harding, George C. *The Miscellaneous Writings of George C. Harding.* Indianapolis: Carlon and Hollenbeck, Printers and Binders, 1882.

Haynes, Dennis E. *A Thrilling Narrative: A Memoir of a Southern Unionist*, edited by Arthur Bergeron, Jr. Fayetteville: University of Arkansas Press, 2006.

Hepworth, George H. *The Whip, the Hoe, and Sword; or, the Gulf-Department in '63.* Boston: Walker, Wise and Company, 1864.

Howard, R. L. *History of the 124th Regiment Illinois Infantry Volunteers: Otherwise known as the Hundred and Two Dozen from August 1862–August 1865.* Springfield, Ill.: H. W. Rokker, 1880.

Howe, Henry Warren. *Passages from the Life of Henry Warren Howe Consisting of Diary and Letters Written During the Civil War, 1861–1865.* Lowell, Mass.: Courier-Citizen Company, 1899.

Irwin, Richard B. *History of the 19th Army Corps.* New York: G. P. Putnam's Sons, 1893.

Johns, Henry T. *Life with the Forty-Ninth Massachusetts Volunteers.* Pittsfield, Mass.: C. A. Alvord, 1864.

Jordan-Bychkov, Terry G., Allen R. Branum, and Paula K. Hood, eds. "The Boesel Letters: Two Germans in Sibley's Brigade," translated by Irma Oglendorf Schwarz. *Southwestern Historical Quarterly*, CII, No. 4 (April 1999), 457–486.

Lane, Walter P. *The Adventures and Recollections of General Walter P. Lane: A San Jacinto Veteran, Containing Sketches of the Texian, Mexican, and Late Wars, with Several Indian Fights Thrown In*, edited by Jimmy L. Bryan, Jr. Dallas: William P. Clements Center for Southwest Studies, 2000.

LeGrand, Julia. *The Diary of Julia LeGrand, New Orleans 1862–1863.* Edited by Kate Mason Rowland and Mrs. Morris L. Croxall. Richmond, Va.: Everett Wadley, 1911.

Lincecum, Jerry Bryan, Edward Hake Phillips, and Peggy A. Redshaw, eds. *Gideon Lincecum's Sword: Civil War Letters from the Texas Home Front.* Denton: University of North Texas Press, 2001.

Lincoln, Abraham. *Collected Works of Abraham Lincoln*, edited by Roy P. Basler. New Brunswick, N.J.: Rutgers University Press, 1953.

Maddocks, Elden B. *History of the Twenty-Sixth Maine Regiment.* Bangor, Maine: Charles H. Glass, 1899.

McCann, Thomas H. *The Campaigns of the Civil War in the United States of America.* Hudson County, N.J.: The Hudson Observer, 1915.

McKinnon, Annie S. "Escape from New Orleans Prison." *The Confederate Veteran* 13, number 1 (January 1905): 19–20.

McLeary, J. H. "History of Green's Brigade." in Wooten, Dudley G., ed. *A Comprehensive History of Texas*, pp. 695–740. 2 Volumes. Dallas: Scarff, 1898.

Moore, Frank, ed. *The Rebellion Record: A Diary of American events with Documents, Narratives, Illustrative Incidents, Poetry, etc.* 12 Volumes. New York: G. P. Putnam, D. Van Nostrand, 1864.

Moors, John Farwell. *History of the Fifty-Second Regiment, Massachusetts Volunteers.* Boston: G. H. Ellis, 1893.

Muenster, Emily Frazier, and Fred W. Edwards, eds., *From Tallow Candle to Television: An Autobiography of Dr. J. M. Frazier.* Belton, Tex.: Mary Hardin-Baylor University, 1981.

Murray, Thomas Hamilton. *History of the Ninth Regiment, Connecticut Volunteer Infantry, 'The Irish Regiment,' in the War of the Rebellion: The Record of a Gallant Command on the March, in Battle, and in Bivouc.* New Haven, Conn.: Price, Lee, and Adkins, 1908.

New York State Division of Military and Naval Affairs: Military History. "161st Regiment New York Volunteer Infantry Civil War News Paper Clippings." Available at http://www.dmna.state.ny.us/historic/reghist/civil/infantry/161stInf/161stInfCWN .htm.

Noel, Theophilus. *A Campaign from Santa Fe to the Mississippi: A Campaign from Santa Fe to the Mississippi: Being a History of the Old Sibley Brigade from Its First Organization to the Present Time; Its Campaigns in New Mexico, Arizona, Texas, Louisiana and Arkansas in the Years 1861–2–3–4.* Shreveport, La.: Shreveport News, 1865.

Nott, Charles C. *Sketches in Prison Camps: A Continuation of Sketches of the War.* New York: A. D. F. Randolph, 1865.

Pellet, Elias P. *History of the 114th Regiment, New York State Volunteers.* Norwich, N.Y.: Telegraph and Chronicle Power Press Printing, 1866.

Plummer, Albert. *History of the Forty-Eighth Regiment M. V. M. During the Civil War.* Boston: New England Druggist Publishing Company, 1907.

Pound, DaNean Olene. "Slave to the Ex-Slave Narratives." M.A. Thesis, Northwestern State University, Natchitoches, Louisiana, 2005.

Powers, George W. *The Story of the Thirty-eighth Regiment of Massachusetts Volunteers.* Cambridge: Dakin and Metcalf, 1866.

Putnam, George Haven. *Memories of My Youth, 1844–1865.* New York: G. P. Putnam's Sons, 1914.

Quien, George. *Reminiscences of the Services and Experience of Lieutenant George Quien of Company K, 23rd Connecticut Volunteers.* Waterbury, Conn., 1906.

Rankin, David C., ed. *Diary of a Christian Soldier: Rufus Kinsey and the Civil War.* New York: Cambridge University Press, 2004.

Sherman, Andrew M. *In the Lowlands of Louisiana in 1863: An Address Delivered by Andrew M. Sherman at the Forty-Second Reunion of the Twenty-Third Connecticut.* Morristown, N.J.: Howard Publishing, 1908.

Simpson, Brooks D., ed. *The Civil War: The Third Year Told by Those Who Lived It*. New York: The Library of America, 2013.

Smith, George G. *Leaves from a Soldier's Diary: The Personal Record of Lieutenant George G. Smith, Co. C, 1st Louisiana Regiment Infantry Volunteers [White] During the War of Rebellion*. Putnam, Conn.: n.p., 1906.

Stanyan, John M. *A History of the Eighth Regiment of New Hampshire Volunteers*. Concord, N.H.: Ira C. Evans, 1892.

Stearns, Albert. *Reminiscences of the Late War*. Brooklyn: Author, 1881.

Taylor, Richard. *Destruction and Reconstruction: Personal Experiences of the Late War*. New York: D. Appleton, 1879.

Thompson, Jerry ed., *From Desert to Bayou: The Civil War Journal and Sketches of Morgan Wolfe Merrick*. El Paso: Texas Western Press, 1991.

Townsend, Luther Tracy. *History of the Sixteenth Regiment, New Hampshire Volunteers*. Washington, D.C.: Norman T. Elliot, 1897.

Vandiver, Frank E. ed., *The Civil War Diary of General Josiah Gorgas*. Tuscaloosa: University of Alabama Press, 1947.

Secondary Sources

Adjutant General of the Commonwealth of Massachusetts, comp., Massachusetts Soldiers, Sailors, and Marines in the Civil War. 9 Volumes. Norwood, Mass.: Norwood Press, 1931–1937.

Allardice, Bruce S. *Confederate Colonels: A Biographical Register*. Columbia: University of Missouri Press, 2008.

The American Annual Cyclopedia and Register of Important Events of the year 1863: Embracing Political, Civil, Military, and Social Affairs, Public Documents; Biography, Statistics, Commerce, Finance, Literature, Science, Agriculture, and Mechanical Industry. Volume III. New York: D. Appleton and Company, 1864. 320.

Arceneaux, William. *Acadian General: Alfred Mouton and the Civil War*. Lafayette: Center for Louisiana Studies, University of Southwestern Lousiana, 1981.

Bailey, Anne J. *Between the Enemy and Texas: Parsons's Texas Cavalry in the Civil War*. Fort Worth: Texas Christian University Press, 1989.

Ballard, Michael. *Vicksburg: The Campaign that Opened the Mississippi*. Chapel Hill: University of North Carolina Press, 2004.

Barnickle, Linda. *Milliken's Bend: A Civil War Battle in History and Memory*. Baton Rouge: Louisiana State University Press, 2013.

Barr, Alwyn. *Polignac's Texas Brigade*. College Station: Texas A&M University Press, 1998.

Barringer, William E. *A House Dividing: Lincoln as President Elect*. Springfield, Ill.: 1945.

Bauer, Craig. *Creole Genesis: The Bringier Family and Antebellum Life in Louisiana*. Lafayette: University of Louisiana at Lafayette Press, 2011.

———. "The Last Effort: The Secret Mission of the Confederate Diplomat, Duncan F. Kenner." *Louisiana History* 22, No. 1 (Winter 1981), 67–95.

Bearss, Edwin Cole. *The Vicksburg Campaign: Vicksburg Is the Key*, Volume I. Dayton, Ohio: Morningside Press, 1985.

———. *The Vicksburg Campaign: Grant Strikes a Fatal Blow*, Volume II. Dayton, Ohio: Morningside Press, 1986.

———. *The Vicksburg Campaign: Unvexed to the Sea*, Volume III. Dayton, Ohio: Morningside Press, 1986.

Bell, Adrew McIlwaine. *Mosquito Soldiers: Malaria, Yellow Fever, and the Course of the American Civil War.* Baton Rouge: Louisiana State University Press, 2010.

Bergeron, Arthur W. *Guide to Louisiana Confederate Military Units, 1861–1865.* Baton Rouge: Louisiana State University Press, 1989.

Bergeron, Arthur W. Jr., "Fort Berwick and Fort Chêne: Guardians of the Attakapas," *Louisiana History*, 47, Number 4 (Autumn 2006), 435–450.

Block, W. T. "Calasieu Parish, La: Hotbed of the Civil War Jayhawkers. Available at http://www.wtblock.com/wtblockjr/calcasie1.htm.

Bragg, Jefferson Davis. *Louisiana in the Confederacy.* Baton Rouge: Louisiana State University Press, 1941.

Brasseaux, Charles A. "Ozeme Carriere and the St. Landry Jayhawkers." *Attakapas Gazette* XIII, no. 4 (Winter 1978): 185–186.

Brasseaux, Carl A., and Keith P. Fontenot. *Steamboats on Louisiana's Bayous: A History and Directory*. Baton Rouge: Louisiana State University Press, 2004.

Butler, Benjamin. *Private and Official Correspondence of General Benjamin F. Butler,* edited by Jesse Aimes Marshall. Norwood, Mass.: Plimpton Press, 1917.

Case, Theodore S. *The Quartermaster's Guide: Being a Summary of Those Portions of the Army Regulations of 1863 and General Orders from the War Department from May 1, 1861 to April 10, 1865, which affect the Quartermaster Department.* St. Louis: P. M. Pinkard, 1865.

Clarke, James Freeman. *Memorial and Biographical Sketches.* Boston: Houghton, Osgood, 1878.

Cornish, Dudley Taylor. *The Sable Arm: Black Troops in the Union Army, 1861–1865.* University of Kansas Press, 1987.

Costello, Brian J. *A History of Pointe Coupée Parish, Louisiana.* Donaldsonville, La.: Margaret Media, 2010.

Cotham, Edward T., Jr. *Battle on the Bay: The Civil War Struggle for Galveston.* Austin: University of Texas Press, 1998.

Current, Richard Nelson. *Lincoln's Loyalists: Union Soldiers from the Confederacy.* Boston: Northeastern University Press, 1992.

Dobak, William H. *Freedom by the Sword: The US Colored Troops, 1862–1867.* Washington, D.C.: Center of Military History, 2011.

Downs, Jim. *Sick from Freedom: African-American Illness and Suffering During the Civil War and Reconstruction.* New York: Oxford University Press, 2012.

Durel, Lionel C. "Creole Civilization in Donaldsonville, 1850, According to 'Le Vigilant," *The Louisiana Historical Quarterly*, 31 (1948): 981–994.

Edmonds, David C. *The Guns of Port Hudson.* 2 volumes. Lafayette, La.: Acadiana Press, 1984.

Finch, L. Boyd. *Confederate Pathway to the Pacific: Major Sherod Hunter and Arizona Territory, C.S.A.* Tucson: Arizona Historical Society, 1996.

———. "Surprise at Brashear City: Sherod Hunter's Sugar Cooler Cavalry," *Louisiana History*, Volume 25, number 4 (Fall 1984): 403–434.

Foner, Eric. *Free Soil, Free Labor, Free Men: The Ideology of the Republican Party before the Civil War.* New York: Oxford University Press, 1970.

Frazier, Donald S. *Blood and Treasure: Confederate Empire in the Southwest.* College Station: Texas A&M University Press, 1995.

———. *Fire in the Cane Field: The Federal Invasion of Louisiana and Texas, January 1861–January 1863.* Buffalo Gap, Texas: State House Press, 2009.

———. "'The Battles of Texas Will Be Fought in Louisiana:' The Assault of Fort Butler, June 28, 1863," *Southwestern Historical Quarterly*, 104 (January 2001), 333–363.

———. *Thunder Across the Swamp: The Fight for the Lower Mississippi, February 1863–May 1863.* Buffalo Gap, Texas: State House Press, 2011.

Freeman, Douglas Southall. *Lee's Lieutenants.* 3 vols. New York: Charles Scribner's Sons, 1944.

Geise, William Royston "The Confederate Military Forces in the Trans-Mississippi, 1861–1865: A Study in Command." Ph.D. Dissertation, University of Texas, Austin, 1974.

Herrington, Fred Harvey, ed. "A Peace Mission of 1863," *The American Historical Review* 46, No. 1 (October, 1940), 76–86.

Hewitt, Lawrence. *Port Hudson: Confederate Bastion on the Mississippi.* Baton Rouge: Louisiana State University Press, 1994.

Hollandsworth, James G., Jr. *The Louisiana Native Guards: The Black Military Experience during the Civil War.* Baton Rouge: Louisiana State University Press, 1995.

———. *Pretense of Glory: The Life of General Nathaniel P. Banks.* Baton Rouge: Louisiana State University Press, 1998.

Kerby, Robert L. *Kirby Smith's Confederacy: The Trans-Mississippi South, 1863–1865.* Tuscaloosa: University of Alabama Press, 1991.

Lackey, Rodney C. "Notes on Civil War Logistics: Facts and Stories." Available at http://www.transportation.army.mil/Historian/PDF/Peninsula%20Campaign/Rodney%20Lackey%20Article_1.pdf.

Levine, Bruce. *Confederate Emancipation: Southern Plans to Free and Arm Slaves during the Civil War.* New York: Oxford University Press, 2005.

Livius. "Civil War Message Decoded: Help is Not on the Way." The History Blog. http://www.thehistoryblog.com/archives/9199.

Lowe, Richard. *Walker's Texas Division CSA: Greyhounds of the Trans-Mississippi.* Baton Rouge: Louisiana State University Press, 2004.

Malone, Ann Patton. *Sweet Chariot: Slave Family and Household Structure in Nineteenth-Century Louisiana.* Chapel Hill: University of North Carolina Press, 1996.

Marks, Paula Mitchell. *Hands to the Spindle: Texas Women and Home Textile Production, 1822–1880.* College Station: Texas A&M University Press, 1996.

Marshall, Michael. *Gallant Creoles: A History of the Donaldsonville Canonniers.* Lafayette: University of Louisiana, Lafayette, 2013.

Marten, James. "A Wearying Existence: Texas Refugees in New Orleans, 1862–1865." *Louisiana History* XXVIII, No. 4 (Autumn 1987), 343–356.

———. "Drawing the Line: Dissent and Disloyalty in Texas, 1856–1874." Ph.D. dissertation, University of Texas, Austin, 1986.

Mathews, James T. "A Time for Desperate Valor: The Confederate Attack on Fort Butler, Louisiana, 1863." *Military History of the West*, 26 (Spring 1996), 23–34.

Messner, William F. *Freedmen and the Ideology of Free Labor: Louisiana, 1862–1865.* Lafayette: Center for Louisiana Studies, 1978.

Moore, Albert Burton. *Conscription and Conflict in the Confederacy*. Columbia: University of South Caroline Press, 1996.

Murray, R. L., ed. *Madison County Troops in the Civil War*. Wolcott, N.Y.: Benedum Books, 2004.

Oakes, James. *Freedom National: The Destruction of Slavery in the United States, 1861–1865.* New York: W. W. Norton & Company, 2012.

Odom, Van D. "The Political Career of Thomas Overton Moore, Secession Governor of Louisiana." *Louisiana Historical Quarterly* 26 (October 1943): 975–1054.

Parrish, Michael. *Richard Taylor: Soldier Prince of Dixie.* Chapel Hill: University of North Carolina Press, 1992.

Parton, James. *History of the Administration of the Department of the Gulf in the Year 1862.* New York: Mason Brothers, 1864.

———. *General Butler in New Orleans: History of the Administration of the Department of the Gulf in the Year 1862*. New York: Mason Brothers, 1864.

Peña, Christopher G. *Scarred by War: Civil War in Southeast Louisiana.* Bloomington, Ind.: Authorhouse, 2004.

———. *Touched by War: Battles Fought in the Lafourche District.* Thibodaux, La.: C. G. P. Press, 1998.

Phisterer, Frederick. *New York in the War of the Rebellion, 1861–1865*. Albany: Weed, Parsons, and Company, 1890.

Pound, DaNean Olene. "Slave to the Ex-Slave Narratives." M.A. Thesis, Northwestern State University, Natchitoches, Louisiana, 2005.

Prichard, Walter. "The Effects of the Civil War on the Louisiana Sugar Industry." *The Journal of Southern History* 5 (August 1939): 315–332.

Prushankin, Jeffrey S. *A Crises in Confederate Command: Edmund Kirby Smith, Richard Taylor, and the Army of the Trans-Mississippi.* Baton Rouge: Louisiana State University Press, 2005.

Raines, C. W. *The Year Book for Texas*. 2 vols. Austin: Gammel Book Company, 1902.

Rein, Christopher Michael. *Trans-Mississippi Southerners in the Union Army, 1862–1865*. M.A. Thesis, Louisiana State University, Baton Rouge, May 2001.

Ripley, C. Peter. *Slaves and Freedmen in Civil War Louisiana*. Baton Rouge: Louisiana State University Press, 1976.

Roland, Charles P. *Louisiana Sugar Plantations during the Civil War*. 1957. Reprint. Baton Rouge: Louisiana State University Press, 1997.

Rothman, Adam. "The Horrors '12 Years a Slave' Couldn't Tell: What a Civil War Soldier's Diary Tells Us about Solomon Northrup's Ordeal." Available at http://america.aljazeera.com/opinions/2014/1/the-horrors-a-12yearsaslaveacouldnattell0.html.

Smith, George Winston "Some Northern Wartime Attitudes toward the Post-Civil War South." *Journal of Southern History* 10, no. 3 (August 1944): 253–274.

Stone, Edwin M. *Rhode Island in the Rebellion*. Providence, R.I.: George H. Whitney, 1865.

Sutherland, Daniel E. "Looking for a Home: Louisiana Emigrants during the Civil War and Reconstruction." *Louisiana History* XXI, No. 4 (Autumn 1980), 341–361.

———. "Abraham Lincoln, John Pope, and the Origins of Total War." *Journal of Military History* 56, no. 4 (October 1992): 568–574.

Taylor, Ethel. "Discontent in Confederate Louisiana." *Louisiana History*, 2, no. 4 (Autumn, 1961), 410–428.

Tsapina, Olga. "Where Solomon Northrup Was a Slave, *Verso*, March 3, 2014. Available at http://huntingtonblogs.org/2014/03/where-solomon-northup-was-a-slave/.

Tunnell, Ted. *Crucible of Reconstruction: War, Radicalism, and Race in Louisiana, 1862–1877*. Baton Rouge: Louisiana State University Press, 1984.

Ullman, Daniel. *Organization of Colored Troops and the Regeneration of the South*. Washington, D.C.: Great Republic, 1868.

———. *Organization of Colored Troops and the Regeneration of the South*. Washington, D.C.: Great Republic, 1868.

U.S. War Department. *How to Feed and Army*. Washington, D.C.: Government Printing Office, 1901.

Vandiver, Frank, "Texas and the Confederate Army's Meat Problem." *Southwestern Historical Quarterly* 47, no. 3 (January 1944), 225–233.

Ward, Susan Hayes. *George H. Hepworth: Preacher, Journalist, Friend of the People, the Story of His Life Told to Susan Hayes Ward*. New York: E. P. Dutton & Company, 1903.

Way, Frederick Jr., *Way's Packet Directory, 1848–1994*. Athens: Ohio University Press, 1982.

Whitman, William S., and Charles H. True, *War for the Union: A History of the Part Borne by Maine Troops in the Suppression of the American Rebellion*. Lewiston, Maine: Nelson Dingley Jr. & Company, 1865.

Williams, George Washington. *A History of the Negro Troops in the War of the Rebellion, 1861–1865*. New York: Harper and Brothers, 1888.

Wilson, Joseph Thomas. *The Black Phalanx: A History of the Negro Soldiers if the United States in the Wars of 1775–1812, 1861–'65*. Hartford, Conn.: American Publishing Company, 1890.

Winschel, Terrence J. *Vicksburg: Fall of the Confederate Gibraltar.* Abilene, Tex.: McWhiney Foundation Press, 1999.

———. *Triumph and Defeat: The Vicksburg Campaign.* Campbell, Calif.: Savas Publishing, 1999.

Winters, John D. *The Civil War in Louisiana.* Baton Rouge: Louisiana State University Press, 1987.

Wood, C. E. *Mud: A Military History.* Washington, D.C.: Potomac Books, 2007.

Wooten, Dudley J., ed. *A Comprehensive History of Texas.* 2 volumes. Dallas: Scarff, 1898.

INDEX

H

T

CPSIA information can be obtained at www.ICGtesting.com
Printed in the USA
LVOW11*2305270215

428658LV00001BC/1/P

9 781933 337630